The Lion's Share

Updated to incorporate a substantial new epilogue considering Brexit and its 'imperial' implications, the sixth edition of *The Lion's Share* remains an essential introduction to British imperialism from its Victorian heyday to the present.

Well-known for its vigorous and readable style, this book presents a broad narrative of events and explores a number of general themes, challenging more conventional and popular interpretations of British imperialism, as well as the simplistic 'for' and 'against' arguments put forward in today's 'history wars'. Bernard Porter sees imperialism as a symptom not of Britain's strength in the world, but of her decline, and he argues that the empire itself both aggravated and obscured deep-seated malaise in the British economy. This sixth edition includes a final epilogue that engages with what Brexit means for British Imperial History, and whether it represents an extension of or final conclusion to Britain's Imperial Career. In so doing, the book offers readers a thorough understanding of the history of British imperialism and its heritage, extending right into the present day.

Supported by maps, images and an updated chronology, *The Lion's Share* is the perfect resource for both students and those interested in British and Imperial History from the Victorian era to the modern day.

Bernard Porter is Emeritus Professor of Modern History at the University of Newcastle upon Tyne, UK. He has also taught at the Universities of Cambridge and Hull, and (as Visiting Professor) at Yale, Sydney and Copenhagen Universities. He is the author of ten books and many articles on a range of subjects, including British imperial history, the history of political refugees in Britain, secret policing, British attitudes to Europe, and Victorian architecture. His *The Absent-Minded Imperialists* (2004) won an American literary prize. He has also contributed to the *Guardian*, the *London Review of Books*, the *Times Literary Supplement*, and *History Today*. He lives in Stockholm and Hull.

The Lion's Share

A History of British Imperialism 1850 to the Present

Sixth edition

Bernard Porter

Routledge
Taylor & Francis Group

LONDON AND NEW YORK

Sixth edition published 2021
by Routledge
2 Park Square, Milton Park, Abingdon, Oxon OX14 4RN

and by Routledge
52 Vanderbilt Avenue, New York, NY 10017

Routledge is an imprint of the Taylor & Francis Group, an informa business

[First edition published by Pearson Education Limited 1975]

[Fifth edition published by Pearson Education Limited 2012]

British Library Cataloguing in Publication Data
A catalogue record for this book is available from the British Library

Library of Congress Cataloging-in-Publication Data
A catalog record has been requested for this book

ISBN: 978-0-367-42699-6 (hbk)
ISBN: 978-0-367-42698-9 (pbk)
ISBN: 978-0-367-85450-8 (ebk)

Typeset in Sabon
by Taylor & Francis Books

Dedicated to those – or their memory – who set me on the path to becoming a historian and a scholar in my early years: Cyril Porter; W. R. Powell; Alan Mould; Peter Watkins; W. E. 'Spud' Barron; John Roach; and R. E. 'Robbie' Robinson

Contents

Illustrations

Maps

Tables

Preface to the sixth edition

When did the British empire come to an end? That's not as easy a question as it may seem. In some ways – described in Chapter 13 of this book – it is still with us, for good or for ill (usually the latter), and continuing to burden, or otherwise, its former subjects. British imperial*ism*, in certain senses of the word, has certainly carried on through to the present, although in weaker forms, and against stiffer competition.

When I completed the fifth edition of this book in 2012, however, I thought that that date would be as good a point as any to bring the curtain down on my narrative. By then, nearly all Britain's formal colonies had gone, and the Iraq War had revealed Britain's weakness by the side of her successor empire, the American. The creature was surely essentially dead. Then, however, came Brexit; not an imperial event in itself, but a phenomenon that seemed to reveal some lingering imperial ambitions among at least a few of its promoters, and which consequently – depending on how it all turns out – needs to be included as either a late extension to the story, or the final stake driven through its heart. The new Chapter 14 of this edition, which is otherwise substantially unchanged from the last one, is about this.

The truth is that old empires, like old soldiers, never properly die, but only fade away; slowly, and always leaving traces, both on the ground, and in people's minds.

I've lost track of the number of publishers whose hands the book has gone through, with takeovers, mergers and the like. Originally it was Longmans, where I was wonderfully handled by Andrew MacLennan, a legend in the publishing industry. Now – as I understand it – it's Taylor and Francis, where I've been well looked after by Zoe Thomson, and – latterly – by my perceptive and ever-cheerful copy-editor Susan Dunsmore, who deserves a bow. (It's a boring and generally unappreciated job.) I should have liked to thank the African who carved and painted the little statue that appears on the cover of this book, but when I bought it at a roadside market near Cape Town some years ago I'm afraid I never learned his or her name. The excellent photograph, however, should be credited to Kevin Greene of Hull. Otherwise my thanks are recorded in the Dedication; and at the end of the Preface to the fifth edition.

Bernard Porter
Stockholm, July 2020

Preface to the fifth edition

This book is about the phenomenon of 'British imperialism' (not just the 'British empire') in the later nineteenth and the twentieth centuries: what it was, how it arose, why it fell, how it worked, what its repercussions and legacies were and are, and a number of other issues relating to it. It is a complex and fascinating story – more so than some simplistic popular reductions of it would have one think. It is also a continuously topical one, in view of the empire's impact, still, on the world and on Britain, and of imperialism's revival – if we are to believe some modern commentators – in very recent years. The final chapters will be about this.

Most of the rest of the book appeared originally in 1975, though it has been updated at intervals since. Things, of course, were very different then. For a start, the British empire was not yet quite dead. Britain had a few significant colonies still, like Rhodesia (Zimbabwe) and Hong Kong. Second, there were many people alive then who remembered the empire in its 'better' days, and were prepared to defend it. They were already coming to seem rather old-fashioned, and even widely ridiculed; but they were there. Third, most established imperial historians were people who were closely associated with the empire, as ex-colonial officials, or running courses for new generations of them. The three major university chairs of imperial history were all named after, and in some cases had been the gift of, prominent imperialists: Rhodes (London), Beit (Oxford) and Smuts (Cambridge). Before *The Lion's Share* most general histories of British imperialism were 'insider' jobs, and broadly sympathetic. The exceptions were those written by Marxists, attacking imperialism as a mere 'stage of capitalism', and generally regarded as too polemical to be recommended widely. That was the background against which this book was originally published.

This was a peculiar time for imperial history in other ways too. There was little general interest in it. It was rather looked down on as an academic subject: not taught as a discrete option in many schools, for example; neglected in most broader 'British' history syllabuses; and afforded a very low status in my own university (Cambridge), where the 'Expansion of Europe' course, as it was called, was widely regarded as an easy option for those unable to cope cerebrally with the alternative and more prestigious 'History of Political Thought' paper. (This was in the 1960s.) This situation was not entirely unprecedented: ever since the days of Sir John Seeley – Regius Professor at Cambridge between 1869 and 1895 – imperialists had regularly complained at the way the empire was marginalised in British history teaching generally,[1] but it undoubtedly got worse during the 1970s. This had a lot to do with the decolonisation that was going on at the time: which first of all *defined* imperialism as *passé*, and consequently not something that 'modern' students and people generally would want to know about; second, provoked a political reaction against the thing itself among the younger generation; and third, may have made it too painful to want to recall on the part of those who had valued the empire in the past. (A prime example is the formerly ultra-imperialist Conservative MP Enoch Powell, who as early as 1964 even tried to persuade himself and others that it had never existed.[2]) I touched on this in the final chapter of my third edition (now Chapter 11). Imperial history was not fashionable; much less so than, for example, social history, many of whose practitioners made a point of spurning it deliberately. (It had nothing to do with 'the common people'.) That made the first edition of this book unfashionable, too. It also made some of my social history colleagues think I must be an imperialist. (They were '*socialists*', after all.) The same is true of the other British imperial surveys that appeared at roughly the same time. (Mine was not alone.[3]) We were all rather pushed to the back of the stage, or even into the wings.

Since then, however, and in the last 15–20 years in particular, imperial history has begun to take on a more leading role. Not only is it featuring more in its own right, with a plethora of new works on it appearing,[4] it is also claimed to be crucial to an understanding of other areas of British history. Now all the talk is of how neglectful earlier generations of British historians were of the imperial aspects of their subject; attributed by some to post-colonial shame or 'denial' (in the psychologists' sense: *vide* Enoch Powell), or even to deliberate deceit: a doctoring of the British or English national myth in order to make Britons feel better about themselves. That is no longer a problem. Most of the generation that had any kind of personal stake in the empire has now gone. Some of the next generation have even begun to rekindle a sense of retrospective pride in it: mistakenly, in my view, as I shall be arguing later. (It is not simply because it was 'bad'.) Others are taking it on board more neutrally. This is inevitable, for once the psychological barriers are taken down, the importance of the empire to Britain becomes obvious. It was a huge enterprise. It must have left marks. Of course, it did. We are seeing them given their due attention now: in scholarly and popular books, films, television documentaries and dramas, the press, and even an excellent museum dedicated to it (opened in Bristol and now relocating to London). No-one will be able to accuse the present generation of 'covering up' for the empire. Indeed, my own complaint, which I developed in another book in 2004, is that in some respects this has gone a little too far.[5]

That refers to the idea that nineteenth- and early twentieth-century British domestic culture was steeped in imperialism, which I do not believe it was, and – which is far more important – I do not believe was *necessary*. This contention is central to the present work as well. The roots of British imperialism were material, not cultural. Specifically, it grew out of the nature of the British capitalism of the time. Politics and society came into it, but they were usually governed by the demands of contemporary capitalism too. 'Culture' (by most of the meanings attached to the word) played the least important part in this process. It certainly was not *responsible* for imperialism, in the sense that the latter emerged because there was a particularly empire-friendly soil it could take root in. I do not wish to elaborate on this point here, as it is covered in that other book of mine; but only to point it out, as a reason why 'culture' plays so small a part in this one, which may surprise modern readers. This book is about the *realities* of British imperialism. Some of those realities, I feel, have been somewhat lost sight of in much recent, culturally biased work on the subject. They need to be restored.

This was a battle I also felt I needed to fight when the book first came out in 1975, though my adversaries then were different. Then, materialistic explanations of history were associated with Marxism. As a result, my book, which adopted a kind of sub-Marxist materialistic line, was generally taken as being critical of the empire in its early reviews. 'Capitalism' was a dirty word in Britain, mainly the weapon of the 'other side'. Traditional imperial historians countered it by downplaying the material aspect of the empire in favour of its 'humanitarian' side; which was nonsense (I believe), but thought to be necessary in order to make it more sympathetic to the poor of the world, including millions of the empire's present and former subjects, who might otherwise be seduced by the communist line. I went against this. I also offended some by my contention – which you will find implied throughout the book – that the empire was not really *very glorious*: was, in fact, a symptom of Britain's weakness and failings, rather than of her successes and strength; and was, as I said in my original Preface, 'moulded far more by events than it moulded them'. On both these matters, of course, opinions have changed utterly since. Nobody any longer minds (do they?) if the empire is belittled. 'Capitalism' is not the term of disapprobation it used to be, so pro-imperialists have no reason to disown it. The reason for this, of course, is capitalism's victory over communism in the great ideological battle of the twentieth century, enabling it to drop many of the disguises it had once felt were crucial to its acceptance. The old demon became openly celebrated in Britain: by Margaret Thatcher, for one. Consequently, to claim a capitalist genesis for imperialism was no longer implicitly to criticise it. This book may have lost much of its supposed anti-imperial sting as a result. But the point is as relevant as ever. The material origins of imperialism still need to be emphasised: this time against the 'cultural' rather than the 'humanitarian' imperialists. This is why I have not changed my line of argument in any fundamental way for this fifth edition. It still stands. Capitalism lay at the root of nineteenth-century British imperialism. Grasp that, and one may also understand the roots of other and later sorts of imperialism (my Chapter 12).

The other thing that distinguished this book when it first appeared was that it was about imperial*ism*, defined rather broadly, rather than 'the empire', as most of its predecessors had been. This arose from the dissatisfaction that many imperial historians had been feeling for some years with the strictly legalistic definitions of the 'e' and 'i' words that had used to be current – empire, imperial, imperialism, imperialist, and so on – which did not, they felt, fully cover Britain's real power and influence in the world during her imperial age. It was from this that the new terms 'informal' and 'cultural' imperialism emerged.[6] The present history was the first general one in the field, I believe, to embrace these other aspects of imperialism, and, indeed, to be structured around Britain's 'real' rather than her merely 'formal' power. This broadened its scope in some respects, but also narrowed it in others. Readers will notice, for example, that colonies like Australia and Canada do not feature as prominently in this book as they generally do in histories of the empire *per se*. This is deliberate. (It certainly does not reflect any disdain on my part for those countries. As it happens, Australia is my favourite place.) As I see it, Britain no longer *ruled* Australia and Canada from the late nineteenth century onwards in any realistic sense. That is why they are rather downplayed here.

While we are on this, certain other aspects of British imperial history are neglected here too, for different reasons. First, Ireland is not included here as a 'colony', although in most ways she certainly qualifies as one (and as a victim of British imperial*ism*, however defined). There is no good excuse for this, beyond the facts that (1) her colonial status was ambivalent: hers was a colonising as well as a colonised people, and (2) the history *of* Ireland is best written by historians *of* Ireland, of which there are many far more competent than me. Second, I have not included very much on social aspects of the history of the colonies – gender, racism, etc. – though I believe that these, like Ireland

and the Dominions, are important. That is because this is a book about British imperial policy and its effects, and not about how people lived and worked in the empire, or related to each other there. It is, in other words, mainly an *Anglocentric* and *political* history, though with economic, social, ideological and cultural factors brought in to explain political developments where appropriate. (I shall be elaborating on this in Chapter 1.) Most of what is called the 'new imperial history', it seems to me, is complementary to this; it does not (or should not) supersede it. My decision not to incorporate the former, which would effectively have meant re-orientating the book, was also taken on the advice of one of the 'readers' my publishers appointed to vet the third edition to tell them whether it was worth reissuing, and how. 'Since … this is what he does best,' he or she wrote, kindly and helpfully,

> my own inclination would be not to [ask him to] try to develop any further the kind of material that the so-called school of 'new imperial history' calls for. I would prefer to have Porter as my political history text and perhaps to assign something else alongside it that speaks to these concerns.

That is what I recommend too. There is a need for a good political history of British imperialism: at this moment in time, I believe, more than at almost any other. This is it. There are plenty of other good books on these other aspects – on 'subaltern' and colonial gender history, for example, imperial cultures, the 'old dominions', Ireland, and so on – to supplement it.

Though my main 'line' has remained constant, however, a number of revisions and additions have been made to the book in its successive editions. In particular, two entire new chapters were added to the fourth edition (2004), and another to the present one. The new Chapter 1 (originally numbered '0' in order to avoid having to renumber the rest, a device which I have abandoned, however, for this edition, I hope without causing too much confusion) sought to furnish a broad philosophical context, suited to the present, for the ensuing narrative. Chapter 12 extended that narrative to cover the *revival* of old-fashioned British imperialism, in some senses, at the beginning of the twenty-first century under Tony Blair and George W. Bush. Chapter 13 represents a rather unusual departure, I think, in histories of this kind: a discussion of the reputation of British imperialism as it has manifested itself in the years after (formal) decolonisation, and some of the possible effects of that reputation (or, more correctly, reputations) subsequently. Great historical events often cast long shadows into the future, not only materially, but also through the myths that they generate or feed. These should be considered to be a part of their histories too.

As well as these major additions to earlier versions of this book, I have taken the opportunity to correct, re-write or amplify some passages of the original; to totally revise the bibliography (though not many of the notes, which remain the *sources* of most of what is written in the text); and to add, at my publisher's suggestion, a section of illustrations, some maps, and a Chronology. I have kept in all the jokes, which I know are generally appreciated, after running them past my partner (a feminist scholar) for possible signs of sexism, which most of us were more prone to in 1975 than we are today. (One we thought might be marginal, but I have left it in.) This Preface is also largely new, subsuming all the previous ones.

There remains the question of my own moral and political attitude towards British imperialism. In 1975, this book was generally taken to be 'anti', as we have seen; today

I understand it is more likely to be criticised for being too soft on the subject. (That is what another anonymous 'reader' told me.) Neither judgement, I think, reflects its real position. Those who regarded it as too critical did so because it was not explicitly supportive; those who see it as too favourable today do so because it does not condemn imperialism openly. In fact. I am not concerned to do either. I have my own views, of course, on both imperialism generally and the British variety as I understand them. For what it is worth – and I should state this here because it may seep through into my narrative unintentionally – I have always considered myself to be an anti-imperialist, and was emphatically so with regard to, for example, the most recent manifestation of Anglo-American imperialism, the 2003 invasion of Iraq. But I do not think you could tell this from my chapter on that. This is because I do not consider that such opinions have any proper place here. History books should help us understand. To understand is *not* necessarily to pardon, despite the old French adage; it may, in fact, furnish better grounds for criticism than ignorance does. But that is no part of my purpose. What this book seeks to do is to try to explain modern British imperialism, not finally and dog-matically – you do not need to be a postmodernist to know that you can never be certain of anything significant in history – but in a way that will alert readers to the complications, ambiguities and even contradictions of it, which were many. Its aim is to *sophisticate* people's understanding of an important historical and current phe-nomenon that is too often viewed simplistically and crudely. They can then make their own minds up – as I do, but not here – about how beneficent or malevolent it was (and is).

The Preface to the first edition acknowledged my original debts in writing this book: to the libraries I used, my college and first teaching university, colleagues, my then wife, and the first of our children, who was tiny then (and did not really help much, I must say) but is now older than I was when I started this book. Looking back, I now realise that I did not appreciate as much as I should have done what really made my writing of it possible, which was the lack of bureaucratic regulation that the universities basked in then. The first edition of this book took me seven years to write (on the top of teaching, of course, and doing my share in the home), which is why I think it is as good as it is; today, under the pressure in particular of the 'Research Assessment Exercise', I would not be given that time. For this latest edition I have fewer people to thank; apart from the hundreds of students in Britain, America, Australia, Sweden and Denmark I have discussed these subjects with over the years; Newcastle University, for allowing me to escape from the stifling bureaucracy there by offering me 'early retirement'; Christina Wipf-Perry at Pearson Education, for suggesting this new edition, and being so con-siderate, especially over the delays; my Swedish friends, for revealing to me just how deeply British imperialism is misunderstood abroad (in their case, arising out of their curious notion that Sweden was innocent of imperialism; but that's a whole new topic); and Kajsa Ohrlander, my essential helpmeet over the past 16 years: for our innumerable discussions of imperialism, usually in relation to modern politics, post-modernism and gender, illuminating I think to both of us; for her understanding of the obsessions of a writer (she is after all one herself); for her advice over my dubious jokes; and for her love.

Bernard Porter
Hull and Stockholm
September 2011

Notes

1 See J. R. Seeley, *The Expansion of England: Two Courses of Lectures* (1883; 2nd edn, Macmillan, 1895), p. 10.
2 J. Enoch Powell, speech at Trinity College, Dublin, 13 November 1964, in Enoch Powell, ed. John Wood, *Freedom and Reality* (Batsford, 1969), pp. 324–5.
3 For example, Ronald Hyam's stimulating *Britain's Imperial Century 1815–1914* (2nd edn, Macmillan, 1993), which complements this book in many ways (it has more on the 'white' Dominions, for example); Colin Eldridge's more thematic *Victorian Imperialism* (Hodder & Stoughton, 1978); and Jan Morris's wonderfully evocative *Pax Britannica* trilogy (Faber, 1968, 1973, 1978).
4 For example, Lewis James, *Rise and Fall of the British Empire* (Little, Brown, 1994); Peter Marshall (ed.), *Cambridge Illustrated History of the British Empire* (Cambridge UP, 1996); Denis Judd, *Empire* (1996); Trevor Lloyd, *Empire* (Hambledon Continuum, 2001); and the massive five-volume *Oxford History of the British Empire* (edited by Wm Roger Louis, Oxford UP, 1998–99).
5 B. J. Porter, *The Absent-Minded Imperialists* (Oxford UP, 2004).
6 The breakthrough here came with J. A. Gallagher and R. E. Robinson's seminal article, 'The imperialism of free trade', *Economic History Review*, vi (1953), 1–15. Robinson was my research supervisor.

Chronology

1850	Discovery of gold in Australia
1850–55	Taiping Rebellion in China
1851–53	Burmese wars
1851	South African (Transvaal) Republic founded
1853–56	Crimean War
1854	Bloemfontein conference, Orange Free State independent
1856	Annexation of Oudh; Natal founded as Crown Colony
1856–60	New Opium Wars with China
1857–58	Indian Mutiny
1858	East India Company's rule comes to an end; British government takes over
1860–70	New Zealand Maori wars
1865	Jamaica (Morant Bay) Rebellion
1866	British North America Act, creating Dominion of Canada
1868	British invasion of Abyssinia; Sir Charles Dilke, *Greater Britain*
1869	Opening of Suez Canal
1870	Diamonds discovered in Kimberley, South Africa
1871	Meeting between Stanley and Livingstone at Ujiji
1873–74	Ashanti War
1874–80	Disraeli is Prime Minister
1875	Disraeli purchases Suez Canal shares
1876	Queen Victoria proclaimed Empress of India
1876–78	Eastern Crisis
1877	Annexation of Transvaal
1878	Annexation of Cyprus
1878–80	Afghan wars
1879	Zulu Wars; Battle of Isandlhwana; Britain replaces Ismael with Tewfik as Khedive of Egypt
1880	Gladstone is Prime Minister
1880–81	First Boer War
1881	British defeat at Majuba Hill; Britain acknowledges Transvaal independence; British North Borneo Company incorporated
1882	Britain bombards Alexandria; occupies Egypt
1883	Sudan evacuated; J. R. Seeley, *The Expansion of England*; Imperial Federation League founded
1884–85	Berlin Africa Conference

1885	Gordon killed in Khartoum; Annexation of Bechuanaland; Penjdeh crisis; Indian National Congress founded; Gold discovered in Witwatersrand, South Africa; Germany annexes German East Africa, Zanzibar
1886	Annexation of Burma to Indian empire; Royal Niger Company charter; Irish Home Rule controversy and Liberal split
1887	Queen Victoria's Golden Jubilee; First Colonial Conference, London
1888	British East Africa Company charter
1889	British South Africa Company charter
1890	Anglo-German agreement over eastern Africa
1891	Anglo-Portuguese treaty on southern Africa
1892	Matabele War
1893	Imperial Institute founded
1894	Uganda becomes British protectorate
1895	Conservative government; Chamberlain becomes Colonial Secretary; British South Africa Company founds 'Rhodesia'; Jameson Raid in Transvaal
1896	'Kaiser's telegram'; Conquest of Ashanti; Abyssinians defeat Italians at Adowa
1897	Queen Victoria's Diamond Jubilee
1898	Battle of Omdurman; reconquest of the Sudan; Fashoda crisis; Britain acquires Kowloon, Wei-hai-wei and Hong Kong 'New Territories'; Boxer uprising in China; US war with Spain over Cuba
1899	Second Anglo-Boer War breaks out
1900	Relief of Mafeking and Ladysmith; Annexation of Transvaal and Orange Free State; Nigeria taken over by British Crown
1901	'Concentration camp' controversy in Boer War; Federation of Australia inaugurated; Queen Victoria dies, Edward VII becomes King
1902	Treaty of Vereeniging ends Boer War; J. A. Hobson, *Imperialism, a Study*; Joseph Chamberlain champions tariff reform and an imperial customs union
1903	Delhi Durbar, for Edward VII's coronation
1904	Anglo-French Entente
1904–05	Partition of Bengal
1905	Liberal government
1906	Landslide Liberal election victory; Responsible government in Transvaal and Orange Free State
1907	Anglo-Russian agreement
1908	Robert Baden-Powell, *Scouting for Boys*
1910	Union of South Africa
1911	Delhi Durbar for coronation of George V
1913	Currah Mutiny against Irish home rule, near Dublin
1914–18	First World War
1915	British conquest of Mesopotamia (Iraq)
1916	Easter rebellion, Dublin; T. E. Lawrence goes to Middle East
1917	Balfour Declaration on Palestine
1919	Peace treaties; British colonial gains; Government of India Act (Montagu-Chelmsford reforms); Amritsar massacre; Gandhi's satyagraha movement begins; Government of India Act
1920	League of Nations Mandates system set up
1921–22	Irish independence
1922	Egyptian quasi-independence British mandate in Palestine begins Chanak crisis

1923	Responsible (European) government in Southern Rhodesia; Devonshire declaration on African paramountcy (Kenya); Halibut Fisheries treaty
1924	First (minority) Labour government; Dominions Office separated from Colonial Office; British Empire Exhibition, Wembley
1925	Empire Marketing Board set up
1926	Imperial Conference defines 'Dominions status'
1929	Second Labour government. First Colonial Development Act
1930	Simon Report (India)
1931	National government under Ramsay MacDonald; Statute of Westminster
1932	Ottawa Imperial Economic Conference
1935	Government of India Act; Italian invasion of Abyssinia
1936	Royal Commission on Palestine
1937	Royal Commission on British West Indies; Royal Commission on Palestine advocates Arab and Jewish states
1938	Japan invades China
1939–45	Second World War
1940	Colonial Development and Welfare Act
1941	Atlantic Charter signed between UK and US
1942	Fall of Singapore; Cripps Mission to India
1943	Great Bengal famine
1945	Labour landslide election victory; Second Colonial Development and Welfare Act
1946	Cabinet Mission to India
1947	India, Pakistan independent
1948	Burma, Ceylon independent; Malayan emergency begins; British withdrawal from Palestine; Israel founded; Riots in Gold Coast
1949	Apartheid instituted in South Africa
1950–53	Korean War
1951	Conservative government
1952	Elizabeth II becomes Queen; Mau Mau Emergency in Kenya begins
1953	Central African Federation created; Constitution suspended in British Guiana
1956	Sudan independent; Suez crisis; Archbishop Makarios (Cyprus) exiled
1957	Malaya, Ghana independent
1958	West India Federation set up; fails
1959	Central African emergency
1960	Harold Macmillan's 'wind of change' speech in Cape Town; Sharpeville massacre in South Africa; Nigeria independent; Cyprus independent
1961	Sierra Leone independent; Tanganyika (Tanzania) independent; Exclusion of South Africa from Commonwealth
1962	Uganda independent; Jamaica independent; Trinidad independent
1963	Central African Federation dissolved; Kenya independent
1964	Labour government; Malawi independent; Zambia independent; Malta independent
1965	(Southern) Rhodesian government declares UDI; Gambia independent; Singapore independent
1966	Lesotho independent; Botswana independent; Guyana independent; Barbados independent
1967	British withdrawal from Aden

1968	British withdrawal from east of Suez announced; Mauritius independent; Swaziland independent
1970	Conservative government; Fiji independent; Tonga independent; Western Samoa independent
1973	Britain joins the EEC; Bahamas independent
1974	Labour government; Grenada independent
1975	Papua New Guinea independent
1976	Seychelles independent
1978	Dominica independent; Solomon Islands independent
1979	Conservative government under Margaret Thatcher; St Lucia independent; St Vincent and Grenadines independent
1980	Zimbabwe (Rhodesia) independent with majority rule
1981	Antigua independent; Belize independent
1982	Falklands War
1983	American invasion of Grenada
1984	Anglo-Chinese agreement for cession of Hong Kong
1989	Pakistan rejoins Commonwealth
1990	Namibia independent; Nelson Mandela released from gaol in South Africa
1991	First Gulf War
1994	South African non-racial election won by ANC; South Africa returns to Commonwealth
1997	New Labour government; Hong Kong reverts to China
1999	Tony Blair's Chicago speech
2000	British military intervention in Sierra Leone
2001	Twin Towers, New York and Pentagon, Washington attacks, 11 September (9/11)
2002	American-British invasion of Afghanistan; Tony Blair's Bangalore speech
2003	American-British invasion of Iraq
2016	Brexit Referendum (23 June)
2017	General Election: inconclusive
2019	Boris Johnson becomes Prime Minister
2020	Britain leaves the European Union

1   Introduction

Everyone knows about the British empire. It was a vast system of conquest, control and exploitation by Britons covering about a quarter of the globe. Two typical images it conjures up are of British men in pith helmets and khaki shorts lording it over half-clothed Africans; and of viceroys, more gloriously attired, riding on elephants in pompous ceremonials in India. It made a hell of a show. It reached its height at the end of the nineteenth century, then came to an end shortly after the Second World War. That was the time of Britain's greatest power in the world ever. During it, the empire dominated British life, and had a huge material impact – for good or ill – on the world outside. Some of its repercussions are still with us, both at home and abroad. It was closely associated with racism, as both effect and cause. It may have experienced a comeback in the early 2000s, in the guise of the 'liberal interventionism' of Tony Blair. Modern American imperialism, so-called (and not just by its opponents), also bears similarities. Despite this, most people, including most Americans, regard it as a Bad Thing. This must be a broadly familiar picture to nearly every reader of this book.

It is by no means an entirely inaccurate one. Most of these statements carry some truth, or could be justified in certain senses, or with qualifications. General judgements about important historical phenomena are usually like this: not easily dismissed – or indeed corroborated – outright, like 'facts'. The most misleading ones are those that *are* plausible, up to a point, but only partially, simplistically, out of context, or without allowing for alternative readings. That is the situation with this popular view of British imperialism. It is not totally 'wrong'; but it is crude, naïve, and consequently misguided in certain important respects. This is an especial problem for those who may want to take 'lessons' from it. (Like most academic historians, I am chary of this.) The aim of the following chapters, therefore, is to present a fuller account of the course of British imperialism over the past 170 years, including its complexities, inconsistencies and mutations, and the all-important domestic and international contexts that gave rise to it, sustained it, transformed it, and aided its (query) revival in the early twenty-first century.

Definitions

First, it needs to be put into the widest possible context. The British did not invent imperialism, of course. Nor for that matter did any other Europeans; or even (probably) humankind. Humans have been at it since the Cro-Magnons spread from Africa into the rest of the habitable world in the 35th millennium BCE, wiping out – if your definition of imperialism requires it to be at the *expense* of somebody – the apparently much nicer Neanderthals. Throughout recorded history peoples have settled amongst, invaded, dominated, ruled, robbed, exploited, civilised, enslaved and exterminated other peoples. So have ideologies, corporations, individuals and one of the two genders. All these carry elements of what today is called 'imperialism'. Then there were the overt empires, those referred to *as* such: Assyrian, Chinese, Mughal, Roman, Ottoman, Spanish ... and so on. The process is still continuing. The latest successful imperialist enterprise in the old-fashioned, full-blooded sense of the term is probably Israel's twentieth-century colonisation – or re-colonisation – of the Holy Land. The American–British invasion of Iraq in 2003 may also qualify.[1] On a more subtle level, modern 'globalisation' has certain imperialist features. It could be argued that the spread of the Christian and Muslim religions, the English language and even Association football have too. Imperialism in these senses appears to be a natural phenomenon; or a normal one, anyway. British imperialism in the nineteenth and twentieth centuries – the subject of this book – was just one major example of this.

It is important to be aware of this broader context, for a number of reasons. Firstly, it highlights some of the semantic difficulties that plague this area. Obviously, the events listed here are not the same phenomenon. If they can all be classed as 'imperialist', then it is by using the word in different ways. Second, and following on from this, it suggests there is no common cause or motivation for them all; unless it *is* human 'nature', which was a popular explanation for imperialism, incidentally, in Britain in her most imperialistic phase. They each had a different genesis. Thirdly, they are not equally reprehensible; if, that is, we are in the business of making judgements of this kind, which a work of history should not really be. The spread of Starbucks is not the moral equivalent of slavery. Even among more conventional kinds of imperialism, some may be more defensible than others. This could be argued, for example, for the foundation of the state of Israel, and the 2003 invasion of Iraq. So 'imperialism' should not be used automatically as a term of abuse, like 'dictatorship' or 'fascism'; or, for that matter, slavery. Indeed (fourthly), it is questionable whether it should be used at all, if its meaning is so shifting, its explanatory value so dubious, and its ethical implications so potentially misleading as we have just seen they are. It does not tell us much about any particular policy or ideology or attitude to know that it was or is 'imperialistic', simply. It is a bit like saying that a person or state is 'aggressive': we still need to know in what ways, and why. Unless (like Robert Ardrey) we take 'aggression' to be a fundamental and irreducible explanation of human behaviour: a kind of *fons et origo*. In fact, both words cover a multitude of quite different phenomena and combinations of phenomena. The chemistry of one brand of 'imperialism' can be quite different from another's. This was often even true within one single brand, like Britain's, which could vary radically from place to place, and at different times. The use of the word – and it is *only* a word – to describe all these varieties is often more obfuscating than otherwise. Lastly, the context tells us that, in creating and sustaining an empire in the eighteenth to twentieth centuries, Britain was not doing anything very unusual. Empires – defined widely and loosely enough – are the rule in human history, not exceptions. This of course is not necessarily to excuse or justify any of them. The same could also be said of diseases, famines and wars.

Defining imperialism is important. Some people, even scholars, do not bother, which can lead to vagueness, confusion and tears. The way to avoid that is to settle on a clear definition, and then stick to it. There are several possibilities. Imperialism has no single, 'right' meaning. It is – to repeat – *only* a word; not a reality (or 'thing'). It has been used in very different ways at different times. In early nineteenth-century Britain it was nearly always associated with Napoleon Bonaparte after he dubbed himself 'Emperor' (1804), which is why the British were so reluctant to apply it to themselves. Hardly anyone talked of a 'British empire' before the 1850s. If they did, they sometimes only meant the British Isles. (Readers of early nineteenth-century literature should beware of this.) Imperialism – the abstract noun deriving from 'empire' – only came to take on something like its modern meaning towards the end of the century. Then it was used rather narrowly. An empire comprised the territories beyond a state's strict boundaries formally ruled by that state; in schematic terms, the countries coloured red on those familiar late nineteenth-century British world maps. Imperial*ism* was the process of expanding those territories; or, alternatively, the ideology that supported that process. The problem with this is that it *only* described the formal, or strict legal, situation, which arguably was merely half the story. It was a little like only counting as 'families' those in which the parents are legally married. It did not cover the whole gamut of Britain's power in the world, which was both more and less extensive than this. (Many marriages are less close than lives lived in what used to be quaintly called 'sin'.) It also distorted the explanations for that gamut, by placing so much emphasis on why British power was *formalised*. (Couples marry for different and sometimes more trivial reasons from the ones that brought them together: to please their parents, perhaps; to 'legitimise' a pregnancy; or as an excuse for a party.) Hence many imperial historians' dissatisfaction, starting in the 1950s, with the red-painted definitions of empire and imperialism. No historian feels they are adequate today.

My own use of the word 'imperialism' in this book will take account of this. The reason I chose 'imperialism' rather than 'empire' for the sub-title of the first edition in 1975, in fact, was that I wanted to describe and explain the *reality* of Britain's power in the world, rather than the somewhat artificial construction that the words 'British empire' represent. This was a novel approach then; it is less so today. It follows obviously – but still needs to be emphasised – that the book is not mainly a history of the empire *per se*. If it were, it would have much more in it about, for example, Australia and Canada, which were indubitably important parts of that empire, but which reflect British imperial*ism* – in the sense of the exercise of British power – rather weakly, in my view, by comparison with many other of Britain's colonies, and even some countries that she never formally colonised. Likewise there is little here about indigenous developments in the colonies Britain did control, except insofar as those developments affected or were affected by the way she controlled them. In other words, this is a Brito-centric history (the more familiar 'Anglocentric' is wrong because Scotland, Wales and Ireland played at least as great a part in the imperial project as England did, however much they may like to dissociate themselves from it now it is unfashionable);[2] defining 'imperialism' in terms of Britain's real power and influence in the world from around 1850 onwards, whether that power and influence were manifested in the formality of empire or not. It is perhaps worth adding, in order to avoid any misunderstanding, that this does not imply any disregard on my part for the ex-colonies themselves. For what it is worth, I feel considerably more empathy with many of their peoples than I do for my own country, Britain. ('Patriotism' – anybody's – is my pet aversion.) But this book is not about them. It is about British imperial*ism*, in the sense just outlined; which is not – again I should perhaps repeat – the only valid sense in which the word can be used.

Of course this raises problems. 'Imperialism' is much vaguer than 'the empire'. Its extent and limits are less definite, and for that reason open to interpretation and dispute. 'Power' cannot be measured exactly. Because it is very rarely a one-way process – you need a certain amount of compliance to give you power (or 'hegemony') – it is rarely a

straightforward quality. Two prime examples relevant to this study are trade and collaboration. The Victorians believed that trade never involved imperialism so long as it was
'free', in the sense that each party was at liberty to buy from and sell to the other:
without, that is, monopolies or other restrictions or duress. Nowadays that kind of
relationship is often counted as an imperial one *de facto*, in view of the discrepancies of
bargaining power between the two sides. (A third-world primary producer might depend
absolutely on the British market for its exports, while Britain had alternative sources of
supply.) The same argument, of course, can be extended to 'globalisation'. Collaboration
muddies the picture because it raises the question of the degree to which Britain controlled even her dependent colonies. Often she worked through native elites because she
could not dominate them completely. What kind of power did this give to them? Did it
compromise Britain's authority? What difference does all this make to the map we might
like to draw, overlying the 'red' one, of Britain's 'real' authority (or 'imperialism') in the
world? Of course Britain *was* an imperial power. None of these observations is meant to
detract from this. The degree and extent of her imperial sway are debatable, however,
once we leave the semantic security of the formal frontiers of the empire, and venture
into these more hidden, but nonetheless genuine, areas of influence and control. While the
definition of imperialism that will be used in this book is *clear*, therefore, it cannot
be *certain*. It depends on assessments made along the way, as to whether particular kinds
of relationship between Britain and other countries were dominating enough to deserve
the appellation 'imperialist', or not. Opinions can differ on this.

They are most likely to differ in the field of 'culture', which is one of the areas of
imperial history where research has expanded enormously since the first edition of this
book appeared. The idea of 'cultural imperialism' is not new. It used to be associated
particularly with Christian missionaries, whose efforts to convert the pagan (usually outside Britain, but not always) can be regarded as imperialist, in our sense, in a number of
ways. First, they were sometimes a prelude to more formal rule. The missionaries went out
initially; then the imperial state stepped in to safeguard their work. Or it could operate
more subtly. Christianisation meant westernisation, which made the converts – whether
they were formally colonised or not – easier for the West to control. Lastly, westernisation
was *itself a* form of imperialism, a way of dispossessing other peoples culturally, whether
or not any further material advantage was to be taken of this. It is this third scenario that
is the most problematical. Missionaries of course disputed that they were dispossessing
anybody; on the contrary, they were merely replacing error by 'truth'. Other kinds of
'enlightenment' can be regarded similarly. 'Freedom', 'human rights', 'rationalism', 'modernity' and so on can be seen as universal values, rather than cultural attributes. (Of course
they are often given a cultural slant.) Sometimes the assumption that these are 'merely'
cultural – exclusively European, that is – hides a kind of racism, as Jack Goody in his study
of 'modern' elements in traditional Indian culture has shown.[3] As well as this, many of
these cultural changes were clamoured for by the receiving societies, rather than being
imposed from without. People all over the world actually *wanted* technology, various kinds
of freedom, the Christian gospel, 'progress' and even (though it is hard to credit this)
McDonald's burgers. (The last are often seen as a vehicle of American 'imperialism' today.)
T. C. McCaskie has coined the word '*in*culturation' (as opposed to *ac*culturation) to
describe this.[4] That complicates the picture; particularly in relation to our chosen definition
of imperialism, in terms of domination and control.

There are other complicating factors. Even where the domination or control was
clearly there, for example, manifested in the most blatant colonial exploitation and

tyranny, it was not always a sign of 'British imperialism' in the most straightforward sense of the term. British imperialism of the 'formal' kind is usually seen in terms of 'Britain' lording it over 'the colonies': as a relationship, that is, in which all the power is on one side of the water, and the powerlessness on the other. But that is not how it usually was in reality. Often the real power on the ground belonged to the colonists, not the British government; especially the power to exploit, rob and massacre native populations, which happened deplorably frequently (it is difficult to avoid moral judgements in this field entirely) in Britain's colonial history. That was rarely part of Britain's imperial policy. Generally, in fact, her stated intention was the opposite: to protect her indigenous subjects from maverick Britons. It is possible that clashes over this were one of the causes of the American War of Independence: the imperial government's attempts to restrain the colonists from expanding further to the west, at the expense of the native Americans.[5] It was a conflict, in other words, between two different kinds of imperialism, 'British' and 'colonial'; of which the 'colonial' was, in this case, arguably the more exploitative. (It is this that makes the common American self-image as a fundamentally anti-imperialist nation at least debatable.) The same situation existed elsewhere, too. The imperialist drive was not all metropolitan. There were imperialists in the colonies too. By the same token, there were also imperial *subjects* – or their very close equivalents – living in Britain. Scottish crofters during the Highland clearances of the nineteenth century, for example, had much in common with the native Americans, far more than they did with their own imperial classes. English workers were more exploited and oppressed by those same classes than most free Australian immigrants. Imperialism was not simply the domination of one nation by another. Dominators and dominated were found on both sides of the geographical divide. If we are looking at British imperialism in terms of real – rather than merely formal – power and control, therefore, we need to take this on board; though it obviously confuses the picture enormously, and may be unsettling for those on both sides of the question who prefer their national historical myths to be more straightforward ('us' *versus* 'them').

Differences

One of the reasons for all this complexity was the peculiar nature of early British imperialism itself. It was genuinely different from other brands. Contemporary Britons insisted on this; it is another of the reasons (apart from Napoleon) why they were so reluctant to use the word to describe their activities overseas for so much of the nineteenth century, which would have invited comparisons they did not feel comfortable with. Of course there *were* comparisons to be made. Most successful empires in history have this in common: they occur in relative vacuums. One society has such an advantage or superiority over others as to make its expansion among them irresistible. The difference can be of various kinds – military, organisational, technological, economic, ideological – largely depending on the state or stage of development of human society as a whole. But it has to be marked, and qualitative. Suddenly a society makes a quantum leap ahead of those around it, making them seem weak and backward by comparison. The natural thing then is for it to expand into that space. This happened to Britain in the eighteenth and nineteenth centuries; just as it had to Rome in the first century BCE, Spain in the sixteenth century AD, and also (one imagines) the Cro-Magnons. So far, so familiar. The *nature* of Britain's leap, however, was different from these others'. It did not involve any great military superiority over her neighbours, for example, though the naval supremacy she achieved during the Napoleonic era certainly helped. The *qualitative* change was in the nature of her economy. She became the first, and for a while virtually the only, manufacturing capitalist economy in the world. It was this that powered her worldwide expansion in the nineteenth century, far ahead of all her rivals; and also *distinguished* that expansion – or 'imperialism', if it had to be called that – from all previous ones. Those were imperialisms of conquest. Britain's was one of settlement and trade. Its main agents were not the British state, but individuals and private companies. It seemed 'natural', not forced. Of course a certain myopia was involved here, as we shall be seeing, not to mention amnesia (of what had gone on in the seventeenth and eighteenth centuries); and yet there was some truth in it too. This *was* less of an empire in the old and literal sense of the word – a centrally directed *imperium* – than most others. This was why less imperial power adhered to the metropole than in those cases, and so much more to the colonists themselves.

This is not to seek to deny or minimise the imperialism that emanated from Britain in the eighteenth and nineteenth centuries in any way. Nor is it the intention to try to exonerate the British state of blame for imperialism's excesses. The colonists, while they still were colonists – before, that is, the American ones broke free – were British subjects, in nominally British territories, and under the ultimate protection of British arms; which made them the British government's responsibility. The latter should have kept them on a tighter rein. That it did not do so was a matter of choice, not necessity. The motive was to save the cost, both human and financial, of policing them properly. Behind *that* was the growing spirit of early nineteenth-century Britain that all government, including policing, should be kept to a minimum, in order to allow enterprise to thrive – the sort of enterprise that had created the colonies in the first place; which would, in truth, have been difficult to gainsay, but not literally impossible. Indeed, the war against the American rebels can be seen as an effort in this direction. Which, however, illustrates the nub of the question graphically: for in order to tame imperialism of one sort (colonial or entrepreneurial), the only solution was imperialism of another (official or paternalistic). Non-imperialism was not an option. In a world full of vacuums, the phenomenon of stronger peoples exploiting and oppressing weaker ones was inevitable. That is why there was so much imperialism in the eighteenth and early nineteenth centuries. State imperialism was only part of this, and as often working *against* the colonial sort, to try to rein it in, as with it. (We shall come across further examples of this.) This demonstrates some of the *varieties* of imperialism that coexisted, even in this one particular (British) case, some of which were hardly even compatible with each other. It is another good reason for using the word itself cautiously, and with discrimination.

This also exemplifies another important point. Imperialism, as it worked out in practice (or 'reality'), was not primarily an ideological or cultural phenomenon, but a material one. People did not go colonising – initially, at any rate – because of any ideas they may have had about glorifying Britain, for example; or bettering the world; or emulating the Romans; or about the superiority of their 'race', or religion or anything else over others'. They did it because they were *able* to (the vacuum); often because they were forced to, for example, by poverty or persecution; and – mainly – to better *themselves*, usually (though not always: *vide* the Pilgrim Fathers) in material terms. The same is true of the traders, like those of the British East India Company, who were responsible for starting off so many of Britain's other eventual colonies. A few years ago this materialist explanation of British imperialism used to be widely contested, because it was felt to be ignoble, and tarred with the neo-Marxist theory that used imperialism's 'capitalist' origins to condemn it; with the result that in the Preface to the first edition of this book I had almost to apologise for it. Today that is no longer necessary. Capitalism is respectable again. Its association with British imperialism seems obvious, and no longer a Marxist smear. Together with other very practical considerations, like security and the 'vacuum', it furnishes an adequate explanation for British eighteenth- and nineteenth-century imperialism on its own, without needing to tease out a specifically imperial or proto-imperial culture in Britain in order to account for it. This needs to be reiterated today, I think, when the essential structure of British imperialism is in danger of being obscured by more 'cultural' approaches. We need to get back to basics. Or – to take a more relativistic approach – to remind ourselves of this other way of regarding the British empire, which has at least as much validity as the culture-based one.

Of course the effect of culture was not negligible. If it had little bearing on whether or not Britain was to be imperialistic, it certainly had an impact on the way her imperialism was regarded at home, and even on the particular forms it took. Most such cultural influences were not imperialistic intrinsically, however; they sprang from other roots. Capitalism was one, creating as it did a system of values that was bound to make British imperialism more mercenary in flavour than other sorts; but also, at the same time, contributing to certain people's resistance against the *idea* of a British imperialism; and, second, provoking in other quarters of Britain's highly polyglot culture the *anti*-capitalist reaction that had a considerable influence ('paternalism') on the way the empire was ruled. Other domestic cultural traits that impacted almost as greatly were liberalism (in various forms), utilitarianism, class, evangelical Christianity and the doctrine of 'progress', among many others. Some of these were also drawn in to *justify* imperialism, after the (material) event; as in fact nearly any cultural trait or ideology can be. (Even 'anti-imperialism' can be harnessed to it, as witness the American imperialism of the turn of the twentieth century.) It was these factors that helped distinguish British expansionism – insofar as it could be so distinguished – from contemporary French imperialism, for example, or the older Spanish, or Roman; or, for that matter, Cro-Magnon. They did not indicate an imperial culture *per se*. Such a culture did emerge, towards the end of the twentieth century; but even then it was not very widespread, or deep. This at any rate is what this book argues. (Some other scholars profoundly disagree.[6]) It was also heterogeneous and inconsistent, much like the varieties of imperialism themselves. In one form, for example, it came close – extraordinarily – to pacifist internationalism. This was because of the continued dominance in British society of other cultures and value systems than any strictly empire-related one. Culture coloured British imperialism, but was not responsible for it, or significantly affected *by* it. Imperialism as *reality* was able to get by perfectly well without imperialism as *sentiment*, certainly before the end of the nineteenth century, and arguably for a while afterwards. The two should not be confused. There is an important rider to this. Things happen in history for contemporary reasons. Britain became an imperial power in the eighteenth and nineteenth centuries because of the material situation *then*. It could have happened to anyone; and did in fact happen in the nineteenth century to several other powers, albeit slightly less spectacularly, for example, Russia, France and the United States. It was President Paasikivi of Finland who admitted in 1940 that even his country *would* have been imperialist if it had been big enough.[7] It depended on circumstances, and not, for example, on nationality or culture or race. Britain was not imperialistic because she was British. It follows from that – this is the 'rider' – that Britons at other periods should not consider themselves in any way *responsible* for the imperialism of their nation's past. Modern Britons are not to 'blame' for the nineteenth-century empire, any more than most of them (anyone born after about 1925) can take any credit for resisting Hitler in the 1940s; events whose only connection with them is that they happen to have been perpetrated by people occupying the same patch of ground as they do today. This is why the present fashion of national leaders 'apologising' for their countries' past sins (right back to slavery) is so intellectually problematical, though there may be other good reasons for it. No-one living in Britain today should feel either proud or ashamed of the old empire; it had nothing at all to do with them. Present-day British imperialism, of course, is something else. Today's Britons can and should all take at least indirect responsibility for the Iraq war of 2003, for example; but not – for goodness' sake! – for the Amritsar massacre.

Difficulties

Hopefully, many readers will be feeling more confused about British imperialism now than they were before they started this book. That is good. The empire *was* a confusing entity. The biggest mistake we can make about it is to regard it as straightforward: monolithic, coherent, mono- (or even bi- or tri-) causal; the sort of thing that by any consistent moral criteria one could be absolutely 'for' or 'against'. It embraced free settlement colonies and cruelly conquered despotisms, with a range of other kinds of jurisdictions in between. Imperial*ism* (by most definitions) brings in trading and missionary stations too. The advocates of one kind of empire could hugely disapprove of the others; few early and mid-Victorian Britons, for example, were proud of having both Australia *and* India; for the simple reason that *they* saw crucial differences between them, even if some present-day commentators cannot. The motives and aims behind these various forms of British overseas expansion could also differ fundamentally. They might not even be complementary. Sometimes they clashed head-on, as when capitalist imperialists came into conflict with more aristocratic ones, who saw their imperial function as protecting their colonial wards *against* the capitalists. That is how confusing it was.

Ideologically the picture is no less so. Imperialism had no real ideology of its own. It raided others; but different ones in different circumstances. Turn-of-the-century imperialism is commonly associated with militarism, nationalism, racism and monarchism (what John MacKenzie calls the 'cluster' of values accreting to it);[8] but it was not invariably or always thus. In the mid-nineteenth century it was more often linked to the spread of British 'freedoms' (like American imperialism today); between the World Wars one important strand of it had strong anti-racist, pacifist and internationalist elements. At most times governments and people differed widely over what it did or should mean. This may be one reason why there were so few genuine '*anti*'-imperialists in Britain at any time during our period (though there were many who called themselves such). Logically it was almost impossible to be one. If you were against one kind of imperialism, it meant that you at least tolerated another, inevitably. In the mid-nineteenth century, for example, 'anti-imperialism' meant giving unscrupulous traders free rein in the world. It was a difficult choice; illustrating the vast complexity of what is often lumped together as British imperialism at this time, but really had almost no common features. Except possibly – the following chapters will argue, albeit tentatively – the underlying material base.

Notes

1 See Chapter 12.
2 See John MacKenzie, 'Scotland and the Empire', *International History Review*, 14 (1993); Keith Jeffrey (ed.), *An Irish Empire? Aspects of Ireland and the British Empire* (Manchester, 1996); David Fitzpatrick, 'Ireland and the empire', in Andrew Porter (ed.), *The Oxford History of the British Empire*, vol. III, *The Nineteenth Century* (Oxford UP, 1999); and Stephen Howe, *Ireland and Empire: Colonial Legacies in Irish History and Culture* (Oxford UP, 2000).

For an example of 'dissociation', see Tom Little in *Scotland on Sunday*, 23 November 2003, quoted in the *Guardian*, 24 November, after England's winning of the Rugby World Cup in Australia: 'I really wanted England to lose … It would be so much easier to support them if they weren't so English … Centuries of pink bits on maps have left them with an out-of-date impression of their own importance.' As if the 'pink bits' were English exclusively.
3 Jack Goody, *The East in the West* (Cambridge UP, 1996).
4 T. C. McCaskie, 'Cultural encounters: Britain and Africa in the nineteenth century', in Porter, *op. cit.*, p. 665.
5 See Fred Anderson, *Crucible of War: The Seven Years War and the Fate of the Empire in British North America, 1754–1766* (Knopf, 2000), p. xviii.
6 These themes are pursued in greater detail in my *The Absent-Minded Imperialists: The Empire in British Society and Culture* (Oxford UP, 2004).
7 J. K. Paasikivi, *Meine Moskauer Mission 1939–41* (Holsten-Verlag, 1968), p. 243. I first came across this reference in Patrick Salmon, *Scandinavia and the Great Powers* (Cambridge UP, 1997), pp. 18–19.
8 John MacKenzie, *Propaganda and Empire: The Manipulation of British Public Opinion, 1880–1960* (Manchester, 1984), p. 2.

2 An empire in all but name
The mid-nineteenth century

The world market

The term 'empire' had its origin in a Latin word associated with notions of 'command' or 'power'. Generally, however, its meaning has been a little more specialised – though not much more. It was never a definitive or generic term like 'republic' or 'democracy'. Its usage was determined more by historical accident than by semantic design. Usually it could mean one of two things. It could mean simply the country presided over or the authority exercised by a ruler who happened to be called an emperor. Or, more helpfully, it could mean the territorial possessions of a state (whose head might or might not be styled 'emperor') outside its strict national boundaries. It was in this latter sense that Britain and her overseas territories in the late nineteenth century together comprised an empire.

On the surface this empire seemed an uneven and inconsistent kind of political entity, as indeed it was. Its different constituents were united in very little apart from their common allegiance to the British Crown. Even the degree of this allegiance, the extent to which the Queen's ministers could presume on a colony's loyalty for help in a crisis, varied in practice from one part of the empire to another. There was no single language covering the whole empire, no one religion, no one code of laws. In their forms of government the disparities between colonies were immense: between the Gold Coast of Africa, for example, ruled despotically by British officials, and Canada, with self-government in everything except her foreign policy, and here London's control was only hazily defined. In between, Nigeria was ruled by a commercial company, the states of Australia by their own prime ministers, Sierra Leone by a governor, Sarawak by a hereditary English rajah, Somaliland by a commissioner responsible to India, Egypt by a consul-general, who, in theory, only 'advised' a native Egyptian cabinet, Ascension Island by a captain as if it were a ship. India was a full-blown oriental autocracy at its outer edges, but with a jumble of 'princely states' cluttering up its interior, where the local nawabs held sway under the protection of a British 'viceroy' responsible to an *empress* – Victoria, who was merely Queen of the British empire, but Empress of this separate empire within it. There was no kind of overall logic – which is chiefly why the British empire held together at all. Government was adapted to local conditions, and the British were happy with the discord of it all so long as the music went on playing.

Underneath this confusion, however, there was a kind of rationality. Fundamentally the empire – true to its derivation – was a manifestation of British power and influence, and whatever strange individual shapes they took, the colonies all shared this common characteristic, that they owed their origins in some way to British economic, political and cultural predominance in the world. This is almost a truism, but there is an important and less obvious rider to it: that the colonies were not the *only* manifestations of that predominance. Other countries outside the empire could be dominated or controlled by one means or another from Britain almost as closely as her colonies – more closely than some. In a way, Argentina was as much a British 'colony' as Canada; Egypt or even Persia more strictly controlled by Britain than Nigeria. British paramountcy was spread over a wide area. The colonies, in fact, were merely the surface outcrops of a much broader geological reef, of a wider system of authority and influence whose frontiers were not at all coterminous with the boundaries of the area painted red on the map. While the empire, therefore, may have been a manifestation of British world power, it was not by itself an accurate reflection of the extent of that power, or a helpful guide to its structure. Conversely, to seek to explain imperial history by reference only to imperial territories is like trying to account for scattered surface rock formations without digging for the connecting bedrock beneath.

The mid-Victorians themselves, or at least some of them, knew how wide their empire was spread. There was much disparaging talk of empire at the time, but generally what was objected to was a particular kind of empire – the old mercantilist relationship with colonies forced to supply Britain's industries with raw materials, forbidden to compete with her in manufactures, and prohibited from trading with other countries. The old American colonies had been in this kind of relationship to Britain, with bitter and long-remembered consequences. The apostles of the 'free trade' creed in the mid-nineteenth century favoured a more subtle kind of empire, a method by which (said a free trader in 1846), 'foreign nations would become valuable Colonies to us, without imposing on us the responsibility of governing them'.[1] The method was to dominate the world by means of a natural superiority in industry and commerce. Twenty-five years later, this had achieved for Britain what Herman Merivale called 'almost an empire, in all but name'.

> By actual possession here and there; by quasi-territorial dominion, under treaties, in other places; by great superiority of general commerce and the carrying trade everywhere, we have acquired an immense political influence in all that division of the world which lies between India and Japan.[2]

This 'informal empire' was the product of Britain's expanding economy. Its dynamism, the way it increased and multiplied the national stock over and over again, was the pride and glory of British capitalism in the mid-nineteenth century: the proof of its virtues, the excuse for its vices. It was the material groundswell beneath the early Victorians' bounding self-confidence in many fields, and beneath their ideal of 'progress'. It also took them into the wider world. Every year the industrial system devoured more raw materials and turned them into saleable commodities, and demanded yet more materials and markets; that its appetite would spread ever wider beyond Britain's national boundaries was therefore natural. 'The need of a constantly expanding market for its products,' remarked the *Communist Manifesto* in 1848, 'chases the bourgeoisie over the whole surface of the globe. It must nestle everywhere, settle everywhere, establish connexions everywhere.'[3] The result was a constant expansion of Britain's world market to match the expansion of her industrial production at home. And because her capitalism was so much more advanced than other nations – unique at the beginning of the century, still ahead by a whisker at the end – it was to Britain's economic blandishments that most of the wider world succumbed, more than to other European nations'.

At the same time, the world market was, in a way, ensnaring Britain too. The proud name she gave herself of 'workshop of the world' might have exaggerated the extent of her economic preponderance, but it did accurately indicate its nature. The way Britain prospered was by manufacturing articles for sale abroad, which her customers paid for in raw materials and food. This international division of labour suited her well, and the pulling down of the tariff barriers against food and other imports in mid-century encouraged it, as it was meant to. By 1860, the value of Britain's trade with the world had tripled in 20 years.[4] Of her visible exports in 1854–57 (measured by volume) 85.1 per cent was in finished goods, only 8.5 per cent in raw materials and 6.4 per cent in foodstuffs. Of her imports, 7.3 per cent was in finished goods, 61.2 per cent in raw materials and 31.5 per cent in foodstuffs.[5] She could not feed herself, and her industry could not function without regular shipments of raw materials from abroad. This was painfully illustrated during the American Civil War when cotton supplies were reduced and many Lancashire textile mills had to stop production. So the polarisation of Britain's trade had rendered her dependent on other countries for prosperity, almost for survival. But those other countries were also in their turn dependent upon Britain, for in many cases there was no other significant customer for their staple products. The ties of dependency therefore between Britain and her trading partners were mutual. (It was this symbiosis which many free traders believed would guarantee world peace, by making war – and the consequent rupture of vital commercial ties – clearly unprofitable and even in some cases suicidal.)

The enormous trading opportunities open to her as the first modern industrial nation, with a virtual monopoly of manufactures, encouraged Britain to concentrate on profitable foreign markets at the expense of an under-exploited domestic market. Consequently her economic involvement with the wider world was even greater than it need have been. In 1859–61, for example, she exported 63.8 per cent of the £77 million worth of cotton goods she manufactured.[6] As well as exporting goods she provided the world with carriage, brokerage, insurance and banking services, whose profits year by year blotted out the regular deficit on visible trade and produced a healthy surplus on the other side.[7] Much of this surplus Britain sent abroad again in the form of capital investments. In the 1860s, she lent half her savings abroad. The sum could well have exceeded the foreign investments of all other countries combined, and the boom had not yet by any means reached its peak.[8] In all these ways Britain became more and more entangled with the wider world.

It was a spontaneous process. The government did not have to push it, indeed it was government policy *not* to push it. Low-born commercial men were generally looked down on by the aristocrats of the Foreign Office. Even if they were swindled, they could not be sure of getting effective consular assistance. 'If persons,' said a governor of the Straits Settlements,

> knowing the risks they run, owing to the disturbed state of these countries, choose to hazard their lives and properties for the sake of large profits which accompany successful trading, they must not expect the British Government to be answerable if their speculation proves unsuccessful.[9]

And at home, governments were of the same mind. 'The traffic with half-civilised peoples,' said the Colonial Secretary sharply in 1862, 'has risks of its own, which are generally compensated by more than ordinary profits.'[10] If a trader wanted security, he should be satisfied with a smaller return. Occasionally the Foreign Office *would* step in, to secure the redemption of a defaulted debt or whatever, in the same way as it would intervene to protect British subjects abroad from any other breach of international law committed against them. There was no reason why it should make distinctions between one kind of injustice and another. But only very rarely did it do anything more positive to encourage the spread of British commerce. It did not, for example, seek commercial or financial concessions for its nationals in foreign countries, except in one or two cases where for political or strategic reasons it was concerned to try to bolster up a regime so unattractive to capital that a carrot had to be dangled in front of it to make it move. Otherwise the government left 'concession-mongering' to the Germans and French, and restricted its broader commercial activities in the diplomatic field to extending the area of free trade. Its fundamental economic aim in negotiating treaties with weaker powers was to secure for all commerce, whatever its source, a 'fair field and no favour' in their markets.[11] But of course Britain was far enough ahead of her rivals to win the prizes in most open competitions. The rules of the game were made for her. The effect therefore was the same as if her government had actively campaigned for trading and financial concessions on her behalf. She expanded economically into the world.

And she did so with an almost missionary zeal. In the mid-nineteenth century a kind of moral halo was given to international commerce by the dominant secular religion in England. For Richard Cobden, trade acted 'on the moral world as the principle of gravitation in the universe – drawing men together, thrusting aside the antagonism of race, and creed, and language, and uniting us in the bonds of eternal peace'.[12] Not all worshippers at the free trade altar would pitch it as high as this. But most English people were convinced that the building of commercial bridges between nations had a civilising, enlightening effect: sufficiently, anyway, to give a prima facie moral sanction to the merchant's activities. On the Niger river, in 1841, trade was employed deliberately by philanthropists (with government backing) as a means of regenerating the Africans. Elsewhere it was pursued for more overtly material motives, but in the happy knowledge that in this field materialism was closely in line with philanthropy, God in harness with Mammon.

Other European countries also traded and invested outside Europe, but none to anything like the same extent. The volume of their foreign business was much more modest than Britain's, and it was always chiefly confined within Europe. Britain's never was. In the 1850s, Europe accounted for not much more than one-third of her imports and exports. The rest of her trade was dispersed all over the world. There was a massive traffic between Britain and the United States (the source of most of Britain's raw cotton and latterly of much of her imported food), and another between Britain and India (a rich market for Lancashire textiles). Trade with other countries was spread much thinner, but together it made up about 30 per cent of the total. With Latin America Britain exchanged her manufactures for wool, hides, sugar, a little cotton, and a great deal of guano (used to fertilise the agricultural revolution). China supplied most of Britain's tea and silk in return for textiles and (Indian-grown) opium (Figure 2.1). From the West Indies, Britain imported sugar; from Indonesia and Malaya, sugar, coffee, tin and rubber; from Ceylon, first coffee and later tea; from Egypt, grain and cotton; from Australasia, most of her wool; and from West Africa, groundnuts and vegetable oils – the latter, made up into lubricants and soap, serving Britain's industrial revolution by oiling its machines and washing the machinists. Then there were those innumerable little trades in the China Seas and the South Pacific, carried on by not very scrupulous merchant captains in small schooners at big risks, not amounting to a great proportion of Britain's total trade, but

Figure 2.1 Commerce. Arrival of tea at the London Docks in 1868.
Source: © Classic Image/Alamy Stock Photo.

supplying certain exotic products in demand at home, and very significant in the life of the islands they traded with: lacquer wares from Japan, nutmeg and mace from the Moluccas, mother-of-pearl from Celebes, sandalwood, coconut oil and tortoise shells from Fiji, and so on. There was hardly any part of the world where British trade had not penetrated by the 1850s. This was the simplest and most common form of economic connection between Britain and foreign countries: the straightforward exchanging of goods with native middlemen on the coasts and in the ports.

Sometimes the connection went deeper. Occasionally Englishmen found that native methods of production were inadequate for their needs – supplied the commodities they wanted too dearly or in insufficient quantities; or else they felt that a new product might be cultivated in a country more profitably than its customary products. In these cases they might take a hand in the production side themselves, buying estates in tropical countries and turning them into plantations, like those in the old American South and the West Indies: growing staple crops on a large scale with native labour. By the 1850s, planting communities had sprung up in Ceylon (coffee), parts of India (tea and indigo), and elsewhere. In more temperate climates the movement of trade was accompanied by a large-scale movement of population. Well over a million people emigrated from the British Isles in the 1850s. Most went to the United States, others went to Canada, Australia, New Zealand, and a few to South Africa. Here they built up useful export trades in staple products like timber and hides and wool, backed up by ties of blood relationship and sentiment. And hard on the heels of the trader, the planter and the settler came the financier. British capital had already helped finance continental Europe's industrial take-off in the early part of the century. Now it was less urgently required in western Europe and was spreading out into the wider world, helping to build railways and other engineering works in eastern Europe, the Americas, India and Australia, and bolstering up governments in South America, the United States, Russia and the Ottoman empire. The great age of foreign investment was yet to come, but already Britain's portfolio was fat and cosmopolitan.[13]

Creeping colonialism

The mere fact that Britain had an economic interest in a country did not make that country her colony or dependency. Otherwise continental Europe and the United States would have to be regarded as colonies, which they clearly were not. On the other hand, a degree of subordination was inevitable in any economic relationship between Britain and one of her less powerful trading partners. In her own view the demands Britain made on the rest of the world were eminently reasonable. All she wanted was to be able to exchange goods with foreign countries fairly and freely. Bargains legitimately concluded must be honoured or legal redress be available. Trade should be open to every nation without discrimination. Foreign lives and property must be secure. Reasonable facilities should be available to all merchant vessels for docking and supplies. Britain was asking nothing she did not offer herself; nothing, in fact, beyond what she regarded as the normal conditions of civilised commercial intercourse. And if another country voluntarily accepted and fulfilled these requirements, as, for example, Argentina did by treaty in 1825, then to the way of thinking of the nineteenth-century free trader, the bargain between her and Britain (like a factory owner's contract with his employees) was a fair and equal one. Both sides had something to sell and something therefore to withhold if an acceptable price could not be agreed (just as an employer could withhold a job or a worker his labour if they could not agree a fair wage). But of course in neither case would the relationship between them be truly equal, because of the disparities in their bargaining positions. Usually Britain's economic reliance on her trading partners individually was less than their reliance upon her, which gave British industrialists the advantage in, for example, negotiating the prices they would pay for their purchase of raw materials. This limited the choice for Britain's trading partners and to this extent subordinated them to the British industrial machine. Their subordination was greater if they depended on London for capital. Whether or not this subordination was 'colonial' depends on the use we wish to make of that word. In one sense, Argentina's economic relationship to Britain was as 'colonial' as Australia's or Canada's. It was 'natural', not forced; both sides accepted the rules – Britain just played the game better. It did not in itself imply any political domination by Britain. It left Argentina some measure of control over the pace and direction of her economic development. And it was voluntary, agreed to by a ruling class in Argentina eagerly responsive to western demands for free trade, security of property, and the rest. Argentina was Britain's perfect satellite economy: a willing servant who did not need to be enslaved.[14]

The growth and dispersal of British trade and finance in the mid-nineteenth century did not necessarily involve any greater degree of imperial control than this. Yet it was rapidly preparing a soil on which imperialism of a more formal kind could flourish. In the first place it was multiplying the number of points in the world where an advanced industrial culture was coming into contact with cultures economically more backward. Such contact, if mishandled locally, could easily give rise to conflict. Misunderstandings were almost inevitable with communities which did not share Britain's commercial assumptions about reasonable access to markets, protection for traders, and so on, and might even be unfamiliar with western concepts of property. Either side could unwittingly offend the other's propriety, or deliberately exploit its weakness. Irritations thus engendered could escalate into more general conflicts – which might eventually provoke intervention from Britain. The chances of this happening were increasing as the areas of potential cultural friction proliferated. In the second place, Britain as a nation was becoming more and more enmeshed in the world's problems. Her commercial expansion was extending the area of her vital national interest outside her own natural boundaries and far into the world. Because she traded with them, and because to a significant extent her industrial life depended on trade with them, what happened in other parts of the world was of material concern to her, more so than to countries whose economies were more self-contained. New Orleans was as essential a part of the British imperial machine as Newcastle, Calcutta as important as Cardiff, the Cape sea-lanes to the east as vital as the Great Northern Railway. This extension of the area of Britain's national interest implied an extension of the area in which her interest might be threatened; of the area, therefore, in which her interest might have to be protected by direct intervention. And intervention could produce a more overtly colonial situation, of British political dominance or control over weaker states.

In the 1840s and 1850s, this sometimes happened, despite the Foreign Office's general reluctance to use the machinery of the state in the service of commerce. When, for example, Latin American republics violated international law by defaulting on their debts or failing to give adequate protection to British traders and their property, then Britain might intervene (if possible in co-operation with other interested powers) to safeguard her economic interests. Usually in these cases the mere threat of force was sufficient to secure the offending country's return to 'civilised' conduct, and direct British involvement in its politics thereafter was unnecessary. In any event, the Foreign Office preferred not to get involved.[15]

Elsewhere, however, a country might require stronger methods to keep it to the path of commercial straight-dealing. China had to be bombarded into submission twice between 1839 and 1860, and then deprived of her territories of Hong Kong and Kowloon, before British merchants could feel really secure there. But China was particularly stubborn in her resistance to foreign trade, and exceptionally barbarous in her conduct – imprisoning British merchants for not handing over their cargoes to be destroyed. Never mind – said Britain – that the cargoes consisted of opium whose import China had expressly forbidden; it was the principle of the thing that mattered, a clear contravention of international law.[16] In China, we have a particularly vivid example of the clash between two totally different kinds of economic cultures, leading by stages to colonial annexation. It should be said that many in Britain were deeply uneasy about this particular case. But there are other, less spectacular examples. At many places on the west coast of Africa, merchants found that the indigenous political structure was too weak to permit a stable commerce without some degree of European control. 'It may be true in one sense,' wrote Palmerston in 1860, expressing the classic mid-Victorian dilemma, 'that trade ought not to be enforced by cannon balls, but on the other hand trade cannot flourish without security, and that security may often be unattainable without the exhibition of physical force.'[17] Usually the force – in this instance, the Royal Navy's anti-slavery squadron – was kept out of sight, a few miles to sea, to act only when called on 'to rescue traders, coerce African rulers, or compel the signature of commercial treaties'.[18] Both traders and officials preferred this arrangement to a more formal colonial one because it was cheaper. It was not always easy, however, to abstain completely from formal control. For some

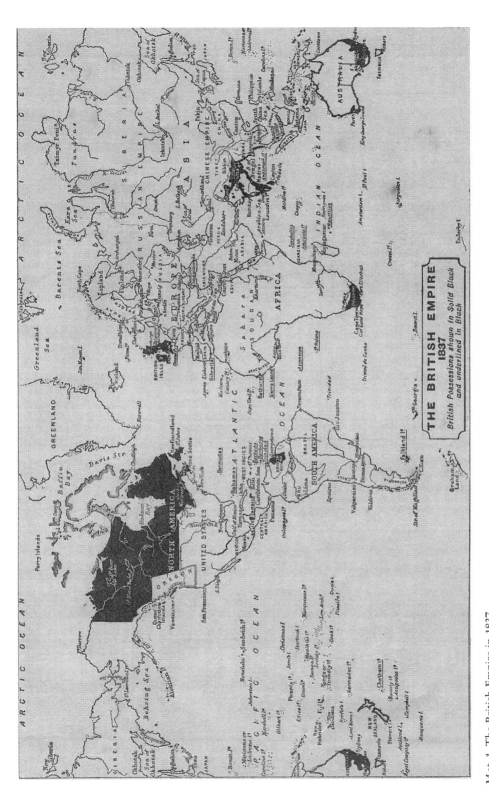

Map 1 The British Empire in 1837

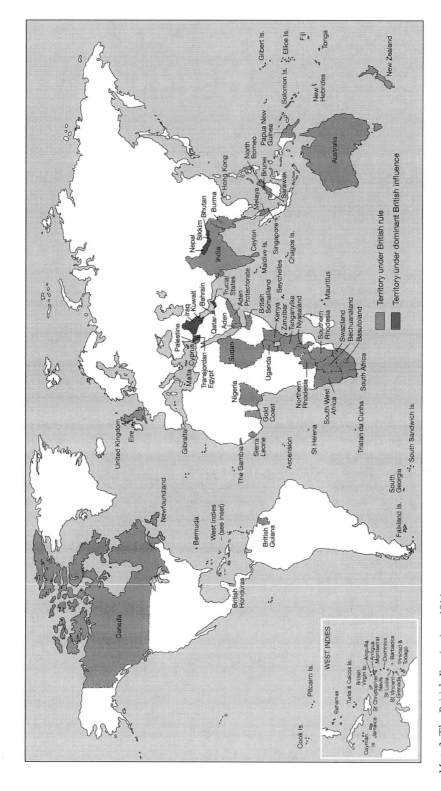

Map 2 The British Empire in c.1914

Gilbert Is.
Ellice Is.
Fiji
Tonga
New Zealand
New Hebrides
Solomon Is.
Papua New Guinea
North Borneo
Brunei
Sarawak
Australia
Hong Kong
Melaya
Singapore Is.
Chiagos Is.
Ceylon
Maldive Is.
Seychelles
Mauritius
Bhutan
Sikkim
Nepal
Burma
India
British Somaliland
Kenya
Zanzibar
Tanganyika
Nyasaland
Southern Rhodesia
Swaziland
Bechuanaland
Basutoland
South Africa
Kuwait
Bahrain
Qatar
Trucial States
Aden
Aden Protectorate
Iraq
Palestine
Transjordan
Egypt
Sudan
Uganda
Nigeria
Gold Coast
Northern Rhodesia
South West Africa
Malta
Cyprus
United Kingdom
Eire
Gibraltar
The Gambia
Sierra Leone
Ascension
St Helena
Tristan da Cunha
South Georgia
South Sandwich Is.
Falkland Is.
British Guiana
British Honduras
Bermuda
West Indies – (see inset)
Newfoundland
Canada
Pitcairn Is.
Cook Is.

Territory under British rule
Territory under dominant British influence

WEST INDIES

Bahamas
Turks & Caicos Is.
British Virgin Is.
Anguilla
Antigua
Montserrat
Dominica
St Christopher Nevis
St Lucia
St Vincent
Barbados
Grenada
Trinidad & Tobago
Cayman Is.
Jamaica

years past the old-established British settlements on the west coast (Bathurst on the Gambia river, the colony of Sierra Leone, the Gold Coast forts and the more recent settlement of Lagos) had shown a tendency to extend their authority and influence inland, by what seemed to be a natural process of frontier encroachment. Governors found that in order to safeguard their settlements and protect the lives of traders who ventured out from them, they had to reach some kind of *modus vivendi* with the adjacent African states. By a mixture of force and diplomacy they did so. On the Gold Coast, the Fante and Ashanti were gently persuaded to accept a form of British suzerainty or protection in the 1830s and early 1840s by the tactful energy of Governor George Maclean.[19] Similar extensions of British commitments took place in Lagos and Sierra Leone. By 1860, a general pattern had been established on the west coast between the Gambia and the Niger: general British paramountcy backed by the contingent strength of the Royal Navy, hardening here and there into areas of indirect influence around coastal spots of direct control.

The pattern was similar elsewhere. In East Africa there was not the same problem with British traders, because there was scarcely any British trade. But still the area was important to Britain's general commercial and strategic interests in the Indian Ocean, and it was to defend those interests against French incursions that she extended her 'informal empire' there. This time it was done, more tidily than in the west, by backing the expansionist ambitions in the area of a single Arab collaborator, the Sultan of Muscat and Zanzibar.[20] In the Malay peninsula, a very unwilling British East India Company found it had to intervene on more than one occasion to protect its trading settlements of Penang, Malacca and Singapore from the effects of native power struggles in adjoining territories. The result, again, was political domination (by treaty) over large areas inland.[21] The island of Labuan, just off the Borneo coast, was annexed in 1846 to make the eastern sea-lanes safe for Britain (and put in the charge of a governor, James Brooke, who was already building up a curious little empire of his own in Sarawak on the mainland). New Zealand (1840) and Natal (1848) were annexed in order to contain friction between British settlers, rival European claimants and the indigenous inhabitants.[22] And in the Near and Middle East, where her commercial and strategic interests were continually being threatened from Russia, Britain's involvement already went far beyond the normal exchange of goods between nations, with treaties, commercial agreements, financial loans and British 'advisers' in key positions.[23] In all this there was no deliberate intention on the part of the Foreign or Colonial Offices to colonise the world in order to make things easier for the British capitalist – rather the reverse. Britain would have much preferred to extend her trade without extending her political control. But things seemed to be taken out of her hands. The area of British economic interest in one or two places hardened into areas of overt colonial or near-colonial domination, by a natural process, almost, of reaction and counter-reaction. Victorians grumbled at the responsibilities thus incurred, but they had about as much right to complain as a reluctant father-to-be. They did not want what happened, but they had wanted the thing which had made it happen in the first place.[24]

The old empire

By the mid-1850s, this process of 'creeping colonialism' had not yet gone very far. Most countries made perfectly satisfactory trading partners with little or no persuasion; the sea-lanes between them and Britain were amply secured by the general supremacy of the Royal Navy. Even so, Britain had a considerable formal empire in the 1850s. It had little to do with her contemporary needs and interests, having been inherited from a previous age when those interests were different. The British West Indies had their origin in a now defunct system of Atlantic trade and a few long-forgotten naval victories. Canada had been secured for Britain by a famous battle in 1759 which the British probably would not have bothered to fight 100 years later (Map 3).

Australia had been taken in the late eighteenth century with less fuss than Canada, mainly because no-one else wanted it (Map 4). The European settlement in South Africa originated in a musty religious quarrel of 200 years before, which few remembered now except the settlers themselves. British India had come into being through an earlier manifestation of 'creeping imperialism', and the cavalier empire-building of a few free-lance adventurers like Clive in the eighteenth century. Other colonies had come as booty from the French revolutionary and Napoleonic wars. These were the largest units of the old empire. It was not a negligible inheritance.

The formal empire posed a constant dilemma to the mid-Victorians. At the time it had been seized it had seemed a good idea, but now it was difficult to justify it from anyone's point of view. Opinions differed as to whether or not it should be retained. For those who said 'no,' the colonies were still tainted by the mercantilist system which had spawned them. Richard Cobden believed they were wasteful: expensive in men and money, a burden therefore to the taxpayer, and affording no reciprocal economic benefit, for trade would continue with them whether they were British or not. (This was the main lesson learnt from the loss of the thirteen colonies.) He maintained that the possession of colonies was detrimental to peace, because it provoked jealousies among other European powers and wars within their frontiers (but, as it happened, so did free trade). Colonies were persisted in, said Cobden, only to enable the English upper classes to find jobs for their younger sons as governors and generals. In logic – the logic of the market, at any rate – there was a lot to be said for this view.

The Cobdenites, however, did not have it all their own way. This was because they were never actually in charge in Britain, however much they dominated the terms of the current debate. Cobden himself was always a dissident, never a member of the ruling establishment, even at this period of greatest apparent triumph for the free trade cause he had so ably led. It may have been that triumph which misled contemporaries – and later historians – as to the real extent of the industrial capitalist influence in mid-Victorian politics, which was always far less than many of them assumed. There were no industrial capitalists in any cabinet before 1877, for example (if we can call W. H. Smith *industrial*); and no majority of them in the House of Commons at any time.[25] There were two main reasons for this. One was that industrial capitalism still did not dominate British *society*, either, but only parts of it: certain industries in certain – mainly provincial – regions, with the rest of the country given over to agriculture, money-making, the professions, and very backward trades.[26] The other is that, even if industrial capitalists *had* been in a position to dominate politics, they would not have wanted to, partly because they did not have the time (running factories was busy work), and partly because they were not greatly impressed by politics in any case. Government was an incubus on wealth creation, so why join in? That left the field to other classes of men. Usually they were broadly sympathetic to the industrial capitalists' demands, but for reasons of their own. Other reasons of their own produced quite substantial modifications of the classic Cobdenite pattern, especially in the realm of imperial policy: partly because *foreign* affairs – directed exclusively by aristocrats – were the least susceptible of all areas of government business to pressure from Cobden and his ilk.[27]

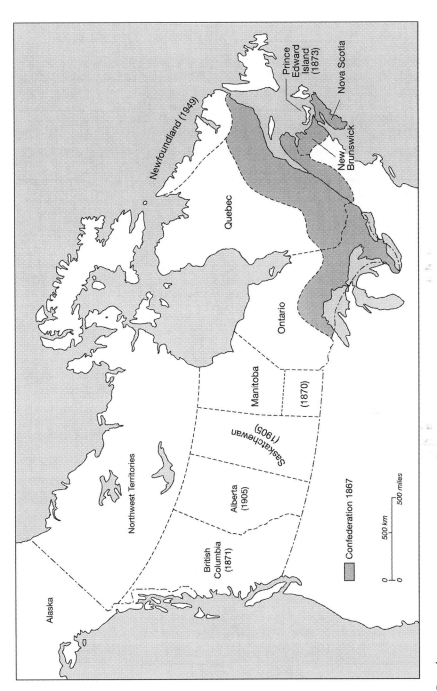

Map 3 Canada
Source: After McIntyre, W. D., *The Commonwealth of Nations* (University of Minnesota Press, 1977, p. 43). Copyright © 1977 by the University of Minnesota.

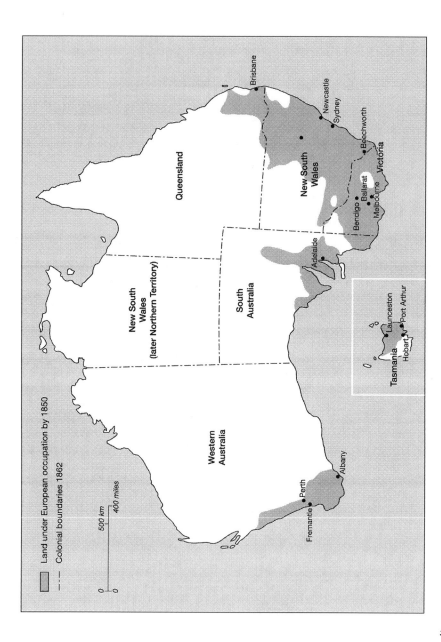

Map 4 Australia
Source: After Marshall, P. J. (ed.), *The Cambridge Illustrated History of the British Empire* (Cambridge University Press, 1996, p. 37). © Cambridge University Press 1996, reprinted with permission of Cambridge University Press via PLS Clear.

This was to persist. The 1850s were probably the time when Britain came closest to being dominated by the manufacturing interest; but even that was not *very* close. The real rulers of the country even then – and they changed very little thereafter – were the southern English upper classes, large landowners, and respectable professional folk. Some of them were also capitalists, but emphatically not of the manufacturing sort. The prejudice against the latter among nineteenth-century 'society' is well known.[28] Finance was different: 'cleaner', both literally and – in this generally honourable age – morally; and so a pursuit a 'gentleman' could dabble in.[29] Most of Britain's rulers did. It was this that gave many of them their personal interest in free trade, which served the export of capital as well as it was supposed to serve the export of goods. But they also had other interests. Their roots and upbringing made them less enamoured of what Thomas Carlyle had called the 'cash nexus' as a determinant of every human relationship than the Bounderbys of the industrial North appeared to be;[30] more mindful of *social obligations*, for example, towards both their inferiors and their kin. Colonies could not just be regarded in a short-term, commercial light. Other factors had also to be taken on board.

One was the *defence* of Britain's commerce, which – argued Lord John Russell in 1850 – required a rather longer view than the Cobdenites' strictly bookkeeping one. Many of Britain's colonies gave 'harbours and security' to her trade, which were 'most useful in times of peace, but ... absolutely necessary in time of war'. That was fair enough, one would think; though possibly not quite enough to justify the number and extent of some of Britain's possessions in the world. A couple of harbours on the North Atlantic run might well be valuable, for example; half a continent and half a hundred islands were not. Elsewhere, however, other parts of the empire might be made highly serviceable to the new pattern of British trade. Cape Colony was a vital refuelling and re-provisioning post for merchant vessels on the long voyage round to their eastern markets. India was even more indispensable, in other ways. It was said that in the past profits from the Indian trade (as well as the slave trade)[31] had provided the spare capital to finance Britain's industrial revolution. Now that revolution was under way India provided it with a vast market for its cotton manufactures, the feeble competition of her own old-established handweaving industry collapsing as her foreign rulers refused it adequate protection by tariffs. In 1850, nearly one-fifth of Britain's exported cotton goods went to India.[32] Outside the United States and possibly Germany, there was no single country with which Britain did more trade. In addition, India furnished Britain with a base from which she could exploit the rest of the Far East – an estate on which to cultivate the opium for the China trade, for example, and a vast barracks which not only quartered troops, but also produced them, like a self-replenishing cup. As the ultimate guarantor of Britain's power in the east, the Indian Army was vital[33] and there could be no Indian Army – or any of these other advantages – without political control over the place.

The other older colonies could not claim the same degree of utility or adaptability to contemporary needs. They appeared uneasily irrelevant to the new structure of British world power, and to many people at the time it seemed surprising that they were still British possessions at all. Canada was a case in point. 'Any man of sense,' the *Edinburgh Review* had said in 1825, 'knows that Canada must, at no distant period, be merged in the American republic.'[34] It did not happen, partly because the Canadians fiercely resisted it; and partly because Britain was able to accommodate their hankering for self-government within an increasingly flexible imperial structure. In January 1848, Nova Scotia was granted responsible government, followed in March the same year by the Province of Canada, and a little later by Prince Edward Island (1851), Newfoundland (1854) and New Brunswick (1855). If they had wanted to rebel now, the Canadians – at least those of British ancestry – had very little to rebel against. In the other settlement colonies Britain loosened the reins in the same way, and retained their allegiance. All the Australian colonies except Western Australia had some degree of responsible government by 1860. So did New Zealand. Cape Colony was given representative (but not responsible) government in 1853. All this looked like 'decolonisation', along Cobdenite lines; and was, in a way. Some people assumed it would lead to entire separation, *à la* United States, eventually. Lord Derby, the Conservative leader, said in 1854 that he 'deeply regretted' this, 'though in the course of time I anticipate it, as the natural result of the growth and progress of democratic principles'.[35] But it was also a way of *retaining* the colonies, and done with that purpose in view. These people – Canadians, Australians, New Zealanders, Cape Colonists – were (most of them) Britons' kith and kin. Blood was thicker than anaemic free marketers took account of. It was also a source of power and influence. 'The possession of a number of steady and faithful allies, in various quarters of the globe,' wrote the third Earl Grey, Russell's Colonial Secretary, 'will surely be admitted to add greatly to the strength of any nation.'[36] Later on scarcely anyone doubted this. Of course, said Benjamin Disraeli, scathingly, in 1863, 'Professors and rhetoricians' would always be able to find reasons for getting rid of the colonies; 'but you are not going, I trust, to leave the destinies of the British empire to prigs and pedants'. Ordinary people knew that 'the best mode of preserving wealth is power', which came with colonies.[37] There was also their value as settlements for emigrants, soaking up the labour surpluses that British capitalism – puzzlingly, to free market zealots – continued to throw up. A man called Edward Gibbon Wakefield campaigned on behalf of them along these lines for years.[38] There was never any danger in the nineteenth century that this kind of colony would ever be given up.[39]

For a time it looked as though Britain's Caribbean possessions might be going the same, devolutionist way. By the mid-nineteenth century, most West Indian islands had legislative assemblies modelled on the British Parliament: lively, independent-minded and with impressive pedigrees, suggesting that, as elsewhere, the effective transfer of power there to European colonists had already taken place, or would shortly do so. But appearances were deceptive here. In the other colonies the recipients of responsible government – the white settlers – were clearly the dominant class within their own societies, economically as well as politically and militarily. Their political control was backed by financial stability and strength. In the West Indies this was not so. The sugar plantation industry on which the European settlers depended for wealth had for some years now been in decline, unable to adapt itself to the new conditions of free (as opposed to slave) labour and free trade forced on it by Britain in the 1830s and 1840s (though the decline had originated long before). Many planters abandoned their estates – or had them confiscated in lieu of debts – and returned 'home' to England. A rival agriculture to the plantations sprang up, as ex-slaves set up as independent proprietors on vacant lands, so creating new communities outside the purview of, and in continuous friction with, the old ruling classes who wanted their labour. The planters who remained to struggle on in the islands found their dominance there seriously threatened. Wealthy 'men of colour' were infiltrating their assemblies, and there was no way for the white planters to stop them short of abrogating their ancient constitutional 'freedoms' and ruling through a white oligarchy. So if the Colonial Office *had* been bent on 'responsible government' for the Caribbean, they could have given it only to parliamentary assemblies of mixed race, or to oligarchies chosen on frankly racial lines. The former could not be entertained. Responsible government, said the Duke of Newcastle in another context, was 'only applicable to colonists of the English race'.[40] At best, a coloured parliament (like a democratic House of Commons in England) would be a very unpredictable polity; there was no precedent, no way of saying how it would behave. The other alternative neither the humanitarians in England nor the government's own good sense would allow. No such tyranny by a handful of incompetent bankrupts over an alienated population would be off its hands for very long. Very soon the settlers would be back clinging to Whitehall's skirts for protection. The settlers themselves were aware of their weakness. It needed just a jolt in the 1860s to have them gladly give up their legislative independence for the cosy security of direct British rule.[41]

Quite apart from these material dangers, there were also Britain's moral responsibilities to bear in mind: not only in the West Indies, but in every other one of Britain's more 'primitive' possessions overseas. This was another reason the third Earl Grey gave for hanging on to them in 1853:

> I conceive that, by the acquisition of its Colonial dominions, the Nation has incurred a responsibility of the highest kind, which it is not at liberty to throw off. The authority of the British Crown is at this moment the most powerful instrument, under Providence, of maintaining peace and order in many extensive regions of the earth, and thereby assists in diffusing amongst millions of the human race, the blessing of Christianity and civilisation.[42]

Patronising and arrogant that may have been; but there is no reason to suppose that it was not genuine, or even possibly true. It stemmed from Grey's and the others' aristocratic roots. Aristocrats – the best of them, at any rate – believed they had duties to the lower orders of humanity. They had exercised those duties in Britain for centuries, looking after their peasants and workers in ways that the new breed of free market individualist had no time for at all. But then, as we have seen, the new breed was not in control in the 1850s. Gentlemen were. It was they – more than the free market *aficionados* – who determined, in particular, how colonies should be *ruled*.

Native policy

Once it had been accepted that a territory was a colony, and would remain a colony for some time to come, it had to be decided what should be done with its people. Where the people were mostly white, or where a minority of whites was economically dominant (as in South Africa), the main line of policy was clear: progress towards self-government. But for the non-whites in these countries, and even more for colonies where large-scale European settlement was impracticable, the problem was not so straightforward. At best, 'coloured' people were thought not to be ready for parliamentary self-government yet; at worst, they were thought to be incapable of it. In either case their needs were felt to be fundamentally different from those of whites. Decisions regarding them were categorised distinctively as 'native policy'. Native policy rarely went far beyond the bounds prescribed by pragmatic convenience – by national self-interest; but within these bounds there was scope for variation. There were in fact very wide variations, in the 1850s, between native policies in the different colonial territories.

India was in a category of her own. Despite the fact that on the surface she was governed by a commercial company, and not by the state, Britain's relationship with her was particularly close. We have seen how valuable she had become to Britain. The reverse was also thought to hold true. Britain was seen as the only sure guarantee of internal stability and unity in India; without the British holding the ring between rival religious groups, the country would probably disintegrate into bloodshed. On both sides this mutual dependence was deepening. Yet it was some time before English people came to recognise it, or to admit it. In the early nineteenth century they saw themselves not as permanent masters of India, but as temporary foster-parents, holding her 'in trust' for a self-governing future.[43] This sense of 'trusteeship' was far more positive and developed here than in the other British colonies. It is in connection with India that the idea of Britain's 'civilising mission' to other races first really takes hold. It began in the first decades of the nineteenth century. Previously the agents of the British East India Company – who governed India under charter from the Crown – had not considered it to be part of their duties to take constructive steps towards the 'regeneration' of the Indians. Many of them respected them and their way of life too much to feel that they needed regenerating. Even where change was needed, they insisted that it should be applied sensitively and tolerantly. There seemed no point in provoking the Indians unnecessarily, and endangering the Company's own position. Their attitude was well expressed in this statement by a governor of Bombay, John Malcolm, in 1826:

> The most important of the lessons we can derive from past experience is to be slow and cautious in every procedure which has a tendency to collision with the habits and prejudices of our native subjects. We may be compelled by the character of our government to frame some institutions, different from those we found established, but we should adopt all we can of the latter into our system ... our internal government ... should be administered on a principle of humility not pride. We must divest our minds of all arrogant pretensions arising from the presumed superiority of our own knowledge, and seek the accomplishment of the great ends we have in view by the means which are best suited to the peculiar nature of the objects ... That time may gradually effect a change, there is no doubt; but the period is as yet distant when that can be expected; and come when it will, to be safe or beneficial, it must be ... the work of society itself. All that Government can do is, by maintaining the internal peace of the country, and by adapting its principles to the various feelings, habits, and character of its inhabitants, to give time for the slow and silent operation of the desired improvement, with a constant impression that every attempt to accelerate this end will be attended with the danger of its defeat.[44]

This was the ideal – or anti-ideal – until the early nineteenth century. But it was never an easy doctrine to implement. Too often the vagaries of Indian custom stood directly in the path of administrative or commercial efficiency, and not all governors had Malcolm's tolerance and patience. In 1793, for example, Lord Cornwallis imposed an English landownership system on Bengal in order to facilitate the collection of revenues. The old school held out as far as they could against this new trend. Sir Thomas Munro, a governor of Madras, complained that 'Englishmen are as great fanatics in politics as Mahomedans in religion. They suppose that no country can be saved without English institutions.'[45] But by now the political 'Mahomedans' were receiving powerful backing in England from evangelical Christians and radical liberals who looked on Munro, Malcolm and the rest as blatant reactionaries, callously tolerating superstition and ignorance where they might be spreading truth and enlightenment. Their confidence in their own particular brands of truth and enlightenment made this seem a betrayal of trust. Their aim, by contrast with the old school's, was radical social change, the total Europeanisation of the subcontinent. William Wilberforce saw this as 'the greatest of all causes' – more important even than his beloved abolition of slavery. 'Let us endeavour,' he said,

> to strike our roots into the soil by the gradual introduction and establishment of our own principles and opinions; of our laws, institutions, and manners; above all, as the source of every other improvement, of our religion, and consequently of our morals.

European laws and institutions, he said, were self-evidently superior to those of Asia, and British ones even more so; they could 'predict with confidence' that when India had been made to exchange its 'dark and bloody superstitions' for 'the genial influence of Christian light and truth', then civil order and security and prosperity would automatically follow, and the Indians would be eternally 'bound ... by the ties of gratitude to those who have been the honoured instruments of communicating them'.[46] The historian Thomas Babington Macaulay, a Law member on the Supreme Council of India, plotted the practical details of the new course. The way to anglicise India, he said, was first to produce a middle class educated in English ways, 'who may be interpreters between us and the millions whom we govern – a class of persons Indian in colour and blood, but English in tastes, in opinions, in morals, and in intellect'. They would be the agents of cultural dissemination. One of the things they would learn and disseminate would be European ideas of political liberty. Macaulay was not afraid to face the implications of this. The 'public mind of India,' he said in 1833 in the House of Commons,

> having become instructed in European knowledge ... may, in some future age, demand European institutions. Whether such a day will ever come I know not. But never will I attempt to avert or retard it. Whenever it comes, it will be the proudest day in English history.[47]

So from the mid-1830s until the governor-generalship of Lord Dalhousie in the early 1850s, the 'reformation' of India was begun. Her land and tax systems, her civil laws, her administration, her higher education, all were moulded in a new, more English image. And during these years too, a new class of Indians was created to Macaulay's specifications: brought up to reject their traditional ways of life, and take on instead the character of middle-class Englishmen. The result was gratifying: a class of men who knew more about English literature and history than most Englishmen themselves, and who admired Britain, 'the bringer of light to the east,' says one commentator, 'more fervently than that country has ever been admired, except by itself, before or since.'[48] The scheme was working famously.

In India, as in every other colony, the room for humanitarian manoeuvre was strictly limited by economic and social realities. Plans for the 'regeneration' of the Indian could not easily have been implemented if they had run counter to dominant European interests there. The champions of the new policy were fortunate that India's particular economic relationship to Britain was one which favoured their schemes. Unlike neighbouring Ceylon, profitable by virtue of its plantation-grown coffee, where the most urgent 'native problem' was how to get more labour for the plantations, or Java, where the Dutch made their profits by squeezing as much tribute as they could from the natives, in India, the British made their profits chiefly by *selling* things to the natives. In theory, therefore, because (in Macaulay's words) 'to trade with civilised men is infinitely more profitable than to govern savages',[49] it followed that it was in Britain's interest to 'civilise' them. Yet even within the limits prescribed by economic self-interest, the standards of probity and duty maintained by India's British rulers in the first half of the nineteenth century were remarkably high. Nominally, political authority was in the hands of a commercial company – an arrangement which in British colonial history has not always been consistent with beneficent trusteeship. The East India Company, however, was unusual in having at this time an administrative structure which clearly separated its commercial from its political functions, and made the political side answerable to higher ideals than economic gain. Since the 1780s, administrators had not been permitted to own land or conduct trade in India, and hence were prevented from having material interests which might interfere with their impartiality. In 1833, the Company lost its commercial side entirely. And its intentions thereafter generally adhered to the principle laid down by Parliament:

> that the interests of the Native subjects are to be consulted in preference to those of Europeans, whenever the two come in competition; and that therefore the Laws ought to be adapted rather to the feelings and habits of the natives than to those of Europeans.[50]

European capitalists complained that the Company was prejudiced against them.[51] Certainly, they were not allowed the scope for exploitation in India that they received elsewhere. A tradition grew up among the administrators of dedication to native Indian interests, as they saw them – the interests of the vulnerable, illiterate masses – which was to continue right through the years of the raj. It was a *very feudal* view; but then this was the British class most of India's new masters came from. And as guardians of this tradition, they managed to a great extent to insulate themselves against contrary pressures from outside, even from their political masters in London. The result was that British India became something more than a mere appendage of British power; it became an empire in its own right with a will of its own. A strange kind of parasitic nationalism developed among her rulers, based on a loyalty not to Britain, and certainly not to the British in India, but to India herself, or rather their own special conception of India and their duties to her. (We are describing the ideal here, of course. In practice it could work out differently.) As well as economic and social policies it evolved strategic, foreign, even colonial policies of its own, sometimes pressed against the wishes of the metropolitan country.[52] Anglo-India was by no means as docile a satellite as the English would have liked.[53]

Elsewhere, official native policy was a good deal more negative. In the case of the white-dominated colonies, the British government, in granting self-determination to them, usually retained in their own hands the ultimate responsibility for their indigenous populations. Partly this was because these colonies were not yet in a position to defend themselves effectively against serious domestic unrest; if they provoked native rebellions, British troops would be called in to settle things, and it seemed impolitic to allow colonists to make messes which they would not have to clear up themselves. But there were humanitarian influences at work too. 'It was,' said the Duke of Newcastle in 1858,

> one of the paramount duties of a good Government, in carrying out colonisation, to interfere as far as possible to prevent those cruelties and horrors that had been perpetuated in the early days of our Colonies where there were a number of aborigines.[54]

In New Zealand and South Africa, such interference was frequently required, and fitfully provided. Most mid-Victorian colonial secretaries had a genuine sense of 'trusteeship' towards the indigenous races of the empire. If they were not altogether successful in fulfilling their trusteeship obligations, it was for two main reasons. First, there was a general sense of impotence when it came to interfering in a self-governing colony's affairs against the wishes of its white inhabitants. 'We have no power to enforce' was the constant complaint,[55] meaning that if a colony was really determined to resist, then intervention could involve disproportionate effort and expense for a government department constantly being reminded of the need for economy and colonial self-sufficiency by a parochial and penny-pinching Parliament at home. The Colonial Office was never free from this feeling of ineffectualness in white-dominated colonies, as we shall see. Second, in the Colonial Office, there was no settled idea of what the goal of native trusteeship should be. Some (the Duke of Newcastle was one) believed that races like the Amerindians were on their way to eventual extinction, and that the aim of trusteeship was merely to ensure a gentle euthanasia. A New Zealand humanitarian said, with reference to the Maoris in 1856, that 'Our plain duty, as good, compassionate colonists, is to smooth down their dying pillow.'[56] It was not always seen in such negative and pessimistic terms, yet the Colonial Office did not have any more constructive plans for the natives in its care. If anything, it regarded their situation as being essentially no different from that of the working classes at home. It was out of the question that they rule themselves; they must be law-abiding and orderly, and work hard when required, for hard work would produce general prosperity. Yet there was also a Whiggish feeling in the Colonial Office that natives should not be left entirely at the mercy of those who wished to exploit their labour, but protected against the grosser abuses of European power. Beyond that, it was up to the missionaries to 'improve' them in whatever way seemed appropriate to them; the Colonial Office would allow them room to work. Overall its role was that of a referee, keeping the ring between the 'improvers' of the native and his exploiters.

The 'improvers' of the natives had very definite ideas about how they should be improved, based on their conception of the demands of their own religion. Christianity is one of the few proselytising religions of the world. At times, its proselytising aspect has been neglected by those whose Christian faith was merely a matter of social convention, or a mark of divine favour, or a licence for the slaughter of non-believers; but in nineteenth-century Britain, there were those whose faith was stronger and whose attitude to those who did not share it was more generous. Convinced of the literal truth of a 2,000-year-old story which appears on the surface highly improbable, and not merely of its truth but also of its exclusive validity and its universal significance, they had for years been trying to persuade the rest of the world to accept it too. It was an uphill task, for the people they preached to already had their own ideas about spiritual matters, and people do not easily abandon their old familiar myths for someone else's. The Christian missionaries did not make it easy for them. They made few allowances for the fact that the social and intellectual environments they found themselves in were totally different from those which had nurtured, or been nurtured by, the particular doctrines they were promulgating. They saw the difference, but they would not admit that it necessitated any adaptation of the doctrine to fit the new environment, for Christianity was an absolute truth whose pure milk could not be diluted for the sake of expediency. If the doctrine could not be altered, the environment must be.

Hence, like Macaulay in India, missionaries tended to favour radical social change. (For this reason, the old pre-Macaulay East India Company had excluded them from its dominions.) They favoured change not only in spiritual matters, or of customs clearly inconsistent with their own Christian morality like human sacrifice and polygamy, but also in a wide range of purely secular matters. Many of them regarded any deviation from European norms, in any field of activity, as a deviation from standards of civilised morality, and they sought to replace native customs all along the line with western ones. Hence the paraphernalia of blouses and tea parties and Methodist hymnals which went along with mission stations and their converts, as 'tokens of civilisation'; and hence also the emphasis placed by many missionaries on the twin blessings of Christianity *and commerce* as the path to salvation for the savage. Partly this Eurocentric attitude arose from an over-simple evolutionary anthropology, which assumed that the stages of development for all peoples took identical forms, and European civilisation was the highest form; partly it was due to an explicit belief that western civilisation and progress were divinely ordained, God's reward for Christian effort. But more often it was the result simply of a failure of imaginative sympathy, which in those early days was not surprising. In Africa and India and the South Seas, there was plenty to shock people whose sheltered upbringing in Britain had taught them what was 'proper', but not that notions of propriety are largely relative. Its total contrast with the stability and prosperity they had left at home was likely to reinforce their regard for European customs and values. Their Christian compassion for the people they were among made them want to strive for their total salvation. And their vocation as missionaries demanded that they do so.

Cultural imperialism

As well as being the main agency of 'native trusteeship' within most British colonies, the missionary movement can also be seen as another aspect of that general extension of western influence in the world outside the boundaries of formal empires, whose commercial and financial aspects have been described already. The British churches exploded into missionary activity abroad at about the same time as British industry exploded into the world market, on the crest of the same wave of national dynamism and self-confident expansionism which came with the industrial revolution and the triumph of 'progress'. Missionaries tried to go everywhere, though they were rigidly excluded from some countries, like Japan and Korea, and made very unwelcome in others – in the New Hebrides they were killed and eaten, in Madagascar, their converts were buried alive.[57] Their impact was mixed. Missionaries required from their converts not only a change of heart on matters concerned with the divinity, but also a change of life-style: the abandonment of traditional everyday customs and the adoption of new ones. Because their demands were pitched so high, their progress was usually slow, especially among peoples already wedded to a great religious tradition like Buddhism or Islam. But for this very reason where they did make progress – usually among minority groups, outcasts and animists – their impact on a society was the more disruptive. It was difficult for a native African or Indian villager to become a Christian and remain a villager: the usual corollary of conversion (except where entire communities were involved) was social alienation. New communities of converts gathered around mission stations, outside the authority of the traditional rulers, inevitably appearing as threats to that authority, rallying points for disaffected subjects. Mission schools taught their pupils to despise the practices of their parents, not always explicitly, but their parents were bound to appear weak and primitive against the wonders being revealed in the white man's books (Figure 2.2).

Figure 2.2 'Opening up' Africa. A missionary brings light to the heathen.
Source: © Chronicle/Alamy Stock Photo.

'Educated natives' affected an air of superiority and aped European middle-class manners in a way which was offensive to their less fortunate brethren. In these ways, tensions were set up between the old traditional cultures and the representatives of the new, even when no interference with local politics was intended by the missionaries. Where there *was* direct interference, the disruption could be worse, with missionaries openly siding with rebels against a ruler, or with one ruler against another, or with a whole native population, perhaps, against Arab slavers or European exploiters.

It was not only the missionary who was trying to change the natives. The European planter was trying to induce them to work steady hours for wages, which threatened their established way of living and working. The respectable trader was trying to get them to change their pattern of agricultural production to meet new market demands. The less respectable trader was selling them guns which altered delicately poised balances of power and expanded the scale of wars. New values, new products, new diseases, occasionally new rulers were being foisted on their people; sometimes whole economies were being remoulded to complement Europe's – to supply her manufacturing industries and attract her capital. Britain's silent ambassadors were ubiquitous: machines made in Oldham and Rotherham, textiles woven in Bradford and Manchester, engine-drivers trained at Crewe, capital saved up by Essex country vicars, theologies learnt at Oxford, manners acquired in Kensington, diseases contracted in Soho. And the natural consequence of this economic and cultural onslaught was friction, pained reactions against it from the native, of which the most famous example was the Indian 'Mutiny' of 1857.

Notes

1 B. Semmel, *The Rise of Free Trade Imperialism* (Cambridge UP, 1970), p. 8.
2 W. D. McIntyre, *The Imperial Frontier in the Tropics, 1865–75* (Macmillan, 1967), p. 11.
3 K. Marx, *The Manifesto of the Communist Party* (1959 edn, Foreign Languages Publishing House), p. 50.
4 B. R. Mitchell and P. Deane, *Abstract of British Historical Statistics* (Cambridge UP, 1962), p. 283.
5 W. Schlote, *British Overseas Trade from 1700 to the 1930s* (Blackwell, 1952), pp. 53, 71.
6 P. Deane and W. A. Cole, *British Economic Growth, 1688–1959* (Cambridge UP, 1962), p. 187.
7 A. Imlah, *Economic Elements in the Pax Britannica: Studies in British Foreign Trade in the Nineteenth Century* (Harvard UP, 1958), pp. 70–5.
8 W. Woodruff, *The Impact of Western Man: A Study of Europe's Role in the World's Economy, 1750–1960* (Macmillan, 1966), pp. 117, 150.
9 N. J. Ryan, *The Making of Modern Malaysia* (3rd edn, Oxford UP, 1967), pp. 122–3.
10 J. D. Hargreaves, *Prelude to the Partition of West Africa* (Macmillan, 1963), p. 33; and cf. McIntyre, *op. cit.*, p. 129.
11 See D. C. M. Platt, *Finance, Trade and Politics: British Foreign Policy, 1815–1914* (Oxford UP, 1968), *passim*.
12 R. Cobden, *Speeches on Questions of Public Policy* (1870), ii, 135.
13 On British foreign trade and investment, see Lance E. Davis and Robert A. Huttenback, *Mammon and the Pursuit of Empire: The Political Economy of British Imperialism, 1860–1912* (Cambridge UP, 1986); P. J. Cain and A. G. Hopkins, *British Imperialism: Innovation and Expansion 1688–1914* (Longman 1993); B. R. Mitchell, *British Historical Statistics* (2nd edn, Cambridge UP, 1988), pp. 313–27; Woodruff, *op. cit.*, Chapters 4 and 7; W. Schlote, *British Overseas Trade from 1700 to the 1930s* (Basil Blackwell, 1952), pp. 156–9; A. Imlah, *Economic Elements in the Pax Britannica* (Harvard UP, 1958); L. H. Jenks, *The Migration of British Capital to 1875* (Knopf, 1927), Chapters 7 and 9; and C. K. Hobson, *The Export of Capital* (Constable, 1914), Chapter 6.
14 See H. S. Ferns, *Britain and Argentina in the Nineteenth Century* (Oxford UP, 1960); and H. S. Ferns, 'Britain's informal empire in Argentina, 1806–1914', *Past and Present*, 4 (1953), 60–75.
15 See Platt, *op. cit.*, Part 3, Chapter 6; W. M. Mathew, 'The imperialism of free trade: Peru, 1820–70', *Economic History Review*, xxi (1968), 562–79.
16 On the 'Opium Wars', see W. C. Costin, *Great Britain and China 1833–60* (Clarendon Press, 1937); M. Greenberg, *British Trade and the Opening of China 1800–42* (Cambridge UP, 1951); J. K. Fairbank, *Trade and Diplomacy on the China Coast* (Harvard UP, 1953); Gerald S. Graham, *The China Station: War and Diplomacy, 1830–60* (Oxford UP, 1978).
17 Hargreaves, *op. cit.*, pp. 36–7.
18 *Ibid.*, p. 29.
19 See G. E. Metcalfe, *Maclean of the Gold Coast* (Oxford UP, 1962).
20 See R. E. Robinson and J. A. Gallagher, *Africa and the Victorians* (Macmillan, 1961), pp. 41–4; K. Ingham, *A History of East Africa* (Longman, 1962), Chapter 3.
21 See C. D. Cowan, *Nineteenth-Century Malaya* (Oxford UP, 1961), pp. 9–20.
22 See K. Sinclair, *A History of New Zealand* (Penguin, 1959; reprinted 1970), Part 1, Chapter 2.
23 See R. W. Bullard, *Britain and the Middle East: From the Earliest Times to 1950* (Hutchinson, 1951), Part 3.
24 On 'Free Trade Imperialism', see J. A. Gallagher and R. E. Robinson, 'The imperialism of free trade', *Economic History Review*, vi (1953), 1–15; D. C. M. Platt, *Finance, Trade and Politics: British Foreign Policy, 1815–1914* (Clarendon Press, 1968); also D. C. M. Platt, 'The imperialism of free trade – some reservations', *Economic History Review*, xxi (1969), 77–91, and D. C. M. Platt, 'Further objections to an "imperialism of free trade"', *Economic History Review*, xxvi (1973), 296–306; Bernard Semmel, *The Rise of Free Trade Imperialism* (Cambridge UP, 1970); D. K. Fieldhouse, *Economics and Empire* (Cornell UP, 1973); John Cunningham Wood, *British Economists and the Empire* (Palgrave Macmillan, 1983); P. J. Cain, *Economic Foundations of British Overseas Expansion, 1815–1914* (Macmillan, 1980); Peter Harnetty, *Imperialism and Free Trade: Lancashire and India in the Mid-Nineteenth Century* (Manchester UP, 1973); Ferns, 'Britain's informal empire in Argentina, 1806–1914'; Mathew, *op. cit.*; and Martin Lynn, 'The

"imperialism of free trade" and the case of West Africa, c.1830–c.1870', *Journal of Imperial and Commonwealth History*, xv (1986), 22–40.

25　W. O. Aydelotte, 'The House of Commons in the 1840s', *History*, xxxix (1954).

26　See B. J. Porter, *Britannia's Burden: The Political Evolution of Modern Britain 1851–1990* (Edward Arnold, 1994), pp. 21–2.

27　See B. J. Porter, *Britain, Europe and the World 1850–1982* (Allen & Unwin, 1983), Chapter 1.

28　M. Wiener, *English Culture and the Decline of the Industrial Spirit, 1850–1980* (Cambridge UP, 1981).

29　On 'gentlemanly capitalism', see P. J. Cain and A. G. Hopkins, *British Imperialism: Innovation and Expansion 1688–1914* (Longman, 1993).

30　Thomas Carlyle, *Chartism* (General Books, [1839] 2012).

31　See Joseph E. Inikori, *Africans and the Industrial Revolution in England* (Cambridge UP, 2002).

32　Woodruff, *op. cit.*, table VII/3 (facing p. 303).

33　Robinson and Gallagher, *op. cit.*, pp. 11–12.

34　Quoted in C. A. Bodelson, *Studies in Mid-Victorian Imperialism* (Constable, 1924), p. 15.

35　Lord Derby in House of Lords, 29 June 1854: *Hansard*, 3rd series, 134, c. 844.

36　Earl Grey, *The Colonial Policy of Lord John Russell's Administration* (1853), i, 12–14.

37　Disraeli in House of Commons, 5 February 1863: *Hansard*, 3rd series, 169, c. 96.

38　A. J. Harrop, *The Amazing Career of Edward Gibbon Wakefield* (Allen & Unwin, 1928).

39　On the self-governing dominions, see W. P. Morrell, *British Colonial Policy in the Mid-Victorian Age* (Clarendon Press, 1969); P. N. S. Mansergh, *The Commonwealth Experience* (Weidenfeld & Nicolson, 1969); J. W. Cell, *British Colonial Administration in the Mid-Nineteenth Century* (Yale UP, 1970); J. M. Ward, *Colonial Self-Government* (University of Toronto Press, 1976); Peter Burroughs, 'Colonial self-government', in C. C. Eldridge (ed.), *British Imperialism in the Nineteenth Century* (Palgrave Macmillan, 1984); P. L. Buckner, *The Transition of Responsible Government* (Greenwood Press, 1985); G. Martin, *The Durham Report and British Policy* (Cambridge UP, 1972); and G. Martin, *Britain and the Origins of Canadian Confederation* (University of British Columbia Press, 1995).

40　*Parliamentary Debates*, 3rd series, 151 (1858), c. 2100.

41　On the West Indies, see H. Parry and P. Sherlock, *A Short History of the West Indies* (3rd edn, Macmillan, 1971), Chapters 13, 14; Morrell, *op. cit.*, Chapter 12; P. Curtin, *Two Jamaicas* (Harvard UP, 1955), Part 2.

42　Earl Grey, *op. cit.*, i, 12–14.

43　F. G. Hutchins, *The Illusion of Permanence: British Imperialism in India* (Princeton UP, 1967), pp. ix–x.

44　E. Stokes, *The English Utilitarians and India* (Oxford UP, 1959), p. 23.

45　*Ibid.*, p. 19.

46　*Ibid.*, p. 35.

47　*Ibid.*, pp. 45–6.

48　V. G. Kiernan, *The Lords of Human Kind: European Attitudes to the Outside World in the Imperial Age* (Weidenfeld & Nicolson, 1969), p. 41.

49　Stokes, *op. cit.*, p. 44.

50　Hutchins, *op. cit.*, p. 95.

51　*Ibid.*, pp. 86–100; and see W. H. Russell, *My Indian Mutiny Diary* (Cassell, 1957 edn), p. 8.

52　K. M. Panikkar, *Asia and Western Dominance* (Allen & Unwin, 1953), pp. 121–2 [2nd edn, 1959].

53　On India before the Mutiny, see Stokes, *op. cit.*, Chapter 1; E. Stokes, *The Peasant and the Raj* (Cambridge UP, 1978); and E. Stokes, *The Peasant Armed* (Clarendon Press, 1986); C. A. Bayly, *Indian Society and the Making of the British Empire* (Cambridge UP, 1988); P. Woodruff, *The Men who Ruled India*, 2 vols (Cape, 1953–4), i, Part 3.

54　*Parliamentary Debates*, 3rd series, 151 (1858), c. 2102.

55　J. W. Cell, *British Colonial Administration in the Mid-Nineteenth Century* (Yale UP, 1970), p. 127.

56　K. Sinclair, *The Origins of the Maori Wars* (New Zealand UP, 1957), p. 11.

57　S. Neill, *A History of Christian Missions* (Hodder & Stoughton, 1964), Chapter 9.

3 Shifts and expedients: 1857–75

Britain at the peak of her unchallenged prosperity in the middle of the nineteenth century did not need extensive colonies (except perhaps India) to provide her with trade or emigration fields or security or glory. In free trade she had found a far better method of dominating the world without paying for it. Free trade was supposed to be nature's own way of dealing with foreign countries, without harmful side-effects. Its beauty was that it avoided antagonising anyone. Unlike conventional imperialism, which profited the imperialists – if it profited them at all – only at the expense of their subjects, free trade profited Britain and her trading partners at one and the same time. The prosperity of the one automatically redounded to the prosperity of the other; economic development was everywhere drawn into the most promising channels. Everyone gained, no country had anything to complain of. Consequently Britain reaped the maximum benefits with the minimum of bad feeling and trouble and expense. That was the theory. And in most parts of the world it seemed to be working, free exchange supplying Britain's wants adequately and cheaply: except in certain countries which resisted the benefits the British were offering them – their commerce, their capital and their culture – and which had to be coerced somehow into accepting them. Where this had already happened, for example, on the west coast of Africa and in China, Britain rightly saw the results – the additions to her formal empire – not as triumphs of diplomacy, but as marks of failure: failure to exert influence in the world the inexpensive way.

After the middle of the century there were many more such failures. As Britain's economy grew, her commercial and cultural involvement in the world grew deeper and more extensive, and came into contact with more peoples who found her demands oppressive or unreasonable, either because they were so, or because the people were not yet industrially mature enough to understand or cope with them. Among these communities the encroachment of the British economy was provoking the kinds of conflicts which nearly always accompany rapid social change, and which were bound to necessitate political intervention if British interests were to be secured. A similar thing was happening in parts of the world where Britain had already assumed political control; involvement provoked local conflicts which, because they threatened Britain's interests, required her to take on more extensive responsibilities than she would have liked. The form the conflict and the response took varied considerably from place to place, but in the third quarter of the century it resulted in a significant expansion and consolidation of the formal empire. In the process, the Victorians were forced to modify a little their ideas about how their colonial responsibilities should be exercised, especially towards the 'subject races' of their empire.

The Indian 'Mutiny'

India was the scene of the most spectacular and violent conflict. India had never accepted without protest the presence of her British predators and protectors, and her history in the first half of the nineteenth century is scattered through with rebellions, army mutinies and civil disturbances.[1] But the most serious of them by far was in 1857–58. It started in May 1857 with a mutiny of native Indian troops at Meerut near Delhi, over a question of religious principle. A cavalry regiment rose in support of colleagues who had been publicly degraded and imprisoned for refusing to use newly issued cartridges coated with grease, which was rumoured (and later confirmed) to be made up of a mixture of pork and beef fat. The cow was sacred to the Hindu, the pig was unclean to the Muslim; the affair, said Lord Roberts later, betrayed an 'incredible disregard of the natives' religious prejudices'.[2] The Meerut mutineers dashed to Delhi, took it with the help of the native regiments there, and proclaimed Bahadur Shah, 82-year-old descendant of the Mughals, 'emperor of Hindustan' – not altogether with his approval. From there the rebellion spread rapidly, but unevenly. It never covered the whole of India. The south gave the British very little trouble. The Madras Presidency in the south-east was quiet, the Bombay Presidency in the west had one or two military mutinies and a Muslim conspiracy to contend with, but nothing it could not manage easily. In the Punjab in the north-west and Bengal in the north-east they held on with difficulty, little volcanoes of mutiny erupting around them, but the civilian population by and large staying aloof. The main trouble was in the north-central part of India – in the North-Western Provinces and Oudh (later called the United Provinces), in Bundelkhand, the Maratha States, Saugor and Narbada to the south, and in the western parts of Bihar to the east (Map 5). Over this sizeable area, covering about one-sixth of India's territory and one-tenth of her population, the British for a time completely lost control. The military mutiny was complemented by civil rebellions, involving in many places nearly all classes of the local population: the aristocracy, small landowners and peasants. In some cases, it was the civilians who started things going. The British were expelled, and successor governments were set up, usually under the old traditional rulers. Their authority was not always very effective, sometimes it was weakened by internal communal discord, and very rarely was there any useful collaboration between the rebel leaders in different parts of the country. But for two or three months at least, their authority was far more convincing than that of the British. For those few months in the middle of 1857 it looked as if the rebellion might possibly succeed. The British had held India with an army of 277,746 men. Of these, only 45,522 were Europeans, the rest were native soldiers or 'sepoys'.[3] Reinforcements had a long way to come. If all the sepoys shook off their old loyalties, how could the raj possibly survive?

The raj did survive, but only after 14 months of the bitterest fighting. On both sides it took on some of the characteristics of a race war. Under pressure, both the rebels and the British tended to regard all persons of the opposite colour as enemies, whether or not they were in fact, and slaughtered indiscriminately. Mutinous sepoys ran through towns and cities killing every European they could lay hands on, and destroying every artifact associated with the English. British troops recapturing a rebel stronghold would hold all Indians found there responsible for the deeds of their fellows, and summarily 'execute' them in hundreds. Each side fed its hatred, and hence its morale, on stories of atrocities perpetrated by the other. The stories were very often true. Indians were shot and hanged

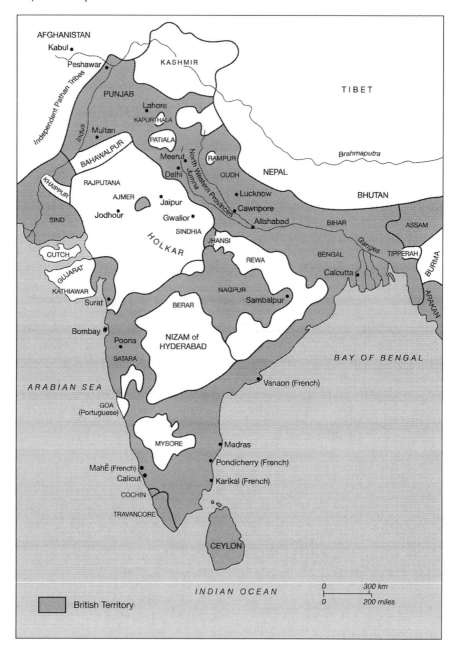

Map 5 India at the time of the Mutiny, 1857–58
Source: After C. C. Eldridge, *Victorian Imperialism* (Hodder & Stoughton, 1978), p. 68.

out of hand, burned alive, and blown from guns by the British (Figure 3.1). For their part, the rebels massacred British women and children. As if this were not enough, the stories were embellished by both sides to appeal to their own particular national forms of moral outrage: on the British side, by reports that their women were 'dishonoured' before

Figure 3.1 Justice. Indian mutineers blown away by guns, 1857–58, as pictured in the American
  Ballou's Pictorial Drawing-Room Companion.
Source: © CORBIS/Corbis via Getty Images.

they were murdered; on the rebel side by reports that Muslims were defiled by sewing
them into pig-skins before execution. Very early on, the war took on the character of a
war of racial revenge, between men defending their most precious taboos. Hence the
ferocity with which it was fought.

It very soon became clear that at the root of all this was something more than the
'greased cartridge' affair which had begun it. 'The decline and fall of empires,' said
Benjamin Disraeli to the House of Commons in July 1857, 'are not affairs of greased
cartridges. Such results are occasioned by adequate causes, and by an accumulation of
adequate causes.' Disraeli's own explanation was the one which almost everyone else
who mattered in Indian affairs was soon to share. The British, he thought, had been too
precipitate in India. They had tried to change the country too quickly and too radically.
The Indians were conservative creatures, like Disraeli himself; they preferred their own
customs and institutions to other people's – especially their own religions and their own
aristocracies. In the old days, the East India Company had realised this, and had realised
too that it was in its own interests to tread carefully in these matters. It was able to hold
India only because the Indians were divided among themselves in religion, race and politics, and because some of them collaborated with the British. If they ever forgot their
differences and combined against them, then the days of British rule were numbered. It
was important not to provoke any such combination; hence the old school's toleration of
Indian customs and institutions; what Disraeli called a 'respect for nationality'. But
recently policy had altered.

> Sir, of late years a new principle appears to have been adopted in the government of India ... one which would destroy nationality. Everything in India has been changed. Laws and manners, customs and usages, political organisations, the tenure of property, the religion of the people – everything in India has either been changed or attempted to be changed, or there is a suspicion among the population that a desire for change exists on the part of our Government.

The conservative instincts of the Indian people were immediately aroused. Communal quarrels were forgotten, the 'powerful classes' turned against the British, and so the two chief pillars of British authority were destroyed. The tinder was dry, the greased cartridge affair set it aflame – but anything else would have done as well. The Company's fundamental error had been to alienate its collaborators by too much zeal for change.[4]

Disraeli made the rebellion sound like an English Tory backlash in defence of the squirearchy and the Church of England – but the analogy was not so far from the truth. When the rebels said why they were fighting or why others should join them, the reason they gave was usually that the British were destroying or intending to destroy their old customs and institutions, and their promise for the future was that they would restore them. Most effective of all the rallying-cries to rebellion was the religious one. 'It is well known,' claimed a rebel broadsheet, 'that in these days all the English have entertained these evil designs – first, to destroy the religion of the whole Hindustani army and to make the people by compulsion Christians.'[5] And there was just enough evidence to make this plausible. The East India Company's official policy was one of toleration and neutrality in religious affairs, but some of its more zealous servants were clearly unhappy under such a tight rein. Their attitudes could be ambivalent, to say the least; for example, during the Mutiny, the chairman of the Company affirmed that

> he had no doubt whatever in his own mind that Providence had been pleased to place the magnificent Empire of India in our hands in order that in due time we might be the instruments of converting the inhabitants to Christianity.

A few weeks later he made it clear that he had not intended to imply that the government of India should take an active part in their conversion; nevertheless 'at the same time the Government ought not to remain inactive in regard to the moral and intellectual advancement of the people'.[6] The trouble was that, in practice, the distinction was impossible to maintain. The 'moral and intellectual advancement of the people' involved doing away with practices which were regarded as stupid or evil; many of these practices were connected with religion, so interference with religion was scarcely avoidable. A great deal of British reforming activity before 1857 came into this category: the abolition of *sati* (or widow-burning), the legalisation of remarriage for Hindu widows, the education of women, subsidisation of mission schools, the prohibition of caste-marks among sepoys, an act permitting converts to retain their inheritances, and much else besides. All these could be justified on social or humanitarian grounds, but they all infringed one religious convention or another. Indians saw them as deliberate challenges to their religions, just as Victorian Englishmen would have done if on humanitarian grounds some 'oriental' (or Mormon) conqueror in London had legalised polygamy. Then there were the missionaries. Until recently they had been excluded from India. Now they were allowed in and by all accounts were preaching more *against* Buddhism and Islam than *for* Christianity, and infiltrating into the native army where, for example, the commanding officer of the 34th Infantry at Barrackpur saw it as his 'aim and end' to convert the sepoy to God, 'or, in other words, to rescue him from eternal destruction'.[7] Even without the greased cartridges it was little wonder that, despite reassurances to the contrary, many Indians entertained a profound suspicion that the British were seeking to subvert their religions, intentionally and systematically.

These fears were largely imaginary, born of miscomprehension of Britain's motives and methods. But in more material affairs, the changes brought by the British, and the displacement they caused, were real enough. Almost every one of their 'reforms' dispossessed, demoted or degraded one class of people or another. The new system of higher education based on English language, literature and science was challenging and superseding the teaching – and therefore the status in their communities – of the old Muslim elite. The British concept of equality before the law was felt to insult the honour of the highest castes: 'when sued by a mean labourer, or a male or female servant, you are summoned without investigation to attend their Court, and are thus dishonoured and degraded'.[8] Free trade had ruined the urban artisan class:

> The Europeans by the introduction of English articles into India have thrown the weavers, the cotton dressers, the carpenters, the blacksmiths and the shoe-makers, etc., out of employ and have engrossed their occupations so that every description of native artisan has been reduced to beggary.[9]

But the greatest changes had come in the countryside, and it was here that Indian resentment against the British was deepest. The British were imposing a new order on the land. In the interests of justice, efficiency and profit, they had introduced new concepts which had hardly existed there before – of individual landownership, fixed money rents, the unrestricted sale of 'encumbered estates' – the whole paraphernalia of modern nineteenth-century land theory, the cleansing wind of 'free market forces', bracing the progressive farmer and blowing away the incompetent. Unable to meet the regular revenue demands of the government, peasants and landlords fell into debt and were forced to sell out, usually to the men they were indebted to. Other landlords – many thousands – were having their lands confiscated by the government because they could not produce adequate documentary evidence of legal tenure. Disraeli pointed out that English landlords would never have stood for this.[10] Others were confirmed in their holdings but deprived by the British of the trappings of their old power. The pattern of rural life was breaking up in many areas: families were forced to abandon lands they had tilled for generations; the old familiar feudal masters were displaced by new ones, sometimes urban moneylenders unsympathetic to rural ways; and the loss of the old elites was regretted, apparently, by their faithful and deferential peasantry. Elsewhere cultivators were disgruntled, not because they were worse off but because they were no better off and their neighbours were. Rural disaffection was particularly serious in those areas where the English revolution had been most recently extended – where the dispossessed still smarted and memories of other days were brightest. Many provinces had only very lately been annexed by the British, and here the manner of their annexation added to the general discontent. Previously guaranteed independence by firm treaty – so it was claimed – their rulers were suddenly pensioned off, deprived of their retinues, their armies and their powers; and often for no adequate reason other than that the governor-general adjudged that they were incompetent, or that the customary rules of Indian inheritance – which allowed inheritance by an adopted son – were no longer to apply. Indians regarded these pretexts as cynical and dishonourable. A host of pretenders, pensioned-off ex-princes and unemployed retainers was added to the general pool of discontent. The latest and most fiercely resented of these annexations was that of Oudh (1856), where, significantly, many of the sepoys of the mutinous Bengal army had their home. 'It is my humble opinion,' wrote a loyal sepoy, Sita Ram, 'that this seizing of Oudh filled the minds of the sepoys with distrust, and led them to plot against the Government.'[11] In Oudh itself, where the British-imposed socio-economic revolution had just begun, rebellious feeling was almost unanimous among the civil population.

After the first few weeks of fighting had exploded the Company directorate's early reassurances as to the Mutiny's insignificance and the general contentment of the Indian population, contemporaries tended to go to the other extreme and exaggerate the extent of the unrest. 'There was disaffection enough in the land,' wrote one of them, 'for half a dozen rebellions.'[12] Yet many Indians, probably the majority, were loyal to their British rulers. Of the native troops in India, fewer than half mutinied. Others took an active part in suppressing the rebellion. Many of the native princes stayed firm despite the disaffection of their subjects: the Nizam of Hyderabad, for example, and the Maharajas of Rajputana. In the south, and in the Punjab, Sind, Bengal and Assam, the civilian population was loyal; even in Delhi, the centre of rebel activities, the townspeople were very reluctant friends of the rebels. Most of these classes remained loyal either because the English revolution had scarcely touched them, or because it had benefited them, or because it had happened sufficiently long ago for its hard edges to have worn down. There were enough Indians profiting from English education and participating in the British commercial nexus in the cities to create large and influential collaborating classes in Calcutta, Delhi, Bombay and Madras. In the countryside, as many landowners gained from the redistribution of estates that followed British rule as lost by it. In Sind, the people 'remembered with gratitude how they were rescued by the British government from the grinding tyranny of the Amirs'.[13] In the Madras and Bombay presidencies and in Bengal, the main social disruption had come many years earlier, the rebellions and mutinies had already taken place, and failed; and now the people were acclimatised to the new order, reconciled to their fate or cowed into submission.[14] The unevenness of the British impact on India provoked an uneven response from the Indians, which helps to account for the failure of the rebellion, and the survival of British India. Over most of the subcontinent, British policies, including the reformist policy of acculturation, had been successful in the sense that in the long run they had proved acceptable, or at least tolerable, to the natives.

Where the flames of rebellion did take hold, it was in a sense a reactionary movement intending to restore old rulers and old institutions – the symbols, perhaps, of a reborn Hindustan nation; but its positive, constructive side was never very strong. What united its participants was not any very clear vision of the future, but a hatred of the British. That hatred was fanned by the recent policies of the East India Company, and also by the manner in which they had been implemented. To the rebels, British policy appeared as a deliberate attempt to seize their lands, humiliate their rulers, impoverish their people, subvert their customary ways of life and destroy their religions, often in the teeth of solemn promises not to do so, by a group of infidels with dubious motives and unpleasant manners. That this was how they saw the intentions of the British denoted, to say the least, a failure of communication between rulers and ruled; but even the best of imperial public relations officers would have found it difficult to disabuse Indians of these ideas, for many of them were true, and indeed were never contradicted by the British. Certainly they admitted – even boasted – their intention to effect very radical changes in the structure of Indian society. They were confident that they knew what was good for India: it was the same as was good for any country, the application of those universal and immutable laws of political economy which they had deduced from first principles, and which had been tested and proven by their own national experience. Perhaps because of their confidence, they grotesquely underestimated the full force and spread of the resentment engendered among Indians against their reforms. They rarely made any attempt to understand the customs and institutions they were trying to supplant, because they did not think them worth the effort. If they did try, more often than not, they failed: 'Even we who live in India for years, who pass our lives there,' admitted one of them, 'obtain at last only a very imperfect and grey twilight knowledge of the natives.'[15] When Indians accused them of issuing the notorious greased cartridges as part of a plot to destroy native religions by defiling their adherents, they gave them too much credit for cunning. If the British *had* wanted to proselytise the Indians by force, it would never have occurred to them to do it this way, because they had little idea that cow and pig fat had this kind of significance for them. Their ignorance caused them to blunder and break things whenever they entered – sometimes without knowing they had entered it – the brittle edifice of Indian religious susceptibilities; it also made their own reforming task in India more difficult for them, by alienating the people they were trying to reform. 'I could not help thinking,' wrote *The Times* journalist W. H. Russell, 'how harsh the reins of our rule must feel to the soft skin of the natives.'[16] The kind of radical and rapid change which Britain envisaged for India, which amounted to an entire social revolution, was a difficult task in the best conditions. The fact that it was imposed from outside, by aliens, made it harder still for the Indians to accept; and the fact that those aliens were almost entirely without tact, frequently contemptuous of the 'nigger's' ways, and not concealing it, made things worse. Possibly the British did not fully realise the social disruption their revolution was causing in India. They did little to make it easier for the Indians, little to soften the impact as they were projected suddenly into the nineteenth century.[17]

After the Mutiny

Eventually the Mutiny was suppressed. Peace was officially proclaimed on 8 July 1858, although guerrilla warfare continued in some places. In Britain, the initial fever of race hatred which had accompanied the first months of the Mutiny – and which had landed the governor-general with the popular soubriquet of 'Clemency Canning' because his revenge was not so bloodthirsty as the people demanded – gave way to a calmer and more thoughtful mood, at least among the arbiters of policy. They blamed themselves for the recent troubles. The missionaries and their patrons, including Gladstone, saw the Mutiny as God's judgement on England for 'keeping back Christianity from the people';[18] it was not the native Christians, they pointed out, who had rebelled. But for most people, the evidence pointed the other way, and the mood of the time, rather less enthusiastic about enlightening the earth than it had been 20 or 30 years before, favoured a more worldly explanation. They had been over-zealous in their efforts to reform the Indians. Some critics believed (with Disraeli) that their reforms were intrinsically mis-guided – too radical, too destructive of the traditional social order in the countryside. Many more were still confident that their intentions, the reforms themselves, were right and good, but doubted now the capacity of the Indians to take them in all at once. Either they were beyond the pale of civilisation, inferior beings incapable of enlightenment, who must always be ruled and led by others, therefore, if they were to progress; or, slightly more charitably, the raw material of civilisation was there underneath, but so deeply encrusted with centuries of superstition and prejudice that the process of enlightenment would take much more time and patience than the *ante bellum* reformers had allowed for. In either case the general moral of the Mutiny was the same. It had been a harsh and costly lesson in the realities of acculturation, bringing home to British people the magnitude and complexity of the task of social engineering they had so lightly undertaken in India.

Aside from the question of whether or not the old 'reforming' policy was good for the Indians, it was generally agreed that it had not been good for Britain. It had alienated the people at whom it had been directed and so threatened the foundation of assent or apathy on which British power in India was built. The post-mortem on the Mutiny uncovered thousands of princes and landowners who had taken part in the rebellion because they had been dispossessed by the British, and thousands more who had remained loyal and acted as 'breakwaters to the storm', in Canning's phrase, because the British had let them alone. The importance attached to the religious issue by the rebels confirmed the correlation which was drawn between European interference and Indian disaffection. If they were to hold on to India, they must not be so quick to interfere, however much it pained them to see the persistence of superstition, vice and inefficiency.

There was no question but that Britain's first priority *was* to hold on to India. Her determination to do so was only strengthened by recent events; injured national pride demanded it, quite apart from the as yet debatable requirements of economic self-interest. To this end, the policies of the years following the Mutiny were directed. In 1858, the government of India was taken out of the hands of the East India Company, and put directly under the British Crown and Parliament. This move was of rather less practical significance than its constitutional form – and the controversy it provoked – suggested. The Company had lost its commercial side long ago, and for some years had been little more than a government agency. But the change was an augury of the government's good intentions to keep India under more continuous surveillance. The same man – Lord Canning – remained in charge in Calcutta, but with the new title of 'Viceroy' added to his old one under the Company of 'Governor-General'. It was his task now to consolidate British rule. The expansion of India's frontiers – which in the past had been a distraction for the English and a provocation to the Indians – was discontinued for a time. The civilian population was as far as possible disarmed. The native element in the army was reduced in numbers, the artillery put entirely in the hands of Europeans, and Hindu and Muslim regiments judiciously mixed in order to play one off against the other if one section threatened mutiny. These were practical actions designed to draw the teeth of any future rebellion. To *prevent* rebellion more fundamental changes of policy were required.

For a start, the missionaries and the Christian zealots among the Crown's officers in India had to be held strictly in check. Recent experience had taught the British how powerful were the Indians' religious prejudices when aroused. So policy after 1858 reverted to the old well-tried path that the Company had followed in the eighteenth century, with the government making a point of avoiding where it could any interference with Indian religion and custom. The Queen's proclamation of November 1858 which formally announced the Crown takeover of the Indian empire unambiguously disclaimed 'the right and the desire to impose Our convictions on any of Our subjects'. Over most of the country the government became ultra-solicitous of their religious susceptibilities, cutting down its grants to Christian mission schools, for example, and dropping almost immediately any 'reformist' plan which threatened to meet with significant resistance from Indian conservatives. This policy was not only thought to be more prudent; by some contemporaries, it was regarded as a more effective way to secure, in the long run, the Indians' spiritual salvation:

> At present it is wiser, I do not say to leave, but to aid, the Hindoo mind to work out its own regeneration, than to force on from without the desired changes, which, to be effectual, must take growth from within.[19]

Still the pre-Mutiny school of Indian reformers objected strongly. Christian zealots like Herbert Edwardes, Commissioner of Peshawar in the Punjab during the Mutiny, regarded promises of religious toleration as 'a most melancholy proof that ... we have greatly retrograded in our principles'.[20] If God had intended England to respect heathen superstitions, he argued, He would not have helped her win the war. But it was done. And not content merely with not offending its subjects, the Indian government set out to win the active support of their leaders. Before the Mutiny, the plan had been to train up a new, western-educated elite to supplant the old one and lead the masses to the light. Unfortunately, the masses had not taken to the new elite. Now the approach was different: the government sought out the already existing 'natural' leaders of old India, those whom the Mutiny had taught them still commanded the people's affections, and hoped, by strengthening them in their privileges, to lead the masses, not towards the light any more, but towards a more loyal attachment to the British raj. If the propertied class of India, wrote an agent of the Punjab government in 1860, could be 'attached to the state by timely concessions ... and obtains a share of power and importance, it will constitute a strong support to the existing government'.[21] So the princes and great landowners were assiduously cultivated as a powerful collaborating class: no longer dispossessed if they were inefficient or unjust or without natural heirs, but confirmed in their holdings, many of them restored to estates they had lost before or during the Mutiny, and represented – the sole native representatives – on the Governor-General's Legislative Council in Calcutta. Again the old school objected. Sir Charles Wood, who had been President of the Board of Control before the Mutiny and was now Secretary of State for India, was shocked by Canning's appeasement of the *talukdars* in Oudh, which had 'upset so completely all that we have been doing in settling the tenures of that country ever since we took it'.[22] But Wood soon changed his mind, the new policy was implemented, and it worked. From 1858, right through to the end of the raj, the traditional aristocracy of India remained faithful to its British patrons. The break in policy was perhaps not quite so sharp as it seemed to men like Edwardes and Wood at the time. Despite the constitutional innovations of 1858, the British personnel in India was not much changed after the Mutiny; many high-ranking officials resisted the new trends, and one of the resisters, Sir John Lawrence, had a spell as viceroy from 1864 to 1869. Yet the emphasis of British policy had very decidedly altered. It had lost a great deal of its old confident, careless idealism, and had become cautious, pragmatic; less concerned with bettering the Indians than with ensuring their docility.

Yet the ambition to 'reform' India was by no means abandoned. It was merely turned into different paths: away from the dangerous and hostile territory of cultural and social change, towards the more familiar terrain of material improvement. The Victorians were far more competent in this field; it required rather less of that quality of imaginative sympathy which they conspicuously lacked. The idea now was to concentrate on enhancing the material welfare of the Indian people: 'the importation of the body of the west without its soul'.[23] The first priority in this field was railway building, because this involved too the security of the raj. During the fighting, W. H. Russell had speculated

> how much blood, disgrace, misery, and horror would have been saved to us if the rail had been but a little longer here, had been at all there, had been completed at another place. It has been a heavy mileage of neglect for which we have already paid dearly.[24]

In 1857, railways in India were insignificant – just 288 miles in three short experimental lines many hundreds of miles apart. In 1859, a network was planned to cover the whole country, 5,000 miles initially, to be built and run by private companies but with their profits guaranteed by the state. The guarantee system got the lines built, but expensively; in the 1870s it was scrapped for a time and the railways were built by state enterprise: 1,588 miles were open to traffic by 1861; 9,891 miles by 1881; and 24,760 miles by 1900.[25] The railways were the proudest achievement of the post-Mutiny era. Progress in other fields was not so dramatic, but irrigation works, the construction of roads, the extension of telegraphic and postal services, the provision of sanitation and lighting, and other public works were pushed ahead steadily. By the turn of the century, 30 million acres of land were irrigated artificially, out of a total cultivated area of 197 million acres; and India had 37,000 miles of metalled and 136,000 miles of unmetalled roads.[26] The progress made in 'modernising' the country bore comparison (a comparison that the Victorians themselves were fond of making) with the achievement of the Roman empire in Europe.

Britain's grasp on India was immensely strengthened by the new network of communications. 'After all,' wrote Lord Roberts in 1897,

> the first condition of improving India is to hold it, and the system of Indian railways in case of concentration, carriage of supplies and munitions, in averting disease and fatigue during sultry marches and sparing the hateful necessity of pressing the carts and oxen of the country people – their only capital – for purposes of service, has revolutionised the military history of India.[27]

But its ultimate purpose was to ease the chronic famine situation in India (which it did to an extent); and to provide the infrastructure for India's economic development. In its efforts to stimulate development, the government was not prepared to go very much further than this. It was not prepared, for example, to promote Indian industries directly, by subsidies or tariffs or state enterprise; partly because of pressure from competing British interests, and partly because prevailing economic dogma was strongly against state intervention. One of the effects of the new railways was to accelerate the destruction of India's indigenous craft industries by exposing more of them to cheap British competition. These industries could have been protected or new infant manufacturing industries fostered by effective tariffs, but British manufacturers – especially the inordinately jealous Lancashire cotton industry – would not tolerate such 'unfair' competition, and economic good sense taught that it was pointless to duplicate in India the manufacture of articles which were better produced elsewhere. What India *should* produce was best left to the ordinary and infallible workings of supply and demand to establish. But it was not difficult to predict what those products would be. With India now part of a free international market dominated by Britain's manufacturing industry, they were likely to be the things

Britain needed and could not produce herself: chiefly subtropical agricultural products. It followed therefore from the logic of India's position under the British Crown that this was the direction her economic development would take – towards the production of foodstuffs and raw materials for export mainly to European markets, in exchange for the clothing and other manufactures she now imported. And this was what happened. The Indian cotton manufacturing industry struggled to a relative prosperity in the 1860s and 1870s (by 1876–77, its exports brought in nearly £2 million). But the staples of the Indian export trade were raw cotton (£13.3 million in 1876), opium (£11.1 million), rice, wheat and other grains (£6.4 million), oil seeds (£5.5 million), hides (£2.9 million), indigo (£2.9 million), jute (£2.8 million) and tea (£2.2 million).[28] The steadiest growth was in the export of tea to Britain, where within the space of a generation a revolution in taste replaced China tea by Indian as the national beverage. Apart from the iniquitous opium trade, which was a government monopoly and in fact the second largest source of state revenue after the land tax, it was left to private enterprise to develop these commodities, with just a little prodding from government.[29]

As the old high-flown aims of moral and spiritual regeneration were gradually superseded by more mundane and practical ones, the *outlook* of the British in India seemed to change too. In the 1830s, Macaulay had looked forward to that 'proudest day in English history' when a grateful India, moulded in a European pattern, would set up on her own as a free country. Macaulay may have been more sanguine than most at that time, but his vision was one which many people had shared or at least professed to share. After the Mutiny, it almost entirely faded. In Britain, one or two men kept it alive: liberals whose faith in the equality and perfectibility of mankind had been resilient enough to withstand the onslaught of the Mutiny. In India, such men were rare. When the Gladstonian Lord Ripon went to India as viceroy in 1880, he found the mood among the white community there set hard against political liberalism.[30] Merchants and planters were notoriously hostile to native advancement, especially the infamous indigo planters of Bengal, some of them recruited from the West Indies and bringing with them racial attitudes nurtured in a slave society. The administrators were more charitable, but their attitudes too had been soured by the experience of the Mutiny. More of them than before were willing to admit openly to a fundamental fatalism about British rule in India which contrasts markedly with Macaulay's happy optimism:

> We cannot foresee the time in which the cessation of our rule would not be the signal for universal anarchy and ruin, and it is clear that the only hope for India is the long continuance of the benevolent but strong government of Englishmen.[31]

The Indian could never be improved; the burden of empire would never be off Britain's shoulders: the administrators' acceptance of these melancholy truths gave to service in India an ethos of stoical self-sacrifice which seemed to sustain them in their work (and which was by no means incompatible with their recognition of India's value to Britain). Indian service was a stern duty to be persevered in, no longer (if it ever had been this) a project of hope to be undertaken in joy. The 'civilians' were still dedicated men (always *men*, of course), but dedicated now to the task itself and not to any future ideal that might come out of it. They took pride in the sufferings it involved: 'long years of exile, a burning sun which dries up the Saxon energies, home sickenings, thankless labour, disease and oft-times death far from wife, child, friend or kinsman'.[32] And they stressed especially the thanklessness of the task, the Indians' sullen rejection of their efforts, which far from discouraging them served only to strengthen their belief in their own indispensability. Kipling captured the note of defiant pride in a poem urging the Americans to follow Britain's example:

> Take up the White Man's burden –
> And reap his old reward:
> The blame of those ye better,
> The hate of those ye guard ...

Before they came to India, their ideals had already been fixed by the environment they had been brought up in, especially the environment of the public schools. These spartan institutions, where the sons of the rich were hardened and purified for lives of service and self-deprivation, set out to inculcate certain virtues and qualities in their pupils, among which the most prominent were courage, self-assurance, honesty, self-sacrifice, and group loyalty. Out of them there poured a race of young men almost identical in their attitudes and opinions, whose individualism and imaginative faculties had been exorcised from them long before. Many of them came to rule India. James Bryce described their qualities: 'a good deal of uniformity ... a want of striking, even marked individualities ... rather wanting in imagination and sympathy ... too conventionally English'.[33] They probably would not have objected to this description. They did not try to be sympathetic or sensitive; these were regarded as feminine, 'unmanly' qualities anyway. They were in India to provide leadership – the leadership of the white race – and to fulfil a duty, a service to humanity. Their womenfolk (wives and daughters) tended to back them up in this.[34] The sense of service seems to have been their prime motivation. In India, they worked tirelessly to prevent famine, build railways, secure law and order, the kind of task that did not require imagination and sympathy; work which was hard, but not emotionally demanding. They knew that they would get very little tangible out of it, certainly not the gratitude of the Indians; no reward at the end of the day, save the knowledge in their hearts of a good work done – and of course the plaudits of their fellows.

Among some civilians this ethos of thankless self-sacrifice may have inculcated a positive hatred of the country they served. The lawyer and political theoretician Fitzjames Stephen claimed that 'no Englishman ever did, or ever will, or can feel one tender or genial feeling' towards India,[35] but his words were written in a fit of pique after the assassination of a viceroy, and they certainly did not accurately describe the general mood in calmer times. Many administrators had a great affection for India and the Indian, but it was affection from a distance. This distance was deliberately cultivated, the studied aloofness of a group of men who saw themselves as a race of Platonic guardians or demigods ruling loftily from above, and were afraid of being too friendly with the natives for the harm it might do to their authority. The way they lived in India widened the gulf between the races. In the depths of the countryside, a lone collector or district officer might cultivate some kind of intimacy with the natives in order to have any social life at all. But in the towns they were able to live their lives totally apart from the Indians. All-white clubs (for drinking and dancing and playing bridge and tennis) provided for them a kind of social life-support system in an alien environment, releasing them from the necessity of coming to terms with that environment and adapting themselves to it (Figure 3.2). In Simla, in the Himalayan foothills, they built a complete English town for themselves, even *looking* like an English town, with gothic revival churches and regency villas, in subtropical surroundings. Their 'society' was the society of other

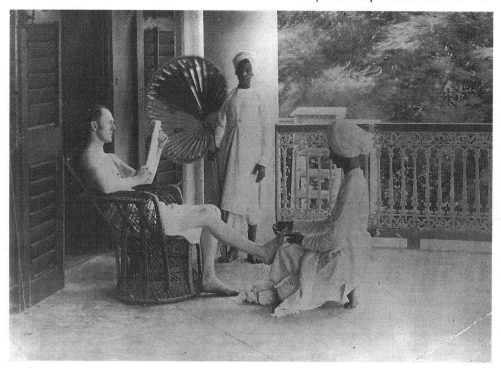

Figure 3.2 Dominion over palm and pine. A typically languid member of the Indian Civil Service
reading his paper while being pedicured (presumably) *circa* 1870.
Source: © Hulton Archive/Getty Images.

Europeans: a man could be among a hundred thousand Indians and still regard himself as 'alone'. They came into familiar contact with Indians only as servants. This situation was not so very different from that in Britain, where among the upper-crust, 'society' was not taken to include the inferior classes, and where an aristocrat's only contact with the proletariat was likely to be with his or her butler or gillie. The main difference in India was that it was very much easier than in Britain to gain entry into 'society' if you were white, but virtually impossible if you were brown.

The bonds of community among this European elite were tightened by a strong sense of group loyalty, which was necessary in a hostile environment where they numbered only some 2,000 among 200 million or 300 million Indians. Their position was precarious, and unity meant strength. Criticism was resented, especially from ignorant radicals in the British Parliament – Kipling's 'Pagett M.P.' – or from 'interfering' independent women. Criticism from within was regarded as treachery, a betrayal of the group and the race. Whether the motivation behind this rigid exclusiveness was a real distaste for Indian culture, or a fear that its attractions might seduce and corrupt the administrators if they were exposed to it, or merely an attempt to conceal the white man's weaker side from the people towards whom he had to appear as a demigod, the effect was to make it more difficult for him to cultivate a genuine sympathy for the Indians. Distance tended to reduce all Indians to a stereotype image, and the form of the stereotype was influenced as much by the Englishman's conception of his own role among them as by direct observation. The Indian had to be inferior in order to justify his subjection; generally his inferiority was supposed to lie not so much in his intellectual calibre, as in his lack of those qualities of 'character' which made the Englishman, by contrast, so much his better. By common consent, the Indian was tricky, devious, untruthful, sensuous and easily corrupted; it was admitted that he could be *deep*, but then so could the devil. This is not to say that the Englishman disliked all Indians, but he tended to appreciate only those qualities in them which were useful to him or flattered him. An English army officer's relationship with his Gurkha sergeant could be of the closest and most intimate kind, but only if the sergeant were a certain kind of man. The virtues an Englishman looked for in an Indian friend, the characteristics he admired, were loyalty, fidelity and 'spirit': the qualities of a good hound. English aristocrats loved their butlers for the same kinds of reasons.

One Indian type they did not entirely appreciate, even if he had all the doggy virtues, was the *babu*, the westernised native. Macaulay in the 1830s had raised up this class – 'a class of persons Indian in colour, but English in tastes, in opinions, in morals and in intellect' – to act as 'interpreters between us and the millions we govern'. In the earlier conception of the British purpose in India, they were to provide the tools for its reformation, and eventually the successors to the English. Now, when the Indians were no longer to be 'reformed' in the same way, and when there seemed little chance that they could take over from the English in the foreseeable future, the westernised Indians were superfluous, redundant. The official attitude towards them was ambivalent. They still represented the ideal, the product which the educational system was geared to turning out. But they did not fit in with the new political policy of rule by collaboration with the traditional Indian elites. Cast in a western mould, they had acquired western ambitions, which included the ambition to be involved in the government of their own country. Theoretically, there was no bar to their entering the service of the Crown if they could pass the Indian Civil Service (ICS) examinations. But those examinations were intrinsically weighted very heavily in favour of Englishmen, and the one or two Indians who did survive them found the going difficult among European colleagues, who regarded them as uncomfortable freaks. After the Mutiny, the westernised Indians advised strongly against the new policies of appeasement and non-interference with the customs and traditions they themselves had shed. The government ignored their advice, it could afford to, for in the short term the loyalty of these cultural quislings was never in doubt: they would be nothing without the British. This whole class of men, created by the British in the 1830s, was deserted by them in the 1860s and 1870s. Very often they were cruelly ridiculed in magazines like *Punch*, which exploited a rich vein of humour by caricaturing their speech and their aping of English manners. The excuse the British gave for not associating them more in government was that they were unrepresentative of the Indian population as a whole, just *because* they were westernised and the 'masses' were not, which was true, but a little hard on the educated Indians, who had been educated in the first place in order to lead the masses in the same, western direction. The British attitude was understandable. They found themselves in the embarrassing position of a manager who had trained up a man to run the firm with him, and then decided he could do the job on his own, and wanted a clerk instead.[36]

Colonial crises: settlement colonies

The Indian Mutiny was the most serious colonial challenge that Britain had to face in the third quarter of the nineteenth century, but it was not the only one. All over the world, local 'crises' in British colonies, or on their edges, or in areas of British influence, were provoking responses from the British government which sometimes led, as in India, to Britain's involving herself more permanently or formally in other countries' affairs.

The local crises could take many forms. They were not always rebellions like the Indian one directed explicitly against British domination, but generally they could be traced back to something the British had done to upset the stability (or at least the customary *in*stability) of established societies and cultures. That such crises happened so often in this period was partly due to the very nature of the method Britain had chosen to extend her influence in the world. In effect, this functioned by delegating the work of expansion, and its expense, to independent agents: commercial firms, adventurers, settlers, missionaries (Figure 3.3). The system was effective, and in the short run cheap, but it was not conducive to good discipline among the agents. Left to pursue their own interests in the world, they could very easily stir up trouble affecting wider national interests of which they were either careless or unaware. The result could be to place unsought-for responsibilities on the government at home: responsibilities it might have avoided had it chosen to exercise a more continuous control over its nationals abroad.

Beyond this, the British government was rarely directly implicated in these colonial crises. Their origins and causes were generally to be found in local factors, in conflicts between established societies and Britons acting independently of the government and its

PIONEERING

Figure 3.3 Pioneering. A hard-working pioneer couple taming nature in Australia, late nineteenth century.
Source: Gordon H. Woodhouse, 1886–1950. Courtesy of the State Library of Victoria. Available at: http://handle.slv.vic.gov.au/10381/76203.

wishes, or *even governors* acting independently of the government. This does not mean, of course, that the government was not responsible for extensions or consolidations of colonial control which took place as a result of these crises. It could have left its nationals to extricate themselves from problems they had brought upon themselves. Usually it did not, but went in to rescue them. Whether the government intervened, and how, depended on a number of considerations: partly on the intrinsic gravity of the crisis, but partly also on the degree to which wider British interests and responsibilities were affected by it, and on its assessment of what measures were necessary to contain it.

Always, however, there was one constant factor in the minds of colonial policy-makers, which was the need for economy. 'Retrenchment' was one of the prime political obsessions of the nineteenth century. To the way of thinking of most politicians, their highest public duty was to save the taxpayer's money, and parliamentary debates on colonial affairs from this period mainly comprised discussions about how to cut down on 'wasteful expenditure'. It was a firmly established principle that existing colonies should stand on their own feet financially, pay for their administrations out of their own resources. Even loans were discouraged: the Indian government was not allowed to borrow money for military building in 1860 because, in the words of the Secretary for India, 'when they are made to feel that they are themselves responsible for every shilling of their expenditure, they will find in it an inducement to economise in their outlay as far as possible'.[37] If money was so begrudged to existing colonies, it was not likely that it would be freely granted to acquire new ones. A powerful current of feeling in Parliament was represented by a Select Committee reporting in 1865 on the British possessions in West Africa, which strongly advised against 'all further extension of territory or assumption of Government, or new treaties offering any protection to native tribes', and which looked forward in the future – but perhaps not very hopefully – to 'our ultimate withdrawal' from three of the four British settlements on the west coast.

> Your Committee think it would have been better if the actual assumption of government had in all cases been at first avoided in countries which the English race can never colonise, and where British law is inapplicable to native customs, which have been connived at, but which might have been eradicated by the gradual influence of commerce without such interference.[38]

Four years previously, a Report on Colonial Military Expenditure had recommended that colonial garrisons maintained at British expense be reduced. Parliament's first instinct was to cut down on foreign commitments for the sake of economy, and it irritated her, therefore, to see Britain drawn into new commitments.

But while parliamentary opinion imposed a certain degree of caution on mid-Victorian governments, it could not halt entirely the process of colonial expansion, still less reverse it. If a government had taken the Commons at their word and actually surrendered a colony, their approval was by no means certain. They might agree in principle that the dog should be drowned, but a degree of odium would still attach to whoever did the drowning. Politicians in office were reluctant to risk this. They could not even stand still. Even in the interests of economy it was sometimes necessary to consolidate British control over certain territories – a paradox which the 1865 Committee itself reluctantly conceded.[39] But anyway, governments had to look beyond the requirements of mere economy: they had wider responsibilities than ordinary MPs, responsibilities not only towards the taxpayer, but also towards the security of the nation and her trade, and towards her subject races. These responsibilities frequently made the accepted ideal of political abstinence impossible to maintain. In the long run, perhaps the chief effect of 'anti-imperialist' sentiment on practical policy in the 1860s and the 1870s was to inculcate a general feeling of resentment against those uncooperative peoples whose recalcitrance had forced Britain to take them over (as it seemed) against her will.

But occasionally 'economy' won out – in areas where a cheese-paring approach was consistent with the maintenance of other essential British interests. In parts of West Africa, for example, local agents – merchants – could be trusted to secure the trade of the rivers, which was what mainly concerned Britain, on their own with only minimal support from home. Similarly, if a colony had a permanent European population strong enough to contain by their own efforts the crises arising within their borders, then Britain could safely economise by delegating the defence of her interests to them. In New Zealand, the whites *were* strong enough (just) to look after themselves, and so Britain retrenched. In the West Indies and South Africa, they were not strong enough. Consequently here the government had to intervene directly, and expensively, to defend its interests, and the frontiers of empire crept forward.

The local 'crisis' in New Zealand was the most common type in the history of colonisation: a conflict over land between an obstinate native population which had more than it could use, and a voracious immigrant population which wanted more than it had. Underlying the immigrants' voracity was a real, material need for more territory to satisfy their growing numbers; a strong cultural obsession – which we shall meet again – that land should not be held on to only to be neglected or misused, and a good deal of straight racial prejudice. Behind the Maoris' obstinacy lay half a century of profound cultural disturbance following their first contacts with white people, which had begun by corroding their institutions and way of life and enticing many of them over to white people's ways, and had provoked the rest of them in the 1850s to a spirited revival and defence of their old culture, refurbished, against the intruders. They made their stand in 1860. A Maori from Taranaki in North Island sold a piece of land to the British government. The Maori irreconcilables denied that an individual member of a Maori tribe had the right to alienate any part of its homeland without the consent of the whole people. Two different concepts of land ownership were involved: the communal concept of the Maoris, the British concept of individual tenure. After prevaricating for a short while, the British decided to take possession of their purchase. The Maoris resisted, and war broke out. It came to an end effectively in 1863 (although the most implacable of the Maoris fought a bitter rearguard action for another ten years). The result was a victory for the settlers' point of view over land. By confiscation and purchase, they managed in the next 30 years to secure for themselves the most fertile areas of North Island.

The British government's role in New Zealand was ostensibly to protect the natives and prevent war. It was British soldiers who had to fight the New Zealanders' wars for them; consequently there was a strong incentive for the Colonial Office to keep a tight hold on native affairs.

> Whilst Her Majesty's Government feel themselves constrained to justify to Parliament the large expense which every year is incurred for the maintenance of a military force in New Zealand for the defence of the colony, and for the better control and regulation of the Native race, they must retain in their hands the administration of those affairs which at any moment may involve the employment of those troops, and the consequences of an expensive conflict.[40]

They tried to. But the task was all but impossible. New Zealand was too far away for detailed Colonial Office supervision of her native policies to be effective, and successive governors sent out to implement Whitehall's wishes on the spot proved aggravatingly independent when they got there, and too easily swayed by settler opinion or hood-winked by local advisers. In any case, the British government's humanitarian resolve was not all that strong, and a good deal weaker than its resolve to economise. In the end, it decided to let the New Zealanders look after their own Maoris, and go to war with them if they liked – and to fight and pay for their wars themselves. Maybe when they were left 'to take the consequences of any false step which they may make',[41] they would tread more carefully in Maori affairs. Many settlers in North Island were outraged at the withdrawal of their free imperial fire service. But it was done; most of the British regi-ments were shipped back home in 1865–66 and the last one a few years later. It did no harm to the settlers, and it did a lot of good to the cost-conscious British government. The crisis in New Zealand was satisfactorily settled without the enlargement of colonial responsibilities, because there the local white population was dominant enough to manage the crisis itself, and preserve the British connection. What was true of New Zealand was even more true of her white neighbours in Australia, who were easily powerful enough to do away with their aborigines.[42]

This was not so, however, in the British West Indies, and the resolution of the local 'crisis' here was not nearly so satisfactory from the Colonial Office's point of view. The West Indian crisis had been brewing for some time. Like the other crises, it was the outcome of European encroachment on non-European societies, but here the encroach-ment had taken place many years before and in another place (on the slave coast of Africa). What was happening in the West Indies was that the system which had originally been devised for controlling the relations between the two racial groups there was breaking down. Traditionally the pattern was one of domination by white sugar planters over black labourers. Circumstances had recently conspired to undermine this pattern, and the ability of the whites to control the situation.[43] Political institutions devised for a slave economy proved deficient in an era of free labour: inadequate, that is, to preserve a satisfactory degree of white planter dominance. They were being infiltrated by men independent of the plantation economy, and hostile to the planters' demands. Attempts to manipulate the constitutions of the islands to retain control in the hands of the planters came up against obstruction from the Colonial Office in London, and from the realities of the planters' own situation – a dwindling group of men, in the main, devoid of enough common ability to run their affairs responsibly, and without the financial and material strength to back up their pretensions.

All this time the situation on the ground was deteriorating in the largest of the islands, Jamaica, whose planters had been hardest hit of all by the economic depression which had followed emancipation and free trade. The cause of their distress, they claimed, was the availability on the island of vacant lands, where the 'lazy' blacks could settle and provide for themselves, thus releasing them from the necessity of recourse to the planta-tions for regular work. On the other islands the same problem was to some degree solved by bringing in Asian immigrants to work the plantations. In Jamaica, the planters tried to force the black settlers off their lands, which provoked riots. Missionaries (particularly the Baptists) encouraged the settlers in their opposition to the planters. In the Legislative Assembly and in the countryside, disaffection grew stronger, tinged with racial overtones. The planters' order was breaking down. Earl Grey had predicted the likely consequences a dozen years before:

No one acquainted with the actual state of society in the West India islands ... can doubt that, if they were left, unaided by us, to settle among themselves in whose hands power should be placed, a fearful war of colour would probably soon break out ... and civilisation would be thrown back for centuries.[44]

In these conditions the only solution left to the planters was to surrender their powers to the Colonial Office. The latter was at least kindly disposed towards them and their method of production, recently it had replied to a petition from a group of poor blacks on the island by castigating their sloth and telling them to return to the plantations to work for wages. The planters preferred to entrust their fate to Whitehall rather than have it decided by militant blacks. Of the latter, they were terrified, mindful of the horrors of the Indian Mutiny and of recent events – a bloody insurrection – in neighbouring Haiti, and only too eager to attribute the same blood-curdling character to their own 'black rebellion' when it came, in 1865. Like the Indian Mutiny, the Jamaica Rebellion was suppressed brutally (and the brutality raised a storm in England). Shortly afterwards the Jamaican assembly voted to relinquish its own powers, and the island's government was taken over by the British Crown. Over the next few years all the other West Indian territories which were not already Crown Colonies followed suit, except one (Barbados). For the planting community, and for the Colonial Office in London, there was no other solution consistent with the preservation of the white man's law and order, with Earl Grey's 'civilisation'.[45]

South Africa occupied an intermediate position between New Zealand, where the whites were adjudged powerful enough now to ride out their own storms, and the West Indies, where they were not powerful enough and probably never would be again. In South Africa, the whites were *not yet* strong enough to manage their own affairs in a way that would ensure the security of Britain's essential interests there, but it was hoped that they would be soon. This was one reason why South Africa's 'crisis' was never resolved in this period, but continued to plague colonial secretaries: a pattern of sporadic wars between whites and Africans interspersed with periods of tension and anxiety, and never at any time looking nearer to being settled. The other main reason was geographical. In Jamaica and New Zealand, and to a lesser extent in India, the boundaries of British suzerainty or responsibility were clearly drawn and accepted. Consequently, their problems, however great, could at least be defined and limited, the competing interests assessed, and the factors involved contained and controlled. They were problems of domestic policy. This was not true of South Africa. There the problems were open-ended, always changing, and affected by developments outside even the theoretical control of the authorities, because the frontiers of British suzerainty were *not* clearly drawn, and it was on the frontiers that all the trouble started. The result was that South Africa remained for years in an interim state, the options as to her future kept open until the situation crystallised, and in the meantime was governed (in the words of Herman Merivale) by 'a succession of shifts and expedients'.[46] For tidy-minded colonial secretaries, this was an irksome state of affairs.

The British official presence in southern Africa centred around Cape Colony and Natal in the south and south-east, and then shaded off towards the north. South Africa's value to Britain, before gold and diamonds were discovered there in the late 1860s, was limited. It did not go far beyond the bay and naval base at Simonstown, a vital staging post for British ships on their way round the Cape to their eastern markets. 'Apart from the very limited extent of territory required for the security of the Cape of Good Hope as a naval station,' wrote the Colonial Secretary in 1852, 'the British Crown and nation have no interest whatever in maintaining any territorial dominion.'[47] Ideally Britain would have liked to restrict her responsibilities to the area of her interests. She could not do so because she was unable to control the activities of her nationals – and other Europeans – up-country.

For many years, white people, independently of any European government, had been penetrating northwards and eastwards into the interior of South Africa. Their contact with the African peoples they found there had produced continuous conflict: not only the conflict of ideas and attitudes which customarily accompanies peaceful culture-contact, but also, overshadowing this, bloody armed conflict for the possession of land. In a way these activities were no concern of Britain's. But she had to make them her concern because frontier conflicts had a habit of spreading and upsetting the security of her settlements at the coast. The problem was exacerbated by the way these frontiers people had organised themselves for their mutual protection – into small, ramshackle and sometimes very transient 'states' acknowledging allegiance to no-one except their own 'presidents' and responsibility towards only their own narrow interests. They did nothing to preserve order on the frontier. Their number only served to multiply the points of potential conflict; their weakness encouraged the powerful African tribes and nations to attack or resist them; and their hopeless lack of cohesion and co-operation dissipated the white man's chances of containing the Africans. There was the danger too that if any of them did ever grow strong enough to control the frontier problem, then they might also be strong enough to threaten British interests directly. This applied especially to the Afrikaner (Dutch-origin) republics to the north of the Orange River; at present near bankruptcy, but thought by many to be the potential growth area in southern Africa, and ambivalent, at the very least, in their attitude towards British 'suzerainty'. These factors beyond their borders immeasurably complicated what was already for the colonists in the south a difficult problem of intercultural relations. In Cape Colony, 100,000 whites lived among 150,000 black Africans; in Natal, 10,000 whites among 100,000 blacks. No solution could be found for their 'race problem' while it could still be so unpredictably affected by what went on to the north. 'No solution' meant, of course, that the British taxpayer was saddled with the expense of policing South Africa in the meantime.

The problem would not solve itself. Natives did not 'die out' in Africa as they were predicted to do, conveniently, in North America and Australasia. They could be a formidable enemy. They had certain advantages: numbers, a home terrain, and usually better and brighter generals than Britain seemed to be able to furnish at this time. That sometimes came as a shock to the British, whose sense of race superiority often led them to underestimate the Africans' tactical acumen. Usually they won in the end, but more often than not by destroying cattle and crops, and so starving their opponents into submission or compromise. That could be said, in fact, of many of Victorian Britain's 'little wars', in New Zealand, for example, as well as Africa, and right through to the end of the century: that she had the worst of far more of them than she admitted to at the time, and eventually came out top only through extra-military means.[48] This certainly applies to the Xhosa and Zulu wars of the mid-century at the Cape and Natal respectively. In the Xhosa case, the colonists were helped enormously by one clear tactical error the Xhosas made in 1857: when they slaughtered their *own* cattle to fulfil a magical prophecy that, if they did so, their warrior ancestors – somehow confused with the Russian army in the Crimea – would rise from the dead and drive the white men into the sea. The result, in fact, was starvation and the end of the Xhosa nation as a political force. But the British obviously could not bank on that happening again.

For this reason, the frontier continued to pose a threat to South African stability; to which the only answer was to exert some kind of discipline and control over it. In effect, this meant extending the area of British territorial responsibility. But it was an open question how exactly this should be done. In this matter, the Colonial Office relied heavily on the judgement of the men it sent out to manage things on the spot. For a time in the 1850s, it gave Sir George Grey his head in a grandiose scheme to pacify the tribal areas on the frontier by annexing them and settling Europeans there, who would 'change inveterate enemies into friends' by releasing the Africans from 'the tyranny of their chiefs' and initiating them into western, Christian ways. The idea was that a de-barbarised and integrated African would be less prone to aggression than a savage.[49] But the scheme did nothing to alleviate the main cause of African hostility, which was land-starvation (this was at the root of the Xhosa episode); and anyway it was costly, its benefits very notional and long-term, and the Colonial Office was never entirely persuaded of its expediency. When Grey left, it was dropped.

In the 1860s, the Colonial Office reverted to less ambitious policies, aimed chiefly at pushing the problem – and the expense – on to the colonists' own shoulders. In 1865 and 1871, it persuaded Cape Colony to take over two large new territories (British Kaffraria and Basutoland) as a prelude, it was hoped, to the withdrawal of imperial troops. But it was done against the strong opposition of the men on the spot: the Governor, Sir Philip Wodehouse, for humanitarian reasons: 'I cannot satisfy myself of the justice or humanity of handing over this large native population to the uncontrolled management of a Legislature composed of those whose habits, interests and prejudices are so entirely different,'[50] and the colonists themselves on grounds of poverty. And it was a fact that on their own the whites in Cape Colony and Natal were nowhere near numerous or prosperous enough to bear an extension of their 'native problem' or the burden of their own defence. The only hope was to persuade them to federate with the other white-dominated states of southern Africa and formulate with them a common native policy. But this idea made little progress in the 1850s and 1860s. If anything, the prevailing tendency on the spot was towards further disintegration, not closer union: Cape Colony, for example, frequently threatened to split in two. The independent republics north of the Orange River were chary of an association with the British colonies which might mean subordination – and Britain certainly intended them to be subordinate. Federation looked a very distant prospect, and meanwhile the 'Kaffir Wars' continued (Figure 3.4).

In the 1850s and 1860s, Britain had been drawn further into southern Africa, but her basic problems there had still not been resolved. As yet, however, there was little urgency in the situation. In the interests of economy (and perhaps of humanitarianism), it would have been nice to have settled the frontier problem, but not, obviously, if this would entail the expenditure of more money than would be saved. There was little of value in the area to justify strong and costly action in its defence, apart from Simonstown, and there was no real danger of losing that. This remained the situation until around 1870, when all was changed by the discovery of diamonds and gold just outside the recognised boundaries of the Afrikaner republic of the Transvaal. Gold and diamonds made South Africa intrinsically more valuable; they also made more real the prospect of some other power – the Transvaal itself or a European intruder – rivalling British predominance if it got hold of the goldfields, and threatening British interests. (The Transvaal did indeed lay claim to the gold- and diamond-bearing territory in 1868, though she very soon had to

Figure 3.4 Derring-do. Heroic deeds in the Zulu Wars, 1879. 'Saving the Queen's Colours' by
        Alfonse de Nauville.
Source: © Peter Newark Pictures/Bridgeman Images.

withdraw.) To the indifferent national interest of economy were added the more compelling ones of potential wealth and security in danger. The stakes had been upped.
Consequently South Africa's frontier problems were to become a matter of urgent
imperial concern. But this was in the future. As yet South Africa's value to Britain did
not justify, or require, more than a moderate effort to secure it.[51]

Colonial crises: tropical colonies

The same can be said of the other parts of the world where Britain had footholds in the
third quarter of the nineteenth century, like South-east Asia, the Pacific, the China coast
and West Africa; although in these areas too, a certain intensification of British interest
and activity can be detected towards the middle of the 1870s. In all of them, except perhaps Fiji, Britain's interests were broadly the same: predominantly commercial, to do
with the exchange of commodities and the shipping and banking services which went
with it; and in all of them her problem was the same: to safeguard or promote those
interests against disruption caused by political trouble inland. To this end in the 1860s
and the early 1870s, Britain intervened in all four areas. But in none of them – initially at
any rate – were her interests important enough, or the political troubles serious enough,
to provoke a very large *scale* of intervention.

The Malay peninsula was probably the most critical of the four areas, more by virtue
of the trade done through it than of the trade done with it. Significant as Malaya was

becoming as a source of tin and spices for the West, it was the role of Singapore as an entrepôt, and to a lesser extent Malacca and Penang, which gave the area its importance to Britain, especially after the Suez route to the east was opened in 1869.[52] Trade, however, required stability, and stability the local Malay rulers were not able to provide. Dynastic wars among the Malays, and clan warfare among the Chinese immigrants who did most of the tin-mining, reduced many areas to virtual anarchy; piracy flourished on the coast and the rivers; and the European settlements on the coast felt themselves threatened directly. The position got worse in the late 1860s and early 1870s, although it was probably never so bad as the local Europeans claimed. Merchants and prospective European tin-miners demanded government intervention; the Colonial Office – which took over the surveillance of the region from the India Office in 1867 – resisted, but somehow could not communicate its distaste for official intervention to the men it sent out to run things on the spot. One after another, the successive governors of the Straits Settlements, as soon as they were confronted by the local situation, became convinced of the need for Britain to rule or at least to dominate the unruly Malay states. (Perhaps it was something to do with their common military background: in a difficult situation soldiers are usually happier and more competent exerting authority than manipulating influence.) Despite repeated reprimands by Whitehall, they managed, within the discretion allowed them by the Colonial Office or by wilfully exceeding it, to extend Britain's influence and responsibility on the mainland, usually in pursuance of pirates. The process was a familiar one: in conditions of civil unrest, British authorities backed whichever party in a local dispute seemed willing and able to co-operate in apprehending the pirates and guaranteeing security for commerce generally. Sometimes this involved them in further complications. In Sungei Ujong, in 1874, Sir Andrew Clarke backed the wrong horse – the weakest of the local contenders for power – and had to send in troops to rescue him. The worst mess was in Perak, where there was no native ruler both willing to co-operate and strong enough to exert his authority locally. The governor (Sir William Jervois) wanted to annex, his local agent was murdered by Malays who resented his interference, and a full-scale colonial war developed in 1875. The situation was out of hand, and before the Perak war the government was persuaded to sanction intervention, if only in the interests of containment. The way they intervened was significantly 'informal' in appearance: not by annexing Malaya, but by planting what were called 'residents' there to 'advise' its rulers. It was well understood on all sides that the residents' advice would be followed. This was the minimum – the least expensive – action that could be taken compatible with the security of British interests in the area. It was realised at the time that the resident system was not so innocent as it looked, that it could escalate into a more formal imperialism in the peninsula. For this reason, wrote the Colonial Secretary in 1874, 'this new phase ... of colonial policy needs very careful watching'.[53]

The problem in Fiji was basically the same as that in Malaya: the islands' inability to cope with the situation imposed on them by their contact with European civilisation and commerce. It was unfortunate that many of the representatives of European civilisation the Fijians came into contact with were not Europe's most worthy ambassadors: a British consul described them in 1870 as 'low adventurers, absconders from the Colonies, and a class of men who are in a chronic state of excitement caused by continual indulgence in alcoholic drinks'.[54] British government agents tried to control these men and their relations with the Fijians, but very unsuccessfully, chiefly because of the absence of any stable native polity to negotiate with or work through. For some time, Fiji had been in the throes of a power struggle between rival kings, neither of whom could gain a firm ascendancy for long. In order to resolve this chaos into some kind of workable system, British consuls, like Malayan governors, tended to exceed instructions and involve themselves in the politics of the islands. When the government at home refused to back them, the local European settlers and freebooters stepped in and established their own, somewhat cavalier order. All this time the British stake in the islands was increasing: a new cotton plantation industry was flourishing and attracting settlers, commerce was growing, and the philanthropists were moving in strength – Fiji was one of the few successful Christian mission fields of the nineteenth century, and the centre too of a notable humanitarian *cause célèbre*, a labour kidnapping racket (called 'black-birding') which was attracting a great deal of public attention and outrage in Britain. For years, the government resisted the pressures on it to annex; instead it considered every expedient short of annexation which might secure the same end: the enforcement of consular jurisdiction over British subjects only; official recognition of one of the native claimants to power; rule by chartered company; even annexation by someone else – an Australian colony, or Germany or Belgium. None of these came to anything. So at length the government relented and formally annexed Fiji to the British Crown: reluctantly, stumbling in on the heels of *local faits accomplis*. The native rulers were persuaded to give their consent; for them, the situation had become as impossible as it was for the British. Fiji became a British colony in 1874.[55]

In West Africa, Britain persevered to the very limit with her traditional policy of safeguarding her interests by means of accommodations with local rulers. Usually this was sufficient. Britain's interests, though significant (especially on the Niger) did not make any greater demands on the Africans than that they be allowed peacefully to sell their produce to British merchants on the coasts and rivers. Generally the local rulers were authoritative enough to be able to guarantee this access, and – sometimes with a little encouragement or pressure – *willing* to guarantee it. Occasionally, however, the accommodation broke down somehow, British interests were threatened and intervention resulted, usually – again – on the initiative of the man on the spot. In 1861, Lagos was annexed for this kind of reason, and Sierra Leone took in one or two new extensions of territory; and the Gold Coast Protectorate was turned into a Crown Colony in 1874, after a brief little war, because the Ashantis had proved impossible – too proud and independent – to coexist with amicably, and their more co-operative rivals too weak to withstand them alone. Here influence and collaboration had manifestly failed, and the only alternative to annexation appeared to be the abandonment of existing British interests. Dedicated as it was to the principle of non-intervention, the Colonial Office rarely pushed it so far as actually to sacrifice an established national interest.[56]

In China, Britain was able to get away with very much less formal control than in South-east Asia, West Africa and the Pacific. China was different: not a backward country unable to supply the conditions of stability and security demanded by western commerce, but a highly sophisticated empire unwilling to admit western commerce. Britain's problem was to persuade her to open her doors. The first Opium War was fought for this end, and the Treaty of Nanking which had ended it in 1842 had established one or two openings for European trade, the 'treaty ports'.[57] Britain hankered after more – direct access to the infinitely promising markets of the Chinese interior; but not enough to risk any political involvement which might burden her with 'another India'. So long as the Manchus kept to their side of the 1842 bargain and provided security for existing trade, Britain left them alone. When they did not, then Britain came down on them, in the second Opium War of 1857–60; and she used the occasion to extend her trading rights (by the Treaty of Tientsin, 1858, and the Peking Convention of 1860). But she was careful not to come down on the Manchus too hard, enough to endanger their hold over their empire; and, in fact, in the 1860s, she helped them when they were threatened internally by the Taiping rebellion. The Taipings were, in a roundabout way, themselves a product of east–west culture contact, an orientalised Jesus Christ movement which for that reason got initial support in Britain as a sign that the Chinese were at last beginning to grope towards the Light. But as it became clear that the Taipings were not going to supplant the Manchus and provide an alternative *pax* for western trade, and British Christians rapidly lost patience with the movement's heretical aspects, all thoughts of cultivating it for Britain's own political and commercial ends were abandoned, and the government instead weighed in on the side of the Manchus. The Manchus were not altogether satisfactory allies – their authority was never completely convincing, and they remained unenlightened on the question of free trade. But they stayed just about in control of things, with a bit of propping up; enough anyway to make the enormous trouble and expense of formal empire in China still unnecessary in the 1860s and 1870s.[58]

The years from 1857 to 1875, therefore, saw a slow, careful building up of the empire, guided by a cool and generally rational consideration of British interests. Governments did not rush blindly into empire, grab pieces of territory merely 'on spec' or because it swelled their hearts to see the Union Jack fluttering over them. But they rarely failed to act to protect existing British interests if they seemed to be under threat. The dynamic of the mid-Victorian colonial movement was provided by the expansion of Britain's commerce and culture, over which governments had very little control. When *they* took action it was to defend or consolidate economic gains already made. The action they took was the minimum necessary to achieve this end. Of course, there could be argument as to what constituted 'minimum action'. Different statesmen differed in their assessments of what was necessary. They relied heavily on local information, and the men on the spot – governors, traders, settlers and missionaries – tended to exaggerate. Consequently there were inconsistencies, and there was certainly no mathematical correlation between the extent of British interests in an area, or any other factor, and the degree of political intervention. Nevertheless there was, throughout this period, a good deal of agreement among colonial secretaries on the general principle that a territory should be annexed only if an existing and legitimate British interest were at stake, and after all other solutions had failed.

Yet towards the end of the period, there were signs of change: not so much a change of policy as of the climate in which that policy was being pursued. In the early 1870s, statesmen were perhaps more sensitive to British interests than before, more quick to smell a threat to them, especially from European competitors. The deciding factor behind the introduction of the resident system in Malaya may have been the intelligence that Germany was planning to step in if Britain did not, and there were similar fears with regard to Fiji and West Africa.[59] There are portents here of that atmosphere of jealous international rivalry which surrounded the later, more competitive period of colonial expansion. Then again, the popular mood in Britain appeared to some to be changing, becoming more enthusiastic towards the extension of the empire for its own sake, instead of merely apathetic or straightforwardly chauvinistic as in the past. Disraeli thought he detected the mood and exploited it in his famous Crystal Palace speech of 1872.[60] His Colonial Secretary, Carnarvon, appeared to share it.[61] The general public certainly gave more attention and adulation than they merited to petty little colonial wars like Wolseley's Ashanti expedition of 1873–74,[62] and by the 1870s, statesmen – whether or not they let it affect their decisions – generally assumed that public opinion was on the side of the imperialists. All this contributed towards a more positive, slightly less apologetic imperialism in the mid-1870s.

The empire itself was beginning to take on a new shape. Most of the annexations of the 1860s and 1870s were of territories peopled mainly by non-Europeans. Of course, there had been vast non-European dependencies before: yet still the empire had been regarded in the mid-nineteenth century mainly as an Anglo-Saxon thing, an empire of 'national settlement', with the tropical colonies not really integral parts of the empire proper but merely supporting it like the butlers at a gentlemen's club. The acquisition of one or two more sizeable non-European dependencies never took away from the settlement colonies their predominance in people's eyes, but it did shift the balance of the empire very slightly away from them. By the 1870s, the empire was beginning to acquire some of that more cosmopolitan and authoritarian flavour which characterised its image in the 1890s and 1900s. The shift in balance had practical implications too. The dimensions of the empire's 'native problem' increased as more and more 'natives' were ruled directly from Whitehall. In Britain, there was as yet little sign that the new responsibilities thus assumed were being taken very seriously, although some colonial secretaries were aware they had them – that (as Lord Carnarvon said) 'annexation has a moral, as well as a material and commercial side' and involved 'duties to be performed to the native races who pass under our protection'.[63] As to what exactly those duties were or how they should be performed, ministers had scarcely any ideas of their own. Approaches to 'native races' generally oscillated between the merely negative, anti-slavery approach of a humanitarianism which had lost most of its vigour since the crusading 1830s, and the simple racist coercionism of the men who put down the Indian and Jamaican revolts. But in the new colonies themselves there were one or two men – like Sir John Grant in Jamaica, Sir George Grey in South Africa and Sir Arthur Gordon in Fiji – who were working out more constructive approaches to the problems of tropical government, and inaugurating a new and pregnant debate on the duties of trusteeship.

The vanguard

While the politicians cleaned up the messes left by previous generations of traders, adventurers and philanthropists, a new generation of traders, adventurers and philanthropists was busy staking out the empire's future frontiers. Britain's expansion into the world in the 1860s and 1870s was only partly territorial and political. Mainly it was economic and cultural.

Between 1857 and 1875, British trade with the rest of the world roughly doubled in value. Exports of cotton goods increased from £39.1 million to £71.8 million; of metal and metal manufactures from £27.4 million to £44.5 million; of woollen textiles from £13.5 million to £26.8 million. Imports of raw cotton increased from £23.9 million to £54.7 million; of corn from £19.4 million to £51.7 million; of meat from £3.5 million to £13.8 million.[64] British shipping and banking also spread, phenomenally.[65] As the volume of trade in commodities and services rose, so its geographical pattern changed. Britain's trade increased with every part of the world, but more rapidly in some areas than others. Europe's relative share of both imports and exports was increasing, in the 1870s, it was around 40 per cent. The Far Eastern market was improving too; for most of this period Asia accounted for about 20 per cent of British exports, as against 10–15 per cent in the previous 20 years. The African and Egyptian markets were beginning to be significant, taking 5–6 per cent of British exports in the 1860s and 1870s. Australia was becoming an important supplier of wool. On the other side, the transatlantic trade was becoming relatively less important. The West Indies were stagnant; Latin America and the United States were both taking a smaller proportion of British exports than in the 1840s and 1850s.[66] But over this comparatively short period, these changes were marginal. With one or two exceptions, Britain's best customers in 1857 were still her best customers in 1875. More important than changes in the direction of British trade was its sheer quantitative increase. The 1860s saw the culmination of the period of Britain's most exuberant industrial and commercial growth, when the plant nurtured by the industrial revolution and then liberated by the free trade legislation of the 1840s came to flower and filled out into the world. With Britain unchallenged by effective competition until the last few years, way ahead of the rest of the world in her technology and industrial organisation, her new cheap products found ready markets almost everywhere, and her demands for food and raw materials eager suppliers. New markets were pioneered and old markets exploited more intensively.

One of the factors which made this commercial expansion possible was the growth of British foreign investment. Very often when a foreign country bought British manufactures – particularly railway stock, machinery and the like – it was with money lent to it by the British. How much they lent is impossible to say. What an Englishman did with his money was his own private affair, a matter between him, his stockbroker and his God, and not for the Treasury to pry into; hence there are no absolutely dependable figures for the export of capital from Britain. The best guess is that, in 1870, she had about £700 million invested abroad overall.[67] That figure was certainly on the rise. Its balance was also shifting. Less of it went to western Europe in 1870 than ten years earlier, either because western European countries were too unstable politically for wary British investors, or because they could now supply their own capital needs out of their own surpluses. British capital sought new pastures, and the areas it chose were generally – but not always – areas either of British settlement, like Australia and Canada, or under British suzerainty, like India.[68] British capital was more venturesome than most, but it still required either a good chance of abnormal profits, or some assurance of reasonable security, before it would venture far beyond the pale of 'civilisation', and a British political connection gave it this security. Where there was no such connection, a British government guarantee would do the trick; very seldom was the government willing to give such guarantees, but just occasionally it might – as, for example, in the case of the Turkish government loans of 1854, 1855 and 1862, which it, in effect, underwrote in order to entice capital into an area whose economic stability and strength were considered vital to Britain's strategic interests.[69] For much the same reason – the minimisation of risk in less developed and therefore less creditworthy territories – British investment in industrial enterprises abroad tended to prefer concerns which, wherever they operated, and by whom, were directly administered from London.[70] Thus, it was predominantly British-based international companies, backed by British capital, which in the 1860s set out to pioneer the industrial development of those distant regions of the world where British trade, British settlers and the British flag had gone before. The contracting firm of Thomas Brassey, for example, which before 1857 had undertaken no work outside western Europe except a very long but ill-constructed and unprofitable railroad in Canada, between 1857 and Brassey's death in 1870 was building railways, docks and waterworks in India, Mauritius, eastern Europe, South America and the Antipodes.[71]

Canada, Australia and other settlement colonies soaked up a great deal of British capital in the 1860s, for railways, urban construction and (in Australia) gold mining ventures. Between 1860 and 1876, loans to their governments alone totalled £75 million.[72] But at this time it was India which offered the most glittering prospects. In India, British investors suddenly discovered that they had in their own possession a continent which was crying out for capital to exploit its potential riches, a country whose very salvation depended on building railways and canals and irrigation works there; and where investment was presented as a patriotic duty as well as a source of safe profit. Encouraged after the Mutiny by a new and uncharacteristically spendthrift government of India, they poured an estimated £150 million into the country between 1854 and 1869. Most of it went into railways, built (as we have seen) expensively but soundly by British contractors (Figure 3.5). The rest went into other public works, the Indian public debt, and private plantation, banking and shipping enterprises.[73]

By 1870, British capital was fast pursuing British commerce into the far corners of every ocean and every continent. Together they worked to open up the world to western civilisation. Helping them in their task was the missionary, slightly aloof from them, but never far away. The 1860s was a time of considerable hope for the missionary. In India, the missionary's labours were thought to have been given new encouragement by the final abolition in 1858 of the old, obstructive East India Company, and by one of that Company's last executive acts – the generous subsidisation of voluntary schools, including mission schools, promised by the Educational Despatch of 1854. In China, the barricades

Figure 3.5 Progress. A locomotive being ferried across the Jumna River, 1887, by an unknown photographer.
Source: © British Library Board. All Rights Reserved/Bridgeman Images.

erected against the incursion of the gospel were pushed further back by the treaties forced on the Celestial Empire by the European powers at the close of the second Opium War. In these two countries, missionary activity was busier in the 1860s and 1870s than ever before. But the great missionary hope now was Africa; and the 'opening up' of that continent, to Christianity and commerce, was in many ways – certainly for the future history of British imperialism – the most significant emanation of mid-Victorian expansion.

The opening up of Africa

To Europeans in the first half of the nineteenth century, Africa was still a virgin continent. They had caressed her coasts but not yet penetrated her interior. There had been little to take them there. Between the Sahara and Kalahari deserts there was nowhere they could settle, except one or two as yet undiscovered highlands. Since the transatlantic slave trade had (ostensibly) come to an end in the 1840s, there were no quick profits to be made there – and anyhow the slave trade had been carried on perfectly satisfactorily at the coasts, with African middlemen. There was ivory further inland, and rumours of gold, but nothing quite valuable or certain enough to make it worthwhile risking disease and death in the interior to get them. (The risk was a substantial one: between 1819 and 1836 the average annual death rate for European troops stationed on the west coast was 20 per cent for officers and nearly 50 per cent for men.[74]) The conditions and motivations which had led Europeans into the Americas, Australasia and the Indies much earlier were not present in Africa; hence the interior was shielded from Europe for an unnaturally long time. Its main geographical features were still a mystery in the 1850s. The source of the Nile was discovered only in 1862; the Great Lake area of central Africa was a blank on the map, sometimes filled with a putative line of mountains from west to east called the 'Mountains of the Moon'. But very slowly the map was being filled in by a handful of lone explorers picking out tortuous paths into the interior: tiny figures confronting a vast unknown, restlessly inquisitive, incredibly courageous, taxed to the limit physically and mentally by the hardships they had to endure; men like Mungo Park in West Africa in the 1790s, and Clapperton and Lander after him; the Germans Krapf, Rebmann, Barth, Rolphs and Nachtigal in Central and East Africa in the 1840s, 1850s and 1860s; John Speke and Richard Burton racing each other to the source of the Nile in the 1860s and 1870s; and David Livingstone in south-central Africa in the 1850s and 1860s.

Exploring Africa might have remained just that: a search after geographical and other kinds of scientific knowledge, fired in the case of East–Central Africa by an obsessive and millennia-old puzzle – where did the Nile rise? – and sustained by the explorers' macho desire to test their bodies and minds against the worst that nature and 'savage' humanity could throw at them; were it not for one other interposing factor. This was the slave trade: not the European Atlantic one, this time, but the Arab African one that long pre- and also post-dated it, and which, in the mid-nineteenth century, was inflicting atrocious horrors on the inhabitants of, in particular, the regions of Africa that were thickest with European explorers just then. This is important to be aware of, especially by those who might otherwise be tempted to assume that Africa was an Arcadia before the European imperialists came. Some of it may have been; much of it was not. Arab exploiters had got there first. Most western explorers were genuinely shocked by Arab slave-raiding when they met it, one of them predicting that the Africans could be 'wiped off the face of the earth' if it were allowed to continue,[75] as well as being inconvenienced, when on their travels they were attacked by the natives on the understandable suspicion that *they* were slavers. (It should be said that they were also greatly assisted by the geographical knowledge that Arab traders of all kinds could provide them with. In truth, the Arabs discovered the 'source of the Nile' before John Hanning Speke.) It was this that led some of them to lobby for British governmental action against the slave trade, in the form of naval patrols off Zanzibar (the main slave market), or by in some way protecting African rulers against the slavers; initially short of overt colonial control, which most of them had too much respect for African cultures, rulers and systems of governance to recommend. For the moment, these appeals fell on deaf ears in Whitehall. Palmerston was typical in failing to see what 'practical usefulness' all these 'discoveries' in Africa could possibly have,[76] but they would not always be so dismissive. Outside government, the eradication of the Arab slave trade became something of a crusade, both in the loose and in the stricter definition of that word, with the Christian missionary David Livingstone in the vanguard of the charge, through his example; and most of the slavers, of course, being Muslims.[77]

Livingstone was not the first to combine exploring with missionary proselytism – that accolade should probably go to the Anglican-sponsored Ludwig Krapf; nor was he, by a long way, the most successful as a missionary, with only a single convert to show for his long years of struggle – and he recanted later. But Livingstone was the one who caught the imagination in Britain, not least through the famous newspaper campaign that sought to 'find' him when he became 'lost' in central Africa, and the carefully staged meeting between him and the newspaper's agent, Henry Morton Stanley, when the latter claimed they merely raised their hats to each other and shook hands – 'Dr Livingstone, I presume' – for all the world as though they were in a London street, rather than the middle of the African bush. Only an Englishman (or, rather, a Scot and a Welsh-American) could have been so restrained. It was a master-stroke; and probably invented by Stanley.[78] The effect of this publicity was to make Africa the new focus of popular vicarious romanticism – which it remained through to the Boer War – and the new target of missionary endeavour. From the University of Cambridge in 1857 dozens of idealistic students rallied to Livingstone's clarion call to them to carry on his work of opening a 'path for commerce' – 'legitimate' commerce, that is, rather than the commerce in slaves – 'and Christianity' among the benighted Africans. A new society – the Universities Mission to Central Africa – was founded as a direct response to his appeal. The work of the older-established societies in Africa – British and foreign, Catholic and Protestant – took on a new lease of life. Tropical Africa was at last joining the other continents within Europe's ambit. As yet, it was early days; the white explorers, missionaries and traders were scattered very thinly over the continent, and most aspects of African life were unaffected by their incursions. But contact had been made at last; the European virus had taken hold, and its further spread was only a matter of time.[79]

For the Africans, this contact was not altogether an unmixed blessing. For as Britons came to know them better, they seemed to respect them less. This had happened in India too, rather earlier. It may have had something to do with their background and education, which encouraged most of them to despise what was strange to them, and to confuse strangeness with inferiority. But it derived far more from their situation in Africa. How Britons regarded Africans, and how they treated them, depended very largely on what they were doing there and how safe they felt – on what was convenient and what was politic. As a rule, the earliest Britons in Africa neither needed nor were able to treat the Africans adversely. Explorers, unless they happened to be the missionary sort, had no need to disapprove of African customs. Some they rather enjoyed, especially the more sexually permissive ones. Their great vulnerability – wandering alone as they did among strange and possibly hostile peoples with little likelihood of support from home if they got into trouble, and no wish for martyrdom – forced them to be tactful, adaptable to their surroundings, in the interests of survival. (There were exceptions, like Henry Stanley, who reputedly bullied his way through central Africa relying on his guns to preserve an illusion of magical authority,[80] but this way was less dependable.) Explorers usually learnt to get along with Africans; as in general did the early west coast traders, who again needed their friendship to survive and prosper, and who throughout the nineteenth and twentieth centuries were among the most easy-going of Europeans in Africa. They frequently found themselves at loggerheads with missionaries who, though they respected the Africans for what they might become, were vocationally committed to changing them and so could not approve of all the things they did. Often the missionaries were more disapproving than was prudent, and consequently met sticky ends. If the male ones had their wives and children with them, they tended to be more disapproving still: fearful that their children might be con-taminated by African talk, which was franker than theirs ('filth unspeakable', said one; 'filth unrecognised as filth by the speakers'[81]); or terrified – though there seemed no grounds for it – by the thought of rape, the Victorians' 'fate worse than death', which sent even the godly Dr Livingstone into a blind rage: 'our blood boils at the very thought of our wives, daughters, or sisters being touched', for they were 'men with human feelings', and if it happened 'would unhesitatingly fight to the death, with all the fury in our power'.[82]

As individuals after knowledge, therefore, Britons were likely to tolerate African cus-toms, or at least to act as if they did. As individuals with a mission to change them, and a duty to protect the virtue of their wives and children, they inclined to be less tolerant. And when they came in groups, with superior force to back them, and a need to justify using their labour or taking their land or ruling them, their attitudes got harder still. In groups, they could afford to respect Africans less, and it was in their interest to: not only in order to justify themselves, but also sometimes to make their task easier. 'It is suici-dal,' said one observer, 'for Europeans to admit that natives can do anything better than themselves. They should claim to be superior in everything and only allow natives to take a secondary or subordinate part.'[83] As in India, it was believed that colonial authority was preserved only at a proper social distance from the Africans. And this was how contact with Africa generally progressed: from the vulnerable individual to the powerful group, from the scientist to the proselytiser and exploiter, from diplomacy to domina-tion. It was a progression which encouraged attitudes towards the Africans which, if they were not downright unfavourable, were at the very best patronising, and became more so as time went on.

Just occasionally, the English were found admiring Africans: generally for the happy (and mythical) simplicity of their 'noble savage' existence; or else for the same 'doggy' virtues which attracted them to the Muslims and Sikhs of northern India too: their loy-alty and courage and strength. 'What splendid fellows!' wrote the explorer Joseph Thomson about some Masai warriors, in terms which could have been used for thor-oughbred horses; 'magnificent specimens of their race, considerably over six feet, and with an aristocratic savage dignity'.[84] More often, the image which was built up of the African was a less flattering one, a stereotype familiar in many situations of race contact – it corresponded almost exactly to the English stereotype of the Irish in the sixteenth century[85] – and not only where Europeans were involved. All people tend to judge others against themselves. In the middle-class British case, the African 'others' seemed dirty, immoral, untruthful, devious and instinctively idle (and so had to be forced to work for their own good). In their own environment they did not need to work, because fruit enough for them and their family just fell from the trees. Consequently they had no ambition, which explained why they had never achieved anything of lasting value that visitors could see. When there was work to be done, they sent their womenfolk out to do it, which was strange and shocking to middle-class Britons whose women were not allowed to work. Africans were imprudent, impulsive and excitable, like children. They had virtues; but even these were not the virtues Englishmen would have liked to have attributed to themselves: kindliness, charity, humour, the 'soft' virtues, not the hard masculine ones. Some believed that Africans were incorrigible. Those who did not tended to regard them as poor souls deluded by superstitions. For this reason they paid very little close attention to African ideas and customs. In a sense they regarded Africans as not having any. 'The Africans,' said one missionary, 'have, so to speak, no fixed belief, but a multitude of bad habits and baseless fears.'[86] The African's nature, wrote another, 'is as plastic and impressionable as a child's – a blank sheet whereon we may write at will, without the necessity of first deleting old impressions'.[87] Which should have made the work of salvation easier for the missionaries than in fact they found it, for it turned out that nearly always they underestimated the resilience and the value of alternative systems of belief to their own. This was a natural tendency, for people coming out of a society as ethnocentric as the British; to look in Africa only for traits they recognised as 'civilised', and to dismiss all others as purely negative factors, intrinsically worthless, indications merely of the degree of 'uncivilisation'. It produced, however, a very negative, and unsympathetic, and at first very ignorant image of Africa, which it took decades to erase.[88]

It was not the best time for Africa to be 'discovered'; what with this, and the general decline of humanitarian interest and activity in Africa, at least among politicians; and the government – all governments – at a loss to know what to make of these new strange peoples they were being pushed up against, and with no plans for them. But this was the time when Africa was 'opened up', to join almost all the rest of the wider world within Britain's commercial and cultural ambit, which now left hardly a corner of the world untouched by the probing fingers of industrial Britain's expanding civilisation.

Other European countries besides Britain were expanding too, though some way behind. As yet, there was room for everyone, and very little conflict between European nations over who should take or settle or trade with whom. It seemed for a time as if Europe had grown out of the bad old eighteenth-century habits of squabbling over colonies, which Adam Smith had shown to be so childish and unprofitable. Mid-nineteenth-century colonial expansion was felt to be different. When Britain took colonies, she took them because they would not or could not play the free trade game fairly. She took them in trust for European civilisation as a whole, used her powers to provide facilities (security and stability) which other European nations were welcome to benefit from too, and did not expect those European nations to complain. Generally, they did not complain, but then most of them were otherwise distracted in Europe – unifying themselves or fighting each other. When the unification and the fighting were finished, it would be a different story. The myth of free trade internationalism would be shattered, and a new era of competitive imperialism would succeed this happier period when Britain could have taken nearly the whole world if she had wanted, but did not want to, because her way was cheaper.

Notes

1 S. B. Chaudhuri, *Civil Disturbances during the British Rule in India (1765–1857)* (W. 1955).

2 F. S., first Earl Roberts, *Forty-One Years in India* (1897), i, 431.

3 H. Chattopadhyaya, *The Sepoy Mutiny, 1857: A Social Study and Analysis* (Bookland, 1957), p. 66.

4 *Parliamentary Debates*, 3rd series, 147 (1857), cc. 440–80.

5 P. C. Joshi (ed.), *Rebellion 1857: A Symposium* (People's Publishing House, 1957), p. 157.

6 *Parliamentary Debates*, 3rd series, 145 (1857), c. 1624, and 147 (1857), c. 532.

7 S. N. Sen, *Eighteen Fifty-Seven* (Luzac, 1957), p. 46.

8 Rebel proclamation quoted in *ibid.*, p. 36.

9 Quoted in Joshi, *op. cit.*, p. 148.

10 *Parliamentary Debates*, 3rd series, 147 (1857), c. 458.

11 Sita Ram, *From Sepoy to Subedar* (Routledge, [1873] 1970), p. 161.

12 J. B. Norton, *The Rebellion in India* (1857), quoted in Joshi, *op. cit.*, p. 63.

13 Chattopadhyaya, *op. cit.*, p. 198.

14 S. B. Chaudhuri, *Civil Rebellion in the Indian Mutinies, 1857–1859* (World Press, 1957), pp. 295–6.

15 Sir Herbert B. Edwardes, *The Speech of Lieut.-Col Edwardes at the Sixty-First Anniversary of the Church Missionary Society* (1860), p. 8.

16 W. H. Russell, *My Indian Mutiny Diary* (Caswell, 1957 edn), p. 194.

17 On the Indian Mutiny, see Chaudhuri, *Civil Rebellion in the Indian Mutinies, 1857–1859*; J. Pemble, *The Raj, the Indian Mutiny and the Kingdom of Oudh* (Harvester Press, 1977).

18 Edwardes, *op. cit.*, p. 6; S. E. Koss, *John Morley at the India Office, 1905–10* (Yale UP, 1969), p. 136.

19 J. W. Kaye (1859), quoted in T. R. Metcalf, *The Aftermath of Revolt: India, 1857–1870* (Cape, 1964), pp. 108–9.

20 Edwardes, *op. cit.*, p. 4.

21 Metcalf, *op. cit.*, p. 165.

22 *Ibid.*, p. 153.

23 P. Spear, *A History of India* (Penguin, 1965), ii, 152.

24 Russell, *op. cit.*, p. 25.

25 R. C. Dutt, *An Economic History of India in the Victorian Age* (Kegan Paul, 1904), p. 548.

26 V. A. Anstey, *The Economic Development of India* (Longman, 1929), pp. 129, 526.

27 Roberts, *op. cit*, i, 438; L. C. A. Knowles, *The Economic Development of the British Overseas Empire* (Routledge, 1928), p. 323.

28 Dutt, *op. cit.*, pp. 347–8.

29 For economic development in India, see Knowles, *op. cit.*, pp. 320–49, 366–83; D. H. Buchanan, *The Development of Capitalistic Enterprise in India* (Macmillan, 1934; reprinted Cass, 1965); M. D. Morris, 'Towards a reinterpretation of nineteenth-century Indian economic history', *Journal of Economic History*, xxiii (1963), 179–207.

30 On Lord Ripon, see A. Denholm, *Lord Ripon, 1827–1909: A Political Biography* (Croom Helm, 1982).

31 Sir John Strachey, quoted in E. Stokes, *The British Utilitarians and India* (Oxford UP, 1959), p. 284.

32 W. Hunter, quoted in M. Edwardes, *Bound to Exile: Victorians in India* (Sidgwick & Jackson, 1969), p. 164.

33 P. Woodruff, *The Men Who Ruled India*, 2 vols (Cape 1953, 1954), ii, *The Guardians*, p. 15.

34 See Mary A. Procida, *Married to the Empire: Gender, Politics and Imperialism in India, 1883–1947* (Manchester UP, 2002).

35 F. G. Hutchins, *The Illusion of Permanence* (Princeton UP, 1967), p. 115.

36 On India after the Mutiny, see Woodruff, *op. cit.*, p. ii (1954); D. Kincaid, *British Social Life in India, 1608–1937* (2nd edn, Routledge & Kegan Paul, 1973); V. G. Kiernan, *The Lords of Human Kind: European Attitudes to the Outside World in the Imperial Age* (Weidenfeld & Nicolson, 1969), Chapter 5; Christine Bolt, *Victorian Attitudes to Race* (Routledge & Kegan Paul, 1971); A. J. Greenberger, *The British Image of India* (Oxford UP, 1969), Chapters 2–4; R. Wilkinson, *The Prefects: British Leadership and the Public School Tradition* (Oxford UP, 1964), Chapter 9.

37 *Parliamentary Debates*, 3rd series, 160 (1860), cc. 1186–7.
38 *Report of the Select Committee on the State of the British Settlements on the Western Coast of Africa* (1865), pp. iii, xiv.
39 *Ibid.*, p. iii, para. 4.
40 Lord Carnarvon, 1859, quoted in W. P. Morrell, *British Colonial Policy in the Mid-Victorian Age* (Oxford UP, 1969), p. 229.
41 Sir Frederick Rogers, 1863, quoted in *ibid.*, p. 289.
42 On New Zealand, see Keith Sinclair, *The Origins of the Maori Wars* (New Zealand UP, 1957); B. J. Dalton, *War and Politics in New Zealand, 1814–1865* (Sydney UP, 1967); Morrell, *op. cit.*, Chapters 7–11; W. H. Oliver (ed.), *The Oxford History of New Zealand* (Oxford UP, 1981); James Belich, *The New Zealand Wars and the Victorian Interpretation of Racial Conflict* (Auckland UP, 1986).
43 See p. 25.
44 Earl Grey, *The Colonial Policy of Lord John Russell's Administration* (1853), p. 14.
45 On the West Indies, see H. Parry and P. Sherlock, *A Short History of the West Indies*, 3rd edn (Macmillan, 1971), Chapters 14, 16; Morrell, *op. cit.*, Chapters 12–13; P. Curtin, *Two Jamaicas* (Harvard UP, 1955), Chapter 9; B. Semmel, *The Governor Eyre Controversy* (MacGibbon & Kee, 1962); G. Heuman, *Between Black and White: Race, Politics and the Free Coloureds in Jamaica, 1792–1865* (Clio, 1981); Thomas C. Holt, *The Problem of Freedom: Race, Labor and Politics in Jamaica and Britain, 1832–1938* (Johns Hopkins UP, 1992).
46 Morrell, *op. cit.*, p. 107.
47 W. M. Macmillan, *Bantu, Boer and Briton*, 2nd edn (Oxford UP, 1963), p. 323.
48 N. Mostert, *Frontiers: The Epic of South Africa's Creation and the Tragedy of the Xhosa People* (Cape, 1992); and see J. Laband, *Kingdom in Crisis: The Zulu Response to the British Invasion of 1879* (Manchester UP, 1992), and J. Belich, *The New Zealand Wars and the Victorian Interpretation of Racial Conflict* (Auckland UP, 1986).
49 J. Rutherford, *Sir George Grey* (Cassell, 1961), Chapters 21–2.
50 Morrell, *op. cit.*, p. 174.
51 On South Africa, see C. W. de Kiewiet, *British Colonial Policy and the South African Republics* (Longmans, Green & Co., 1929); J. Rutherford, *Sir George Grey* (Cassell, 1961); J. S. Galbraith, *Reluctant Empire* (University of California Press, 1963); A. E. Atmore and S. Marks, 'The imperial factor and South Africa', *Journal of Imperial and Commonwealth History*, iii (1974), 105–39.
52 G. C. Allen and A. G. Donnithorne, *Western Enterprise in Indonesia and Malaya* (Allen & Unwin, 1957), pp. 38–9; C. N. Parkinson, *British Intervention in Malaya 1867–1877* (Oxford UP, 1960), pp. 36–9.
53 W. D. McIntyre, *The Imperial Frontier in the Tropics 1865–75* (Macmillan, 1967), p. 299. See also C. D. Cowan, *Nineteenth Century Malaya* (Oxford UP, 1961); Parkinson, *op. cit.*, *passim*.
54 McIntyre, *op. cit.*, p. 227.
55 See *ibid.*, Chapters 7, 8, 11, 12; J. D. Legge, *Britain in Fiji 1858–1880* (Macmillan, 1958).
56 See McIntyre, *op. cit.*, Chapters 3, 4, 9; J. D. Hargreaves, *Prelude to the Partition of West Africa* (Macmillan, 1963).
57 The first Opium War (1839–42) comes outside the strict remit of this book, but an excellent recent account of it by Julia Lovell, *The Opium War: Drugs, Dreams and the Making of China* (Picador, 2011), also deals at length with its aftermath in our period.
58 See J. S. Gregory, *Great Britain and the Taipings* (Routledge, 1969).
59 McIntyre, *op. cit.*, pp. 73–4, 95–6, 105, 124, 202–5, 252; Cowan, *op. cit.*, pp. 166–72.
60 R. Koebner and H. D. Schmidt, *Imperialism: The Story and Significance of a Political Word* (Cambridge UP, 1964), p. 112.
61 McIntyre, *op. cit.*, p. 332.
62 Hargreaves, *op. cit.*, p. 169.
63 Legge, *op. cit.*, p. 137.
64 B. R. Mitchell and P. Deane, *Abstract of British Historical Statistics* (Cambridge UP, 1962), pp. 283, 298, 303–4.
65 P. J. Cain and A. G. Hopkins, *British Imperialism: Innovation and Expansion 1688–1914* (Longman, 1993), pp. 170–3.
66 W. Schlote, *British Overseas Trade from 1700 to the 1930s* (Blackwell, 1952), pp. 156–9.

67 Cain and Hopkins, *op. cit.*, p. 173; D. C. M. Platt, 'British portfolio investment overseas before 1870', *Economic History Review*, xxxiii (1980), 1–16.

68 C. K. Hobson, *The Export of Capital* (London School of Economics, 1914), pp. 121–40; H. Feis, *Europe, the World's Banker 1870–1914* (Council on Foreign Relations, 1931), pp. 17–19; L. H. Jenks, *The Migration of British Capital to 1875* (Cape, 1927; revised 1938), pp. 195–6.

69 D.C.M. Platt, *Finance, Trade and Politics* (Clarendon Press, 1968), p. 199.

70 Jenks, *op. cit.*, p. 195; Hobson, *op. cit.*, p. 125.

71 Jenks, *op. cit.*, pp. 419–20.

72 *Ibid.*, p. 231.

73 *Ibid.*, pp. 206–31; Hobson, *op. cit.*, pp. 135–6; and see L. E. Davis and R. A. Huttenback, *Mammon and the Pursuit of Empire: The Political Economy of British Imperialism, 1860–1912* (Cambridge UP, 1986).

74 P. D. Curtin, *The Image of Africa* (Macmillan, 1965), p. 362.

75 John Hanning Speke, quoted in Tim Jeal, *Explorers of the Nile: The Triumph and Tragedy of a Great Victorian Adventure* (Faber & Faber, 2011), p. 127.

76 *Ibid.*, p. 190.

77 See *ibid.*, *passim*; and also Tim Jeal, *Livingstone* (Heinemann, 1973), and Tim Jeal, *Stanley: The Impossible Life of Africa's Greatest Explorer* (Faber & Faber, 2007).

78 Jeal, *Explorers*, p. 270.

79 On the European penetration of Africa, see R. I. Rotberg, *Africa and its Explorers* (Oxford UP, 1970); M. Perham and J. Simmons (eds), *African Discovery* (Faber & Faber, 1942); A. Moorhead, *The White Nile* (Hamish Hamilton, 1960), and A. Moorhead, *The Blue Nile* (Hamish Hamilton, 1962); R. Oliver, *The Missionary Factor in East Africa* (Longmans, Green & Co., 1952); E. A. Ayandele, *The Missionary Impact on Modern Nigeria 1842–1914* (Longmans, 1966); Stuart Piggin, 'Halévy revisited', *Journal of Imperial and Commonwealth History*, ix (1980), 17–37; A. N. Porter, 'Religion and empire: British expansion in the long nineteenth century, 1780–1914', *Journal of Imperial and Commonwealth History*, xx (1992), 370–90; Philip Curtin, *Death by Migration: Europe's Encounter with the Tropical World in the 19th Century* (Cambridge UP, 1989).

80 See Jeal, *Stanley*.

81 H. A. C. Cairns, *Prelude to Imperialism* (Routledge, 1965), p. 59.

82 *Ibid.*, p. 60.

83 R. Symonds, *The British and Their Successors* (Faber & Faber, 1966), p. 76.

84 Cairns, *op. cit.*, p. 107.

85 See D. B. Quinn, *The Elizabethans and the Irish* (Cornell UP, 1966).

86 Cairns, *op. cit.*, p. 164.

87 *Ibid.*, p. 165.

88 On British attitudes to Africa, see Curtin, *The Image of Africa*; Cairns, *op. cit.*; Christine Bolt, *Victorian Attitudes to Race* (Routledge & Kegan Paul, 1971), Chapter 4; D. Lorimer, *Colour, Class and the Victorians* (Leicester UP, 1978); V. G. Kiernan, *The Lords of Human Kind: European Attitudes to the Outside World in the Imperial Age* (Weidenfeld & Nicolson, 1969), Chapter 6.

4   Conquests forced on us: 1875–90
The European challenge

Throughout the reign of Queen Victoria the broad motives behind Britain's acquisition of colonies altered very little. Annexation was never undertaken lightly, and very rarely as a means of extending British interests and influence into new areas of the world. In almost every case the interests and influence were already established there, independently of government, and political annexation was intended merely to safeguard or defend them when they appeared to be threatened. Always annexation was regarded as a last resort. This was as true of the 1880s and 1890s, when the empire spread like a measles rash, as it was of the more restrained 1860s and 1870s. The difference between the two periods was that in the latter period the last resort had to be resorted to more often. The reasons for this lie partly in the objective situation of the time – especially political and economic developments in Europe; and partly in people's subjective assessments of this situation. In the last quarter of the nineteenth century, British interests in the world seemed to be threatened more and more, and people in Britain were becoming more aware of this and more vigilant. Consequently more colonies were annexed.

In the earlier period, where British interests were threatened, it was generally by recalcitrant 'natives' on the spot. Natives continued to be recalcitrant during the 1880s and 1890s, but by then the main threat came not from them but from European rivals. Before the 1880s there was very little European colonial rivalry because continental Europe had more urgent political priorities. The revolutionary era and the settlements which followed it had left her somewhat artificially and unsatisfactorily divided politically, and she spent most of the nineteenth century trying to shake herself down into viable nations – nations, that is, united by language and common customs rather than dynastic ties or strategic convenience. This was achieved only around 1870, with the unification of Germany and of Italy. While this was going on, Britain was the only European nation of any size that was able to remain aloof from continental affairs, apart from a brief foray eastwards in 1854; and Britain too, though she had her internal troubles in the 1840s, was spared the full effect of Europe's revolutionary movement of 1848. Britain remained united, stable and at peace during most of these years, and consequently had been able to take advantage of the disorder and disunity on the continent to do more or less what she liked outside. In the 1870s, all this was changing. Continental Europe had gelled at last into modern nations. The shapes which had emerged were not satisfactory to everyone – France in particular felt mortally aggrieved by the loss of Alsace-Lorraine to Germany; but they looked fairly permanent, for the foreseeable future. Europe could afford to look outwards once again. Sixty-odd German states, or six or seven Italian ones, could never have been conceived of as colonial powers, but a unified Germany and a unified Italy could. And France, where this process of nation-building had been felt most severely, and whose European ambitions seemed frustrated at every point, appeared to have no alternative, if she were to recover her prestige, but to do it outside Europe.

Europe was settling down politically; she was also expanding demographically and commercially, though her progress was uneven. Between 1850 and 1900, the population of Europe increased by 50 per cent: Britain's from 28 million to 42 million, Germany's from 36 million to 46 million, Russia's from 60 million to 111 million, and the Netherlands' from 3 million to 5 million. (France was the strangely infertile exception, with an increase of only 3 million to 39 million.[1]) At the same time continental European countries were at last beginning to close the economic gap between them and Britain, and doing it fast. By 1880, Germany had more railway mileage than Britain, and France almost as much; and Russia had built, almost from nothing, over 10,000 miles of railways in twenty years.[2] They were becoming more mechanised. Between 1850 and 1870, while Britain's steam-engine capacity increased from 1,290,000 to 4,040,000 horse-power, Germany's went from 260,000 to 2,480,000, France's from 370,000 to 1,850,000, and Russia's from 70,000 to 920,000.[3] Industrial growth was reflected too in fast rising trade and investment figures. Between 1860 and 1880, the value of Britain's exports rose by 36 per cent, from £164 million to £223 million; and her imports rose by 96 per cent, from £210 million to £411 million. By comparison, the continent's foreign trade was increasing faster (Table 4.1).

Figures for capital investment abroad are more notional, but it has been estimated that France's share was £204 million in 1855, £510 million in 1870 and £673 million in 1885: about half of Britain's.[4] By most yardsticks for measuring expansion, therefore, Europe was an expanding society, although in different countries expansion took different forms, and some countries lagged behind.

An expanding society was not necessarily a colonialist one. There were one or two European countries besides Britain with a recent tradition of empire-building: France in North Africa and South-east Asia, the Netherlands in the East Indies, and Russia on her own southern and eastern borders (and at one time over as far as California). Yet this was not, yet, a time when empires were regarded with unmixed enthusiasm by any of them; for most other countries, and for many French, Dutch and Russians too, their value was dubious at the very least. Bismarck in 1871 was quite emphatic: 'I will have no colonies. For Germany to possess colonies would be like a poverty-stricken Polish nobleman acquiring a silk sable coat when he needed shirts.'[5] This was the dispassionate view of colonialism. But there were signs then, in the 1870s, that it might lose favour

Table 4.1 Comparative European trade, 1860–80

	Exports (£million)			Imports (£million)		
	1860	*1880*	*Increase (%)*	*1860*	*1880*	*Increase (%)*
France	91	139	53	76	201	164
Germany	n/a	142	–	n/a	136	–
The Netherlands	30	53	77	27	71	163
Belgium	24	49	104	21	67	219
Russia	35	81	133	33	79	251[1]

Note [1] W. Woodruff, *The Impact of Western Man: A Study of Europe's Role in the World's Economy, 1750–1960* (Macmillan, 1966), pp. 300–32; P. I. Lyaschenko, *History of the National Economy of Russia* (Macmillan, 1949), p. 518.

soon. In the first place Europe was already, in a sense, overspilling her borders: well over a million continental Europeans emigrated to other continents in the 1870s (mostly from Germany), and 12 million over the whole second half of the century.[6] More significant was the emigration of their goods and capital. As foreign trade increased, so in proportion did the amount of it going outside Europe. France had always been strong outside Europe, especially in North Africa and the Mediterranean. In 1840 £7.7 million of her export and £9.2 million of her import trade was done outside Europe; in 1880, the figures were £38.4 million and £73 million. Other countries' extra-European trade was slighter, but still significant and increasing.[7] Europe's economic contacts with the wider world were multiplying, much as Britain's had been doing for years. In Britain's case this process of commercial penetration had in many places led her to acquire colonies in the interests of commercial security; it might do the same for France and Germany. Many European statesmen and industrialists wanted to hurry the process up, secure colonies before they strictly needed them. Their reasoning was that European markets might soon become glutted, and a nation's economic survival depends on its being able to offload its surplus products elsewhere. Jules Ferry in France and King Leopold of the Belgians both argued in this way. And even Bismarck eventually was brought to realise the value of colonies for securing (in his words) 'new markets for German industry, the expansion of trade, and a new field for German activity, civilisation and capital'.[8]

This affected Britain in two ways. First, of course, Europe's new interest in colonial expansion brought her into direct competition with Britain, and in many parts of the world might bring them into conflict. In the past, Britain's hegemony over the wider world had been maintained with relatively little effort, because she had more or less a clear run of it. Now she had to take account of foreign rivals: the old traditional ones of France and Russia, whose fitful expansion was becoming more resolute and vigorous and in several places meeting Britain's own; and the newer rivalry of a Germany out for a 'place in the sun' for whatever reason – because she really wanted one, or because it was a way to bother Britain. Continentals argued that there was room for them both. Britain's colonial possessions did not cover the whole world; there were plenty of spaces between them where other countries could expand without encroaching. From Britain's point of view, however, it was not so simple. Her national interests were spread much wider than the limits of her colonial empire. Consequently they could be damaged even in 'neutral territory': on the East African coast, for example, which was nominally independent and therefore fair game for a predatory imperialist, but where there existed very definite British interests which could be put at risk if a predator pounced. This was the immediate and obvious challenge. Clearly it had to be met or accommodated in some way. If Britain stood still, there was a danger that she might in effect lose ground.

But it went deeper than this. Europe might have kept clear of colonies altogether and still presented a threat to Britain which had implications for her colonial policy. Her *commercial* rivalry in itself was enough to set many people worrying and reaching for their maps. In a way, of course, Europe's rise to industrial maturity meant, for Britain in common with all exporting countries, a more prosperous European market. But that was not how the worriers looked at it. What struck them more forcibly was the threat it presented to her existing export trade, and to her whole manufacturing supremacy. There were one or two Cassandras prophesying economic doom as early as 1870,[9] and the trade depression of the later 1870s and 1880s seemed to show that they were not conjuring fears out of nothing. The chief feature of the depression was falling profits. It was easy to show that profits were falling because too many manufactures and too much capital were chasing too few markets, and it seemed likely that markets were scarce because foreigners were grabbing them – especially, said a Royal Commission reporting on the causes of the depression in 1886, the more persevering and enterprising Germans.[10] If this diagnosis was not altogether correct, it at least provided a scapegoat, especially when it was suggested that the competition from foreigners was, by the free trade rules, not altogether fair:

> We are disposed to think that one of the chief agencies which have tended to perpe-
> tuate this state of things is the protectionist policy of so many foreign countries ...
> The high prices which protection secures to the producer within the protected area
> naturally stimulate production and impel him to engage in competition in foreign
> markets. The surplus production which cannot find a market at home is sent abroad,
> and in foreign markets undersells the commodities produced under less artificial
> conditions.[11]

In effect, they were cheating. The implication was that there was nothing much that British industrialists could do by their own unaided efforts to counteract foreign competition, and this, and the whole emphasis on foreign markets, suggested to some people that the answer might be to make sure of their export outlets by securing them politically.[12]

It was this that made the empire apparently even more vital to Britain than it had used to be, despite the threats against it that now loomed. Joseph Chamberlain, later to be a forceful Colonial Secretary, and later still a protectionist, but neither of these just yet, pointed out some of the advantages in a speech he gave in 1888:

> We have suffered much in this country from depression of trade. We know how
> many of our fellow-subjects are at this moment unemployed. Is there any man in his
> senses who believes that the crowded population of these islands could exist for a
> single day if we were to cut adrift from the great dependencies which now look to us
> for protection and which are the natural markets for our trade? ... If tomorrow it
> were possible, as some people apparently desire, to reduce by a stroke of the pen the
> British Empire to the dimensions of the United Kingdom, half at least of our popu-
> lation would be starved.[13]

It was a highly dubious argument, but a common one. It carried weight at a time when there was considerable concern in Britain about what was called 'the social problem', the time when Charles Booth was quantifying the desperate condition of London's poor, and when strikes and riots and 'outrages' were pointing to an alarming moral for the middle classes. Colonies appeared to be one very obvious way to relieve poverty. In arguments reminiscent of the 'colonial reformers' of the 1840s, a young radical called Edward Jenkins showed, first, how the poor could find work there, and second, how by working and earning they would provide a growing market for British manufactures, and hence employment at home for those who did not emigrate.[14] General Booth's final solution to the problem of what to do with the folk the Salvation Army saved from damnation was to send them to colonies abroad.[15] James Froude, an imperial propagandist writing in the 1870s and 1880s, saw it as a question of racial vigour. In the overcrowded slums of England, he asked, 'Was it to be supposed that a race of men could be ... reared who could carry on the great traditions of our country?' Rome had gone under because

city-living had enervated her people; Britain might suffer the same fate. But she had a remedy in her colonies of settlement,

> where there was still soil and sunshine boundless and life-giving; where the race might for ages renew its mighty youth, bring forth as many millions as it would, and would still have the means to breed and rear them strong as the best which she had produced in her early prime.

In this gigantic free-range farm for breeding better Britons, she had 'all she needed to eclipse every rival that envied her'.[16]

It was the rivalry which made the matter urgent. Other countries were being quite deliberate in their efforts to oust Britain from her pre-eminent position among trading nations, as, of course, they were entitled to do. Britons were beginning to doubt their own capacity to rise to the challenge, economically and also militarily. (A pamphlet published in 1871 called *The Battle of Dorking* gave a convincing picture of how the Germans could overrun England, and 'naval scares' were regularly worked up by the press throughout the 1880s.) And on a higher level of speculation, the problem was serious because it was not merely a question of German commercial competition or Russian military ambition, but more fundamental: to do with hard facts of geography. The point was that once Germany had begun to exert her full industrial strength, she *had* to overtake Britain, because she was bigger, more populous and had better natural resources. And if this was true of Germany, it was even more true of Russia and the United States. Europe's population was expanding in the nineteenth century, but theirs was expanding even more: North America's from 6 million in 1800 to 81 million in 1900, Russia's from 37 million in 1800 to 111 million in 1900.[17] Their natural riches were limitless. 'Germans, Russians, and Americans,' wrote Froude, 'were adding yearly to their numbers, and they had boundless territory in which millions could mature into wholesome manhood.'[18] To anyone with an instinct for what later became called 'geopolitics', the signs were clear that Europe's days were numbered. The historian John Seeley wrote in 1883:

> If the United States and Russia hold together for another half century, they will at the end of that time completely dwarf such old European States as France and Germany, and depress them into a second class. They will do the same to England, if at the end of that time England still thinks of herself as simply a European State.[19]

The choice – as Benjamin Disraeli put it to his audience at the Crystal Palace in 1872 – was between 'a comfortable England, modelled and moulded upon Continental principles and meeting in due course an inevitable fate' and empire.[20] The latter required a positive and vigorous effort.

What is significant about most of the new arguments for imperialism is the vein of pessimism which ran through them. The suggestion now being made was that Britain *had* to expand in order to stay alive. The language was the language of Nemesis. 'This is what England must either do, or perish,' said John Ruskin in 1870; 'she must found colonies as fast and as far as she is able.'[21] Fear probably made more people into imperialists than anything else did, whether it was fear for economic survival, or for the future of the race; or just a general, unformulated anxiety that things were not quite so easy for Britain as they had been once, and that maybe she ought to prepare herself for a harder time to come. However widespread this feeling was, it was certainly growing towards the end of the century. The ebullient self-confidence which had characterised the mid-nineteenth century, among its middle classes, was waning as the rising graph of economic prosperity levelled out a little, and the middle classes seemed to have their horizons clouded, their future rendered less infinitely promising, by the cold spectre of diminishing profits. Loss of confidence naturally produced a more defensive frame of mind – less self-assured, less trustful of others, less willing to take risks. To some people, as we have seen, it suggested that the solution to Britain's problems lay in building up the empire dramatically. Such recommendations never had very much practical effect, certainly not in the 1870s and 1880s. The men who made practical policy were generally cooler-headed, or just cautious of grandiose schemes. Very rarely was an out-and-out imperialist given his head and an effective say in things; when one was, as Froude was in South Africa and Lord Lytton in India, the result was not always to his liking. Colonial policy remained an *ad hoc* business, of governments responding to certain specific political situations which seemed to have some bearing on British interests, and responding to them, ideally, with an aristocratic detachment from emotional rumblings beneath them. Yet they could not be entirely detached, and if 'imperialism', in the imperialists' sense of the word, had little effect on their decisions, yet the general political mood of which it was a symptom must have done. It was all part of the background. With things looking not quite so rosy all round in international affairs, a Russian advance in central Asia or a German commercial challenge in Africa could not be regarded with the same equanimity as it would if Britain had felt basically secure. Even if they did not share it themselves, governments ignored the general unease at their peril. Gladstone was crucified by journalists, and by a cantankerous old Queen, for truckling too much to foreigners and letting the country slide. It was an anxious time for all.

One symptom of this prevalent disquiet was a revival of protectionist economics in Britain in the last quarter of the nineteenth century, on the grounds that the time was past when Britain could afford to be so charitable to her rivals as to allow them free play in her markets – as she did – while they excluded her from theirs. The orthodox free trade position, of course, was that this was ultimately self-defeating; that, as *The Times* put it in 1881 in reaction to a new French tariff, 'Protection … brings its own punishment. We are safe, therefore, in leaving its adherents to the stern teaching of facts. Nature will retaliate upon France whether we do so or not.'[22] But at a time of depression such reassurances seemed less and less convincing. The protectionist countries did not seem to be suffering overmuch for their sins. Britain, on the other hand, could be courting destruction. It was a big gamble to take on a theory. Faced with this situation some people turned against the theory altogether, and became protectionists themselves. 'It is strange,' commented a London newspaper in 1878, 'after thirty years of silence, to hear – issuing as it were from the tomb – the assertions and fallacies … which most people supposed were buried beyond hope of resurrecting.'[23] The new protectionists' main point was that free trade was 'unfair' while it was so one-sided. They founded a 'Fair Trade League' in 1881 to press for the reintroduction of tariffs: selective tariffs to retaliate against foreign protectionists, or, more ambitiously, a whole system of tariff preferences to bind the empire into a great customs union (modelled on the German) which would give Britain the commercial security – safe markets and sources of raw materials – which in a hostile world free trade could no longer guarantee. 'With the markets of the world closing up before our eyes,' said a newspaper in 1885, 'it becomes clear that the livelihood of our population may depend on keeping Australia, and Canada, and South Africa open to our traders. An Anglo-Saxon *Zollverein* has come within the purview of the most "practical" politician.'[24] And it was this policy which a member of the 1886 Royal Commission claimed would cure the depression, by giving 'fuller employment to our working classes at home ... thus increasing the healthful activity of the home trade, as well as the import of raw materials for our various industries to operate upon'.[25] Basically, it was a crisis of confidence. For protectionists, the free trade seas had become rather perilous of late, and they wanted more sheltered waters to sail in.[26]

That campaign failed in this period, and indeed for 40 years afterwards. This was because no political party could be found to espouse it; industries were split over it, mainly according to whether or not they felt seriously threatened by the competition; and the gentlemen of 'the City' – the financial interest – saw nothing in it for them.[27] That may have tilted the balance decisively, at a time when finance and the service sector of the economy (banking, insurance, shipping) were rising sharply in importance, by comparison with – possibly even at the expense of – manufacturing industry. That trend was to continue. It probably had an effect on the decisions taken by Britain's political leaders. The contemporary imperial critic J. A. Hobson thought so. He thought that finance was somehow manipulating events to its own profit, but against the interests of the nation as a whole.[28] Two historians – P. J. Cain and A. G. Hopkins – have shown that it did not require anything as crude as 'manipulation' to persuade government ministers to go along broadly with the City's views. Most of them were stockholders; and they shared a common culture with the financial class.[29] That marked them off from Joseph Chamberlain, for example, whose conversion to protectionism in the early 1900s may have had something to do with his very different origin, from industrial capitalist stock. Most of his top colleagues disagreed with him over this. They did not go for tariffs. But they shared in the general worry over Britain's prospects in the latter part of the nineteenth century which the tariff reform movement was part and parcel of.

This, then, created a new situation in the 1870s and 1880s. The political and economic transformation of continental Europe had raised it to a position where it was believed to threaten Britain's interests throughout the world. The apprehension with which Britain regarded both this, and the internal economic and social dangers she attributed to it, affected her response to those threats, and in some areas perhaps caused her to over-react to them. In the ominous political and economic atmosphere of the 1880s and 1890s, established British interests in the world appeared more vulnerable, and so the measures taken to secure them were more drastic. Sometimes they might have been more drastic than was strictly necessary. But in the situation of the time it often seemed best to annex first, and ask questions afterwards. Otherwise the European vultures might swoop.

India's frontiers and Russian expansion

British statesmen – the men who actually reacted to the crises and made the decisions – had their own pet fears; some vultures they saw bigger than others. The main one in the 1870s, as it had been ever since Bonaparte had fallen out of the reckoning, was Russia. Russia and the United States together were the fastest-expanding powers of the mid-nineteenth century, both of them fortunate in having promising outlets for their expansionary urges in their own back yards. America's expansion was not of any great concern to Britain. But Russia's was, because her back yard at one or two points abutted on to British possessions or areas of British interest. In the mid-1860s, a sudden surge of Russian military activity in central Asia accumulated for her a plethora of new provinces and protectorates in and around what became Russian Turkestan, and brought her uncomfortably close to Afghanistan, described by an old diplomat as 'the walls of the Indian garden'.[30] Her advance continued into the 1870s and 1880s. By 1885, Russia controlled most of the country to the north of Afghanistan – and was perhaps (as Lord Salisbury feared in 1875) plotting at the Afghan court to 'throw the Afghans upon us'.[31] It was a source of great agitation among British statesmen. This north-western frontier was British India's most vulnerable flank. If an enemy picked his moment – another mutiny, for example – he could cause a great deal of trouble there for a British defending force thinly dispersed over difficult terrain. Or he could use his position (as one influential propagandist warned) to fan into 'a chronic conflagration' the discontent which, because she was a conquered country, 'must be ever smouldering' in India.[32]

The Russian threat was not confined to the mountains and steppes of central Asia. Further to the west, Russia had designs on the Ottoman empire – checked by her reverses in the Crimean War, but revived again in the 1870s; and those designs endangered India's security in another way. The defence of India, because it was undertaken or at least officered by British soldiers, depended vitally on swift and safe communications between her and Britain (Map 6). There were two ways of getting from London to Calcutta. The first – the long, slow, safe way – was around Africa and across the Indian Ocean by ship. The other was through the Mediterranean, then across into one or other of the main inlets into the Arabian Sea – the Red Sea or the Persian Gulf – to Bombay. After the completion of the Suez Canal in 1869 the Red Sea route became the most popular, because it could all be done by boat. Compared with the Cape route, it was very much quicker, and therefore more useful in emergency: but it had drawbacks, mainly arising from the fact that it did not all belong to Britain the way the open oceans did. Most of the way it was safe enough – impressively policed by the Mediterranean fleet and the naval bases at Gibraltar and Aden – but not all the way. Whichever of the short routes you took to India, the Ottoman empire stood across your path, which meant that at that point you depended on the good faith of a foreign power to let you through. The Ottomans did not try to prevent Britons from travelling to India but only because they were too weak, and that weakness also meant that on their own they were vulnerable to predators like Russia. If Russia defeated the Ottomans, the British empire's lines of communication would be threatened, and India would be in very serious danger. For this reason, a tottering and corrupt Turkish regime had been propped up for decades by Britain; but it was not an altogether satisfactory arrangement, least of all to a strong body of opinion in Britain who objected to the way their Turkish protégés slaughtered Christians.

These two areas – central Asia and the Middle East – were the empire's soft spots. In both of them the threat was mainly from imperial Russia. And both of them involved the security of India, which, when all was said and done, was the only part of the empire which was really essential to Britain's well-being, and becoming more so.

Not everyone took fright at the Russian threat to the same degree. In general, the British in India tended to worry more than the British in Britain; soldiers more than civilians; Conservatives more than Liberals. It was the mid-1870s, in fact, which saw the beginnings of a real partisan approach to colonial and foreign policy, at least on the level of the debating platform. When it came to actual practice, as we shall see, Conservatives and Liberals acted more alike than they said they did, because the national interest was broadly the same for both of them, and the same external dangers threatened each alike. Nevertheless Conservatives tended to spot the danger sooner. This was certainly so in the case of Afghanistan.

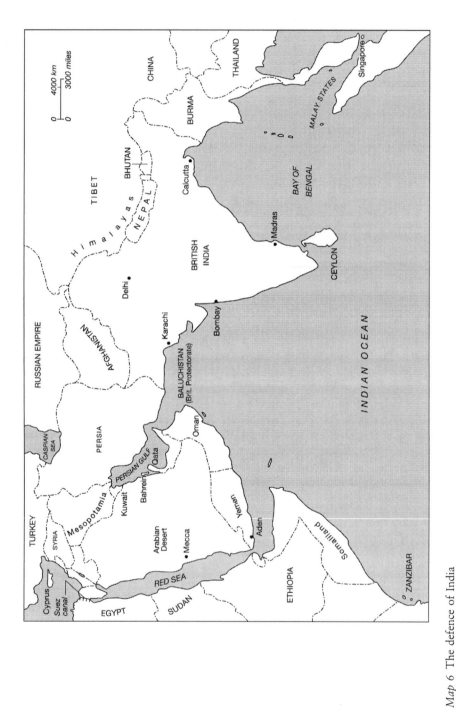

Map 6 The defence of India

Source: After McIntyre, W. D., *The Commonwealth of Nations* (University of Minnesota Press, 1977, p.96). Copyright © 1977 by the University of Minnesota. All rights reserved. Reprinted by permission of the University of Minnesota Press.

For years Whitehall had been happy with a situation on the North-West Frontier whereby Afghanistan was left to her own devices, on the principle that she had not given any trouble yet and it was pointless to go looking for it. The policy was nicknamed 'masterly inactivity'. Then, in 1874, a Conservative government came to power, immediately smelt Russian intrigue at Kabul, and decided that a more direct surveillance was necessary over Afghanistan to make India secure. Initially its policy was cautious: merely to persuade the ruling Amir to admit British agents into his country (as Salisbury put it) 'to guide the Ameer, and to watch'.[33] But things escalated. The Amir, distrustful of this departure from the old policy, obstinately refused access to the agents. Consequently to suspicious British noses the Russian smell got stronger. Disraeli's new appointment to the viceroyalty of India, Lord Lytton, chosen because he was bold, proved to be bolder than Disraeli bargained for, tried to force an entry into Afghanistan with a regiment of Lancers in September 1878, and was turned back. Lytton's initiative was against orders, and it was made at the very moment when Disraeli thought he might have averted the Russian threat by diplomacy at St Petersburg. Disraeli was angry: 'when V-Roys and Comms-in-Chief disobey orders,' he said, 'they ought to be sure of success in their mutiny'.[34] But the damage was done, there was an insult to be avenged and prestige to be reasserted on a dangerous frontier: and so (in November 1878) Disraeli declared war. General Roberts, in the first of his many notable campaigns in the service of the empire, went in and beat the Afghan forces. A British envoy was installed at Kabul in July 1879, and a new Amir persuaded to accept British control of his foreign policy, which should have settled the matter. But then in September the envoy was murdered by mutinous Afghan soldiers, the army had to come in again to punish them (with the summary and wholesale hangings which were the customary British response to 'outrages' of this kind); and it looked as though Britain might have to take a closer grip on Afghan affairs. Lytton wanted to break it up into smaller, weaker states, others wanted to annex it. But before they could do either, Disraeli's government was ousted in Britain in April 1880, and a new Liberal government came to power which had recently scored a lot of propaganda points over the Afghan affair: 'an unjust war', Gladstone had called it; 'a war as frivolous as ever was waged in the history of man'.[35] Even for the Liberals, however, considerations of Indian security made a return to the *status quo ante bellum* impossible. A new Liberal viceroy, Lord Ripon, guaranteed Afghanistan's integrity against foreign invasion, but, of course, the guarantee was only given for a price, and the price (as before) was British control over her foreign relations. In effect, Afghanistan became a British protectorate, a client state. That did not solve the Afghan problem, or entirely secure that part of the frontier. Afghanistan continued to give trouble in the 1880s and 1890s, and ultimately there could be no guarantee that if Russia made it worth their while, the Afghans would not still renege and help her invade India. Even if they did not, it was uncertain whether Britain could defend them against a Russian attack. Happily this was never tested, though in 1885 it nearly was, when the Russians defeated an Afghan army at Penjdeh – but then were prevailed upon to stop. At the very best, Afghanistan was a weak crutch to lean on.

Nevertheless, the arrangement with Afghanistan endured, and British policy turned to plugging the gaps around her. Methods varied. To the south of Afghanistan, down to the Arabian Sea, Baluchistan was tamed in the 1880s – quietly and gradually, almost by stealth, avoiding the drama (and the expense) of large-scale confrontation. First, British access to the area was secured by treaties with the local rulers, then that access was used skilfully by a local British agent, Sir Robert Sandeman, to discipline and organise the tribes into an integral part of British India, one of the 'native states'. To the west of Afghanistan and Baluchistan, Britain depended on Persia to keep the Russians away. Here she used diplomacy, and not altogether successfully, for the Russians were generally more seductive and generous diplomats there, and the Persians not reliable. Still, Russia never reached the Persian Gulf, which was Britain's main concern. To the east of Afghanistan, where Russia came closest to India – but in most inhospitable terrain – again it was diplomacy, in the mid-1890s, which made sure they never actually met by establishing buffer zones between them. Within the areas secured for Britain the most unruly of their new subjects – Pathans, Waziris, Chitralis – were subdued in a series of spirited little wars in the 1890s. Over to the other side of India, where the threat, if any, came from the French rather than the Russians, Upper Burma was invaded and incorporated into the Indian empire in 1885–86, because its ruler would not otherwise accept the vassal or puppet status Britain required of states on her strategic borders.

The territorial gains which accrued to Britain from this activity – all in the interests of 'security' – by the end of the century were considerable. All along India's land border her influence and control had thickened: in some places, it became outright where control was indirect before, but elsewhere indirect, where there was nothing before. Burma and Baluchistan had been annexed. Within the existing frontiers of the empire a loose, informal kind of suzerainty had been replaced by more direct forms of control, in the tribal territories of the north and north-west. Beyond the frontiers, nominally independent states were bribed or cajoled into becoming tributaries or 'buffers', as what had previously been the great political vacuum or no-man's-land between India and Russia filled up with Russian generals and troops, and Britain could no longer rely on the mere neutrality or ineffectiveness of her weaker neighbours to keep her enemies away. India was being braced for the impact with Russia, though it was an impact that never came.[36]

The occupation of Egypt

British India was in quite a lot of trouble in 1877–78. As well as the Afghan War, a famine which killed 5 million, and what *The Times* called 'an ominous restlessness' among the natives which provoked an Act censoring the vernacular press in 1878,[37] she was menaced by another war some 3,000 miles to the west, which did not involve India directly, but affected her interests more than those of any other non-participant. In 1877, the Russians were marching towards Constantinople. This was dangerous. If Russia took Constantinople and the Straits, wrote a contemporary observer in Britain, then 'we should lose the protection afforded to our Indian possessions by the fact of the lands lying east and west of the channel dividing Europe and Asia being under the dominion of a friendly, inert, and unprogressive power'.[38] They might also lose a trade with the Middle East which averaged £30 million a year in the 1870s, 5 per cent of their total foreign trade.[39] We have seen already how Britain did not give up her established interests easily. Consequently, when Russia got the better of her war with Turkey, Britain stepped in to make sure that the 'friendly, inert, and unprogressive power' was not too heavily bruised by the encounter. When Russia and Turkey signed a peace treaty at San Stefano in March 1878, Britain browbeat Russia to revise it (at the Congress of Berlin) in a way which still guaranteed Ottoman control of the Straits. At the same time she took Cyprus for herself as a kind of insurance. It was not the first time Britain had acted as Turkey's guardian angel, nor would it be the last. Turkey had to be supported against Russia. If it could have been a modern, enlightened Turkey it would have been better – and in the 1840s Britain had tried hard to make Turkey modern and enlightened. But failing that, it would have to be a corrupt Turkey – a Turkey which in fact contravened nearly every one of the Victorians' criteria of international respectability. Until Gladstone in the 1880s started bringing extraneous considerations like 'morality' into foreign policy, this kind of thing never gave the Foreign Office many qualms. They already supported a 'corrupt' China and a 'corrupt' Afghanistan. The important thing was that Turkey was not strong enough to be dangerous to Britain, and she stood against a power which was.

Britain's involvement in the Ottoman empire was financial as well as commercial and diplomatic. In 1854 and 1855 (during the Crimean War) and again in 1862, the British government lent varying degrees of support – in one case a formal guarantee – to flotations for Turkish government loans. British interests required a stable Turkey, Turkey required foreign investment to make her stable, and her own credit was far too bad to attract investment. Hence Britain had to underwrite the risks; and when the risk turned out to be a bad one, and Turkey went bankrupt in 1875, she was obliged to step in (with other interested European countries) to act as receiver.[40] After that she shied away from further financial or political involvement in Turkey proper, except to ensure that no other power got exclusive financial control over the country.

In Egypt, which was nominally a tributary of the Ottomans, Britain went very much further. By European standards, Egypt was more 'enlightened' than Turkey. Her ruler from 1863 to 1879, Ismail Pasha, wanted nothing better than to make Egypt into a modern, civilised, European-type state. Unfortunately, he tried to do it too quickly, borrowed money unwisely and at frightening interest rates, and by the mid-1870s had landed his country in much the same condition as Turkey: hopelessly in debt to European bondholders, mainly British and French, and with most of her revenues mortgaged to them as security for her debts. In a quasi-imperial kind of way she was already in the power of western Europeans, though not yet of western European *governments*, because they were not yet directly involved there in the way Britain and France were in Turkey, for example, by the terms of the 1855 guaranteed loan. The British government had little hand in Egypt's progress towards bankruptcy. But she had to be affected by that bankruptcy, if it happened. Bankruptcy produced insecurity, and insecurity spelt danger to Britain's national interests, especially to the Suez Canal, 80 per cent of whose traffic was British. By 1875, therefore, Britain's interest in Egypt, though it was not identical to the bondholders', did go along with theirs; and by the end of that year Disraeli had established a British government bondholding interest there too. The Khedive was now directly facing bankruptcy, on the tail of the Turkish collapse. He had one valuable asset left, which if he mortgaged or sold it might bail him out: his shares – 44 per cent – in the Suez Canal Company. Disraeli, unexpectedly and dramatically, bought the shares for Britain for £4 million in November. The reason he gave for doing it was to prevent the French getting them, in which case 'the whole of the Suez Canal would have belonged to France, and they might have shut it up!'[41] This was not strictly accurate. (If anything, France could only have controlled the Canal *Company*, which did not entitle her to control the *Canal*.) Neither was *The Times*'s assertion, that he had acquired for Britain 'a heavy stake in the security and well-being of another distant land'.[42] Her 'stake' in Egypt had already been there before the purchase of the shares, and the purchase had done nothing to increase it. What it had done, apart from giving Britain some say in the running of the Canal, was to put her interest there on a more regular and legitimate footing; for as Disraeli's Lord Chancellor pointed out, if it came to war to protect British interests there, without the shares, 'it must have been war to destroy or take possession of the property of others; now it will be war to defend our own property'.[43] Whether or not this was the reason for the purchase – to give Britain a pretext to invade – when Britain did invade, she had this new plea to sustain her.

This was just the beginning of the British government's official involvement in Egypt. Disraeli's transaction with the Khedive saved Egypt for only a few months. The weight of her debt proved too much for her, and she followed Turkey into bankruptcy in May 1876. This created just the conditions of uncertainty and instability Britain most feared. Egypt's creditors took over the running of the country, through various international commissions and authorities set up to administer her revenues and finances. France was a leading light on all of them. Britain at first wanted no part in sorting out Egypt's mess, but decided that as France was participating she ought to too. Egypt's new *de facto* rulers set about making the country a better place for western capital. Its old Khedive (Ismail) was ousted in 1879 and a new collaborationist one (Tewfik) put in his place. Drastic reforms were instituted designed to make Egypt solvent again. Thus far, Britain went along with France and her other allies only with misgivings about the proportion of Egypt's revenues which was being channelled to pay off her debts. When these measures provoked a nationalist uprising in Egypt against its foreign bondholder masters, and British national interests became more directly threatened, she acted more resolutely. It had always been her policy *not* to rescue individual capitalists whose greed tempted them to risky undertakings for inordinate profits, yet to protect established national interests where they were threatened by internal instability or foreign intervention. The security of the Suez Canal was certainly a vital national interest, and it was threatened in 1881 both by internal instability and foreign intervention. The instability was the uprising by over-taxed peasants, 'fanatical' Muslims and out-of-work soldiers led by Arabi Pasha which ousted Tewfik in September. The foreign intervention was France's. Without France, Britain would very likely not have invaded Egypt, but left it to Turkey to march in and reassert her old control. This would be an adequate safeguard for British interests. But France would have none of it. Concerned for the effect an extension of Turkish power might have on her own nearby Muslim dominions of Tunisia and Algeria, and perhaps more solicitous than Britain for the bondholders, France, by the end of the year, was all for intervening herself. And if France intervened and Britain did not, then the worst might happen and a strong foreign power be established, alone, around the Canal. Britain consequently had to keep close on France's tail. When France took action, Britain stayed with her.

Ironically, the only effect of their actions was to goad the nationalists to more extreme rebellion, which endangered the Canal further. When France opted out, her prime minister overruled by a parliament less convinced of Egypt's value to them, things had gone too far for Britain to pull out too. Arabi was clearly irreconcilable, in control of Egypt, and making things hot for the foreigner. The British navy had already engaged with Egypt by bombarding Alexandria in July 1882. That action had to be followed up on land to make it effective. So Britain went in alone with troops (under Wolseley), defeated Arabi's army easily at Tel-el-Kebir in September, and found herself with a new protectorate on her hands. It was Gladstone, the 'anti-imperialist', who had invaded Egypt; which shows, perhaps, how compelling the national interest was. He himself presented it differently, as an action taken less for national than for international reasons: on behalf of what he liked to call 'the Concert of Europe', or the then 'civilised' world. There is also another possible view of this. Gladstone himself owned Egyptian bonds, to the tune of 37 per cent of his total portfolio in 1882. That gave him a personal interest, which a cynic could make much of. Alternatively it may simply – as Cain and Hopkins charitably put it – have enabled him 'to see the creditors' point of view with greater clarity if it could be presented as … in the wider public interest'.[44] The wider public interest was certainly involved too: threatened in this case by the way the bondholders' activities had placed a greater burden on an economically unsophisticated regime than it could bear, and broken it, and by the actions of the French.

Turkey and Egypt were both areas of vital interest to Britain. Both went through similar crises in 1875–76 which provoked British action in defence of those interests. But only Egypt became a British protectorate. There were good reasons for this. In the first place, Britain would not have been allowed by the other European powers to make Turkey a protectorate. Second, the internal threat to British interests – Arabi – was more dangerous in Egypt. Turkey was more passive than Egypt after the powers had intervened there; more willing to collaborate in a way which amply safeguarded British interests, or less able to resist. Third, although Turkey still had a prominent place in British calculations of their foreign strategy right into the 1890s, by the 1880s, Egypt was more important: Britain's commerce with her bigger, and expanding; her capital investment there larger; and her strategic priorities – as Disraeli's 1875 coup emphasised – very firmly centred now on the Suez Canal. Over Turkey, Britain's informal influence in the 1880s and 1890s remained stable, or even waned; over Egypt, it increased. Gladstone found he could not get out, though he wanted to, or said so. The difficulty was a simple one: Egypt would have to be left in the hands of a popular, liberal, pro-British native government, and the only popular, liberal native – Arabi – was anti-British. So a 'temporary' occupation became less and less temporary. Not only was it difficult to leave Egypt, it was also difficult to avoid being dragged in further – into the Sudan, for example, where the Khedive's authority was being subverted by a national-religious rebellion under 'the Mahdi' (Muhammed Ahmad), and which the Khedive desperately wanted to win back. The British government believed that Egypt could not afford such a project in her present financial state, but it was not easy to persuade the Khedive so, or the press and public opinion in Britain. Gladstone in fact handled the whole affair disastrously. In January 1884, he sent to evacuate an Egyptian force beleaguered in Khartoum a Christian zealot and popular hero – General Gordon – who, when he got there saw it as his duty to save the whole city from the Mahdi, and stayed. Gladstone bowed to public pressure and sent a second expedition out to relieve him, but it arrived too late. Gordon was killed, and immediately apotheosised in Britain as a Christian martyr (Figure 4.1). Gladstone was vilified as his 'murderer', which was a heavy charge to bear for another's insubordination. Nevertheless Gladstone stayed out of the Sudan, and Britain managed for a time to limit her liability in North Africa. The respite was only temporary. The forward movement of British imperial encroachment in those parts of the world where local power structures were too weak to resist was beginning to seem inexorable, and necessary, if certain basic assumptions as to the requirements of British strategy were accepted. Gladstone's partial resistance to it, his refusal to sail with the tide of events and the wind of opinion as far as they seemed to be taking him, was a brave but in the end unsuccessful gesture.[45]

The first Boer War

Just as the bondholders, independently of any government's control, had created the occasion for British government intervention in Egypt, by the effect their activities had on

Figure 4.1 A great imperial myth. 'General Gordon's last stand.' An iconic (and almost certainly
    misleading) representation by G. W. Joy, 1885.
Source: © Leeds Museums and Galleries/Bridgeman Images.

local politics, so in South Africa it was the capitalists – this time seeking gold and diamonds in the hinterland – who sparked off a new phase of imperial expansion there
which, eventually, was to lead to the incorporation of two erstwhile independent Boer
republics in a new South African Union, and the creation of another batch of colonies to
the north. In South Africa, these developments came less out of the blue than in Egypt.
For several decades the country had been teetering on the brink of some dramatic extension of imperial control, which it was thought would most likely take the form of a
confederation of all the European settlements under the British flag, on the Canadian
model. But although this had been talked about for years, it had not been achieved before
the 1870s, because the matter had not been urgent enough and the cost was too prohibi-
tive to make it worth the effort. Then came the gold and the diamonds. The first diamond strikes were made in Griqualand, on the western borders of the Orange Free State,
in the late 1860s. As their value and extent were realised, they changed everything. They
made southern Africa what she had never been before: potentially an economic asset. Her
trade nearly trebled in ten years; her debts melted away; and investment there from
abroad boomed spectacularly. Whatever one's purpose in the country, this had to make a
difference. For those out for profit, it made the prize richer. For those who wished to turn
South Africa into another happy Canada, it would give her the means to support herself.
For those concerned with the security of the sea-lanes round the Cape to the east, it could
pose a threat to them from the hinterland, if someone else got the diamond fields. For
those solicitous for the welfare of the natives, it had placed among them a horde of
10,000 fortune hunters whose own interests were likely to conflict with theirs – and

consequently it had added to the turmoil on the frontier. The discoveries had compounded South Africa's old problems, and given them a new urgency.[46]

The British government could not be indifferent to this. It was a Liberal ministry which annexed Griqualand West in 1871 (after a British colonial governor acting as arbitrator had decided that it did not belong to the Boers). This made sure that the diamond fields did not fall into rival hands. But it did nothing to resolve South Africa's main problem for Britain, which was her chronic instability, arising ultimately from the Europeans' relations with the native African peoples around them. In the mid-1870s, the problem was as serious as it had ever been. As the native population was squeezed into smaller and smaller areas of fertile land to make way for the Europeans, the resulting congestion made them resentful, and the Europeans apprehensive at the way they were 'massing' on their borders. There was talk of a final confrontation looming between the races. In newly acquired Griqualand West there was continuous friction between the Griquas and their European diamond-seeking visitors, greedy for their land and labour and having good money and guns to offer in exchange. There was trouble with the Nguni around the Kei River, and in Natal to the north-east where the settler government over-reacted (as they often did) to a minor piece of insubordination by the Hlubi chief Langalibalele. In Transvaal the Boers were fighting little wars all the time, not always successfully, and constantly anticipating the big one: the large-scale invasion for which the Zulu king Cetewayo was preparing a formidable army from his capital at Ulundi. The 'native problem' was not only no easier than before; it seemed to be coming to a head.

It was clear that things could be made easier for the European settlers in southern Africa, and for British interests there, if there were some strong, centralised, overall responsibility for relations with the natives. Both parties in Britain came to believe that federation was the only solution. For Lord Carnarvon, who became Disraeli's Colonial Secretary in 1874:

> The advantages of Federation are very obvious. European immigration and capital flow slowly into countries under small and isolated Governments whose financial solvency is questionable, and where there is no adequate security for property and no confidence in prudent legislation. Federation would greatly improve and cheapen the administration of affairs in almost every branch and greatly lessen the probability of a demand for aid in the shape of Imperial money or troops. But the most immediately urgent reason for general union is the formidable character of the native question, and the importance of a uniform, wise, and strong policy in dealing with it.[47]

Carnarvon was convinced that federation had to come at once. By a combination of bad intelligence (some of it coming from James Froude) and wishful thinking, he persuaded himself that the South Africans wanted it too. In reality, the British colonies were at best very lukewarm, and the independent Afrikaner republics probably hostile. But Carnarvon pressed on. In April 1877, the natural resistance of the Transvaal republic was at its lowest: at the end of her financial resources, in a state almost of political anarchy internally, and encircled by hostile and powerful African armies. This also happened to be a time when the importance of the Cape sea-route to the east, on which affairs in the Transvaal were supposed to have a bearing, was being highlighted by the Russian threat to the other one. It was this moment that Carnarvon chose to bluster the Transvaal into the British empire. She was annexed on 12 April 1877, as a prelude (Carnarvon hoped) to incorporation into a South African federation.

The annexation had the very opposite effect. For the Boers it was the culmination of a decade of wrong. First Basutoland had been snatched from them, then Griqualand, and now their own independence. Very quickly the Afrikaners – both in the Transvaal and in the British colonies to the south – began to cultivate a fierce and enduring nationalism whose very last wish was for federation, unless it were a federation dominated by themselves – the majority among the whites. Britain's brief autocratic rule over the Transvaal did nothing to make the Boers love her more. Her most valuable achievement from the Boers' point of view was probably to bring to a head the confrontation with Cetewayo's Zulus which had been threatening for some time, and finally to subdue them in July 1879. Even this was a mixed blessing for Britain. It was done in order to win the Boers' gratitude and loyalty. But it worked the other way: with the Zulus tamed, the Boers no longer needed the British. Furthermore, it was done very incompetently, against orders from London, and with a humiliating defeat along the way, at Isandhlwana in January 1879 when the British lost 1,600 soldiers. This only damaged Britain's prestige in the eyes of the Boers, and sapped the patience of the British public.[48]

The Boers expected Gladstone to give them back their independence, as he had all but promised in his Midlothian campaign. But when he came to power in 1880, he was seduced as much as his predecessors by the prospect of federation as a final solution to South Africa's ills, and as misinformed as they were about the Boers' view of it. So the Boers had to take their independence themselves. At the end of 1880, they rebelled, and in February the next year beat a British army in a famous skirmish at Majuba. Gladstone hardly needed to be persuaded that the policy of confederation through coercion had broken down. He had never been happy anyway about the morality or the expediency of the Transvaal annexation. He had sued for peace before Majuba, although the message had not got through to the Boers in time. Majuba made his decision more difficult to take – conciliation would look like surrender – but he took it all the same. In March 1881, his hands full with Irish troubles, he decided to give the Transvaal back her independence, rather than risk another Ireland there. The position reverted to the *status quo ante* annexation, except that Britain retained a vaguely defined 'suzerainty' over the Transvaal, which she now believed might suffice to guarantee her interests there. For a while it did. From a security point of view, the Boer republics did not yet present a great enough threat to Britain to justify her holding them against their will, once the depth of their opposition to British rule had been revealed.

The full danger materialised over the next decade. In the 1880s, the Transvaalers became more self-assertive, and better able to back up their self-assertion with real power. Majuba had done two things for them: it had convinced them that Britain was weak, and it had supplied them with a new legend to stoke the fires of their nationalism. They quickly resumed their encroachments on African lands beyond their borders, to the west in Bechuanaland and to the east in Zululand. They tried all they could to secure an outlet to the sea which would free them commercially from the British ports to the south. In 1884, their isolation looked as if it might soon be ended, when Germany suddenly appeared on the scene by annexing Angra Pequeña, on the west coast just north of the border of Cape Colony, with unsettling implications for Britain. In 1886, vast deposits of gold-bearing rock were discovered on the Witwatersrand in the Transvaal, and the Transvaal suddenly became rich – richer than the Cape. Previously the Dutch in South Africa had had the numbers but not the money; now they had the money too. It was not long before they could afford a railway to Delagoa Bay – and the sea – in Portuguese Mozambique, away from the British. Very rapidly the position for Britain was being transformed. Her difficulties in South Africa were taking on a new dimension. Before it had been chiefly a problem of stopping Europeans on the frontier stirring up the native tribes and endangering the security of the Cape. Now it had very little to do with the natives. In the well-established areas of white settlement south of the Limpopo and Orange rivers, most of the more powerful African polities had been broken down one by one during the 'Kaffir wars' of the 1870s and 1880s. Tribesmen had been tamed into peasants and proletarians. The 'native question' was no longer one of relations with external autonomous nations, but a question of domestic land allocation and labour recruitment. The old frontier problem was on its way to being solved. Britain's problem now was one of power rivalries between the European groups in South Africa. In 1884, the War Office had advised the cabinet that, because it was 'impossible, for political reasons, to create a Gibraltar out of the Cape Town peninsula', in order to retain that peninsula, they would have to maintain 'British ascendancy in all South African colonies'.[49] British ascendancy now appeared to be threatened directly by one of those colonies, the richest one, with powerful foreign friends waiting in the wings.

Britain's response to these developments in the 1880s was further territorial expansion and consolidation, but not yet to the extent of re-annexing the Transvaal. She was careful in fact not to put the Transvaalers' backs up too much, for she preferred if she could to seduce them into a commercial union with the Cape, rather than repeat the expensive mistake of 1877. Hence when she annexed southern Bechuanaland in 1885 to prevent the Transvaal meeting up with the new German colony of Namaqua-Damaraland in the west, she surrendered to the Boers (at the London Convention of 1884) her residual protective powers over the natives of the Transvaal to sugar the pill; and when she took over the remaining parts of the Zulu coastline between Natal and Mozambique in 1885 and 1887 to stop the republicans reaching the sea, she let them have as much as she could of the inland region of Zululand, for the same reason. The encirclement of the Transvaal was completed at the end of the decade, when the diamond millionaire Cecil Rhodes (who always had British colonial interests more at heart than the British Colonial Office) formed a commercial company to occupy Matabeleland and Mashonaland to the north. The idea was that the company should take over the administration of the country in return for its profits. There was opposition to the scheme from humanitarians, worried by the implications of a situation whereby native Africans were governed by their exploiters. But for a parsimonious government, it was a tempting bargain. The profits to be got from the country were as yet merely notional, whereas the expense of governing them was predictable. So the company got its royal charter in October 1889. In this way, Rhodesia was born, and for the British government another potential counterbalance to Afrikanerdom secured at almost no expense.

On the map the extensions of British dominion which had taken place in southern Africa in the 15 years after 1875 looked – and were – spectacular. From the standpoint of Britain's essential interests in that area, however, the net result of all this activity was minimal. Overall Britain had managed just about to hold her own. In the face of a growing challenge to her supremacy, she had succeeded, by dint of these annexations, in containing the threat. But that was all. In 1890, she was no nearer a final solution to her South African problem than she had been in 1875. Still British interests in that country – commercial and political – were not completely secure. They could not be so while the richest province in the country was independent of Britain and hostile to her; and while the loyalty of a very large proportion of Britain's white South African subjects, bound to the Transvaalers by linguistic, cultural and racial ties, was doubtful. For years, the ideal solution to the South African problem had been seen as federation, originally to give co-ordination to frontier policy, now to disarm the Afrikaner challenge by absorption. Two methods of achieving this federation, the voluntary and the coercive, had been tried and failed. The current hope in the 1890s was that (in Lord Salisbury's words) by impressing the Afrikaners with 'the pressure of English activity all around them', they might 'be compelled to fall into line and to join the great unconscious federation that is growing up'.[50] It was still an open question whether this method would work any better than the others.

Meanwhile one constant factor in British policy, except for a short time under Carnarvon in the late 1870s, was that British interests in South Africa should be secured as cheaply as possible. As much as in mid-century, national interest had to be balanced against national economy; and ways could generally be found of reconciling the two. This was one of the purposes of the federation policy, and of the constant efforts of British governments to persuade the colonists themselves to assume responsibility for new territories annexed. It was also a reason why Rhodes's offer was so eagerly accepted in 1889. One result of this, however, was a kind of paradox: that in order to maintain cheaply a general British supremacy over southern Africa, Britain was tending to lose her particular authority there – her authority over the white colonists' conduct of their domestic affairs, including, of course, their 'native policies'. As yet, the concept of British imperial trusteeship for native races was not quite dead, and the humanitarian lobby in Britain won some minor victories, where it did not cost much in money or local good-will. Where larger interests were at stake, however – agreement with the Boers at the London Convention, containment of the Boers by Rhodes in 1889 – trusteeship could make little headway. Slowly Whitehall's powers were devolved upon the men on the spot, to secure their co-operation and spread the burden. Consequently as the area of the British empire in southern Africa expanded, so its real effective control there diminished.[51]

German rivalry in the tropics

The late 1870s and the 1880s were a period of considerable pressure – commercial, diplomatic and military – on British interests abroad. For the governments in Whitehall that were faced with these pressures, there were certain priority areas, areas where they, the government (merchants and missionaries might have different priorities), felt Britain had most at stake. Throughout this period they comprised that broad belt of land from the Middle East to the Himalayas which divided Russia from India and her supply lines; and, to a lesser extent, southern Africa. These were the areas in which the pressure was greatest, and in which it was most resolutely resisted, but they were not the only pressure points in this period. In the mid-1880s, in particular, British interests elsewhere came increasingly under challenge from European rivals. The challenge was spearheaded by Germany: a newly outward-looking Germany, pursuing a deliberate policy, it seemed, of bearding the British lion in all his favourite commercial dens all over the world – the Levant, the Pacific, the Far East, South America, Africa; even in his own colonies; and in Africa, Oceania and the Far East ambitious for colonies of her own to rival Britain's. Her own colonial effort, when it came, was swift and spectacular. Between 1884 and 1886, besides Namaqua-Damaraland (South-West Africa), Germany took the Cameroons, Togoland and Tanganyika in tropical Africa, and in the Pacific north-eastern New Guinea and dozens of small islands to the north and east. She had her eye on other places too, like Samoa and the China coast. And she was instrumental in establishing King Leopold of the Belgians as proprietor of the Congo at the Berlin Conference of 1884–85, and in encouraging the French to expand *their* colonial interests in West Africa. This sudden intrusion seemed to take the British completely by surprise. Granville, Gladstone's Foreign Secretary, said in September 1884 that he would have taken more notice of what the Germans were doing if he had known that they were serious about colonies – 'but I had constant assurances from Munster and from Ampthill' (Germany's and Britain's ambassadors to each other) 'that the reverse was the case'. Gladstone assumed that Bismarck's change of face was only an electoral gimmick.[52] But Germany's colonial challenge was a serious matter. It introduced an unknown factor into colonial affairs, a new member of the club, in addition to the familiar faces of France, the Netherlands and Russia. And it introduced it into areas where Britain had previously regarded herself as having a near monopoly, or at least a pre-emptive right, of vigorous empire-building.

By the prevalent international morality of the day, which regarded colonial annexation as something akin to the enclosure of waste land, Bismarck's colonial ambitions were not unreasonable: not so large as Britain's, and not necessarily in conflict with hers. Gladstone professed to welcome them: 'If Germany is to become a colonizing power, all I say is "God speed her!" She becomes our ally and partner in the execution of the great purposes of Providence for the advantage of mankind.'[53] Yet there *was* thought to be a threat to British interests here, especially to those interests which had been established only informally, by dint of commercial or other ties not yet translated into overt colonial control. In West Africa, for example, where British trade was substantial if not spectacular (£34 million between 1873 and 1882), the area of that trade was only very partially covered by the flag, most of it being conducted through foreign-owned ports, or depending on intricate connections with African trading networks far beyond British political control, which might be seriously disrupted by a foreign presence. Foreign annexations also carried the danger of foreign tariffs, squeezing out British trade from its established markets.[54] So there was ample cause for alarm. In East Africa similarly there was no firm guarantee that British interests would be able to resist a strong foreign challenge. Established British interests there were much thinner on the ground than in West Africa (a small coastal trade and some ivory hunting and missionary soul-saving inland) but they were increasing every year, and there were hopes of more to come – dreams of a vast potential wealth, as yet untapped, in the hinterland, which gave East Africa a number of influential champions in London. As yet these interests were secured by means of an arrangement with the Sultan of Zanzibar, which was satisfactory only so long as it was not vigorously contested. In the Pacific, protection of British (and Australasian) commercial and financial interests was entrusted to a 'High Commissioner of the Western Pacific' and a 'Consul-General for the Pacific', who happened to be the same man, and Governor of Fiji too; and whose powers were minimal and thought to be inadequate, at least by the Australian governments to the south who were ever petitioning Whitehall to let *them* annex the areas of their interest before the Germans stepped in.[55] In each of these areas the guarantees of security for British trading and financial interests were fragile, effective in a former age when the pressure was off, but not now; and there were people in England to tell the government so.

The nature and extent of the government's response to these challenges were strongly influenced by what was happening elsewhere. In part, it was a simple question of logistics. Britain's latest series of foreign wars – Afghanistan, the occupation of Egypt, the Zulu War, the first Boer War – had stretched her resources more than she liked. Because her colonial empire, the biggest in the world, and her wider commercial empire, had been to a large extent accumulated and consolidated in an era when she did not have to compete seriously for them, she had not yet acclimatised herself to the new situation in which they might now have to be defended against serious competition. Her land forces had never been extensive. Consequently, in using them against any one country, she always had to keep a weather eye open for the reactions of others. 'Once at war with Russia,' wrote Granville in 1885 when it appeared that such a war might be imminent, 'we shall be obliged to toady Germany, France and Turkey.'[56] The occupation of Egypt increased Britain's dependence on other powers, her need to cultivate their goodwill, because it was not a *total* occupation. Until 1904, Britain had to share certain functions in Egypt with other European powers, including a measure of control over her finances (Maps 7 and 8). This meant that other powers could make her administration of Egypt difficult if they

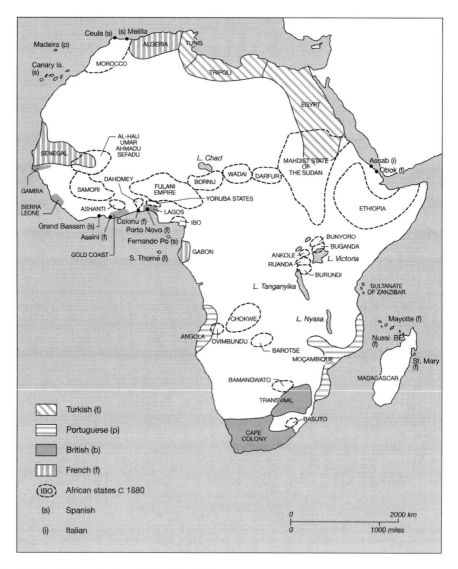

Map 7 Africa before the 'scramble', *circa* 1870s

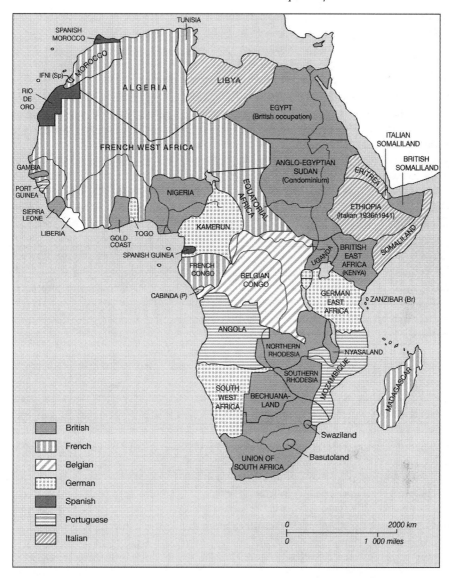

Map 8 Africa after the 'scramble', 1880s–1914
Source: After Eldridge, C. C. (ed.) *British Imperialism in the Nineteenth Century* (Palgrave Macmillan, 1984, p. 92). Reproduced with permission of Palgrave Macmillan via Copyright Clearance Center.

liked – and especially if Britain proved obdurate elsewhere in the world. Gladstone attributed Bismarck's antagonism to Britain at the London Conference on Egypt of 1884 to his annoyance over initial British resistance to his designs in South-West Africa: it was 'a return slap for Angra Pequeña'. Thereafter, 'close-co-operation with Germany' was a cardinal tenet of his foreign policy during the most difficult Egyptian years.[57] Salisbury was not very different, conciliating Bismarck in, for example, East Africa, then using the 'credit' he piled up in this way 'to get help in Russia and Turkey and Egypt'.[58] This kind of factor, together with the natural reluctance of politicians of both parties to repeat all over the world 'forward' policies which had not been without their drawbacks in southern Africa, the Middle East and on the North-West Frontier, made them look very carefully before over-reacting to challenges in areas of lower priority to them. In general, they restricted their actions to merely protecting existing local interests, as in the past; occasionally taking stronger measures to serve what were conceived to be broader imperial interests; and always trying to do it in ways which would as far as possible spare the government trouble and expense, by delegating the responsibility to others.

In this latter regard, British governments were fortunate. The wide dispersal of British commerce and culture in the world worked two ways. On the one hand, if it had not been there it would not have been necessary for governments to intervene to protect it. On the other hand, however, it could provide the means by which this intervention might be exercised. Because of the many thousands of Britons and British organisations that had established themselves in far-off places long before governments feared to tread there, it was seldom difficult for governments, if they wanted to, to find people to delegate to. In the Pacific, it could be the governments of the Australasian colonies; in southern Africa, the government of the Cape. Elsewhere a favourite instrument of vicarious colonial administration in the 1880s was the chartered company, like Rhodes's in South Africa. The disadvantages of giving commercial companies licence to rule colonial territories were that they discouraged free competition; and that their exploitative functions might not always be compatible with their subjects' welfare – although current economic orthodoxy tended to assume that profits arising from exploitation did filter down. The great advantage of the chartered company was that it disburdened the British taxpayer of the cost of colonial administration. The Liberal and avowedly anti-imperialist Chancellor of the Exchequer Sir William Harcourt was reported in 1892 to have said that 'even Jingoism is tolerable when it is done "on the cheap"' in this way,[59] and indeed for old-fashioned Liberals not yet reconciled to a new spendthrift imperialism, this seemed a good way of meeting new exigencies without too much violence to their old shibboleths.

Delegation was the rule wherever it was practicable. In the Pacific, it was practicable. British intervention there was moderately extensive in the 1880s, but generally it was indirect. More often than not it took the form of giving to the local factions who demanded it the responsibility for effecting their own salvation. North Borneo, most of New Guinea and the Cook Islands came under the British flag in the 1880s, and the southern Solomon Islands in 1893. North Borneo from the beginning was delegated to the chartered company which had proposed its acquisition. From the British government's point of view, the advantage of having North Borneo was that it could provide a naval station to protect the China trade: the advantage was marginal, but the government would not be paying for it, so the charter went through in 1881. (Gladstone claimed it was without his noticing it.) New Guinea was partitioned between Britain and Germany in 1884, for the benefit of the Australian colonies and at their insistence; three years later its administration, and most of the cost, were transferred to the Queensland government. In April 1886, a convention between Britain and Germany demarcated their respective spheres of influence in the rest of the western Pacific, which left Britain free to ignore her own sphere without fear of Germany's taking advantage of her quiescence. In fact, she was not entirely inactive. The Gilbert and Ellice Islands, for example, were made a formal protectorate in 1892, and a Resident put in charge of them at an annual salary of £500 – which sum he would easily raise himself on the spot. And the British share of the Solomon Islands was proclaimed a protectorate in 1893: again, administrative costs were kept to a minimum. Further to the east, in an area not covered by the 1886 Convention, the Cook Islands were made a protectorate in 1888, and ruled for a time from Whitehall, but eventually (in 1901) annexed to New Zealand. Other acquisitions in this period were trifling: tiny islands, mostly uninhabited, on or around the equator, which provided guano or could house land stations for a new projected Pacific cable. The Pacific never held a very high place in Britain's scale of priorities. It rated very high, of course, in Australia's and New Zealand's. When there were conflicting claims there between European powers, Britain tried as far as possible to reach amicable settlements with her rivals. Australia and New Zealand thought she was far too amicable, but then (claimed Lord Derby in 1883), they would have annexed the planets if it had been feasible.[60] Britain's acquisitions there were the minimum compatible with the preservation of local British interests and colonial goodwill, and the maximum compatible with economy and foreign goodwill.[61]

It was not so very different in tropical Africa, despite the fact that British economic interests here were so much greater. In West Africa in the 1880s, all the running was made by Germany and France: France extending her power eastwards from Senegal over the western Sudan, and active too establishing colonies in Dahomey and on the north bank of the Congo River; Germany swooping quite suddenly on Togoland and the Cameroons in 1884. Britain did not sit back and watch it all happen. She protested, rather ineptly; and she pushed Portugal's somewhat musty claims to some of the newly colonised territories. But she took little direct action herself, for fear of antagonising France and Germany at a diplomatically inopportune time by thwarting them.

The one exception was on the Niger, where Britain's commercial interests (buying palm-oil with guns and liquor) were greatest or most promising, and where there was an agency at hand, as in Borneo, to carry the burden of administration. Sir George Taubman Goldie's United African Company had been formed in 1879, an amalgamation of three other trading enterprises, with one main purpose: to raise profits for European traders on the Niger by eliminating the competition which at present was forcing palm-oil prices up to uneconomic levels. It did not work. Goldie's prices were still being bettered by rivals, including some French. In a seller's market there was no way of excluding competition unless it was done artificially, politically; and so Goldie set himself to try to secure this, a politically engineered monopoly of trade over the region. Two authorities could give it to him: the local African rulers, by refusing to sell to anyone else; and the British government, if they took over the territory and gave to his company political powers which would enable him to enforce a monopoly of his own. Goldie worked on both. With the chiefs he made a great deal of progress; with the government, at first, less so. In 1881, he explored the idea of getting a charter like the North Borneo Company's, but made no headway. He reconstituted the Company under a new name (the National African Company) in 1882, and persuaded an ex-Liberal Home Secretary and friend of Gladstone's, Lord Aberdare, to take on the chairmanship. In 1885, he was luckier. By that time there was a real possibility of Britain's losing the Niger altogether: to the French, or to an 'International Commission' proposed at the Berlin Conference of 1884–85 to supervise the Niger trade. In these circumstances Goldie worked desperately to strengthen his hold over the Niger, and his government's claim to it. In July 1886, after some clever politicking, he was finally granted his charter by a Liberal government frightened of being accused of extravagance if they annexed the Niger basin, and of pusillanimity if they did not, and grateful for this means of ducking both charges. With his charter Goldie got his monopoly. The monopoly was not explicit: monopoly on the Niger was expressly forbidden by an Act which Britain had proposed and the other powers accepted at the Berlin Conference in 1884. But the administrative functions of the Royal Niger Company (as it became) required it to levy taxes, and taxes could be framed to eliminate competition. This Goldie did, and he got away with it, because there was no-one to stop him.

From then until the end of the century, the Royal Niger Company was the effective ruler of a large portion of the palm-oil-producing region of present-day Nigeria, behind the Niger delta. Although the government would have liked to, it did not rule the delta itself, because the British traders already established there would not let it. Consequently the delta (the Oil Rivers Protectorate) was ruled by a consul, directly from London, on a shoestring. Together the presence of British officials in the Oil River and of the chartered company inland also established Britain's claim to a very much wider area to the north, whose boundaries were not yet settled, and which for a long time was hardly touched by any real British authority. It was a very minimum occupation, but it was enough for the purposes of the British government, who had not, after all, taken the lower Niger because they had any particular plans for it.[62]

The German coup in East Africa seemed to be as much of a surprise to the government as their exploits in the west. At one moment there was no danger, everything quiet and calm, the coastal areas dominated by the Sultan of Zanzibar and, sheltering behind him, the British. The next moment, in February 1885, the Germans were there, claiming all the mainland behind Zanzibar as theirs, and able to hold up a dozen treaties with African chiefs to prove it. Gladstone tried to pretend it did not matter, but it clearly did, because at a stroke it destroyed the basis of British supremacy and security in the area. The Sultan of Zanzibar was no longer the dominant authority on the East African coast, and so he was no use any more as a puppet. Britain's bluff in East Africa had been called.

Her reaction to this crisis was similar to her reaction to the West African one. She did not quarrel with the Germans over what they had taken: diplomatically, she was not in a good position to, as she needed German support over Egypt. If anything, she helped Germany, for instance, by persuading her protégé the Sultan of Zanzibar (in what to him seemed a gross betrayal of trust) not to resist. But she did do something to retrieve the position elsewhere, and to delimit the area of German expansion so as to prevent her becoming (in Salisbury's words) 'the monopolists of the Big Lakes market'.[63] It was done very quickly and amicably by agreement between the two countries, for neither Bismarck nor Salisbury felt very strongly about East Africa. In November 1886, it was agreed that the offshore islands and the coast to a depth of 10 miles should stay with the Sultan, and the rest – the hinterland from the Juba River in the north to the Ruvuma River (and Portuguese East Africa) to the south – should be split between Britain and Germany, Britain taking the northern part, Germany the south, plus a little piece of coast beyond Witu in the far north (which she later swapped for the island of Heligoland in the North Sea). These were to be 'spheres of influence' only, not colonies but areas which it was agreed the respective tenants could make into protectorates if they wanted, with other powers keeping out. And that was as far as the British government wanted to go. For a time they would not even entertain the chartered company idea for East Africa, although a company existed, at least on the drawing board, which wanted to take on the work. William Mackinnon's East African Association had plans to develop the whole region up to and beyond the Great Lakes, whose proprietorship was not yet established, and where German agents threatened to move in. Mackinnon worked hard to consolidate British control in the British sphere of influence, for example, by persuading the Sultan to lease the northern part of the coastline to him in May 1887, and by signing treaties with

African rulers inland. His efforts won the approval of the Foreign Office, but not, as yet, a charter. Lord Salisbury considered his Association too insecure financially and its plans too nebulous to merit one. The North Borneo and Niger Companies (he said) had both had far more solid achievements behind them.

What made Salisbury change his mind, as he did during the course of 1888, was partly the appearance of financial solidity which Mackinnon was able to give to his company during that year – with a large capital subscription and an impressive board of directors; and partly the government's own reassessment of the dangers which threatened Britain's national interests in East Africa. In 1888, Salisbury became convinced that the Sultan of Zanzibar was in real danger of having what remained to him of his dominions taken from him by Germany. British interests there had to be safeguarded, and the best way to do this seemed to be to underwrite Mackinnon's arrangement with the Sultan. In addition, there was considerable disquiet in the Foreign Office about what was happening in Uganda in the Lakes region. The German explorer Karl Peters was threatening to take it; Bismarck denied that Germany was officially interested in the area, but only a few years back she had not been interested in the Cameroons or Zanzibar either. The lakes were the source of the Nile, which gave life to Egypt. Whoever had control of the Lakes could cut the Nile off, or divert it, or flood it. Mackinnon's company promised to occupy the Lakes region for Britain.

In September 1888, Mackinnon got his charter. In November 1889, with some prodding from the government, he sent an expedition to Uganda under Frederick Lugard to win the country for Britain. The expedition was a success: Lugard established the company's authority over Uganda – but a side-effect was the ruination of the company. For in Uganda it was not just a question of over-awing petty African chieftains to put crosses on treaties; the rulers there were powerful, already deeply involved with Europeans, and struggling among themselves for supremacy, which complicated matters. The struggle itself had initially been sparked off by European penetration (mainly by missionaries); it was a struggle between two rival nations – Buganda and Bunyoro – who saw themselves as representing, on the one hand, acceptance of European rule, and, on the other (with Muslim help), resistance to it. By the time Lugard arrived, however, the Europhiles had split between a Catholic and a Protestant section, and the dispute had the grotesque appearance of a seventeenth-century European religious war – which was carrying the acceptance of western 'civilisation' *too* far. Lugard's contribution to the affair was to help Buganda finish off Bunyoro, then to help the Protestant party in Buganda smash the Catholics. He returned to the coast with treaties signed by both parties in April 1892 accepting the suzerainty of the Imperial British East African Company. But the whole exercise had been expensive, and the company had already decided it could not bear the expense any longer. They told the government so, hoping for a subsidy; instead the government took Uganda out of the company's hands. In April 1893, the Company relinquished its rights over the country to a government agent; the next year Uganda became a formal British protectorate. The Imperial British East Africa Company collapsed in March 1895.

In East Africa, the British government's policy of minimum involvement, of rule by proxy, was least successful of anywhere. The reason was that the agency they chose to delegate their authority to was not solidly enough based to fulfil the functions the government required of it. Unlike the Niger and Borneo Companies, Mackinnon's company had been granted its charter on the basis of prospective plans rather than realised achievement; unlike Rhodes's South Africa Company, it had no millionaire chairman and no lure of gold about it to tempt the confidence and enthusiasm of investors – or of Lord Salisbury – when its capital was spent. Spurred on by government pressure, and by his own grandiose imperial ambitions, Mackinnon overstretched his resources. The government had to take over because it could not stomach the idea of subsidising a commercial concern, and had little faith in this one anyway; because once Britain's interest had been declared in the region, non-action would have been tantamount to withdrawal, or defeat; and because a reappraisal of British interest in the area in the early 1890s, by looking at the country in relation to Egyptian strategy rather than its coastal trade, gave it a higher priority than before.[64]

Reluctant imperialists

'It is not the habit of the English people to set out with their eyes open on a career of conquest and annexation. The conquests which we make are forced upon us.'[65] This was how the *Manchester Guardian* explained the Liberal government's colonial acquisitions of the 1880s, which must have bewildered many Liberals who thought Gladstone had originally been voted into power to stop this kind of thing. The plea of 'self-defence' was a common one. There was no aggression: Britain was only protecting what was hers already, under pressure from other European powers; so went the argument. For the native inhabitants of the countries she took, this could carry very little comfort or even conviction. It sounded cynical, especially when Britain's rivals were making exactly the same claims. It was the kind of thing all of them would say whether it were true or not, because no country ever liked to admit to aggression. Britain was certainly the aggressor on them, the natives, whose land it was, and who had done little themselves to offend her. But of course natives were not taken much into account when Britain talked of her 'rights' and 'interests' in Africa. 'All coloured men seem to be regarded as fair game', said another newspaper in April 1884; the principle was 'that no-one has a right to any rule or sovereignty in either hemisphere but men of European birth or origin'.[66] The contest at this stage of the story was between European powers, and from this point of view, regarding only the challengers and not the spoils, there was something in Britain's claim, that her actions were not aggressive, or if they were, then they were at least a *pre-emptive* kind of aggression. When she took a country, she said, it was only when she had good cause to fear that someone else would take it if she did not, and stop her doing whatever it was she did there before – trade or preach or travel through. She would have preferred not to have to do this kind of thing, but to carry on as she had in the past, picking the world's commercial apples wherever she wanted without owning the orchards, because this way had served her well until now, but others were not going to let her. There was a note of resentment in it. Britain certainly regarded herself throughout this period as more under attack than attacking, and most of her colonial exploits had more the character of salvage operations than movements of genuine aggrandisement.

Disraeli and Carnarvon had been different in that they had taken initiatives in these matters, and they had also seemed to take a positive delight in adding new jewels to the Queen's imperial crown. But in real territorial terms they had added very little: Cyprus and the South African Republic, and the latter was lost again almost immediately. Their successors in the 1880s, Liberal and Conservative, acquired much more, but were far less cavalier about it. By that time, the pleasure had gone out of empire-building. British governments felt themselves to be on the defensive. The initiative was being taken by other powers, and the task of statesmanship now was to decide when to respond to this initiative and when not to. The responses which both Gladstone and Salisbury made were not the maximum responses they thought they could get away with, but the minimum responses compatible with the national interest as they read it. Both were concerned to avoid what Gladstone called mere 'annexationism', which meant annexing a country merely because it was there to be annexed. Salisbury knew the cost of colonies as well as Gladstone: 'you must divide victories by taxation if you wish to know in solid figures the real worth of Empire', was how he put it in 1900.[67] Both Gladstone and Salisbury were very firm on Egypt, because it was vital to so many national interests. Even in Egypt, as a Liberal weekly put it in 1884, 'They say they intend to retire, and they say it honestly; but whenever the retirement begins ... Destiny, or Providence, or the stream of events, interposes with an imperative order to remain.'[68] Beyond Egypt, they tried as far as possible to avoid acquiring new responsibilities. In tropical Africa and the Pacific, colonial questions were dispatched with almost indecent haste: not out of a desire to grab as much as was going, but out of a wish (in Gladstone's words) to 'wind up at once these small colonial controversies'[69] which neither statesman set much store by, and which were proving annoying impediments to an understanding with Bismarck over Egypt.

With this general bias in British policy against annexation outside the strategically sensitive area of the Middle East, people who wanted Britain to take over a country had to show a good case for it. The onus of proof was on them. What constituted a good case could vary from place to place and from minister to minister. But there were certain general rules. First, there had to be a real, tangible British interest there to be defended – commercial, financial, spiritual or strategic. Occasionally it could be a *potential* interest – possibilities there which Britain wanted to explore before other countries did – but governments did not often throw money after eldorados. Sometimes the interest was colonial (Australian or South African) rather than metropolitan. Of course it could happen that governments were over-generous in their assessment of British interests, and neglectful of those of other European nations, but this did not often happen. Certainly, they did not accept uncritically the claims their traders and missionaries made about the extent of British influence anywhere: sometimes they seemed embarrassed by them. Second, the mere existence of a 'national interest' was not sufficient on its own to warrant British intervention. It also had to be shown that that interest was under threat from outside and would likely be lost if something positive were not done to secure it. There were still plenty of national interests in the world which Britain did *not* enclose because she did not feel she needed to: 'Why should we marry the lady,' said Cecil Spring-Rice of Russia's attitude to Persia, but it could apply to Britain's, 'when we can have her without the ceremony?'[70] (This may be thought a revealing metaphor.) And, lastly, it was an advantage to those who advocated imperial intervention in the defence of national interests if they could show that it could be done cheaply. The smaller the cost, the less convincing the case on other grounds need be.

Retrenchment was still a cardinal tenet of British colonial and foreign policy, and it did not only affect the decision of whether to intervene or not. It came out in the way Britain ran her new acquisitions once she had them. By and large she was not interested in 'developing' or 'civilising' them (though others were welcome to do this if they liked, at their own expense); only in holding them, and limiting her liability. Of all the new acquisitions made in the 1880s only one – British Bechuanaland – was annexed outright and could strictly be called a 'colony'. The rest were 'protectorates' or 'spheres of influence'. The distinction became blurred later on, but it was important then; it allowed Gladstone to believe, for example, that he had successfully kept out of the scramble for

Africa. 'Colonies' were run from a metropolitan country, which was responsible for them, had to provide their administrations, and so on. In a 'sphere of influence' the metropolitan country was under no obligation to do anything at all. Spheres of influence usually originated in friendly agreements between two powers, and were designed to forestall quarrels over territories neither of them thought were worth quarrelling over. They were means *of avoiding* colonial annexation. In a 'protectorate' the metropolitan country had some responsibilities, but not many. The word implied that some indigenous authority did the actual ruling, but with the privilege of being able to call on the metro-politan country's help and protection if they were needed. Protectorates were generally legitimised by treaties between both parties to this effect. In practice, the 'protection' afforded by Britain took a number of guises, and in some cases it was a legal fiction covering what was in effect a piece of political puppetry. Nevertheless the intention was always the same: to minimise Britain's responsibility, ensure that when she felt she had to take a country over in the imperial interest, she did not have to rule it imperially, and expensively.

All this coolness and imperial self-control did not meet with everyone's approval. Gladstone got a very rough passage for it, not because his outlook on colonial affairs was markedly different from Salisbury's at this time, but because he made more of an issue of it. It is doubtful whether public opinion in the 1880s cared very much about colonies and empire. But it did care about murdered heroes and defeated redcoats; and it was on emotive issues like these – General Gordon, Majuba – that Gladstone made his stand. The result was predictable: on the Gordon affair, the abuse he had to suffer was the kind usually reserved for assassins and adulterers. He had besmirched his country's honour, sent Gordon to his death, looked on while women 'were murdered in cold blood and little children were spitted on the Arab spears in pure wantonness';[71] one Member of Parliament even saw in him 'that Anti-Christ whose advent was foretold as the prelude of the end of the world'.[72] How far this unpopularity went is uncertain. A section of the press put it around that it was universal, that Gladstone's name was 'held up to execra-tion this day wherever the English language is spoken';[73] and gave the impression that the country was far ahead of Gladstone in its 'imperialism', but the true picture was prob-ably calmer. The *Spectator* pointed out between crises how quiet the provinces were: 'The candidates are talking about the Lords, taxes on corn, the depression in trade, local taxation; anything except the humiliation of the country and the necessity of war. There are no warlike public meetings.' Even the ordinary run of war news was greeted with indifference: 'Our people hardly watch or listen unless some favourite officer falls dead.' When Gordon did fall dead, the *Spectator* tried to set a balance against the furore:

> British journalism often gives a really false impression of the true drift of British opinion. ... There is no greater chasm than the chasm between the opinions of the sensational newspapers and the judgment of the British Public. The former are often fierce, frothy and fickle; while the latter is slow, calm, and steady.[74]

Probably popular opinion was more volatile than this, and jingoism stronger, but it was intermittent, soon blew past; and it gave no clue at all to how the public regarded the broad lines of Gladstone's colonial policy, his stand on the issue of 'imperialism'. Jingoism was a new word (new in 1876), but the phenomenon it described, popular xenophobia, was at least as old as the city life which spawned it. Its association with imperialism in the 1880s was purely accidental. Jingoism fed on heroes and wars, and it just so happened that most of Britain's heroes murdered then were murdered in the cause of empire, and most of her wars or quarrels were over colonies. It could not be said yet – if it could be said ever – that the British people were 'imperialist' in any positive or constructive way, despite their flashes of feeling at some of the more spectacular episodes of empire.

But whether or not the 'people' shared their concern, the political classes, as reflected in their newspapers, worried inordinately in the 1880s about the state of the British empire: and it was not all simple party politicking. For Liberals as well as Conservatives, it was apparent that Britain had struck a bad patch in her national history, not only abroad with Egypt and the Russians in central Asia and the Germans in Africa, but also at home, with the trade depression, and Ireland, and London terrorised by anarchist bombs. All governments must feel that their problems are uniquely serious, but the Liberal governments of the 1880s had more than most to contend with, and they had no more desire than the Conservatives to gloss over them. Where the Conservative Party differed from the Liberals was in believing that the Liberals' problems were partly of their own making, and could have been avoided by 'firm action': in foreign affairs by more obduracy in resisting the demands of other nations, backed up by a bigger army and a stronger navy. In all the anti-Gladstone press comment of the 1880s the dominant note is that of wounded pride, the sense of national humiliation, the fear of dire consequences if Britain continued to show pusillanimity to her enemies. 'The shock of the fall of Khartoum,' said the *Statist*,

> will be felt far beyond the limit of the African desert. Wherever a handful of Englishmen are performing the daily miracle of our Imperial rule, and controlling and administering a subject Eastern race, with no other force than that of their own character and of their national prestige, there the triumph of the Mahdi will work embarrassment and create difficulty and danger. There is the danger that not only in Africa, not only in Asia, but throughout the world, the idea should take root that England is too weak or too indifferent to hold her own.[75]

And the *Pall Mall Gazette* commented more generally:

> We have avoided trouble hitherto by knuckling down humbly all round the world. We have brought all this trouble in Egypt on our heads out of the desire to oblige France, which dictated the Joint Note; and still our neighbours are not satisfied. Prince Bismarck orders us out of the north-eastern corner of New Guinea, and we take up our hat and go. France tears up our own financial proposals, and we humbly accept her alternative scheme … With the cream of our available fighting force locked up in the Soudan, what can we do but give in here, give in there, and give in everywhere all round the world until at last we are sharply brought up by some demand to which we cannot give in – and then! How are we prepared for that eventuality, which will come as certain as the summer sun?[76]

'Popular' imperialism is usually associated with national self-confidence. In the 1880s, it could equally well be associated with national self-doubt.

All this was perhaps too gloomy. But it was a natural reaction to the colonial crisis of the time, which was a very real one to Britain. For what was happening in the 1870s and 1880s was something more than just a few minor setbacks in her foreign relations. It was a major upheaval of her position in the world. Before the 1870s, Britain's world supremacy had been based on a kind of natural monopoly of influence and power outside Europe. Now that monopoly was being slowly eroded away. The *Pall Mall Gazette* spotted the general trend most clearly. 'Our old position is lost – irrevocably', it said in 1885; nothing could restore to Britain 'the conditions under which we lorded it over one-half the world'.

> In times past ... we did what we pleased, where we pleased, and as we pleased. The whole of heathendom, to use a comprehensive term, was our inheritance, and the salt sea our peculiar possession. All that has changed. Europe has overflowed into Africa, Asia, America, Australasia and the Pacific. At every turn we are confronted with the gunboats, the sea lairs, or the colonies of jealous and eager rivals ... The world is filling up around us ... Europe, no longer distracted by intestine feuds, throws off ever increasing swarms to settle in other continents, and whereas, since Trafalgar, the Englishman has never found himself confronted by any other opponent but the savage with his spear, or the pirate in his prah, we now find every ocean highway furrowed by European ironclads, while over many a colonial frontier frowns the cannon of Continental rivals.[77]

Confronted by this new situation, Britain had to adapt. If she complained about it, it was not out of any real reluctance to safeguard or extend her interests in the world, but out of resentment at the means she now had to use to do it, which was the 'enclosure' of certain areas where she had had free rein before, the fencing off of bits of the common garden. She had to do this in order to salvage anything of her old ascendancy. 'Spheres of influence' could no longer be taken for granted: they had to be marked out on the map. The end result of all this was twofold. In the first place, and most obviously, the area of Britain's formal empire expanded, most of all in Africa. But at the same time, and intimately connected with this expansion as both cause and effect, her old 'informal empire' was contracting; in Turkey and Persia, for example, she was losing her political influence, and in Africa and the Pacific her commercial predominance. Consequently the expansion of the British empire in the 1880s was a reflection not so much of Britain's growing power in the world as of her slow decline, or at least the anticipation of it.

Twenty or thirty years before, in the 1850s and right up to the 1870s, Britain's formal empire had been only a manifestation of her power and strength, not a definition of its extent. It was the visible core of a vast structure of ascendancy in the world, which stretched far beyond the empire's boundaries. In the 1880s, this was changing. The frontiers of Britain's 'informal' empire were shrinking, and as they did so the frontiers of her 'formal' empire expanded to meet them. They never did meet exactly; but the formal British empire was beginning to identify and delimit the extent of Britain's world dominance more closely than it had. The pressures of the 1880s had forced the British to declare their hand in the world outside Europe, and had translated a vague ascendancy over the whole of it into a more definite proprietorship over just part of it, albeit the biggest part still. The empire had been there for some time but it needed the very special conditions of the 1880s to reveal it.[78]

Notes

1 W. Woodruff, *The Impact of Western Man: A Study of Europe's Role in the World's Economy, 1750–1960* (Macmillan, 1966), p. 104.
2 *Ibid.*, p. 253.

3 D. S. Landes, *The Unbound Prometheus: Technological Change and Industrial Development in Western Europe from 1750 to the Present* (Cambridge UP, 1969), p. 221.
4 Woodruff, *op. cit.*, p. 150.
5 M. E. Townsend, *Origins of Modern German Colonialism* (Columbia UP, 1921), p. 18.
6 Woodruff, *op. cit.*, p. 106.
7 *Ibid.*, pp. 318–31.
8 Townsend, *op. cit.*, p. 181; and see H. Brunschwig, *French Colonialism 1871–1914* (Pall Mall Press, 1966), pp. 74–85; W. L. Langer, *European Alliances and Alignments 1871–1890* (American Book Supply Co., 1931), pp. 286–7.
9 C. A. Bodelsen, *Studies in Mid-Victorian Imperialism* (Constable, 1924), p. 82.
10 *Final Report of the Royal Commission on the Depression in Trade and Industry* (1886), para. 75.
11 *Ibid.*, para. 67.
12 See R. J. S. Hoffman, *Great Britain and the German Trade Rivalry 1875–1914* (Pennsylvania UP, 1933); Langer, *op. cit.*, Chapter 9.
13 W. L. Langer, *The Diplomacy of Imperialism 1890–1902*, 2 vols (Harvard UP, 1935), i, 77.
14 Bodelsen, *op. cit.*, p. 103.
15 William Booth, *In Darkest England and the Way Out* (1890).
16 J. A. Froude, *Oceana* (1886 edn), pp. 8–9, 174.
17 Woodruff, *op. cit.*, pp. 103–4.
18 Froude, *op. cit.*, p. 174.
19 J. R. Seeley, *The Expansion of England* (1895 edn), p. 88. For precedents for this argument, see Bodelsen, *op cit.*, p. 173, n. 2.
20 R. Faber, *The Vision and the Need: Late Victorian Imperialist Aims* (Faber & Faber, 1966), p. 54.
21 *Ibid.*, p. 64.
22 B. H. Brown, *The Tariff Reform Movement in Great Britain* (Oxford UP, 1943), p. 3.
23 *Ibid.*, p. 9.
24 *St James's Gazette*, 15 January 1885.
25 *Final Report of the Royal Commission on the Depression*, pp. 138–9.
26 On tariff reform, see Brown, *op. cit.*; J. E. Tyler, *The Struggle for Imperial Unity 1868–1895* (Longmans & Co., 1938); B. Semmel, *Imperialism and Social Reform* (Allen & Unwin, 1960), Chapters 4, 5; P. J. Cain and A. G. Hopkins, *British Imperialism: Innovation and Expansion 1688–1914* (Longman, 1993), Chapter 7.
27 *Ibid.*, Chapter 7.
28 J. A. Hobson, *Imperialism: A Study* (Nisbet, 1902), Part I.
29 Cain and Hopkins, *op. cit., passim.*
30 A. P. Thornton, *For the File on Empire* (Macmillan, 1968), p. 136.
31 G. Cecil, *Life of Robert Marquis of Salisbury*, 4 vols (Hodder & Stoughton, 1921, 1921, 1931, 1932), (1921), ii, 72.
32 H. C. Rawlinson, *England and Russia in the East* (1875), p. 147.
33 W. F. Monypenny and G. E. Buckle, *The Life of Benjamin Disraeli* (John Murray, 1920), v, 434.
34 R. Blake, *Disraeli* (Eyre & Spottiswoode, 1966), p. 662.
35 R. J. Moore, *Liberalism and Indian Politics* (Edward Arnold, 1966), p. 25.
36 On Indian defence, see D. P. Singhal, *India and Afghanistan 1876–1907* (University of Queensland Press, 1963); D. R. Gillard, 'Salisbury and the Indian defence problem 1885–1902', in K. Bourne and D. C. Watt (eds), *Studies in International History* (Longmans, 1967); A. P. Thornton, *For the File on Empire* (Macmillan, 1968), Chapters 14–16; R. L. Greaves, *Persia and the Defence of India 1884–92* (Athlone Press, 1959); G. J. Alder, *British India's Northern Frontier 1865–96* (Longmans, 1963).
37 *The Annual Register*, 1878, p. 254.
38 Edward Dicey, 'Our route to India', *Nineteenth Century*, i (1877), 666.
39 B. R. Mitchell and P. Deane, *Abstract of British Historical Statistics* (Cambridge UP, 1962), pp. 315–16.
40 D. C. M. Platt, *Finance, Trade and Politics: British Foreign Policy 1815–1914* (Oxford UP, 1968), pp. 199–207.
41 Monypenny and Buckle, *op. cit.*, v, 449.
42 L. H. Jenks, *The Migration of British Capital to 1875* (Cape, 1927; reissued 1938), p. 235.

43 Blake, *op. cit.*, p. 586.

44 Cain and Hopkins, *op. cit.*, p. 365. Gladstone's Egyptian shares were discovered by H. C. G. Mathew.

45 See R. E. Robinson and J. Gallagher, *Africa and the Victorians* (Macmillan, 1961), Chapters 4, 5; Langer, *European Alliances and Alignments*, Chapter 8.

46 See W. H. Worger, *South Africa's City of Diamonds: Mine Workers and Monopoly Capitalism in Kimberley, 1867–1895* (Yale UP, 1987); R. V. Turrell, *Capital and Labour on the Kimberley Diamond Fields 1871–1890* (Cambridge UP, 1987).

47 C. W. de Kiewiet, *A History of South Africa, Social and Economic* (Oxford UP, 1941), p. 101.

48 For the Zulu Wars, see A. Duming and C. Ballard (eds), *The Anglo-Zulu War: New Perspectives* (University of Natal Press, 1981); J. Laband, *Kingdom in Crisis: The Zulu Response to the British Invasion of 1879* (Manchester UP, 1992).

49 D. M. Schreuder, *Gladstone and Kruger: Liberal Government & Colonial Home Rule 1880–85* (Routledge, 1969), p. 15.

50 Robinson and Gallagher, *op. cit.*, p. 242.

51 On the 'scramble' for southern Africa, see *ibid.*; C. W. de Kiewiet, *The Imperial Factor in South Africa* (Cambridge, UP, 1937); D. M. Schreuder, *The Scramble for Southern Africa 1877–1895* (Cambridge UP, 1980), and *Gladstone and Kruger* (Routledge & Kegan Paul, 1969); John Benyon, *Proconsul and Paramountcy in South Africa: The High Commission, British Supremacy and the Sub-Continent, 1866–1910* (University of Natal Press, 1980).

52 A. Ramm (ed.), *The Political Correspondence of Mr Gladstone and Lord Granville 1876–1886* (Oxford UP, 1962), ii, 249, 251.

53 Langer, *European Alliances and Alignments*, p. 308.

54 C. W. Newbury, 'Trade and authority in West Africa from 1850 to 1880', in L. H. Gann and P. Duignan (eds), *Colonialism in Africa 1870–1960*, 5 vols (Cambridge UP, 1969), i.

55 On Australian 'sub-imperialism', see Roger C. Thompson, *Australian Imperialism in the Pacific: The Expansionist Era, 1820–1920* (Melbourne UP, 1980).

56 Langer, *European Alliances and Alignments*, p. 313.

57 Ramm, *op. cit.*, ii, 246, 309.

58 Cecil, *op. cit.*, iii, 230.

59 A. G. Gardiner, *The Life of Sir William Harcourt* (Constable, 1923), ii, 199.

60 Langer, *European Alliances and Alignments*, p. 295.

61 See *The Cambridge History of the British Empire* (Cambridge UP, 1959), iii pp. 142–5, 149; K. G. Tregonning, *Under Chartered Company Rule: North Borneo 1881–1946* (Oxford UP, 1958), Chapter 2; W. P. Morrell, *Britain in the Pacific Islands* (Oxford UP, 1960), Chapters 9–12; John M. Ward, *British Policy in the South Pacific* (Australasian Publishing Co., 1948), Chapter 28.

62 See Robinson and Gallagher, *op. cit.*, pp. 163–89; J. E. Flint, *Sir George Goldie and the Making of Nigeria* (Oxford UP, 1960).

63 Cecil, *op. cit.*, iii, 230.

64 See J. S. Galbraith, *Mackinnon and East Africa 1878–95: A Study in the 'New Imperialism'* (Cambridge UP, 1972); Robinson and Gallagher, *op. cit.*, pp. 189–202; R. Oliver and G. Mathew, *History of East Africa* (Oxford UP, 1963), i, Chapters 10–11; R. Coupland, *The Exploitation of East Africa 1856–90: Slave Trade and the Scramble* (Faber & Faber, 1968 edn), Chapters 15–20.

65 *Manchester Guardian*, 7 April 1884.

66 *Pall Mall Gazette*, 23 August 1884.

67 D. Dilks, *Curzon in India*, 2 vols (Hart Davis, 1969, 1970), i, 136.

68 *Spectator*, 6 December 1884, p. 1607.

69 Ramm, *op. cit.*, ii, 343.

70 Dilks, *op. cit.*, i, 130.

71 *Pall Mall Gazette*, 11 February 1885.

72 *Manchester Guardian*, 6 March 1885.

73 *Yorkshire Post*, 7 February 1885.

74 *Spectator*, 3 and 24 January 1885.

75 *Statist*, February 1885.

76 *Pall Mall Gazette*, 10 February 1885.

77 *Pall Mall Gazette*, 4 February 1885.

78 On colonial expansion *c.* 1860–75 see Paul Knaplund, *Gladstone and Britain's Imperial Policy* (Allen & Unwin, 1927); J. D. Hargreaves, *Prelude to the Partition of West Africa* (Macmillan, 1963); W. D. McIntyre, *The Imperial Frontier in the Tropics* (Macmillan, 1967); F. Harcourt, 'Disraeli's imperialism, 1866–1868: a question of timing', *Historical Journal*, 33 (1980), 87–109; and F. Harcourt, 'Gladstone, monarchism and the "new" imperialism, 1868–74', *Journal of Imperial and Commonwealth History*, xiv (1985), 20–51; C. C. Eldridge, *England's Mission: The Imperial Idea in the Age of Gladstone and Disraeli, 1868–1880* (Macmillan, 1973); John S. Galbraith, 'The "Turbulent Frontier" as a factor in British expansion', *Comparative Studies in Society and History*, 2 (1966), 150–68.

5 Struggles for existence: 1890

Britain under siege

If one intention of the colonial activities of the 1870s and 1880s – the wars, the diplomacy and the annexations – had been to allow statesmen at home in London to sleep more soundly in their beds, then they singularly failed. In the 1890s, the prevailing political gloom among statesmen was as deep as ever, probably deeper. The picture had not significantly changed, of Britain under challenge from European rivals and forced to expend more and more of her energy and resources resisting it. In many ways the picture had got worse, as Britain's resources diminished, her responsibilities increased, and her rivals grew bolder. In the 1890s, she became an 'imperialistic' power in a self-conscious kind of way she had not been before (at least since Disraeli): flaunting her empire like a cock-bird blowing up his feathers to assert his dominance to rivals. From the impression she gave – the bragging of her favourite poets and her press, the public celebrations of might and glory like the Jubilee procession of 22 June 1897 – she had never been greater or more powerful in the world than now. But this impression was misleading. Beneath the display there was fear, behind the self-assertion a feeling of vulnerability which could not entirely be hidden, either from herself or from the rivals she was seeking to impress. Britain was weaker in the world in the 1890s than she had been 20 years before, and that despite the vast size of her empire and its recent expansion. There were very few politicians who by 1900 at the latest did not have some sense of this.

The facts of the matter were simple and ominous. Economically Britain was falling back in the world in the 1890s, as she had in the 1880s. The trade depression lifted a little in the mid-1890s, but her economy never was to regain the health and vitality it had had in the mid-nineteenth century. Year by year the gap narrowed between Britain and her industrial competitors. In foreign trade Britain was having to struggle to maintain even a moderate rate of growth, while her rivals bounded ahead in theirs. Between 1880 and 1900, her trade increased by only 25 per cent. France was doing worse than she was, but other western European countries were doing better, and one or two, like Germany and the Netherlands, spectacularly better (Table 5.1).[1]

Symbolic of the new state of affairs was the decline in Britain's old export staples of cotton and woollen textiles. In 1875, they accounted for 35 per cent of her total exports, in 1900, for only 27 per cent.[2] In the 1880s, Britain was overtaken in steel production by the United States, and in the 1890s by Germany.[3] In 1900, Britain was still overall the greatest manufacturing and trading power in the world but her lead over others was being cut back remorselessly year by year. As a result, the balance of her trade was beginning to look distinctly unhealthy, as the great developed markets of Europe and North America increasingly provided for themselves the things Britain had used to make

Table 5.1 European trade (£million)

Country	Exports			Imports		
	1880	*1900*	*Increase (%)*	*1880*	*1900*	*Increase (%)*
Britain	223	291	23	411	523	27
France	139	164	18	201	180	−10
Germany	142	231	63	136	293	107
the Netherlands	53	144	172	71	167	137
Belgium	47	77	56	67	89	33

Source: Woodruff, W. *The Impact of Western Man: A Study of Europe's Role in the World's Economy, 1750–1960* (Macmillan, 1966), pp. 314–31.

for them, and began piling up payments surpluses against her. By the late 1890s, Britain was regularly recording import figures of 50 per cent above her exports.[4] These massive deficits were bridged partly by the interest on her capital investments abroad – which was not unusual; it had been the way things were done for decades – but even foreign investment was going through a bad patch in the 1890s, after a series of worldwide defaults and crises at the beginning of the decade.[5] Britain was sending far less of her new surplus capital abroad in the 1890s than before or afterwards: perhaps 3.2 per cent of the national income in the period from 1890 to 1904, compared with 6 per cent in the 1880s and 7.8 per cent between 1905 and 1914.[6] The economic picture, therefore, was far from rosy, at least so far as Britain's involvement in the wider world was concerned (Table 5.2).[7,8]

The empire did something to help the situation, but not much. Marginally less of Britain's trade was with the empire in the 1890s than in the 1880s (27.5 per cent as compared with 28.5 per cent), and most of that trade was with the 'old' dominions of Canada, Australia and India.[9] Similarly, the empire exerted no significant long-term pull on foreign investment – or no more than in the 1870s and 1880s – and again, the new tropical colonies virtually none at all.[10] What was helpful, however, was that trade with the empire was predominantly an export trade, and this went some way towards counterbalancing the import surplus elsewhere. The empire accounted for 22.3 per cent of Britain's imports in the 1890s, but for 33.7 per cent of her exports,[11] and it was the 'new' or under-developed colonies which made the difference. As the balance of trade ran into deficit with the 'advanced' countries of Europe and North America, so it ran into credit with the 'backward' territories of Asia and Africa: not enough to make up the difference, but significantly (Table 5.3).[12]

Table 5.2 UK trade: annual averages (£million)

Dates	Europe and North Africa			USA and Canada		
	Imports	*Exports*	*Re-exports*	*Imports*	*Exports*	*Re-exports*
1870–79	147.8	87.1	44.0	81.8	33.4	4.7
1880–89	165.2	78.0	42.6	102.3	39.3	10.7
1890–99	192.2	37.4	120.0	29.7	15.4	
1900–09	241.6	119.0	41.9	151.8	36.1	24.0

Source: Mitchell, B. R. and Deane, P., *Abstract of British Historical Statistics* (Cambridge UP, 1962), pp. 316–19.

Table 5.3 UK trade: annual average (£million)

Dates	Tropical and southern Africa			Asia		
	Imports	*Exports*	*Re-exports*	*Imports*	*Exports*	*Re-exports*
1870–79	8.3	6.9	0.8	52.6	37.4	2.0
1880–89	8.6	8.8	0.9	56.4	47.9	2.6
1890–99	9.4	15.0	1.3	45.7	48.3	1.6
1900–09	12.3	25.8	2.2	55.7	71.0	1.8

Source: Mitchell, B. R. and Deane, P., *Abstract of British Historical Statistics* (Cambridge UP, 1962), pp. 318–19.

The contribution of these countries to Britain's prosperity was important, but overall it was not yet decisive. In the 1890s, for example, Britain still did more trade with Belgium than with the whole of Africa. If any British statesmen, manufacturers or speculators had ever believed that new colonies would make a big difference to trade, then they were disappointed. By and large, trade and capital investment followed old, well-worn paths, to and from countries with prosperous European populations, and left the primitive underprivileged tropics well alone.

Politically the new colonies were little help to Britain either, and, in fact, in many ways they could be said to be making matters worse. The ignorant saw the size of Britain's empire in the 1890s as a sign or even a source of strength in the world: politicians and military men were less euphoric. A bigger empire, and especially a scattered empire like Britain's, meant more frontiers to defend and longer supply lines. With colonies like Canada and Australia – the old colonies of white settlement – this was compensated for by the existence within the frontiers of loyal populations willing to help defend them: the two factors more or less cancelled each other out. With the new colonies accumulated in the 1880s and 1890s, this was not so. They were generally filled with peoples who had no particular loyalty to Britain, no desire to defend her hold over them – indeed, might welcome foreign hostility if it came and take advantage of it for ends of their own. For this reason, they could be serious liabilities strategically, points of instability which, far from adding to Britain's strength, might drain it dangerously at any moment of crisis. And this was true also – as it had always been – of India. Lord Roberts in 1884 described India's frontier as 'impossible', and Britain's chances of holding on to the country in the event of any full-scale attack as hopeless, for:

> It must … be remembered that, whereas the invasion of any country is usually met by the determined opposition of all classes of the inhabitants … with the British in India, the conditions would be vastly different. At the best, we could only expect the natives to remain passive, while the first disaster would raise throughout Hindustan a storm, compared with which the troubles of 1857 would be insignificant.

'A discouraging result,' he said, 'of more than a century's rule.'[13] In fact, for those who wanted to look for them, the empire was full of weak spots in the 1890s. Lord Kitchener, who was Roberts's successor as Commander-in-Chief in India, and his Viceroy Lord Curzon both worried inordinately about their northern frontier and the Russian hordes glowering over it: Kitchener saw as inevitable a contest with Russia 'in which we shall have to fight for our existence', and was not sure that the Indian army was competent to meet it.[14] South Africa could not be secure while the Boers were so numerous and their republic so rich and hostile. The Middle East was safe only while Britain held Egypt, and holding Egypt made her vulnerable elsewhere. John Morley's conclusion from all this in 1906 was that Britain's 'vast, sprawling empire' presented 'more vulnerable surface than any empire the world ever saw'.[15]

To defend this empire, it was by no means certain that Britain had anything like sufficient armed forces. Her army was certainly inadequate, although its inadequacy until now had been obscured by the lack of any opportunity really to test it. It needed the first disastrous months of the Boer War to point up its failings: 'I think all my colleagues feel, as I do,' wrote Lord George Hamilton, the Indian Secretary, in November 1899, 'that this war makes self-evident that our Empire is in excess of our armaments, or even of our power to defend it in all parts of the world.'[16] Of course the Army had never been Britain's strongest point. Her real security was supposed to rest on her naval supremacy: or as Winston Churchill put it – 'As to a stronger Regular Army, either we had the command of the sea or we had not. If we had it, we required fewer soldiers, if we had it not we wanted more ships.'[17] The Navy's special and peculiar importance to Britain was emphasised by Lord George Hamilton in 1894: 'The freedom of sea communications between Great Britain and the outer world is as essential to her existence as the passage of air through the windpipe of any human being is to the preservation of his life.'[18] The Navy was Britain's first (and to some people her last) line of defence. For this reason, perhaps, people scarcely stopped worrying about it in the 1890s. In 1889, the government had adopted the 'two-power standard' of naval strength (that the naval establishment should always exceed that of the next two strongest European navies combined), and a programme of naval building had been inaugurated to bring the Navy up to that standard. But big ships took a long time to build; meanwhile other nations were pushing their own targets up, and in the early 1890s the Navy was still below par. Arthur Balfour was shown some tables of comparative naval strengths at the end of 1891, which revealed Britain still some way behind France and Russia combined in the number of ships built and under construction; 'I confess,' he wrote, 'that the perusal of these Tables fills me with anxiety.'[19] Anxiety was fed throughout the 1890s by Admiralty experts who never would admit to their political masters that they had enough ships to win a war, and by pressmen and politicians wanting to make party capital out of public unease. 'The panic mongers are abroad,' said the *Daily News* in 1893, 'and venerable Admirals are joining juvenile politicians in their attempts to prove that the British fleet, if it has not already gone to the dogs, is at least on its way to them.'[20] One of the casualties of this particular scare was Gladstone, who resigned the premiership rather than give in to 'militarism'.[21] But still expenditure on the Navy went up year by year, and doubts remained as to its strength and efficiency. Until it had undergone a test like the Army's in South Africa, those doubts would never be entirely allayed.

What made things worse for Britain – what made it necessary for her, for example, not only to have the world's biggest navy, but also to have one which would vanquish all comers in any combination – was that she had no friends. Her diplomatic isolation in the world was called 'splendid' at the time, as if it were an aloofness deliberately chosen and born of strength. But many statesmen regarded it with considerable unease. Lord Rosebery took a hard look at Britain in 1899 and saw only

> [a] little island ... so lonely in these northern seas, viewed with so much jealousy, and with such hostility, with such jarred ambition by the great empires of the world, so friendless among nations which count their armies by embattled millions.[22]

'So long as you are isolated,' Joseph Chamberlain asked the Commons in 1898, 'can you say that it is not possible, can you even say that it is not probable, that some time or another you may have a combination of at least three Powers against you?'[23] This was always the fear, that other countries would combine against Britain: possibly Germany and France, as Germany intended in 1897; more probably France and Russia, between whom an alliance looked in the offing from the beginning of the 1890s, though it was not openly acknowledged until 1895. It was widely believed that the Franco-Russe alliance would soon turn against Britain,[24] and almost as widely held – and by experts – that if a war did come, Britain would lose it. 'To meet such a combination single handed,' wrote the Second Sea Lord in 1895, 'our resources are, at present, seriously inadequate ... England is in a very unfit state to undertake war, even against France alone.'[25] Queen Victoria in 1893 worried that the Franco-Russe 'may lead to a combination which might prove disastrous to our small forces'.[26] On a more popular level, there was a brief fashion in salutary novels (the best known was William le Queux's *The Great War in England in 1897*, published in 1894), which described hypothetical invasions of Britain in much the same way as *The Battle of Dorking* had done twenty-three years before.[27] The blackest days of the Boer War rekindled the fear that other nations would take advantage of Britain's isolation at a time when (as it appeared to W. T. Stead) 'the Empire, stripped of its armour, has its hands tied behind its back and its bare throat exposed to the keen knife of its bitterest enemies'.[28]

That those enemies would use their knives if they could was almost axiomatic. It was natural that they should be jealous. 'I never spent five minutes in enquiring why we are unpopular,' wrote Curzon in 1900; 'The answer is written in red ink on the map of the globe.'[29] Out of jealousy they would do all they could to humble Britain or even destroy her. The growth of foreign navies in itself was suspicious, because foreign countries were supposed to have no legitimate need for navies: having 'no great commerce, no transmarine empire like ours to protect', said the naval propagandist H. W. Wilson in 1896, their navies 'must be destined for offensive action against ourselves'.[30] Commercial competition was part of the same pattern. A widely read book alerting the nation to the dangers of German trade competition in 1896 accused Germany of entering 'into a deliberate and deadly rivalry' with Britain, 'battling with might and main for the extinction of her supremacy'.[31] 'An actual state of war against England began some time ago,' wrote another commentator in February 1898; 'war has long been organised and in progress upon military lines.'[32] Joseph Chamberlain took up the cry:

> There has been for some time past a combined assault by the nations of the world upon the commercial supremacy of this country, and if that assault is successful our existence would be menaced in a way in which it never has been threatened [since Bonaparte].[33]

For the *Contemporary Review*, the plot was clear:

> What our pushing rivals are now seeking to accomplish is this: figuratively they are constructing a cage or palisade around the British Empire, within which we shall have freedom of motion for a time, but whose dimensions ... we shall have outgrown in a certain number of years.[34]

Some detected a broader, more fundamental pattern to all this. The vogue philosophy of the time, 'Social Darwinism', saw foreign hostility and rivalry as a biological imperative:

> The foreign policies of nations ... are anticipation of, and provision for, struggles for existence between incipient species ... The facts are patent. Feeble races are being wiped off the earth and the few great, incipient species arm themselves against each other. England, as the greatest of these – greatest in race-pride – has avoided for centuries the only dangerous kind of war. Now, with the whole earth occupied and the movements of expansion continuing, she will have to fight to the death against successive rivals.[35]

'The truth is,' wrote another in 1896, 'that what we call national rivalry is to all intents and purposes part of the universal scheme that makes Nature "red in tooth and claw".'[36] This was rather strong liquor for most ordinary people. But many imperialists, including, for example, Lord Salisbury, who was not the most rabid of them, shared its view of the world as a jungle – 'in which each one obtains his rights precisely in proportion to his ability, or those of his allies, to fight for them'.[37] In a famous speech of May 1898, which alarmed and offended many foreign governments, he spelt out the implications of this view for the world as it was then:

> Nations may roughly be divided between the living and the dying ... For one reason or another – from the necessities of politics or under the pretence of philanthropy – the living nations will gradually encroach on the territory of the dying, and the seeds and the causes of conflict among civilised nations will speedily appear. These things may introduce causes of fatal difference between the great nations whose mighty armies stand opposite threatening each other. These are the dangers, I think, which threaten us in the period which is coming on.[38]

It was a *very predatory* view of international affairs. But in the climate of the time, especially in the years 1898–99 when the auguries of international conflict were most alarming, it seemed a likely prognosis, and the one which it might be expedient to accept and act on. The 'scramble' for the world which had begun in the previous decade was still going on; after the supply of vacant land dried up, what would happen? 'Where fifty years ago we had every liberty of movement to go where we chose,' wrote Curzon in 1895, 'we have had within the last twenty years scarcely walking-room; where we had walking-room, now we have scarcely elbow-room; and now, where England has hardly elbow-room, she will very soon have hardly room to move.'[39] If the scramble went on, it could be only at the expense, first, of weaker empires, and then at the Great Powers' mutual expense, which meant war. This was the way the signs seemed to be pointing.

There were many, of course, for whom such talk appeared alarmist. A school of Liberals still survived who steadfastly refused to regard all foreigners automatically as rivals or enemies, who persisted in believing that nations, like individuals, could be moral and co-operate together peacefully without being forced to,[40] but this voice was growing smaller. The governments of the 1890s, which were mostly Conservative governments, made a special virtue of 'realism', which meant, in their case, acknowledging the evil, or at least the amorality, of the world. Foreign nations might behave in a decent Christian manner, but it was dangerous to trust them to do so. Considerations of morality which were mandatory in dealings between individuals had no place in international affairs, because in relations between nations, there was no supranational body to compare with the paraphernalia of the law on a national level to ensure that morality was not penalised or taken advantage of. 'As a collection of individuals,' wrote Lord Salisbury, 'we live under the highest and latest development of civilisation ... As a collection of nations we live in an age of the merest *Faustrecht*.'[41] Consequently, in foreign policy, it was best to 'recognise distinctly the unfriendliness of other nations', and 'remember that we have no-where to look for support but to ourselves'.[42] 'Patriotism is only selfishness on a large scale', was how it was put by one man who called himself 'An Old Tory'.[43] A 'realistic' foreign policy consisted in suspecting every other nation as a potential aggressor, and building up defences and resources against the day when they would become *actual* aggressors. Britons never felt quite so insecure in an unfriendly world as when their territorial empire seemed at its glorious zenith.

Not everyone was so gloomy: not the ostriches who refused to believe in the possibility of war, nor, at the other end of the political spectrum, the hawks who found the prospect positively exhilarating. If imperialists expected the challenge to come soon – the war for the survival of the fittest – not all of them by any means were afraid of it. 'In the end,' wrote the patriotic poet W. E. Henley, 'it is a certainty; for it is written, or so it seems, that the world is for one of two races, and of these the English is one', but the English were equal to it. 'We are not one of the "dying nations", we! Our tradition is alive once more; our capacities are infinite.'[44] Sir Edward Grey told Theodore Roosevelt in 1906:

> Before the Boer War we were spoiling for a fight. We were ready to fight France about Siam, Germany about the Kruger telegram, and Russia about anything. Any Government here, during the last ten years of last century, could have had war by lifting a finger. The people would have shouted for it. They had a craving for excitement, and a rush of blood to the head.[45]

The 1890s saw a spate of literature which not merely defended war as a necessity, but glorified it as a good in itself, usually for the qualities of character it brought out in the participants, and for its purgative effect on nations which might otherwise grow 'effeminate'.

> The stimulus of a great patriotic excitement, the determination to endure burdens and make sacrifices, the self-abnegation which will face loss, and suffering, and even death, for the commonweal, are bracing tonics to the national health, and they help to counteract the enervating effects of 'too much love of living', too much ease, and luxury, and material prosperity ... Strength is not maintained without exercise.[46]

Some imperialists certainly took their imperialism all very light-headedly: conquering the whole world from their armchairs, revelling in their powers and their 'manifest destiny' with the carefree arrogance of a Siegfried. The braggadocio of empire was a strident voice in the 1890s. But by and large it was not the voice of those imperialists who mattered. Men of action and responsibility – the Roseberys, Curzons and Chamberlains – did not relish the prospect of a European war, because they had the navy lords close to them to warn them of the possible consequences. On a broader level too, their interpretation of the past and their reading of the future told them how fragile was the basis of their power in the world. Imperialists were particularly fond of detecting 'broad currents of history' and on the basis of them mapping out paths for the future. One of the things Curzon disliked about Salisbury was that while he was 'an adept at handling the present ... the future to him is anathema'. This was not the way to run an empire: 'We must take stock, must look ahead, must determine our minimum and our maximum and above all must have a line.'[47] With the scramble for the world hotting up soon, and with most of the geopolitical advantages lying with the great continental powers (and the imperialists were remarkably prescient in their predictions of future world trends), they could not afford to sit back and bask in the glory of the empire as it was. They had to make plans.

The 'new imperialism'

The plans they made were ambitious. For men like Chamberlain, Rosebery, Curzon, Milner and Rhodes, their imperialism was a serious matter: in a very literal sense a matter of life and death. It was a question of fitting Britain for survival, preparing her, as Lord Rosebery put it, 'for the keen race of nations'.[48] Consequently it would involve quite drastic changes in Britain as well as abroad; all agreed, or said they did, that a true imperialism began at home. 'An Empire such as ours,' wrote Rosebery to *The Times* in 1900,

> requires as its first condition an Imperial Race – a race vigorous and industrious and intrepid. Health of mind and body exalt a nation in the competition of the universe. The survival of the fittest is an absolute truth in the conditions of the modern world.[49]

And that meant *everyone*. This was another corollary, for most imperialists, of the requirement of imperial strength. 'No single class can sustain it,' wrote Lord Milner in 1913.

> It needs the strength of the whole people. You must have soundness at the core – health, intelligence, industry; and these cannot be general without a fair average standard of material well-being. Poverty, degradation, physical degeneracy – these will always be. But can any patriot, above all can any Imperialist, rest content with our present record in these respects? If he cares for the Empire, he must care that the heart of the Empire should beat with a sounder and less feverish pulse.[50]

For Milner, that implied widespread social reform. Other imperialists even dared to suggest the need for social*ism*,[51] though they generally meant something different by that than more regular socialists did. This link between imperialism and social reform became an influential one later.[52] For the moment, it was a sign of the seriousness with which the coming imperial crisis was perceived.

Most imperialist prescriptions were more conventionally reactionary – though often no less radical – than that. One or two, indeed, specifically rejected social reform as a solution, on the grounds that what had been achieved already on that front merely softened people up. The reason why so many of Britain's young men were weak and stunted, argued Lord Meath in 1908, was that the weak and stunted were now being allowed to live. That went against nature.[53] One or two even advocated 'eugenic' solutions – sterilising the less fit in society – as a slightly more humane alternative to the one implied by Meath.[54] A number of imperialists, led by Lords Roberts and Milner, saw the solution in universal military conscription, as a way both of involving all Britain's citizens in the imperial enterprise, and also of counteracting the baleful influence of socialism (the regular sort) among the proletariat. It would also, wrote Sidney Low in 1899, have the inestimable advantage of sending back into the factories a working class imbued with the 'alertness, the docility, and the disciplined promptness' of the German artisan; which was just the thing needed to strengthen Britain on the *industrial* front.[55] This was part of the explicit agenda of Baden-Powell's Boy Scout movement (1907), too.[56] Another commonly perceived problem was 'effeminacy', at the level both of individuals (the 'Oscar Wilde tendency' was seen as a definite national threat), and of the state as a whole. Imperialists worried inordinately about the political rise of women in the later nineteenth century. That is why so many imperialists were found, later, in the ranks of the anti-suffragists.[57] Empires were masculine institutions: potent, penetrative, tough. It would be fatal to entrust their fate to women. By agitating for this, women were undermining the empire in other ways. They were being distracted from producing and nurturing boy babies, which was their proper imperial role. 'Women's true place,' wrote one imperialist, a woman herself, 'is in the background', serving their husbands and sons. 'Patriotism is what we want in women ... not suffragism.'[58] It is possible that this factor – the 'masculinism' clearly associated with imperialism – was one reason for the very notable lack of progress made by the women's suffrage movement at this time. Some imperialists wanted not only to exclude women from politics, but to ban politics altogether. Milner, for example, advocated abolishing parliament – 'that mob at Westminster', he called it[59] – and replacing it by some other form of governance. Most imperialists saved their criticism for *party* politics, however, which divided the nation, they said, and so sapped its strength. In 1900, Rosebery floated the idea of a new 'centre' party to overcome this. But even he, the most liberal of all the leading imperialists of the day, was too disillusioned with 'democracy' to want to persist in this.

Two threads ran through all these attitudes, from 'social imperialism' through to anti-democracy. The first, obviously, was imperial patriotism. The second was the pursuit of what was known at the time as 'national efficiency'. Only by becoming 'efficient' could the empire survive in the ominous future that was now foreseen for it. Efficiency involved harnessing all the country's resources to this essential task: intelligence, capital, labour, men's muscles, women's wombs. It also required changes in the nation's leading institutions. The legislature was one. Public schools were another that came under some imperialist scrutiny, partly because they were expected to supply the empire's officers; with calls for less Latin and more geography, for example; less cricket and more rifle-shooting: more *useful* pursuits, in fact, to nurture professionalism by the side of good character.[60] The point of all this was to toughen and temper Britain into a proper imperial nation, or 'race', as it was usually put then. To the most avid imperialists of the 1890s and 1900s, she was very far from being this yet.

The task also went beyond that. The empire itself had to be reformed. As well as Britons needing to be fitted to defend it, it had to be fitted to make it an instrument of strength for Britons: a source of security for them in a hostile, predatory world. To this end even greater changes were required. The empire was vulnerable because it was incomplete and (that word again) 'inefficient'. To make it secure, there had to be more of it, and better use of what there was. So imperialists also bent their efforts to that.

Some of them, it seemed, would never be fully satisfied until the whole world was British. Only when there *were* no foreigners would Britain be entirely *secure* from foreigners. This was the ultimate in imperialist paranoia. Cecil Rhodes as a young man envisaged Britain taking over and settling

> the entire Continent of Africa, the Holy Land, the valley of the Euphrates, the Islands of Cyprus and Candia, the whole of South America, the islands of the Pacific not heretofore possessed by Great Britain, the whole of the Malay Archipelago, the seaboard of China and Japan.

the whole process to be completed by 'the ultimate recovery of the United States of America as an integral part of the British Empire'; and *this*, he concluded, would 'render wars impossible'.[61] This was clearly over-ambitious, but it was a common desire of imperialists to want to make existing colonies secure by surrounding them with more. Curzon, for example, wanted Afghanistan, Persia, Tibet, Arabia and Siam turned into a great series of buffer states around India; and there were many who saw Egypt's frontier stretching south as far as Uganda, and South Africa's boundary way beyond the Zambesi. There were supposed to be other reasons why it was imperative, in the interests of national survival, to take more colonies. The most common one given was the economic one: an old familiar argument for imperialism, but given a new urgency – sometimes a sense of panic – by the prevailing climate of fear:

> If we mean to hold our own against the efforts of all the civilised powers of the world to strangle our commerce by their prohibitive finance we must be prepared to take the requisite measures to open new markets for ourselves among the half-civilised or uncivilised nations of the globe, and we must not be afraid if that effort, which is vital to our industries, should bring with it new responsibilities of empire and government.[62]

That was the sober and sensible Lord Salisbury in 1895. Cecil Rhodes in the same year was quoted even more sensationally on this, as if the survival of the capitalist system itself depended on it:

> In order to save the 40,000,000 inhabitants of the United Kingdom from a bloody civil war, we colonial statesmen must acquire new lands to settle the surplus population, to provide new markets for the goods produced by them in the factories and mines. The Empire, as I have always said, is a bread and butter question. If you want to avoid civil war, you must become imperialists.[63]

There was little firm evidence for the special economic value of colonies, certainly not the evidence of the past 10 or 15 years. This did not much matter. Imperialists said that it was too soon to tell. In the immediate future new colonies might be worthless, but imperialists were looking much further ahead. 'We are engaged at the present moment, in the language of the mining camps, in "pegging out claims for the future",' said Rosebery in 1893.[64] No doubt it would have been better to wait and make sure the claims were worthwhile, but in the frantic 1890s that was impossible. It was a question of hedging your bets. The economic case for colonialism was never proved beyond dispute. But while the case *against* seemed equally in doubt, and other nations were more willing to risk their arm on the off-chance that it would do them some good, it might seem impolitic even to more cautious statesmen to stand by still debating the question while the best potential plums were taken from under their noses. To an imperialist with the siege-warfare mentality of a Curzon or a Rosebery, it would seem criminal for Britain not to expand while she still had the chance.

Expansion on its own was not enough, however. As it was, the empire was enormous; it was estimated to comprise one-quarter of the world's land area and one-fifth of its population. The potential there was vast; the trouble was that it was not being used as well as it could be. Politically and constitutionally, for example, the empire was the most confusing structure in the world, with no real common policy between any of its self-governing components, no agreed central direction, no 'permanent binding force,' said Milner, 'or rational system',[65] and this dissipated its strength and sapped its efficiency. United as a single political and military unit, it could defy the world. Imperial federation, said *The Times* in 1891,

> is the great task which lies before the British statesmanship of the future. With the colonies massed around us we can hold our own in the ranks of the world Powers ... Without them we must sink to the position of a merely European kingdom – a position which for England entails slow but sure decay.[66]

Like-minded men started up associations to work for empire unity: the Imperial Federation League in 1884, the British Empire League in 1894. Most federationists wanted to see the empire united commercially too. Joseph Chamberlain first campaigned for what he called an imperial *Zollverein*, or customs union, in the 1890s, but the idea had been in his mind, and in others', for 10 or 15 years before. A *Zollverein* would make the empire self-sufficient, which was clearly an advantage in a world of enemies. Then it should be exploited more intensively, to make it richer. 'It is not enough to occupy certain great spaces of the world's surface,' said Chamberlain in March 1895, 'unless you can make the best of them, unless you are willing to develop them'.[67] His favourite analogy was with estate management:

> Great Britain, the little centre of a vaster Empire than the world has ever seen, owns great possessions in every part of the globe, and many of these possessions are still almost unexplored, entirely undeveloped. What would a great landlord do in a similar case with a great estate? If he had the money he would expend some of it at any rate in improving the property.[68]

It was Chamberlain's ambition, when he came to the Colonial Office in 1895, to do just this with Britain's 'imperial estates'.

Ideas like these were widespread among self-styled 'imperialists' in the 1890s. Behind all of them it is possible to detect a certain unease, which derived from a common analysis of the contemporary world situation and of Britain's place in it. Britain was under threat on a number of fronts, and the way to resist that threat, as the imperialists saw it, was for Britain to dig in, rally her colonies around her, and prepare for the siege. Of course, it was not all fear and stark realism. Imperialists would not have been so anxious to defend their empire if they had not thought that it was intrinsically worth defending. Fundamentally, they believed in their own abilities, were confident that they had it in them to run a great empire – that they were, if they organised themselves properly, *fit* to rule a quarter of mankind. 'We happen to be,' said Cecil Rhodes, 'the best people in the world, with the highest ideals of decency and justice and liberty and peace, and the more of the world we inhabit, the better for humanity.'[69] Many others doubtless shared his patriotic self-esteem, but it was not common to voice it so crudely, and it was in any event not necessary to the imperialist's case to believe that his 'race' was overall and absolutely superior to others. What late Victorian imperialists did like to claim was that they were better at *governing* than others: better at the practical and pragmatic science of managing the affairs of other people. In this they fancied themselves greatly. 'I believe,' said Joseph Chamberlain in 1895, 'that the British race is the greatest of governing races that the world has ever seen',[70] and the proof of this for him could be measured in money:

It is interesting to notice that we alone have been successful, astonishingly successful, in making these acquisitions profitable. Every addition to the colonial possessions of France, or of Germany, adds immediately, and continues to add, to the latest date, a heavy burden upon the taxpayers of the mother country, whereas, in our case, all our colonies are either self-supporting from the first, or become so in a very short space of time.[71]

For others, the proof lay in the undoubted happiness and prosperity of the people of the British empire themselves. For while very few imperialists ever tried to maintain that the *motive* for imperial expansion was philanthropy, most of them believed, or claimed, that philanthropy was a by-product; that the result of it all was the betterment of mankind:

> The imperialist feels a profound pride in the magnificent heritage of empire won by the courage and energy of his ancestry ... He is convinced that the discharge of the duties of his great inheritance has an educational influence and a morally bracing effect on the character of the British people, and that the spread of British rule extends to every race brought within its sphere the incalculable benefits of just law, tolerant trade, and considerate government.[72]

This was imperialism's more positive, enthusiastic side; and for those who needed a degree of idealism, or sense of self-righteousness, to sustain them in their defence of the empire, it gave it to them. It sustained Curzon: 'To me the message is carved in granite, hewn of the rock of doom: that our work is righteous and that it shall endure.'[73] The British empire, he said, was 'under Providence, the greatest instrument for good that the world has seen'.[74] Such grandiose claims for it were common among imperialists. Rosebery called it 'the greatest secular agency for good that the world has seen'[75]; and before the end of the century was wondering whether it could in fact be so secular: 'How marvellous it all is! Built not by saints and angels, but the work of men's hands ... Human, and yet not wholly human, for the most heedless and the most cynical must see the finger of the divine.'[76] Others were fond of comparing the British empire with the Roman,[77] which, in view of what had happened to the Roman empire, was perhaps as salutary as it was flattering.[78]

Imperialists also liked to believe that they had 'the people' behind them, that (as one propagandist put it) 'the instincts of the British public are those of an imperial race'.[79] During the late 1890s they were able to sustain this impression quite easily. Even anti-imperialists accepted it, dispiritedly, though they believed the people were the worse for it. For a time it appeared that imperialism might provide the cement the Conservatives had been looking for since Disraeli to heal social divisions and meld all classes of society into his 'one nation': this appeal to patriotism which would raise men, especially working men, above their sectional interests to a common national purpose. In Parliament, which was supposed to be representative of the people, avowed 'anti-imperialists' were a very small minority, even in the Liberal Party; although 'imperialists' could come in many different shapes and sizes. In 1900, the Unionists fought an election on the issue of an imperial war and won it. And the fundamental solidity of popular imperialism was reckoned to be amply demonstrated when the patriotic working classes took to the streets during the Boer War – or seemed to. On the night of 18 May 1900, vast crowds all over Britain rowdily celebrated the relief of Mafeking after a seven-month siege. On numerous occasions thereafter mobs attacked houses of suspected anti-imperialists and broke up 'pro-Boer' meetings. Very few people questioned that these were clear signs of popular imperialism. Liberal pro-Boers certainly did not, but contented themselves with explaining it away. Usually they blamed the press for misleading the people and stirring them up. In fact, the press may have fooled the Liberals more than it fooled the people. For the working classes who participated in Mafeking night, the whole occasion was probably little more than a celebration of the safety of their comrades in uniform. Many of the more violent manifestations of 'popular imperialism' may not have been so 'imperialistic' or so 'popular' as appeared at the time; often the 'imperialism' was a mere unthinking hooliganism, and the 'working-class mob' turned out to be a crowd of medical students or Conservative clerks. It is likely that the working classes were considerably less imperialistic, and less *interested* in imperialism, than the middle classes. Generally, 'imperialism' in the abstract meant little to them, and when it was translated into something specific – like the Boer War – was important to them only in so far as it involved them or their friends as soldiers, or was supposed to be taking money which could better be used for social reform.[80] Nevertheless imperialists were able for a time to claim convincingly that they represented the mood of the nation. Their opponents let them. Divided, ineffectively led, without a firm parliamentary basis on which to build a spirited opposition (the Liberal Party was sitting on the fence, the Labour Party hardly yet born), the anti-imperialists and the pro-Boers never gave the imperialists a fair fight of it. They let their opponents take all the initiatives, and themselves reacted defensively, or even declined to react at all, in the hope that the storm would soon pass over – which it did. Until it did, the imperialists appeared to have it more or less their own way.[81]

This may have been one reason for the inflated sense they had of their own importance. Another was that many of them were, in fact, very important figures in British political life. For years there had existed in Britain a school of imperialists who had believed that the expansion of the British empire was desirable for its own sake: that it should be a central aim of British policy, and not merely accepted as a by-product (as it was then) of policies directed towards other ends. 'Imperialists', in this sense of the word, had always been there, but until now they had never been so numerous, or so voluble, or so very close to the centres of power. Chamberlain at the Colonial Office, and the top men in South Africa and India – Milner and Curzon – were all imperialists in this mould, as was at least one of the decade's three prime ministers, Lord Rosebery; and there was a fair scattering of them among the lower echelons. For this reason, it was difficult at the time, and is difficult now, to avoid making those men responsible for the colonial policies of the 1890s, and explaining British imperialism solely by reference to their motives. They gave *their* reasons why they thought the empire should be expanded or consolidated. When it *was* expanded or consolidated they, and other people too, tended to assume that it was for the reasons they had given. But it was not necessarily so. The fact was that the imperialists, when in power, were subjected as much as other men to the limitations of power. They could not do all they wanted to do because circumstances would not allow them to do so. 'Circumstances' included external factors, such as – for example, if an imperialist planned to annex a territory – the strength and disposition of British troops, the niceties of European diplomacy, the resistance of native populations. It also included the opinions and interests of other people in Britain: not 'the people' necessarily, for Britain was as yet a very imperfect democracy, but the dominant classes and interests within the country. In the 1890s, as at other times, the normal constraints of elective government applied: that ministers, and more indirectly pro-consuls, ultimately derived their power from others, who could put them out; and that, in order to implement their policies, they required the co-operation of others. However powerful the imperialists were, they could never be sufficiently powerful to *impose* policies on an uncooperative country for long. It was a very rough-and-ready sanction, but it had some effect. It meant that the imperialists' policies, before they could be carried through, had to be consistent with broader, more generally accepted, and possibly quite different assessments of the 'national interest' from their own. It meant that their influence was less significant than their eminence suggested.

Imperialists had a whole lot of things they wanted to do to make Britain and her empire secure and prosperous. In the end, some got done and some did not. The list of their failures is a long one. Chamberlain failed in his lifetime with his *Zollverein*. The empire never got federated, chiefly because the colonies did not want to be. British imperialists constantly got this wrong: misunderstood the nature of their expatriates' affection for the mother country, and underestimated their pride in their own fledgling nationalities.[82] Curzon was not allowed his string of buffer states around India until 1919, and then only briefly. Milner had wanted parties and Parliament abolished: neither was, not even in wartime. Roberts never saw his dream of a peacetime conscript army realised. All of these things imperialists had maintained at one time or another were essential to the preservation of the empire, and none of them was achieved, which was why, perhaps, the empire ultimately was not preserved. These measures failed because, despite the political eminence of their advocates, they were not accepted as necessary by the people and interests in whom lay ultimate authority, and the imperialists were not strong enough to override them. When a measure of theirs *was* successfully implemented, it was sometimes because, in that particular matter, they *were* strong enough to override them (for a time, for an accumulation of such measures might be said to have contributed to the Unionist Party's electoral defeat in 1906). But more often it was because there was less resistance to it from the country, because it corresponded with the general assessment of Britain's interests in other ways as well as the imperialists' assessment of those interests. The imperialists had one conception of what was good for Britain; the 'nation' had another. The points in the imperialists' programme which were implemented were most often those which satisfied both.

The national interest

The 'new imperialism' gave an edge and a flavour to the colonial policy of the 1890s which had not been there before, but it did not dictate its course. Colonial policy still grew out of the broader interests of Britain in the world – not her real 'national interest' necessarily, for that might have been better secured by her not having colonies at all; but at any rate a wider spectrum of special interests than those represented by the loudest imperialists.

In the 1890s, those interests were not so very different from what they had been in the 1860s. Britain's dependence on her economic ties with the wider world was as great as ever, and still far greater than other nations'. This dependence was a fundamental fact of British life and had been for years, since the time when Britain had chosen, under the persuasion of *The Wealth of Nations*, to concentrate her productive capacity on the things she produced best. The result of this, and it was an intended result, had been to make her into a highly specialised economy, unbalanced to a degree which some considered dangerous, dependent on foreign markets to consume the things she produced, and on foreign suppliers, not only for the luxuries of life, but for some of its necessities too.

Throughout the second half of the nineteenth century, Britain had been manufacturing far more textile goods than she could consume herself, and from materials she could not grow herself; and she had been leaving much of the food she ate to other nations to supply. If it had ever happened that her trade with other nations had been cut off, she could not have survived except at a terrible cost. World trade was not just a luxury to her, an exchange of the morsels left over at the end of the day when her own people had been catered for. In a very real sense, she lived by it.

As the century wore on, this trend accelerated, and the imports, especially, came flooding in through Britain's open doors. In 1900, she imported £523 million worth of goods, which was double her annual average in the 1860s.[83] And although she never had any trouble paying for them (in no year between 1847 and 1926 did Britain ever have a balance of payments deficit, and usually the account was very substantially in the black – by £50 million a year in the 1890s), the way she paid for them was significant. For she was never able to do so with visible exports of her own: in nearly every year from the beginning of the nineteenth century, the balance of visible trade showed a deficit, and that deficit was increasing from one decade to the next. Before the 1890s, she had made up the difference with invisible exports – insurance, banking services and the rest. On top of this, profits from overseas investment had made a nice little bonus. From the 1890s onwards, however, invisible exports on their own were unable to make up the deficit on her visible trade. From then on, interest on foreign investment took up the slack (Table 5.4).[84]

This meant that now, for the first time, Britain was unable to support herself by the goods and services she sold abroad. To complete the payment on her immense import bill she was relying on interest earned on the re-investment abroad of profits from previous enterprises. In a way she had begun living off the achievements of the past.[85]

To some contemporaries, this was a matter for concern. Easy profits from abroad were allowing Britain to import more goods than on present industrial performance she strictly deserved, which could be unhealthy as well as parasitic. The point was, wrote one economist in 1899, that interest from foreign investment directly benefited only the very small group of people who received it, and indirectly a few more who were 'in their pay or ministered to their luxuries'; it did not *employ* people in Britain. In the meantime, home industry, which did, and which for that reason was a sounder basis for prosperity, was starved of capital and 'choked' by the 'stream of wealth' from abroad. When the stream dried up, as it must, they would learn their lesson: that 'the gain which the moneyed class draw from their investments abroad … cannot possibly last for ever, and cannot compensate us for the misfortune which will overtake us if we allow our great national industries to be sacrificed'.[86] There was a good deal of sense here, although the nemesis predicted seemed a very distant one in 1899.

Table 5.4 Annual average balance of payments (£million)

Dates	Visible trade	Invisible trade	Overseas investment earnings
1870–79	−84.9	+88.5	+50.9
1880–89	−97.1	+94.0	+70.8
1890–99	−133.4	+94.4	+96.1
1900–09	−159.7	+121.7	+125.5

Source: Mitchell, B. R. and Deane, P., *Abstract of British Historical Statistics* (Cambridge UP, 1962), pp. 334–5.

Undoubtedly the best thing Britain could have done to correct this situation would have been to make her export industry more competitive – improve her methods of manufacture and marketing in order to sell more abroad. That this on the whole was not the way she chose was due to a number of factors, not the least of which was that it was not really a matter of 'choice' anyway: no government could decide that it wanted a more competitive industry and then pursue policies to that end, because direction of industry was not a proper part of a government's function. The efficiency or otherwise of industry depended on 'natural' causes, and mainly on the material incentive which existed for manufacturers to improve their products and for investors to invest in progressive industries. In the late nineteenth century, that incentive appears to have been lacking. Steady profits could still be made without improving production. And among the reasons for this was that markets were still relatively easy to come by for the old unimproved products in Britain's colonial empire and elsewhere, and that rich opportunities for investment abroad were enticing capital away from risky new undertakings at home. It was too easy to make money without much effort, so the effort was not made. A kind of vicious circle had been set up, with domestic industry lagging because capital was going elsewhere, and capital going elsewhere because industry was lagging.

This was the trouble: there were still easy ways out. The overall payments account could always be balanced with invisibles and investment earnings; surplus manufactures which could not be found buyers in the demanding and closely fortified European and American markets could always be pushed onto the under-developed world. From this emerged two compelling economic needs, which could be presented as 'national interests'. The first was the need to maintain and extend Britain's overseas markets, because her export capacities were rapidly falling behind what was demanded of them. The second was the need to maintain and extend her fields of investment abroad, because they were rapidly becoming more important in making up for the deficiencies of the first. And from these two 'national interests', so-called, there followed a particular emphasis on countries outside Europe and America – those parts of the world whose industries were mainly agricultural or extractive, or which were just beginning to set up manufactures, what might be called the 'developing' countries, though not all of them were developing very rapidly. The special significance of the developing world was threefold. First, in so far as it was developing, and not merely stagnant, it followed that it required more capital than it could provide itself, and this, Britain could supply. In the 1890s, 92 per cent of the new capital Britain invested abroad went outside Europe, and half of it to the developing countries of Africa, Asia and Australasia.[87] Second, from the commercial point of view it was a market which overall bought more from Britain than it sold – just,[88] and such markets were becoming very rare. Third, it was a market which, in so far as it had not been cornered by European rivals and surrounded by their tariffs or saturated with their capital, was still 'open'. 'Open' markets were getting hard to find in the protectionist 1890s; but if Britain's products were to be sold abroad at all, those that were still open had to be kept open. And this was where politics might come in, because here there was still time and room for politics to be effective.

So there was an argument from 'national interest' (albeit a short-sighted conception of the national interest) for employing the political powers of the Foreign and Colonial Offices to further British commercial and financial interests in the developing world. The argument, however, justified political action only within certain limits, which were the limits imposed by Britain's continued adherence to the general principles of free trade. The government might give British commerce and finance assistance; it could not give them any special *advantage* over the commerce and finance of other nations – could not, for example, restrict just to British traders markets won by British diplomacy. Protectionism as a consistent fiscal policy was almost as unthinkable in the 1890s as it had been in the 1880s; for many important sectors of industry, most politicians and virtually the whole of 'the City', there seemed no need for it yet. The economy was a little sickly, but not chronically so; if British industry, commerce and finance could be assured of the same freedom and equality with the industry, commerce and finance of other nations that they had been accustomed to in the middle of the nineteenth century, there was no reason why they should not continue to hold their own in the more competitive conditions of the later nineteenth century. This was the generally accepted opinion in the 1890s, and it left no room for any radical departure from free trade policy.[89]

It did, however, leave room for little departures. It rested on the proviso that other nations played fair with Britain – allowed her the latitude she allowed them; and the special problem in the 1890s was that in matters of international commerce and finance, other nations were *not* playing fair. Bounties, protective tariffs, and the use of the diplomatic powers of the state to secure exclusive concessions in foreign markets for their own nationals: by such means, foreigners were loading the dice against Britain. How could an honest free trader, with only the quality of his goods to recommend him, hope to compete against the resources of the German Reich? In these circumstances new tactics might be called for: tactics not altogether consistent with a purist's reading of free trade doctrine. For while the British economy was fundamentally sound enough not to require special surgery, it might not be so strong as to be able to look on unconcerned while foreigners, by means which Britain regarded as illicit, deliberately set out to cripple it.

Considerations like these gave governments excuses to deviate a little from the straight free trade path if they wanted to. The remarkable thing is that they were so very reluctant to do so – even Conservative governments, which were supposedly not so doctrinally committed to free trade as Liberal ones. Chamberlain persuaded a couple of colonies – Canada and South Africa – to institute systems of preference towards British goods, but he had to do it that way, there was never any question of his instituting colonial preference at the British end. When foreign bounties on beet sugar made the West Indies' case for retaliation almost unanswerable, and urgent, the British government at last in 1902 relented and threatened to impose countervailing duties if the bounties were not lifted – which worked; but that (a threat) was the nearest Britain ever got in this period to a retaliatory tariff, though the question was much discussed. That was about the sum total of British efforts (outside of India) to manipulate tariffs in the interests of British trade: at the end of the day, the lady's virtue was left almost intact. Dogma may have had a lot to do with this, and veneration for the good work free trade had done for Britain in the past. Curzon in Parliament in August 1895 complained that Britain had to meet foreign competition 'with one hand tied behind its back, because our fiscal system compelled us to enter it without anything to give, to promise, or to threaten', but he still believed that it was 'the intrepidity and enterprise of their individual traders' that had made them great, not 'the protection or activity of Governments', and should be still.[90] Lord Salisbury exhorted the faint-hearted

> to believe that which all past history teaches us – that, left alone, British industry, British enterprise, British resource is competent, and more than competent, to beat down every rivalry, under any circumstances, in any part of the globe, that might arise.[91]

There were sound economic reasons too for believing that Britain could continue to exist and prosper as a lone free trader in a protectionist world. As economists and politicians were always pointing out, the bounty system worked two ways: German steel 'dumped' on the British market did little good to the British steel industry it was undercutting, but it gave a bonus to the British shipbuilding industry, for example, which could build cheaper ships with it; and foreign sugar subsidies, while they might hurt the West Indies, also meant cheap sugar for the British housewife, and at someone else's expense. Likewise the beguiling logic of free trade taught that Britain could live with foreign tariffs. 'The purpose of all protectionists', wrote the president of the Cobden Club in 1898, was 'to export without importing'. This was clearly impossible because their customers must pay for their imports with exports of their own. There had to be a balance; if it was not bilateral, then it had to be multilateral. 'Continental Europe exports to England, and obstructs the importation of English goods, but at the same time imports from the east. England, in her turn, exports goods to the east, and thus pays indirectly for what Europe sends her.'[92] It came to the same thing in the end. For these reasons, and for the more compelling reason that retaliatory tariffs would mean higher prices, which was electoral suicide (as was proved in 1906), Britain persisted in playing to the old rules, though almost every one of her rivals had abjured them.

The limits of Britain's willingness to employ the offices of state to back her commercial interests in the world were set by this. Except in very special circumstances, the furthest she was prepared to go was occasionally (as in China in 1898) to use her consuls as salesmen where other countries were doing the same; and more broadly, to try to keep as much as possible of the developing world's trade free. As in the past, her adherence to this apparently self-denying ordinance gave her most aggressive actions a virtuous, or self-righteous, flavour: annexing a country to prevent a protectionist rival taking it was made to sound almost like buying a slave to set him free – or at least to share him with other slave-owners. Lord Salisbury claimed that 'we only desire territory because we desire commercial freedom',[93] and Joseph Chamberlain was constantly pointing out how Britain's imperialism was not as other nations':

> We, in our colonial policy, as fast as we acquire new territory and develop it, develop it as trustees of civilisation for the commerce of the world. We offer in all those markets over which our flag floats the same opportunities, the same field to foreigners that we offer to our own subjects, and upon the same terms. In that policy we stand alone, because all other nations, as fast as they acquire new territory ... seek at once to secure the monopoly for their own products by preferential and artificial methods.[94]

Which was true, though hardly as philanthropic as it was made to seem. The preservation of free trade was as far as Britain, in her own economic interest, needed to go.

She did not need to do *this* everywhere. Britain relied greatly on the developing world to off-load her surplus manufactures and capital; but some parts of the developing world were better markets than others. Most of the best were in Britain's pocket already. One-third of her exports went to her own colonies in the 1890s; as another half went to Europe and the United States, it left very little over for the rest of the world.[95] Foreign investment likewise seemed quite happily employed in countries where Britain was already looking after it, or where it could look after itself. The territories left over to trade or invest in outside the existing empire were either in the hands of other countries, or of relatively stable governments of their own; or they were more or less barren of any real economic potential. The big exceptions were the South African Republic and China. The South African Republic's potential was already realised, with a booming gold-mining industry drawing British capital to it like a magnet, but threatened (or so some of the gold-miners claimed) by a hostile political regime. In China, the opportunity was even greater, and the threat more real: with 400 million potential customers, if only they could be reached; their obstructive government rapidly crumbling; and rivals waiting on the sidelines restless to intervene. There were high stakes to play for in both China and South Africa. But these two countries apart, what was left of the underdeveloped world to scramble for in the 1890s was pretty dry bones. The benefits of places like Central and East Africa were merely notional; meanwhile (said Lord Farrer), 'there must be obviously still an immense outlay before a return can be expected, and what that return may be no-one can tell'.[96] There were good reasons why no-one had bothered to appropriate such places until now: one of them was that there was nothing there to make the effort and the risk worthwhile.

Yet despite their intrinsic worthlessness, their annexation could be made to appear 'in the national interest', if that same national interest – in preserving Britain's economic ties with the wider world – were viewed more broadly. For the preservation of British economic interests required defence in depth: this was a clear lesson from the foreign rivalries of the 1880s and 1890s; and if a territory was so barren as to be of no direct economic use to Britain at all, yet still it might be seen as valuable indirectly as a place from which to defend territories that were. After all, there was little profit in India's North-West Frontier Province either. In themselves, Uganda, the Sudan and Rhodesia were almost worthless, though all kinds of dazzling futures were dreamed up for them. But when the focus was widened, they took on a greater significance, as buttresses to a more imposing building. That building was Britain's established and substantial interest in Egypt and South Africa, and in the sea-lanes to India and the east which passed through them. Egypt was fed by the Nile, which rose in Uganda and watered the Sudan. British South Africa had Rhodesia as a northern outpost and a counterweight to Afrikanerdom. It may seem – and to some at the time it did seem – over-vigilant, almost neurotic, for governments to be so concerned as Rosebery's and Salisbury's appeared to be with frontiers so distant, and interests so indirect, but it was consistent with the mood of the time.

Capitalists

Of course, the criterion of 'national interest' was not always consistently applied in policy; it could not be. In the first place, governments very often relied on others to implement their policies, and there were a dozen ways in which this could affect and divert the outcome. Lord Salisbury, who was constantly alive to the imperfections of the tools he had to work through, told of one way in 1890:

> When once you have permitted a military advance, the extent of that military advance scarcely remains within your own discretion. It is always open to the military authorities to discover in the immediate vicinity of the area to which your orders confine them, some danger against which it is absolutely necessary to guard, some strategic position whose invaluable qualities will repay ten times any risk or cost that its occupation may involve. You have no means of arguing against them. They are

upon their own territory and can set down your opposition to civilian ignorance; and so, step by step, the imperious exactions of military necessity will lead you on into the desert.[97]

South Africa provided another kind of example in 1895. Policies had to be implemented by people, and they were sometimes people over whom governments had little effective control once they had given the orders, because they were out of earshot, or just wilful. But there was room for error much earlier, too. Policy was *made* by people: and people were fallible and corruptible. The concept of the 'national interest' was anyway so equivocal as to leave wide scope for misreading or for deliberately perverting it, by statesmen and by the men whom statesmen relied on to brief them. When in any given political situation it came to interpreting and assessing the degree to which the 'national interest' was involved or threatened, these men were not always the most calm, objective and accurate of assessors. Hence they could often exaggerate threats to British interests, as they may have done in the Sudan and southern Africa; or they could overestimate the value of countries, which again they may have done for Rhodesia and Uganda. The first was a quite natural effect of the 1890s' obsession with security, which has been described already. The second might have been due to gullibility, or to venality. In the 1890s, governments did seem somewhat less discriminating than they had been in the past: less critical of fabulous prospectuses put out by rogues or optimists promising riches from the desert if their particular areas of interest were taken under the British flag. Twenty years before, they would act to safeguard only British interests which were established. Now they backed hopeful pioneers, took 'promising' territories and built speculative railways on trust. Possibly it was just that the world's vacant lots were running out, so that there was less time for cool assessments of the pros and cons of those that were left. Or the politicians might have been corrupted and manipulated by people with more nefarious, special interests. This was what contemporary critics suspected.

The question of corruption or manipulation arose only where 'national' and 'sectional' interests overlapped, and they did not overlap everywhere. Just as the capitalist's world was wider than the statesman's – the emphasis of British trade and investment very largely outside the area contemporary diplomacy concentrated on – so the statesman's world was much wider, in other directions, than the capitalist's. We have seen how statesmen customarily looked further than capitalists in their defence of the national interest, because their way of viewing things was necessarily more provident. Capitalists were not found pressing for Waziristan to be annexed, because there was little trade done with the Waziris, but statesmen did, because of the danger to India (where there *was* trade and investment) if they did not. Over vast areas, therefore, diplomats diplomatised without even sniffing a promissory note or a bond: maybe in defence ultimately of the capitalist's interests, but unbidden by him. But in many places, like South Africa and China and Nigeria, the two were found suspiciously together, and there was a case, a prima facie case at least, to answer.

There are three ways of looking at these connections. The first is to regard them as evidence of British policy's being manipulated, or corrupted, by the capitalist lobby. Statesmen either pretended, or fooled themselves, that they were pursuing actions for altruistic purposes, when in fact more sordid motives lay beneath. Sometimes those sordid motives could be their own: as may *perhaps* be inferred from Gladstone's holding of Egyptian bonds in 1882.[98] Or they could be hoodwinked by the lies of others, out to line their pockets at the public expense. Second, it could be a matter of simple coincidence. Politicians pursued policies for one set of reasons; capitalists for another, but they just happened to converge. This was bound to occur. No policy, however disinterestedly formulated, ever profits *no-one*. That does not make the profiteer automatically responsible. The South African situation in the 1890s is sometimes claimed to have been like that. Both capitalists and government wanted the same end – control over the Transvaal – but for totally distinct reasons. That may have been so.

A more subtle explanation is that statesmen pursued policies mainly out of consideration for the national interest; but with their conception of that national interest influenced – if not governed – by the general capitalist ethos that surrounded them. That has the advantage of not requiring solid evidence of corruption to prove it, but the disadvantage of not being susceptible of final proof at all. Ethoses are imbibed imperceptibly, and then simply *assumed*. They have to be read between the lines of politicians' speeches and writings, according to our estimate of how they were *likely* to have thought about things, in view of their upbringing, and whom they moved among. Statesmen of the 1890s could scarcely have avoided being thoroughly imbued with the values of what Cain and Hopkins call 'gentlemanly capitalism' – the capitalism, that is, of finance and services, conducted mainly by the southern upper classes, rather than of industry – at the schools, universities and clubs they shared with the gentlemanly capitalists.[99] It would not have occurred to them that there might be a *conflict* between what was good for this sort of British capitalism generally and what was good for the country, though they might be wary of *particular* capitalist interests; and would almost certainly have maintained that the national interest took in a wider range of factors than financial profit alone. They were instinctive capitalists, even those of them (if there were any) who owned no stocks at all; and consequently likely – even bound – to favour policies which conduced to the capital wealth of the nation, while at the same time – and why ever not? – enriching individual capitalists too. This was why they pursued the policies they did: in the national interest, but the national interest perceived through a particular (and, it has to be said, possibly dangerously distorting) capitalist lens.[100]

This is not to say – far from it – that such motives alone determined what Britain actually achieved in this field. She was also subject to constraints. One obvious one was her fragility in diplomatic terms, of which everyone actually concerned in the making of colonial policy in the 1890s was only too well aware. Imperialist politicians might – and did – reap easy patriotic cheers and votes by telling the nation that it was mightier than ever, but it was transparently not. Joseph Chamberlain struck a more sobering note in 1898: 'We are the most powerful Empire in the world,' he said, 'but we are not *all-powerful*.'[101] The Army and Navy scares of the 1880s and 1890s, and a host of diplomatic incidents, underlined this. It was Chamberlain's view that Britain had to find an ally if she were not to be constantly plagued by the fear of being set upon, alone, by two or three enemies. In the Victorian era, his advice was ignored. Britain survived, but her isolation left its mark on her foreign policy. Because the whole world was set against her, any responsible statesman, like Lord Salisbury assuredly was, had to tread warily. He had to conserve his military resources carefully, not over-commit himself on too many fronts, or leave any of them dangerously exposed. He could not go for everything, but had to arrange priorities, make choices between different national interests and objectives. 'There are certain things we can do and certain things we cannot do,' said a foreign under-secretary in the spring of 1898, admitting that they had been weak in China; and he promised, truthfully as it turned out, that 'we shall retrieve ourselves completely in the Sudan'.[102] This was the kind of dilemma that ministers were faced with throughout the

1890s, which 'national interest' to stick on, which to give up. It was a kind of salvage operation. That they salvaged as much as they did was more a tribute to Salisbury's diplomatic artistry than a sign of Britain's bargaining strength. That she was not really strong enough to bear the burdens which had accrued to her over the last 30 years was tacitly acknowledged when she finally abandoned isolation early in the new century. But until then she went it alone, and precariously.

The history of British foreign and colonial policy in the 1890s sometimes took strange and unpredictable turns. But there was a kind of consistency about it. Very rarely did it stray beyond the boundaries set, on the one hand, by a concept of the 'national interest' which had as its central imperative the preservation of Britain's capacity to trade and invest as freely and as widely as possible, especially in the developing countries; and, on the other hand, by the prevalent apprehensions of the time about the threats to that capacity from other nations. Within these very broad bounds, policy varied considerably, according to how the chemistry of each separate situation was mixed: how valuable the 'national interest' there was, or might become; how far it was threatened; what extraneous pressures were there (especially from private financial interests) to affect policy; and – most important in the over-stretched 1890s – the means the government had in its hands to deal with it, and its preoccupations elsewhere.

Notes

1   W. Woodruff, *The Impact of Western Man: A Study of Europe's Role in the World's Economy, 1750–1960* (Macmillan, 1966), pp. 314–31.
2   *Ibid.*, p. 302.
3   M. Barratt Brown, *After Imperialism* (Heinemann, 1963), p. 82.
4   B. R. Mitchell and P. Deane, *Abstract of British Historical Statistics* (Cambridge UP, 1962), p. 283.
5   H. Feis, *Europe, the World's Banker 1870–1914* (Council on Foreign Relations, 1931), pp. 12, 20; C. K. Hobson, *The Export of Capital* (London School of Economics, 1914), pp. 149–57; M. Simon, 'The pattern of new British portfolio investment 1865–1914', in A. R. Hall, *The Export of Capital from Britain 1870–1914* (Methuen, 1968).
6   Barratt Brown, *op. cit.*, p. 108.
7   See A. L. Friedberg, *The Weary Titan: Britain and the Experience of Relative Decline, 1895–1905* (Princeton UP, 1988).
8   Mitchell and Deane, *op. cit.*, pp. 316–19.
9   Barratt Brown, *op. cit.*, p. 111.
10 Simon, *op. cit.*
11 N. Schlote, *British Overseas Trade from 1700 to the 1930s* (Blackwell, 1952), pp. 160–3; Barratt Brown, *op. cit.*, p. 111.
12 Mitchell and Deane, *op. cit.*, pp. 318–19.
13 R. L. Greaves, *Persia and the Defence of India, 1884–1892* (Athlone Press, 1959), p. 197.
14 D. Dilks, *Curzon in India*, 2 vols (Hart Davis, 1969, 1970), ii, 115, 182.
15 A. Lamb, *The McMahon Line* (Routledge, 1966), i, 59.
16 Dilks, *op. cit.*, i, 126.
17 A. J. Marder, *The Anatomy of British Sea Power* (Putnam, 1940), p. 78.
18 *Ibid.*, p. 84.
19 C. J. Lowe, *Salisbury and the Mediterranean 1886–1896* (Routledge, 1965), p. 87.
20 Marder, *op. cit.*, p. 174.
21 *Ibid.*, p. 203; P. Stansky, *Ambitions and Strategies* (Oxford UP, 1964), Chapter 2.
22 R. R. James, *Rosebery* (Weidenfeld & Nicolson, 1963), p. 412.
23 J. L. Garvin, *The Life of Joseph Chamberlain* (Macmillan, 1934), iii, 302.
24 Marder, *op. cit.*, pp. 20–1 and Chapter 6.
25 *Ibid.*, p. 233.

26 *Ibid.*, p. 194.
27 *Ibid.*, p. 215n.
28 *Ibid.*, p. 377.
29 Dilks, *op. cit.*, i, 153.
30 Marder, *op. cit.*, p. 241.
31 E. E. Williams, *Made in Germany* (1896), p. 8.
32 Frederick Greenwood, 'England at war', *Nineteenth Century*, xliii (1898), 174.
33 J. A. S. Grenville, *Lord Salisbury and Foreign Policy* (Athlone Press, 1964), p. 169.
34 *Contemporary Review*, lxxiii (1898), 462.
35 W. L. Langer, *The Diplomacy of Imperialism 1890–1902*, 2 vols (Harvard UP, 1935), i, 87.
36 Frederick Greenwood, 'Sentiment in politics', *Cosmopolis*, iv (1896), 341.
37 M. Pinto-Duschinsky, *The Political Thought of Lord Salisbury* (Constable, 1967), p. 122.
38 A. L. Kennedy, *Salisbury, 1830–1903: Portrait of a Statesman* (John Murray, 1953), p. 277.
39 Dilks, *op. cit.*, i, 54.
40 See B. J. Porter, *Critics of Empire: British Radical Attitudes to Colonialism in Africa 1895–1914* (Macmillan, 1968), pp. 92–3.
41 Pinto-Duschinsky, *op. cit.*, p. 122.
42 *Annual Register* (1900), 110.
43 T. E. Kebbel, 'England at war', *Nineteenth Century*, xliii (1898), 339.
44 W. E. Henley, 'Introduction', in C. de Thierry, *Imperialism* (1898), pp. xiv–xv.
45 Marder, *op. cit.*, p. 20.
46 Sidney Low, 'Should Europe disarm?', *Nineteenth Century*, xliv (1898), 523; and see Marder, *op. cit.*, p. 19n.
47 Dilks, *op. cit.*, i, 128.
48 Marquess of Crewe, *Lord Rosebery* (Murray, 1931), ii, 575.
49 B. B. Gilbert, *The Evolution of National Insurance in Great Britain* (M. Joseph, 1966), p. 72.
50 Viscount Milner, *The Nation and the Empire* (1913), pp. 139–40.
51 For example, T. J. Macnamara, 'In Corpore Sano', *Contemporary Review*, lxxxvii (1905), 248.
52 See Gilbert, *op. cit.* On 'social imperialism' generally, see B. Semmel, *Imperialism and Social Reform* (Allen & Unwin, 1960); G. R. Searle, *The Quest for National Efficiency* (Blackwell, 1971); Anna Davin, 'Imperialism and motherhood', *History Workshop Journal*, 5 (1978), 9–65.
53 Lord Meath, 'Have we the "grit" of our forefathers?', *Nineteenth Century*, lxiv (1908), 425.
54 On eugenics, see Matthew Thomson, *The Problem of Mental Deficiency: Eugenics, Democracy and Social Policy in Britain, c. 1870–1959* (Oxford UP, 1998).
55 Sidney Low, 'The future of the great armies', *Nineteenth Century*, xlvi (1899), 390–2.
56 On the Boy Scout movement, see J. Springhall, *Youth, Empire and Society* (Croom Helm, 1977); Michael Rosenthal, *The Character Factory: Baden-Powell and the Origins of the Boy Scout Movement* (1986); T. Heal, *Baden-Powell* (Hutchinson, 1989); R. H. MacDonald, *Sons of the Empire: The Frontier and the Boy Scout Movement, 1890–1918* (University of Toronto Press, 1993).
57 B. Harrison, *Separate Spheres: The Opposition to Women's Suffrage in Britain* (Croom Helm, 1978).
58 M. Barry, 'Women and patriotism', *National Review*, 53 (1909), 303.
59 C. Headlam (ed.), *The Milner Papers* (Cassell, 1933), ii, 291.
60 E. C. Mack, *Public Schools and British Opinion since 1860* (Methuen, 1941), Part 3.
61 J. G. Lockhart and C. M. Woodhouse, *Rhodes* (Hodder & Stoughton, 1963), pp. 69–70.
62 B. H. Brown, *The Tariff Reform Movement in Great Britain* (Oxford UP, 1943), p. 83.
63 Quoted in V. I. Lenin, *Imperialism, the Highest Stage of Capitalism* (Left Word, 2000), p. 97; but it may be unreliable. See Bernard Porter, *The Absent-Minded Imperialists* (Oxford UP, 2004), Chapter 8.
64 James, *op. cit.*, p. 284.
65 Headlam, *op. cit.*, ii, 288.
66 Brown, *op. cit.*, p. 88.
67 R. V. Kubicek, *The Administration of Imperialism* (Duke UP, 1969), p. 68.
68 Garvin, *op. cit.*, iii, 19.

69 R. Faber, *The Vision and the Need: Late Victorian Imperialist Aims* (Faber & Faber, 1966), p. 64.
70 Garvin, *op. cit.*, iii, 27.
71 J. Chamberlain, *Foreign and Colonial Speeches* (1897), p. 145.
72 J. Lawson Walton, 'Imperialism', *Contemporary Review*, lxxv (1899), 306.
73 Dilks, *op. cit.*, ii, 137.
74 G. N. Curzon, *Problems of the Far East* (1894), p. v.
75 Faber, *op. cit.*, p. 64.
76 James, *op. cit.*, p. 419.
77 Raymond F. Betts, 'The allusion to Rome in British imperialist thought of the late nineteenth and early twentieth centuries', *Victorian Studies*, xv (1971).
78 On the 'new imperialism' generally, see W. L. Langer, *The Diplomacy of Imperialism* (2nd edn, Knopf, 1951), i, Chapter 3; R. Koebner and H. D. Schmidt, *Imperialism: The Story and Significance of a Political Word* (Cambridge UP, 1964), Chapters 7, 8; A. P. Thornton, *The Imperial Idea and Its Enemies* (Macmillan, 1959); Faber, *op cit.*; H. John Field, *Towards a Programme of Imperial Life: The British Empire at the Turn of the Century* (Greenwood Press, 1982); B. J. Porter, 'The Edwardians and their empire', in Donald Read (ed.), *Edwardian England* (Croom Helm, 1982); John M. MacKenzie (ed.), *Popular Imperialism and the Military, 1850–1950* (Manchester UP, 1992); Richard Jay, *Joseph Chamberlain: A Political Study* (Oxford UP, 1981); Gordon Martel, *Imperial Diplomacy: Rosebery and the Failure of Foreign Policy* (Mansell Publishing, 1986).
79 Edward Dicey, 'After the present war', *Nineteenth Century*, xlvi (1899), 694.
80 J. A. Hobson, *The Psychology of Jingoism* (1901), Part ii, Chapter 1; C. F. G. Masterman *et al., The Heart of the Empire* (1901), pp. 339–40; Richard Price, *An Imperial War and the British Working Class* (Routledge & Kegan Paul, 1972), *passim*.
81 On 'popular' imperialism, see *ibid.*; H. Pelling, *Popular Politics and Society in Late Victorian Britain* (Macmillan, 1968), Chapter 5; B. J. Porter, *Critics of Empire* (Macmillan, 1968), S. Koss, *The Pro-Boers* (University of Chicago Press, 1973); M. D. Blanche, 'British society and the war', in Peter Warwick (ed.), *The South African War* (Longman, 1980); John MacKenzie, *Propaganda and Empire: The Manipulation of British Public Opinion, 1880–1960* (Manchester UP, 1984); John MacKenzie (ed.), *Imperialism and Popular Culture* (Manchester UP, 1986); and Porter, *The Absent-Minded Imperialists*, Chapters 6 and 9.
82 See C. Berger, *The Sense of Power* (University of Toronto Press, 1970); J. Eddy and D. Schreuder (eds), *The Rise of Colonial Nationalism: Australia, New Zealand, Canada and South Africa First Assert Their Nationalities, 1880–1914* (Allen & Unwin, 1988).
83 Mitchell and Deane, *op. cit.*, p. 283.
84 *Ibid.*, pp. 334–5.
85 On British foreign investment, see M. Edelstein, *Overseas Investment in the Age of High Imperialism: The United Kingdom, 1850–1914* (Methuen, 1982); A. N. Porter and R. F. Holland (eds), 'Money, Finance and Empire', special issue *of Journal of Imperial and Commonwealth History*, xiii (3) (May 1985); L. E. Davis and R. A. Huttenback, *Mammon and the Pursuit of Empire: The Political Economy of British Imperialism, 1860–1912* (Cambridge UP, 1986).
86 'Ritortus', 'The imperialism of free trade', *Contemporary Review*, lxxvi (1899), 284–5.
87 Simon,, *op. cit.*, p. 42.
88 See above, p. 107.
89 See S. B. Saul, *The Myth of the Great Depression* (Macmillan, 1969), especially its bibliography; Barratt Brown, *op. cit.*, Chapter 3; S. B. Saul, 'Britain and world trade 1870–1914', *Economic History Review*, vii (1954), pp. 173–92.
90 *Parliamentary Debates*, 4th series, 36 (1895), cc. 1272–4.
91 H. Birchenough, 'Do foreign annexations injure British trade?', *Nineteenth Century*, xli (1897), 993.
92 Lord Farrer, 'Does trade follow the flag?', *Contemporary Review*, lxxiv (1898), 833 (punctuation altered).
93 Kennedy, *op. cit.*, p. 207.
94 Chamberlain, *op. cit.*, p. 144.
95 Schlote, *op. cit.*, pp. 156–63.

96   Farrer, *op. cit.*, p. 814.
97   G. Cecil, *Life of Robert Marquis of Salisbury*, 4 vols (Hodder & Stoughton, 1921, 1921, 1931, 1932), iv (1932), 327.
98   See Chapter 4, p. 84.
99   P. J. Cain and A. G. Hopkins, 'Gentlemanly capitalism and British expansion overseas', *Economic History Review*, 2nd series, 39 (1986), 501–25, and 40 (1987); and P. J. Cain and A. G. Hopkins, *British Imperialism: Innovation and Expansion, 1688–1914* (Longman, 1993), Part 2.
100 On 'capitalist imperialism', see J. A. Hobson, *Imperialism: A Study* (James Nisbet & Co., 1902); Lenin, *op. cit.*; D. K. Fieldhouse (ed.), *The Theory of Capitalist Imperialism* (Longmans, 1967); W. G. Hynes, *The Economics of Empire: Britain, Africa and the New Imperialism 1870–95* (Longman, 1979); Cain and Hopkins, *British Imperialism: Innovation and Expansion 1688–1914*; J. S. Galbraith, *Mackinnon and East Africa 1878–95: A Study in the 'New Imperialism'* (Cambridge UP, 1972); J. E. Flint, *Cecil Rhodes* (Hutchinson, 1976); Robert I. Rotberg with Miles S. Shore, *The Founder: Cecil Rhodes and the Pursuit of Power* (Oxford UP, 1988).
101 Langer, *op. cit.*, p. 509.
102 *Ibid.*, p. 537.

6 A limited area of heather alight: 1890–1905

Britain in Asia

The critical problems of British diplomacy in the 1890s were nearly all concentrated in a broad band of contiguous territory which ran from South Africa up the eastern half of Africa to Egypt and the Levant, then eastwards across southern Asia along the northern border of India to China. This band took in several areas of great economic profit to Britain and to individual Britons, like the Transvaal, Egypt and the Yangtse valley, and some areas rather less profitable in between. Its importance consisted partly in its intrinsic value, partly in the value of neighbouring territories, like India, which it was felt to shield. Its prominence in the diplomacy of the 1890s arose from the fact that it was disputed territory, in the sense that it had not been finally settled how it should be split between the imperialist powers. Hence the activity there, as Britain and her rivals jostled for position.

In Asia, Britain's main rival was Russia, followed some distance behind by France and Germany. In Africa, it was Germany and France. The Russian threat in Asia was more real and more dangerous than the German and French threat in Africa, which was why Britain was more chary of fighting in Asia than in Africa. Russia presented a threat to British interests from the Mediterranean right through to the East China Sea. That was the extent of her land frontier with British colonies or satellites. Along that frontier she could always presume to have the advantage over Britain for simple reasons of geo-politics: on her side of it she was relatively compact and secure, on the other side, Britain was extended, precarious, and a long way from home. What scanty military forces Britain could spare from keeping the Indians down were hardly enough to defend even part of the frontier if Russia attacked, and along most of its length the Royal Navy could be of little help unless it learned to sail over mountains. In Asia, fears for Britain's safety were not merely the professional pessimism of the military: she really was vulnerable.[1] In British cabinets there was universal agreement on this, but disagreement over the remedy. Joseph Chamberlain wanted Britain to enter into alliance with someone – almost anyone – to ease the burden. Lord Salisbury saw only the disadvantages of alliances, and instead sought to avert or minimise the Russian threat by means of clever diplomacy and agreements for limited objectives. His view prevailed until about 1900 because for most of that period he was both Foreign Secretary and Prime Minister. The result was that Britain stayed vulnerable in Asia, and had to defend her interests there circumspectly. In Africa, on the other hand, she could afford to be more combative.

Britain's problem was felt to be particularly delicate on the two flanks of her long frontier with Russia. On one of them stood Turkey, on the other China: both of them ancient empires which were assumed by almost everyone to be stumbling towards extinction, with

Russia in a good position to pick up the choicest pieces. In both Turkey and China, British policy had hitherto staked a lot on the preservation of their 'integrity', or neutrality, and there seemed no way in which Britain could gain by their disintegration. 'Whatever happens will be for the worse,' said Salisbury (of Turkey) in 1887, 'and therefore it is our interest that as little should happen as possible.'[2] To the extent that Salisbury's diplomacy prevented things happening, Britain managed to avoid new colonial or semi-colonial commitments. At times it was like playing Canute, but he had some success. The neutrality of Turkey was preserved until the time – early in the 1890s – when Salisbury decided that, with Egypt having taken over from her as the lynch-pin of Britain's eastern Mediterranean policy, her neutrality was no longer particularly vital to Britain anyhow. (Even then Turkey never did collapse, and Russia never made any great gains there, though Germany did.) In effect, Britain solved her near eastern problem by ducking it.[3]

The Far East was less easily disposed of. This was partly because Britain's interest there was mainly commercial, and there were no easy substitutes for it. Not that Britain's China trade was particularly voluminous, but it was of a rather special kind. For the beginning of the 1890s, it was something of an anachronism. Everywhere else, the world Britain traded with had changed almost out of recognition over the previous 30 years. On the whole the changes had not been to Britain's advantage: the fierce rivalry from other European powers, the expensive cordoning off of great expanses of territory into competing empires, the restrictions this placed on existing enterprise, and the slow whittling down of new opportunities: none of this was entirely made up for by the glorious new territorial empire Britain had received in compensation. Looking back, the age of free trade, backed only by minimum force, when British merchants could go anywhere the locals would allow them, and second-rate commercial powers like France and Germany were content to play the game as Britain played it, seemed a golden age, from which the present day was a sad decline. It may have been the fact that it was almost the last place on earth where the old golden conditions still seemed to hold good in the 1890s – where trade was still free and the political apparatus needed to support it was minimal – which in the eyes of many Britons at this time gave China its great importance. For the actual size of Britain's trade with China scarcely seemed to justify the fuss that was made over her – £2.5 million of imports and £5.5 million of exports in 1900, and a capital investment of perhaps £30 million, or little over 1 per cent of Britain's total investment abroad;[4] nor could it be said of China, as it could of almost everywhere else, that she stood on the route to somewhere where Britain's economic stake was bigger, for she stood, in fact, at the very end of all the trade routes. China's commercial and financial value to Britain was potential rather than actual. The potential was obvious just from her numbers; 'What must be the commercial advantages to this country,' Palmerston had enthused in 1864, 'if it can have an unimpeded, uninterrupted commerce with one-third of the human race!'[5] Thirty years on, the potential had been very slow to realise itself. Curzon wrote in 1894 that they were still 'only standing on the threshold of Chinese commercial expansion'. But it was still there, and there was nowhere else with quite so much promise that had not yet been gobbled up by others. This was its importance to the 'national interest'; 'It is only in the East,' said Curzon again, 'and especially in the Far East, that we may still hope to keep and to create open markets for British manufactures.'[6] At the beginning of the 1890s Britain was doing this in China by the 'informal' methods of a generation before, and to her great advantage.

But it could not last; and the imminent dissolution of what was called the 'open door' in China hovered like a storm cloud over Britain's Far Eastern policy throughout the 1890s. There seemed to be a pattern in the decline of ancient polities and empires in the late nineteenth century which was inexorable – the pattern Salisbury had referred to in his 'dying nations' speech of May 1898; and China, like Turkey and Persia, appeared to be conforming to it exactly, step by step. The eventual outcome had to be the partition of the Chinese empire among living nations like Britain, France, Germany, Japan and the United States, and this could not be good for Britain. In the first place, even if out of the partition as much as half of China went to her, her relative position vis-à-vis the other powers would be worse, because at present a good deal more than half of China's foreign trade was in her hands. (Contemporary estimates varied between 60 and 80 per cent.) In effect, she would be exchanging possible access to all of China for exclusive control over part of it – and as she was against exclusive trading, she would not be utilising that part of the bargain anyway. In the second place, to everyone except the special champions of the China trade it was arguable whether it was worth going to the lengths of partitioning China for it, if partition meant more controls, more political involvement, and the cost that this would entail. The China trade – actual and potential – was indubitably worth defending cheaply, which was how it was defended at present. It was another question whether it was worth defending expensively. British policy, therefore, was never very consistent or confident in China, because, as in Turkey, there was no way in which it could improve Britain's position there short of resisting changes which seemed inevitable. In practice, it pursued two lines which were contradictory, to the confusion of the men on the spot: resistance to the new trends so far as was possible, coupled with participation in them when it was not.

The threat to Britain's position in China had started in the 1880s, when other countries got involved in the China trade more – especially Germany, whose superior efficiency and 'pushfulness' were widely remarked there as elsewhere.[7] So long as the threat merely involved simple commercial competition, Britain never minded it, or would not admit to minding it. When the other competitors started breaking the rules, for example, by using their consuls and ambassadors to tout for orders for them, it unnerved her a little, but this was easily dealt with, without too much violence to free trade dogma, by retaliating in kind. In 1885, Lord Salisbury authorised British ministers abroad to push British trade if foreign ministers were pushing theirs, although in practice the British consular service as yet still kept its hands pretty clean of commerce.[8] The real danger to Britain's position came when the competition stopped being really 'competitive' at all, when rivals began to exploit the Manchus' crumbling authority by inveigling *exclusive* concessions out of them; which happened to an extent in the 1880s (especially with the French in the south), but much more after 1895. In that year, China was badly defeated in a war with Japan, and partially occupied by enemy troops, but then rescued from the occupation by Russia and France, who persuaded Japan to accept a £30 million indemnity instead. Of course, China could not raise the money (or the money she owed for war expenditure) from current income, and had to borrow – almost for the first time in her history. And her need to borrow forced her into the kind of position the Ottomans had got themselves into in the 1870s, where she had to mortgage resources as security. The danger here, from Britain's point of view, was that her creditors might secure too much in mortgage: concessions which excluded, or could be used to exclude, the British altogether, perhaps even territorial empires like Britain and France had acquired from Turkey. In 1897–98, there was a frantic scramble among the powers to lend China the money she needed, and to establish themselves there with ports, railways, banks, mining rights, control of customs revenues, and other tangible means of influence. The picture which began to emerge was of a clear territorial division of China into 'spheres' (Map 9): Russia in the north down

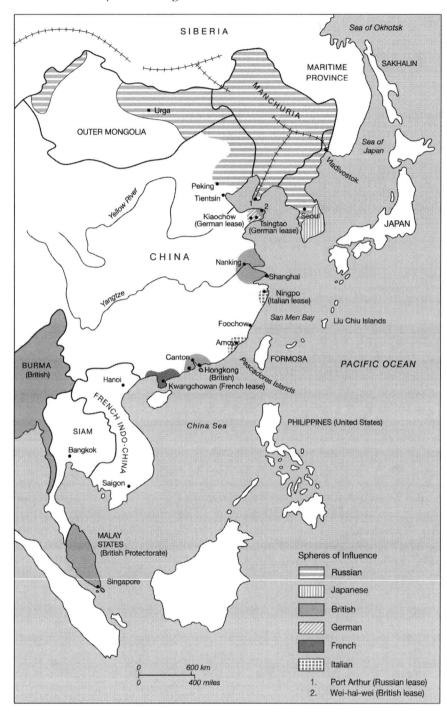

Map 9 The scramble for China
Source: After Eldridge, C. C, *Victorian Imperialism* (Hodder & Stoughton, 1978, p. 203).

to Peking (the seat of government), France in the south bordering her South-east Asian empire, and Germany in Shantung, below Peking, striking westwards. Britain was being left with the Yangtse valley, which was perhaps the commercial plum of China – but not so tasty as the whole banquet she had been able to nibble at before.

To attempt to stop this process, said *The Times* in July 1898, was like 'trying to keep out the ocean with a mop'.[9] Britain had perforce to join in. When other powers grabbed little pieces of territory, she grabbed some too: the port of Wei-hai-wei in the north in April 1898, to keep company with Germany's and Russia's recent acquisitions in the same area; and more of Kowloon (behind Hong Kong) in June after France had taken Kwangchow 200 miles to the south. And so as not to be left out of the scramble for concessions, Salisbury sent the local British minister Sir Claude MacDonald 'touting' for them like other governments did, but against all the traditions of the British diplomatic service. In this instance, open government backing for specific capitalist enterprises seemed the only way to secure a *national* economic interest, and so it was done. Almost any wildcat capitalist scheme was supported so long as it was British, and its tenders were backed up by recommendations, and sometimes threats, from Whitehall. By November 1898, Britain had secured more concessions than her capitalists could use, including 2,800 miles of railway contracts. Initially the idea was to go for a wide scattering of concessions and acquisitions all over China, to break the pattern which was forming of 'spheres', but it soon became clear that Britain would have her work cut out just to save the Yangtse for herself. Reluctantly she had to accept the way things were going, and tried to make the best of it: first, by making sure that if China had to be partitioned, it was done amicably, without any disputes – to this effect, she came to agreements with Russia in April 1899 and Germany in October 1900; second, by limiting its significance: trying to ensure that China as a territorial entity survived, was not subsumed by foreign empires; and that the different 'spheres' into which she was divided were not too exclusive: 'spheres of influence' at the most, if possible, a lesser degree of dominion still, which Balfour termed 'spheres *of interest*', though the distinction was a subtle one.[10] It was not an ideal arrangement, but at least it saved Britain the expense of a more formal imperial one.

And it lasted fairly well, considering the depth of resentment the Chinese themselves felt at this cat-and-mouse treatment of them, and their violent reaction against it in 1900 – which might have been expected to provoke a wholesale colonial grab by the powers, as similar situations had countless times in Britain's imperial experience in the past. The Chinese were renowned (perhaps unjustly) for their chauvinism: 'from the bottom of their hearts they hate us all,' wrote MacDonald in 1899, 'as the devil hates the holy water'.[11] This kind of feeling, of course, was not peculiar to the Chinese; we have seen it to be a common ingredient of culture-contact situations in the nineteenth century. To the ethnocentric West, it was supposed to arise out of the natural preference of the ignorant for their superstitions or the depraved for their vices: the superior attractions of darkness over light. But in fact the Chinese had good rational cause to dislike the foreigner for the harm he had done to their polity, their economy and their society. Their grievances were legion: against British opium 'pushers', of course; against the governments of the powers for their appropriation of China's dominions – Turkestan, Burma and Tonkin in the 1880s, now the northern ports; against the indiscipline and excesses of their 'punitive' soldiery, especially Germany's; against their merchants for what their cheap manufactures had done to her native industries; against their missionaries for their assaults on her religions and (more important) their insensitive interference in her laws and customs. The file was bulky, and it got bulkier as contact intensified during the period of concession-hunting. Resentment smouldered, and then, at a time of drought and plague in northern China at the end of the 1890s, it flared up in an outbreak of terrorism known in the West as the Boxer rising, though it was more of a national revolt; a movement which, when its adherents laid siege to the foreign legations in Peking in June 1900, became a matter of serious diplomatic import for Britain. Western reprisals were inevitable: if they further undermined the power of the Chinese court, which was involved with the Boxers, all pretence of Chinese territorial integrity would be destroyed and a formal partition would follow as a matter of course. For the time being, Britain was lucky that Germany and Russia did not want this to happen either. They agreed to put down the rebellion in concert, and to maintain the Manchus still. This exercise in imperialism by co-operation, however, could not be depended on to last. Russia used the Boxer crisis to intensify her influence in Manchuria, and the present *modus vivendi* looked as brittle as it had ever been. Lord Salisbury was widely attacked in Britain (and in his own cabinet) for his weakness over China all along; and indeed Britain's position there was not strong, and could not be until she had found some more positive way of countering Russia's growing preponderance. This she did in 1902, after Salisbury had gone from the Foreign Office, in a famous alliance with Japan, who in 1904–05 (by defeating Russia in war) proved to be a capable counterweight indeed. And so the territorial integrity of China, like that of Turkey, was maintained in theory, for its European masters to do what they liked with in reality; until its Manchu rulers finally crumbled under the weight of a new movement of national resentment in 1911, and Europe had to seek new accommodations from new and less pliable styles of leaders.[12]

In China, Britain had not ventured as boldly as many would have liked. And elsewhere along the long frontier which divided Britain-in-Asia from Russia, except in the territories she controlled directly, her policy was much the same: cautious, conciliatory towards Russia, and on the whole regressive. In the view of Lord Curzon, who was Viceroy of India between 1899 and 1905, it was dangerously inadequate to safeguard India, but Curzon was not so impressed as the cabinet was by the Russians' strength at that moment, and thought they could be stopped. The cabinet appears to have thought they could not; Russia's advance in Asia, wrote Lord George Hamilton in 1900, was 'like that of a glacier, slow but omnipotent'.[13] Consequently, in the complicated game of influence and intrigue which was played out in – or at the expense of – the buffer states of Persia, Afghanistan and Tibet in the 1890s and 1900s, all the initiatives seemed to be Russia's, most of the gains made were hers, and Britain's achievement was confined mainly to defining more exactly the limits of her advance. In Persia, for example, she scarcely tried to stop Russia 'steadily swallowing the Persian artichoke leaf by leaf', as Curzon put it,[14] allowing her all manner of commercial and financial victories in the north and middle of the country, before deciding in 1902 to make a stand on what was left to her by threatening the Persians with all kinds of dire consequences if they let Russia anywhere near the Persian Gulf, and finally, in 1907, splitting the country into formal 'spheres' with Russia. Likewise in Afghanistan, where Russia's agents were supposed to be almost as rife but more covert, and her formal claims were advancing closer to Kabul, little was done except (in 1895) to fix its frontiers in the north at the line the Russians had advanced to. Only in Tibet was resolute action taken to counter Russian intrigues – a military expedition sent in 1904 to reassert British predominance there – and even then, when it succeeded at the cost of some hundreds of Tibetan lives, the government seemed more embarrassed by it than otherwise, and almost tried to disown it.

In India's own frontier provinces, Britain was less inhibited, because there were few diplomatic problems involved, and she had got down to a fine art the purely military game of subduing and punishing rebellious tribes. The 1890s were enlivened, for cravers after vicarious excitement back home and for army officers in India, for whom it was a welcome change from polo and pig-sticking, by a regular series of tribal risings and punitive forays in the mountains around the Khyber Pass, culminating in a general frontier conflagration in 1897 which was of more serious import, and from which, when it had been put down, useful lessons were learnt. The main lesson was not to be so free with British troops in the area, because they merely irritated and provoked the natives, but instead to persuade the tribes to police themselves, and keep the Indian army hidden in reserve – but on hand – in case they did not. This Curzon did when he came to India in 1899, with the result that the North-West Frontier – in 1900 organised into a new Indian province – quietened down, and what the Indian army lost in excitement the Indian government gained in security.[15] It remained the uneasy suspicion of many, however, that this security was ultimately only on the sufferance of Russia, who when she saw the opportunity could still disrupt India at will. 'She won't try to conquer it,' wrote Salisbury in 1900; 'It will be enough for her if she can shatter our government and reduce India to anarchy.'[16] This suspicion remained right through to the 1940s.

The Nile valley

One of the reasons why Britain was not quite so tough in Asia as people like Curzon would have liked was that, in her present military condition, she could not afford to be tough in two broad areas at once, and she had already decided to be tough in Africa. For Curzon, it was a curious set of priorities that put the dark and impoverished continent of Africa before the treasure-house of Asia,[17] but this was how it appeared. Lord Salisbury, especially, underwent a dramatic transformation when he moved from Asia to Africa. The Asian mouse, meekly submitting in Persia and Turkey and China, immediately became the man, and a very John Bull-ish kind of man, when he had an African swamp to defend or a desert to take. But he had his reasons. The first reason was that Africa was not really so valueless by contrast with Asia; South Africa especially was rapidly becoming a treasure-house itself with its diamonds and gold and the prospect of much more to come, and, from British India's point of view, it, and Suez at the other end of the continent, were as essential as ever for access to Britain. A second was the presence there of a very clear-cut humanitarian issue to justify western intervention – or to use as a cynical excuse. This was the Arab slave raiding that had terrorised and devastated the Lakes region of Africa for decades now, revealed by the early European explorers (chief among them Livingstone and Stanley), and picked up on in a big way by liberal and religious opinion in Britain, whose agitation for government action against it would, at the very least, blunt the sharpness of the anti-imperial objections that would generally be expected from that side.[18] The third reason, however, was that Britain's African interests were easier for Britain to defend anyway. None of her rivals there had the natural advantages Russia had in Asia – except perhaps the Afrikaners, and they were underrated; Britain's naval strength could count more there, and her military weaknesses need show less in skirmishes with Africans or European expeditionary forces than in wars with standing armies; and there was no India to fall apart there at the first touch of trouble. Africa was a coat more suited to Britain's military cloth than Asia, and for this reason Britain could be braver there.

The decision to be brave in eastern Africa was taken around 1890, and it was a very enticing logic that forced the decision on a government which, only a few years before, had regarded Uganda and Kenya as negotiable if anything could be got for them,[19] and persisted in treating its occupation of Egypt as a temporary one.[20] Indifference to this part of Africa was defensible so long as Egypt *could be* thought of as a transient responsibility, but this was never really on, and ministers probably knew it. The man they had sent out to rule Egypt, Sir Evelyn Baring (later Lord Cromer), told them why: it was because there was no-one there to hand over power to, no-one, that is, who was sufficiently strong, sufficiently popular among his own people, and sufficiently compliant to the demands of Europe. 'Really, the more I look at it,' he wrote to Salisbury in 1889, 'the more does the evacuation policy appear to me to be impossible under any conditions.'[21] If ministers had still been minded to risk it, they would at least have required to be allowed to take over again if things went wrong. This right of 're-entry' Salisbury, in lengthy negotiations during 1887, tried to get Turkey's assent to as the price of evacuation, but France scotched that. Without a right of re-entry, and with the stakes as high as they were – Egypt, the Canal, and Britain's massive traffic to the east – the gamble was far too great. And the stakes were getting higher. With Turkey crumbling, and Britain unable – or so the Sea Lords said – to prevent Russia taking Constantinople if she wanted to, Egypt was becoming more vital to Britain year by year: not quite Turkey's successor as the guarantor of Britain's interests in that part of the world, for she had not quite abandoned Turkey yet; but rapidly becoming so. In 1889, Salisbury's attitude over Egypt hardened. In June, he broke off negotiations with the French over evacuation, even though they now seemed willing to consider a right of re-entry.[22] Egypt had been accepted as a permanent responsibility, and a first priority in British policy.

It followed that the territories to the south of Egypt were a high priority too, as indeed they would have been considered before 1890, had they ever been seriously threatened then by European rivals. The vast territory of the eastern Sudan, and the Great Lakes region further down, impinged on Egypt's welfare because they straddled the upper Nile, and the Nile fed Egypt. 'Whatever Power holds the Upper Nile valley must,' wrote Baring in 1889, 'by the mere force of its geographical situation, dominate Egypt'[23] – because it could cut off the Nile, or flood it, or divert it. The possibility had been mooted for centuries; Sir Samuel Baker reckoned it had been done before, in Old Testament times, to cause the seven years' famine in Egypt; and an eminent French hydrographer in 1893 showed his countrymen the way to do it in detail.[24] It could be done, of course, only by a scientifically sophisticated people (whatever had happened in Old Testament times), so it did not matter if the upper Nile continued to be occupied by dervishes. Lord Salisbury advised Baring to go easy on the dervishes for this very reason, while they were in control it meant that no-one cleverer was.[25] The danger came when they began to show signs of weakening, as they seemed to in 1888–89,[26] and when Europeans began to look covetous. From then onwards Salisbury made it his job to look after the upper Nile: first, to keep it neutral, then to make it British. It was (he wrote in October 1897), 'the only policy which it seems to me is left to us'.[27]

The earliest threats to the upper Nile came from Italy and Germany, but they proved to be not altogether whole-hearted ones, and were easily parried. Germany's recognition of Britain's title over Uganda and the upper Nile was secured by agreement in July 1890, at a price which included the cession to Germany of Heligoland (which irritated Queen Victoria, whose simple philosophy it was that 'Giving up what one has is always a bad thing').[28] In March the next year, Italy was bought off in return for a recognition of her (dubious, and very short-lived) claims in Abyssinia.[29] In June 1894, Rosebery's government declared Uganda a British protectorate. In May the same year, the Congo (in the person of its proprietor, King Leopold) recognised Britain's title in southern Sudan, and leased part of it from her by an arrangement which Britain hoped would stop the French marching across from the west. For it was the French who were by this time the main threat. Smarting since 1882 from their self-inflicted exclusion from Egypt, they hoped by occupying the Sudan themselves to prise the British out[30] – and they were not easily put off by all this diplomatic activity around them. France would not agree that, because three other countries recognised the Sudan as British, it was so. Nor would she abide the Congo's plotting with Britain against her. In August 1894, she persuaded Leopold not to occupy most of the territory he had leased, which left the way open again for Frenchmen to approach the Nile.[31] It was clear that France had ambitions in the eastern Sudan which were not going to be easily diverted by diplomacy. Britain resorted therefore to force, or the threat of it. In March 1895, the Foreign Under-Secretary, Sir Edward Grey, told the House of Commons that if rumours of a secret French military expedition to the Nile valley were true, Britain would construe it as 'an un-friendly act' – which, in the familiar diplomatic litotes of the time, constituted a clear warning. France disregarded it. When the expedition that had given rise to the rumours failed to make headway, she sent another one out via the Congo under Captain Marchand. At the same time Britain was preparing to invade from Egypt, with a sizeable army under General Kitchener, whose ultimate objective was left contingent on circumstances, but which Salisbury himself – against Baring's advice, and the opinion of many of his cabinet colleagues – saw as the eventual conquest and occupation of the Sudan. His view now was that treaties were no substitute for solid possession. In 1896, Kitchener marched south to subdue the dervishes, slowly and methodically. Marchand started out later but moved more quickly. What would happen when they met was anyone's guess.

Their actual meeting, at the fort of Fashoda, 400 miles upriver from Khartoum, in September 1898, was like an encounter between rival male animals, when a display of strength between them establishes the dominance of one without the need of a battle. From France's point of view it came at the worst possible time, when her naval strength was at its lowest ebb: the most pessimistic of British admirals would have felt cheered if they had known what chance the French gave to *their* fleet.[32] France's hand was very much weaker now than when Marchand had left, thanks partly to some clever diplomacy by Salisbury. When Marchand arrived, and while he sat at Fashoda waiting for the British to come, Delcassé in the French foreign ministry was fervently hoping that he had not got there at all, in case the meeting sparked off a war.[33] In the outcome he was grateful to avoid this, at least. The two soldiers met, fraternised, agreed to differ, and then sat back and waited for London and Paris to sort it all out. The solution that London and Paris arrived at was in accordance with the realities of the situation in the Nile valley at that time. Britain, with an army on the spot and a string of military conquests to confirm her title, stayed there. France, who had got there first, retreated. 'We have nothing but arguments,' said Delcassé, 'and they have got troops.'[34] France agreed that the Nile was Britain's. Salisbury had got the fourth and decisive European signature to his claim, and there the argument – except over details – ended.[35]

It was a bloodless victory in itself, but on his way to it Kitchener had lost some hundreds of his own troops in battles with the Sudanese, and killed many thousands of theirs. His relentless progress up the Nile was notorious at the time for the extremity of its methods, which Kitchener justified on grounds of military necessity. ('The most arbitrary and unjust man I ever met', was Cromer's description of Kitchener.[36]) In the biggest battle of all, at Omdurman near Khartoum on 2 September 1898, 11,000 dervishes were killed, many of them as they lay wounded on the ground, which shocked some British Liberals, and even caused Kitchener some misgivings about the 'dreadful waste of ammunition'.[37] After it all he decided to rub home the lesson to the dervishes by exhuming the remains of their Mahdi and scattering them, which shocked British Liberals even more. (It was supposed to 'make a deep impression' on the Sudanese, said John Morley; did then the slaughter not make a deep enough impression?[38]) In its determination to hold its own on the Nile in the difficult, crisis-filled, late 1890s, British imperialism was not prepared to give any quarter.

West Africa

But it was not so uncompromising elsewhere in tropical Africa. In the Sudan, Britain was clearly the dominant power: she had made sure she would be, because – mainly for strategic reasons – she valued the Sudan highly. In West Africa her position was rather different. Her interest there was an established one, and moderately valuable; Sierra Leone, the Gold Coast, Lagos and the Niger were important sources of essential tropical products, and together did a trade with Britain of around £4 million a year. But it was strictly a commercial interest, kept up by the government for merchants, to the extent, only, that they required to carry on their commerce; and in one case (the Niger) actually secured and administered by the merchants themselves. The West African colonies had no value to Britain beyond the trade that was done with their people: they had no strategic importance, and no pretensions (except in the eyes of one or two eccentrics) ever to joining up and becoming parts of a larger contiguous British province. Britain was not going to try to make more of them when there was no demand to from her nationals there; she could not spare the forces, nor did she have the diplomatic resources to do so anyway. The only question was how far their hinterlands should go. France, on the other hand, had great ambitions in West Africa. The area of her effective control here was larger than Britain's, though much of it was desert. It was, or could be made to be, contiguous: a vast empire straddling the Sahara from the Mediterranean in the north to the Gulf of Guinea in the south – and perhaps, if they were lucky, down to the lower Congo and across to the upper Nile and the Red Sea; all joined up together, and engulfing and dwarfing the separated British, German, Spanish and Portuguese enclaves on its edges. And the French had armies there champing at the bit to fight for such an empire; the same basis of military strength, in fact, centred on Algeria, as Britain had for the upper Nile in Egypt. France, in other words, was more *committed* in West Africa than Britain; Britain was not disinterested, but the nature of her interests there, and the reality of her power, suggested more limited objectives. It may have been, too, that she saw West Africa as a possible sop to France, to buy the upper Nile with, or to mollify her with when she had seized it.

Over most of West Africa Britain did not fight very hard. The boundaries of Sierra Leone and Gambia were drawn very tight around them, in agreements concluded in 1889 and 1891; later the Gold Coast was delimited a little more generously, but not much. Merchants complained, but really they had no cause to feel robbed of anything, except a potential field for commerce in the hinterland which they had done nothing to tap yet. On the Niger it was different; the writ of Goldie's Royal Niger Company ran far inland, and could be made to appear to run even further than it did. Here there was a real, firm claim for the government to negotiate on, and a flourishing agency to make the claim good for it. 'In this matter,' Salisbury told the man he appointed to negotiate its boundaries with the French in 1890, 'the interests of this country are the interests of the Royal Niger Company.'[39] Joseph Chamberlain was willing to go to war for it.[40] So on the Niger the government and the Company worked together to resist the French, who launched a formidable campaign here, and to push the frontiers of Nigeria as far as possible upriver and towards the Sudan. It was an exhilarating game for the Europeans; a bewildering one for the Africans, who found themselves being fought over like a bride by two jealous suitors – except that the suitors fought *them* instead of each other; and it finished up with honours about even. In June 1898 (just in time to prevent it interfering with Fashoda), Nigeria's boundaries were fixed, not quite as far up the Niger as Britain would have liked, but further in other directions than her actual occupation really justified. It would have been a satisfactory outcome for the Company, if the Company had not itself been one of the casualties of the process. As the spearhead of expansion on the British side, it was clearly no match for a French army. It overstretched itself, and towards the end had to be helped out by the government. Chamberlain did not see why they should bear the expense of getting Nigeria, and then have Goldie 'step in and enjoy without cost all the security that we have gained for him'.[41] He decided to buy out the Company, revoke its charter, and turn its territories into a Crown Colony. This was done formally on the first day of 1900.[42]

By 1898, then, the Niger question had been settled, for Britain satisfactorily. Almost as important was the mere fact that it had been settled at all. At the beginning of the 1890s, Africa had been full of open sores – boundaries undelimited or in dispute, where pressure could be applied and irritation caused by foreign powers when Britain was taken up with important matters elsewhere. By the end of 1898, most of these sores had been healed, the frontiers of the rival powers' influence defined right across tropical Africa. The medicine had even been extended to the Portuguese colonies of Angola and Mozambique, where it was felt that new sores might break out soon when Portugal (another 'dying nation') crumbled. In August 1898, it was agreed between Britain and Germany who was to take which part of the pickings, before it even happened.[43] This whole process of African settlement left Britain free, now, to concentrate on the south, where the issues and interests at stake were vastly more important than those in Nigeria and central Asia, or even the Sudan and the Far East. South Africa saw the biggest and (until 1914) the last of Britain's major colonial wars. It needed her full attention; and after 1898 it could get it. South Africa was also the place where 'national' and 'sectional' interests, imperialism and capitalism, were most closely intertwined.

South Africa: the second Boer War

The development and exploitation of a country's resources by capitalists on capitalist lines were, in the late nineteenth century, a normal and natural accompaniment of imperial rule. Everywhere in the world where the British flag flew, the capitalist stood under it, alongside the administrator and the philanthropist, usually having been there before either of them and before the flag; for the real original agents of the expansion of British influence in the world, if not necessarily of formal British imperialism, were, as we have seen already, the merchant and the money-lender. The association of capitalism with imperialism, therefore, was commonplace, but nowhere in the late nineteenth-century British empire, with the possible exception of Egypt, was the association quite so close or so blatant as in South Africa in the 1890s. In South Africa, the tissue of industrial capitalism, grafted late, had taken hold firmly in the 1880s and spread phenomenally thereafter; by the mid-1890s, for those who believed capitalism should be kept in its place and that place was outside politics, it was clearly out of control. The cause of this was the domination of the South African industrial scene by Cecil Rhodes, a man whose conception of financial and political power would not admit of any necessary demarcation between them, a man who believed that what was good for his Consolidated Gold Fields was good for South Africa, and would buy political power to achieve that good. Rhodes was the reason why South African capitalism in the 1890s became a force on the side of British imperialism. It was not naturally imperialistic. Capitalists in general do not mind where they make their wealth, so long as they are allowed to make it and to keep it when they have made it. To welcome the protection of an imperial power, they have to feel thwarted without it, and convinced that they would do better with it. Of the handful of big European capitalists scrapping for riches among the gold reefs of the independent Transvaal in the late nineteenth century, only a tiny minority believed that their interests would be furthered by an extension of British rule there; most of them – Beit, Barnato, Robinson – were happy digging for gold under the auspices of the relatively ordered, if not very friendly, government of the Afrikaners, or, if they wanted change, wanted it under their own control and not another country's. Rhodes was exceptional partly because his financial interests were spread over more of southern Africa than theirs, and partly because he had very special imperial visions of his own; *his* capitalism *was* imperialistic, though at first not unambiguously so. In the late 1880s and early 1890s, there took place a somewhat insalubrious struggle between wealthy capitalists for supremacy – hegemony if possible – over southern Africa's mineral resources. It was Rhodes who eventually came to the top of the pile, though if the luck had gone another way, it could have been one of the others. Rhodes's victory was a victory for imperialistic capitalism – capitalism harnessed to imperial ends – over the sort of capitalism which had more limited horizons. The consequence was that, in the imperial history of southern Africa in the 1890s, the forces of industrial and financial capitalism played a more prominent role than they would have done otherwise.[44]

Rhodes's influence in South African affairs was partly the outcome of his wealth and the use he made of it, partly the result of the favour shown to him by British government ministers for reasons of their own. The two things were connected, of course: Rhodes used his wealth to cultivate ministers' favour, and ministers favoured him partly because of the power he wielded through his wealth. The threads of politics and finance were finely entangled, but they were distinct. Rhodes's power had been built up out of the Kimberley diamond fields, which he came to monopolise in 1888, and the gold reefs of the Witwatersrand, which he never could control absolutely, but which he shared with two or three other great magnates in the 1890s. With the wealth from these two gigantic concerns at his back, and with winning ways with all kinds of men which none of his rivals could begin to compete with, he established for himself a predominant position in South African politics. In 1890, he became Prime Minister of Cape Colony at the head of a party which preached and practised co-operation between the white races, and which practised, though it did not preach so loudly, co-operation too between politics and capital: of his dual role as company director and premier, 'I concluded,' he wrote, 'that one position could be worked with the other, and each to the benefit of all.'[45] As well as a parochial predominance at the Cape, he had friends in higher places. Sir Hercules Robinson, who became High Commissioner for the second time in 1895, was an old friend and a director of his diamond monopoly; and in England he had the admiration of the Queen, the backing of Lord Rothschild – who also happened to be Lord Rosebery's father-in-law – and the support of at least two influential journalists: the notorious W. T. Stead, probably the best-known newspaperman of his day, and Flora Shaw, who as colonial correspondent of *The Times*, was one of the most prestigious. This kind of influence was of great assistance to him when he directed his sights northwards towards the greater gold reef which was supposed to lie beyond the Limpopo, and in 1889 secured from the Liberal government a charter to carve a whole country in his own commercial image[46] – an even more intimate wedding of financial and political power than existed at the Cape. In the early 1890s, his company took possession of its inheritance, swindled and shot the Matabele and Mashona peoples who lived there into a sullen subservience, and dug for the promised gold but failed to find it. It was when the prospect of big dividends – or even of any dividends at all – receded in 'Zambesia' that he turned his full attention, and the powers – legal and illegal – that his wealth gave him, towards making the Transvaal British.

Rhodes always insisted that he valued riches not for their own sake but for the power they gave him to help extend and consolidate the British empire, which grand ambition, he held, justified any use he might make of those riches – 'you must judge of my conduct by the objects that I had in view'.[47] The imperial implication of his failure to find gold in Zambesia was that it made virtually certain the Transvaal's eventual domination of southern Africa, because no other part of the country could overbid it in gold. It followed for Rhodes that, for southern Africa to be secured for the British empire, the Transvaal must become part of it; and he believed that he had the means to help this on. His assessment of the situation was not very different from the government's in London, although he was quicker, perhaps, to read a crisis into it than London was. On some matters there could be no dispute: that the Transvaal *was* becoming richer than the Cape; that it was trying its hardest to sever all ties of dependence on the Cape; and that it was doing this to the considerable detriment of the Cape's economy. When the Rand's gold had first been discovered, the Cape had reaped some profit from it by transporting it to the sea. By 1894, however, the Transvaal could export and import goods without touching British territory at all, by means of a new, independent railway just completed to Delagoa Bay in Portuguese East Africa; and she was fighting a crude tariff battle with the Cape to siphon the Rand's traffic away from there entirely. There were rumours too that Paul Kruger, the Transvaal President, was planning a republican takeover of the whole of South Africa – and there were enough of his blood-brothers in the British colonies to make the plan, if it was true, perfectly feasible. And from 1894, there were more solid reports of German involvement in the Transvaal, with the Transvaal's encouragement, which gave the situation a more sinister look still. Ministers in London were worried, but not worried enough yet (or else too scrupulous) to make them want to take overtly aggressive action against the Transvaal. 'Every nerve should be strained,' said the Colonial Secretary in 1894, 'to prevent such a disgrace as another African war.'[48] Rhodes, however, had more urgency, fewer scruples, and the power to make an African war almost on his own.

Rhodes's decision to use his considerable powers to incite revolution in the Transvaal, to abet it when it came, and to use it to try to force the Republicans into some kind of compliant union with the British colonies, arose from his conviction that a rebellion was going to break out in the Transvaal anyway, and that it had better be turned into a British imperial direction by him than into another direction, less favourable to the

British, by others. For years there had been unrest among the largely foreign mining community on the Rand, the 'Uitlanders', who were daily subjected to innumerable aggravations and disabilities by a dominant people they regarded as rude and inferior, and who regarded *them*, with rather more justice, as a threat to their whole national way of life. For a rather shorter time this unrest had been encouraged and exploited by some of the great gold magnates, who by the mid-1890s were beginning to chafe under a form of indirect taxation which was particularly galling to them: state monopolies over some of their basic necessities, like gunpowder and rail haulage, which the Afrikaners saw as a just tribute for the general good, but the capitalists as fetters which were becoming increasingly irksome as the mines went deeper and their costs rose. During 1894–95, there was talk of armed rebellion on the Rand: wild talk, as it turned out, from the ordinary Uitlanders, but more serious from some of the big capitalists, who took measures – like gun-running – actively to promote it. Rhodes's involvement in this plotting would ensure that the revolution, if it came and succeeded, would be to the advantage of the empire.

It also led the British government to be dragged into the affair, not necessarily because it approved of Rhodes's cloak-and-dagger ways of solving its South African problem, but because it was coming to accept his diagnosis of that problem, and because his power and prestige in South Africa made him the readiest means at hand, if not the best, towards a solution. This was another instance – there were many before and afterwards – where the freedom of action which Britain theoretically exerted in South Africa by virtue of her ultimate sovereignty there was in fact limited by the choice of tools she was presented with; Rhodes was the agent she was given to work through, and Rhodes had ideas of his own. Before the autumn of 1895, he secured the co-operation he needed from the British government to put his plot into effect: troops, a friendly High Commissioner, and a strip of land on the western border of the Transvaal he could start an invasion from. Joseph Chamberlain, when he succeeded the rather less enthusiastic Ripon at the Colonial Office, played along with Rhodes, with misgivings but not serious ones, because the plan as it was presented to him was not blatantly illegitimate: it did not involve an invasion on no pretext at all. His connivance in Rhodes's schemes rested on the assumption, which was made on the best authority, that an Uitlander rebellion would take place, which would be or could be made to seem spontaneous. In that event, intervention by Britain, or by a British colonial in Britain's name, could be presented as a response to a situation generated independently of her, made in order legitimately to safeguard her nationals in the Transvaal. What ruined things for the government was that the Uitlanders never rebelled, yet the intervention took place regardless. On 29 December 1895, Dr Leander Starr Jameson rode into the Transvaal at the head of a band of 500 mounted troops and carrying the Union Jack, to aid a rebellion which never happened. He was easily stopped. The results of this fiasco were disastrous for everyone except the Boers. Bereft of the veneer of respectability and legality that the 'spontaneous rising' had been supposed to give them, the colonial troops, which had been intended to turn a success to Britain's advantage, instead implicated her in a failure to her very great disadvantage. Chamberlain tried to cover the traces of imperial involvement, but could not even to his compatriots' satisfaction, and certainly not to the Afrikaners' or the world's. To all intents and purposes, Britain was implicated in a squalid conspiracy against a foreign state. The fact that her implication was vicarious did not absolve her from responsibility for employing such unscrupulous and incompetent vicars. The result of the Jameson Raid was the complete opposite of what had been intended. Instead of weakening Kruger, it strengthened him; instead of persuading him to compromise, it made him more intransigent; it justified the Republicans' suspicions of the past five years, and it prolonged them for another five. At the time men said that it made war inevitable between the British and the Boers, though it was so only if it was assumed that Britain had to have the Transvaal. After the Raid, the Boers would make sure that she did not have it *without* a war.

The lesson of the Jameson Raid for the British government was that it could no longer pursue its policies in South Africa on the coat-tails of capitalists. Rhodes and the government had done a great deal for each other in the past, and Chamberlain was convinced that Rhodes could do something for him still in the future – but in the north, where his buccaneering methods were likely to be more successful against black Africans than against white Afrikaners, and less likely to arouse strong feelings at home or diplomatic repercussions abroad. In any case he was badly needed there. Before he had raided the Transvaal, Dr Jameson had been Rhodes's viceroy in Zambesia; in this capacity, he had managed to provoke the Matabele, and even their neighbours the Mashona, who had always been supposed to be meeker, to seething unrest; and then when he took time off with his Company police for the Raid, they both rebelled, reasserted their old sovereignties, and put 'Rhodesia' – and the value of Chartered Company shares – in very real danger. Rhodes had to restore the authority of the Company or his whole world would have collapsed, and this he did during the course of 1896 in one of the bloodiest and most ferocious of southern Africa's 'punitive' wars, capped – when it was clear the Africans were not going to be tamed by force alone – by a remarkable exercise by Rhodes in peaceful persuasion. In the north, therefore, Rhodes was left to repair his own breaches, but in the south he was, for the time being, a spent force, too discredited to be of use to any political cause, unless he kept very much behind the scenes. The British government had perforce to disown him, and to secure its South African salvation by its own efforts – as it should have done all along.

British interests in South Africa had not grown any the less during the Raid, nor had the government's resolve to secure them; and the threat to them was thought to have increased considerably as a direct result. Kruger refused to talk with the British government about their differences, unless the talks were about ending British suzerainty over his country, which would mean giving him the right which was denied him then (by the Pretoria Convention of 1881) to treat with foreign powers. Intelligence from the Republic suggested that he was pushing for complete independence and plotting with Germany to get it. A telegram of congratulation from the Kaiser to Kruger after the failure of the Raid strongly suggested that Germany was not averse to helping the Transvaal to her own diplomatic advantage. Agitated ministers read into all this the possible loss of everything in South Africa to a German-backed Afrikaner republic spreading south – by force, by the impetus its mineral wealth gave it, and by its natural, racial appeal to the Afrikaner minority at the Cape.[49] Even if this fear proved groundless and there were no threat at all to the British position in the Cape and Natal, still it was a depressing thought that those colonies in the future would have to get along in the shadow of a Transvaal which was already (said the Colonial Under-Secretary) 'the richest spot on earth', and was likely to be soon 'the natural capital state and centre of South African commercial, social and political life'.[50] The aftermath of the Raid had made it more necessary than ever for Britain to get hold of the Transvaal somehow; it also seemed to make it less likely than ever that this could be done except by force. At the same time it made the exercise of force a more hazardous proposition for Britain. In the first place the enemy was stronger – the Transvaal was arming heavily in response to the Raid, and in

1897 the Orange Free State joined in a military alliance with her. In the second place, Britain's support was much shakier. The High Commissioner reported in April 1896 how the feeling of the Cape Dutch had 'undergone a complete change since the Jameson Raid', and how 'they would now neither sympathise with nor support any forcible measures undertaken by the Imperial Government to secure the redress of the Uitlanders' grievances'.[51] Chamberlain pointed out in a speech the next month that a war in South Africa would be 'in the nature of a Civil War ... a long war, a bitter war, and a costly war'; and a war, too, which it would be difficult to find a good, convincing justification for to rally the doubtful.[52] There would be support, of course, among the Uitlanders, but a disorganised kind of support, and at present without the open participation of the big capitalist magnates. Even in Britain the ground was not certain: in November 1897, the Chancellor of the Exchequer felt it necessary to remind the Prime Minister that it was colonial wars which had lost their party an election in 1880.[53] And there were strong diplomatic reasons for caution: 'a war with the Transvaal,' wrote Salisbury to Chamberlain in April 1897, 'will have a reaction on European politics which may be pernicious. ... It might mean the necessity of protecting the North-East of England as well as the South.'[54] Britain was stalemated. She could neither persuade the Transvaal to join the empire nor force her into it: neither seduce her nor try to rape her. Consequently, for two years after the Raid she held back, remonstrating with the Transvaal continuously but not threatening her; all the while feeding soldiers and arms to the Cape for the time when the stalemate might be broken.

The stalemate was broken, slowly, in 1897–99, as the British government rebuilt for itself a position strong enough to threaten from. In August 1898, Balfour got the Germans to agree to keep out of South Africa as part of the deal which shared the Portuguese colonies out between them. Chamberlain nursed public opinion in Britain on to his side in a series of speeches calculated to make it hostile to Kruger. And in South Africa he got what he needed most: a handle to turn his policy by, to fill the gap left by Rhodes's departure. The 'South African League' was formed in 1896 to rally imperialist opinion in the two British colonies and the Transvaal. It was strong – stronger than any of the political associations that had gone before; its policies were Rhodes's, and in April 1899, Rhodes himself returned from the political wilderness to become its president. This time, however, it was not Rhodes who would take the initiatives. That duty lay firmly with the 'officials' – with Chamberlain and with his new High Commissioner, Alfred Milner. The combination of these two men was enough to tilt any diplomatic balance with the Boers in favour of war, without local freelances being needed to do so. Chamberlain himself probably was not bent on war. But he was bent on threatening war, because he thought Kruger would succumb to threats: 'If they see we are in earnest, I believe they will give way, as they have always done.'[55]

Milner was more positively for war. A self-declared 'British Race Patriot', he could not conceive of the Afrikaners of the Cape being loyal to the empire while there remained an independent nation of their 'race' to the north to divert their loyalties; while their loyalties were so much in doubt, the empire was in peril, and he could not see the Transvaal forfeiting her independence without war. In any case, she should be pushed to the limit, mainly on the issue of the Uitlander franchise – because it was a genuine grievance, and because if Kruger did give satisfaction on it, Britain's position in South Africa would be automatically secured: Uitlanders out-numbered Boers, most of them were British, and it was assumed that, if Britons were given the vote, they would use it imperially. Consequently, from the beginning of 1898, Milner devoted his energies to bringing on a crisis which could be exploited to this end[56] – if necessary, without support from home: 'If I can advance matters by my own actions, as I still hope I may be able to, I believe I shall have support when the time comes.'[57] For 18 months he worked doggedly along these lines, in South Africa and in England. In England, he used almost all his holiday leave to propagandise and persuade, though he found 'the attempt to interview *all* the leading politicians and pressmen … and to stamp on rose-coloured illusions about S. Africa … a most exhausting one'.[58] In South Africa, he spent all his time organising the faithful, in close collaboration with the loyalist press and the capitalists who owned the press: using them, as he saw it, to pursue his imperial aims.[59] By the summer of 1899, he was satisfied that he had 'absolutely rallied all our forces on the spot', though he was unsure about England.[60] On the diplomatic front he did what he could to prevent a reconciliation with the Boers: for apart from London 'ratting' on him and turning pacifist, his other constant fear was that Kruger might make reasonable concessions which he would have to accept, which would take from him the pretext for grabbing all he wanted. At a conference with Kruger at Bloemfontein in June 1899, he had to work hard to avoid a peaceful settlement.[61] But he succeeded, and the war he desired at last broke out, on an ultimatum from the Boers, in October (Map 10).

It was Milner who forced the pace in South Africa, sometimes to the disquiet of the government in London, which tried on one or two occasions to restrain him.[62] The government's aims, however, were no different from his: all ministers agreed on the importance of bringing the Transvaal to heel in order to uphold British supremacy – to make sure that 'we, not the Dutch, are Boss', as Salisbury put it to Selborne.[63] Where Milner and his political masters disagreed over tactics, it was because ministers – being representative politicians with wider responsibilities – constantly had to be sensitive to the reactions to their policies of the people they represented, and the repercussions of their policies on other British interests elsewhere, and to adapt accordingly. Milner wanted to rush in when he considered the time was ripe in South Africa. Salisbury was concerned to get the boards clear of other troubles first: 'We cannot afford to have more than a limited area of heather alight at the same time.'[64] And all ministers were concerned about public opinion. Throughout 1898 and most of 1899, they felt the country would not stand for a war. In the summer of 1899, Goschen wrote to Milner, 'I *think* this has now given way to a change towards a much firmer attitude. But it is impossible to say that a war in the Transvaal may be popular.'[65] With public opinion so uncertain – and it was the public who would have to fight the war – it was important that the thing looked right: the negotiations genuinely conciliatory and the *casus belli* just. In the event, the fact that it was the Boers who issued the ultimatum and not the British (the British had one prepared in case the Boers failed to) made it easier. The ultimatum, said Salisbury, had 'liberated us from the necessity of explaining to the people of England why we are at war.'[66] 'Middle opinion' fell into line: people and interests who (like most of the Rand capitalists and the City of London) had been more in favour of negotiating while negotiation had seemed possible, but who, when it was presented as a choice between taking all and losing all in war, chose to take all.[67]

Yet the government had been right to anticipate difficulties with a full-scale war in South Africa. That broke out finally on 11 October 1899. It seemed well supported initially, both in Britain, and among those in South Africa on whose loyalty the British felt they could reasonably count. They included many black and 'coloured' Africans, who expected more liberal treatment from the British when they won. Thousands of them volunteered for service, usually in auxiliary capacities.[68] In the end – two and a

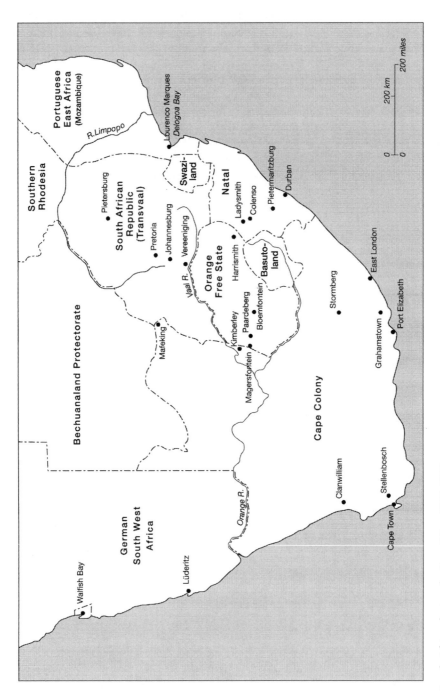

Map 10 South Africa during the Boer War, 1899–1902

Source: After Eldridge, C. C., *Victorian Imperialism* (Hodder & Stoughton, 1978, p. 208).

half years after the outbreak of the war – the Boers surrendered, which had to be counted a British success. By the time the success came, however, few Britons felt like rejoicing at it. 'We have always felt,' wrote one commentator, 'that the Boer was a preposterously little fellow, and the work of crushing him ... was not in itself an essentially pleasant or heroic thing to carry through.'[69] It had been a dispiriting war in many ways. It had shown up more weaknesses in the British soldiery – who had vastly outnumbered their enemies – than strengths. It turned into a pretty grim kind of war after the first four months, with the British (as usual) owing their victory more to farm- and crop-burning, and a new policy of 'concentrating' Boer women in camps – condemned by the Liberal leader in 1901 as 'methods of barbarism'[70] – than to military bravery or skill. That further alienated the Afrikaners, which was not promising for the imperial connection in the longer term. The war also seriously tested the loyalties of the 'Uitlanders', who turned out to be less enthusiastic about it than all the British propaganda about rescuing them from their Boer oppressors had led people to expect; and of black Africans, who were disappointed by its results for them.[71] Back home, people tired of it. The 'jingoism' of its early months soon waned. When Sir Henry Campbell-Bannerman made his remark about 'methods of barbarism', he knew it would touch a sympathetic nerve. 'Anti-imperialism' was growing confident – confident enough to declare itself, without fear of reprisal – and strong. The Boer War seemed to have exhausted the imperial enthusiasm of the British people. It was just about as much imperialism as they would take.[72]

The government – still a Conservative one until December 1905 – took these signals to heart. It was careful not to make such demands on the people again. In Turkey and China, for example, it allowed Britain's position to crumble quite drastically, rather than risk more imperial wars there. With the Japanese alliance of 1902 and then with a new entente with France in 1904, which settled their differences over Egypt, it tacitly abandoned the pretence that Britain could go it alone any more. All this was a natural outcome of the diplomatic and military ferment of the years 1898–1902, and especially the South African war, which had very clearly demonstrated the strengths and the limitations of Britain's power in the world in the 1890s: the measure of her imperial resolve at home, as well as of her military resources abroad.

Native policy

Milner did not consider his job done in South Africa when he had (in his own words) 'saved the British position' there.[73] There was much more to do yet before its safety was assured for the future. He advised his successor in April 1905 that 'to make it certain requires years of strong, patient policy':[74] policy designed in the first place to reconstruct South Africa's economy – which meant getting the gold mines running again – and in the second place, to keep her loyal. His own ideas as to how this latter should be done were very definite, and characteristic of that school of 'forward' imperialism which had flowered so bountifully in the 1890s. When they came to run colonies – and they ran one or two important ones around the turn of the century – 'forward' imperialists brought with them the same mood of gloomy realism which had made them want to *acquire* colonies: the same expectation of foreign enmity, the same reluctance to trust people who were not of their 'race', the same compulsion to build their defences high. It gave a particular flavour to their administration of non-British colonial subjects: made it in many ways tougher and less charitable, as we shall see, than that of their less 'forward' successors. In South Africa, for example, the Boer would always be an enemy and a threat to the empire until his nationality was utterly crushed and his numbers exceeded by Anglo-Saxons: until it was so, Milner, for one, would never feel quite secure. Consequently, he was full of schemes for deposing the Afrikaans language because it was an agency of Afrikanerdom,[75] making the history taught in Boer schools more 'impartial' and imperial than it was,[76] and – most urgently of all – inducing 'loyal' Britons to emigrate to South Africa: 'If, ten years hence, there are three men of British race to two of Dutch, the country will be safe and prosperous. If there are three of Dutch to two of British, we shall have perpetual difficulty.'[77] It followed, of course, that responsible government was out of the question as yet. 'Absolutely everything,' he wrote home in November 1901, 'depends upon starting the new self-governing Confederation with a British-minded majority. We must wait for Federation and self-government until that majority is assured.'[78] For the defence of their interests in the world, the British had only their own 'race' to rely on.

If non-British whites were so distrusted, Africans and Asians could be trusted even less. Imperialists justified their denial of power to non-whites on grounds of racial incompetence. In India, Curzon maintained that 'the highest ranks of civil employment ... must be held by Englishmen for the reason that they possess ... the habits of mind and the vigour of character which are essential to the task'.[79] Lord Salisbury's biographer told why they did not even entertain the idea of Africans ruling themselves:

> The reason is not far to seek. That generation had contemporary knowledge of what 'Africa for the Africans' stood for before civilization entered – the dead, effortless degradation which it represented, broken only by interludes of blood-lust, slaughter, slavery, and unspeakable suffering. It was impossible for them to feel doubt – far less scruple – as to replacing it, wherever occasion served, by white dominion.[80]

Needless to say, the picture they painted of the pre-colonial African was a grotesquely distorted one. For all their vaunted devotion to science and reason, in the human and social sciences, the late Victorians were curiously prone to jump from skimpy evidence to false conclusions when it suited their preconceptions. African society was non-society because it was not *their* society; Africans had no artistic culture because there were no cathedral spires in the Kalahari; they were primitive because they were naked and Britons had been naked when *they were* primitive; they had always been 'backward' because they were 'backward' now; if they advanced, it would take them centuries because it had taken Europe centuries: the Briton's image of Africa at the end of the nineteenth century was built up out of such non-sequiturs, and out of a disposition always to measure African civilisation against his or her own, treating differences, therefore, as merely negative qualities, shortfalls. The missionaries in their search for funds played up the 'degradation'; so did administrators and capitalists if it justified their designs; and the ingrained ethnocentrism of the Briton did the rest: Africans were not fit to rule themselves. But beyond this there was another reason for ruling autocratically, and this was that it was obvious that British dominion could not be preserved *except* autocratically, for 'natives' would certainly not support it out of love. In the last resort, the sanction of Britain's sovereignty in Asia and Africa was that of force, and its guarantee was not the loyalty of her subjects but, as a great imperial soldier saw, quite simply and brutally their 'respect based on fear'.[81]

This was not to say that 'natives' were not supposed in their heart of hearts to know what was good for them. The trouble was that those who did were constantly being misrepresented and malignly influenced by agitators out for their own ends: in India, middle-class nationalists who merely wanted the chance to exploit the people themselves. 'The noise comes forth as the voice of India,' said Curzon of the Indian National Congress. 'But if you go to the other end of the funnel, you find that it is nothing of the sort.'[82] All over the empire there was general agreement that nationalists did not matter – were 'unrepresentative' – and that the people who did matter, the 'silent millions', much preferred good government to self-government, or ought to if they had any sense. 'To these people,' said Curzon again, '... representative government and electoral institutions are nothing whatever ... The good government that appeals to them is the government which protects them from the rapacious moneylender and landlord.' As Indian government became more parliamentary, so it would become 'less paternal and less beneficent to the poorer classes of the population'.[83] In Egypt, Lord Cromer insisted similarly that if you treated the fellaheen right and, in particular, kept his taxes low, he would love you far more than if you let his 'nationalist leaders' lord it over him.[84] And Sir Alfred Milner regarded Africans as 'children, needing and appreciating a just paternal government' rather than the incongruous political rights demanded for them by ignorant philanthropists at home.[85] Turn-of-the-century imperialists had no doubts at all that they knew best what was good for the masses – just as those of them who were country squires back in England knew best what was good for their tenants; and they were only a little less confident that the masses knew it too. A corollary of this was that the more they did for the masses, the more the masses would thank them. The seeds of nationalist agitation could only flower in a soil of mass discontent. They could not avoid breeding demagogues, said Cromer: 'but we may govern in such a manner as to give the demagogue no fulcrum with which to move his credulous and ill-informed countrymen and co-religionists'.[86] Curzon preened himself that this was just what he was doing: 'I hold the scales with exasperatingly even hand, but this is the last thing that they desire ... They prefer the open sore which can always be kept angry by a twist of the goad.'[87] The nationalist sting could be drawn by keeping the masses happy, and they could be kept happy without giving them power.

What kept them happiest, or was best for them, could be a matter for dispute. What Lord Milner's Africans needed most, apparently, were to be 'well-treated', 'justly governed', and encouraged to work in gold-mines: 'undoubtedly the greatest benefit that could be bestowed upon them ... would be to teach them habits of regular and skilled labour'.[88] Cromer's Egyptians were happier with solid finances, low taxes, administrative honesty, and better irrigation.[89] Curzon put the emphasis on justice and racial tolerance: the way to counter nationalist demands, he wrote in 1903, was

> to rally round the Government all the more stable and loyal elements of the community: to pursue the path of unwavering justice: to redress, wherever they are found, a grievance here or an anomaly there: to make the government essential to the people by reason of its combined probity and vigour: to insist upon a juster and more generous recognition of India in the plans of British governments and in the policy of the Empire; and to be perpetually building bridges over that racial chasm that yawns eternally in our midst, and which, if it becomes wider and there are no means of getting across it, will one day split the Empire asunder.[90]

Different national circumstances dictated slightly different variations: but the theme was the same all over – a familiar Tory theme, which was echoed in a contemporary work on 'Conservatism':

> A nation's dominion is a divine vicegerency; to the extent of that dominion it must labour for the good of men, establishing order, keeping peace, doing justice, enlightening ignorance, making smooth the path of religion, to the end that the earth may be full of the knowledge of the Lord as the waters cover the sea.[91]

A conspicuous absentee from this catalogue was freedom, or the preparation for freedom; and it was absent too from the philosophies of most of the great proconsuls of the 1890s and 1900s. This was unusual; in the past, lip-service at least had generally been paid to the idea that colonies were being trained up to rule themselves – a real 'paternalism' – but at this time it was hardly mentioned at all. For a short while at the turn of the century imperialists seemed seriously to believe that the empire might last for ever, though they hardly dared to mouth the words.[92] In place of the older, and perhaps insincere, ideals there were found others more suited to a permanent guardianship.

The purest expression of this philosophy – and the most vivid demonstration of its shortcomings – was Curzon's India. For years, India had been ruled as if she were to be ruled for ever, a ward whose majority was never contemplated: the attitudes of her ruling class made this clear, if the pronouncements of her viceroys and secretaries of state did not. In the early 1880s, a Gladstonian viceroy had tried to nudge her into a more liberal current, with the 'Ilbert Bill', for example, which would have enabled Indian judges to try Europeans; but the weight and virulence of entrenched Anglo-Indian opinion was too much for him, and he failed. By Curzon's time, the continual frustration of Indian political and social pretensions had provoked a significant, but moderate, nationalist reaction. Curzon ignored it because he believed that he could do so with impunity, so long as he retained the loyalty of 'the great mute pathetic cultivating class – the back-bone of the country'.[93] Consequently, everything he did he claimed to do with them 'in the background'.[94] As they were 'mute', it was difficult to tell what they wanted. But it was assuredly not what the nationalists wanted. Curzon did his best with a series of reforms contrived in the main to make the administration of India cheaper and more efficient; they included the institution of more effective machinery for famine relief, a large-scale irrigation programme, university and police reform, municipal reform in Calcutta, and the division of the province of Bengal into two. When nationalists complained at some of these – in particular, the Calcutta reforms (which reduced their participation in its government) and the partition of Bengal – he dismissed their agitation as 'mere froth'; 'it only floats on the surface, and I have little doubt that when my time comes to go, I shall find that deep and tranquil waters have all the time been running below'.[95] He was wrong; he had stirred up the depths more than he knew – or else the froth was more potent than he thought. His successors were to reap the consequences. But Curzon could not give nationalists any quarter, because they had no place at all in his plans for India. India, he believed, was already on its way to acquiring a nationality of its own. But it was a nationality with British rule 'rivetted'[96] firmly on it: like China under the Manchus, perhaps, or India under the Mughals long ago. India was rapidly being lifted 'from the level of a dependency to the position which is bound one day to be hers, if it is not so already, namely that of the greatest partner of the empire'.[97] At every opportunity Curzon pressed India's separate political and economic interests against Britain's; he was more energetic than almost anyone before him in preserving and restoring the relics and the literature of India's historic past; and the great Delhi Durbar he summoned in 1903 was intended to display her 'unity and patriotism'.[98] But the nationality all these things were meant to strengthen was an Anglo-Indian nationality, not a native Indian one. This was the nationality he wanted to foster in the masses, and he believed he was succeeding: 'the people of all India are, I think, filled with more loyal sentiments … at this juncture than at almost any previous time'.[99] It was an autocratic, almost oriental ideal; and with it the western liberal ambitions of the nationalists were clearly incompatible.[100]

Even in Egypt, which could not be treated quite so proprietorially because she was not supposed to belong to Britain, there was a kind of permanency about the way she was run. Cromer, like Curzon, could not really see his subjects ever ruling themselves: 'free institutions in the full sense of the term', he wrote, 'must for generations to come be wholly unsuitable to countries such as India and Egypt', and perhaps even for all time: 'it will probably never be possible to make a Western silk purse out of an Eastern sow's ear'.[101] It was something to do with what he called the 'oriental mind'. In any case, 'orientals' did not want it. Those who did were 'demagogues' and 'agitators', a bourgeois minority wanting power merely to lord it over the poor, unprotected proletariat.[102] That proletariat had better sense. All it wanted was to be governed justly and benevolently. If it sometimes succumbed to the blandishments of the 'agitators', it was only because it had 'genuine' grievances which made it think that they could do better for it. 'Genuine' grievances were material grievances, about taxation and land and food and labour, which were all that the ordinary Egyptian was really interested in. No-one could get really worked up about nationalism if he or she was well fed. Consequently, the way to spike the nationalists' guns was by 'attention to material interests', which is what Cromer concentrated on, and claimed thereby to have reconciled the ordinary Egyptians to British despotism, and reduced nationalism to 'a mere splutter on the surface'.[103] The Egypt Cromer left behind him in 1907 was financially more healthy, better irrigated, more justly taxed, and quieter than he had found it and as illiberal as ever.[104]

If it could not be liberal, however, a permanent empire had to try to be tolerant – or it would not long be permanent. No-one realised this better than Queen Victoria. 'We shall never really be liked in India,' she wrote to Curzon in 1900, 'if we keep up this racial feeling, and some day real danger may result from it.' She regarded it as her special concern, an essential part of the 'Great White Queen' role she enjoyed so hugely, to plead for her black and brown subjects, though she could not do much for them in practice (Figure 6.1). In Africa, she saw the natives being regarded by the English as 'totally different beings to ourselves, fit only to be cursed and shot down'; in India, she constantly cavilled at the 'snobbish and vulgar overbearing and offensive behaviour' of its British rulers towards the Indians which, she believed, gave them a quite unnecessary sense of humiliation: 'they must of course *feel that* we are masters, but it should be done kindly and not offensively, which alas! is so often the case'.[105] Salisbury, Cromer and Curzon all concurred.[106] Chamberlain in 1898 declared that it had always been a 'tradition' of the empire that no distinction was made 'in favour of, or against, race or colour';[107] all the leading imperialists seemed anxious to temper the race prejudice which they saw undermining their good works everywhere, but it was an uphill struggle to stop it, especially against the entrenched racialism of the South African whites and of the Indian civil and military services. Milner gave up the fight in South Africa, both for the Africans and for the Asiatics whose treatment aroused more feeling because of the bad press it gave in India to the empire; in effect, he felt constrained to swim with local white prejudices

Figure 6.1 The Queen Empress. Victoria works at her dispatch boxes (in England) with Abdul
Karim, her Indian servant, 1893.
Source: © Historic Images/Alamy Stock Photo.

because it was the local whites whose affection and loyalty the empire most badly
needed.[108] In India Curzon tried a lot harder, and got into trouble for it. More than one
Indian regiment was penalised by him for covering up outrages committed by their men
on Indians, and in a famous incident at the Delhi Durbar, one of them, the 9th Lancers,
provoked a rowdy demonstration in their favour by the Europeans there which emphasised the hopelessness of his cause. Curzon never was able to achieve his ideal of a beneficent autocracy which was just and tolerant at all levels; and no doubt for him it would
have been this, rather than its autocracy, which accounted for its ultimate impermanence.

Because they condemned certain manifestations of racial insolence and intolerance
among white people in the colonies, it did not follow that the leading imperialists of the
1890s and 1900s were not racialists themselves: just as opponents of cruelty to animals do
not necessarily hold that budgerigars are men's brothers under the skin. Curzon's attitude
towards Indians was much the same as his predecessors'; the types he admired were the
faithful, soldierly ones, and he did not believe they were equal.[109] Milner's view of the
Africans was not really very different from that of the white colonials he was trying to
restrain: they were 'aboriginals' with different 'capacities' from white people, many centuries behind them in evolution, and most of them unlikely ever to catch up.[110] Cromer
was constantly wondering at the incorrigible contrariness of the 'oriental' mind.[111] These
people did not go so far as to admit to a belief in the biological and ineradicable inferiority of other groups, which made them less than extreme racists; but they were

impressed by 'racial' or cultural differences, and they believed too, generally more than their predecessors, that colonial policies should take account of these differences. This was one reason why self-government was supposed to be unsuitable for non-Europeans: it had been evolved for a different racial or cultural type. They should beware, said Cromer, of the disposition 'to transport institutions, whose natural habitat is Westminster, to Calcutta or Cairo'.[112] But another side of this same emphasis on cultural differences was a more positive one, which the humanitarian Aborigines' Protection Society insisted on too: that indigenous cultures and structures ought to be respected more than in the past, as being peculiarly suited to the people among whom they had evolved. It was a principle which was accepted by Milner for the Africans: 'that native institutions should not be unnecessarily interfered with; that their existing system of communal tenure and of tribal government, and their traditional customs, so far as they are not in gross conflict with civilised ideas, should be respected'.[113] It was a convenient doctrine for those who wanted to keep the native down, and unenlightened, so, certainly, old-fashioned Liberals of the Macaulay school would have said. But it was also, or could be the makings of, a more sensitive approach to problems of colonial government; and it caught on.

In itself, the preservation and utilisation of indigenous social and political institutions by conquering imperial powers was not a new idea. Pontius Pilate had given Christ over to a subject people to be tried by their own tribal laws; almost every empire in history has kept and worked through local hierarchies where they have proved amenable, replacing only the top men: it was the common-sense way to run an empire, with the minimum of disturbance and expense. To a certain extent, the rulers of India had learnt this after 1857, when they decided to stop interfering needlessly and to try to rule through the princes where they could; and in parts of the tropical empire where the resources of the Colonial Office were more stretched, it was the only way to manage a colony at all. What was new was the elevation of this expedient into a principle of policy – still only used, perhaps, because it was expedient, and *where* it was expedient, but justified now on higher grounds, and for its supposed benefits to subject as well as to ruler. The point had occurred to broad-minded and sympathetic colonial governors before, like, for example, Sir Arthur Gordon in Fiji: that there were other paths to 'civilisation', and even to salvation, than the narrowly Anglo-Saxon one. But it was first widely noticed in northern Nigeria, where Sir George Goldie had from the 1880s pursued a systematic policy of 'ruling on African principles through native rulers', which Sir Frederick Lugard when he went to Nigeria in 1900 inherited, and over the next few years developed and extended and turned into a theory, which he called 'indirect rule'. 'Indirect rule' became the orthodox British colonial philosophy of the twentieth century, although under the same title there appeared many variants of the original, and more often than not colonial practice paid little or no attention to colonial philosophy anyway. As yet, while Lugard was still easing himself into Goldie's saddle, there was little to show for it. But the seed had been sown in the 1890s, and fertilised then in a mixture of soils: in humanitarianism with its concern to protect the native in his milieu; in the 'new' imperialism with its open abandonment of the old liberal westernising mission; in the hardening of racial attitudes, possibly; and in the practical pressures faced by a Colonial Office with many millions of new subjects to rule, and neither the staff nor the resources to westernise them with.[114]

For the time being, however, 'native policy' was not a thing the Colonial Office gave very much thought to, though it was constantly being prodded to by the humanitarian societies. The basic, and almost the only, requirement it made of its governors in the field was that they kept order. The details of how they kept order were a matter for them to work out for themselves, adapting their experience to the varied materials they were presented with, with the proviso, only, that they should not overstep certain bounds of decency and humanity in the punishments and penalties they meted out.[115] Beyond this, the field was theirs.

'Constructive imperialism'

What the Colonial Office did become concerned with in the 1890s was the material, economic side of colonial administration. In a way, it always had been concerned with economics; concerned, that is, to keep down the cost of running colonies, so as not to trouble the British taxpayer. But with Joseph Chamberlain's arrival, its purpose became more positive than this: to make the colonies profitable. For Chamberlain, colonies were first and foremost an economic proposition, an enormous potential source of national wealth and economic security. It was a potential Britain had scarcely begun to tap as yet. 'Cases had already come to my knowledge,' he said two months after coming to the Office, 'of colonies which have been British Colonies perhaps for more than a hundred years in which up to the present time British rule has done absolutely nothing.'[116] With his businessman's distaste for resources going to waste, he wanted to exploit them, use the soils and the natural products of the colonies to their best advantage; for it was in no-one's interest that they should be neglected, least of all, he believed – as a Victorian capitalist was bound to – to the advantage of the inhabitants of the colonies themselves. For Britain, the proper exploitation of her colonial estates could mean prosperity and a contented (because fully employed) proletariat; more than that, it could bring her ultimate security, the kind of security which only economic self-sufficiency could guarantee:

> here we have an Empire which with decent organisation and consolidation might be absolutely self-sustaining. Nothing of the kind has ever been known before. There is no article of your food, there is no raw material of your trade, there is no necessity of your lives, no luxury of your existence which cannot be produced somewhere or other in the British Empire if the British Empire holds together and if we who have inherited it are worthy of our opportunities.[117]

But it had to be exploited properly, its exploitation encouraged and directed wisely from above: for Chamberlain, as well as being a businessman, had been a 'municipal socialist' once, and believed that the state had a vital part to play in economic development. In the tropics it could best help by providing capital and credit. There were golden eggs there to be had, but the geese would not lay without a stimulus, and the best kind of stimulus was a national commitment, with the nation's money, to open them up to private trade and industry. At the beginning of his reign at the Colonial Office, Chamberlain was full of the revolution he meant to work in colonial affairs. It would be, he told a deputation of West African interests, 'in a certain sense a new policy'.

> It is a great policy. It is indeed open to criticism, for you cannot undertake a policy of this kind without a certain amount of risk. But if the people of this country are not willing to invest some of their superfluous wealth in the development of their great estate, then I see no future for these countries, and it would have been better never to have gone there.[118]

The economic development of the empire, in the interests of all its members and subjects for perpetuity, would be the crowning achievement of the 'new imperialism'.

Like many revolutionaries, Chamberlain was ahead of his time, but only by a decade or two. What he actually achieved fell far short of a revolution, chiefly because the British taxpayer, represented by the Chancellor of the Exchequer, was not in a revolutionary frame of mind. He was not yet ready for a full-blown programme of state-aided colonial development, and not at all sure that taxes should be used for this kind of thing anyway. Chamberlain had to struggle to get anything at all past the vigilant and sceptical eye of the Treasury, and some favourite schemes he never tried to, for example, a plan to take over Rhodesia for the Crown, which he kept to himself because the Treasury, he said, 'would never give me the money that would be required to place the administration on a proper footing and at the same time to develop the estate'.[119] The idea of 'developing' colonies at all was unfamiliar and unwelcome, except in the case of 'developments' which were considered essential on grounds of security. Uganda was showered with money for a railway, though the trade it would bring was thought to be derisory, because the area could not be defended or administered easily without one. By contrast, colonies which wanted money merely to improve themselves had to make do with pittances. The sugar islands of the West Indies got £860,000 in grants between 1897 and 1905, and one or two big loans besides. But most of this was to save them from ruin, and went to settle debts. Very little of it – perhaps £280,000 – was used for anything more constructive, like agricultural research, new roads and shipping. Elsewhere outright grants were much more rare, and the rule was to lend, at around 3 per cent. In 1899, Chamberlain steered a package of £3 million worth of colonial loans through Parliament. Thereafter, the financial demands of the South African war made money tighter.

Another factor also came into play here, adding to Chamberlain's difficulties. His own people, by and large, did not share his visions and designs. His was a business morality, applied to the empire; but few of his minions – under-secretaries and other staff at the Colonial Office, colonial governors, district officers – had the same or even a similar cast of mind. There was a simple reason for that. Business people in Britain generally went into business, not into administering colonies. The latter was not a rational choice for them. It offered no scope – no honourable scope, at any rate – for making large amounts of money, and it was not supposed to be a useful occupation in any case. Administration in general – government, bureaucracy, state interference – was the bane of capitalists. So they kept out of it. When Britain needed men to run her empire, therefore, she had to look elsewhere. She needed people dedicated to serving others, not creating wealth; paternalists rather than narrow economic individualists. She found them first of all among the old paternalistic *classes* of Britain, the remnant – quite a substantial one, even in this industrial age – of her pre-capitalist aristocracy and its hangers-on; and then set about breeding new ones, in the great public schools which revived and proliferated from the 1860s on. Of course, this was not done consciously. There was no political *decision* taken to use the public schools as forcing-grounds for governors. The schools were merely responding to a demand. That is why it is foolish to *blame* them, as is sometimes done, for diverting Britain's elite and consequently distorting her dominant values away from the entrepreneurial channels they might have flowed into otherwise.[120] That result – if it was one – followed partly from the demands of the empire, which grew as time went by, for what a later public school headmaster called 'prefects' to run them, rather than 'pirates',[121] which was ironic if it was true – as we have seen it substantially was – that it was piratical motives that had been responsible for the acquisition of the empire in the first place.

Paternalists were generally conservatives when it came to the economic exploitation of their bailiwicks. They did not welcome change, especially when it threatened – as capitalist industrial development invariably did – indigenous social structures they relied on and usually respected. Their instincts and upbringing, for example, put them against treating people simply as an economic resource. As well as this, practical experience had taught them it might be dangerous. Half of Britain's troubles in India over the past century had been arguably sparked off by various measures of 'modernisation', taken in the interests of making the country more amenable to development. In Sierra Leone, in 1898, the imposition of a 'Hut Tax', requiring people to work to earn money wages, provoked a rebellion which had to be put down by military force. Britain's available military force for coping with this kind of upset was limited. She could not afford to stir her subjects up. Capitalist development threatened to do just that. So it was best avoided, in the interests not only of the 'natives', as the prefects insisted, but also of themselves.

All this stood in Chamberlain's – and capitalism's – way. Some state schemes nonetheless got through. The West Indies were given protection for their sugar industry to prevent its going under completely, for example, until the cause of its distress – foreign bounties on beet sugar – had been eradicated by international agreement in 1903. Cyprus got whole new irrigation and railway systems out of the 1899 Colonial Loans Act. The first railways were built in Sierra Leone, Lagos and the Gold Coast. Two Schools of Tropical Medicine, one in London and the other in Liverpool, were founded on Chamberlain's initiative, to study the diseases which hampered progress in the tropical empire; and numerous institutes to research into better methods of colonial agriculture and husbandry. This was something; but it did not measure up to Chamberlain's best hopes.

The purpose of it all was to ease the way for private capital to go in and develop the tropics more intensively. This proved a disappointment, too. Chamberlain felt very let down by the reluctance of capitalists to go where he wanted them to go – always excepting, of course, his faithful Rhodes. When it was a matter of gold or diamonds in South Africa or Australia capitalists flocked in, but South Africa and Australia hardly needed to be encouraged to develop. The countries which required capital most, and whose development in the long run was most vital to Britain – the primary producing, manufacture-importing regions of the tropics – were avoided in general, except by traders. Traders were all very well, but they only purchased the products of estates, they did not develop them. What Chamberlain wanted were industrial capitalists to organise tropical production on a large scale with modern methods. Occasionally, in the 1890s and the early 1900s, it was tried; there were cocoa plantations in Nigeria, for example, copra plantations in the Pacific islands, and rubber plantations in Malaya. None of these ventures came to anything except the last, and that not for some time. A lukewarm bureaucracy was partly to blame for this. West African production stayed in the hands of an inefficient native peasantry; Malayan industry in the hands mainly of the Chinese. In Chamberlain's time at the Colonial Office, the capitalists – and his minions – let him down rather. But it was only for a short while. Chamberlain had not been wrong about the capitalists' needs; he had merely anticipated them a little. In the new century, after or shortly before he left the Colonial Office in 1902, world shortages in certain primary products sent them searching again, and more urgently, for new sources and more efficient means of production; and the spadework Chamberlain had done in the tropical empire began to pay off. Rubber worked in Malaya, and became a flourishing staple industry. European gold-mining started up again on the Gold Coast when Chamberlain's railways were built. Around 1902, the soap manufacturer William Lever began looking into the possibility of farming palm trees for palm-oil in West Africa. In the same year Lancashire textile interests set up a British Cotton Growing Association to start cotton plantations in Africa. The idea of large-scale capitalist development in the tropics caught on, and the times caught up with Chamberlain.[122]

Chamberlain, however, had resigned meanwhile. Perhaps he had lost heart with the way colonial development had gone in his time. But anyway he was consumed now with a much grander vision: a new imperial programme which would subsume all the rest. His resignation from the Colonial Office was meant to leave him free to preach it to the country:

> a policy of Imperial Preference and Empire development, by means of which the resources of the Empire would be gradually and surely developed, so that the essentials for life, industry, and trade within the Empire should be available for the Empire.[123]

But this campaign, his last, was a failure. The City did not like it. Nor did most of Chamberlain's cabinet colleagues. More to the point, perhaps, the British electorate was persuaded that imperial preference entailed a sacrifice: to give tariff preferences to colonies Chamberlain would have to reimpose tariffs elsewhere, which would mean the corn laws back, and a dearer loaf. The people were not going to stand for that. Consequently the government Chamberlain had left, but which was still tainted by his views, was defeated at the polls in 1906, by the biggest margin within living memory. And with the government, by coincidence or design, also went Curzon and Milner, the foremost exponents of 'forward' imperialism.

Reaction

The ideals and the visions which men like Milner, Curzon and Chamberlain represented were sideshoots off the main stem of late nineteenth-century imperialism; they were not responsible for it. Before ever Milner, Curzon and Chamberlain had come properly on to the imperial scene, most of Britain's empire had been accumulated already, and not much of what was accumulated thereafter, saving perhaps the Boer republics, was because of them. Theirs was a minority view of the empire – or if it was not so in the 1890s, it certainly proved to be after the turn of the century. During the course of the Boer War, the Unionist government, which was closer to the national pulse than Milner in Pretoria or Curzon in Delhi could ever be, and had never been confident that the 'people' would take to a real imperial war anyway, became aware of the disaffection in the country, which a natural war-weariness, uneasiness at the methods which were being used to snuff out the enemy, and a growing suspicion that it might have been engineered by Jewish capitalists after all, was engendering. The superficiality of 'jingoism', its total dissimilarity to a real, solid imperial patriotism, was revealed as it waned when the glorious episodes of the war – the victories and the raising of sieges – dried up. There was not the kind of feeling here which would sustain any more constructive and ambitious kind of imperialism: an imperialism, for example, which threatened a dearer loaf of bread as the price to pay for a closer imperial unity. Despairing of the patriotic line, some imperial propagandists tried to persuade the people that in the long run imperialism would be good for social reform too; but it was a sophisticated argument, and never caught on. Milner found himself at his wits' end trying to find ways to 'explain to these d—d fools' – the British public – why they needed an empire, and he never succeeded properly.[124] Imperialists and the people were out of tune with one another, at variance in their assessments of what was good for the nation and for them.

Worried by the turn of public sentiment, and the ominous implication they saw in it for their chances at the next election, the government tried to soft-pedal a little, to Milner's and Curzon's consternation. In December 1902, Lord George Hamilton, fearful that Curzon was going to start something in Afghanistan, wrote to tell him of the position at home:

> The fact is that the reaction, after our recent outburst of warlike ardour, had already begun to operate, taxation is exceptionally high, trade is on the wane, distress is rife in our large towns, the weather is exceptionally cold, and all these circumstances in combination make the vast majority of the Cabinet look with apprehension and dislike on any movement or any action which is likely to produce war or disturbance in any part of the British Empire.[125]

Of all the imperialists in the field, Lord Milner was the one who was most aware of the growing isolation of his species. In September 1902, he acknowledged that he was 'out of touch with the predominant sentiment of my countrymen, the trend of opinion which ultimately determines policy'. For him, it was confirmation of the 'rottenness' of the system which allowed 'an ignorant people' to 'play with' the fortunes of an empire. Why bother, he wrote, to labour to 'keep an Empire for people who are dead set on chucking it away?' 'Representative Govt. has its merits, no doubt, but the influence of representative assemblies, organised on the party system, upon administration – 'government' in the true sense of the word – is almost uniformly bad.'[126]

When he left South Africa – in time, he hoped, for a sound man to be appointed in his place before the Liberals came in – he made himself the leader of those imperialists who wished to free colonial policy from the shackles of the party system and British democracy, and to promote the imperial union which had been Joseph Chamberlain's most disappointing failure. With his detestation of politics, he was not the most effective politician, and with his contempt for the people, he was not the most sympathetic of popular speakers. But he tried hard in both roles: an imperial Messiah in the wilderness, waiting and working patiently for the imperial mood to come upon Britain again, and for the Call, which, for him and Curzon, was to come.

Other *fin-de-siècle* imperialists did not take defeat so badly. Lord Cromer in particular was more level-headed. He saw the events of 1905–06 – the Unionists' defeat at the polls, the rejection of imperial preference, the betrayal of Milner in South Africa and Curzon in India – for what they were: not necessarily a repudiation of imperialism whole and entire, but a choice of one variety of imperialism over another. 'Anti-imperialism' was a devil almost of Milner's own conjuring: 'Few, if any, pronounced anti-imperialists exist,' Cromer wrote in 1913; 'but a wide divergence of opinion prevails as to the method of giving effect to an imperial policy.'[127] This was becoming more and more so, as political Radicals who before 1900 would have rejected all kinds of imperialism now came to accept it, when it had stopped being expansionary and expensive, lost its brief association with protectionism, and begun to be an administrative rather than a diplomatic matter. In the early twentieth century, there was more broad agreement on imperial questions than for a long time, now that its contentious aspects were out of the way; more common ground between political parties, and a wider acquiescence in the fact of empire.[128] This may have been because colonial policy was once more in tune with the 'national interest', which, for a time in the 1890s, it had not been.

Notes

1   D. R. Gillard, 'Salisbury and the Indian defence problem 1885–1902', in K. Bourne and D. C. Watt (eds), *Studies in International History* (Longman, 1967), pp. 236–48.
2   C. J. Lowe, *Salisbury and the Mediterranean, 1886–1896* (Routledge, 1965), p. 1.
3   See J. A. S. Grenville, *Lord Salisbury and Foreign Policy* (Athlone Press, 1964), Chapters 2, 4; Lowe, *op. cit.*
4   W. Woodruff, *The Impact of Western Man: A Study of Europe's Role in the World's Economy, 1750–1960* (Macmillan, 1966), pp. 152, 315, 317.
5   A. R. Colquhoun, *China in Transformation* (1899), p. 151.
6   G. N. Curzon, *Problems of the Far East* (1894), pp. 304, 421.
7   See G. C. Allen and A. G. Donnithorne, *Western Enterprise in Far Eastern Economic Development: China and Japan* (Allen & Unwin, 1954), pp. 44–5; and Colquhoun, *op. cit.*, p. 144.
8   D. C. M. Platt, *Finance, Trade and Politics: British Foreign Policy, 1815–1914* (Oxford UP, 1968), pp. 271–4.
9   W. L. Langer, *The Diplomacy of Imperialism 1890–1902*, 2 vols (Harvard UP, 1935), ii, 679.
10 L. K. Young, *British Policy in China, 1895–1902* (Oxford UP, 1970), pp. 61, 91–4.
11 Grenville, *op. cit.*, p. 305.
12 On the 'scramble' for China, see L. K. Young, *British Policy in China 1895–1902* (Clarendon Press, 1970); Grenville, *op. cit.*, Chapters 6, 13, 14, 17; W. L. Langer, *The Diplomacy of Imperialism* (2nd edn, Knopf, 1951), Chapters 6, 12, 14, 15, 21–3; Chester C. Tan, *The Boxer Catastrophe* (Columbia UP, 1955, reprinted 1967); Victor Purcell, *The Boxer Uprising* (Cambridge UP, 1963); Edmund C. Wehrle, *Britain, China and the Antimissionary Riots, 1891–1900* (University of Minnesota Press, 1966); Joseph W. Esherick, *The Origins of the Boxer Uprising* (University of California Press, 1987).
13 D. Dilks, *Curzon in India*, 2 vols (Hart Davis, 1969, 1970), i, 132.
14 S. Gopal, *British Policy in India, 1858–1905* (Cambridge UP, 1965), p. 243.
15 See F. Kazemzadeh, *Russia and Britain in Persia, 1864–1914* (Yale UP, 1968), Chapters 4–7; D. P. Singhal, *India and Afghanistan, 1876–1907* (University of Queensland Press, 1963), Chapters 9–11; *Cambridge History of India* (Cambridge UP, 1932), vi, Chapters 23, 25; Dilks, *op. cit.*, i, Chapters 5–7, ii, Chapters 2, 3, 6.
16 Grenville, *op. cit.*, p. 296.
17 Dilks, *op. cit.*, i, 68.
18 See Tim Jeal, *Explorers of the Nile: The Triumph and Tragedy of a Great Victorian Adventure* (Faber & Faber, 2011).
19 G. Cecil, *Life of Robert Marquis of Salisbury*, 4 vols (Hodder & Stoughton, 1921, 1921, 1931, 1932), iii (1931), 230.
20 R. E. Robinson and J. A. Gallagher, *Africa and the Victorians* (Macmillan, 1961), Chapter 8 *passim*.
21 Cecil, *op. cit.* (1932), iv, 139.
22 Robinson and Gallagher, *op. cit.*, p. 282.
23 *Ibid.*, p. 285.
24 Langer, *op. cit.*, pp. 103–8, 127.
25 Cecil, *op. cit.* (1932), iv, 332.
26 G. N. Sanderson, *England, Europe and the Upper Nile, 1882–99* (Edinburgh UP, 1965), p. 43.
27 K. Bourne, *The Foreign Policy of Victorian England* (Oxford UP, 1970), p. 452.
28 G. E. Buckle (ed.), *The Letters of Queen Victoria*, 3rd series (John Murray, 1930), i, 615. There is controversy over the significance of the Nile in the Anglo-German agreement of 1890. See D. R. Gillard, 'Salisbury's African policy and the Heligoland offer of 1890', *English Historical Review*, lxxv (1960), 631–53; G. N. Sanderson, 'The Anglo-German agreement of 1890 and the Upper Nile', *English Historical Review*, lxxviii (1963), 49–72; D. R. Gillard, 'Salisbury's Heligoland offer: the case against the "Witu Thesis"', *English Historical Review*, lxxx

(1965), 538–52; R. O. Collins, 'Origins of the Nile struggle', in P. Gifford and W. R. Louis (eds), *Britain and Germany in Africa* (Yale UP, 1967).

29   See G. N. Sanderson, 'England, Italy, the Nile Valley and the European balance, 1890–91', *Historical Journal*, vii (1964), 94–119.

30   See C. M. Andrew, *Théophile Delcassé and the Making of the Entente Cordiale* (Macmillan, 1968), pp. 21–5, 41ff., Chapter 5.

31   See A. J. P. Taylor, 'Prelude to Fashoda: the question of the Upper Nile, 1894–5', *English Historical Review*, lxv (1950), 52–80.

32   Andrew, *op. cit.*, p. 102.

33   *Ibid.*, p. 92.

34   Robinson and Gallagher, *op. cit.*, p. 371.

35   See *ibid.*, Chapters 8–12; Sanderson, *England, Europe and the Upper Nile*; Langer, *op. cit.*, Chapters 4, 9, 16.

36   Roger Owen, *Lord Cromer* (Oxford UP, 2004), p. 303.

37   P. Magnus, *Kitchener: Portrait of an Imperialist* (John Murray, 1958), p. 128.

38   *Parliamentary Debates*, 4th series, 72 (1899), c. 342.

39   Cecil, *op. cit.*, iv, 320.

40   J. W. Garvin, *The Life of Joseph Chamberlain* (Macmillan, 1934), iii, 211.

41   *Ibid.*, p. 210.

42   See Robinson and Gallagher, *op. cit.*, Chapter 13; Garvin, *op. cit.*, iii, Chapter 55; J. E. Flint, *Sir George Goldie and the Making of Nigeria* (Oxford UP, 1960).

43   See Langer, *op. cit.*, pp. 522–32.

44   On capitalism in South Africa, see S. Marks and R. Rathbone (eds), *Industrialisation and Social Change in South Africa* (Longman, 1982); and C. van Onselen, *Studies in the Social and Economic History of the Witwatersrand 1886–1914*, 2 vols (Longman, 1982).

45   J. G. Lockhart and C. M. Woodhouse, *Rhodes* (Hodder & Stoughton, 1963), p. 189.

46   See above, p. 87.

47   S. G. Millin, *Rhodes* (Chatto & Windus, 1952), p. 346. On Rhodes, see also P. Maylam, *Rhodes, the Tswana, and the British: Colonialism, Collaboration, and Conflict in the Bechuanaland Protectorate, 1885–1899* (Greenwood Press, 1980); A. Keppel-Jones, *Rhodes and Rhodesia* (McGill-Queens UP, 1983); R. I. Rotberg with M. S. Shore, *The Founder: Cecil Rhodes and the Pursuit of Power* (Oxford UP, 1988).

48   Robinson and Gallagher, *op. cit.*, p. 419.

49   *Ibid.*, pp. 434–7.

50   *Ibid.*, p. 434.

51   *Ibid.*, p. 433.

52   Garvin, *op. cit.*, iii, 138.

53   Robinson and Gallagher, *op. cit.*, p. 444.

54   Garvin, *op. cit.*, iii, 141.

55   *Ibid.*

56   C. Headlam (ed.), *The Milner Papers* (Cassell, 1933), i, 222.

57   *Ibid.*, i, 302 (January 1899).

58   *Ibid.*, i, 299 (December 1898).

59   A. Porter, 'Sir Alfred Milner and the Press, 1897–9', *Historical Journal*, xvi (1973), 323–39.

60   Headlam, *op. cit.* (July 1899), i, 473.

61   G. H. L. Le May, *British Supremacy in South Africa 1899–1907* (Oxford UP, 1965), pp. 19–21.

62   *Ibid.*, pp. 13, 21.

63   A. Porter, 'Lord Salisbury, Mr Chamberlain and South Africa, 1895–9', *Journal of Imperial and Commonwealth History*, i (1972), 19.

64   Grenville, *op. cit.*, p. 122.

65   Headlam, *op. cit.*, i, 473; and see E. Stokes, 'Milnerism', *Historical Journal*, v (1962), 55–6.

66   Le May, *op. cit.*, p. 28.

67   On the South African war, see Andrew Porter, *The Origins of the South African War* (Manchester UP, 1980); Ian R. Smith, *The Origins of the South African War, 1899–1902* (Longman, 1996); Peter Warwick (ed.), *The South African War* (Longman, 1980); Robinson and Gallagher, *op. cit.*; John Benyon, *Proconsul and Paramountcy in South Africa: The High Commission, British Supremacy and the Sub-Continent, 1866–1910* (University of Natal Press,

1980); J. van der Poel, *The Jameson Raid* (Oxford UP, 1951); J. S. Marais, *The Fall of Kruger's Republic* (Clarendon Press, 1961); Le May, *op. cit.*; Rotberg with Shore, *op. cit.*; Peter Warwick, *Black People and the South African War, 1899–1902* (Cambridge UP, 1983); Diana Cammack, *The Rand at War, 1899–1902* (James Currey, 1991); and later works listed in Further reading.
68 Warwick, *Black People and the South African War, 1899–1902*; W. R. Nasson, *Abraham Esau's War: A Black South African War in the Cape, 1899–1902* (Cambridge UP, 1991).
69 *Fortnightly Review*, o.s. 78 (1902), p. 3.
70 J. A. Spender, *The Life of the Rt. Hon. Sir Henry Campbell-Bannerman* (Hodder & Stoughton, 1923), i, 336.
71 Cammack, *op. cit.*; J. Krikler, *Revolution from Above, Revolution from Below: The Agrarian Transvaal at the Turn of the Century* (Oxford UP, 1993).
72 See B. J. Porter, *Critics of Empire: British Radical Attitudes to Colonialism in Africa, 1895–1914* (Macmillan, 1968); S. Koss, *The Pro-Boers* (University of Chicago Press, 1973).
73 Headlam, *op. cit.*, ii, 103.
74 *Ibid.*, p. 550.
75 *Ibid.*, p. 42.
76 *Ibid.*, p. 134, and see Eliza Riedi, 'Teaching empire: British and Dominion women teachers in the South African War concentration camps', *English Historical Review*, cxx (2005), 1316–47.
77 Headlam, *op. cit.*, ii, p. 242.
78 *Ibid.*, pp. 279–80.
79 R. Symonds, *The British and their Successors: A Study in the Development of the Government Services in the New States* (Faber & Faber, 1966), p. 37.
80 Cecil, *op. cit.*, iv, 342–3.
81 Lord Roberts, quoted in Dilks, *op. cit.*, i, 103.
82 *Ibid.*
83 Lord Roberts in Dilks, *op. cit.*, ii, p. 258.
84 Lord Cromer, *Political and Literary Essays* (1913), pp. 50–1; and see Roger Owen, *Lord Cromer* (Oxford UP, 2004).
85 Headlam, *op. cit.*, ii, 312.
86 Lord Cromer, *op. cit.*, p. 51, and cf. *ibid.*, pp. 255–6.
87 Dilks, *op. cit.*, i, 237.
88 Headlam, *op. cit.*, ii, 35, 307.
89 Lord Cromer, *Modern Egypt* (1908), ii, Part 6.
90 Dilks, *op. cit.*, i, 105.
91 Lord Hugh Cecil, *Conservatism* (1912), p. 211.
92 F. G. Hutchins, *The Illusion of Permanence* (Princeton UP, 1967).
93 Dilks, *op. cit.*, ii, p. 256.
94 R. J. Moore, *Liberalism and Indian Politics* (Edward Arnold, 1966), p. 76.
95 Dilks, *op. cit.*, i, 104.
96 *Ibid.*, i, 237.
97 *Ibid.*, ii, 133.
98 P. Woodruff, *The Men who Ruled India*, 2 vols (Cape, 1953, 1954), ii, *The Guardians*, 199.
99 Gopal, *British Policy in India 1858–1905* (Cambridge UP, 1965), 266.
100 On India from 1880 to 1905, see *ibid.*, Chapters 3–5, and S. Gopal, *The Viceroyalty of Lord Ripon, 1880–1884* (Oxford UP, 1953); Moore, *op. cit.*, Chapters 3–5; Woodruff, *op. cit.*; A. Seal, *The Emergence of Indian Nationalism* (Cambridge UP, 1968); Dilks, *op. cit.*; Nayana Goradia, *Lord Curzon: The Last of the British Moghuls* (Oxford UP, 1993).
101 Cromer, *Political and Literary Essays*, p. 25.
102 *Ibid.*, pp. 28, 256.
103 *Ibid.*, pp. 253–5.
104 See Afaf Lufti al-Sayyid, *Egypt and Cromer* (John Murray, 1968); J. Marlowe, *Cromer in Egypt* (Elek, 1970); Lord Cromer, *Modern Egypt*, and *Political and Literary Essays*, Chapters 1 and 13.
105 Dilks, *op. cit.*, i, 64, 240; J. H. Lehmann, *The First Boer War* (Cape, 1972), p. 30.
106 Dilks, *op. cit.*, i, 65, 105.
107 W. K. Hancock, *Survey of British Commonwealth Affairs* (Oxford UP, 1942), ii, Part 2, p. 3.

108 Headlam, *op. cit.*, ii, 311–12, 466; R. A. Huttenback, 'Indians in South Africa 1860–1914', *English Historical Review*, lxxxi (1966), 286.
109 Dilks, *op. cit.*, i, 227; Gopal, *British Policy in India 1858–1905*, p. 227.
110 Headlam, *op. cit.*, ii, 307–13, 466–70.
111 Cromer, *Modern Egypt*, Chapter 34.
112 Cromer, *Political and Literary Essays*, p. 350.
113 Headlam, *op. cit.*, ii, 307.
114 See J. D. Legge, *Britain in Fiji 1858–1880* (Macmillan, 1958); Flint, *op. cit.*, pp. 94–5, 258–63; M. Perham, *Lugard* (Collins, 1960), ii, Chapters 7–8.
115 See R. V. Kubicek, *The Administration of Imperialism* (Duke UP, 1969), pp. 34–7.
116 Garvin, *op. cit.*, iii, 19–20.
117 L. C. A. Knowles, *The Economic Development of the British Overseas Empire* (Routledge, 1928 edn), i, 46–7.
118 Garvin, *op. cit.*, iii, 20.
119 Kubicek, *op. cit.*, pp. 90–1.
120 M. Wiener, *English Culture and the Decline of the Industrial Spirit, 1850–1980* (Cambridge UP, 1981).
121 John Rae, quoted in *The Observer*, 6 April 1980.
122 On 'tropical development', see W. K. Hancock, *Survey of British Commonwealth Affairs* (Oxford UP, 1942), ii, Part 2, Chapter 2; S. B. Saul, 'The economic significance of "constructive imperialism"', *Journal of Economic History*, xvii (1957), 173–92; Kubicek, *op. cit.*, Chapters 4 and 6; A. G. Hopkins, *An Economic History of West Africa* (Longman, 1973); Michael Havinden and David Meredith, *Colonialism and Development: Britain and its Tropical Colonies, 1850–1960* (Routledge, 1993).
123 Sir P. Fitzpatrick, reporting Chamberlain, in [J. L. Garvin and] J. Amery, *The Life of Joseph Chamberlain* (Macmillan, 1951), iv, 529.
124 A. M. Gollin, *Proconsul in Politics* (Blond, 1964), p. 106.
125 Dilks, *op. cit.*, i, 186.
126 Headlam, *op. cit.*, ii, 421, 446, 448, 263, 364, 505.
127 Cromer, *Political and Literary Essays*, p. 246.
128 Porter, *Critics of Empire*, Chapter 9.

7 An essential compromise: 1905–14

The empire in 1905

When the Liberal Party took over the running of the empire from the Unionists in December 1905, the expansionist hurricane had already, some years back, blown itself out. 'Now,' Sir Edward Grey told President Roosevelt, 'this generation has had enough excitement, and has lost a little blood, and is sane and normal.'[1] They had got as much empire as they were going to get for a while: as much as they could manage, and more than Britain needed by most ways of calculating it. Responsible Unionists felt this as well as Liberals. The time for expansion was past; now was the time for consolidation, for making the best of the empire as it stood. That 'best' was still thought to be consider- able – and not any the less for being less shouted about. Indeed, in the twentieth century, when it was lost, we shall find the empire becoming in many ways more vital to Britain than in the nineteenth century, when it had been won. Liberals were as aware as anyone of the value of the empire, and they acted accordingly.

In 1905, it was clear that the empire was at least as necessary to Britain as it had ever been. The needs which had prompted its acquisition still remained – the need especially to succour trade and investment. In addition, years of possession had added new ties, new commitments, new layers of dependency to the original ones, all of which strength- ened the need to stay. The empire had arisen originally out of Britain's economic in- volvement in the wider world. She was still involved economically in the wider world: still living on the profits from her foreign trade and investment, and indeed living rather better on them than in the recent past. The years between the Boer War and the Great War were boom years – which was partly why Chamberlain's protectionist schemes, which were designed for a desperate situation,[2] never caught on. Between the 1880s and the 1890s, imports had increased by 11 per cent and exports by only 3 per cent; between the 1890s and the 1900s, imports shot up by 31 per cent and exports by 32 per cent, and the increase continued, at a faster rate still, until 1914. By 1910, Britain was regularly balancing her trade accounts again (goods and services), quite apart from the interest from her foreign investments.[3] And at the same time, foreign investment was booming too, reaching new record levels after 1907.[4] These increases were general ones; the British empire played no significantly larger part in British trade and investment after 1905 than it had before: Europe and America were, as always, the staples (Europe for trade, America for investment). But still the British empire's contribution was a very large and vital one, and more than kept pace with the rest of the world's. The trend, which we noted before, for most of Britain's export trade to be with 'underdeveloped' countries, continued into the 1900s, with nearly 70 per cent of exports going there in 1909–13, which was more than ever before. The proportion going to the countries of the British empire rose slightly, from 33.6 per cent in the 1890s to 35 per cent in the 1900s. Africa in particular began to fulfil the promise Chamberlain had seen for it in the 1890s, doubling its trade with Britain between 1900 and 1913.[5] Foreign investment was more empire-orientated than trade – which was not surprising because most of the empire was 'underdeveloped', and underdeveloped countries need to borrow capital more than they can afford to purchase goods. Between 1900 and 1914, new capital investment abroad climbed from £45 million to £200 million, and 42 per cent of it went to British colonies.[6] All of which did nothing to reduce the intrinsic importance of the empire to the British economy; or the extrinsic importance of those parts of it, like Suez and Simonstown, which were considered strategically essential to guard Britain's trade with the rest of the world.

Nothing had changed since the 1890s to loosen the bonds between Britain and her empire. Britain still needed overseas outlets for her trade and investment, and certain of those outlets she needed as much as ever to control to make them politically and economically secure. It could be disputed whether her economic interest had *ever* required this kind of security, but it could not be claimed that she needed it now any less than before. And as time went on, and people grew accustomed to using and depending on the colonies for certain things – Malaya for rubber, India for tea, Egypt for cotton, West Africa for cocoa (all of these were commodities whose large-scale production had been a consequence of the establishment of British rule) – the bonds grew stronger and tighter. The dependence of his constituency on Egyptian cotton, for example, made an imperialist of at least one Liberal Member of Parliament: to supply Bolton's looms with raw material they were 'bound to remain' in Egypt: 'You may say that we in Lancashire are selfish. But we have got to look after our business.'[7] The British economy was becoming geared to colonial markets and products: not wholly or predominantly, but significantly and intricately. Maybe if at a stroke the empire could have been got rid of, and India, Malaya and the rest become independent countries, trade and investment there would have carried on as before, and the repercussions on Britain would have been negligible or even beneficial (as the precedent of the American colonies suggested). Yet it would have required an enormous act of faith to act on this hypothesis. As Britain's interests became more and more closely bound up with those of her colonies, the less likely she was to want to chance any other kind of arrangement – to risk opening the cage door in the hope that the canary would still co-operate. From the extent and the complexity of her economic involvement in her colonies the inference had to be that if the empire were got rid of, then the ramifications would be widespread and immensely damaging, and would require an enormous and complex readjustment to cope with them.

And that – if it had occurred – would not have been an end to the upheaval, for the empire was important to Britain in other, less material ways too. As any institution, evolved for whatever purpose, becomes established and customary, there develop other bonds between it and the people involved in it, which may be incidental to its main function, but which are nonetheless real, and tend to become powerful factors in support of its conservation. The empire did more for people than merely profit them: some of them it gave jobs to, or honours, or their authority, or a mythology, or a sense of purpose, or a feeling of pride and superiority; these had not been significant motives for acquiring the empire in the first place, but they could be strong reasons for not wanting to abandon it. It was the empire which had created these needs, visions and ideals in the first place; having been created, they in turn needed the empire to satisfy them. How deep this symbiosis went – just how emotionally and vocationally necessary the empire was to how many people – was never easy to gauge. It was some time, and perhaps only when the connection had weakened a little, before the social effects of breaking it could be even hazily observed. But it was clear in 1905 that the empire had bitten fairly deeply into certain sections of British society.

Some people it bit so deep that they migrated there. Between 1870 and 1900, more than 7 million had emigrated from the British Isles; in the next ten years over 3 million more. Not all of them went to British colonies, but more did during this last decade than ever before, about three-quarters.[8] They mostly left kin back in Britain who thus maintained a personal, family link with the overseas empire. And this was not the limit of the empire's demand on British manpower. It employed directly about 20,000 men as colonial admin-istrators, 146,000 as soldiers permanently garrisoning the colonies (8,000 officers and 138,000 men),[9] and many more as clerks, agricultural advisers, forestry officers, education officers, engineers, surveyors, policemen, doctors and the like, besides countless others engaged in directing and supplying them at home. The empire, therefore, was a source of employment and a means of satisfying ambition. Nearly all the men it employed except the non-commissioned soldiers were from the upper and middle classes. Many of them were good at what they did, but good for little else, which made their dependence on the empire even greater. That will have been emphasised by the empire's other attractions, which soon turned into necessities once the upper classes got used to them. It was a tre-mendous source of excitement, for example; of adventure in exotic settings, which appealed to young men in particular, as can be seen from the juvenile literature of the time,[10] and against which scarcely any occupation in dull unbending Britain could hope to compete. Big-game hunting was probably the apotheosis of this.[11] Some of the excite-ment was sensual. The empire offered opportunities for various kinds of physical attachment which, while by no means absent in Britain, were becoming more and more frowned upon towards the end of the nineteenth century (it was then, for example, that the most draconian Victorian laws against homosexuality were passed), and in any case could be indulged in far more freely, openly and with more desirable partners overseas. The evidence for widespread philandering by Britons in the colonies is incontrovertible. One or two historians have tentatively suggested that it may have been an original *cause* of Britain's imperial expansion: 'surplus sex-urges', rather than 'surplus capital'. Ronald Hyam believes it may explain how young male Britons could be found to stay and run the empire, in circumstances which would otherwise – despite the adventure – have been 'intolerable'.[12] Jobs, adventure and sex together comprised a powerful cement, bonding the upper classes of society in Britain to the empire they served (Figure 7.1).

The empire also had a wider importance. Certain British institutions came to depend on it, albeit indirectly. The public schools are the obvious one: revived and transformed in the later nineteenth century, as we have seen, very largely in order to cater for the empire's needs, their whole ethos – superiority, authority, service – requiring the existence of colo-nial subjects to feel superior to, exact authority over, and serve.[13] The British monarchy gleaned obvious prestige from the empire. It may have been vital to the preservation of Britain's very nationality: this great extra-national enterprise in which English, Scots, Welsh and some Irish could all proudly share.[14] The Christian churches, of course, were deeply involved. More generally, albeit vaguely and unquantifiably, it attracted 'ordinary' people, many of whose lives must have been enriched, albeit vicariously, by the empire and its various popular cultural accretions: the boys' adventure stories, the patriotic poems, the songs and marches, the thrice-told tales of the heroes of empire; all of which broadened

Figure 7.1 Loyal sons. This music-hall song from 1890 lauded the fidelity of the self-governing
colonies towards their 'mother country', which was good to know at a time when
Britain was becoming so vulnerable at home. Similar songs celebrated the loyalty of the
'Macs', 'Paddies' and even the Indians.

horizons, and puffed out loyal breasts. If popular literature was any guide, the empire by
1905 was well knitted into the fabric of British culture.[15]

This was new. Before the 1880s, at the earliest, the empire had not figured high among
most Britons' priorities, and with the large majority of them, possibly not at all. It can be
argued that they were fundamentally pro-empire nonetheless, with their true imperial
feelings coded, and so needing to be teased out of contemporary cultural productions (by
'cultural theorists', usually); but this is a controversial procedure, and its findings too
tenuous to have merited inclusion in the earlier chapters of this book.[16] What we can say
is, first, that overt references to the empire are very rare indeed in mid-Victorian culture
at all levels: take Dickens, for example, who appealed to a wide range of readerships, but
whose interest in the British empire seems infinitesimal beside his fascination with the
European continent; and, second, that if the fundamental premise of this book is correct,
there is no *need* to posit an imperial or imperialist culture in Britain in order to explain
how (practical) imperialism arose. Material factors are sufficient on their own. Culture
followed on, and, in fact, quite a distance behind. It is only in the 1880s that you find
significant 'empire' genres starting to appear in literature, painting, architecture and
music (again, at all levels), and not until the 1900s that they really make their presence
felt. Their peaks probably came in the inter-war period, or even just afterwards, curiously, when the British empire was already doomed. (The same, incidentally, is found in

all other European countries with colonies.[17]) In the 1890s and 1900s, we have Kipling; Elgar's famous 'imperial' marches; G. A. Henty's most imperialist books for boys (before then he had mainly taken historical themes); the most 'imperial' examples of English monumental architecture (that is, neo-Roman); and the 'jingoistic' music-hall songs that so depressed the anti-imperial theorist J. A. Hobson in 1901.[18] Imperial culture had become difficult to ignore.

But it is still possible to exaggerate it, even in this hothouse period. So far as 'high' art was concerned, imperial subjects were disapproved of by the *cognoscenti*, who rated softer and domestic themes rather more highly, and consequently tended to look down their noses at Kipling's and Elgar's 'vulgarities'. (Kipling was even too strong for Elgar.[19]) Sir Arthur Sullivan, who wrote more imperial works than Elgar,[20] was similarly sniffed at, though in his case the flippant character of much of his other music (the Savoy operas) will have played a part. Painting imperial battle-scenes, rather than rural land-scapes, still lifes, portraits or female nudes, almost guaranteed rejection by the Royal Academy. Architectural critics were similarly sniffy over the imposing but dour new main front of Buckingham Palace, for example, preferring – by this time – less pretentious Queen Anne, free-style Gothic, Arts and Crafts or 'eclectic' architectures. Of course we should not read too much into this. Arty people were a class apart.[21] But if imperialism was as knitted into British culture to the extent that the political noise it was making might lead one to expect, it should surely have shown up more in these 'higher' reaches.

Even in the 'lower' ones, there is little evidence that it percolated very deeply, despite the efforts of middle-class propaganda organisations to spread the imperial gospel there. Those jingoistic music-hall songs, for example, represented only a very small proportion of the total number that were sung on the boards even at times of great imperial excite-ment, like the Boer War; they are matched by songs that can be seen as implicitly critical of empire, those that bewailed the treatment of the poor 'Tommy' who was called on to sustain it, for example; and were hardly found at all in less exciting times. The ubiqui-tous children's literature featuring the empire was usually foisted on them by middle-class authors, like Henty and Bessie Marchant (for the girls), partly in order to wean working-class kids away from what were seen as the baleful effects of their own 'penny dreadfuls', which still, however, enjoyed large sales. Whether the formers' imperialist lessons really took hold on their young readers is impossible to say. (There were working men who denied it, but they were mainly socialists, and so may have been less susceptible.) Adult popular literature, and the people's theatre, steered clear of imperialism (apart from the odd allusion) in probably 95 per cent of cases.[22] So it was possible to avoid. In the case of a large proportion of the working classes, with more material priorities to concern them (like where their next meal was coming from), and alternative ideals to attract them (like socialism), it was easy enough, especially after the hothouse had cooled down, *circa* 1901.

Whatever the cultural record suggests, however, there can be little doubt that for many of the upper and middle classes – not all, and possibly not even a majority, but a lot all the same – the empire was popular, and did a great deal, for their souls and spirits as well as their pockets. Without the empire, the public schools and the monarchy and the churches would doubtless have adapted (as they did later), and the middle classes might have found new spiritual and sexual sops. There is no reason to think that the empire was in any real sense 'essential' to the middle classes, just as there is little empirical evi-dence that it was 'essential' to the survival of their capitalist economic system. It could have disappeared, and both survived. But it would have been a wrench. The empire had insinuated itself into many aspects of the British way of life; merely by existing, therefore, it was strengthening its claim to exist. The longer it existed, the more Britain became entangled with it, and the less easy it became to contemplate disbanding or losing it.

This being so, it was fortunate that there appeared for the moment to be no prospect of losing it. For perhaps the first time in 30 years the empire appeared relatively secure in 1905; safe, in any event, from external threats. In the 1890s it had seemed for a time that Britain's grasp of her empire might just be prised from her by besieging rivals, but she had stood firm, and in the 1900s, the advancing troops appeared suddenly all to have fallen back. The far eastern 'scramble' which nearly everyone predicted never transpired: Russia's military credibility was toppled by Japan before she could ever test it on Britain, and Britain was in alliance with the victor to provide an adequate insurance there. Elsewhere the main points of friction with her two main colonial rivals, France and Russia, were gradually smoothed away by agreement before they could explode into conflict: Persia divided between Britain and Russia in 1907, the Middle East and North Africa similarly demarcated between Britain and France in 1904. Victory over the Boers had guaranteed security in South Africa, for a time. The 1900s were not by any means a carefree time for Britain, but the cares she had were not by and large colonial ones. If France and Russia receded into the background as potential enemies, Germany soon loomed larger to take their place; but the German threat was primarily a naval and European one, requiring to be met in a European ambit, and only very indirectly a threat to Britain's colonial position. The threat was provided for by the Foreign Office, the War Office, the Admiralty, and the Committee for Imperial Defence; the Colonial Office did not need to trouble its head over it. The pressures in the 1900s, therefore, were different, centring on Europe. If the empire had to be fought for, it would have to be fought for there. In the world at large – on the frontiers of the empire itself – the pressures had eased off.[23]

On the frontiers Britain had things under control; within the frontiers of the empire, too, little appeared to endanger her hold: nothing in the way of rebellion or disaffection that could not comfortably be contained. Yet here the impression of power and security which Britain's huge, powerful empire gave was not altogether a true one, for it was something more – or less – than power which was the real source of Britain's control. It seemed a marvel: so many millions of people, scattered so wide, ruled over by such a mere handful of Britons, but it was a marvel of diplomacy, of political dexterity, rather than of real power.

There was, in truth, very little of that. Britain had too few soldiers ever to hold down the whole empire forcibly, as her difficulties during the Boer wars had graphically shown. She was unhappy about relying on soldiery to do it in any case, because of its tyrannical connotations, and its tendency – as she had learned from her own domestic experience early in the nineteenth century – to provoke more unrest than it subdued. This was why the military had long been withdrawn from regular public order duties in Britain, to be replaced there by a supposedly more consensual 'police'. That was tried in the colonies too in the later nineteenth century, with police forces fashioned on London Metropolitan principles being set up and recruiting locally, in order to soften the sharpest edges of the colonial relationship, but not altogether successfully. Often it was something of a sham, the word 'police' merely masking a cruder kind of force, as in Canada, in 1869, for example, where the early 'Mounties' were seen by their founder as a kind of cavalry really, 'not … *expressly* military, but … *styled* police' in order to make them more acceptable to the local community; or in those colonies where the very different 'Irish' model of policing – much more military, armed, alien – soon came to oust the London pattern. In any case, most locally recruited colonial policemen turned out to be of low quality, because of the stigma that attached to the job in their own communities; and were far too thin on the ground to be able to control things on their own.[24] They were not the chief reason for the relative stability of the British empire at this time. That was more subtly achieved.

It was done mainly through accommodation: adapting to circumstances, and, in particular, to the wishes of local people who the British thought could be of use to them. This, of course, had always been Britain's way. Without some degree of collaboration, she could never have won her empire in the first place: whether it be the collaboration of individual quislings, or of kings and princes seeking help against neighbouring rivals, or her own people's willing collaboration as settlers. Her techniques of accommodation were brilliantly successful; she made her colonial control tolerable enough to enough of her subjects, first, to justify her claims as to its beneficence – it was true that a large number of her subjects were content to be ruled by her; and second, to restrict disaffection to an amount which could easily be contained by the force she had at hand. But there was a further corollary to this policy, which was that Britain's effective control over her empire was limited, her freedom of action restricted, to those actions which would keep her collaborators content. To this extent – and it was a considerable extent – she did not in fact control the empire which in theory she was sovereign over; she could not do anything she liked in, with or for it. And the limitations to her imperial power, in the first decade or so of the new century, were as important determinants of her colonial policy as was the power itself.

The Liberals

This was the empire the Liberals inherited from the Unionists in December 1905. What they would do with it was a matter for conjecture. Their past record on Ireland, the Sudan and South Africa still dogged them, and hardly recommended them to Imperialists. Some Conservatives were persuaded by their own propaganda that they were a bunch of tender-minded Little Englanders who would give the empire away as soon as blink. But the Liberals assuredly were not that, and if one thing was certain in December 1905, it was that the empire would not be given away. It was, as we have seen, too valuable to Britain to give it away; there was no pressing need to; and anyway the Liberal Party did not want to.

Liberals had different ideas about the empire from those of the Unionists. But they were not against it. During the Boer War some of them had put up a show of opposition which the Unionists regarded (as all criticism of governments in wartime tends to be regarded) as unpatriotic. But very few of these were in any general sense 'anti-imperialist', and those who were, were easily outnumbered by a group on the further wing of the party which refused all but the most respectful and innocuous criticism, and believed that 'imperialism' was at least as apposite a creed for a Liberal as for a Conservative, and as consistent with his or her tradition. After all, Palmerston had been a Liberal, and Chamberlain at one time. And Sir Charles Dilke, who was widely credited with having started off the whole imperialist movement with a travel book he wrote in the 1860s, and Lord Rosebery, who had sustained it as Prime Minister after Gladstone, still were. Ideologically imperialism could be squared as easily with Liberalism as with Conservatism: if a Liberal felt strongly enough about his Liberalism, it was arguable that he should want to bestow it on others. Some of the keenest imperialists had always called themselves Liberals, spreading 'enlightenment' by conquest; Conservatives never had such an inspiring incentive, for who wants to spread a status quo? It may not have been a good argument, but it sustained perhaps a third of the Liberal Party in its 'Liberal imperialism'. 'Liberal imperialists' like Richard Haldane, Sir Edward Grey and Herbert Henry Asquith were men, whom all but the most hidebound Conservative imperialist could trust; and when the new Liberal Cabinet announced on 10 December included these three in it, it should have been enough to reassure anyone that the empire was not going to be disbanded without a struggle, even with Lloyd George, Morley and the ambiguous Campbell-Bannerman also there from the other wing. The new Colonial Secretary, Lord Elgin, had never been an active member of the Liberal-imperialist group. But he was surely safe too: educated at that seminary of imperialism Balliol College, Oxford, and until recently Viceroy of India, which it was difficult to be and *not* be an imperialist. His under-secretary, Winston Churchill, had not long defected from the Tory camp. Perhaps the only real worry was John Morley, a radical put in charge of India. His true colours had yet to be revealed. But Morley apart, the new cabinet of 1905, in the posts where it mattered, was pretty well tarred with the imperialist brush.

Where the Liberals differed from the Conservatives was in the means by which they felt the empire would be best secured. They disapproved of the Conservatives' imperialism: especially that of Curzon, who could not feel secure in India until his ramparts stretched across to the Caspian Sea and beyond, and of Milner, for whom the only loyal Briton had to be of British 'race', and the only safe non-Briton was a subordinate one. Milner's demise was especially sweet to the Liberals: a vote they passed against him in the Commons in March 1906 was deplored by his biographer as 'a mean and pitiful exhibition of party spite'[25] – but, as an anti-democrat, Milner could have expected little better from the democracy. They rejoiced in the fall of Milnerism, but then they – or those who were interested enough – set to work to make the empire better (as they believed) without him. For it was not the empire they opposed so much as the methods the late government had employed to get it – what Campbell-Bannerman in 1899 called 'the vulgar and bastard imperialism of irritation and provocation and aggression, of clever tricks and manoeuvres against neighbours, and of grabbing everything even if we have no use for it ourselves';[26] and also the methods its proconsuls had employed to run it, which the Liberals held were less likely to preserve and strengthen it than to weaken it, by creating tensions within it. More alive than the Conservatives to the underlying fragility of Britain's imperial authority, they were wary of trying to impose security by force alone. Less suspicious, too, than Conservatives tended to be of the designs of foreign powers on the colonies (which anyway, as we have seen, were not so ominous in their time as in the 1890s), they saw less *need* to impose security by force. And more sanguine than Conservatives about mankind, even non-Anglo-Saxon mankind, they were prepared to consider alternatives to force to achieve security.

It was sometimes said that the Liberals were less realistic and more idealistic than the Conservatives. This was not so. The Conservatives – or some of them – had their idealism, which was an imperial idealism. Sometimes that could be a highly unrealistic thing. And the Liberals were aware of realities, but of different realities: less aware of the reality of foreign enmity and malevolence, which was the only reality Conservatives tended to see; more aware of the reality of Britain's vulnerability, of the sheep's body under the wolf's skin, which they believed could not support the weight the Conservatives had heaped on to it. No less than the Conservatives, the Liberals were affected by what was politic, as much as by what was right.

It was for this kind of reason that the Liberal government rejected, in the first place, the expansion of the empire, because they saw no need for it. 'Nobody,' wrote Morley, '... means to give anything up', but the new cabinet would be 'in the highest degree jealous both of anything that looks like expansion, extension of protectorates, spheres of influence, and the like; and of anything with the savour of militarism about it'.[27] The only place where expansion was still going on – in Somaliland – the Liberals stopped it. They also of course vetoed Chamberlain's schemes for imperial federation and tariffs, which, they believed, were likely to defeat Chamberlain's own purpose. The best way to cement imperial unity, they argued, was not to institutionalise it. The tighter the formal bonds, the more damaging would be the tensions between widely scattered nations with divergent interests. This was the British government's theme at the Colonial Conference (of the dominions) held in London in 1907. They felt the same, of course, about Ireland. To use an analogy the Edwardians would not have approved of: Britain and her dominions were living together amicably; if they got formally married, the relationship would be far more likely to break down. Certainly Britain should not try to *force* her colonies to marry her – impose imperial unity from the centre, as the Conservatives were doing in South Africa: coercing the Boers into the empire and by so doing alienating them. Instead she should rely on loyalty born of trust and liberty to create a natural bond of sentiment between her and her colonies. 'Liberals will not cease to believe,' wrote Herbert Samuel in 1902, 'that the only guarantee of an empire's unity is the contentedness of the peoples who compose it.'[28] The only way to get lasting imperial loyalty was to make the colonies *want* to remain united to Britain; and to get this loyalty, she had to show she trusted them. The Liberals had done this in Canada half a century before, reconciled both the British and the French there to the empire by giving them self-government; and Canada was still part of the empire: more secure than South Africa, more secure even than Ireland, where the Conservatives had not shown this same kind of trust. To a lesser extent they applied the same kind of reasoning to the dependent empire: if they could succeed in securing the Indians' loyalty and confidence, said Lord Ripon in 1885, then 'we may contemplate without fear the intrigues of foreign foes or the efforts of internal opponents'.[29] Liberals were fully aware, therefore, of the essential collaborative nature of British imperial authority; the importance, to its survival, of compromise and accommodation.[30]

Between 1905 and 1914, therefore, things were quieter on the colonial front: as the main tide of the great contemporary debate about security and foreign policy shifted again to Europe and the Army and Navy, and left the empire alone, except to ask how it could help. Interest in the empire narrowed down to a few specialists and parliamentary crotchet-mongers. The conduct of the colonies' affairs was left to lesser, or less dynamic, men than before, for a more pragmatic approach to their problems, and a gentler one. The dynamic men had had great visions of the empire they were building. Their successors had none: 'I can answer for today,' said their first Indian Secretary; 'I can do pretty well for tomorrow; the day after tomorrow I leave to providence,'[31] and the deepest thoughts of Lord Crewe, who at different times was both Colonial Secretary and Indian Secretary in the Liberal government, were along the same lines:

> What will be the future of India, fifty, sixty, or a hundred years hence, need not, I think, trouble us. It is on the knees of the gods, and all we have to do is to provide, as best we can, for the conditions of the moment, having, of course, an eye to the future, but not troubling ourselves about what may happen in days when, to use Sheridan's words – 'all of us are dead and most of us are forgotten'.[32]

Consequently there was little attempt in the 1900s to force the empire into any pattern. Rather it was allowed to go its own way: the pressures which existed in one direction or another in its different provinces left to express and resolve themselves with little attempt on the part of Whitehall to stop or divert them in the interest of any extraneous ideal or plan. Not even the demands of humanity, or liberalism, were allowed to stand in their way if the price was the creation of another tension, another obstacle to collaboration. The Liberals' chief humanitarian act in the colonial field was to put an end to the importation of Chinese indentured labourers into South Africa to work the gold mines – the thing for which Milner was censured; which was easy enough because Chinese labour was widely resented in South Africa anyway: the current was running with the Liberals.[33] On other South African matters, such as the native franchise, it was not; and the government spent only a very little time trying to battle against it before turning around and swimming, regretfully, the other way.

South African union

In South Africa, collaboration had to be with the white communities there, because it was the white communities whose loyalty Britain needed for an easy passage. As yet the favour of the African communities could be of no political value to her, and that of the Indians in South Africa hardly more. Consequently the Europeans were appeased at the expense of the Africans and Indians.

The loyalty of its own people in South Africa the British government presumed it could count on. But the Afrikaners were a different matter. Their incorporation in the British empire had been extremely unwilling. The likelihood was that it was still resented. For many Liberals in 1905, the whole unhappy affair of the war, the way it had been conducted in its later stages, the annexation of the two republics, and the way they had been run since, had not only not improved matters in South Africa but had made them worse, by sorely trying the loyalty of the very large Afrikaner population in Cape Colony. Between them Chamberlain and Milner had stirred up so much bad feeling in South Africa that it could lose them all they had gained, and very likely more.[34] The 'only hopeful policy', thought Lord Ripon, was the old Canadian strategy: to try to court white South Africa's affection by magnanimity.[35] The two Boer republics should have their self-government restored to them – now, while Britain could gain credit from the concession and still guarantee the most fundamental of her interests there. If they waited, wrote Churchill, what they might have given on their own terms would only at some later date be 'jerked and twisted from our hands' on terms which would lose them everything.[36]

So, in December 1906, in a dramatic reversal of previous policy, the new government restored full responsible self-government to the Transvaal, and six months later to the Orange Free State. In May 1910, they reaped the first reward: the prized ambition of British colonial diplomacy for decades – a new Union of South Africa, which the two new colonies agreed to join with the Cape and Natal. It was a Union two provinces of which – the new ones – specifically excluded non-Europeans from their franchise. In another, Natal, they had only a paper franchise. At the Cape the franchise was less racially restricted, but the effect of Union was to dilute its effect. Membership of the Union parliament was limited to 'British subjects of European descent'. Non-Europeans, therefore, got a raw deal from the South African policy of the Liberal government; many Liberals, and many Liberal South Africans, saw and deplored this. Non-Europeans would always be a majority in South Africa, said the Cape Boer Jan Hofmeyr; in the interests of white South Africa's own security, they should try to 'reconcile them with our political institutions'.[37] John Merriman, another South African, remarked that as a 'safety-valve' the Cape franchise in the past had been a great boon: 'our natives have increased both in wealth and in habits of industry and civilization. They have given little or no trouble.'[38] Sir Charles Dilke in England warned that an empire based on white domination would be certain to come to a bad end.[39] Even the British Colonial Secretary, the cautious old Elgin, was aware of the implications of refusing political rights to three-quarters of the population of South Africa: 'the time must come when there will be danger of a collision between the white and coloured races unless the relations between them are fair and equitable'.[40] Some time in the future the non-whites would have to be conciliated, but for the moment – and it was only the 'conditions of the moment' which Liberal Colonial Secretaries felt they could properly act for – the Afrikaners needed conciliating more. 'We on this side,' said Winston Churchill, 'know that if British dominion is to endure in South Africa it must endure with the assent of the Dutch.'[41] They were too many, and too proud, permanently to be held in subjection.

The assent of the Boers to remain within the British empire was not easily secured. The offer of self-government to them was magnanimous, but by itself not enough. The settlements of 1906 and 1910 were grimly bargained for. The Boers' constitution had to be of their own making, not one imposed on them by Downing Street. In particular, they would not accept self-government at the expense of their own deeply and religiously held conviction, uncompromisingly and unambiguously laid down in the first constitution of the old Transvaal Republic (1858), 'to permit no equality between coloured people and the white inhabitants either in church or state'. When they had surrendered to the British at Vereeniging in May 1902, one of the conditions, which the latter had agreed to, was that this question was theirs to settle. For the Transvaal, therefore, the British government could not in honour insist on equality. Whether it could for the Union was another matter, but the Afrikaners in discussions with British commissioners sent out in 1906 to negotiate a basis for self-government, and despite the representations of the Cape Liberals, made it clear that they were adamant on this too: no colour-bar, no Union. And as Jan Smuts said in 1908, while 'the political status of the natives is no doubt a very important matter' (though he never showed signs of conviction in this), '... vastly more important to me is the Union of South Africa'.[42] It was to Liberal ministers too. The Europeans-only clauses in the South Africa Bill were 'regretted' by the government, but they were 'part of an essential compromise'; if they were struck out, 'the Union would be smashed'.[43] They put the best face they could on it by expressing the hope that a more liberal attitude must prevail in the northern states when they were made to feel more secure in a Union, and brought in the lee of a more egalitarian south wind from the Cape. They also did something to compensate for their surrender on the main issue: they did not let the South Africans have Swaziland, Bechuanaland and Basutoland, but retained them as protectorates under direct Colonial Office control; they imposed a clause on the Union constitution reserving to the British government any South African legislation which was racially discriminatory; they provided that four nominated senators in the Union parliament should be experts in native affairs; and they tried to 'entrench' the limited Cape coloured franchise by making its abrogation dependent on a two-thirds majority of both houses.[44] They would have liked to do more: disapproval of South African racial politics was hardly less fashionable then than in the later days of apartheid. But they felt it was impossible: by which they meant that to impose a Liberal solution on an unwilling people was too costly politically to contemplate. 'I would earnestly appeal to the House,' said the Colonial Under-Secretary in 1909, 'and to every man who hears me, to look the facts in the face, and realise that we cannot get our way, that we have no power to get it, and to pass the Bill and trust to the people of South Africa.'[45]

The illiberalism of the South Africans' constitution, however, did not derogate from the Liberal credit the government got for the decision to grant it to them. Self-government, Churchill admitted to the House of Commons in February 1906, was not a 'moral principle', and when it clashed with moral principles – and he was thinking of the principle of racial justice – he believed that sometimes it should be 'over-borne'. But self-government was 'a fundamental maxim of Liberal colonial policy'; it was 'the master-key of many of the problems which embarrass and perplex us'; it was 'one of the most precious gifts we can bestow'.[46] For the Liberals' faith in self-government, their South African policy was a great triumph and a great vindication. When it was proposed, Balfour had denounced it as 'the most reckless experiment ever tried in the development of a great colonial policy',[47] and Milner described himself as doing 'nothing but … write letters, … and mutter curses, … at the appalling mess which these bunglers are making of South Africa'.[48] Neither man could conceive of a trustworthy Boer. But the immediate outcome only showed how wrong they could be, and had been all along, not to trust their enemies. Most of the Boer leaders were reconciled; from sniping at British cavalry from behind *kopjes*, some of them even became British imperialists: 'I fought against the British,' said Botha, 'but I am a firm upholder of the Commonwealth.'[49] One of them in 1917 became a member of the British War Cabinet. And their loyalty was demonstrated beyond doubt when at the outbreak of the Great War, they put down a nationalist rebellion of Afrikaners, their own people. The Liberals' 'reckless experiment' in fact strengthened the empire materially. It bound South Africa to Britain far more closely than Milner's policy of repression and racial gerrymandering had done. It secured the Navy's long route to India, and the wealth of the Witwatersrand, to Britain for 50 years. And it restored to British imperial policy some of that moral kudos which Liberals had seen ebbing away from it in the frantic years of 'jingoism' and *realpolitik*. The South African Union was the Liberals' proudest achievement in the colonial field.

Yet South Africa was never quite the model prodigal. She was too wayward, and Britain's effective powers of discipline almost non-existent. It was usually on racial matters that South Africa offended, especially in her conduct towards Indian immigrants, who had a powerful voice for their grievances, a protest movement led by the young Gandhi; and a vast sensitive audience for them in India. Natal's treatment of Indians was a constant embarrassment to the British government, with Gandhi there displaying the most devoted loyalty to the empire in word and in deed (in the Boer War, he had organised an ambulance corps which served it with great distinction and bravery; he did the same to help British forces put down an African rebellion in 1906; and in 1914 was to support the British war effort powerfully) – and then calling on its protection against the Natal whites; and with the Viceroy of India, too, to back his case.[50] That Britain felt she could do little to help was a measure of the real weakness which lay under the illusion of her imperial authority. In 1906, she did try once to assert her authority over Natal (which Churchill called 'the hooligan of the British Empire') to stop her executing 12 African rebels tried under the most dubious judicial procedures. The Natal government replied by resigning *en masse*, and the Colonial Office had to retreat.[51] Thereafter Britain was chary of as much as criticising the actions of South Africans. They could so easily resort to the blackmail of mass resignation, the only counter to which would have been for Britain to step in and take over direct control of the country once more, which, as well as being expensive, would have upset the delicately cemented accommodations of 1906 and 1910.

A future Colonial Under-Secretary, Colonel J. E. B. Seely, commented sadly in April 1906 that 'A spirit seemed to have grown up in the last year or two that the British Empire was a thing which had no common principle, that it was to be bound together by other means or by no means at all.'[52] This was true, and it was dictated by circumstances. In theory, the British flag stood for certain standards of conduct which Britain had the right to enforce on her self-governing subjects. In practice, as *The Times* said in 1913, 'If the Government were to make any attempt to enforce this policy, the breakup of the Empire would follow'[53]; or as the Colonial Secretary in 1914 told the Commons more picturesquely: the empire was held together by a silken cord: 'twist this cord into a whiplash' and 'the crack of that lash would be the knell of your Empire'.[54] The empire was as fragile as this. Seely, while he was still a backbencher, professed that in that case he did not want it: 'If they were to abandon the principles upon which the Empire was founded, better a thousand times the Empire were shattered in pieces.'[55] But they were empty words. On cooler consideration, Seely and the Liberal Party preferred to compromise their principles, and keep the empire.[56]

Egypt and India: Morley–Minto

From one point of view, conciliation in South Africa had not been too hard a pill to swallow. Afrikaners were very rude Europeans, but they were Europeans still. For racially conscious British people in the 1900s, therefore, collaboration with them was acceptable. With 'orientals', however, it might be a different matter. The common stereotype of the 'oriental' in the 1900s, especially the ambitious, educated one, was that he was incompetent and untrustworthy. For years the British empire had had perforce to collaborate with such people but generally it had been with the conservative, and hence less demanding, classes of them – Indian princes, the Manchus in China, and the like. For a time this had sufficed, and in some colonies it sufficed still. But in others the traditional ruling classes could no longer command the loyalty they had boasted before from their subjects – eroded away, perhaps, by their collaboration – and were consequently losing their value to Britain. In India and Egypt, notably, the forces of nationalism were growing and filching support from the collaborators: and so it was these forces which needed conciliating, or else repressing, now. The prospect of being nice to the classes of 'natives' the British always affected to despise most was a distasteful one, and distasteful especially to the men on the spot, the colonial officials. But in both Egypt and India the Liberals considered it necessary to widen the basis of collaboration, and tried it. Their purpose was, by granting timely concessions, to win over moderate nationalists to co-operate with the British, and hence to isolate the extremists.

In Egypt, it did not seem to have this effect. Partly this was because its implementation was inept, partly because the forces of Egyptian nationalism were too strong. In Egypt, which was never called a colony and was supposed to revert to the Egyptians after its finances had been put in order, the nationalists' expectations were high, and not to be placated by sops. Nationalist feeling was stimulated by revolutionary example in neighbouring Turkey, and angered by certain insensitivities perpetrated by their British rulers: an infamous injustice at Denshawai in 1906, when a misunderstanding provoked a village riot which was brutally suppressed; statements and actions which appeared to favour Coptic Christians at the expense of Muslims; a proposal in 1909 to delay for a further

40 years after 1968 the Suez Canal's reversion to the Egyptian state: nationalism fed hungrily on such insults. Its more general complaint against the British was that, while they had done wonders for the material condition of Egypt and her people, they had done nothing to further their political progress. By 1907, nationalism in Egypt was, according to one of its English rulers, 'very active and intensely virulent'.[57] Lord Cromer was slow to see this, but did after the Denshawai affair, and at the end of his career took some steps to win over the more moderate of the nationalists: appointing one of them to head his Education Ministry, and encouraging them to form a political party which (he wrote) 'might be a set-off against the extremists'.[58] His successor in 1907, Eldon Gorst, pursued a slightly different tack: increasing the participation of Egyptians in local government, and at the centre strengthening the powers of the Khedive, the traditional authority, who had been thrown together with the nationalists by their common antagonism to Cromer, but had had nothing else in common with them then, and nothing at all now that he had made it up with the British. None of this was enough to mollify the nationalists, or to pacify the country. In a very short time, Gorst was forced to adopt more drastic measures: a press censorship act, and a 'Relegation Law' to imprison criminals without trial, which went beyond anything Cromer had ever found necessary, and were a sad commentary on the government's Liberal professions. In 1911, he was forced by ill-health to resign, and was replaced by a man to whom such measures came much more naturally. Lord Kitchener's effort to mix the carrot with the stick – an enlargement of the powers and the representation of the Egyptian Legislative Assembly – did not stop the nationalists complaining, but only gave them a bigger stage to complain on. If nationalism was dampened down at all in Egypt, it was by coercion. Egypt was the one clear vindication in the 1900s of the old imperialists' conviction – which South Africa and India seemed to belie – that concessions to 'babus' only undermined the authority of the 'dominant race', and laid up trouble for the future.[59]

But the field the Liberal government set more store by, and took more interest in, was India. India was a much more challenging test of their imperial mettle. It was inherited by the Liberals from Curzon, who was third only to Milner and Chamberlain in the Liberals' imperialist rogues' gallery. Curzon's effect on India was considered to have been almost as poisonous as Milner's on South Africa. Curzon had had many great qualities, said his successor Lord Minto, but few people knew 'the legacy of bitter discontent he left',[60] and Minto's wife described him as having 'strained the patience of his subjects almost beyond endurance'.[61] His last important political act had been to partition Bengal without consulting the Bengalis, provoking a widespread agitation which was a cold wind to greet Minto's arrival. 'Never,' said the nationalist leader Gokhale, 'was discontent in India more acute and widespread',[62] and John Morley, the Liberals' new Indian Secretary, looking back from 1917, remembered 'the vision of a wave of political unrest from various causes, partly superficial, partly fundamental, slowly sweeping over India'.[63] It was not all Curzon's fault – some of it he had inherited – but he had passed it on with interest. Here was a task indeed for Liberal statesmanship.

Indian national protest was nothing new; the British were used to agitation and riots and obstruction and a seditious press. What was new was the strength of it now, and the direction which some sections of it were taking. It had been a notable feature of Indian protest in the last decades of the nineteenth century that it had been generally moderate, constitutional, almost fawning in its insistent loyalty to the British connection: a tribute to the esteem in which the protesters held the British, from whom they had learnt how to criticise autocracy as well as how to suffer it. In the 1890s, however, another strain of protest began to flourish by its side, fed by a revival of Hindu religion and literature and, on a different level, by the stubborn, popular conservatism which had always been a bugbear to the raj: a strain of nationalism which rejected European values wholesale, and constitutionalism among them. It demanded not just more say for Indians in their government but complete national independence. It was ably led by men like Bal Gangadhar Tilak and Lala Lajpat Rai, and looked to be gaining over the more moderate wing as the honest efforts of the moderates to effect change by merely asking for it were continually and contemptuously frustrated: 'No one,' inferred Tilak, 'gets anything by begging.'[64] Its leaders took heart, and the British took warning, from the success that bolder methods had had elsewhere. 'As time goes on,' predicted Morley, 'Indian discontent or alienation or whatever we like to call it, will be sure to run into the same channels of violence as Italian, Russian, Irish discontent.'[65] Neither could it any longer be dismissed as 'mere froth', the sulky whinings of an unrepresentative Indian elite: it went 'far beyond the *Babu* class', wrote Minto; 'the most loyal supporters we have are coming under its influence'.[66] A wide-ranging boycott organised in protest against the partition of Bengal, of British 'offices and associations'[67] as well as of British goods, though only moderately effective was an augury of the disruption which could be caused. By India's rulers, and also by those Indian politicians who distrusted its reactionary rejection of what they had been taught to see as progressive and Liberal, the new tide was regarded with apprehension.

The flowering of extremist, atavistic nationalism threw together moderate Liberals from both countries: men like Gopal Krishna Gokhale in India, and John Morley in England. Gokhale expected much of Morley: 'Large numbers of educated men in this country,' he told the Indian Congress in 1905,

> feel towards Mr Morley as towards a master, and the heart hopes and yet trembles as it had never hoped or trembled before. He, the reverent student of Burke, the disciple of Mill, the friend and biographer of Gladstone, – will he courageously apply their principles and his own to the government of this country?[68]

And Romesh Dutt wrote to Morley of his people's expectations: 'They *will not* believe that in these days of political progress all over the world, the most Liberal government which England has seen within thirty years will leave India in discontent and despair.'[69] It was Morley's Liberal record which gave them cause for hope; more to the point, perhaps – for from his public and private utterances it seemed that his Liberalism was a somewhat faded flower in 1905[70] – was his brand of Liberal realism, which told him that the Indian National Congress was there to stay anyway, and had to be accommodated. To Minto, he wrote that

> It will mainly depend upon ourselves whether the Congress is a power for good or for evil. There it is, whether we like it or not (and personally I don't like it). Probably there are many questionable people connected with the Congress ... All the more reason why we should not play their game by harshness, stiffness, and the like.[71]

Gokhale had shown him the nationalist movement's more moderate side, which, if it could be appeased, might 'draw the teeth of the Extremists'.[72] Gokhale's group was gradualist and legitimist in its methods; for its aims it accepted 'the British connexion as ordained, in the inscrutable dispensation of Providence, for India's good. Self-government within the Empire … is their goal.'[73] There could be little danger to the empire in collaborating with such men. The danger in *not* collaborating with them, as Gokhale himself warned Minto, was that they might be driven into the revolutionary camp too, and 'the whole younger generation of India' go over to the extremists.[74] 'Reforms may not save the Raj,' Morley wrote to Minto in 1908, 'but if they don't nothing else will.'[75] The path of prudence was clearly marked.

But Morley and Minto were obliged to tread it carefully. They needed the co-operation of moderate Indians, but they needed more the co-operation of the Indian civil service (ICS), the bureaucracy which actually ran the country. Indian civil servants were not known for their sympathy to *any* brand or colour of Indian nationalism. Minto commented that they tended to assume 'all political expressions of an advanced nature to be seditious; in many cases they were very far from being so'.[76] But he understood and partly shared their attitude: 'The feeling of personal danger throughout India,' he wrote to Morley, 'is a quite justifiable one, and the haunting apprehension of what may happen to women and children is I am certain not understood at home.'[77] Morley should remember that 'we are here a small British garrison surrounded by millions composed of factors of an inflammability unknown to the western world, unsuited to western forms of government, and we must be physically strong or go to the wall.[78] The advice he continually got from the ICS, and passed on to Morley, was to put down protest, show that 'agitation' did not pay, stand firm on 'law and order': Morley commented that he was as firm on 'law and order' as the next man, but 'don't forget that "law and order" without common sense and a sense of proportion, are responsible for most of the worst villainies in history'.[79] Such policies, he said, played right into the hands of their enemies: 'I believe that, just as you approach Russian methods of repression, so in precisely the same proportion do you bring down Russian ferocious methods of reprisal.'[80] If the Mutiny were ever repeated, then the blame would lie entirely with those 'over-confident and overworked Tchinovniks who have had India in their hands for fifty years past'.[81] There lay the obstacle to any kind of progress. Theoretically the servants of the government of India, which was itself responsible to Parliament at Westminster, they were in effect very nearly a law to themselves. Morley was always conscious of this limitation; despite his supposed authority, he found that 'at this distance' he could not 'effectively control the Government of India's action'.[82] He felt 'like a man in a nightmare, intent on striking out, but powerless to lift his arm'.[83] Always if he was cautious, in his actions or his words, this was the excuse for his caution: that he had to reassure the officials, for India could not be run without them.

The salvation of British India appeared, to men of Morley's persuasion, to lie in moderation and conciliation, yet the pressures in India all seemed to be the other way. The ICS and the nationalist extremists worked to compound each other's folly, the one side urging and the other side provoking repression and coercion, the actions of each reinforcing the attitudes of the other. In this atmosphere it was difficult to be conciliatory: 'the morrow of a carnival of bomb-throwing,' said *The Times* in the summer of 1908, 'is not a convenient occasion for proclaiming concessions'.[84] At the very beginning Morley and Minto got off on the wrong foot by categorically refusing to revoke the partition of Bengal: 'I expected nothing better from him', wrote Tilak, for whom it only went to show the futility of the 'mendicant' approach of the moderates.[85] Thereafter Minto's viceroyalty was punctuated by bomb blasts and assassinations: one of the latter even in London, where the high Indian official Sir William Curzon Wyllie was shot on the steps of the Imperial Institute by an Indian student in July 1909, which were in their turn met by coercion from the other side: deportations, press laws, laws to curb public meetings, and the like: all of which Morley regretted, some he thought mistaken, but which he seemed powerless to avoid. They did not initially weaken the extremists or strengthen the hands of the moderates, who by their collaboration with a coercive government were likely to incur much of the latter's odium.[86] Nor did they create the best atmosphere for collaboration. What concessions Morley and Minto were able to make to moderate Indian opinion were minimal in their immediate effect – though Morley claimed they were revolutionary in their implications – and were partly vitiated by the repression which accompanied them, and by certain suspicions which attached to one of them. Yet in their basic aim they succeeded.

The 'Morley–Minto reforms' announced in 1909 were designed to increase the participation of Indians in the government of India. At its highest level, an Indian was appointed for the first time to the Viceroy's executive council in India, and two to the Secretary of State's Indian Council in London. All three were nominated by the British government, chosen from among loyal Indians, and without regard to the representativeness of their views. More Indians were added too to the Imperial Legislative Council in India, some of them elected. On a local level, provincial legislative councils were filled with more Indian members, elected directly, and out-numbering the official, nominated members. On the imperial and on some of the provincial legislatures, a proportion of elected seats was reserved for Muslims, who claimed that they would be under-represented otherwise. The imperial and the provincial legislatures were permitted for the first time to debate budgetary matters, to move amendments and to call for divisions. None of these measures affected the *responsibility* of government, which was still firmly in British hands. What they did was to give wider opportunities for Indian opinion to be heard, which might guarantee that it were listened to, but not that it were acted upon. Morley claimed a great deal for his reforms, usually in the vaguest of terms: they were 'destined in the fullness of time,' he said in 1911, '… to prove themselves changes of the first order in their effects upon Indian policy in all its most extensive bearings'.[87] But never did he claim that they were *democratic* in their implications, and indeed he persistently disavowed any 'intention or desire to attempt the transplantation of any European form of representative government to Indian soil'.[88] Their purpose was benevolent but still autocratic: not to undermine British rule, but to reconcile the Indians to it: 'to enable Government,' said Morley to Minto in 1908, 'the better to realise the wants, interests, and sentiments of the governed, and, on the other hand' – which was significant – 'to give the governed a better chance of understanding, as occasion arises, the case for the Government, against the misrepresentations of ignorance and malice'.[89]

The reforms were mild enough to reassure Minto, the ICS, and most Conservatives in Britain – from all of whom Morley got a rather easier passage than he had anticipated. In India, their reception was in general favourable. There were points of contention, the main one being the provision of separate electorates for Muslims, which many Indians suspected was designed to split the nationalist movement to make it more manageable. If this was a motive – and the supposed political advantages of setting Islam against Hinduism were certainly known to the government of the time[90] – it misfired in the long run by stoking the anger of the Hindus, and doing little to secure the permanent loyalty of the Muslims. (More deliberate 'divide and rule' strategies were probably those which set princes against 'babus', and moderate nationalists against extremists.) There were also disappointments arising out of the reforms: that they did not mark an end of repressive legislation, and that Indian initiatives on legislative councils frequently got no further to being implemented than they had ever done.[91] Nevertheless the moderates in Congress welcomed the package, perhaps because they preferred to disregard Morley's disclaimers of democratic intention, and to see it for what they could make of it – if the government were willing – rather than for what in cold reality it contained. Gokhale, who had staked his reputation on Morley and the policy of collaboration, dutifully supported the reforms; more than this, he accepted them as reason enough to give his tacit support too to other legislation – like the draconian Press Act of 1910 – which privately he deplored. Even Tilak in later years came to have more confidence in the goodwill of the government which had passed the reforms.[92] As for the irreconcilable extremists, for the moment at least they were repressed almost out of sight: their leaders deported, their meetings forbidden, their propaganda suppressed. In 1910, the government of India was able to persuade itself, as Minto's private secretary assured the King, that the situation was better, the nationalists appeased, the anarchists 'isolated'.[93] And little happened during the next four years, when Morley and Minto were both gone, to alter this picture; indeed, by reunifying Bengal in 1911, the next Viceroy, Hardinge, took away one of the major obstructions in the 'loyal' nationalists' gullets, and cemented the bonds of collaboration harder. India was not such a triumph for the policy of conciliation as South Africa, for there were still too many important and antagonistic interests there to conciliate them all. But until the war it worked, far better at least than the abrasive overrule of the previous regime.[94]

Tropical development

Other parts of the dependent empire did not evoke anything like the same degree of political interest in Britain as South Africa and India, or of party dissension. But they had their problems too, to which there were found 'Liberal' solutions which differed from Conservative ones, though the differences may not have been so stark or so provocative. The differences were not generally over the question of political control, because the tropical African, Caribbean, Pacific and South-east Asian colonies were universally considered to be at a far too primitive stage of development for any question of political control to arise. If, in the popular and almost literally taken metaphor of the turn of the century, Canada, Australia and New Zealand were grown adults, South Africa had reached her majority, and India was going through a kind of adolescence, then the other colonies were still very much children, and wise Edwardian parents did not allow the question of giving power and responsibility to children even to be considered. There was some debate over the best ways of making them obedient. But most discussion was about their welfare, and how it related to their material development: on which matters there was room enough for disagreement.

Liberals (and for that matter many Tories) had never fully understood Joseph Chamberlain's enthusiasm for tropical colonies, although in some areas they might accept the necessity for having them. For Chamberlain, they had been part of a grandiose scheme for a vast imperial estate, with granaries and coal fields as well as workshops of its own, which would be a self-sufficient economic unit commanding and integrating all the factors of production, and be developed to that end. Few Liberals ever shared this vision (although Churchill was to flirt with it[95]) because they never saw the virtue of or the need for self-sufficiency, national or imperial, especially if it involved obstructions (like tariffs) to the natural division of international labour. Consequently they lacked Chamberlain's sense of constructive purpose when it came to the tropics. In practice, however, this made less difference to policy than might have been supposed, for two reasons. In the first place, Chamberlain had never been able to get as far with his 'constructive imperialism' as he wanted, because of lack of co-operation from the Treasury and his capitalist friends. If his Liberal successors wanted to erase the damage, therefore, there was little damage to erase. In the second place, because the Liberals were blind to the *imperial* need for tropical 'development', it did not follow that they opposed tropical development altogether. From Britain's point of view, there were clear advantages in producing many of the raw materials she needed in the colonies. From the colonies' point of view there might be advantages too. It was a question which still had to be decided, on its merits.

Edwardian Britain, no less than Victorian Britain, needed oil and metals and foodstuffs from the tropics: in fact, she needed them more, for many of them were becoming in very short supply. 'The progress of electrical science,' Sir Charles Dilke told the Commons in 1910, 'of motoring, and even of sports, had caused an enormous advance in rubber; cotton is very short of the world's requirements; and cocoa has gone up in price.'[96] For all these commodities Britain looked greedily to the tropics, and she had a perfect right to. In hardly anyone's political morality in the 1900s was it considered proper for a country's resources to go to waste when other countries could use them; consequently, there was no intrinsic ethical obstacle to the exploitation of one country by another. Socialists and trade unionists, especially if they came from parts of Britain where the commodities were badly needed, campaigned as vigorously for it as Conservatives; one imperialist during a debate on East African development in 1912 commented gleefully on the 'rapid progress of imperialistic ideas' in cotton-starved Lancashire.[97] Approval of 'exploitation' was almost universal; but in no-one's morality did this imply a right to exploit regardless of the interests of a colony's indigenous people. At its very minimum, an exploiter might be content to assume that his exploitation benefited them automatically, by providing them with employment, money wages, new markets and new skills, and needed no special safeguards. Or the benefit might go to the natives in the form of a tax on his profits which could be used to provide hospitals and schools and good government. On the negative side, although there was a strong prejudice among exploiters that it did people good to be made to labour (the advantage of a poll tax in East Africa, said one of them in 1908, was that it would force 'lazy young natives who now only took to drink to do a useful day's work'[98]), there was general agreement too that this should not be done too brutally, or too directly. But until the end of the nineteenth century, this was felt to be about the limit of an exploiter's responsibilities to the people of the country he was exploiting.

At the beginning of the twentieth century, some people were beginning to wonder whether something more might not be required. Still very few doubted that the exploitation of the tropics was a good thing. But they began to have a more discriminating regard for the means that were employed. Cases came to light around the turn of the century of the most shocking abuses of trust by exploitative concerns. One was Cecil Rhodes's conduct in Zambesia in the 1890s. But the worst was the Congo Free State, entrusted to King Leopold of the Belgians by the Berlin Conference of 1884, where the most horrific tales of systematic massacre and mutilation in the search for profits were revealed to the European public in the 1900s, and provoked a widespread agitation which eventually was to lead to Leopold's surrender of his Congolese kingdom to the Belgian parliament in 1909.[99] Rhodes and Leopold together made Liberals highly distrustful of capitalists in the tropics, and especially of capitalist *monopolies* with title over vast expanses of territory, which were the cause of the worst abuses. This distrust was shared by Colonial Secretaries, and permeated the Colonial Office, which had always, as we have seen, been chary of 'development', for a number of quite different reasons,[100] which these events simply added to. All of which posed something of a dilemma. Capitalists claimed they needed monopolistic rights to make it worth their while going into the tropics at all. If the Colonial Office refused them, they might go elsewhere, which would free a British colony from a possible source of abuse, but also deprive it of capital, without which its progress would be stifled. 'In the case of an undeveloped country,' said Elgin, 'beyond a doubt the first thing is to attract capital.'[101] If capital did not come from capitalists, it was hard to know whom it could come from. The natives were too poor, in most colonies rich settlers and traders were too few, and the Treasury was hardly more spendthrift in these matters than it had been in Gladstone's time. In these circumstances the capitalists' offers were seductive.

There was, however, another way. Certain parts of West Africa had for years been producing an export surplus, without needing capitalists at all except the mercantile capitalists who bought it from them. Palm-oil, rubber, groundnuts, cocoa, ginger were grown by African peasants on their own lands, and sold to African middle-men, who took them to the coast or the rivers to sell to European factors, whose only involvement in the process was to provide the demand, and perhaps some credit, to stimulate production. If it were encouraged, and assisted with technical advice to improve methods and railways to facilitate marketing, this system might provide a viable alternative basis for development. The development might not be so rapid as if the industrial capitalists were given their way. But it would be safer, less open to abuse, and less disruptive of African life and society. For this reason the system of 'peasant proprietorship' had powerful advocates in the 1900s, including of course the mercantile interest, but also the anti-Congo lobby, and a number of prominent colonial governors, for whom it fitted in very neatly with the philosophy and technique of 'indirect rule' they were beginning to develop in northern Nigeria and elsewhere. Liberals liked the combination of 'indirect rule' and 'peasant proprietorship' because it seemed a conciliatory, devolutionary kind of policy much like their policies for Ireland and South Africa, likely to cause less friction with natives than the alternatives, and hence less likely to rock the imperial boat. It satisfied too those radicals and socialists on the Liberal side in Parliament who were beginning to question the wisdom of imposing everything western, including western industrial slavery, on the rest of the world: indirect rule was gentler, less arrogant, more sympathetic. It was also supposed to cost less. The government consequently flew to it: not without some capitulations to the sirens of industrial and financial capitalism, but stronger in their anti-concessionaire resolve as the years went on.

Chamberlain had pleaded to capitalists to come and develop his estates for him, but by and large they had turned a deaf ear. Now, at a time when their vital raw materials were in short supply and fetching high prices, they listened and answered the call: and were surprised and indignant to find the government looking their gift horses in the mouth. Sir William Lever applied in 1907 for facilities to farm and process his own palm-oil in British West Africa, to the unquestionable benefit, as he thought, of the latter. He was repeatedly turned down, and moved down to the Congo in 1911, where the authorities were less choosy. It did not happen every time, but it happened enough times for the Colonial Office to acquire a reputation for being against tropical development. Of course, it was not. In the amount of assistance it gave to, for example, railway projects in the colonies, or research into tropical agriculture – the infrastructure of development – the Liberal government's record compared very favourably with Joseph Chamberlain's, though the latter made more of a song and dance about it.[102] The fact was, however, that in West Africa, at least, the method of peasant proprietorship, assisted by rigid laws against land alienation to Europeans and a vigorous programme of technical assistance, appeared to work well enough to render Lever's mode of development superfluous:; certainly in the production of cocoa, cotton and some minor tropical products. In 1905, the Gold Coast and Nigeria produced 6,098 metric tons of raw cocoa, or 4 per cent of the world's total output; in 1915, they produced 87,774 metric tons, or 23 per cent of the world's output.[103] Overall the value of West Africa's trade quadrupled between the last years of the Conservative government and the last years before the Great War,[104] which suggests that if the government's stand against capitalist concessions retarded development, it did not retard it very greatly, and if the industrial world's demand for raw materials was still unsatisfied, then it was insatiable. The debate about the relative efficacy of the two methods of production was to continue beyond the war. But for the moment, in so far as it was put into practice, peasant proprietorship did not appear to be doing much harm.[105]

Liberals and other interested parties were perhaps too impressed by the virtues and successes of their new-found colonial philosophy to notice the limits to which it was in practice being applied. The great virtue of British colonial policy, as opposed, for example, to French colonial policy, was supposed to be its 'pragmatism'; the 'philosophy' of indirect rule itself was in a way simply an idealisation of pragmatism, but even indirect rule was not pragmatic enough to apply everywhere. The way British colonies were actually run depended much more on circumstances than on 'policy'; even under Chamberlain, who had a plan, this was so; under the Liberals, who had no plan, it was more so. Of all Britain's tropical colonies, only northern Nigeria could really be said to be run on indirect rule principles, because it was run by the indirect rule's inventor. Even there Lugard's principles more often than not got adapted and diverted when they met, in the field, the rocks of practical expediency.[106] Elsewhere there were colonies whose governors found they had been applying indirect rule for years, simply because it had been expedient to do so: places like the Federated Malay States, whose system of rule by 'advice', taken from India, was supposed to be the self-same thing; or Egypt, which Britain ruled through a native khedive and ministry; or the British High Commission territories (Basutoland, Bechuanaland and Swaziland) in South Africa, whose almost total neglect by the British government surely merited the name. Other colonies, however, were for the time being unsuited to any definition of indirect rule: either because they were too old and set in other ways, or too young and still being 'tamed'; or because the human material in them was somehow unadaptable to it – because the indigenous native society, perhaps, was insufficiently hierarchic and centralised for native rulers to be found to rule through, as in eastern Nigeria;[107] or, more often, because of the presence of European immigrants. A very large part of the empire was covered by such conditions. It tended to drift in whatever direction local expediency pressed, with the government concerned or able neither to lead nor even to monitor it.

So the West Indies, for example, were allowed to continue the limping decline which the economic facts of life had decreed for them, with even the wretched crutch which Chamberlain had given them, of protection for their sugar exports against foreign bounties, taken from them in 1908 because it was only 'prolonging their dying agony',[108] and if they did not die, it was no thanks to the British government. So also Southern Rhodesia and Kenya were allowed to develop into 'white men's countries', despite very considerable Liberal doubts about the quality of the small white minorities there. In Southern

Rhodesia, the government had at the front of their minds the cost which the white men were saving the government, by paying for its administration out of their own pockets; and also the possible help they might be to the British cause in South Africa, as a reservoir of British blood against the Boers.[109] In Kenya, where their options were very much more open, for the settlers were not completely entrenched as yet, the government was nevertheless prevailed upon to condone a rapid takeover of the most fertile parts of the country, at a heavy cost in African lives and livelihoods, by a white settler organisation which was small but determined, and (to a Liberal mind) outrageous in many of its frontier attitudes and opinions. Whitehall was not helped by the weakness or the downright collusion of the governors they sent out there to keep the settlers in check. With kith and kin against them, and their own servants, the government was content to bend to the prevailing wind.[110]

Elsewhere the administration of colonies went on much as before, determined by their governors; good or bad, dynamic or passive, according to the *quality* of their governors; with Whitehall taking little part in their affairs except as a source of loans for uncontroversial projects, like railways, or occasionally as a court of appeal against blatant injustices and tyrannies. Colonial governors themselves managed to act as best they could with the often scanty resources at their disposal, their own ability and room to act within their own colonies often limited in much the same way as was Whitehall's in the empire as a whole by a lack of real power to back their theoretical authority: 'Here we are,' wrote one of those sent out to tame Kenya,

> three white men in the heart of Africa, with 20 Nigger soldiers and 50 Nigger police, 68 miles from doctors or reinforcements, administering and policing a district inhabited by half a million well armed savages … the position is most humorous.[111]

In such circumstances, which were not unusual on the tropical frontier, colonial government could only be carried on either by bluff or by compromise, and the bluffs were frequently being called. Consequently it was very often not in an official's power to do more than choose whom to collaborate with. In the new colonial territories (those taken in the previous 20 years), this was a common occurrence. In the Sudan, for example, the British collaborated with the anti-Mahdists; in Uganda, with the Ganda aristocracy; in northern Nigeria, with the emirs: and so on.[112] When it was collaboration with a ruling class, it was called 'indirect rule'. If they chose their collaborators wisely, three white men *could* hold half a million 'savages'. But to the extent that a regime depended on collaboration to sustain it, its freedom of action was stifled. This was the Liberal government's problem all over the empire.

Nationalists and imperialists

Judged, however, from the point of view of imperial security, the Liberals' policy was a great success. As Liberals were not particularly concerned to do anything with the empire anyway, the restriction on their freedom of action did not matter much to them. The important and triumphant point was that friction within the empire was greatly reduced, and it seemed a happier place, and cheaper to run. A comparison between the last ten years of Conservative government and the first ten years of Liberal government in the colonies was an illuminating lesson in the virtues of collaboration. It was a lesson the Liberals were never reluctant to point out.

Yet they had not conciliated away *all* opposition to their colonial rule. Resistance was endemic in the colonial situation, though there were many different strains of the disease, and many different symptoms. Only relatively rarely between 1905 and 1914 did opposition break into armed insurrection or violence. Egypt and India had their bombs and assassinations and the occasional riot. There were urban riots in British Guiana. There was a rebellion in Sokoto, in the north-west of Nigeria, in 1906, which cost the rebels 2,000 lives.[113] In the East African Protectorate (Kenya), which was the least 'pacified' of Britain's colonies in the 1900s, there was considerable resistance to the extension of British rule, and many African lives lost in the process: 1,117 Nandi people killed in battle between 1905 and 1906, 407 Embu in 1906, and over 200 Kisii between 1905 and 1908, which Churchill thought looked 'like a butchery'.[114] He was as disturbed by the aftermath of the Zulu rebellion in Natal in 1906–08, in which over 3,500 Africans were killed, 7,000 gaoled and 700 (reportedly) had their backs 'lashed to ribbons' for their defiance.[115] Another kind of rebellion in the same part of the world was one by 10,000 inveterate Afrikaner republicans against the British in 1914. Yet such violent resistance was exceptional, and on nothing like the same scale as in, for example, Germany's African colonies, where, between 1905 and 1907, two-thirds of the Herero people of south-west Africa were exterminated, and 75,000 'Maji-Maji' rebels in Tanganyika. Opposition to the British was in general less desperate, but in most places it was there. It could be seen in certain religious, cultural and industrial movements as well as overtly political ones. The Hindu revival in India, the Gaelic League in Ireland, the Mumbo cult in south-western Kenya, Dutch Calvinism in South Africa, neo-Mahdism in the Sudan, were all to some degree symptoms of, or vehicles for the expression of, strong anti-colonial feeling. Politically, there were sophisticated and influential secular nationalist movements in India and Egypt, as we have seen. In tropical Africa, straight political agitation was much slower to grow, chiefly because Africans had hardly yet been shown what politics was. But in South Africa the political scene by 1914 was fairly teeming with activity by the three racial groups there who felt excluded: Afrikaner republicans had a new 'National' party under General Hertzog, Africans a new 'Native National Congress', and Indians their old Natal Indian Congress under Gandhi. So the colonial animal was not tamed yet.[116]

The world at large, outside the empire, was becoming much more familiar with anti-European, anti-colonial feeling. Japan's rise to world power, the Chinese revolution of 1910 against the collaborating Manchus, the Young Turk revolution of 1908, the black nationalism of Marcus Garvey in America: all these were in different ways powerful expressions of a revolt against European domination. They gave a kind of context to colonial resistance movements, however small or isolated they were; a community of sentiment in which they could join and feel strengthened. Doubts about the justice and efficacy of colonialism were growing in Europe too: and one particular strain of criticism, against its supposed capitalist genesis, was finally, in the version Lenin made of it in 1917, to serve the rebels with an ideological rallying point thereafter.[117] Things might seem relatively peaceful for the British empire now. But the preconditions were being laid down for a stormier future.

On the other side of the fence, the committed imperialists, those with plans for the empire, were getting restless too. When the Liberals came to power, some of them had thought that all was lost. That the Liberals continued to hold the imperial fort was a relief to some of them, and it obviated the need for any drastic retrieving action, except on Ulster. But the young John Buchan, an admirer of Milner who had worked for him in South Africa, found these years – to anyone else surely as interesting as any in British history – 'rather an empty patch', during which it seemed that 'both the great parties were blind to the true meaning of empire', and the spartan imperial virtues were on the decline:

> The historic etiquette was breaking down; in every walk money seemed to count for more; there was a vulgar display of wealth, and a *rastaquouère* craze for luxury. I began to have an ugly fear that the Empire might decay at the heart.[118]

At the very least, opportunities were being missed to realise the imperialist dream, which Buchan dreamt of, 'a world-wide brotherhood with the background of a common race and creed', and a 'high conscientiousness' towards those who did not share that race and creed, all 'consecrated to the service of peace'.[119] At its worst, which was how Milner tended to look on it, it was 'a desperate mess', a 'tyranny',[120] a new Dark Ages during which it would need dedicated men to keep the flame alight. And dedicated men were found. While the Liberals marched on, a kind of underground movement flourished on the right wing of British politics, organised in a plethora of secret or overt, but always exclusive, societies, designed to do just this. Prominent in them were generally to be found Lord Milner and his old South African disciples, known at the time as 'the Kindergarten'. The 'Confederates', who were supposed to include Chamberlain and Milner in their ranks, were organised 'to drive the enemies of tariff reform out of the Conservative Party';[121] the 'Compatriots', started by Leopold Amery, were to push for tariff reform and (said Amery) 'lots more ... from compulsory service and the demolition of the Treasury to the construction of an Imperial Council and the putting of the House of Commons in its proper place';[122] and the more significant and lasting 'Round Table' group existed to preach, through a journal of that name, the ideology of imperial consolidation.[123] The campaign was mainly one of persuasion – persuasion on the highest level, of cabinet and ex-cabinet ministers, colonial statesmen, and newspaper editors, rather than of the 'people' – who, it was confidently assumed, would turn out all right if given the right leadership. But the imperialists were not committing themselves to continue to be entirely scrupulous and democratic in their methods. Balfour's statement in 1906, that it was the duty of everyone to see that 'the great Unionist Party should still control, whether in power or in opposition, the destinies of this great Empire',[124] could be read many ways, some of them ominous. On one occasion, during the Irish Home Rule crisis of 1912–14, it looked as though they might be prepared to pursue their aims by treasonable methods, when the situation called for it. Milner, for one, felt no sense of loyalty towards Parliament when that Parliament challenged the Englishman's wider 'loyalty to the Empire and the Flag'.[125] Home Rule for Ireland was the Liberals' first overt betrayal of a part of the empire since they had come to power; consequently, all the stops, including illicit and unconstitutional ones, had to be pulled out to prevent it. Fortunately, for Milner and the Ulstermen, the war intervened, and Home Rule was shelved before their real imperial mettle could be tested.[126]

Apart from the Ulster crisis, the influence of the irreconcilable imperial consolidationists appears to have been minimal before 1914. A radical journalist in 1913 explained why he thought 'Milnerism' would never catch on in Britain:

> The fundamental fact about Lord Milner is that he is a German – born in Germany, the son of a German professor by an English mother, cradled in Germany, educated in German schools and German ideas ... When this fact is fully realised, his entire

divorce from the English spirit is readily understood. He stands for German, or rather Prussian ideas in English politics. In him we see the Bismarckian policy as well as the Bismarckian spirit in being … A drilled and disciplined proletariat is their hope against an insurgent democracy.

It is a vain hope. If Lord Milner's career proves anything it proves conclusively that Bismarckism cannot be successfully engrafted upon the tree of English liberty … The prison plant will not live in British air …

And so he stands, a forlorn, solitary figure in our midst, with no thinkable future.[127]

But the immediate future for Milner, and for Milnerism, was to turn out brighter than this, as the result of a very exceptional situation which few could have foreseen, but which, in the field of colonial policy as in others, was to cut right across the trends of the past decade.[128]

But those trends anyway were not very pronounced. The Liberals during their guardianship of the empire had done nothing really but stay with it. Their years were quieter years than the Conservatives' partly because they did not feel strongly enough about the empire to want to force it anywhere. Their policy was in the nature of a holding operation. They held it by trimming their sails to the prevailing winds. Because they were Liberals, they could accept and stay with Liberal winds, winds which seemed ultimately to be blowing in the direction of self-government, which Conservatives had been unwilling to sail with. This distinguished their seamanship from the Conservatives'. But there had to be a prevailing wind in that direction: they would not act liberally gratuitously; they would not sail very far along that tack if they did not want to; and they were willing to take other, less Liberal winds. Because they were Liberals, too, they had no clear idea of the direction they were sailing, or their ultimate destination, because they did not have one of their own in mind. This left the options for the empire still very much open in 1914. No great positive steps had been taken for the future, except to confirm southern and East Africa as 'white men's countries', to give moderate encouragement – whether intended or not – to nationalist ambitions in India and Egypt, and to proceed with the development of the tropics as satellite economies of industrial Europe. Anything could come out of it. What might have come out of it, but for the Great War, was anyone's guess.

Notes

1   A. J. Marder, *The Anatomy of British Sea Power* (Putnam, 1940), p. 20.
2   See L. S. Amery, *My Political Life* (Hutchinson, 1953), ii, 261–2.
3   B. R. Mitchell and P. Deane, *Abstract of British Historical Statistics* (Cambridge UP, 1962), pp. 283–4, 334.
4   M. Simon, 'The pattern of new British portfolio investment, 1865–1914', in A. R. Hall, *The Export of Capital from Britain 1870–1914* (Methuen, 1968), p. 41; M. Edelstein, *Overseas Investment in the Age of High Imperialism: The United Kingdom, 1850–1914* (Methuen, 1982).
5   W. Schlote, *British Overseas Trade from 1700 to the 1930s* (Blackwell, 1952), pp. 82, 160–3.
6   Simon, *op. cit.*, p. 41.
7   *Parliamentary Debates*, 5th series, 19 (1909), c. 1576.
8   W. Woodruff, *The Impact of Western Man: A Study of Europe's Role in the World's Economy, 1750–1960* (Macmillan, 1966), p. 106; M. Beloff, *Imperial Sunset* (Methuen, 1969), i, 94n.
9   *Statistical Abstract for the United Kingdom*, Cd 3092 (1906), p. 349; *Statistical Abstract Relating to British India*, Cd 2754 (1906), pp. 216–17. The figures comprise the British Army

establishment serving abroad (including India), and British officers and men of the Indian army, but not 'natives'.

10 J. Richards (ed.), *Imperialism and Juvenile Literature* (Manchester UP, 1989); W. R. Katz, *Rider Haggard and the Fiction of Empire* (Cambridge UP, 1987).

11 J. M. MacKenzie, *The Empire of Nature: Hunting, Conservation, and British Imperialism* (Manchester UP, 1988).

12 R. Hyam, 'Empire and sexual opportunity', *Journal of Imperial and Commonwealth History*, xiv (1986), 53; and see R. Hyam's *Empire and Sexuality* (Manchester UP, 1990). Hyam's first airing of this interesting idea, in R. Hyam, *Britain's Imperial Century* (Batsford, 1976, pp. 135–48), came closer to suggesting it as a causal theory of imperialism; as does L. Stone, *The Family, Sex and Marriage in England 1500–1800* (Weidenfeld & Nicolson, 1977), pp. 52–4, 379–80.

13 On the public schools, see E. C. Mack, *Public Schools and British Opinion since 1860* (Methuen, 1941), Parts II and III; D. Newsome, *Godliness and Good Learning* (John Murray, 1961), Chapter 4; R. Wilkinson, *The Prefects* (Oxford UP, 1964), Chapter 9; J. A. Mangan (ed.), *Benefits Bestowed: Education and British Imperialism* (Manchester UP, 1988); P. J. Rich, *Chains of Empire: English Public Schools, Masonic Cabalism, Historical Causation, and Imperial Clubdom* (Regency Press, 1991).

14 L. Colley, *Britons: Forging the Nation, 1707–1837* (Yale UP, 1992), pp. 129–30.

15 H. Ridley, *Images of Imperial Rule* (Croom Helm, 1983); J. Kruze, *John Buchan and the Idea of Empire: Popular Literature and Political Ideology* (Edwin Meller, 1989); J. S. Bratton *et al.*, *Acts of Supremacy: The British Empire and the Stage, 1790–1930* (Manchester UP, 1991); J. MacKenzie, *Propaganda and Empire: The Manipulation of British Public Opinion, 1880–1960* (Manchester UP, 1984).

16 The subject is treated exhaustively in Bernard J. Porter, *The Absent-Minded Imperialists* (Oxford UP, 2004).

17 See John MacKenzie (ed.), *European Empires and the People* (Manchester UP, 2011).

18 J. A. Hobson, *The Psychology of Jingoism* (Richards, 1901).

19 See, for example, Percy M. Young (ed.), *Letters of Edward Elgar* (Geoffrey Bles, 1956), p. 55.

20 See Bernard J. Porter, 'Edward Elgar and empire', *Journal of Imperial and Commonwealth History*, 29(1) (January 2001), p. 33, no. 106.

21 Jeffrey Richards makes this point, in his *Imperialism and Music* (Manchester UP, 2001).

22 See Further reading, 'Culture and empire' section.

23 See Beloff, *op. cit.*, i, Chapter 4.

24 D. M. Anderson and D. Killingray (eds), *Policing the Empire: Government, Authority and Control, 1830–1940* (Manchester UP, 1991), p. 93 (italics added), *et passim*.

25 C. Headlam (ed.), *The Milner Papers* (Cassell, 1933), ii, 560.

26 G. B. Pyrah, *Imperial Policy and South Africa, 1902–10* (Oxford UP, 1955), p. 23.

27 J. Morley, *Recollections* (1917), ii, 158, 163.

28 Pyrah, *op. cit.*, p. 3.

29 T. R. Metcalf, *The Aftermath of Revolt: India, 1857–1870* (Cape, 1964), p. 236.

30 See Pyrah, *op. cit.*, Chapter 1; R. Hyam, *Elgin and Churchill at the Colonial Office, 1905–8* (Macmillan, 1968), Chapter 3.

31 S. E. Koss, *John Morley at the India Office, 1905–10* (Yale UP, 1969), p. 181.

32 Hyam, *Elgin and Churchill at the Colonial Office*, p. 543.

33 See P. Richardson, *Chinese Labour in the Transvaal* (Macmillan, 1982). In fact, its abolition was anticipated by the new Transvaal government.

34 G. H. L. Le May, *British Supremacy in South Africa, 1899–1907* (Oxford UP, 1965), Chapter 7.

35 Hyam, *Elgin and Churchill at the Colonial Office*, p. 57.

36 *Ibid.*, p. 116.

37 E. A. Walker, 'The franchise in Southern Africa', *Cambridge Historical Journal*, xi (1953), 106.

38 P. N. S. Mansergh, *The Commonwealth Experience* (Weidenfeld & Nicolson, 1969), p. 88.

39 *Parliamentary Debates*, 4th series, 162 (1906), c. 772.

40 Hyam, *Elgin and Churchill at the Colonial Office*, p. 375.

41 Le May, *op. cit.*, p. 186.

42 Mansergh, *op. cit.*, p. 93.

43 *Parliamentary Debates*, 5th series, 9 (1909), cc. 958–9.

44 Walker, *op. cit.*, pp. 104–7; R. Hyam and P. Henshaw, *The Lion and the Springbok: Britain and South Africa since the Boer War* (Cambridge UP, 2003), Chapter 4.

45 *Parliamentary Debates*, 5th series, 9 (1909), c. 1602.

46 *Ibid.*, 4th series, 152 (1906), cc. 1238–9.

47 Le May, *op. cit.*, p. 189.

48 W. Nimocks, *Milner's Young Men: The 'Kindergarten' in Edwardian Imperial Affairs* (Hodder & Stoughton, 1970), p. 62.

49 Pyrah, *op. cit.*, p. 238.

50 R. A. Huttenback, 'Indians in South Africa, 1860–1914: the British imperial philosophy on trial', *English Historical Review*, 81 (1966), 273–91.

51 Hyam, *Elgin and Churchill at the Colonial Office*, pp. 237–62.

52 *Parliamentary Debates*, 4th series, 155 (1906), c. 254.

53 Huttenback, *op. cit.*, p. 291.

54 *Parliamentary Debates*, 5th series, 58 (1914), c. 378.

55 *Parliamentary Debates*, 4th series, 155 (1906), c. 254.

56 On South African union, see Pyrah, *op. cit.*; L. M. Thompson, *The Unification of South Africa, 1901–10* (Clarendon Press, 1960); W. M. Macmillan, *Bantu, Boer and Briton* (Faber & Gwyer, 1929); Le May, *op. cit.*, Chapters 7–8; Hyam, *Elgin and Churchill at the Colonial Office*, Chapters 4 and 7; John Benyon, *Proconsul and Paramountcy in South Africa: The High Commission, British Supremacy and the Sub-Continent, 1866–1910* (University of Natal Press, 1980); Hyam and Henshaw, *op. cit.*, Chapters 3–5.

57 J. Boyd, in Alef Lufti al-Sayyid, *Egypt and Cromer* (John Murray, 1968), p. 179.

58 *Ibid.*, p. 177.

59 See Lord Lloyd, *Egypt since Cromer* (Macmillan, 1933), i, Chapters 3–12; P. J. Vatikiotis, *The Modern History of Egypt* (Weidenfeld & Nicolson, 1969), Part III; P. Mansfield, *The British in Egypt* (Weidenfeld & Nicolson, 1971), Chapters 15–18; al-Sayyid, *op. cit.*, Chapter 8.

60 Koss, *op. cit.*, p. 184.

61 M. Gilbert (ed.), *Servant of India* (Longman, 1966), p. 23; Mary, Countess of Minto, *India, Morley and Minto, 1905–10* (Macmillan, 1934), p. 49.

62 S. A. Wolpert, *Morley and India, 1906–1910* (Cambridge UP, 1967), p. 231.

63 Morley, *op. cit.*, ii, 149.

64 S. A. Wolpert, *Tilak and Gokhale: Revolution and Reform in the Making of Modern India* (University of California Press, 1962), p. 171.

65 M. N. Das, *India under Morley and Minto* (Allen & Unwin, 1964), p. 21.

66 *Ibid.*, p. 14.

67 Wolpert, *Tilak and Gokhale*, p. 195.

68 S. R. Wasti, *Lord Minto and the Indian Nationalist Movement, 1905–1910* (Oxford UP, 1964), p. 21n.

69 Wolpert, *Morley and India*, p. 145.

70 R. J. Moore, *Liberalism and Indian Politics, 1877–1922* (Hodder & Stoughton, 1966), Chapter 6; but see Wolpert, *Morley and India, passim*.

71 Morley, *op. cit.*, p. 171; Wasti, *op. cit.*, p. 23.

72 Morley, *op. cit.*, ii, 186.

73 Wolpert, *Tilak and Gokhale*, pp. 159–60.

74 Mary, Countess of Minto, *op. cit.*, p. 109.

75 Koss, *op. cit.*, p. 201.

76 *Ibid.*, p. 98n.

77 Gilbert, *op. cit.*, p. 168.

78 Wolpert, *Morley and India*, p. 131.

79 *Ibid.*, p. 102.

80 Gilbert, *op. cit.*, p. 150.

81 Morley, *op. cit.*, ii, 265.

82 Wolpert, *Morley and Minto*, p. 99.

83 *Ibid.*, p. 109.

84 Koss, *op. cit.*, p. 153n.

85 Wolpert, *Tilak and Gokhale*, p. 181.

86 See Gokhale quoted in *ibid.*, p. 229.
87 Koss, *op. cit.*, p. 210.
88 Mansergh, *op. cit.*, p. 249.
89 S. R. Mehrotra, *India and the Commonwealth, 1885–1929* (Allen & Unwin, 1965), p. 50.
90 For example, see Gilbert, *op. cit.*, p. 202; Das, *op. cit.*, pp. 147–62.
91 For example, Gokhale's Education Bill 1911: Wolpert, *Tilak and Gokhale*, p. 247.
92 *Ibid.*, pp. 264–5.
93 Gilbert, *op. cit.*, pp. 216, 219.
94 See Wolpert, *Tilak and Gokhale*, and Wolpert, *Morley and India*; Wasti, *op. cit.*; Das, *op. cit.*; Koss, *op. cit.*; Moore, *op. cit.*
95 Hyam, *Elgin and Churchill at the Colonial Office*, p. 350.
96 *Parliamentary Debates*, 5th series, 18 (1910), c. 987.
97 *Ibid.*, 5th series, 40 (1912), c. 134.
98 *Ibid.*, 4th series (1908), c. 1305.
99 See R. Slade, *King Leopold's Congo* (Oxford UP, 1962); B. J. Porter, *Critics of Empire* (Macmillan, 1968), Chapter 8.
100 See above, p. 155.
101 Hyam, *Elgin and Churchill at the Colonial Office*, p. 466.
102 *Ibid.*, pp. 196–7 and Chapter 12.
103 W. K. Hancock, *Survey of British Commonwealth Affairs*, ii, Part 2 (Oxford UP, 1942), 338.
104 A. McPhee, *The Economic Revolution in British West Africa* (G. Routledge and Sons, Ltd, 1926), p. 313.
105 See Hancock, *op. cit.*, ii, Part 2, 173–200; Hyam, *Elgin and Churchill at the Colonial Office*, pp. 390–404.
106 See R. Heussler, *The British in Northern Nigeria* (Oxford UP, 1968).
107 H. A. Gailey, *The Road to Aba* (University of London Press, 1971), pp. 5–6.
108 Hyam, *Elgin and Churchill at the Colonial Office*, pp. 457–9.
109 *Ibid.*, pp. 287, 388–9.
110 See G. Bennett, *Kenya: A Political History* (Oxford UP, 1963), Chapters 3–4; G. H. Mungeam, *British Rule in Kenya 1895–1912* (Oxford UP, 1966); Hyam, *Elgin and Churchill at the Colonial Office*, pp. 405–19; V. Harlow and E. M. Chilver (eds), *History of East Africa*, 2 vols (Oxford UP, 1965), ii, 1, 2 *et passim*.
111 T. O. Ranger, 'African reactions to the imposition of colonial rule in East and Central Africa', in L. H. Gann and P. Duignan (eds), *Colonialism in Africa, 1870–1914*, 5 vols (Cambridge UP), i (1969), 295.
112 See *ibid.*; and R. E. Robinson, 'Non-European foundations of European imperialism', in E. R. J. Owen and R. B. Sutcliffe (eds), *Studies in the Theory of Imperialism* (Longman, 1972).
113 M. Perham, *Lugard* (Collins, 1960), ii, Chapter 12.
114 Mungeam, *op. cit.*, pp. 173 *et passim*.
115 S. Marks, *Reluctant Rebellion: The 1906–8 Disturbances in Natal* (Oxford UP, 1970), pp. 237–8 *et passim*.
116 See R. Rotberg and A. Mazrui (eds), *Protest and Power in Black Africa* (Oxford UP, 1970); E. A. Ayandele, *The Missionary Impact on Modern Nigeria* (Longman, 1966), Chapter 8; and E. A. Ayandele, *'Holy' Johnson* (Cass, 1970).
117 See V. I. Lenin, *Imperialism, the Highest Stage of Capitalism* (English edn, 1922).
118 J. Buchan, *Memory-Hold-the-Door* (Hodder & Stoughton, 1940), pp. 126–8.
119 *Ibid.*, p. 125.
120 A. M. Gollin, *Proconsul in Politics* (Blond, 1964), p. 135.
121 A. Gollin, *Balfour's Burden* (Blond, 1965), pp. 224–5.
122 Gollin, *Proconsul in Politics*, p. 105.
123 *Ibid.*, pp. 161–7; Nimocks, *op. cit.*, *passim*.
124 R. Blake, *The Unknown Prime Minister* (Eyre & Spottiswoode, 1955), p. 53.
125 Gollin, *Proconsul in Politics*, p. 184.
126 *Ibid.*, Chapters 8–9.
127 *Ibid.*, pp. 170–1.
128 See Gollin, *Proconsul in Politics*, and Gollin, *Balfour's Burden*; Nimocks, *op. cit.*; Amery, *My Political Life*, i, Chapters 11–15.

8 Everything becomes fluid: 1914–20

The Great War

The Great War, when it came, was no surprise to imperialists, who had been expecting something like it for years. It stood to reason that the period when European nations could expand freely was coming to an end, that there would soon be no more unclaimed territory to expand into, and that the only way left to expand would be at other European nations' expense. The country which stood to lose most when this colonial rivalry turned cannibalistic was Britain, because she had most colonial flesh on her. It was becoming equally obvious that Germany was the rival most likely to threaten her: the Great Power whose colonial appetite had been least satisfied over the past 30 years, and the one whose face recently had carried the hungriest and most bellicose expression. British imperialists persisted in regarding German imperialism as 'aggressive', their own as not; German imperial ambitions, wrote Leopold Amery, were 'essentially artificial and not, like our own overseas policy, deep-rooted in the instincts of the nation'.[1] But artificial or not, Germany's colonial pretensions were clear and unambiguous in the 1900s, and to them the British empire stood as a constant provocation. Via Turkey and Morocco and the Balkans, Germany since the 1890s had steered a steady course, which was bound eventually to bring her into collision with Britain. Imperialists had been warning their countrymen of this for some time.

Whether or not the Great War really was, *au fond*, the result of colonial rivalries does not concern us. If it was, then it was Germany's rivalry to Britain that caused it, and not Britain's to Germany. It is unlikely that Britain in 1914 had either the desire or the need to expand her already vast colonial empire at the risk of a European war. There was little to tempt her in the German colonies, which had not made money since they became German colonies, and did not look like doing so ever. But of course there was a great deal to tempt and provoke the Germans in the British colonies, and the prospect of colonial aggrandisement might have weighed with them. In regard to colonies, Britain was one of the 'Haves' among European nations and Germany a 'Have-not'. It is generally in the interests of Have-nots to change things, of Haves to preserve the status quo. Britain's motive in going to war with Germany was to preserve the status quo, which she regarded as being threatened by Germany all over the world. It was not to get more colonies. Which is not to say that, if the opportunity arose, she would not use the occasion of the war to do just that. War motives and war aims had been known to diverge in the past, and they were likely to do so again.

In any event, the war when it broke out was clearly, among other things, a war for the preservation of the empire, in the sense that if Britain had lost, she could not have retained her empire. But it was a European war in the sense that the decisive battle was in France, and not in the colonies. There were campaigns outside Europe which were overtly colonial: in the Pacific, where it took only four months for Australian and New Zealand troops with Japanese allies to seize everything German; in East and South-west Africa, where it took a mainly South African force just a little longer; and in the Middle East against Germany's ally, the Ottoman empire. This last campaign was important in diverting enemy troops from Europe, boosting morale at home during the western war's congealed phase, and ensuring some profit from the war afterwards if the Allies won. But the most fervent champions of the Mesopotamian campaign never saw it as more than a 'side-show', strictly subordinate to the main effort in the west. 'From the point of view of the British Empire,' minuted the Cabinet War Committee in December 1915, 'France and Flanders will remain the main theatre of operations';[2] and the War Cabinet spelt it out more fully in April 1918: 'The security of India or of any other subsidiary theatre must not weigh against the successful prosecution of the war at the decisive point – France.'[3] It was a simple equation: if Britain won on every other front, but lost in Europe, she would not long retain her colonies; likewise if she lost on every other front, but won in Europe, she would get them back. The survival of the empire, therefore, rested in France.

But what kind of empire survived the war would likely be decided outside France. The war put tremendous pressures on the different parts of the empire; it also presented great opportunities to them. By the nature of both would the future character of the empire be determined.

The opportunities which the war opened up for the empire were thought at the time to be considerable. In the first place there was the clear chance it offered for expansion. The war made uncertain the position not only of the Allies' possessions but also of the Central Powers'. If the Allies won, large areas of the under-developed world would come again on to the open market: the German colonies, and the remaining dominions of the Ottoman empire. 'Now everything becomes fluid,' said H. G. Wells's Mr Britling when war broke out; 'we can redraw the map of the world.'[4] Put more bluntly, it meant that the British empire could get bigger.

In the second place, the war made the empire she had more valuable to Britain: valuable as a source of fighting men, and of necessary imports. The manpower contribution of the colonies and dominions to the Allied war effort is illustrated by their casualty figures: 62,056 Indians killed, 59,330 Australians, 56,639 Canadians, 16,711 New Zealanders, 7,121 South Africans, about 2,000 East Africans (black men were never counted so carefully as whites), 1,204 Newfoundlanders, 850 West Africans. In all, about 2.5 million colonials fought for Britain, and thousands more served as non-combatants.[5] Economically too, the empire's contribution was crucial. Some of the colonies made direct grants of money. But more significant were the material goods they supplied. A nation at war is always more dependent on its own resources than a nation at peace, partly because it needs more resources and partly because some other countries' resources are cut off from it. Many of Britain's resources – raw materials vital for war production – lay in her colonies, and still more lay in the wider world market which it was part of the colonies' purpose to defend. Britain's war economy gobbled up imports during the years of fighting, at a rate which in peacetime would have been considered disastrous to her balance of trade: £1,161 million a year between 1915 and 1919, compared with £714 million a year during the five years before. The United States, to their great profit, contributed by far the most but the colonies played their part too (Table 8.1).[6]

Every colony was affected, because (Winston Churchill told the Commons after the war) 'the commodities which they produced were in many cases vital to the maintenance of the industries, and particularly the war industries, of Britain and her Allies'.[7]

Table 8.1 British extra-European imports, 1910–20

	Value of imports (annual average in £million)	
Source of imports	1910–14	1915–20
USA	131	393
Canada	29	86
Australasia	58	94
Asia	89	164
Sub-Saharan Africa	21	47
West Indies	6	23

The proven value of the colonies stimulated proposals during the war to capitalise on it afterwards. The old school of Chamberlainite imperialists found their faith in the empire's economic potential confirmed, and all their old ideas suddenly catching on. From a dozen quarters – from imperialists in the government, from a Dominions Royal Commission set up in 1912 but still sitting to discuss imperial economics, from an unofficial 'Empire Resources Development Committee' (ERDC) formed in 1917, and from a host of pamphleteers and propagandists – there came a flood of proposals during the war, reminiscent of the great Joe (Chamberlain), to exploit the empire like an estate under siege: to which a government distracted by more immediate matters gave its approval probably without thinking much about them. Developed and worked to the national or imperial advantage – the ERDC suggested by a monopolistic consortium of capitalists – and safely lodged behind a wall of tariffs; self-sufficient in everything, but controlling the world's whole supply, perhaps, of some things; with her empire organised like this, Britain's future was assured. The empire had 'vast potentialities', Milner was reported as saying in 1917; if it could 'link up closely', it would be 'strong enough to defy all comers' and to keep Britain 'out of European complications'.[8] The response of the dominions to Britain's call during the war seemed to promise that they would play ball too. The war had provided, at many levels including the highest, a sampler of what could be done by the colonies co-operating and acting as one; 'in the course of it,' wrote Amery, they 'achieved a greater measure of effective imperial unity in its direction than statesmen had ever contemplated before'.[9] The flavour was exciting, even intoxicating. If they could build on it after the war, there was no saying what the empire could become.[10]

As the war dragged on, their chances of being in a position to build on it became rosier. For in order to win the war, the government, which started as a Liberal one, found it had to co-opt warriors; those warriors by the end of the war came to dominate; and they turned out to be some of those rather old-fashioned imperialists, with very special, and illiberal, war aims of their own. The 'new imperialists' of the 1890s (who were now older imperialists) had been waiting since 1906 for a better day to dawn: now at last the sun rose for them. One by one, they were spirited into the government, which became less Liberal, and more congenial company for imperialists, as the war went on. Curzon and Balfour joined the government in May 1915, Milner in December 1916, and a colonial Prime Minister, Jan Smuts from South Africa, in June 1917: Milner and Curzon in the streamlined, five-man inner cabinet which Lloyd George instituted in December 1916. One by one, also some less well-known but dedicated younger imperialists gathered around them in influential advisory posts, including a good section of Milner's old 'Kindergarten'. The Prime Minister had three of them, Waldorf Astor, Lionel Curtis and

Philip Kerr, in his personal secretariat, one of them (Kerr) as his 'expert on imperial and foreign affairs'. Two more, Leopold Amery and Mark Sykes, were in the cabinet secretariat to advise on Eastern and Middle Eastern affairs; another, John Buchan, was deputy director of a new Information Ministry created to brief ministers. It was a remarkable resurrection of a school of imperialism which had been thought to be dead and buried for years, spurned by successive electorates since 1906. In ordinary times it would have remained mouldering under the ground. But the very extraordinary circumstance of the war had acted like an earthquake, throwing up the coffin and breaking it open, and so Joseph Chamberlain walked the earth again.[11] And the imperialists were clear what they wanted to do with their new-found authority. Leopold Amery's 'first and foremost' war aim was 'the immediate security and, still more, freedom for the development and expansion of the British Commonwealth in the world outside Europe'.[12] A Cabinet Committee on 'Territorial Desiderata' chaired by Curzon in 1917 recommended that this expansion be concentrated in East Africa and the lands between Egypt and India.[13] It was plain what the imperialists' counsels would be, if they still prevailed when the war was over.

But all these opportunities were in the future. For the present, there were dangers to the empire in the war too. The Great War was a total war, and it stretched Britain's resources as they had never been stretched before. Even while she was at peace, she had not been able to hold her empire by force alone, and had had to resort to collaboration and concession to keep the challenge to her power within manageable bounds. Now she was much less able to hold the empire by force: to keep tied up in the colonies troops which were so badly needed in Europe, or to count on reinforcing them in an emergency. In India, for example, the number of British troops dwindled at one stage to 15,000, which was 23,000 fewer than on the eve of the Mutiny. The perils of the situation were clear, and could only be met by compromising with any emergency or threat that might arise: a course whose prudence was also indicated by the attitude of the United States, upon whom Britain came to rely more and more as the war continued, and who disliked, or professed to dislike, being harnessed with imperialists. Concession was a way for Britain to retain her control over her empire: but it was a way to dilute that control too. She would obviously have preferred not to do it, but she was hardly her own mistress in these matters. The war forced her into all kinds of actions which, in the long term, were unwise or unsatisfactory, but the sort of war it was made this inevitable. It put the government under very special kinds of pressure, which affected and often distorted the decisions it took. In wartime, there could be no coherent long-term policy for the empire. Everything, including what was happening in the colonies, was overshadowed by the war in France. Every decision had to be taken with that in view, and not with a view to the interest either of the colonies themselves, or even of the whole British empire itself, except in so far as the latter's fate was bound up with that of the Western Front. Consequently, colonial policy decisions could not be other than pragmatic, unplanned, short-term, often inconsistent. Quite often they came to be regretted afterwards. Especially regretted were the promises made during the war, in order to curry favour from various quarters, to nationalists in India and the Middle East.[14]

The promises: India, the Middle East

In India, the promises came very slowly, because for a long time it looked as though they might be done without. The war caught India at a relatively tranquil moment: a time when opposition to British rule was deeply divided; its charismatic extremists silenced by imprisonment and by expulsion from their own Indian National Congress; and its moderates content for the moment to trust to the good intentions of a Viceroy, Lord Hardinge, who in four years in India had done nearly all the right things: reunified Bengal, supported the cause of the Indians in South Africa (to the embarrassment of the Colonial Office), and come out in favour of political reforms – in the direction of provincial self-government – which went some way beyond the ambiguities of Morley–Minto. India's tranquillity was not immediately disturbed by the war: indeed, it was surprising to many people how loyal Indians were to their masters, how they refrained from exploiting their difficulties, so that Britain did not *need* more than 15,000 troops to control them. Perhaps for this reason the government thought that concessions could be delayed for the moment, although one or two, like Hardinge himself, his successor Lord Chelmsford, and Edwin Montagu, who had been Indian Under-Secretary before the war and wanted now to be Viceroy, were keen to announce reforms from the beginning. Another reason was that one of the concessions that was contemplated, India's representation at Imperial Conferences with the 'white' self-governing dominions, met with considerable opposition from the latter on the grounds (which were irrefutable) that India was neither 'white' nor self-governing. They were overruled, however, and India was admitted at the beginning of 1917. Promise of political reforms came a little later, in August.

Both concessions were late enough to suggest that they were born of fear more than persuasion. For in the months before, the nationalists had healed both their main breaches: between Congress and the Muslim League by the Lucknow Pact of December 1916, and between moderates and extremists when a chastened Tilak was released from gaol in 1914, was readmitted to Congress at the end of 1916, and captured it soon afterwards. In 1916, the nationalists went on to the offensive under him and the Englishwoman Annie Besant ('It is her activity', wrote Montagu later, 'which has really stirred the country up'[15]); by 1917, they looked threatening enough to persuade the Indian government to intern Mrs Besant in June, which provoked further agitation. In July, the Viceroy wrote home that the situation was urgent, and that any further prevarication would be 'fatal'.[16] It was at this moment that Montagu, who had returned to the India Office as Secretary of State in July, was allowed to make a declaration – which all the same was watered down a little by Curzon – of the government's intent for India. That intent was to provide for 'the increasing association of Indians in every branch of the administration, and the gradual development of self-governing institutions with a view to the progressive realisation of responsible government in India as an integral part of the British Empire'. Montagu followed his declaration up with a trip to India in the winter during which were gestated more specific reform proposals which were announced in August 1918. The Montagu–Chelmsford Report recommended significant progress towards responsible government in the provinces in certain matters, which included education, public health and agriculture. The British governors were still to control finance and law and order, and the word 'dyarchy' was coined to describe the division of responsibility between the two kinds of authority.

The Montagu–Chelmsford reforms, or very similar ones, had been in the minds of successive Indian Viceroys for some years, and of many British politicians for longer: mostly Liberals but also some 'Round Table' imperialists who could not see Indians being satisfied for long with less, and feared that if they were not satisfied, they might be lost altogether to the empire. To attribute the sudden manifestation of these proposals in 1917–18 to the pressures of war was hard on men like this, but it may have been true that only the pressures of war gave them the chance to implement their ideas against the weight of official inertia at home, and of stubborn prejudice among officials in India. Lord Morley had not felt strong enough, or confident enough in his Liberalism, to challenge the serried ranks of the ICS frontally; when Hardinge and Montagu before the war showed more courage, the outcry against them was as violent, if not as widespread, as the outcry over Ireland, and the Secretary of State, Lord Crewe, had to devote most of his parliamentary time to making disclaimers. 'Oh! for six months as a viceroy,' once exclaimed Montagu, who found, exactly as Morley had done, that 'in a supreme position the instrument through which one has to work thwarts one's purpose'.[17] But the war changed this situation, in two ways. First, it impressed many people in Britain with the Indians' loyalty and service to the empire, both at home and on the fighting fronts, which were supposed to indicate their political maturity and also to deserve some reward. Second, and in seeming contradiction to this, it impressed others with the depth of the Indians' discontent and *disloyalty*, which at this critical stage in Britain's fortunes, if the loyal Indians were not rewarded, might be disastrous for her hold over them. Until now Britain had never liked to declare officially that self-government was her aim – even her most distant aim – for India. Morley had denied it; one of Crewe's disclaimers had called it 'a world as remote as any Atlantis or Erewhon that ever was thought of by the ingenious brain of an imaginative writer'.[18] Montagu was able to utter the words 'responsible government' in 1917, even though it provoked a storm in the House of Lords and a flurry of resignations in India, because the situation then was more desperate: nationalist opposition more widespread, the need 'to arrest the further defection of moderate opinion' (said Chelmsford) more urgent, the country (said Montagu) 'rolling ... to certain destruction'.[19] This, the war had done.

But the war had also made it less likely that the promise of Liberal reforms to India, when it did come, would suffice (as Morley–Minto had done) to stem the nationalist tide. Indian nationalism was fired enormously by the war: its grievances compounded, its following augmented, its organisation greatly improved, its expectations increased; 'a seething, boiling, political flood', was how Montagu described it in November 1917, 'raging across the country'.[20] For a while the Montagu Declaration and the Montagu–Chelmsford Report had held it back; if he had done nothing else, wrote Montagu in February 1918, 'I have kept India quiet for six months at a critical period of the war.'[21] But he had done much more, as he had intended to. The reforms represented the biggest concession Britain had yet made to the demands of the nationalists. Whether it was big enough to keep pace with them was yet to be seen.[22]

The same could be said of Egypt, where the promise was made much earlier, but much more evasively. Egypt's status had been somewhat irregular for 30 years, and was too irregular for Britain's purposes in 1914, when (in October) her nominal suzerain, Turkey, came into the war on the German side. In December, Britain made an honest woman of her at last by declaring a protectorate over her, and dared Turkey to prove otherwise. It was politically necessary, but it was a snub to the Egyptian nationalists, whose ambitions for their country were not for it to become more colonial, but less. To sugar the pill, Britain promised to give consideration, after the war, to the question of Egyptian self-government. This was the first of her pledges in the Middle East: a cautious one, but liable to prove troublesome. It was hardly likely after the war that the nationalists would feel that the pledge had been honoured if Britain gave consideration to the question, and said no.

That was not the end of things in the Middle East. The Ottoman threat was not neutralised merely by changing Egypt's status. In the Middle East a whole gamut of British interests which previously had rested fairly heavily on Turkish neutrality was imperilled, chief among them, of course, the Suez Canal, which the Sultan's lines were dangerously close to, and the oil fields of the Persian Gulf which (said Curzon in 1919) 'are worked for the British Navy and ... give us a commanding interest in that part of the world'.[23] Beyond this, Indian Muslims were likely to be troubled, and their loyalties diverted, by the spectacle of Britain fighting a Muslim power; and the sudden non-neutrality of the Middle East reopened all those rivalries among the allies which its neutrality had been intended to prevent, in particular, the old Anglo-French squabble which had lain dormant since 1904. Turkey's hostility was an irritation – perhaps not much more – which the British empire could have done without and it demanded action. Military action was tried: fronts set up in Iraq (pushing north-west from the Persian Gulf) and Palestine (pushing north-east from Egypt), but neither made very much headway. In 1915, Churchill persuaded the government to let him attack Gallipoli in the Straits, a campaign which was meant to mop the Middle East up once and for all but that failed. Most of the Allied casualties in that adventure were brave Australians, which created a running sore for years. Part of the trouble was that Britain could not spare the troops from the more crucial Western Front. Something else was needed: help from people on the spot. To get their help, they had to be promised something in return.

Certain Arab groups in the Middle East had been planning a revolt against the Turks since 1914, and they had requested British backing then. Towards the end of 1915, with the Gallipoli adventure floundering, the British government decided it might be worth a small bet. In October, the Egyptian High Commissioner, Sir Henry McMahon, promised, with reservations, that Britain would 'recognise and support the independence of the Arabs', in order to get the revolt going, which it did, with British military and financial help, in June 1916. With the Arabs, the British were very much more successful than without them; by December, under Allenby, they had taken Jerusalem, and by September the next year, overrun Palestine and Syria. Further east, General Maude (with mainly Indian troops) used the opportunity to advance into Iraq. The Arab revolt helped to turn the military tide for Britain in the Middle East, and so take the pressure off the Suez Canal and the oil fields for the duration of the war.

But this did not solve all Britain's problems. In particular, it did not solve her long-term problem of how to safeguard her Middle Eastern interests now that the old Turkish buffer was gone; or the short-term problem connected with it, of how to avoid quarrel-ling with her friends over it. To settle these problems, she came to a secret arrangement with France in April 1916 – the Sykes–Picot Treaty – which was supposed to determine how the Ottoman empire would be partitioned after the war. Most of it Britain and France earmarked for themselves, either in the form of outright possessions (for Britain, most of Palestine and much of Iraq and the Persian Gulf), or of 'spheres of influence' (Britain's to stretch across from the Jordan to the Gulf). Included in these projected spoils was some territory like Palestine – which the Arabs understood had been pledged to *them* by McMahon.

Sykes–Picot was, on the face of it, a blueprint for a cynical piece of imperialistic plunder, and Britain was embarrassed by the look of it both to the Arabs, who got to know of it when the Russian Bolsheviks found it and revealed it to the world towards the end of 1917, and to the Americans, who had to be told of it when they came into the war in April 1917. America preferred to believe that she was fighting for democracy and lib-eration, and the Arabs obviously wanted to be fighting for themselves. To reassure both, and the mounting number of their critics in Britain, the government stepped up its promises to the Arabs, in a series of 'declarations' (the Hogarth Message in January 1918, the Declaration to the Seven in June, and the Anglo-French Declaration in November) which became progressively more ardent, though not very much more specific.

At the same time, the government committed itself as firmly to the Zionists, who did not exist as a Middle Eastern nation as yet, but wanted to. The Balfour Declaration of November 1917 gave the British government's blessing and support to 'the establishment in Palestine of a national home for the Jewish people'. It was the kind of commitment which could have been made only in wartime: when political geography was so fluid that such an artificial creation could be considered; when the government was so pressed and distracted as to be able to ignore or neglect its patent drawbacks and dangers; and when the need for it could arise. For British ministers, there were a number of substantial arguments in favour of such a declaration, which included a genuine Zionism on the part of some, and a devious but ingenious imperialism on the part of others, which Leopold Amery, who was not a minister but claimed he drafted the declaration, acknowledged as *his* main motive:

> I confess that my interest was, at first, largely strategical. I was keen on an advance into Palestine and Syria on military grounds, and the idea of consolidating that advance by establishing in Palestine a prosperous community bound to Britain by ties of gratitude and interest naturally appealed to me. I already had doubts as to the permanence of our protectorate in Egypt.[24]

But the chief reason was probably less grandiose, and more immediate: the need to court support among American and Russian Jewry to put pressure on their governments to keep them in the war, or even among German Jewry to turn them against their government. Balfour said:

> The vast majority of Jews in Russia and America, as indeed, all over the world, now appeared to be favourable to Zionism. If we could make a declaration favourable to such an ideal, we should be able to carry on extremely useful propaganda both in Russia and America.[25]

Lloyd George used the same word – propaganda.[26] It was a big long-term risk to take for a short-term propaganda point but the government was desperate.

By the end of the war, the Middle East was a tangle of promises which Britain had made to the Arabs, to the Jews, to France and to herself. They were contradictory, although no-one knew quite how contradictory, or how intentional the contradictions had been. There was a great deal of room for honest confusion in them. Words like 'self-determination' and 'independence' were capable of different degrees of interpretation: the British, for example, believed that Arab 'independence' was quite consistent with a 'sphere of influence' over them, and Curzon just after the war said that he was quite happy to accept 'self-determination' because 'I believe that most of the people would determine in our favour.'[27] In one of the reservations to Arab independence contained in the McMahon Letter, there was a genuine ambiguity in one Arab word, which could mean a district or a province, and on the difference depended whether the Arabs were promised Palestine or not. Later pledges to the Arabs were no less ambiguous, promising greater degrees of 'independence', but not saying exactly where. The most ambiguous term of all was the Balfour Declaration's 'national home in Palestine', which Balfour clearly intended to mean a Jewish state of Palestine,[28] but which on the face of it could mean a number of other, and lesser, things. Yet no-one pretended that even the most ingenious diplomatic puzzle-solver could have pieced all the promises together to make them fit, except in his own mind: Curzon, for example, who was sure that McMahon had promised Palestine to the Arabs,[29] by defining the 'national home' small; Balfour, by reading Palestine into one of McMahon's 'reservations'. There were contradictions; and inevitably they led, after the war, to betrayals.

All the promises had the mark of expediency about them, being designed to reap some short-term advantage or respite, or to curry somebody's favour. Whether or not those who made them intended at the time to break them is uncertain. T. E. Lawrence ('Lawrence of Arabia') claimed that it was evident to *him* that Britain's promises to the Arabs would be 'dead paper' after the war, and confessed himself to misleading them deliberately: 'I risked the fraud, on my conviction that Arab help was necessary to our cheap and speedy victory in the East, and that better we win and break our word than lose.'[30] But to those higher up who made the promises, the 'fraud' might not have been so clear, simply because little thought was given to whether the cheques they wrote out so freely could be redeemed. They were written out usually under pressure; from day to day, things changed rapidly – October 1915 was a century away from November 1917, the world a different place, the necessities which pressed on government of a different order. The future, when the cheques would come in for payment, was unknown, and not a fraction so urgent as the present moment. On the present moment depended whether there might be a future for Britain and her empire at all; it was vital therefore to do all that could be done *for* the present. How ironic it would be if all were lost out of a too scrupulous regard for a hypothetical morrow. This was the kind of consideration which weighed with those ministers who had grave doubts about some of the pledges – with Balfour, for example, who strongly opposed the Montagu Declaration, and with Curzon and Montagu, who were as disapproving of the Balfour Declaration.[31] In calmer times governments would have broken up over such large questions. In wartime they had to stay together, and the dissidents to give way under a more pressing necessity. In such circumstances it was not surprising that promises and declarations were made, not purposely or knowingly inconsistent, but with little regard to whether they were consistent or not; in other words, irresponsibly.

The peace

In themselves, the pledges Britain made during the war did not determine anything that happened afterwards. Britain gave no-one self-government after the war simply because she had promised it to them. She might keep her promise; very often she did. Sometimes it was because the promise had raised expectations among its recipients that could not be denied – made them stronger and more resolute claimants. But if it had not had this effect, and if Britain could prevaricate or break a promise with impunity, she would. The colonial settlement when it came after the war, and as it was modified subsequently, was determined much more by the conditions of that time – the interests, strengths and weaknesses of different parties then – than by pledges and declarations made, cynically or irresponsibly, in the past.

The conditions of 1919 determined that, initially, Britain would get a great deal out of the war for herself. In the first place, she and her allies had won the war, and Germany and Turkey had lost. This meant that there were, suddenly, a large number of colonies going begging in the world, with only Britain, France, Italy, the United States and Japan in a position to snaffle them up, which effectively meant Britain and France, because Japan would be satisfied with the north Pacific, America did not want any colonies, and Italy, whose contribution to the Allied victory was negligible, was not thought to deserve any. Togoland, the Cameroons, South-West Africa, Tanganyika, Samoa, the Bismarck Archipelago, Kaiser Wilhelmsland, Iraq, Persia, Palestine, Arabia, Lebanon, Syria – all these were gift horses for Britain and France if they wanted them, which they did. Britain would probably have wanted her share under any government, but the fact that her government in 1919 was the same imperialist-infiltrated government which had fought the war made her desire the keener. In December 1918, a 'Khaki' election had returned the wartime coalition with an unstoppable majority; Balfour, Curzon and Milner were all in it (Milner as Colonial Secretary), and these were not the kind of men in this situation to exercise colonial self-restraint – as neither were the leaders of the Dominions which had fought. Lloyd George was not bothered much about the empire either way, and put up little resistance to his imperialists' accepting what fell into their laps. In case he had felt like resisting, Leopold Amery soothed his conscience with a statement of what they were doing, which was convincing, and in part true; their battle, he wrote to Lloyd George at the end of the war,

> had been over Europe; but *incidentally*, on behalf of that cause, as well as in defence of our existence, we shall find ourselves compelled to complete the liberation of the Arabs, to make secure the independence of Persia, and if we can of Armenia, to protect tropical Africa from German economic and military exploitation. All these objects are justifiable in themselves and don't become less so because they increase the general sphere of British influence … And if, when all is over … the British Commonwealth emerges greater in area and resources … who has the right to complain?[32]

Which was probably the version most people in Britain shared. So the will and the opportunity for colonial aggrandisement were there; and for the time being, there was little reason to suppose that the strength to hold on to new acquisitions was not there too. Consequently, the first result of the war for Britain was a considerable augmentation of her empire. The Middle East was divided up almost *à la* Sykes–Picot. The Arabs for their efforts were given the Arabian desert. Britain took for herself Palestine, Transjordan, the Persian Gulf states and Iraq, which, together with her existing protectorates in Egypt, Cyprus and Aden, made up a tidy little Middle Eastern empire (Map 11). It almost fulfilled Curzon's old dream of a continuous belt of influence or control between the Mediterranean and India, which *was* fulfilled in August 1919 when the final link in the chain, Persia, was secured by means of a one-sided, and widely resented, treaty. The year 1919 was one for dreams to come true: another one which did was Cecil Rhodes's 'Cape to Cairo' scheme, when Britain took Tanganyika from Germany and so completed that chain too. In the west of Africa, the Gold Coast and Nigeria were extended at the expense of parts of Togoland and the Cameroons, and further down the Union of South Africa took over the administration of South-West Africa.[33] In the South Pacific the spoils were divided between Australia and New Zealand. With Britain's existing colonies remaining intact despite the disruption of the past four years, and all these additions, the British empire in 1919 was more extensive than it had ever been.

Of course, it was not quite as straightforward as that. Palestine and the rest were not *called* annexations, or even colonies. The climate of opinion of the time, the new

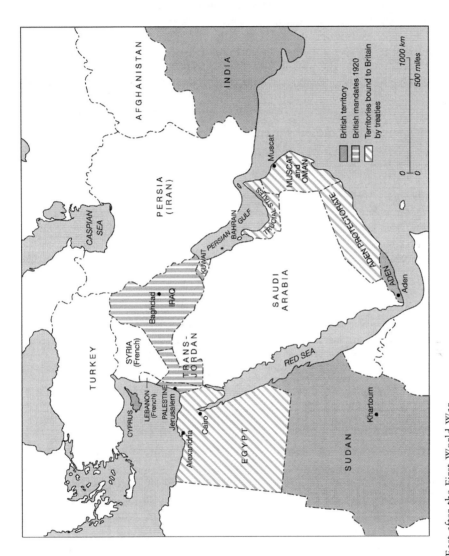

Map 11 The Middle East after the First World War
Source: After Marshall, P. J. (ed.) *The Cambridge Illustrated History of the British Empire* (Cambridge University Press, 1996, p. 83). © Cambridge University Press, reprinted with permission of Cambridge University Press via PLS Clear.

disfavour which was felt or professed for imperial conquest, especially among Americans, would not admit of annexations pure and simple. All these acquisitions were called 'mandated' territories, which meant that they were entrusted to Britain by the League of Nations to administer in the interests of their inhabitants, and with a view to their eventual independence. But this was a limitation which British ministers did not feel they had to worry much over. They did not baulk at the mandate principle when it was proposed; neither did they regard or treat their new mandated territories, when they got them, any differently from their existing colonies. It looked cynical, and was seen by many critics as such ('the crudity of conquest', the historian H. A. L. Fisher called it, 'draped in the veil of morality'[34]). But for an imperialist, it was not necessarily so. In essence, said Amery, the mandate was 'nothing more than a formal obligation to the League of Nations to follow certain principles already in force in our other African colonies':

> I do not think that the Mandate is likely to impose upon us any conditions which we would not impose upon ourselves or which we have not been in the habit of imposing upon ourselves whenever we dealt with subject peoples.[35]

If anything, the mandate principle was accepted by Britain with a certain irritation. It went without saying that she would treat her colonies kindly. She did not need to be told.

The real limitations which existed to Britain's imperial power after the war did not stem from the League of Nations or the mandate system, or indeed from outside the empire at all. They came from within. Imperialists were too euphoric to notice it at first, but in fact while the war had added new colonies to Britain's collection, it had also weakened her grip in her old ones. In the self-governing dominions, the co-operation with Britain which imperialists gloried in was misleading. That they had co-operated in wartime did not necessarily signify that they wished to be shackled in peace. In all of them, the experience of war stimulated local nationalisms as much as a common imperialism, and in some, notably in South Africa among the Afrikaners and in Canada among the French, it had provoked fierce resentments, which their governments would have to take account of after the war.[36] In Ireland and some of the dependent colonies, the effect on local nationalism was similar, and more damaging. The Great War was a war which Britain only just won, and with many defeats along the way: in itself, this damaged her prestige and authority. This was to show in the long run, but in the short run it had already shown in the concessions which her vulnerability had forced from her. During the war she had had to pay a heavy price for the collaboration on which her power had always rested: the promise to Egypt, the McMahon Letter, the Montagu Declaration, and all the other more general commitments she had made to the principle, which she scarcely believed in, of 'self-determination'. Even before they were honoured, they were a stimulation to colonial nationalism; if they were not honoured, they would be a provocation, as were some other things Britain had done during the war. Irish nationalism was stirred beyond hope of collaboration by the scale of reprisals that Britain had found it necessary to take after the Easter rebellion of 1916 in Dublin, which made a popular cause out of a minority and faintly ridiculous adventure, and drowned the old, accommodating Home Ruleism of before the war. In Egypt, the fellaheen suffered from Army commandeering and private profiteering, which alienated them from the government and made them ripe fodder for nationalists. In India, the war had given the Muslim League over to Congress, and Congress over to extremists. On all these fronts the war had provoked, or provided an opportunity for, a more vigorous assertion of nationalism; and a nationalism with a harder edge than before. Before the war, there had been violence and terrorism, but the mainstream of colonial nationalism had been represented by Gokhale's Congress or Redmond's Irish Home Rule Party: moderate in their aims, which generally did not embrace absolute national independence, and also in their methods, which were constitutional. Sinn Fein and Gandhi-ism, though poles apart in other ways, were similar in this: that they both worked unconstitutionally, outside the system. Sinn Fein in Ireland almost swept the board in the 1918 election – but refused to take its seats. In India, Gandhi's distinctive contribution to the nationalist armoury was 'non-co-operation'. The nationalist struggle had gone into a higher gear, and this spelt danger for the empire: danger which even in peacetime it might not be able to contain.

With the troops back from the Western Front, and available, the empire should have been more able to contain trouble. Its armies, if they could have been kept in uniform, were big enough. But they could not be kept in uniform: because of the expense, which middle-class taxpayers cavilled at, and because of the danger – a real one – of mutiny among the working-class troops. When they had beaten Germany, the British soldiery felt they had done their job. They had not joined up to police the empire. Many of them were restless at not being demobilised immediately, and there were strikes and mutinies – small ones – in France and in England. The government had little choice but to demobilise fast.[37] By 1922, the Army had dwindled to 200,000 men, who, if they were spread all over Britain's world responsibilities, would be spread very thin. Over certain kinds of terrain Britain found she could save on ground troops by a brand new method of counter-insurgency, which was to bomb or strafe rebel villages from aeroplanes. But that had its disadvantages. It could not be employed in Dublin or Calcutta, for example (though Sir Hugh Trenchard, Chief of the British Air Staff, probably did not see this; on one occasion in 1921, he suggested that strikers in Britain be bombed into submission in this way).[38] Even in semi-deserts it was a somewhat indiscriminate method of public control, difficult to target the real villains, as opposed to women and children, and for that reason unpopular with many of the pilots themselves. It was just not cricket. Morality was not always a sure guarantee against atrocity in the British empire, but it could sometimes exercise an inconvenient constraint. For all these reasons, the empire in 1919 was undoubtedly more vulnerable than it looked. The main threats were internal. One it could contain, possibly two. But what would happen if it were challenged by nationalists on three or four fronts at the same time?

The aftermath: Ireland, India, the Middle East

In 1919, it happened. In March, Egyptian nationalists, inflamed by Britain's refusal to allow them to put their case at the Paris Peace Conference and by the arrest and exile of their leaders, began demonstrating, rioting, sabotaging and assassinating British army officers. In April, there was a rash of rebellions in the Punjab serious enough to convince at least one British general that the Indian Mutiny was about to be repeated, which persuaded him to open fire on a crowd of unarmed Indians in a public square in Amritsar, and to continue firing into their backs until his ammunition ran out, killing at least 380 and wounding 1,200 (Figure 8.1). In April, came the first serious Arab–Jewish clash in Palestine. In May, Britain was at war with Afghanistan, and about to go to war again, it seemed, with Turkey. Iraq exploded into full-scale rebellion in July the next year, which cost Britain more than she had spent on all her wartime operations in the Middle East to

Figure 8.1 Atrocity. The Amritsar Massacre of 1919, as seen by the German satirical paper, *Simplicissimus*
Source: © Chronicle/Alamy Stock Photo.

put down, and more than 400 soldiers' lives besides. In Persia, she had to contend with bitter resistance from nationalists to the treaty they felt she had forced on them, and with infiltration and, on occasion, direct invasion from Russia. And all this time, nearer home, Ireland was coming to the boil: insurgents proclaiming a republic and setting up a provisional government, attacking police stations, carrying on a guerrilla war of terrorism and assassination against the English, which it took 30,000 troops to contain.

Here at last was the concerted colonial uprising which imperialists had long been frightened of, and which only good fortune had prevented before. One conflagration could have been kept under control; so many at the same time was rather stretching the resources of the imperial fire service. 'Our small army is far too scattered,' wrote the Chief of the General Staff in May 1920; 'in no single theatre are we strong enough – not in Ireland, nor England, not on the Rhine, not in Constantinople, nor Batoum, nor Egypt, nor Palestine, nor Mesopotamia, nor Persia, nor India.'[39] The means were not there; some said that the motive was not adequate either: 'Neither on the grounds of obligation or on grounds of interest,' said Asquith, had they any stake in the Middle East which was 'at all commensurate with the demands that are being made upon the sorely tried British taxpayer'.[40] The latter was represented at this time by the new 'Anti-Waste League', which managed to get three MPs elected in 1921, and targeted Iraq specifically. It is at times like this, when it involves sacrifice, that a people's will to keep an empire is really tested, and the government in 1920 calculated, probably rightly, that there was just not enough solid imperial resolution in Britain to bear the full and enormous burden of retaining it all. The imperialists had miscalculated, and overgorged. It was clear that they would have to back down.

And back down they did, but selectively, cutting losses and retaining, so far as possible, the more essential of what they regarded as Britain's vital national interests in the east. The way they did it was reminiscent of the old 'informal' imperialism of years before. What was sapping Britain's strength and resources were the colonial bureaucracies and military establishments she had to maintain in countries that did not want them. If she could withdraw these, but still retain under-cover control or surveillance over what was most valuable to her in these countries, it would be less provocative, cheaper, and, one hoped, as effective. So in Iraq, for example, Britain dismantled her short-lived Indian-type administration in 1921, and established a national government there which was 'independent', but committed, by a treaty signed in October 1922 and subsequent military and financial agreements, to toeing Britain's line (which was not demanding) in return for her protection and advice. She made a similar arrangement with Transjordan. Likewise Egypt was granted what was called independence in February 1922, thanks to Lord Allenby, now her High Commissioner, who threatened resignation if she were not, but Egypt's foreign and military affairs, and the affairs of her foreign residents, were kept in British hands, and a British garrison stayed there to guard the Canal. Persia was abandoned, the treaty with her tacitly repudiated; but the Persian Gulf states and their oil still held on to tightly. Arabia Britain had already given over to the Arabs, except for the strategically important south coast, which remained under British protection. Right across the Middle East, therefore, apart from Cyprus where British control was tightened, and Palestine, British supremacy was shaded in more lightly, but (for 20 years at least) adequately for what she wanted. What she wanted, said Balfour, and what she got, was 'supreme economic and political control, to be exercised no doubt ... in friendly and unostentatious co-operation with the Arabs, but nevertheless, in the last resort to be exercised'.[41]

In India and Ireland, where the ties of interest and sentiment were stronger, and the stakes higher, the government's strategy was different, and less successful. That concessions to nationalists would have to be made there had become obvious; what was less obvious was how far those concessions would have to go to satisfy them. The government still hoped that they could play 'moderates' off against 'extremists', which had worked before the war, and might work again. In both Ireland and India, they pursued a dual policy of concession to moderate nationalists, those who wanted less than complete emancipation from colonial control, in order to strengthen their hands against the extremists, and thus preserve the imperial connection; together with fierce repression of what was called 'sedition', in order to placate red-necked imperialists at home. But the two things mixed very badly. Ireland might possibly have accepted old-fashioned 'Home Rule' – self-government in domestic affairs only, which had satisfied John Redmond in 1914 – if it had not been for the punitive executions carried out after the Easter Rising, and the infamous 'Black and Tans' sent out by Lloyd George to police the Irish in 1920. In India, the equivalent – 'dyarchy' – *was* accepted, and implemented, and seemed for a short time to be going well, until again the repressive side of British policy manifested itself in the Rowlatt Acts, which severely attenuated judicial procedures in suspected conspiracy cases; in the Amritsar massacre; and even more, perhaps, in the reaction to that massacre in Britain, where its perpetrator, General Dyer, was mildly censured by the Army, then virulently defended by his superiors, by the House of Lords, by much of the press, by most Conservative MPs, and by a large number of ordinary people who subscribed £26,000 in a month to a fund set up on his behalf by the *Morning Post*. (To be fair, however, the majority opinion was probably against this.[42]) The effect of all this on

Indian nationalist opinion was disastrous. Gandhi made it the occasion for his first non-co-operation campaign. In both Ireland and India, repression only undid the gains made by the policy of concession.

India Britain was able to hold on to for a while. Non-co-operation failed, Gandhi was arrested. But not Ireland. The Irish nationalists refused to be compromised with *or* suppressed. Guerrilla warfare made Ireland a death-trap for British troops, who were unused to it. Britain's resources were strained, her will to win undermined by Liberal and clerical criticism at home of the excesses of the Black and Tans. In February 1920, the Conservative Lord Chancellor, Lord Birkenhead, said that he would have liked to try 20 years' coercion again in Ireland: but he knew that he did not have the material means or the popular support to do it.[43] So Lloyd George negotiated with the rebels, concluded a treaty with them in 1921, and in 1922 handed Ireland over to Sinn Fein. This was Britain's first foray down a twisting path which was soon to become familiar: a nationalist movement first branded by her government as 'a small nest of assassins' (Lloyd George's phrase), and resisted by a privileged settler minority; then negotiated with; and finally given self-government within what was now beginning to be called no longer an empire but – and the word acknowledged the dispersal of her power – a 'Commonwealth of Nations'. Ireland was where the colonial rot really set in. That Britain could not keep firm hold even of her 'Other Island' was ominous. Colonial nationalists looked on, and drew their own conclusions.[44]

Imperial morale, 1920

For those who administered the British empire, and for the classes which sustained and supplied them at home, all this could not have been good for morale. That morale before the war had been compounded of a number of elements, among them self-confidence, a sense of duty, a certain idealism, an 'illusion of permanence',[45] material well-being; and a corporate experience of all these things, by a ruling cadre whose chief strength had lain in its social and ideological homogeneity, its *esprit de corps*. All these things had been under constant attack before the war, but gently and gradually, so that they could adapt and maintain equilibrium. The impact of the war and its aftermath was more violent, and probably more damaging.

The war's general effect on the culture and ethos of the young privileged classes in Britain is well known from the accounts of men like Robert Graves and Siegfried Sassoon.[46] Graves and Sassoon may have been atypical, but they were not alone in finding, as the historian E. L. Woodward did, that 'the horrors of the war of attrition, repeated again and again by the commanders to whom all the Great Powers had handed over the destiny of youth, stunned and deafened the imagination'.[47] Some reacted more strongly than others. 'Every junior officer', said George Orwell,

> looked on the General Staff as mental defectives ... People who in a normal way would have gone through life with about as much tendency to think for themselves as a suet pudding were turned into Bolshies just by the war.[48]

The young men's reaction against their seniors turned into a reaction against what their seniors had stood for: 'so far as the younger generation was concerned, the official beliefs were dissolving like sand-castles'.[49] This mood produced fascists and pacifists, Mosley and Neville Chamberlain, nihilists and free lovers: all from the ranks of the ruling classes.

It would have been surprising if it had not produced anti-imperialists too, and made some dent in the morale, the certainties, of those who ran the empire.

In fact, those who ran the empire were very likely the most resistant of all the ruling classes to the new strains. Those who stayed ruling the empire while the war was on were isolated from its most harrowing experiences, and so relatively unaffected. Those who were exposed to the war in Europe, but still joined the colonial services afterwards, were likely to be immune by inoculation. Those whom the war set against imperialism altogether were not likely to join in the first place. So the empire continued to be run by men with their imperial visions intact, with these differences only: that they were likely to be less representative of their class in Britain than they had been before, because their class as a whole had shifted away from them; that they were likely to be harder to find than before, for the same reason; and that all the time they would be subjected to criticism from home, more than they had been used to before, which might be expected at some points to cause doubts, if not total disillusion. It is likely that colonial administrators after 1918 were a little less confident than before, both of the rightness of what they were doing, and of its permanence.

This was true of India, where a great deal had happened since 1914 to undermine the morale of its civil service. There was the Montagu Declaration, and then the Montagu–Chelmsford Report and the 1919 Act. There were the nationalists, and terrorism and rioting, and the danger – many thought – of another 1857; and the British government's shabby treatment of brave General Dyer when he nipped it in the bud. Lastly there was the wholesale takeover of the Indian Civil Service by Indians which the Lee Commission proposed in 1917, and to which a start was made in the 1920s, as well as a start to the Indianisation of the Army's officer corps. The whole stability of the Indian civil servant's life was imperilled by these changes: his rationale, his career, even his physical safety. Those who felt most threatened, and most outraged, resigned. The new post-war intake of Indian civil servants knew what they were coming in to, and adapted. In the 1930s, the service had far fewer 'die-hards' in its upper echelons: a fact which Winston Churchill angrily attributed to a deliberate government plot to promote only 'people who are supposed to be modern-minded'.[50] There was consequently less disillusion and bad feeling among Anglo-Indians than there might have been. But the old spirit of the ICS, the old self-assurance, the old complacency, the old satisfactions, were gone. The decline in morale was perhaps reflected in the slow dissolution of the Anglo-Indian's social life, and especially of its chief pillar, the Club. It was reflected in the literature of Anglo-India, into which had crept a critical, sometimes downright condemnatory note, most wounding (because most sensitive) in E. M. Forster's *A Passage to India* (1924). Some Anglo-Indians may have shared the condemnations; George Orwell, who from 1922 to 1928 was himself one of them in Burma, found Englishmen 'all over India ... who secretly loathe the system of which they are part',[51] but it was more usual to defend it, albeit sometimes apologetically. That it needed quite so much to be defended was dispiriting; what dispirited the rulers most of all was that their *moral* case could no longer be taken for granted – 'and they had been used on the whole to feeling rather self-righteous'.[52] Morale is most difficult to sustain among troops in retreat, and the ICS was assuredly in retreat, whether it welcomed it or not: giving ground all the time to native Indians, its years numbered, its judgement day in sight. Service in India was becoming less and less attractive as a career, because less assured. Consequently, and because it needed a rarer type of young man to be willing to work to make himself dispensable, recruitment fell off after the war, and the ICS found it difficult in Britain to fill its quota. Before the war this had been unheard of.[53]

But the Indian Service's loss was the Colonial Service's gain. The decline in morale was by no means universal, and in tropical Africa, for example, where the war had had nothing like the same impact as in India, and British rule still looked to have a future, Britons could still get the same warm, assured feelings that had used to sustain them in India, without qualms of doubt or of resentment. In the 1920s, under the guidance of a dynamic Colonial Secretary and a far-seeing recruitment officer, the Colonial Service, which before the war had been very much a poor sister to the ICS, accrued to it some of the latter's lost prestige: and overtook it as the favourite career for young paternalists out of Eton and Oxford. This did not happen automatically. In an age when anti-imperialism was rife and virulent, a young colonial guardian's morale had to be deliberately and carefully nurtured. In the inter-war Colonial Service it was so nurtured, recruits looked after and propagandised and trained as never before. The result was a sturdy and confident plant, more healthy by far than its fading and withering sister.[54]

And so the empire, and its officers, in the short term survived the shock of the war and its aftermath. It remained to be seen for how long.

Notes

1 L. S. Amery, *My Political Life* (Hutchinson, 1953), ii, 104.
2 P. Guinn, *British Strategy and Politics, 1914 to 1918* (Oxford UP, 1965), p. 126.
3 M. Beloff, *Imperial Sunset* (Methuen, 1969), i, 197.
4 H. G. Wells, *Mr Britling Sees it Through* (1916), p. 197.
5 C. E. Carrington, 'The empire at war', in *The Cambridge History of the British Empire* (1959), iii pp. 641–2.
6 B. R. Mitchell and P. Deane, *Abstract of British Historical Statistics* (Cambridge UP, 1962), pp. 319–20, 325–6.
7 *Parliamentary Debates*, 5th series, 144 (1921), c. 1621.
8 A. M. Gollin, *Proconsul in Politics* (Blond, 1964), p. 529.
9 Amery, *op. cit.*, ii, 32.
10 See W. K. Hancock, *Survey of British Commonwealth Affairs* (Oxford UP, 1942), ii, Part 2 pp. 94–109; V. H. Rothwell, *British War Aims and British Diplomacy, 1914–1918* (Oxford UP, 1971), Chapter 7; Beloff, *op. cit.*, i, 225–8.
11 See Guinn, *op. cit.*, pp. 191–2; Beloff, *op. cit.*, i, 212–17.
12 Amery, *op. cit.*, ii, 160.
13 Rothwell, *op. cit.*, p. 71.
14 On the empire in the Great War generally, see Carrington, *op. cit.*, Chapter xvi; Guinn, *op. cit.*; W. R. Louis, *Great Britain and Germany's Lost Colonies* (Clarendon Press, 1967), Chapter 2; Melvin E. Page (ed.), *Africa and the First World War* (Macmillan, 1987); F. W. Perry, *The Commonwealth Armies: Manpower and Organization in Two World Wars* (Manchester UP, 1988).
15 E. S. Montagu, *An Indian Diary* (Heinemann, 1930), p. 57.
16 S. R. Mehrotra, *India and the Commonwealth, 1885–1929* (Allen & Unwin, 1965), p. 102.
17 Montagu, *op. cit.*, pp. 194, 364.
18 Mehrotra, *op. cit.*, p. 63.
19 *Ibid.*, p. 100; Montagu, *op. cit.*, p. 8.
20 *Ibid.*, p. 66.
21 *Ibid.*, p. 288.
22 See Mehrotra, *op. cit.*, Chapter 2; R. J. Moore, *Liberalism and Indian Politics, 1872–1922* (Hodder & Stoughton, 1966), Chapter 7; H. F. Owen, 'Towards nationwide agitation and organisation: the Home Rule Leagues, 1915–18', in D. A. Low (ed.), *Soundings in Modern South Asian History* (Weidenfeld & Nicolson, 1968); Montagu, *op. cit.*, *passim*; C. H. Philips (ed.), *Select Documents on the History of India and Pakistan* (Oxford UP, 1962), Part 2.
23 E. L. Woodward and R. Butler (eds), *Documents on British Foreign Policy, 1919–1939*, first series, iv (HMSO, 1952), p. 1121.

24 Amery, *op. cit.*, ii, 115.
25 S. H. Zebel, *Balfour: A Political Biography* (Cambridge UP, 1973), p. 247.
26 *Report of the Palestine Royal Commission*, Cmd 5479 (1937), p. 23.
27 W. R. Louis, *Great Britain and Germany's Last Colonies* (Oxford UP, 1967), p. 6.
28 Woodward and Butler, *op. cit.*, iv, 1276–7.
29 P. Knightley and C. Simpson, *The Secret Lives of Lawrence of Arabia* (Panther, 1969), p. 106.
30 T. E. Lawrence, *Seven Pillars of Wisdom* (Penguin, [1926] 1962), p. 24.
31 D. Judd, *Balfour and the British Empire* (Macmillan, 1968), pp. 260–3; Zebel, *op. cit.*, p. 246.
32 Amery, *op. cit.*, ii, 161.
33 B. Digre, *Imperialism's New Clothes: The Repartition of Tropical Africa, 1914–1919* (Peter Lang, 1990).
34 H. A. L. Fisher, *A History of Europe* (Edward Arnold [2 vols, 1936], 1960 edn in 1 vol), p. 1275.
35 Amery, *op. cit.*, ii, 360; *Parliamentary Debates*, 5th series, 118, c. 2175.
36 See Beloff, *op. cit.*, i, 191–4; P. N. S. Mansergh, *The Commonwealth Experience* (Weidenfeld & Nicolson, 1969), Chapter 6; *Cambridge History of the British Empire*, iii (Cambridge UP, 1959), Chapter 16.
37 R. Graves and A. Hodge, *The Long Weekend* (Faber, 1941), pp. 25–6; M. Howard, *The Continental Commitment* ([M. T. Smith, 1972], Penguin, 1974), p. 78.
38 D. Omissi, *Air Power and Colonial Control: The Royal Air Force, 1913–1939* (Manchester UP, 1990), p. 41.
39 C. E. Callwell, *Field-Marshal Sir Henry Wilson* (Cassell, 1927), ii, 240–1.
40 *Parliamentary Debates*, 5th series, 144 (1921), c. 1529.
41 A. P. Thornton, *The Imperial Idea and its Enemies* (Macmillan, 1959), p. 168.
42 See Derek Sayer, 'British reaction to the Amritsar massacre, 1919–1970', *Past and Present*, 131 (1991), 130–64.
43 Thornton, *op. cit.*, p. 181.
44 On the post-war imperial 'crisis', see John Gallagher, *The Decline, Revival and Fall of the British Empire* (Cambridge UP, 1982); Keith Jeffery, *The British Army and the Crisis of Empire, 1918–22* (Manchester UP, 1984); John Darwin, *Britain, Egypt and the Middle East: Imperial Policy in the Aftermath of War, 1918–1922* (Macmillan, 1981); E. Monroe, *Britain's Moment in the Middle East, 1914–71* (Chatto & Windus, 1981), Chapters 2–3; E. Kedourie, *Britain and the Middle East: The Vital Years, 1914–21* (Bowes & Bowes, 1956); John Charmley, *Lord Lloyd and the Decline of the British Empire* (Weidenfeld & Nicolson, 1987); R. Furneaux, *Massacre at Amritsar* (Allen & Unwin, 1963).
45 F. G. Hutchins, *The Illusion of Permanence* (Princeton UP, 1967).
46 Robert Graves, *Goodbye to All That* (Cape, 1929); Siegfried Sassoon, *Memoirs of an Infantry Officer* (Faber & Faber, 1930).
47 E. Llewellyn Woodward, *Great Britain and the War of 1914–18* (Methuen, 1967), p. xxv.
48 G. Orwell, *Coming Up for Air* (Penguin, [1939] 1962), p. 123.
49 G. Orwell, *Inside the Whale* (Penguin, [1940] 1962), p. 23.
50 *Parliamentary Debates*, 5th series, 276 (1933), c. 1048.
51 G. Orwell, *The Road to Wigan Pier* ([Gollancz, 1937] Penguin, 1962), p. 127.
52 P. Woodruff, *The Men Who Ruled India*, 2 vols (Cape, 1953, 1954), ii, *The Guardians*, 250.
53 See D. Kincaid, *British Social Life in India, 1608–1937* (G. Routledge and Sons, 1938), Chapters 10–12; A. J. Greenberger, *The British Image of India* (Routledge, 1969), Chapter 5; Woodruff, *op. cit.*, ii, *The Guardians*, Part ii, Chapters 1–3.
54 See R. Heussler, *Yesterday's Rulers* (Syracuse UP, 1963), Chapter 11.

9 Difficult times: 1920–39

Recovery through empire

Britain's troubles of 1919–21 in India, the Middle East and Ireland, though they were largely attributable to the extraordinary circumstances of the war, were at the same time symptomatic of a more fundamental and long-term trend, which was her relative political and economic decline in the world. Since the 1870s, this decline had been apparent, though at that time not very worrying because she had some way to decline yet before her lead was taken from her; and to a great extent Britain's empire-building after that time had been a direct response to that decline and its manifestations. The most prescient imperialists in the 1880s and 1890s had foreseen that this decline would have to continue, if the British empire did not organise itself more efficiently to cope with the inevitable challenge, latent as yet, of industrially young, naturally favoured countries like Germany, the United States and Russia. The war had in some ways staved off the challenge: by Germany's defeat, Russia's confusion, and the United States' retreat into her isolationist shell afterwards, but Britain's victory was a pyrrhic one. The setbacks of 1919 to 1921 showed how little able Britain was to capitalise on it, even with her rivals wounded or sulking. As it turned out, the war had weakened her permanently.

Between the wars, the decline continued, though slowly enough not to be perceived by everybody or construed by them as irreversible. For the 1920s and 1930s were abnormal times by most criteria, not easy years for any country; and Britain, though she no longer led the world, stayed among the front runners, and perhaps needed only a slight change of fortune to put her into the lead again. This was how some felt, but the bare economic facts of the time were gloomier. Production in Britain's old staple industries was stagnant, or (as in textiles) actually declining; or if it was rising (as it was in steel), it was doing so sluggishly and at a lower rate of profit.[1] This was serious for the present; what was more ominous for the future was that Britain was lagging in some of the most promising new growth areas of industry too, which meant that as the old export staples declined, there would be nothing to take their place.[2] Britain's foreign trade, though it kept just ahead of her rivals', was declining both relative to theirs (in 1938, her share of world trade had slumped to 14 per cent, from 17 per cent in 1913 and 25 per cent in 1860)[3] and relative to her total production: she was exporting a smaller proportion of what she manufactured. Partly this was due to her own difficulties, partly to an overall drought of world trade in the 1920s and 1930s. Worse still, her overseas investments, on which she had depended in the past to balance her books, never wholly recovered from her massive sale of them recently to pay for the war, so that, in 1930, for example, they were £1,000 million down on the 1914 figure, and reaping less interest too.[4] In the 1930s,

Britain's balance of payments, even with invisibles and investment earnings counted in, began to go very badly into the red, for the first time in over a century.[5]

All this spelt a sad decline from the halcyon days of the 1860s, or even from the breezier time before the war. But more than this, it spelt a quite dramatic change in the balance of Britain's national interest in the wider world. In the first place, between the wars Britain was trading with and investing in the wider world to a lesser degree than before. In 1935–39, her import trade represented only 19 per cent of her national income, compared with 33 per cent in 1910–13; her export trade 10 per cent as against 22 per cent; her foreign investment 3.9 per cent as against 8.6 per cent.[6] Of course, this did not signify necessarily that foreign trade and investment had become less important to Britain (a crust might be as important to a hungry man as a loaf, if it is all he can get), but it did signify that they now played a smaller part in her total economic activity than before. But, second, within this shrinking asset, the empire's share at the same time was getting larger. Between 1910 and 1914, 25 per cent of Britain's import trade and 36 per cent of her export trade had been with her colonies. After 1920, both increased considerably (Table 9.1)

The trend was the same for foreign investment: 46 per cent going to the empire in 1911–13, 59 per cent in 1927–29.[7] Such figures were vivid proof that, although it was fashionable in progressive circles to decry it, from Britain's material point of view, the empire was very far from being an anachronism; that, on the contrary, it was only just beginning to pay the dividends its old champions had always expected from it, and handsomely.

For some, the dividends were higher than for others. They were especially high for the giant British-based industrial and commercial combines and cartels which the war and the Depression, by weeding out their smaller, weaker competitors, had left in control of many of the empire's most valuable resources: concerns like Unilever, which had started the trend and had its fingers everywhere, but particularly in West Africa where it had bought out most of the old trading companies; Dunlop, which had massive interests in Malaysia; Tate and Lyle in the West Indies; and the like. To a large extent now, British industry not only bought its raw materials from the colonies but was directly involved in growing them there too, which further cemented the bonds between British capitalism and the empire. The benefits of the empire were spread unevenly, but to some degree or other they were supposed to filter down to everyone. 'At the bottom of his heart,' wrote George Orwell in 1937, no Englishman wanted to lose the empire; for 'apart from any other consideration, the high standard of life we enjoy in England depends upon our keeping a tight hold on the Empire, particularly the tropical portions of it such as India and Africa'.[8] This had been true for some time, but it was especially true of *this* time, as the importance of the empire increased steadily, in an overseas trade which overall was diminishing.

Table 9.1 Empire trade between the Wars

Dates	Imports (%)	Exports (%)[9]
1920–24	27	37
1925–29	28	42
1930–34	31	42
1935–39	39.5	49

This trend had fundamental implications for British foreign policy. Throughout the nineteenth century and a good way into the twentieth century, the empire had not been the exclusive or even the main focus of foreign policy, because it had not been the exclusive or main repository for Britain's economic interests. Always she had traded more with the world outside her formal possessions; always therefore her main interest had lain in maintaining the widest possible geographical scope for her trade and investment, and never in favouring or protecting exclusively one part of it. Consequently, for example, the arguments for an imperial *Zollverein* had never carried total conviction, because they had seemed to sacrifice a boundless market for an extensive but limited one; consequently, also the extent of her concern and involvement in the world had never been confined to, though of course it had embraced, her formal imperial interests. With the empire now comprising so much more of her interest, her priorities in the world were naturally different. In the first place, because her national economic interests were now less extensive than they had been, her political involvement in the world was likely to be less extensive too; and of course she was in any case not strong enough to defend the range of interests she had defended before. The wider world was becoming less Britain's oyster, more its own or someone else's; Britain's oyster was becoming smaller and more closely defined. In the second place, to the extent that it *was* becoming more closely defined, the means by which it could best be defended were seeming to change. Britain's wider and expanding world market of the nineteenth century had best been maintained – almost everyone agreed – by free trade, leaving as much of the world as possible as open as possible for British commerce and finance to win on their own. This had been the function of British fiscal policy before the war, and one of the preoccupations of foreign policy too. The more restricted nature of Britain's new trade between the wars seemed to require a different approach. The frontiers had been set, their bounds clearly marked; it was no longer a question of finding new worlds to conquer, but of digging in and defending those she had. Such a change of emphasis, if it did not automatically suggest tariffs and free trade areas and the like, at least made them more attractive propositions than before. Every slight swing in Britain's trading figures away from the wider world, and towards the empire, weighted the national interest against free trade, and on the side of imperial preference.

Whether or not this would be the lesson drawn from the consolidation of Britain's commercial boundaries around her empire between the wars depended on how the trend was explained, and whether it was thought to be endemic. In reality, it was a perfectly natural trend, and not really a departure – though it seemed to be – from pre-war. The diminution of trade was new, but in a way it was only continuing a familiar trend for Britain: the trend which, since 1870 or before, and for whatever reason, had made her industry increasingly less competitive in world markets; which after 1918 was only just beginning to bring on it the nemesis it deserved. Before the war we noted a tendency for Britain to export less and less to industrialised countries and more and more to 'underdeveloped' countries, which was a reflection of her increasing inability to compete with other nations in the production of sophisticated goods for sophisticated markets. The underdeveloped world was an easy refuge for inefficient or hard-pressed entrepreneurs, and its existence itself perpetuated their inefficiency. After the war, the same trend continued: in 1927–29, over 75 per cent of British exports went to non-industrial countries, compared with 69.6 per cent in 1909–13 and 58.5 per cent in 1867–69.[10] The growing preponderance of the empire between the wars was in part an aspect of this trend, for the empire consisted mainly of underdeveloped or agricultural markets, which for that reason, as well as reasons of familiarity and sentiment, would be likely to remain when others fell away. They were the easiest markets, the last ditches of British commercial defence, consequently, in times of difficulty, they were likely to form a larger proportion of a small trade than in good times they did of a big trade.

But the moral of this situation – its bearing on the 'national interest' – could be read two ways. The flourishing nature of imperial trade could be looked at for itself, with satisfaction; or as a symptom of a more general commercial ill-health, with concern. The inference of the first diagnosis would be to encourage and develop imperial trade – the healthy sector – more. The result of the second diagnosis would be to concentrate on the disease which was crippling the rest of the commercial body: do something to make British trade more competitive, in markets which did not fall so easily to it as colonial ones. In fact, there was never any doubt as to which of those courses the country would choose. The second would have required interventionist measures no government of that time could have contemplated. If they had involved expenditure, the Treasury would have objected. Industry – the chief beneficiary – had less clout in government circles than finance, which had no need for this kind of thing. Besides, with colonial markets still so available, there was insufficient *pressure* for so drastic a change. So Britain took the first, easier, possibly more natural path, though – it has to be said – with no particular conviction or resolution. The end result was to allow her relative economic decline to continue, masked and cushioned more and more by the empire; and to give the empire a few last years of prominence, and imperialists a few last years of dreaming, before the prominence and the dreams were both finally dissolved by reality.[11]

The imperial solution to Britain's economic problems was a seductive one because it seemed to lie in Britain's *power*. 'Nothing this House can do,' a Conservative MP told the Commons in 1925, 'will have the slightest effect on the amount of goods that the foreigner will purchase from us.' That was why it was

> absolutely essential to develop our own Imperial markets, to foster the privileges we enjoy in our Dominion markets, to increase the amount of exports from our Crown Colonies, to help our factories at home, and to increase the demands from our Crown Colonies for our manufactured goods.[12]

For the most ambitious imperialists the whole beauty of their schemes – which we have met before – was that they could put Britain's destiny altogether in her own hands again, and put an end to her dependence on others. This had been Chamberlain's dream, and it was shared by his disciple Leopold Amery, who was Colonial Under-Secretary under Milner from 1919 to 1921, and Colonial Secretary himself from 1924 to 1929. Amery had a plan:

> an imperial economic policy based on the mutual development of our common resources of nature and human skill, and on the maintenance of a standard of living which we set for ourselves, and are not simply content to have set for us by the unlimited and unregulated competition of the world outside.[13]

The plan was not a new one, but it looked to stand more chance in the 1920s, when the world seemed much closer to that of Chamberlain's imagining than had Chamberlain's own. It involved closer imperial political union if possible, imperial tariff preference, state aid for emigration to the colonies, and the 'development' of the tropical dependencies. And it had other purposes and perspectives than the economic one. It had a social perspective: state-aided emigration was supposed to relieve unemployment in Britain in two ways – first, by taking away some of the unemployed to where they were wanted, and, second, by setting up a new demand (from the emigrants) for British goods, which would reinvigorate British industry and so provide more work at home.[14] It had a political perspective: such schemes were presented as a way to 'kindle the imperial idealism of the British working man' and so seduce him from the false gods of socialism.[15] And it also had a grand, geopolitical perspective. This again was familiar. The geopolitical trend of the times against Britain, and in favour of America and Russia, had been spotted by imperialists long ago; in the 1920s, it was clearer than ever. Amery reiterated it in 1928, in terms which read today like a prophecy, but were meant as a warning:

> We are face to face with the gradual emergence of a new type of greater unity, economic and political, in the world's affairs. We have to realise that what we shall be confronted with is, on the one side, the immense standardized mass production of the United States. On the other hand, we may have, through the gradual coming closer together of Europe and its colonies, another great unit of over 400,000,000 people with nearly 10,000,000 square miles of territory to develop. At the back of these, potentially capable of organization on American lines, lie the Russian Empire, with its 150,000,000 people and 9,000,000 square miles, and the Chinese Empire ... In these conditions there are only two alternatives. One is to drift on, with the certain result that, from a position of ever-increasing relative weakness, Great Britain, on the one side, will eventually have to be absorbed inside the European Economic Union, while the Dominions will gravitate, as subordinate economic dependencies, towards the great American Union. In the long run, that can mean nothing but the break-up of the Empire. The other alternative is that the nations of the Empire should get together effectively in order to make use of their resources.[16]

The key to survival in the coming age of continental superpowers lay in the empire. More specifically it lay in creating a worldwide federation of great, white, self-governing dominions, victualled by a vast estate of non-white and non-self-governing dependencies: the whole united in security and self-sufficiency against a malevolent world.

This was the broad plan. Of course, it did not fit all the empire – not India, for example, because they could not be sure which category of colony she came in. But India, against the general trend, was losing her value to Britain in the 1920s and 1930s, partly because the latter's cotton exports were finding it difficult to surmount India's new tariff barriers (the right to erect them had been another bribe for her loyalty in 1917),[17] and India was not Milner's or Amery's responsibility or even concern in any case. Nor could the plan be implemented all at once. Amery's priorities were set by what seemed realistic at the time. Chiefly he concentrated, first, on pulling the 'white' dominions together; second, on carving a new 'white' dominion out of East Africa – and perhaps another one in Palestine; third, on 'developing' the non-white dependencies. His progress in all three areas was painfully slow, but never totally discouraging. In 1939, the old imperial vision, though a distant one, was still not entirely unrealistic. Britain's supremacy in the world might yet be salvaged by a judicious marshalling and husbanding of her imperial resources.[18]

The Dominions

It was in the Dominions that Amery put his best hopes, but the Dominions that let him down worst. During the war, expectations had been raised that the co-operation they had shown then might carry on into peacetime, and lead them to look again and more favourably at all those 'closer union' ideas the imperialists had been holding out to them for years, but it did not happen this way. 'Closer union' had been designed to fit the empire to withstand a siege. In 1914, the siege had come, and the merits of the scheme had shone out. But as soon as the siege was lifted, those merits receded again, and people put out of their minds the possibility that there might be sieges again in the future.[19] Imperial union no longer appeared in the Dominions' interests, or, to most Britons, in their own: or at any rate, not *urgently* enough in their interests to generate momentum. The common cause of victory in war was replaced for the Dominions by the separate and divergent national interests of peacetime. Resolution was dissipated, resistance reared up again, and inertia set in. Amery, with his wider vision, in the years of power given to him did something to push the cause on a little further. But all the time he was fighting a battle against the dead weight of apathy and obstruction.

The Dominions would never stomach anything which detracted from their national sovereignties, which was why most of the old schemes for political federation were dead letters from the start. Certainly, they would not be content, for example, any longer to have wars declared on their behalf by the King in England without their sanction, which was how it had been done in 1914. The imperialists hoped that nevertheless something might be achieved to give the Commonwealth a united voice in world affairs: perhaps a kind of democracy of foreign policy, whereby diplomatic lines were agreed among themselves by the Dominions and acted on together. That hope never died in the 1920s and 1930s, but nothing concrete ever came of it; and the tendency was for the Dominions to go their own ways, and apart from Britain if they wanted. In September 1922, two Dominions (Canada and South Africa) categorically refused to back British policy in defending the Straits at Chanak against Mustapha Kemal, and a third, Australia, wavered. In 1923, Canada, for the first time, concluded a treaty with a foreign power (the Halibut Fisheries Treaty with the United States) without reference to Britain. There was little doubt that in foreign policy the Dominions – despite their imperial pride, which was undoubted – regarded themselves as equal partners with Britain, and in some matters not even partners. The trend here was fissiparous, and Britain did not have it in her power to reverse it. In the endless constitutional debates about the Dominions' status which ran through successive imperial conferences in the 1920s and 1930s, the problem was always to define a partnership to which none of the partners wanted materially to commit herself. The best that could be done was Balfour's formula of 1926, which was notable more for the obligations it disavowed than for those it delimited: by it, Britain and the dominions were stated to be

> autonomous Communities within the British Empire, equal in status, in no way subordinate one to another in any aspect of their domestic or external affairs, though united by a common allegiance to the Crown, and freely associated as members of the British Commonwealth of Nations.

In the end, with feeling in the Dominions as it was, perhaps imperialists should have been happy that, although imperial unity had not been furthered in any significant way between the wars, it had not been precluded either.

And the old imperialists were able to make small advances along other lines of attack. They had a measure of success with state-aided emigration, though not enough to satisfy its champions or, certainly, to cure the Depression. An Empire Settlement Act was passed in 1922 to help it on, and in all a little over 400,000 emigrants were assisted before the early

1930s, when emigration from Britain virtually dried up. Imperial preference had a slower and stormier passage. The main obstacle here was a simple but massive one. Imperial preference meant imposing lower duties on empire imports than on foreign imports, which presupposed that foreign imports paid duties. But by and large, they did not, which meant that the proponents of imperial preference, before they could start cutting duties, had to get some imposed first, and this was a much more contentious matter.

In 1915, a breach had been made in Britain's long-standing free trade edifice when, to raise revenue for the war, a tariff of 33.3 per cent had been levied on imports of certain luxuries. After the war, these tariffs were never abolished, but they were not extended significantly either because both the Liberal and Labour Parties were still faithful to free trade, and on this matter public opinion seemed to be on their side. In 1922, the Conservative Party pledged itself not to alter its fiscal policy without an electoral mandate; when it sought this mandate in December 1923, it was badly defeated; and although it got into power again the next year the man it chose as its Chancellor was Winston Churchill, whose free trade convictions in the past had been strong enough to make him desert to the Liberals. In 1930, therefore, there was little sign of hope for the preferencers: 83 per cent of British imports paid no duty at all,[20] and these included most foodstuffs, which for the empire were the items that mattered most. Any preferences secured in the 1920s, therefore – and there were some – were of marginal importance.

The 1930s, however, saw things change a little. They changed mainly because during the Depression it sank in how sick was Britain's trading capacity, but how relatively healthy was the imperial part of it, which certainly weakened the overwhelming case that free trade had once had, and strengthened the imperialists'. First of all, when the Depression was at its worst, in 1931–32, as a kind of last resort *in extremis*, free trade was scrapped, which was the big step. The Import Duties Act of February 1932 put a 10 per cent tariff on most imports, and allowed for increases and preferences if required. After that, the imperial preferencers had it relatively easy, though not altogether so because less committed men, like Prime Minister Baldwin, did remember that if the empire took *nearly* half of Britain's exports, that still left the rest of the world taking *more* than half.[21] At an Imperial Economic Conference held at Ottawa in 1932, a number of reciprocal preferential arrangements were negotiated between the different Dominions which, though they by no means made up an 'Imperial *Zollverein*' or anything like it, did go some way to satisfying the imperialists. Whether they contributed significantly to the continuing growth in the empire's share of British trade after 1932 is doubtful. If they did, it is even more doubtful whether they did Britain any good. A discriminatory tariff is more likely to reduce trade to the countries it is discriminating against, than increase trade to the countries it is discriminating for; consequently, if the Ottawa agreements did anything to augment Britain's imperial trade, it was very likely at the direct expense of the rest of her trade. This anyway was the trend in the 1930s: that British trade relied on imperial markets more and more and on foreign markets less and less – abjured the open and stormy sea of world competition for more sheltered waters. Which, though it might have saved the commercial vessel from floundering – which was one of the imperialists' intentions – did not encourage its builders to build it strong.[22]

A new Dominion? Rhodesia, Kenya, Palestine

At every step in the field of imperial consolidation the imperialists' ambitions were dogged by parochial pressures and jealousies in the Dominions, by prejudice and inertia at home, and, most fundamentally, by their lack of control over the scattered political units they wished to consolidate. From this tangle of frustrations it should have been a relief to escape into one of their other major projects: to make East and Central Africa into another great dominion for the Anglo-Saxon race to breathe and breed in; for at least in East–Central Africa most of the strongest pressures were working for them, and not against them, and, in theory, control over it was still uncompromisingly theirs. The East–Central Africa scheme was the kind imperialists loved best of all, especially those imperialists who had missed the heady days of the 1880s and 1890s: it recalled the heroic ages of the empire, and stirred the blood again. There were practical points in its favour too, such as the economic advantage of securing and exploiting the region's mineral and agricultural resources, and the possible political advantage of setting up a counterweight to Afrikanerdom, which was increasingly asserting itself in the south. Amery, predictably, made the scheme his own.

His agents were to be the white settlers. White settlement in that part of Africa had for years been encouraged by all governments: by Conservative governments for the positive reason that it was a way to extend the empire, by Liberal governments for the negative reason that it was a cheap way. For 30 years, therefore, the settlers had had things more or less their own way, and had been using their power and influence to secure some of the best African lands for themselves, on the grounds that they would make better use of them; and then to pressure the Africans to work for wages on them, on the grounds that they would not be able to use them profitably otherwise. Their needs were real ones. Some settlers had got rich quickly in East–Central Africa and wanted cheap labour only in order to boost an already luxurious standard of living, but such men were exceptional. Many, perhaps most, of the early settlers had had to struggle hard to make ends meet. The British South Africa Company, which had opened up the Rhodesias, had paid no dividends to its shareholders ever. Lord Delamere, the picturesque father-figure of the Kenya settlers, reputedly lost his fortune twice over in Kenya farming, experimenting with new crops and stock to find out which ones would survive the climate. The settlers were struggling to open up a new frontier in conditions of considerable difficulty; the territory was virgin, success not assured. 'These are men up against the wilderness,' said Churchill in 1921:

> They have mostly sunk every penny they possess in their holdings, and they are engaged in a struggle, comparable only to actual war, to keep themselves alive and to make a home; fighting against the wilderness, the wild beasts, the loneliness, and the difficulties of these new, wild lands.[23]

If it did not justify them, this at least explained their hunger for the good land and cheap labour, which is what they hoped political power would give them more of. With some justice they claimed that colonial secretaries had promised them 'self-government' all along. Amery certainly agreed.

The flies in the settlers' ointment were the non-Europeans in East–Central Africa, who everywhere overwhelmingly outnumbered the whites, and to whom some people believed Britain had commitments which were incompatible with the settlers' ambitions. Amery could never see why white supremacy should ever conflict with native 'trusteeship', and neither, of course, could the settlers. But there was a large body of informed opinion in Britain which disagreed, and a larger one in Africa. So Amery and the settlers had a battle on their hands, although for one of the provinces of Amery's projected dominion, it turned out to be a very easy one.

The settlers won in Southern Rhodesia because they had all the economic and strategic aces in their hands. Since 1889, when it was founded, Britain had never directly administered the country, but allowed a capitalist company to, because that way she had got it done for free. Under the company the settlers had fairly quickly become used to ruling themselves in most matters, through a legislative council, which in 1908 they had come to dominate numerically. It had always been understood that when the time came for the Company to pull out of Southern Rhodesia, it would be they who would take over formally. And when the time did come, just after the war when the Company decided it could no longer continue administering at a loss, they were there waiting for their inheritance, and indeed demanding it.

From the point of view of the humanitarian lobby in Britain, there was a good reason why the Southern Rhodesian settlers should not be given control of their destiny, which was that tied up with that destiny was the destiny of the colony's African population too. 'If you give self-government to the present council with the present franchise,' a Labour Party spokesman pointed out in 1921, 'it means that practically the whole of the franchise will be in the hands of the white settlers'; and, that, he said, was not fair to the natives.[24] Yet it was doubtful whether the settlers would willingly accept anything less. And it was doubtful too whether, in order to do better by the natives, Britain would be willing to bear the cost of administering Southern Rhodesia herself, which would involve not merely its running cost from that moment on, but also the Company's accumulated debt from the past, which had been put (by an official Commission) at £4.5 million. The cost of any settlement, in fact, was one of the main reasons why Britain at first favoured the idea of Southern Rhodesia's incorporation into the Union of South Africa, which could underwrite the debt. Another compelling reason was that a new Rhodesian province might have done something to redress the British balance in South Africa against the Dutch. But this plan came to nothing, because a Rhodesian referendum (of white voters) in November 1922 decided against it; and so the choice remained between the Colonial Office and the settlers.

There was never any real doubt as to which way the British government would decide. It was a very familiar situation: Britain's imperial designs needed the collaboration of the Rhodesian whites; she could not afford to alienate them, and possibly could not have controlled them if she had wanted to. The only difficulty was that if a settler government took over, and then found it could not meet the Company's bill, the British taxpayer might after all be saddled with it, but this problem was cleared away in 1923 when the Company agreed to waive part of the bill in exchange for Britain's confirmation of some of its more dubious claims to lands and mineral deposits in Northern Rhodesia. In the end, Britain had to pay only £1.5 million, which delighted even her humanitarians, who of course were taxpayers too. In October 1923, Southern Rhodesia passed into the hands of its white Legislative Assembly. Strictly speaking, the country was not yet constitutionally 'self-governing', and there was a host of reservations placed on the kinds of laws the Assembly might enact, mainly designed to safeguard African rights. But similar reservations had been made to the South African Constitution in 1910, and they were worth just as much – or as little – now. After 1923, Southern Rhodesia went the way of South Africa, albeit more slowly. In 1930, she passed a Land Apportionment Act which was blatantly discriminatory, and the Colonial Office, which in theory had the right, in practice, did not have the power or the will to stop it. The reality of the situation was that Southern Rhodesia belonged to her settlers, to do with her as they willed.

This was a first step towards the imperialists' 'Great White Dominion', and it looked for a time as though it might very soon be followed by a second. In Kenya to the north, the white minority was as ambitious and vocal as in Rhodesia, buoyed up with past promises, backed by their governors, and if anything more willing to go to violent extremes in support of their demands. But they did not have quite the hand of cards the Rhodesians had. In the first place they were fewer than in Rhodesia: only 9,651 among 2.5 million Africans, as against 33,620 Southern Rhodesian whites among 865,000 Africans, and while it was perhaps no more moral for one man to rule 25 men than for one man to rule 250, it was more practical, which might give even the most favourable British government reason for pause. Then Kenya did not have Rhodesia's strategical cards either; or her mineral wealth; and she *had* had a Colonial Office administration of sorts to govern her in the past. Again, resistance was stronger in Kenya, and in Britain on behalf of Kenya. Kenya became in the early 1920s a focus of humanitarian, missionary and political attention in Britain, the battleground on which they chose to defend what they conceived to be the cause of colonial 'trusteeship', against the assaults of white exploitation; and it was a battle they persisted in throughout the inter-war years. They were aided, too, by increasing and effective pressure coming out of Kenya itself: from mavericks among the white settler pack, who provided a steady stream of informed and lethal ammunition in books and articles and pamphlets; and from the Africans themselves, who at the beginning of the 1920s began to organise themselves into political associations which Europeans would recognise as such, and comprised an increasingly effective resistance thereafter. And, lastly, in Kenya there was a complication that Rhodesia did not have, which was the presence there of a large number of Asian immigrants (23,000 in 1921), who outnumbered the whites, and were no more content to be dominated by them than (probably) were the Africans. The Asians were politically organised too, and, as ever, they had not only themselves but also the Indians in India to support them, and the government of India which was always sensitive to the treatment of its subjects abroad. It was a more formidable line-up than the anti-settlers could claim in Rhodesia, and consequently the battle was more equal.

Nevertheless, the settlers in Kenya and their champions in England could probably have won, had they been quicker. They were slowed down at first by the Asian problem, which was the initial cause of conflict in Kenya; and then by what Amery regarded as the culpable vacillations and temporising of his colleagues in the Conservative government of 1924–29. It was the vociferous opposition of the Indian community after 1919 which prevented a devolution of power to the Europeans at the same time as power was being devolved to their kin in Southern Rhodesia, and, in fact, did more. In 1923, a White Paper on 'Indians in Kenya' contained this declaration, which was intended mainly to avoid a decision one way or the other on the question of whether Indians should share representation with Europeans, but which clearly had much wider implications:

> Primarily, Kenya is an African territory, and His Majesty's Government think it necessary definitely to record their considered opinion that the interests of the African natives must be paramount, and that if, and when, those interests and the interests of the immigrant races should conflict, the former should prevail.

Furthermore, said the White Paper, their obligations to the Africans could not be delegated or shared: 'This paramount duty of trusteeship will continue, as in the past, to be carried out ... by the agents of the Imperial Government, and by them alone.'[25] It seemed uncompromising and final. Yet Amery, when he became Colonial Secretary, did not accept it as such. In 1927, he issued another White Paper which proposed to do what the

1923 declaration had expressly forbidden: to share the 'trust' with the settlers.[26] And when there came out of Africa a new campaign, this time on a broader front, to bring all the East–Central African colonies (Kenya, Tanganyika, Uganda, the Rhodesias and Nyasaland) into a 'closer union' dominated by Southern Rhodesia (his 'Great White Dominion'), he gave it his support.

But, in 1927, the climate in Britain was different, colder for the settlers; and it affected the Conservative cabinet too. Instead of pushing right ahead, first, with giving responsible government to the Kenyan settlers and then with 'closer union', the cabinet put the whole problem to a Royal Commission under Sir Edward Hilton Young, and the Commission, when it reported in 1929, took – from Amery's point of view – the wrong view of the matter entirely. In the first place, it saw the point of closer union as being to unify native policy, which was not its point for Amery. In the second place, it did not see native policy as best entrusted to white settlers, which scotched the Great White Dominion idea.[27] For Amery, it was valuable time wasted, and there was no more time left to him. In May 1929, the Conservative government resigned and Amery left the Colonial Office. They were superseded by Labour, and by the Fabian Sidney Webb (Lord Passfield). 'Only those who have been in governments,' wrote Amery after it all, 'know how exasperating, and often fatal, can be the delays created by one's colleagues' unconsciousness of the flight of time, and by a Prime Minister's conviction that the less a Government does the better.'[28]

Webb was not able to do anything very positive for East Africa; but what he did do was reaffirm the 1923 declaration and the Hilton Young Report, which stemmed the tide of white supremacy.[29] Though the white settlers still grumbled and plotted and agitated against what they called the 'Black Papers' of the Labour government, in the 1930s they did not again have the opportunity they had had in the 1920s, when Amery was in and the opposition struggling. It was a negative achievement by Webb, but perhaps a vital one; a holding operation for the future, when the battle would be joined again.[30]

Apart from East Africa, Amery was continuously on the lookout for new white dominions, though it was not easy to find suitable candidates. Malta, he thought, might have made a good one, if it were not so small; and he toyed once with the idea that Greece, who shared a contentious interest with Britain over Cyprus, might be persuaded to join the Commonwealth of her own free will.[31] Both were populated by Europeans, which for Amery was an essential qualification for membership. This would be the advantage too of a new Jewish state in Palestine, which was another of Amery's ambitions in the 1920s.

Zionism was always a popular cause among British imperialists, though it was not supported by all British imperialists (not, for example, by Lord Curzon, or anyone associated with India); nor was it supported by any means by imperialists alone. It had many virtues, but two which endeared it especially to imperialists. First, it was thought to be a means of safeguarding British imperial interests in the Middle East, especially now that the imperial hold over Egypt was looking so insecure.[32] Second, Zionism, if you took away its religious aspect, seemed to be a typically imperialist way of running and developing 'primitive' countries: by a European settler population with the energy and expertise to make more of them than the natives. The history of Palestine in the 1920s and 1930s, in fact, closely resembled in many ways Kenya's, with the differences that the settler minority was always very much larger in Palestine than in Kenya; that it had greater and better organised support outside, including apparently God's, and that what was seen as the 'moral' question at issue, between the settlers' claims and the natives' rights, was muddled by another and more taxing moral question, which loomed larger as time went on, arising out of the particular and peculiar dilemma of the Jews elsewhere. The Kenya settlers could have done with some of the sympathy the Jews earned so tragically during Hitler's persecution of them.

Yet there was resistance from the Palestinian Arabs; and there was also the subsidiary duty enjoined on Britain by the mandate to safeguard the 'civil and religious rights of non-Jewish communities in Palestine',[33] which prevented an immediate handover of the country to the settlers, even if there had been enough of them to hand over to. So the first years of Britain's mandatory rule in Palestine were devoted to trying to reconcile Zionist and Arab claims, with no success but with no urgency either, because by and large after 1921 there was very little trouble there. The political trouble started after 1929, when an Arab uprising against Jewish immigration, and Jewish retaliation, led the new Labour government in Britain to appear to repudiate the Balfour Declaration. That was an illusion; but what Passfield's White Paper of 1930 did do was threaten to restrict Jewish immigration and the sale of Palestinian lands to Jews, which was provocative enough. It was greeted with a furore of protest from Zionists worldwide, from Conservative imperialists in Britain and from some Labour MPs, which enabled the Zionists to sweep away this hurdle as the Kenya settlers had not been able to sweep away the fence Passfield had put up to block *them*. The government quailed beneath the storm and submitted.

This was a crucial decision because, although afterwards pro-Zionist feeling in Britain was never again as strong, in the 1930s it did not matter. Things were taken out of Britain's hands. The Jewish population of Palestine, which had increased only from 150,000 to 172,000 between 1926 and 1931, more than doubled (to 384,000) by 1936,[34] and with most of them fleeing from Hitler, and doors closed to them elsewhere (including Britain and the United States), it seemed all the more heartless to deny them refuge in Palestine. The greater their numbers, the better they were able to assert their own claims, which they did, forcibly, and Britain's role was reduced to policing an increasingly intractable situation, with less and less relish. In the 1930s, she tried continuously to find 'settlements', but failed. What determined the outcome in Palestine – the creation of the state of Israel on the left bank of the Jordan in 1948, and her subsequent expansion – was the balance of strength between Zionists and Arabs on the ground, which at the time was in the Zionists' favour.[35]

Between the wars, however, Palestine remained a British mandated territory; and because the British were unable to delegate their responsibilities there to the Zionists, as some wanted, it remained in that state which in the ordinary (non-mandated) British empire was called 'dependent': a colony ruled autocratically from Downing Street. Kenya was in the same category – although in practice, while her fate was still uncertain, she occupied a kind of limbo between that state and the higher one; as did those other colonies in East–Central Africa whose settler populations were too small to form viable governments yet: Uganda, Tanganyika, Northern Rhodesia, Nyasaland. For this dependent category of colonies, the imperialists had different kinds of plans.

Tropical development

Amery's schemes for the dependent empire were, in their broadest outlines, less controversial than any of his other plans. 'The economic possibilities for us in the development of that tropical Empire,' he told the Commons in 1925, 'are perhaps greater than those available to us anywhere else in the world. We have there immense territories with immense natural resources.'[36] Against the vague idea that these imperial estates should be 'developed' there was very little resistance in the 1920s and 1930s from any quarter. That they should be developed simply in Britain's interest *would* have been resisted, but it was rarely put as crudely as that, though it had been by some capitalists during the war.[37] Lord Lugard wrote in 1922 that Britain's 'mandate' in her colonies was a 'dual' one: on the one hand. on her colonial subjects' behalf, on the other hand on 'the world's'. On her colonial subjects' behalf, she had the duty to promote their 'moral and educational progress'; on 'the world's' behalf, she had the right to exploit their 'abounding wealth'.[38] Very few people dissented from this formula, either from the duty or from the right. 'The prime object, of course, of that development,' said Amery in 1919,

> must be the welfare of the inhabitants of those regions … But I am as sure as I stand here that we cannot develop them and help them without an overspill of wealth and prosperity that would be an immense help to this country in the difficult times that lie ahead.[39]

It was a point which was reiterated continually, mainly for the benefit of Labour, but it hardly needed to be. When the Labour government in July 1929 introduced to the House of Commons a bill to finance 'colonial development on a very large scale – development which will in turn provide work for our people in this country', it described the measure as 'non-controversial'.[40] Which by and large it was: though the means by which colonies were to be developed were less so.

Amery's main problem was that, although the desirability of colonial development was accepted on all sides, until the Depression had got as bad as it did in 1929, his colleagues in government could not be persuaded that it was necessary to spend taxpayers' money on it; and afterwards, despite the 1929 Act, they could not be persuaded that they had the money to spend. The prejudice against government spending was a strong one. In part, it derived from the old and persistent axiom of British colonial policy, that colonies – because it did *them* good as well as the British taxpayer – should be 'self-supporting'. In part, and in so far as colonial development was proposed as a panacea for unemployment at home, it arose out of the contemporary Treasury-led shibboleth, which is notorious, that the way out of Depression was not to spend money but to save it. Amery was continually kept short of money for his schemes, and consequently was not able to do everything he wanted for those territories (as he put it again in 1919) 'whose boundless potentialities call urgently for development in the interests of their own inhabitants, of the British Empire as a whole, and of the impoverished and wasted world'.[41] But he did enough to give him some satisfaction. He got one or two railways built in East Africa, for example, which otherwise might not have been built; some roads in Nigeria; and important harbours at Kilindini in Kenya, Takoradi on the Gold Coast, and Haifa in Palestine. He did a great deal to improve research facilities for the dependent colonies, especially into tropical medicine and agriculture, by setting up, for example, a Colonial Medical Research Committee in 1927 and an Agricultural Advisory Council a little later. A pet scheme of his was to try to sell the empire to people, encourage them to buy imperial, through an Empire Marketing Board set up in 1926 and an imaginative campaign of public advertising. All this was a poor substitute for his bolder schemes for a more systematic exploitation of the imperial estate with tariff preferences to guard and encourage it, but it was all grist to the mill.

All this cost relatively little. If the railways and harbours got any government assistance at all, it was in the form of loans, and research and advertising cost perhaps £1 million overall in ten years. Expenditure was small, and it was very strictly limited to the infrastructure of economic development: to providing services (communications, research, marketing facilities) which anyone could use. The nearest government got to subsidising or aiding a more specific commercial enterprise was in setting up the Empire Cotton Growing Corporation in 1921, and even then, the Corporation was not allowed actually to grow cotton commercially itself, but only to research, advise and guarantee. Even the 1929 Colonial Development Act, which broke new ground by giving outright grants to projects in the colonies, in the first place gave very *little* money away (only £1 million in the first three years); and in the second place gave nearly all of it for communications and research. Any real agricultural, industrial or commercial development by colonies had to be initiated and financed by the colonies themselves, or by private enterprises. Which at a time of Depression – a depression the tropical colonies were feeling more keenly than most because of their reliance on single staple products – was asking a great deal of colonies and of businessmen.

Consequently, the 'development' of the dependent colonies progressed between the wars with very little help from the Colonial Office. Quite often it was, if anything, retarded by local colonial governments, some of which, as we have seen, were against capitalist exploitation on principle. This was partly because they saw what it could do to the social fabric of the African societies they governed – making them less *governable*, exactly as had happened when capitalist exploitation had been let loose on Britain more than a century before. Surprisingly, perhaps, they were often supported in this by the agricultural experts sent out from Britain to advise on 'development', who, whatever their preconceptions may have been at the beginning, soon came to regard African ways as superior in agricultural terms. One of them characterised plantation methods, for example, as not 'farming' at all, but 'soil exploitation'.[42] Most of them favoured 'peasant proprietorship'. That, however, might produce the goods, or might not. In the other cases, where capitalists or other agents of western enterprise (like settler-farmers) were given a freer hand, the progress of tropical development followed ordinary market forces, like the abundance of capital and world prices, which also, of course, had an effect on peasant-produced commodities, which had to be sold. Because those market forces were so unpredictable in the inter-war years, and commodity prices especially, the progress of tropical development tended to vary greatly. In the 1930s, as demand from the industrial countries fell, colonial production and export of materials dropped drastically; or else the prices they fetched did, which had the same effect. The production in British West Africa of raw cocoa, for example, increased from 144,000 metric tons in 1920 to 240,000 metric tons in 1930 and 396,000 metric tons in 1939, but as at the same time its price fell – at Liverpool from 81s per cwt in 1920 to 37s 11d in 1930 and 23s 2½d in 1939[43] – it was not clear that the increase benefited anyone, except cocoa drinkers. Most tropical colonies shared in the world's Depression, and suffered; they 'suddenly discovered', said the Labour MP Josiah Wedgwood, 'that they are merely cogs in a gigantic trading machine which has suddenly collapsed and left them, their raw materials, their produce, and their living on their hands stranded and useless'.[44] Because the government would not help, any kind of 'development', on anyone's behalf, was delayed for 20 years.

As colonial budgets could not greatly increase, so expenditure on social welfare tended to lag, which gave to this whole period of tropical colonial administration an air of stagnation. It was not absolutely stagnant. Budgets could be redistributed, and where they were, it was generally in favour of health and education and the like. Uganda, for example, whose revenues were fairly stable between 1928 and 1938, still managed to improve its hospital facilities a little, but the increase was painfully slow, and the total progress made was pitiably small when measured against the problem: 1,300 hospital beds provided in 1938 for an African population of 3 million, and the position was worse elsewhere. By 1938, still under 5 per cent of Nigerian children went to school, and between 10 and 15 per cent of Kenyan African children. (In white supremacist Southern Rhodesia, where the writ of the Colonial Office no longer ran, and where the problem was smaller, the figure was much better; as it was too in the West Indies.[45]) Overall government expenditure on economic development and social welfare in 'black' Africa was never more than a few shillings per head of population per annum: in 1936–37, typically between 3*s* and 8*s*, with Nyasaland, Tanganyika, Nigeria and Sierra Leone getting substantially less, and only Zanzibar, Bechuanaland and Swaziland getting more.[46] For the West Indies, a Royal Commission set up in 1938 painted an almost identical picture of past neglect: the social services still 'all far from adequate for the needs of the population', schools ill-staffed, hospitals impoverished, housing 'deplorable', sanitation 'primitive in the extreme'.[47] In 20 years, almost nothing had been done to fulfil what Britain always claimed was her 'positive trust' to her colonial subjects: little to justify the claim. A governor of Tanganyika described his colony as lying 'in mothballs' between the wars,[48] and the description fits nearly everywhere. In very few meanings of the term was 'colonial development' at that time anything more than a pious wish.[49]

The problems of imperialists

The inter-war experience demonstrated how powerless any Colonial Secretary was, even so determined a one as Leopold Amery, to make progress in any direction in the sluggish political and economic waters of the time. For the Dominions, Amery found his own volition a weak thing against the pressures of colonial particularism and Treasury conservatism. On Kenya, Amery and Passfield, who wanted opposite things, found themselves both forced to adhere to the same uneasy stalemate, because the pressures from both sides were so powerful. In the dependencies, it was not intentions – good or bad – which determined whether things would get done, but money, or the lack of it. 'However willing may be the spirit,' said the Colonial Under-Secretary in 1921, 'the flesh, interpreted in terms of ready money and rigidly bound by economic laws, is sadly weak.'[50] The imperialists' most grandiose design, for an imperial economic system which would – among other things – make Britain strong again, cure the Depression, and foil the socialists, scarcely left the drawing-board. As in other aspects of British policy at this time, statesmen seemed cowed by circumstances; they allowed themselves to be transfixed by fears and doubts, and to be persuaded by those who counselled caution in the face of them, so that, in the 1920s and 1930s, almost nothing was done which was bold and imaginative and positive. If anyone asked, then it was the Depression which was to blame.

If Amery had had greater support from his colleagues, he still might not have achieved much more than he did, but the fact that he did not have that support made his position impossible. For his brand of imperialism was not that of the rest of his party, or of the country; during the war it had seemed to be, but as the war receded into the past, it became less so. Milner, when he left the Colonial Office in 1921, wrote to Amery regretting leaving him 'rather alone, among people who have very little real sympathy with the things which we both care about'.[51] In Baldwin's government Amery did not stand entirely alone, but he had the Treasury against him and 'its imperious chief (Churchill), and a Prime Minister who let things slide; and that was enough'.[52] In Parliament too, the mood was not propitious. There was a general feeling rife perhaps of imperial pride – the kind which one MP described as 'surging in the bosoms' of the members of an all-party imperial tour as they 'realised that we could travel round the world always landing on British soil, except for an hour or two at Honolulu',[53] but this was a vague, amorphous thing, nothing which could be necessarily translated into an imperial *policy*. Of the old kind of imperial 'arrogance and self-satisfaction', a Conservative MP in 1923 regretted that it had almost gone, replaced now 'by a habit of disparaging and belittling all British ideas'.[54] On the Labour side, MPs tended to be, if not unequivocally 'anti-imperialist', at least suspicious of the imperialists' motives – especially their keenness to 'emigrate other people's children to distant countries' when things could be done for them at home, and critical of 'development' schemes which seemed designed, as many did, merely to 'make the nigger work' or to 'benefit ... exploiters in this country'.[55] On the Conservative side, though there may have been many who shared Amery's visions, there were few who were prepared to fight for them. 'Who is for the Empire?' asked Lord Beaverbrook's *Sunday Express* in 1929; 'The answer is all men and no one. For while all men are willing to register the sentiment of goodwill towards the Empire, the practical side of Imperial development has been forgotten.'[56]

It was not 'anti-imperialism' which was Amery's problem at all, but the fact that not even rampant imperialists could agree among themselves on the road their imperialism should follow. Before the war there had been a rift – perhaps not a clear one – between Curzon's type of imperialist, for whom India was the empire's centre, its sun, and who thought very little of Africa, and Milner's and Chamberlain's type, for whom the empire consisted of the white Dominions and the tropics, and who concerned themselves hardly at all with India. After the war, this rift persisted, perhaps widened, and was complicated by the parallel development of at least one other offshoot from the imperialist stem, which was the new tradition which had grown up during the war, associated with the 'Round Table' group, which sought to nurse the empire into a multi-racial commonwealth. Amery and Lord Birkenhead were both 'imperialists', and both Conservatives, but there was virtually nothing in common between Amery's down-to-earth imperial realism, and this:

> Although Birkenhead had never visited India [wrote his son], he was well read in its history and strongly imbued with its atmosphere. The story of India had always appealed to his imagination as a record of romance, of strident colours and the clash of virile peoples, of stately Indiamen riding at anchor in the mists of Gravesend, making ready for their six-month voyage, of the wild Maharatta hordes scouring the table-land of the Deccan, and of the columns of the Company's armies winding through parched hills to the relief of distant fortresses ... He had the 'feel' of the country in a manner unusual in one who had never visited it, and he attributed this to an intensive reading of Kipling's Indian books with their wonderful descriptive passages.[57]

Winston Churchill's imperialism was as strong, but it came from the same stable, and it helped him not at all to understand what Amery was at. This division and mutual obstruction among the imperialist forces reflected the prevailing uncertainty of the times about what the empire was becoming. It also ensured that whatever it did become, it would not be what any one group of them wanted it to become.

Outside Parliament Amery found the ground harder, if anything, than inside. It was not that people were against the empire, more that, they were imperially ignorant. During the war H. G. Wells estimated that 'nineteen people out of twenty, the lower class and most of the middle class, knew no more of the empire than they did of the Argentine Republic or the Italian Renaissance. It did not concern them.'[58] After the war the imperialists tried to do something about this: Beaverbrook with his press crusades, Amery with his emigration schemes and his Empire Marketing Board. They had a whole army of regiments behind them: like the Royal Empire Society, the British Empire Union, the Empire Day Movement, the British Empire League, the Overseas League, the Victoria League, the Patriotic League of Britons Overseas: all devoted to propagandising the empire among the people – regiments of officers looking for men. As ever, a good proportion of the working classes proved impervious to Empire Days, Empire Songs, Empire Essay Competitions, Empire Meals on Empire Day, and all the other ingenious ploys of the imperialists; 'in spite of unremitting efforts for a number of years,' bemoaned the chairman of the Empire Day Movement in 1931, 'there are still many dark corners in Great Britain, especially in the industrial areas, where the rays of our Empire sun have not yet been able to penetrate.'[59] As an alternative to the more immediate attractions of socialism, which it was part of the empire movement's purpose to wean the working man away from,[60] or as an alternative to plain apathy, imperialism stood little chance of success.

It failed to catch on widely because people could not be convinced that it was in their interests – either because it was really not in their interests, or because they were too short-sighted to see it. As a cure for the Depression, sending capital abroad for colonial development and the like did seem a little roundabout, compared perhaps with a bigger dole or a road to work on at home; for much of industry too, it was at best a very long-term solution to their troubles, to discriminate between customers, when (as they thought) they could make themselves all round more competitive by the simpler expedient of reducing wages. Joseph Chamberlain before had found that the social imperialist argument, whether it was sound or not, was just too sophisticated to be a popular one; which was why, in the 1920s too, it never gathered behind it any electoral weight. That it was not popular was not absolutely fatal to its chances, but it did not help.

But possibly what was so especially unattractive about Amery's kind of imperialism, and what foiled it in the end, was, quite simply, its amorality. It is a bold claim to make that any gainful course of action has ever been rejected by a nation because it was not *moral*, and of course the new imperialism might not have been really 'gainful' at all, but Englishmen in the past had been used to thinking that their empire was based on a wider and higher morality than the morality of national self-interest, or power, and it is possible that by now they *needed* to think this. A feature of the old free trade imperialism had been that it had not sought exclusive advantages anywhere. When Britain had taken a country, she had opened its trade to everyone; allowed any ship to steam through the Suez Canal, or to put into her colonial harbours. She did this because it suited her, and not at any sacrifice of her own interests at all, but it did enable her convincingly to justify her actions very piously. In theory, the whole world was supposed to gain from her empire, not just Britain alone; the empire was not created at anyone's *expense*. The Victorians had believed that the difference between this, and an empire run for the purely selfish advantage of a country, was a crucial one: the difference between seizing a playground for your own children only to play in, and seizing a playground to run for everyone's children.

This sense of moral justification, which other countries, who saw *only* the selfish motives behind Britain's empire-building, found objectionable and hypocritical, ran right through nineteenth-century British imperialism, as it ran right through the nineteenth century's particular brand of capitalism. People got accustomed to it, and were not at all accustomed to cruder justifications of imperialism, with arguments merely from national interest or *realpolitik*, with which other countries may have been more familiar and come to terms. Against this old-established habit of thinking came the 'new' imperialism, which *was* cruder – perhaps more honest. The new imperialists justified their schemes very much in national terms; almost their whole case was that they would make Britain strong against the world, give her advantages, weaken her rivals. Their highest sanction was the interest of the nation; there was nothing, beyond that, for the world. Perhaps people's stomachs for this kind of thing had been weakened by so many years of a milkier morality.

Even the old imperialism was losing some of its shine. Socialists and nationalists were making their voices heard in Britain as well as in the colonies, and raising all kinds of doubts about the justice of Britain's imperial methods: not only about the excesses, like Amritsar, but also about the assumptions which lay beneath the ordinary day-to-day administration of the empire. There was more talk of the rights of non-Europeans, as well as of their protection; doubts about the morality of even the kindest and best-intentioned paternalism; doubts, long-standing but bolstered most recently by the war, as to whether Europeans, who had just perpetrated such an atrocity among themselves, had any cause to regard themselves as superior in any way to those they were supposed to be 'raising' to their level. Things which were swallowed easily enough before by most people, like the right of white emigrants to settle where they pleased and take over countries from their *indigènes*, now began to stick in some gullets. It began to be noticed that some 'virgin' territories were not so virgin after all, but had people living in them who merited no less consideration just because they were inefficient. Such feelings were not strong enough yet to save the Rhodesian Africans or the Palestinian Arabs from having other people carve new countries out of their lands, but they did save Kenya for a while. And, more generally, the very possession of an empire was, among more and more people, beginning to be regarded as alien or at least irrelevant to the best ideals of the twentieth century; imperialism losing what pure idealists it had, to socialism or pacifism or isolationism or the League of Nations, or to some other deity which was not so tarnished as yet. To quantify such a change in the climate of opinion would be impossible, still more to speculate on its effect. But there can be little doubt that empire and imperialism had a surlier, less carefree, more anachronistic and defensive image between the wars than before.

The problems of the anti-imperialists

Yet if the schemes of the 'new imperialists' did not get very far between the wars, neither did the hopes of those others – who included some imperialists as well as anti-imperialists – for the evolution of the empire into something freer and friendlier: the early advocates of a multi-racial commonwealth. The idea of the empire as a training academy for self-government had a very long lineage in British political thought, especially with regard to India. The idea that successful pupils, after their graduation, would remain within the empire as voluntary members, and the empire transform into a kind of Oxbridge college fellowship, with its senior members but no unequals, was of more recent growth, emerging slowly in the late nineteenth century when it was discovered that the academy's first graduates, at least, did not particularly want to leave. These first graduates had been of European origin, tied to Britain filially as well as politically, and so their fidelity was perhaps not surprising. It was a big step from the idea of a self-governing commonwealth of common racial origins, to one which embraced non-Europeans. That step was taken, falteringly, in 1916–17, when India was first admitted to the Imperial War Conference on an equal footing with the 'white' Dominions. She was represented then by her British rulers and their collaborators, which obscured the racial implications of the change. But then followed the promise of responsible government to India, which made things plainer. India was the first of the non-European dependencies to be given a firm promise that ultimately she would be free and equal with Australia and South Africa. The racial barrier had been breached.

Some men in Britain welcomed the breach, and its implications for other non-white dependencies. They included a few imperialists as well as socialists and Liberals. Socialist policy on this question was always quite explicit. 'The question before us really is this,' said Josiah Wedgwood to the Commons in 1920:

> is the British Empire going to be purely a white Commonwealth, spreading all over the world, but confining its citizenship to white people; or are you going to follow the wider plan of absorbing into the British Commonwealth all the races who can be absorbed and are willing to be absorbed into it? ... The Labour Party stand for the wider view of Empire.[61]

And the Round Table group of imperialists had believed for some time that the empire could not endure long into the twentieth century, if it excluded countries from its self-governing upper echelon on the mere ground of colour.

But between the wars sentiments like this were all very theoretical. Nothing could be done towards a multi-racial, self-governing commonwealth while the circumstances were not right, and in the 1920s and 1930s, except in India and one or two lesser places, they were not. In the first place, there was as yet no urgent pressure for political progress in the colonies, outside India and the Middle East. Winston Churchill, with more attention to style than to strict accuracy, overpainted the contrast in 1921:

> In the African Colonies you have a docile, tractable population, who only require to be well and wisely treated to develop great economic capacity and utility; whereas the regions of the Middle East are unduly stocked with peppery, pugnacious, proud politicians and theologians, who happen to be at the same time extremely well armed and extremely hard up.[62]

The Africans were neither as docile nor as tractable as he made out. There was trouble in the African colonies after the First World War as there had been before – disturbances in Kenya and Northern Rhodesia just after the war, for example, which were almost rebellions; strikes of Sierra Leone railway workers in 1919 and 1926 and Rhodesian copper miners in 1935, which were treated as rebellions; religious cults and sects which contained strong elements of rebellion in them; and a variety of 'Native Associations', 'Welfare Associations', 'National Congresses' and 'African Associations' all over British Africa, formed in response to discontent.[63] But the organisation of discontent in Africa was as yet very embryonic, easily suppressed or disregarded locally, and it caused the

British little trouble – much less, for example, than the organisation of discontent among the Europeans and the Indians in Kenya. The same was true elsewhere in the dependent empire. In places like Somaliland and Aden, order was easily kept by the new cruel expedient of strafing rebel camps and villages from fighter planes (in 1921 and 1926); and in Cyprus in 1931 more conventionally by troops and ships. The West Indies had strikes and riots in the late 1930s, which were less easily tamed, but no really effective political organisation until after those riots. Most of the empire outside India and the Middle East was quiet in the 1920s and 1930s – quieter even than it had been before (Figure 9.1). And without urgent pressure from below, it was unlikely that political reforms would be granted gratuitously. An old Liberal had pointed out in 1908 how 'there never was an extension of political rights and political freedom made to any people in the world by the mere spontaneous goodwill of the ruling class'.[64] In Britain's case the colonies were still too valuable to her for her to want to give them up, or to loosen her control over them, unless she had to.

Other reasons were given for withholding political responsibility from colonial sub-jects. A common one was that colonial subjects were incapable of ruling themselves: either altogether incapable, or incapable just yet. For some, this applied even to the Indians, despite the promise of 1917: 'To me it is frankly inconceivable,' said the Secretary of State for India, Lord Birkenhead, eight years after that promise, 'that India will

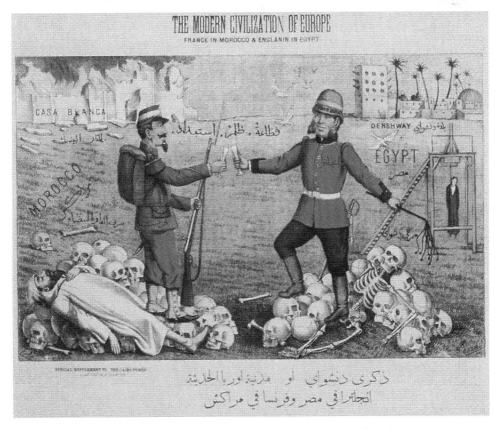

Figure 9.1 The view from below. An Arab view of British and French colonialism.
Source: Photo by Library of Congress/Corbis/VCG via Getty Images.

ever be fit for dominion self-government.'[65] It applied much more to Africa, where even socialists believed (in 1943) that their aim of self-determination was not realisable 'for a considerable time to come'.[66] The rationale which Leopold Amery offered for this was typical. It was not, he said, a matter of intelligence: Africans were intelligent enough for self-government. But self-government required more than this: it required 'a widely diffused social conscience and sense of responsibility both in the electorate and in its would-be leaders'. And,

> while the intellectual knowledge is easily acquired against a background of mere ignorance – often all the more easily by the freshness of minds which have lain fallow – the social sense is something instinctive, traditional and acquired in the home from infancy. It is something not easily changed by teaching, even in individuals. To change it in a community is a matter, not of a few years, but of generations. Yet, if it is lacking, both in leaders and in led, their intellectual knowledge and the self-confidence that goes with it are a constant temptation to the former to play upon the ignorance and irresponsibility of their fellow countrymen for purely selfish and mischievous purposes.[67]

So self-government should be held back while Africans acquired – Amery never said how – their 'social sense'. In fact, this eventuality scarcely ever occurred to imperialists in Britain. Between the wars, wrote Amery again, 'the future emergence of the dependent Empire into the higher status of equal free partnership, if not rejected altogether, was at any rate relegated to a dim and remote future'.[68] And it was relegated there by the colonies' friends as well as by their enemies.

To accept fully the idea that Nigeria, or even India, would one day be ruled by its own 'natives' on equal terms with Canada and Britain, required a revolution in basic attitudes which some members of the imperial governing class were unable to make. Imperial philosophy had long professed a belief in race equality, and at the heart of the empire, in Britain, there had not for a long time been any institutional racial discrimination. In the colonies themselves, however – especially the colonies of white settlement – things had long been very different: in South Africa most notoriously, but elsewhere too; and until 1942 the ranks of the Colonial Service were closed to anyone of non-European descent.[69] Where there was not administrative or legal discrimination, there was a great deal of social discrimination. Sir Charles Dilke in the nineteenth century had remarked on 'the antipathy exhibited everywhere by the English to coloured races';[70] the Indian Civil Service and the South and East African settlers, especially, were notorious for it. In India, it was generally confined to the pettier officials (and their wives); the big men, whose more overall view revealed the harm it was doing, usually deprecated it. Lord Salisbury had believed that, together with red tape, the 'damned nigger' attitude was 'threatening our rule in India'; Queen Victoria feared that 'some day real danger may result from it'; Curzon thought it might 'one day split the empire asunder'; Edwin Montagu saw it 'at the bottom' of their troubles in 1917.[71] Similarly critics of the settlers in Kenya were always warning of the harm that their prejudices were doing the empire.[72] Race prejudice, and the habit of authority, made it difficult for many colonial officials to take seriously the prospect of non-Europeans governing themselves, still less to contemplate serving under them. Montagu once had the idea of setting an example himself by demoting himself to Under-Secretary for India and getting an Indian appointed above him.[73] But it probably would not have moved them. The British long ago had formulated their stereotype images of the 'races' they ruled, in the main, derogatory stereotypes, devised perhaps partly to justify their rule. Now those stereotypes had got hold of them, and were helping to perpetuate their rule. Their erosion, when and if it came, would be slow.[74]

This tendency towards inertia in the matter of political progress for colonial subjects was compounded by the fact that there was no unwavering commitment to it among the friends of those colonial subjects either. The official statements of socialist organisations, for example, except the communists, were ambiguous: self-government was always an aim, but sometimes a very far-off one. The weight of informed British opinion, even benevolent opinion, was against it. For very many years now it had been an axiom of British colonial thinking that European institutions, including the paraphernalia of parliamentary democracy, were unsuited to non-Europeans – 'can no more be carried to India by Englishmen,' wrote Ramsay MacDonald in 1898, '... than they can carry ice in their luggage'.[75] This was not necessarily because those institutions were too good for non-Europeans, although, for many Britons, that might immediately follow. The crux of the matter was supposed to be this: that different peoples and different environments gave rise to different cultural institutions which were uniquely and especially suited to them, and which were not likely to be bettered by other institutions evolved in different environments. Indeed, the attempt to replace customs and institutions by others imported from outside was thought to be directly harmful, to which the Indian Mutiny and a host of minor upheavals since were still supposed to bear witness. The particular lesson to be drawn from this was that 'politics' in the Western sense was not necessarily suited to non-Westerners. The general lesson was that *nothing* was suited to them which had not been evolved or at least carefully adapted by themselves. This was the ideological justification for 'indirect rule'.

How indirect rule worked out in practice varied widely according to local circumstances, but usually it tended to the side of conservatism and stasis. The idea of it was supposed to be to 'raise' primitive societies from their own foundations. But it was always easier to see the foundations than it was to know how, or in what direction, to raise them; and as more and more came to be known about those foundations, mainly through the efforts of an enthusiastic little band of 'social anthropologists' who went out and studied them, the more oppressive the problem became. As they looked deeper into (mainly African) cultural systems, the more anthropologists were impressed by what they called the 'functional interdependence' of institutions, customs and values: the fundamental importance of even the most bizarre of them in cohering and stabilising societies. 'Tradition is a fabric,' wrote the best known of the functional anthropologists, Bronislaw Malinowski, 'in which all the strands are so closely woven that the destruction of one unmakes the whole';[76] and anthropologists could point to societies in which – they claimed – this had happened: whole populations reduced, even, merely by interfering with the social mechanism.[77] Which counselled extreme caution, or, rather, justified the caution which many colonial administrators already instinctively favoured. Anthropologists did not rule out change, but they believed it had to be done gradually and on a broad level. 'In reality,' said Malinowski again, in advocacy of indirect rule, 'all social development is very slow, and ... it is infinitely preferable to achieve it by a slow and gradual change coming from within',[78] which was exactly the official's sentiment: 'The danger of going too fast with native tribes,' said Lugard, 'is more likely to lead to disappointment, if not to disaster, than the danger of not going fast enough.'[79] Not only was slowness advocated by indirect rule; the inherent difficulties of the system made it slower. If colonial societies were not to be Europeanised, then the Europeans had no sure blueprint to tell them where to go; and it was clearly much more difficult, for example, to educate a whole population broadly, than it had been in the past to educate a small elite piecemeal. All these things obstructed progress, quite apart from lack of money, and lack of will.

Indirect rule may have been an empirically derived system with no other purpose than to help colonial peoples to progress painlessly, but it was mistrusted. It was convenient how it tended to perpetuate colonial rule, to prevent 'enlightenment', to legitimise indigenous feudal rulers who could be collaborated with; and it was coincidental that it should back up so many of the prejudices – for example, against the 'babu' or 'educated native' – which Britons had had long before it had been thought of. Some people believed it was a cynical ploy to 'keep the native down'; to some South Africans, for example, 'indirect rule was welcome as an excuse for leaving the African very much as he is, and leaving him to deteriorate in his own way'.[80] Others who may have accepted its good intentions still quarrelled with its conclusions, especially the 'educated natives' themselves, who had no place in a system built on a society they had been educated away from, and no satisfaction for their political ambitions, but also others.[81] Indirect rule, said one of its British critics who was more in favour of the missionary way of doing things, 'tends to stereotype customs and institutions which are associated with a backward race, and which are not consistent with the progress of that race towards a higher state of civilisation'.[82] But the pros and cons of indirect rule could be debated until doomsday. It operated where it could – where there were still coherent indigenous societies to preserve, and even occasionally where there were not and they had to be resurrected. And where it operated, it was a force – with all the others – on the side of inertia.[83]

Almost everything, but especially this immobility on the political front, seemed to work for a sense of stability and solidity in colonial affairs between the wars; a feeling of permanence, of room and time to work in, which, whether or not it was good for the colonies, did wonders for the confidence and morale of those who administered them. The 1920s and 1930s were the heyday of the Colonial Service, the time when it felt most certain and wanted, and most prestigious; by contrast with earlier, when it had been still immature and confused, and later, when it became rushed and harassed. It had an ethos and a unity about it which had not been there before, consciously inculcated by Amery and his lieutenants, and especially encouraged by the separation off from the Colonial Office in 1925 of Dominion affairs, which were of a different nature entirely and had been distracting. Unity and morale were fostered too by the quality and kind of men who were recruited to the Colonial Service between the wars, who, on the whole, were better than before in the sense that they were chosen from a larger pool of the sort of people that the service liked to choose from, the sort of people who formerly had preferred the more prestigious ICS. Most of them were public school men, because the public schools were supposed to encourage the qualities of 'character' the colonies needed. Education in any other sense was rather looked down upon. New recruits to the Colonial Service tended as a result not to be the brightest of their generation, but were generally solid, paternalistic in their attitudes, honourable, and resourceful within certain narrow limits. They tended to be unimaginative. Reading their reports, one is also struck by the instinctive racism of nearly all of them. These were the sort of people that Sir Ralph Furse, the main Colonial Service recruiter from 1919 to 1948, preferred. He was a great believer in the interview (and particularly the handshake) as a means of summing them up. The result was the sort of social and moral homogeneity in the service that made for good morale, though also, of course, for a degree of cliquishness.[84] Their womenfolk, when they took them with them, came from the same class, and in the main supported them loyally, as conventional middle-class women of that time were supposed to do. If their more 'enlightened' sisters back home expected any different perspective from them on the imperial relationship, they were disappointed. Colonial wives, and other women in the colonies (doctors, nurses, after 1925, a very few administrators) were not generally feminists.[85] They did little therefore to upset the prevailing stability, which – so far as nearly all these expatriates were concerned – looked as though it would last for a long time yet. In 1939, the Colonial Service was still recruiting 21-year-olds, who fully expected to see their careers out in the colonies, governing natives for their good and Britain's.[86]

Egypt and India

But while the Colonial Office ran *its* empire in blithe ignorance of what was to come, the Foreign and India Offices could not be so complacent about Egypt and India. There the auguries were clear, and ominous. India looked set for self-government after the Montagu Declaration of 1917 and the Act of 1919; Egypt after 1922 looked to have it already. The trend could not be mistaken; for imperialists who wanted to hold on to Egypt and India, the task was to halt or reverse it.

In both countries they succeeded at least in slowing it down. In Egypt, despite big talk of 'independence', Britain had retained what she needed most in 1922, and in 1939 still retained it: control over the Suez Canal and her route to the east. The 1922 'independence' Declaration had reserved to Britain ultimate control over Egyptian defence, the Canal, the Sudan and the protection of foreign interests, which made Egypt not very much more independent than she had been under Gladstone. Nationalists resented the reservations, and reacted against them, sometimes bloodily. Yet Britain was able to resist them: first, by force, then by accommodation. In the 1920s, contraventions of the 1922 Declaration by nationalist (Wafdist) governments, and more extreme actions by nationalist terrorists like the assassination in 1924 of the Sirdar of the Egyptian Army, Sir Lee Stack, were met with British gunboats off Alexandria and strict ultimata, which complaining but irresolute Egyptian governments felt compelled to submit to. It was effective, but Britain would have preferred a friendlier method of preserving her imperial interests, and more so in the 1930s, when there was a fresh prospect of a real military threat to Britain's position in that part of the world from fascist Italy, which was Egypt's neighbour in Libya, and was about to take Ethiopia. Fascist Italy worried the Egyptians too: and, in 1936, after years of fruitless negotiation, the two sides managed to agree on a treaty to replace the unilateral arrangement of 1922. The Anglo-Egyptian Treaty removed most of the old reservations on Egypt's formal independence, except for the British military presence on the Canal and her colonial presence in the Sudan. It lasted, and for Britain's purposes was adequate, until 1956.[87]

India was a less tractable problem, because there was more to fight for there: more for the nationalists, who had not yet got the degree of self-government the Egyptians had; and for many imperialists, who – despite her diminishing trade with Britain – valued India more. It was over India that the romantic, Churchillian type of imperialist most regretted the concessions he felt had been forced on them during the war. Lord Birkenhead, who was Secretary of State for India from 1924 to 1928, told his Viceroy Lord Reading in November 1924 for his 'secret information',

> that this cabinet, as is natural, is in my analysis under the influence of a considerable reaction from the Montagu reforms. It has a general impression that under the

Coalition, and since, too much has been given away, I will not say through weakness, but through the general malaise which succeeded the war in India, Ireland and Egypt.[88]

On India, the old imperialists fought their most determined rearguard action. But the fight did not begin in earnest until the 1930s, when the possibility sank in that India really might be lost.

Before the 1930s, it never looked likely. There was an alternative to self-government, which was to continue the present practice of provincial 'dyarchy', if not for ever, at least for a good time yet. Dyarchy could be read as fulfilling already Britain's promise of 'responsible government' within the empire, though it was only just barely consistent with the letter of that promise, and not at all with its spirit. In India itself, there was the desire for more but no really effective pressure for more. The new provincial governments were set up, and mostly worked, despite being boycotted by Congress, whose understanding of them was very like the imperialists'. The nationalists were in disarray. Congress and the League had split apart again, and much nationalist energy was wasted trying to reconcile them. Their failure was reflected, between 1924 and 1928, in the worst spell of communal rioting for some years. (This, said Lord Birkenhead, was the real guarantee against India's ever governing herself: 'you cannot bridge the unbridgeable'.[89]) Gandhi's new peaceful method of mass protest, civil disobedience or *satyagraha*, had got out of hand and been abandoned disconsolately by Gandhi himself. Gandhi was imprisoned and (in the opinion of Viceroy and Secretary of State) his sting drawn.[90] In India, there was nothing really to startle imperialists, to force independence from them. The only threat to British India was, or was thought to be, the British Labour Party, which said it wanted to emancipate her.

It was to pre-empt this threat that Birkenhead – two years before he needed to, in 1927 while the Conservatives were still in power – set up the Statutory Commission which had been enjoined by the 1919 Act to inquire into its workings.[91] In the event, the Simon Commission did more than anything else to provoke Indian nationalism into some kind of effective activity, not because it was early but because it had not a single Indian on it. It was, said one meeting of Indian Liberals,

> a deliberate insult to the people of India, as not only does it definitely assign to them a position of inferiority, but what is worse, it denies them the right to participate in the determination of the constitution of their own country.[92]

This feeling was widespread, and widely expressed. As the Commission travelled around India during 1928–29, it drew after it a trail of boycotts and demonstrations and riots. In its wake Indian nationalism began to revive and regroup and reform. An all-party committee under Motilal Nehru drew up the Indians' own constitution for an independent India in August 1928, which in the end was not accepted by all parties because it could not satisfy the Muslim League on the matter of communal electorates, but was nevertheless presented to the British government as an alternative to whatever the Simon Commission might propose. At the end of 1929, when the British Labour government, from whom the Indians expected much, had still not pronounced on the Nehru constitution, it was decided to go on to the offensive. The government and the Liberal Viceroy Lord Irwin proposed a 'Round Table Conference' to discuss the next step for India; Congress refused to take part unless it was committed actually to framing a self-governing constitution. In March 1930, Gandhi inaugurated his civil disobedience movement proper, by marching from Ahmedabad to the coast to make salt illegally. And this time the movement took hold. It was partly intended to provoke, and it did. Sixty thousand resisters were imprisoned, among them Gandhi and (on other charges) Motilal Nehru.

It was the instinct of the Labour government, and also of Lord Irwin, to appease the Indian nationalists at least part of the way. In October 1929, Irwin had tried to reassure them by spelling out again the government's commitment to achieving 'Dominion status' for India. When the Simon Report was at last published in June 1930, and turned out to be as conservative as had been expected, the government (in effect) rejected it. At the first Round Table Conference, which was held in November without Congress but with 74 other Indians, Ramsay MacDonald proposed full autonomy for the Indian provinces, and progress towards self-government at the centre. In January 1931, Irwin – who admired him – let Gandhi out of gaol, and signed a pact with him (in March) by which the others were released too, and *satyagraha* called off. In September 1931, Gandhi participated – alone among Congress members – in the second Round Table Conference. It was a glimmer, at last, of progress.

The problem with all this conciliation was that it made others, on both sides, restless. Gandhi's submission to Irwin, for little tangible gain, was mistrusted by most and resented by many, and he became the butt of hostile nationalist demonstrations in India himself. To imperialists in Britain, Irwin was supposed to be the one to have debased himself. 'It is alarming and also nauseating,' said Winston Churchill,

> to see Mr Gandhi, a seditious Middle Temple lawyer, now posing as a fakir of a type well known in the East, striding half-naked up the steps of the viceregal palace, while he is still organising and conducting a defiant campaign of civil disobedience, to parley on equal terms with the representative of the King-Emperor.[93]

Imperialists by now were thoroughly alarmed. British India appeared to be imperilled not only by agitators in India and appeasers in Britain, but also by the old enemy, Russia, on the North-West Frontier. In August 1931, a new 'National' – but effectively Conservative – government came to power which put an end to some of it. Irwin's successor as Viceroy, Lord Willingdon, could not get on with Gandhi as Irwin could, which put an end to the spectacle that had so 'nauseated' Churchill. When Gandhi started up another civil disobedience campaign in 1932, it was resisted stoutly – Congress leaders arrested, Congress outlawed, public meetings and processions forbidden – and it collapsed. Firm action paid off: 'Order has been largely restored throughout India,' Churchill complimented the government in March 1933: 'The Civil Disobedience Movement is broken. Mr Gandhi, upon whom the Prime Minister and Lord Irwin lavished their caresses, has been in prison ... for more than a year ... Hardly anyone has been killed or severely hurt.'[94]

On the constitutional front, the Secretary of State, Sir Samuel Hoare, had at last made it clear that 'in view of British public opinion, Conservative anxieties in Parliament, and not least, Communal fears in India', Dominion status was for the moment unthinkable.[95]

The constitutional reforms the government proposed for India, and which were contained in a Government of India Bill which finally passed into law in 1935, took full account of all these pressures. The bill extended responsible government in the provinces, where now the imperial authorities (the Governors) could act independently only in very exceptional circumstances. At the centre there was a new bicameral legislature which

represented a federation of those provinces and of the princely states. What was conservative about the federal legislature, and what Congress objected to, was that the
princely states – traditionally the element of 'stability', or collaboration, in India – were
grossly over-represented in it, by members not elected democratically but nominated by
the princes; and that the legislature was not fully sovereign anyway. As they had been in
the provinces before, now on the federal level, certain matters were 'reserved' to the
Viceroy, who needed to consult no-one in the actions he took on them; these included
India's defence, her foreign affairs, and certain 'special responsibilities' like protecting
minorities and preventing tariffs on British imports. India as a whole, therefore, was not
yet a self-governing state. Some British ministers, like the Indian Secretary himself,
claimed that this was nevertheless a step towards it. Many Conservatives thought so too.
It marked 'the definite decline, and even disappearance, of our authority in India', said
Churchill; the desertion of 'our children' to 'carnage and confusion';[96] Britain had 'as
good a right to be in India as anyone there'; her government was 'incomparably the best
Government that India has ever seen or ever will see'; and to prefer self-government
above it was 'an infatuation of the Liberal mind'.[97] The diehards fought hard alongside
Churchill to wreck the bill, and in the event delayed it probably for two years. But if the
diehards thought the bill marked the beginning of the end, Indian nationalists were not so
sure. They tried to work the provincial part of the Act, which was implemented in 1937.
But the federal part was mistrusted. It was a scheme, wrote the nationalist Subhas
Chandra Bose, 'not for self-government, but for maintaining British rule in the new
political conditions, through the help of the Indian princes and sectarian, reactionary and
pro-British organisations'.[98] Which for some of its authors and supporters it may well
have been. The Muslim and princely cards were, like the Orange card in Ireland years
back, strong ones to play for those who wanted excuses to deprive the Indian majority of
self-government.[99] But they were strong cards because many others felt that Muslims and
princes had a good case on their own, and deserved safeguarding anyway. Conservatives
had reasons for being cautious and slow, other than the hope that it might stop things
altogether.[100]

An empire still

But whether or not the 1935 Act was intended as a real stage towards Indian self-
government, its caution, and the opposition it aroused from the right, suggested that
Britain was not able to look on the prospect of losing India with equanimity yet. The
diehards were determined that it would not happen at all: 'There will be no "Lost
Dominion",' Birkenhead thundered to the House of Lords, 'until the moment – if ever it
comes – when the whole British Empire, with all that it means for civilization, is splin-
tered in doom.'[101] Birkenhead was an exceptional case: but exceptional only in that he
was willing to face the prospect that the empire might come to an end, and resist it.
Others dared not think about it. Those who wanted and welcomed it, as the Labour
Party said it did, did little to hurry it on. Most people took it that it was a long way off
yet. 'We may ... assume,' wrote the chronicler of colonial Nigeria in 1937, 'that for a
people so backward and so divided that day' – when Nigeria would become self-governing – 'will be very distant.'[102] That gave them *time*; and it partly explained why there
was so little political advancement in the colonies between the wars, and so little economic development: none at all in the direction of making colonial economies self-reliant
and national, rather than dependent and colonial. Over the whole field of policy between

the wars, almost nothing was done by any government to prepare the colonies to live without Britain, or to prepare Britain to live without the colonies. Everything was done – or not done – on the assumption that the British empire would, as far ahead as needed to be foreseen, continue as an empire.

Or – as something not *quite* an empire, and so the more likely to buck the general trend of empires, which was – of course – to 'decline and fall'. It was in this inter-war period that the word 'commonwealth' began seriously to displace 'empire' as a term for it; in school history books, for example, where it accompanied a wholesale revision of the version of 'empire' that was taught to schoolchildren, de-emphasising its strictly 'imperial' (dominating) aspects – the battles, conquests, and so on – and presenting it rather as a great exercise in friendly, familial co-operation, and even 'internationalism': the new fashionable word of the time. To read some of these new accounts, one might think that India, Kenya and the rest had all joined the British empire voluntarily.[103] 'It is no figure of speech,' claimed one of these textbooks as early as 1919, 'to call Great Britain and her colonies a family circle.'[104] This will have confused the general public, and may have fooled them, too, that the Empire-Commonwealth could still run and run. All empires like to think they are different from – generally more benevolent than – those that have gone before them. In Britain's case in the 1920s and 1930s, this extended to a belief, for popular consumption at least, that hers was not really an empire at all. Hence its supposed resilience.

This assumption dominated Britain's broader foreign policy too. Britain in the 1920s and 1930s had very few doubts that she was still, as she had been in the nineteenth century, a world power and not – or not merely – a European power.[105] In 1921, she conceived the idea of building a huge, and supposedly impregnable, naval base at Singapore, which was completed in 1938 at a cost of £60 million, and which would hardly have been conceivable if she had had serious doubts about her world role. Because she had a world role, and world interests and commitments, her concern for Europe was not as close as it could have been, and certainly not as close as the French would have liked. It was this which embittered Anglo-French relations between the wars – the French never believing that Britain, with her eyes roving outside Europe, saw the German menace clearly. And it could have been this which inclined Britain in the 1930s to appease, where others would have resisted. Britain had her imperial front to look to, as well as her European, and not the resources, it was thought, to resist on both: 'we cannot provide simultaneously,' wrote Neville Chamberlain in 1934, 'for hostilities with Japan *and* Germany'.[106] If she had been given a free choice, she might have appeased Japan, and resisted Germany; that she acted the other way around may partly have been due to the influence of America, whom she was coming to rely on a lot; and of the Dominions, who were not threatened by Germany but were by Japan, and would not (they made clear in 1937) come to Britain's support if she fought Germany over Czechoslovakia.[107] In any event the dilemma would not have arisen if Britain had considered herself firmly a part of Europe. To defend her empire, it seemed, she gave way in Europe; which seemed ironic after the Second World War; whose result was to prise her from her colonies, and throw her closer to Europe.

Notes

1   D. S. Landes, *The Unbound Prometheus* (Cambridge UP, 1969), pp. 451–80.
2   W. A. Lewis, *Economic Survey 1919–39* (Allen & Unwin, 1949), pp. 78–9.

3   W. Woodruff, *The Impact of Western Man* (Macmillan, 1966), p. 313.
4   *Ibid.*, p. 150; Landes, *op. cit.*, pp. 362–3.
5   B. R. Mitchell and P. Deane, *Abstract of British Historical Statistics* (Cambridge UP, 1962), p. 335.
6   M. Barratt Brown, *After Imperialism* (Heinemann, 1963), p. 108.
7   *Ibid.*, p. 110.
8   G. Orwell, *The Road to Wigan Pier* (Penguin, 1962), pp. 139–40.
9   W. Schlote, British Overseas Trade from 1700 to the 1930s (Blackwell, 1952), pp. 156–9; Barratt Brown, op. cit., p. 111.
10   Schlote, *op. cit.*, p. 82.
11   See I. M. Drummond, *British Economic Policy and the Empire 1919–39* (Allen & Unwin, 1972), Chapter 1; Barratt Brown, *op. cit.*, Chapter 4.
12   *Parliamentary Debates*, 5th series, 187 (1925), c. 172.
13   *Ibid.*, c. 80.
14   *Ibid.*, cc. 74–80.
15   L. S. Amery, *My Political Life* (Hutchinson, 1953), ii, p. 299; also pp. 208, 241, 292–3.
16   *Ibid.*, ii, 471–2.
17   P. J. Cain and A. G. Hopkins, *British Imperialism: Crisis and Deconstruction, 1914–1990* (Longman, 1993), pp. 181–2; Mitchell and Deane, *op. cit.*, p. 326.
18   See Drummond, *op. cit.*, Chapter 2; W. K. Hancock, *Survey of British Commonwealth Affairs* (Oxford UP, 1942), ii, Part 1, Chapter 2; Amery, *op. cit.*, ii; W. R. Louis, *In the Name of God, Go! Leo Amery and the British Empire in the Age of Churchill* (W. W. Norton, 1992), *passim*.
19   Hancock, *op. cit.*, ii, Part 1, 94.
20   *Ibid.*, pp. 140–1.
21   *Ibid.*, p. 219.
22   On imperial unity, see R. F. Holland, *Britain and the Commonwealth Alliance, 1918–39* (Macmillan, 1981); Drummond, *op. cit.*; Hancock, *op. cit.*, ii, Part 1, Chapters 2–3; Forrest Capie, *Depression and Protectionism: Britain between the Wars* (Allen & Unwin, 1983); Philip Williamson, *National Crisis and National Government: British Politics, the Economy and Empire, 1926–1932* (Cambridge UP, 1992); Tim Rooth, *British Protectionism and the International Economy: Overseas Commercial Policy in the 1930s* (Cambridge UP, 1993).
23   *Parliamentary Debates*, 5th series, 144 (1921), c. 1624.
24   *Ibid.*, cc. 1581–2.
25   *Indians in Kenya*, Cmd 1922 (1923).
26   *Future Policy in Regard to Eastern Africa*, Cmd 2904 (1927).
27   *Report of the Commission on Closer Union of the Dependencies in Eastern and Central Africa*, Cmd 3234 (1929).
28   Amery, *op. cit.*, ii, 362.
29   *Memorandum on Native Policy in East Africa*, Cmd 3573 (1930).
30   On East–Central Africa, see C. Palley, *The Constitutional History and Law of Southern Rhodesia, 1888–1965* (Clarendon Press, 1966); Richard Gray, *The Two Nations: Aspects of the Development of Race Relations in the Rhodesias and Nyasaland* (Oxford UP, 1960); G. Bennett, *Kenya: A Political History* (Oxford UP, 1963); R. G. Gregory, *Sidney Webb and East Africa* (University of California Press, 1962); E. Huxley, *White Man's Country* (Macmillan, 1935); Robert M. Maxon, *Struggle for Kenya: The Loss and Reassertion of Imperial Initiative, 1912–1923* (Oxford UP, 1993).
31   Amery, *op. cit.*, ii, 118–96, 369.
32   See above, pp. 198–9.
33   Mandate printed in J. Marlowe, *The Seat of Pilate* (Cresset, 1959), appendix.
34   *Ibid.*, p. 108.
35   On the Palestine mandate, see *ibid.*; C. Sykes, *Cross Roads to Israel* (Collins, 1965); Martin Kolinsky, *Law, Order and Riots in Mandatory Palestine, 1928–35* (Macmillan, 1993); Tom Bowden, *The Breakdown of Public Security: The Case of Ireland, 1919–21, and Palestine, 1936–39* (Sage, 1977).
36   *Parliamentary Debates*, 5th series, 187 (1925), c. 84.
37   See above, p. 193.

38 F. Lugard, *The Dual Mandate in British Tropical Africa* (Blackwood, 1922), p. 18.
39 *Parliamentary Debates*, 5th series, 118 (1919), c. 2182.
40 *Ibid.*, 230 (1929), c. 471.
41 *Ibid.*, 118 (1919), c. 2174.
42 Quoted in Helen Tilley, *Africa as a Living Laboratory: Empire, Development and the Problem of Scientific Knowledge, 1870–1950* (Chicago UP, 2001), p. 167.
43 Hancock, *op. cit.*, ii, Part 2, 338, 340.
44 *Parliamentary Debates*, 5th series, 156 (1922), c. 238.
45 V. Harlow and E. M. Chilver (eds), *History of East Africa* (Oxford UP, 1965), ii, 484–5; L. H. Gann and P. Duignan, *Burden of Empire* (Pall Mall Press, 1968), p. 278; *West India Royal Commission Report*, Cmd 6607 (1945), p. 97.
46 Lord Hailey, *An African Survey* (2nd edn, Oxford UP, 1945), p. 1433.
47 *West India Royal Commission Report*, 1945, p. 424.
48 H. Stephens, *Political Transformation of Tanganyika* (Praeger, 1968), p. 30.
49 See Hancock, *op. cit.*, ii, Part 1, Chapter 2; Part 2, Chapter 2; Amery, *op. cit.*, ii, Chapter 11.
50 *Parliamentary Debates*, 5th series, 144 (1921), c. 1555.
51 Amery, *op cit.*, ii, 212.
52 *Ibid.*, ii, 355, 505.
53 *Parliamentary Debates*, 5th series, 208 (1927), c. 499.
54 *Ibid.*, 167 (1923), c. 557.
55 *Ibid.*, 187 (1925), c. 148; 128 (1920), cc. 938, 940.
56 R. Graves and A. Hodge, *The Long Weekend* (Faber & Faber, 1941), p. 251.
57 Frederick, 2nd Earl of Birkenhead, *F.E.: The Life of F. E. Smith, First Earl of Birkenhead* (Eyre & Spottiswoode, 1960), p. 506.
58 H. G. Wells, *Mr Britling Sees it Through* (1916), p. 207.
59 T. R. Reese, *The History of the Royal Commonwealth Society 1868–1968* (Oxford UP, 1968), pp. 156–7, and see p. 142 and Chapter 10 *passim*; J. MacKenzie, *Propaganda and Empire: The Manipulation of British Public Opinion, 1880–1960* (Manchester UP, 1984).
60 Reese, *op. cit.*, p. 145.
61 *Parliamentary Debates*, 5th series, 128 (1920), cc. 944–5.
62 *Parliamentary Debates*, 5th series, 144 (1921), cc. 1626–7.
63 See R. I. Rotberg and A. A. Mazrui (eds), *Protest and Power in Black Africa* (Oxford UP, 1970); R. I. Rotberg, *The Rise of Nationalism in Central Africa* (Harvard UP, 1966), Chapters 5–7; M. Crowder, *West Africa under Colonial Rule* (Hutchinson, 1968), Part 7.
64 *Parliamentary Debates*, 4th series, 179 (1908), c. 418.
65 S. R. Mehrotra, *India and the Commonwealth, 1885–1929* (Allen & Unwin, 1965), p. 216.
66 The Labour Party, *The Colonies* (1943), p. 2.
67 Amery, *op. cit.*, ii, 359–60.
68 *Ibid.*, i, 15.
69 R. Symonds, *The British and Their Successors* (Faber & Faber, 1966), p. 128.
70 R. Faber, *The Vision and the Need* (Faber & Faber, 1966), p. 67.
71 D. Dilks, *Curzon in India*, 2 vols (Hart Davis, 1969, 1970) i, 65, 105, 240; E. S. Montagu, *An Indian Diary* (Heinemann, 1930), pp. 4, 75.
72 *Parliamentary Debates*, 5th series, 167 (1923), cc. 544–5, 579–80.
73 Montagu, *op. cit.*, p. 104.
74 See A. J. Greenberger, *The British Image of India* (Routledge, 1969); R. Gray, *The Two Nations Aspects of the Development of Race Relations in the Rhodesias and Nyasaland* (Oxford UP, 1960); P. Woodruff, *The Men Who Ruled India*, 2 vols (Cape, 1953, 1954), ii; V. G. Kiernan, *The Lords of Human Kind* (Weidenfeld & Nicolson, 1969); R. A. Huttenback, *Racism and Empire* (Cornell UP, 1976); B. Rich, *Race and Empire in British Politics* (Cambridge UP, 1986); P. Fryer, *Black People in the British Empire* (Pluto Press, 1988).
75 B. J. Porter, *Critics of Empire* (Macmillan, 1968), p. 187.
76 B. Malinowski, 'Ethnology and the study of society', *Economica*, ii (1922), 214. On anthropology and Africa, see Tilley, *op. cit.*, Chapter 6.
77 For example W. H. R. Rivers (ed.), *Essays on the Depopulation of Melanesia* (Cambridge UP, 1922).
78 B. Malinowski, 'Practical anthropology', *Africa*, ii (1929), 23.

79   A. P. Thornton, *For the File on Empire* (Macmillan, 1968), p. 352.
80   *Journal of the Royal Society of Arts*, lxxxii (1934), 703.
81   *Ibid.*, pp. 699, 704–7.
82   *Parliamentary Debates*, 5th series, 128 (1920), c. 920.
83   The classic texts on 'Indirect Rule' are Lugard, *op. cit.*; M. Perham, *Native Administration in Nigeria* (Oxford UP, 1937); and L. P. Mair, *Native Policies in Africa* (G. Routledge and Sons, 1936).
84   See Anthony Kirk-Greene, *Britain's Imperial Administrators, 1858–1966* (Macmillan, 2000); Finlay Murray, 'The making of British policy on Tropical Africa', PhD thesis, University of Newcastle upon Tyne, 2001.
85   See H. Callaway, *Gender, Culture and Empire: European Women in Colonial Nigeria* (Macmillan, 1987); M. Strobel, *European Women and the Second British Empire* (Indiana UP, 1991); N. Chaudhuri and M. Strobel (eds), *Western Women and Imperialism: Complicity and Resistance* (Indiana UP, 1992).
86   See R. Heussler, *Yesterday's Rulers* (Syracuse UP, 1963); C. Jeffries, *The Colonial Office* (Allen & Unwin, 1956); R. D. Furse, *Aucuparius: Memoirs of a Recruiting Officer* (Oxford UP, 1962).
87   See P. Mansfield, *The British in Egypt* (Weidenfeld & Nicolson, 1971), Chapters 22–3; P. J. Vatikiotis, *The Modern History of Egypt* (Weidenfeld & Nicolson, 1969), Chapter 12.
88   H. Montgomery Hyde, *Lord Reading* (Heinemann, 1967), p. 382.
89   Frederick, 2nd Earl of Birkenhead, *op. cit.*, p. 507.
90   Montgomery Hyde, *op. cit.*, pp. 380, 389.
91   Frederick, 2nd Earl of Birkenhead, *op. cit.*, pp. 511–12.
92   S. C. Bose, *The Indian Struggle, 1920–1942* (Asia Publishing House, 1964), p. 145.
93   R. Payne, *The Life and Death of Mahatma Gandhi* (Robert Payne, 1969), p. 404.
94   *Parliamentary Debates*, 5th series, 276 (1933), c. 1040.
95   Samuel, first Viscount Templewood, *Nine Troubled Years* (Collins, 1954), p. 58.
96   *Parliamentary Debates*, 5th series, 276 (1933), cc. 1035, 1038, 1058.
97   *Ibid.*, 297 (1935), cc. 1651, 1654.
98   Bose, *op. cit.*, p. 324.
99   R. J. Moore, 'The making of India's paper federation, 1927–35', in C. H. Philips and M. D. Wainwright (eds), *The Partition of India: Policies and Perspectives, 1935–1947* (Allen & Unwin, 1970), p. 68.
100 On 1930s India, see B. N. Pandey, *The Break-Up of British India* (Macmillan, 1969), Chapters 4, 5; Judith Brown, *Modern India: Origins of an Asian Democracy* (Oxford UP, 1985); B. R. Tomlinson, *The Indian National Congress and the Raj, 1929–42* (Macmillan, 1976); R. J. Moore, *The Crisis of Indian Unity, 1917–40* (Clarendon Press, 1974); D. A. Low (ed.), *Congress and the Raj* (Heinemann, 1977).
101 Mehrotra, *op. cit.*, p. 226.
102 Perham, *op. cit.*, p. 361.
103 See Bernard Porter, *The Absent-Minded Imperialists* (Oxford UP, 2004), Chapter 11.
104 E. A. Hughes, *Britain and Greater Britain in the Nineteenth Century* (Cambridge UP, 1919), p. 282.
105 See A. Clayton, *The British Empire as a Superpower, 1919–39* (Macmillan, 1986).
106 D. C. Watt, *Personalities and Policies* (Longman, 1965), p. 91.
107 See *ibid.*, Chapters 4, 7, 8; R. Ovendale, *Appeasement and the English-Speaking World* (University of Wales Press, 1975).

10 Moving quickly: 1939–70

The Second World War

In wartime, the empire never was the source of strength to Britain that in peacetime the 'new imperialists' had sought to make it. When war had looked imminent in the later 1930s, the empire was widely regarded, among those who were responsible for the security of Britain, as a strategical and military burden, an impossibly extended frontier which stretched Britain's resources further than they would go, and consequently weakened considerably her diplomatic hand against the dictators. When the war really got going in 1940, the empire brought Britain some benefits, but as many liabilities. The Dominions and colonies contributed 5 million fighting troops to the war effort, half of them from India, which was considerably more than they had contributed in the First World War.[1] But many of them were employed in defending their own lines, and could not have done *this* without American help; and overall the defence of the empire tied up more British troops than the war in Europe used colonial troops, so that the total military account of the empire was in debit (a debit which, however, for the other advantages Britain continued to get from the empire, it was still worth her while paying). There was too little muscle, too much fat, on the imperial body, which had served a purpose in peace as a source of warmth and energy (and perhaps to preserve an illusion of greatness), but was debilitating in more rigorous times. Britain survived the test, but suffered from the burden; and after the war the damage showed.

Yet it was surprising, and perhaps a little wonderful, that her empire was not more crippling a weight than it turned out to be: that the dominions (except Ireland) came so readily to Britain's aid, though they were no longer obliged to; and that even the dependencies did not take more advantage of Britain's embarrassment than they did. In 1940, Britain had her back to the wall; then if ever (said Winston Churchill three years later) was surely the moment for the empire to break up, for the Dominions

> to seek safety on the winning side … to throw off their yoke and make better terms … with the conquering Nazi and Fascist power. Then was the time. But what happened? It was proved that the bonds which unite us, though supple and elastic, are stronger than the tensest steel … In that dark, terrific, and also glorious hour we received from all parts of His Majesty's Dominions, from the greatest to the smallest, from the strongest and from the weakest … the assurance that we would all go down or come through together. You will forgive me if on this occasion … I rejoice in the soundness of our institutions and proclaim my faith in our destiny.[2]

Not only the self-governing Dominions proved loyal, but the dependent colonies too – those that Britain *denied* self-government to, which was the greater miracle. 'I think it is significant,' said a former Colonial Secretary, Malcolm MacDonald, in 1940,

> that these 60,000,000 people, scattered over 50 different territories, who are not yet free to govern themselves, who are governed by us, recognised instinctively ... that we are the true guardians of the liberties and the happiness of small peoples.[3]

Which was one in the eye for Hitler, who had expected the empire to crumble at the first nudge; and a tribute to the resilience of Britain's colonial methods.

It was a little later on in the war that the weak points began to show, as they were bound to. The military experts had been right when they had predicted that the empire just could not be defended if it were challenged by Japan as well as Germany, and in the early 1940s her colonies in the east toppled one by one before the Japanese wind: Hong Kong in December 1941; then Malaya – with her people apparently not lifting a finger to stop it, which put a damper on Britain's euphoria;[4] then, in February 1942, that great new 'invulnerable' imperial bastion in the east, Singapore (allegedly because its guns were all pointing out to sea and the Japanese came in from the land); and then Burma. With the Americans after Pearl Harbor taking over the main burden in the Pacific, Britain was able to hang on to what remained: but at a price. Everywhere there were strains. As in the First World War the main stress points were the Middle East and India, where by now Britain's hold was very tenuous anyway. Both proved somewhat wilful and unruly horses to ride to war on.

The Middle East swarmed with British battalions once again: for all the old strategical reasons, and for a comparatively new one – oil. Sometimes the troops were there under clauses in treaties which allowed Britain this facility in this kind of crisis, sometimes not. In either case, their presence was generally resented locally. The North African campaign had to be fought all the time from a base, Egypt, whose loyalty was always in doubt, which would have welcomed Rommel had he come, and where a collaborationist government was only kept in power by intimidation. In Iraq, there was an army rebellion against the British garrisons in May 1941, which was successful for a while. Persia was invaded by Russia and Britain in concert to safeguard her oil. And Palestine was throughout the war a running sore, bubbling over into violent conflict between Arabs and Jews, neither side any longer willing to be used by the British as they had been in the Great War, and both communities occasionally turning on their distracted British guardians murderously. Since 1918, the Middle East had gone very sour on Britain.[5]

India was only a little less amenable. Although most Indian nationalists probably sympathised with the British case against Germany on its merits – Gandhi and Nehru did[6] – they were irritated by the fact that they were given no choice in the matter, but merely told one morning by their Viceroy that they were at war. Congress's line was that before they fought in the cause of democracy, they wanted democracy themselves. Denied this, they refused to co-operate. Throughout the war there were rumblings of discontent in the subcontinent, and worse: mass resignations by all the provincial ministries at the start; a civil disobedience campaign inaugurated by Gandhi in October 1940, which filled the prisons with 14,000 protesters six months later; serious riots and disorders all over India, killing 900, in August 1942; and a small but steady stream of defectors, reputedly 42,000 altogether, to the ranks of the 'Indian National Army', fighting on the Japanese side, after the fall of Singapore. Disaffection increased during the Great Bengal Famine of 1943–44, which raised inevitable doubts over whether the raj could discharge even the most basic duties of any government there. (Between three and four million Bengalis died in this, which was comparable to the toll of the contemporary European Holocaust. Clearly the motives behind these two events were different, but the scale of the horror must have been the same, and British historians' neglect of the former more culpable.[7]) All this had to be put on the other side of the account against the troops and the money raised in India for the war (neither of which anyway, claimed Congress, could be 'considered to be voluntary contributions from India'[8]). For a time – while the Japanese were in Burma and aiming towards Assam – the end of British India looked very near indeed: a fact which was recognised by the British cabinet, who were moved in desperation to make their most generous advance to the Indian nationalists yet – the Cripps offer of March 1942; and by the nationalists, who felt confident enough to refuse it. With the restoration of the Allied position in South-east Asia, the initiative passed away from the nationalists again, and the concessions which were actually implemented in India were very small. But the damage was lasting.[9]

Even the quietest parts of the empire were unsettled by the war, though less directly or immediately. From the empire's very beginnings Britain's control over her colonies had always rested on a delicate admixture of power, or the illusion of power, and collabora-tion: the latter depending largely on the former, as an acknowledgement of British power was an encouragement for politic men to collaborate. Britain's reverses in the Far East were damaging here. Even the normally loyal Australians resented what they saw as Britain's half-hearted efforts in this theatre, which was, of course, the critical one for them. For a time, Menzies, the Australian Prime Minister, and Churchill were hardly on speaking terms.[10] Other colonial subjects could not fail to be shocked by the ignominious spectacle of Singapore, which probably did more than any other single event to prick the bubble of Britain's 'prestige'. For the Indians, there came a constant reminder of the les-sons of Singapore from the propaganda radio stations the Japanese could now set up in Burma; for other colonial subjects, those lessons were perhaps delayed, but nonetheless distinct when they seeped through. Back to Africa and the West Indies after the war came black soldiers who had served in Burma or elsewhere, side by side with white men, and so knew about Britain's soft spots at first hand. As well as this, they came back with new ideas and expectations. A Conservative MP, who had served with the West Africa Fron-tier Force during the war, warned how it would be:

> We shall see after the war a very large number of Africans going home, who are trained or part-trained artisans, with a sense of discipline, with a knowledge of English, and educated, in a broad sense, by travel. Now they will be going home, in some places, to distant villages and remote districts, and to the old life, but seeing it with very different eyes.

This could be, he said, 'a big force for good or for bad'.[11] In the Gold Coast just after the war, it was a force for bad: or so it appeared to a Commission inquiring into riots there in 1948:

> Such Africans by reason of their contacts with other peoples, including Europeans, had developed a political and national consciousness. The fact that they were dis-appointed with conditions on their return, either from specious promises made before demobilisation or a general expectancy of a golden age for heroes, made them the natural focal point for any general movement against authority.[12]

For those who stayed at home and did not meet any returning soldiers, or any of the British or American soldiers stationed in bases among them, the war acted in other ways to disturb them. As in the First World War, it put a premium on tropical products, which stimulated colonial industries and hence the mobility and the urbanisation and (for some) the relative prosperity which are the normal concomitants of industrial growth. Travel and contact and new expectations prompted new political activity. Concessions and promises made during the war gave fuel to that activity – concessions, for example, of regional councils in Northern Rhodesia, and of new constitutions to the Gold Coast and Nigeria; promises like that contained in the Atlantic Charter of August 1941, which proclaimed (regardless of Churchill's efforts to get the British empire excluded) 'the right of all peoples to choose the form of government under which they live'. Stirrings were just visible in parts of British Africa during the war. There was another serious and violent strike on the Northern Rhodesian copper belt in 1940; trouble with the Kikuyu Central Association in Kenya, which was proscribed because it was thought to be plotting with the Italians; new political parties in Nigeria (the National Council of Nigeria and the Cameroons) and in Nyasaland (the Nyasaland African Congress), both founded in 1944; and on a different level, a new campaign, which met with some success, by white Kenyans to use the war to further *their* political aims in East Africa. But the chickens really came home to roost after the war, when the troops returned home, and other Africans too who had been spending the war educating and organising themselves in Europe and America; and when Africans could take stock of the new climate and the new realities of power. 'When the balloons come down for good,' predicted Sir Ralph Furse in 1943,

> the curtain will go up on a colonial stage set for a new act ... When the lights are turned full on, we may well find that what we are watching is not so much a new act but, as it were, a new play in some great trilogy.[13]

Things would assuredly never be the same.[14]

That Britain eventually came out of the war still in the colonial saddle was due largely to the help of her allies, and in particular Russia and the USA: which more than anything underlined the incongruity of her position. To save her empire, she had required the assistance of powers who were opposed to her having it, which because it had suited their immediate purpose during the war had been forthcoming then, but was a precarious guarantee for the future. Russia's fulminations against imperialism Britain could disregard, because her motives were suspect and because the Russian alliance was never widely regarded as more than a temporary *mariage de convenance*. But America's ill-will Britain could not afford so well, because the American alliance was more vital to her, both at the time against Japan and Italy and Germany and afterwards – in all probability – against Russia. America was needed badly, and America – or so it appeared from the utterances of certain of her statesmen and her press – was not going to be used, as she had been in the First World War, to maintain imperialism: 'one thing we are sure we are not fighting for,' said *Life* magazine in 1942, 'is to hold the British Empire together.'[15] From some accounts it appeared that the Americans were 'making the liquidation of the British Empire one of their war aims'.[16] It was like getting a policeman to help you defend stolen property against another thief: it was going to be difficult to persuade him to let you keep it afterwards.

There were two kinds of response in Britain to American wartime criticism of her imperial conduct. The first was self-righteous rejection, which was common enough, and did not help Anglo-American relations at all, but merely confirmed (said Leonard Barnes, a leading left-wing writer on colonial affairs) 'in our critics' minds the worst that can be said against us'.[17] A notable feature of the Second World War, however, was that this was not the only kind of response, and that, in general, British propagandists pleaded a far more sympathetic case to their American protectors, which was that although the property *was* stolen, they had in general looked after it well, and intended anyway to give it back eventually in better shape than they had found it. Past colonial sins were admitted, or at least some of the more venial ones, and especially sins of omission. In the future, if they were allowed to, they would do better.[18]

It was all very humble and contrite, and it was not all empty words. For while smugger imperialists like Churchill were congratulating themselves on the 'soundness of our institutions' as reflected in the empire's loyalty, there were some others who were working hard to *improve* their colonial institutions, and by 1945 solid plans for a new colonial deal, adequate or otherwise, were well under way. Before the war broke out, there had been already a genuine resolution on the part of some politicians and colonial civil servants, provoked and stimulated by the West Indian riots of the late 1930s, to make something more of Britain's professed aim of 'trusteeship' than had been made of it hitherto. Wartime gave the movement some impetus. In 1940, a bill was introduced in Parliament to give grants to colonies for their 'development and welfare', on the lines of the 1929 Act but more generous. It had been thought up before the war, and its sponsors were at pains to discount any idea that it was intended as 'a bribe or a reward for the Colonies' support in this supreme crisis',[19] but it was undoubtedly helped along by such considerations. Conceived, perhaps, in the purest altruism, it still (like its predecessor) needed an appeal to urgent material interest for it to be born; and its supporters were full of how it would cement colonial loyalties, pre-empt foreign criticism, and (one or two suggested) stimulate the production in the colonies of certain vital war materials.[20] Though very little of the money actually granted was ever spent (only £3 million in its first four years, out of a possible £20 million), it was a start: a precedent for a much more substantial Colonial Development and Welfare Act in 1945, and a signpost for future policy.

Other things were done too. New labour laws were enacted, universities projected, research committees set up. On the constitutional front, Ceylon in 1943 was promised internal self-government, and by the end of the war had worked out a constitution for herself and got it substantially approved by a visiting British Commission. Malta too was promised self-government. Jamaica was granted full adult franchise for her House of Representatives in 1944, and Trinidad and British Guiana got new constitutions. The Gold Coast was given an African majority on its legislative council (though it was a majority largely picked by the chiefs). Kenya's legislative council got its first African member. Then for India – or so it was assumed, despite its rejection by Congress and withdrawal by Britain – the Cripps offer still stood on the table, to set up an Indian assembly immediately after the war to determine with Britain the form which an independent India would take, and then to devolve power as quickly as possible to it. And for those who set store by such things, there was the more general pronouncement made by the Colonial Secretary in 1943, that the government was 'pledged to guide colonial people along the road to self-government within the British Empire', which was there for the record, however many ambiguities there might be in it to seize on later.

Enough had been said and done during the war, therefore, to promise a radically new departure in colonial policy afterwards: unless, of course, the British government reneged on it as it had tried to do after the First World War. It might conceivably have done this if Churchill had stayed in power. Churchill's position was similar in some ways to Milner's in the First World War: an imperialist who had never had very much of a following before the war, but had been called to power during the war because it was thought (rightly, as it turned out) that he could win it better than any of those who had. He was no fonder of colonial reform than he was of social reform, but had been forced into sanctioning both by the exigencies of wartime, under protest, and was delighted when, for example, the Cripps mission failed. One of the most celebrated of his wartime pronouncements had been (in 1940, in reply to an American who had advocated putting the British colonies under the United Nations) that he had not become Prime Minister in order to preside over the liquidation of the British empire, and had he remained in power after 1945, it is possible that he might have kept his word, or tried to. The promises made during this war were no more impressive, for their time, than those made during the First World War, and many of the promises of the First World War had not been honoured.[21] But there were differences now. The first was that neither Churchill, nor his coalition, nor his party was returned to power to undertake the work of reconstruction as Lloyd George's coalition had been in 1918. The second difference was that the world situation and the balance of power now were utterly changed.[22]

Labour's empire

That there was in July 1945 a Labour government, with a majority in the House of Commons for the first time ever, and the kind of mandate that wartime and pre-war memories gave it to sweep clean the old political stables, was significant in the history of the empire, but not decisive. In almost every field of policy it was a long time now since anyone had been able convincingly to label the party, as some had managed to get it labelled in the 1920s, as a 'revolutionary' party, except by a very alarmist definition of the word 'revolutionary'; and in colonial affairs, in which Labour as a whole had displayed relatively little interest ever, it was likely to be less radical than in domestic social affairs, which concerned it most of all. In its policy towards the empire between 1945 and 1951, Labour in fact played the game very much within the old rules, bounded by the limits of a very broad agreement which interested and 'moderate' sections of both parties had established in wartime; a bipartisan approach which was possible now because during the war many Conservatives had moved quite a considerable way towards the 'moderate centre' on colonial questions, and Labour had never been very far away from that centre. Most of the Labour Party's supporters were ignorant of the empire and apathetic towards it, which had always been the case in Britain though only now, with the development of techniques to sample popular opinion, could the extent of popular ignorance be gauged. In 1948, three-quarters of the population did not know the difference between a dominion and a colony, and half could not name a single British colony,[23] which was a pathetic return for all the effort that had in the past been put into propagandising the empire, and an indication that colonial affairs would cut very little electoral ice. Labour MPs shared the people's broad apathy towards imperial questions, which effectively allowed a free hand to those in the party who *had* pondered them. Surprisingly, perhaps, these people turned out to be not half as *anti*-imperialist as most Conservatives feared.

   This was because they shared many imperialist values. This should not be a surprise. It appears so only if British politics at this time is conceived in irreducibly partisan terms. In fact, the two main party leaderships agreed on a great deal. One thing was the need to uphold Britain's material interests in the world, so far as was possible; and what seemed possible to Ernest Bevin – Labour's Foreign Secretary – was still quite a lot. It included the preservation of the empire in some form or another; for 'if the British Empire fell ... it would mean the standard of life of our constituents would fall rapidly'.[24] That does not sound like a conventional socialist view. But then Labour was not conventionally socialist in this field. The reason for this in Bevin's case was that he was a patriot before he was anything – including a socialist. For others in his party, the imperialism arose out of the socialism itself.

This is where partisan categories are misleading. They make almost no sense in this field. Labour and Conservatives were not in opposite halves of a spectrum; both covered the same spectrum, though in subtly different ways. Labour went from anarchism to statism, the Conservatives from libertarianism to paternalism: the similarity is striking, and enabled unconventional liaisons between the parties, so long as the whips did not get in the way. Statists and paternalists came together over the welfare state in the 1950s, for example; and before that, during the war years, over the question of the way the empire should be run. The main institutional link between them was the Fabian Society, a gradualist socialist sect, whose constructive interest in imperial matters went back to the time of the South African War, when – breaking ranks with just about every other socialist body – it had issued a pamphlet advocating that the empire be not abolished, but preserved and transformed into one great worldwide welfare state.[25] The Fabians even had one colonial governor (Lord Olivier) as a leading early member.[26] (It may be worth mentioning here that another, Clement Attlee, Labour's leader in the 1940s, had been educated at Haileybury, which had been originally *founded* to train boys in the service of the empire.) When the Fabians set up a 'Colonial Bureau' in 1940 to discuss these things, therefore, even Conservative governors found the forum a perfectly congenial one. It was here, in fact, that much of the practical colonial policy of the 1940s and 1950s was actually thrashed out, by paternalistic imperialists working together with socialist imperialists, and away from what they both regarded as the merely destructive influence of Labour anti-colonialism, and the Conservative free market tendency.

The policy that was thrashed out in this way owed much to an old concept, which we have met before, of 'trusteeship'. It was this, for example, which infused the two new Colonial Development and Welfare Acts of 1940 and 1945. Its central emphasis was that it was the duty of colonial government, before it thought of giving self-rule to any colony, to work to establish the infrastructure of 'good' government there, which meant educational and welfare and medical and administrative services, but chiefly the economic prosperity which would make all these things possible and the new polity stable. 'It is economic development,' said Arthur Creech Jones, Labour's first post-war Colonial Secretary (and another Fabian) in 1940, 'which in the long run makes possible social services and welfare, and the ability of the Colonial peoples to stand on their own feet.'[27] In 1945, he besought socialists not to let their distaste for imperialism, or 'some sentimental inclination to "liberation"', mislead them into too hasty a colonial retreat: 'To throw off the colonial empire in this way, would be to betray the peoples and our trust.'[28] Britain was forever trying to get this point home to her international critics, too. Of course, a government official explained patiently to an American delegation in May 1950, 'If self-government were the aim without qualification, it could be granted to every Colony tomorrow, but the result would simply be political chaos in the territories concerned.'[29] There was a lot in that. It was also, it has to be said, a very convenient argument: in political terms because it kept both imperialists and anti-imperialists quiet.

It anticipated the end of empire, but not too soon. As well as that, as one Labour enthusiast put it, it 'neatly dovetailed idealism with [British] economic needs'.[30] Most of all, perhaps, the concept of 'development and welfare' was seductive because its effect was to sanction what was expedient now, while at the same time seeming to endorse most of what had been done in the past. A too hasty colonial retreat would have been a tacit admission of the error of past imperial policy, and made a mockery of the old professed aim of trusteeship, which had always provided its justification. Trusteeship implied that Britain was in Africa and Asia for the Africans' and Asians' good: that her aim was to 'develop' them to a stage where they could fend for themselves. The corollary was that she could not withdraw, just because it suited her, before she had 'developed' them to that stage. Otherwise there would be no retrospective justification of her colonial rule, and trusteeship would be seen as a sham.[31]

Labour's problem in 1945 was that trusteeship *had* been a sham in the past, in any positive, constructive sense. Parsimony and neglect were fond traditions in British colonial policy, things which generations of Englishmen had prided themselves on: that 'there has probably never been,' as a Colonial Under-Secretary put it in 1922, 'any Empire in the world's history that was so economical in its encroachments upon public cost or public time'.[32] Economic development in many colonies had been minimal, or where it was more than minimal, had not generally conduced to the growth of viable national economies which could stand on their own (although this latter problem had hardly occurred to anyone before: not to Conservative imperialists because their ideal economic unit had been not the nation but the empire; nor even to anti-imperialist Liberals, because theirs had been the whole world). Britain had a lot of leeway to make up to compensate for past neglect (Figure 10.1).

The 1945 Colonial Development and Welfare Act provided some of the means for a final effort. The colonies were given £120 million to spend over ten years, which was immensely more than in 1940 or 1929. That probably reflected not only the situation in the colonies, but also the new economics ethos – Keynesian, less subject to deflationary dogma – of that time. On this occasion, most of the £120 million was actually spent, and in a more systematic, ordered way than before, with carefully devised five- and ten-year plans, and public development corporations to implement them. Many colonies were brought along quite rapidly: roads, houses and hospitals built, university colleges established, grand new economic schemes pursued with energy and enthusiasm – occasionally too much enthusiasm, as with the notorious Tanganyikan groundnuts scheme of 1948, which wasted £36 million trying to make groundnuts grow where they would not. To top up the coffers, further Colonial Development Acts were passed in 1949 and 1950. Not all colonies benefited equally: not, for example, the poorer colonies who were not thought to have any resources worth developing, and who used their share of the money merely to cancel their overdrafts. Neither was anything done yet (or ever) to make colonial economies balanced, less dependent on single products for any prosperity which might come their way, which was a common complaint afterwards. Nevertheless enough was done, just, to save the faces of those liberal imperialists who had always claimed that they ruled the Africans and the Asians for their own good, but who had had almost nothing to show for it, hardly a shred of evidence for their claims, before 1945.[33]

To all this, the Conservative opposition offered scarcely a breath of criticism, which was scarcely surprising. The idea of colonial development had a good Conservative pedigree as well as a radical one. The means which Labour employed might have been a little socialistic and bureaucratic for some, not kind enough to free enterprise capitalists, but

The Abyssinian Delegate
*Jomo Kenyatta asked for an Act of Parlia-
ment making discrimination by race or
colour a criminal offence.*

The Nigerian Trade Unionist
*Chief A. S. Coker, represents unions with
a membership of half a million workers. He
demands full franchise for the negro worker.*

The Liverpool Welfare Worker
*Mr. E. J. Du Plau, is responsible for hostels
and centres for negro seamen. "Negroes are
social exiles in Britain," he maintains.*

AFRICA SPEAKS IN MANCHESTER

**Delegates from many parts of Africa and the United States to the first Pan-African Conference talk for a week—
of freedom from the White Man, of the colour bar, of one great coloured nation, of force to gain their ends.**

Photographed by JOHN DEAKIN

THE dance was a mixed affair—mixed in trade, from the stoker to the anthropologist; mixed in class, from the £3 a week labourer to the rich cocoa merchant; mixed in dress, from the baggy grey flannels to the suit of tails. But above all it was mixed in colour, from the blonde white to the midnight black. This dance, held at Edinburgh Hall, on the corner of one of Manchester's drab and soot-blackened streets, was the first gathering of delegates to the Pan-African Conference. They chose Manchester because its people have less curiosity or hostility to colour than the people of any other English city. Certainly, there was no self-consciousness among the white women who part-nered their negro husbands or friends through 'jive' to the last romantic waltz. Their attitudes varied. Some had approached the colour bar problem intellectually, others from a Christian viewpoint and others from simple human values.

Typical of the last attitude is the mixed marriage of Mary Brown to John Teah Brown, and before the conference got down to the more serious prob-lems of the negro peoples, I went to their home to see a successful black and white marriage in its own domestic setting. Mary Brown was left stranded in Liverpool with her child when she met John Brown, a donkeyman on a merchant ship. He married her, gave her overwhelming affection, and saw that her child was properly educated.

I listened to John Teah Brown's story—a story which in many ways put in terms of one human being the resolutions and speeches of the whole week's conference. John Teah Brown was born in Sierra Leone and is a member of the Kroo tribe. He was educated at a mission and brought up a Roman Catholic. He was devout and sincere in his religion until one day in a church at East London, South Africa. He went in to pray but a priest came up to him and told him it was a white man's church and he must get out. He has not been inside a church since, though he remains true to the Christian faith, practising it, he thinks, with rather more sincerity than the priest who turned him away from the altar.

He left Sierra Leone at the age of fifteen, for he
Continued overleaf

A Mixed Marriage That is a Success
*Mr. John Teah Brown, with his white wife, Mrs. Mary Brown, in their Manchester home.
He says the negro must earn the respect of the white man to merit full citizenship.*

19

Figure 10.1 Colonial nationalism comes to Manchester
Source: From *Picture Post*, 10 November 1945. Photo by John Deakin/Picture Post/Hulton Archive/
Getty Images.

this was only to be expected of the government which had nationalised the coal mines and set up the welfare state. Their ultimate aim too – self-subsistence and self-govern-ment – might have been objectionable to many Conservatives, but that aim was by no means implicit in the policy of colonial development, which could equally well be harnessed, as it had been by Chamberlain and Amery, to very different imperial purposes. Colonial development was uncontroversial as between imperialists and anti-imperialists, because it did not actually give any colonies away.

All this, however, was for the quieter parts of the empire. In Africa (where colonial development was largely concentrated), Britain seemed under no great pressure to decolonise yet. 'It is clear,' concluded a government committee in 1947, 'that in Africa the period before self-government can be granted will be longer than in most other parts of the Colonial Empire': so long, indeed, that the ultimate date was not worth speculating about. 'At least a generation' was the usual rough estimate.[34] This was because Africa was so politically underdeveloped at present. Elsewhere, however, the situation was clearly different. The Middle East and South and South-east Asia were the most problematical areas. Scarcely anyone of either British party disputed that there would need to be some fairly swift belt-tightening there. Palestine and India were the obvious first candidates for freedom. Beyond that, however, there was room for uncertainty and doubt.

The greatest uncertainty surrounded colonies that were deemed to be important strategically to Britain: useful, that is, for defending what was still regarded as her 'world role'. The Attlee government was seriously divided over this. Attlee himself was for scuttling, but was overruled by his powerful Foreign Secretary, Bevin, whose clinching argument was probably his warning that if Britain abandoned these places, the Russians would simply step in.[35] There was, of course, something in this. The Soviet Union was a powerful and aggressive entity at this time. This complicated the general picture in a number of ways. It introduced another motive into the defence of colonies, especially those colonies – like Malaya – where the opposition to empire was clearly communist-led. Eventually even the anti-imperialist United States, took this on board.[36] It was also, incidentally, a factor behind the policy of colonial development, which was pursued – much as welfarism was in Britain – partly in order to reduce the poverty which was supposed to be communism's best ally. Bevin was wedded to both policies: welfare, plus resistance, to prevent the Soviets advancing either by seduction or by force. Underneath this, of course, there was a bottom line. If ex-colonies did go over to the enemy, it would be not only their own misfortune, but also Britain's. She depended on their goodwill economically. By the beginning of the 1950s, for example, Middle Eastern oil had come to be vital to her. She could not afford to let her colonies go to the devil. Hence her rear-guard action – despite Attlee's doubts – over Cyprus, the Persian Gulf (though not Persia itself – Iran – which *was* 'scuttled' in 1951), Malaysia; and anywhere else where it was not self-evidently a lost cause.

The transfer of power in India

India was the big exception. Not everyone regarded it as such. That was partly because of the romantic attachment many British Conservatives had to the old raj: a love, an obsession, almost it seemed sometimes an emotional necessity. For some of them the withdrawal from India, when it happened, hit very hard. At the head of the party, Winston Churchill hated it, and spoke against it. At the very foot of the party, the young Enoch Powell, who was not an MP yet, walked the streets all night 'trying to digest it. One's whole world had been altered.'[37] Yet they let this through too, without doing anything – like forcing a division in Parliament – really to embarrass the government in its designs. Partly this may have been because India was no longer – had not been since the First World War – centrally important to Britain's economy as she had been in the nineteenth century. More powerful a reason was probably that, after the first euphoric months of victory at least, it no longer looked practically feasible to stay in India: not with India considering herself to be just on the brink of freedom, and likely to turn nasty if disappointed; and with no help or sympathy from any other quarter if Britain found the task of hanging on beyond her.

In 1946, it became obvious that Britain did not rule India in any meaningful sense anyway. Communal riots and massacres which broke out in August of that year in Calcutta, and soon spread throughout Bengal and Bihar and elsewhere, reduced parts of the country very quickly to near anarchy. The Indian police became implicated, and there were fears that communalism might spread to the army, which would destroy finally any hope of preserving the impartial enforcement of law, and hence control.[38] The situation was a self-aggravating one. What the Muslim community, who started it, feared most was their domination by Hindus in an independent India, when the power of the raj, which was at the very least impartial towards them, had gone. There had been communal tensions in India for many years; possibly they had been exploited in the past by the British to cement their rule, but there can be little doubt that the presence of the British there in another way kept them down, for the simple reason that while the power lay outside either community, it did not matter which of them 'dominated'. With the prospect of self-rule, and consequently the problem of the distribution of power between them, looming nearer, the stakes were raised, and so fears and rivalries were heightened and transmuted into violence. As the violence increased, so Britain's ability to control the situation diminished and the prospect of self-rule loomed nearer still, which fired up communal tensions further.

On the political level, the two main nationalist organisations could not agree between themselves how power was to be shared. The Muslim League demanded, as it had done since 1940, a separate Pakistan nation. Congress was cast in the role of the Hindu party, but had always hotly denied it, and stood out for an 'all-India' which would subsume all religious and cultural groups. Britain's solution, which was put to them by a 'Cabinet Mission' early in 1946, for a loose all-India federation with a complicated system of safeguards, seemed to win acceptance in principle, but then foundered on details, and on the composition of the transitional administration which would precede the new union. The failure of this solution sparked off the violence, and the breakdown of law and order. A more desperate expedient was called for. 'Unless these men were faced with the urgency of a time limit,' wrote the Prime Minister, Clement Attlee, afterwards, 'there would always be procrastination.'[39] So a date was set for independence before agreement was reached. Lord Mountbatten, who suggested the time limit, was to act as midwife for a new independent India, or more than one India if that proved inevitable. He was to arrange things as well as he could for the birth. But if he could not arrange things well, the baby was to be born regardless.

Once the date had been set (in February 1947 for June 1948), and once Mountbatten had departed for India (in March 1947), there was very little more that the British government could do for or with India. It was the Conservatives who pointed out, ruefully, that the time limit policy prevented Britain bargaining with India to retain anything of her rule, because it left her nothing (except perhaps aid) to bargain with.[40] Britain, of course, was an interested party in her discussions with the Indians about their future: she wanted her nationals and her economic interests safeguarded in India, and independent India's political goodwill, if she could get it. The time limit, however, gave her very little leverage, beyond what powers of persuasion Mountbatten could summon from his own resources of character: in terms of real authority, he was little more than an intermediary. After February 1947, there was no longer any possibility that Britain would try to hold on to India by any means. Any interests she wished to retain in India could be retained only by the voluntary agreement of the Indians themselves. The final decision had been taken in February, and Britain's effective rule in India, her control over her destinies, ended then.

But the setting of the time limit itself greatly affected the outcome. In the first place, the Muslim League knew now that they needed only to hang on to secure what they wanted, which was a separate Pakistan state. With the situation in the Punjab and Bengal as chaotic as it was, a Congress-dominated Indian government would have been no more able to control it than the British, which Congress leaders recognised. Both parties agreed therefore – one of them very reluctantly – to partition India. Second, the announcement of a time limit itself accelerated things further: the breakdown of order, the decline of a doomed administration, the scramble for seats of power by politicians and interest groups before the music stopped: and in the end, to put a brake on this tumble into anarchy, the day of demission itself was brought forward. 'India in March 1947,' recalled Mountbatten's chief of staff,

> was a ship on fire in mid-ocean with ammunition in the hold. By then it was a question of putting the fire out before it actually reached the ammunition. There was in fact no option before us but to do what we did.[41]

India and Pakistan became independent on 15 August 1947, which was ten months earlier than originally intended. The demarcation between them was not satisfactory, as it could not have been after two centuries during which the 'natural' divisions between India's peoples, if they were such, had been obscured and cushioned and allowed in some places to run into each other under the vast, protective and essentially artificial blanket of the old raj. For months after devolution, there were massive, panic-stricken and bloody adjustments to the new gravity: wholesale exchanges of population east and west between the borders of the new states, running into millions; riots in Delhi and elsewhere which killed more than half a million; almost immediately a war between India and Pakistan, which the United Nations had to step in to settle; and running disputes over contentious territories to the present day. Pakistan in the awkward bisected shape which 1947 had put it in survived only for 25 years. It was all something of a shambles but a shambles was scarcely avoidable. To those who charged the government with betraying Britain's trust in India because it had not stayed there long enough 'to clear up all these things before we go', Attlee replied sharply (and it could equally have applied to Africa and elsewhere) that 'if that trust is there, it ought to have been fulfilled long ago'.[42] It did not prevent the Labour Party, and those imperialists who had managed to reconcile themselves most happily to the new realities, from preening themselves on their achievement, and on the goodwill – which must have surprised some of them – which their erstwhile subjects still expressed for them, even after it was all over. What flattered them most of all was that India and Pakistan both chose to remain in the Commonwealth, though the Commonwealth had to be altered a little to accommodate them.[43] By a slightly demoralised Britain this was taken – however it was meant – as a tacit but welcome vote of thanks.[44]

On India's heels into the ranks of newly independent nations came Burma in January 1948, and Ceylon in February. Both of them had far too much independence already at the end of the war for the full thing to be denied them now. In June 1948, Palestine west of the Jordan was not so much granted self-government as abandoned to whoever was stronger there, who turned out – after some bloody fighting and a mass exodus of Arab refugees – to be Israel.[45] Ceylon remained in the Commonwealth, Burma did not. For Israel, who after Balfour had had very little to thank Britain for, it would have been unthinkable. And so the first stage of Britain's decolonisation came to an end: with the letting go of what, after the war, just could not be held.

The nationalist challenge

India over the previous 100 years had been regarded as the keystone of the British empire; the *raison d'être* of much of the rest, like Egypt and East Africa and the Transvaal, which were supposed to have been secured to guard Britain's sea-lanes there. With India gone, the rationale for the whole empire might seem to have gone, but some did not see it like this. Traumatic as it was, the demission of power to India and Pakistan was not necessarily the beginning of the end, for the empire's rationale in the last two or three decades had changed quite considerably from what it had been in the nineteenth century, and could accommodate now what then would have been rather like the removal of its heart. In the 1920s and 1930s, as we saw, some of the most practical imperialists had come to centre their attention and their designs almost exclusively around the Colonial Office's dependent empire, and primarily around Africa, which, in the 1950s, was as valuable to Britain as it had ever been, and consequently a seductive focus for imperialists' attention still. In addition, the inevitability of general decolonisation – if it was inevitable – was obscured for many by the adhesion of India and Pakistan to the Commonwealth, which at this time was a very uncertain quantity, but might still develop into something an imperialist could use: as if nothing had really happened to the empire more significant than the promotion of one or two of its NCOs to officer rank. Of course, in 1947, they saw the danger signs, but not necessarily the death-knell for imperialism – for Britain as a world power, and a colonial power in much the old style. In various ways they tried throughout the 1950s to cling on to their imperial ermine: at first, by resistance to nationalist demands, then by compromise, then at last (if they could) by giving away the trappings of power, and keeping back the substance. For those colonies who wished to pursue India to independence, it was not simply a question of following closely along a path beaten flat by her. The hurdles she had knocked down Britain erected again for the others. To become free, they would need to fight.

What was chiefly standing in their way was their economic value to Britain. That value was not quite the same as it had been. Over the previous few years Britain had plummeted quite disastrously in the world's league table of great economic powers. She no longer had a significant surplus to send abroad. Her proportion of the world's exports in manufactured goods in 1960 was only 18 per cent (and 13 per cent five years later), down from 33 per cent in 1900. She owed far more money than was owed to her. She no longer needed foreign markets and fields for investment for quite the same reasons that she had needed them before. Yet still she did trade and invest abroad; and her trade and investment, though it might not have been spread so thickly as it had once been, was still spread as *wide*. In 1960, 67 per cent of her exports went outside Europe, and as much as 92 per cent of her foreign investments.[46] If Britain was already destined to become a 'European' power after the war, these figures gave little clue of it. For the empire they appeared even more impressive. Just before the war, the empire had accounted for

Table 10.1 Post-war empire trade

Dates	Imports (%)	Exports (%)
1946–49	48	57.5
1950–54	49	54
1955–59	47	51

39.5 per cent of Britain's imports and 49 per cent of her exports. After the war, the imperial proportion of what trade she still had left was even greater (Table 10.1).

Of Britain's capital exports, 65 per cent went to the empire between 1950 and 1954, and 60 per cent between 1958 and 1960.[47] If Britain no longer had a credible world role, however, she still had worldwide interests. She had a special interest in the Middle East, because it supplied 82 per cent of her mineral oil, which was her principal import. She depended on Australasia for 66 per cent of her imported wool, 50 per cent of her imported butter, and 29 per cent of her imported meat; on South Africa and Canada together for 50 per cent of non-ferrous metals; on India for 81 per cent of her tea; on Canada for 54 per cent of her imported grains; on the West Indies for sugar; on Malaya for rubber; on tropical Africa for metals and vegetable products.[48] Her leading exports (machines, aircraft, cars) similarly depended largely on extra-European markets: especially on North America, which took 19 per cent of them, Asia (17 per cent), Africa (12 per cent) and Australasia (12 per cent).[49] The pattern had not really changed very much from pre-war, though the colours were now a little faded.

It followed that Britain's political interests in the world were not so very different either, though her capacity to safeguard them may have been. Britain still had stakes in certain parts of the world, like Africa and South-east Asia, where security or stability seemed to depend on her maintaining a political presence there, or nearby. In addition, these stakes and all Britain's others in more reliable parts of the world, like North America and Oceania, together made up a network of interests which was thought to require continued political presences elsewhere to safeguard it: forts and garrisons at strategic points to protect the traffic between Britain and the world. For a colonial people ambitious to be free, either of these interests, or both, could be a formidable obstacle to them: for Northern Rhodesians, Britain's interests in their copper; for Cypriots, her concern for the strategy of the east Mediterranean which derived from her broader interests; for Malays, both kinds of interest. There was a great deal to keep Britain in her colonies; a great deal, therefore, to keep nationalists well occupied.

In the tropical colonies, which now formed the bulk of her dependent empire, Britain's interests were as vital as ever, or more so. The tropics were not (and never had been) the main suppliers of her imports or recipients of her exports. What they did do was to supply her with a large quantity of very vital metals (copper, tin, cobalt, gold, uranium), vegetable products (rubber, palm-oil) and foods (cocoa, coffee, groundnuts), all of which were exploited more voraciously in the post-war years than ever before, and by bigger and more powerful European industrial monoliths. From the purely economic point of view, the 1950s may have been the time when the ties between Britain and her tropical colonies were closest of all: between British industry and capital, on the one side, and colonial products and (to a lesser degree) markets, on the other. To a great extent this more intensive exploitation of her colonies by Britain tightened her grip on them, or at least her incentive to grip them. But it had another, contrary, effect too.

The fact that workers massing together in factories and towns are more prone than peasants scattered in fields and hamlets to dissent and rebellion was well known from British domestic experience, though it might be attributed variously (to the realisation of latent 'class consciousness', or to the work of 'agitators'). It happened too in Africa. Industry on the scale in which it was conducted in tropical Africa in the 1940s and 1950s needed large concentrations of population. All over Africa such concentrations appeared: mining settlements like the Northern Rhodesian copper belt, which was the biggest and employed 30,000 Africans as early as 1930;[50] factories like the United Africa Company's complex of timber mills and plywood factories at Sapele in Nigeria, which employed 10,000 men in 1950;[51] and the expanding towns and cities which were the badges of tropical Africa's new rise to commercial favour, like Lagos which in 1910 had contained 74,000 people and now (the mid-1950s) contained 270,000.[52] In the cities and the mining settlements, people from different backgrounds, freed from the binding restraints of traditional rural societies, confronted with alternatives and hence stimulated to think and to question, could meet together and exchange ideas, discuss common grievances, perhaps form common associations (like trade unions where they were legal); the environment provoked inquiry, fired ambitions, stimulated material and political expectations; and provided the physical conditions which accelerated the spread of ideas, and facilitated combination. Towns and town-dwellers had always made colonial rulers uneasy: urban living was supposed to denature Africans, make them something they should not be, give them a style and pretensions above their station, which was why the Briton's racial prejudice was rarely directed against the happy tribal African, but much more often against the urban semi-sophisticate, the 'West Coast educated native', the 'babu', the 'westernised oriental gentleman' or 'wog'. The British were right to fear them. It was in the towns of West Africa and in industrial concentrations like the Central African copper belt and the South African gold reef that the earliest expressions of modern African nationalism had manifested themselves before the war. After the war, nationalism flourished as the soil for it spread. In a way colonialism was breeding its own antidote.

In the years after the war, African nationalism sprang very suddenly and very rapidly into full growth. Out of the plethora of welfare associations, tribal associations, community leagues, friendly societies, youth movements, trade unions and all the other vehicles for African discontent which had proliferated before the war (and which had included a few overtly nationalist associations, but very weak ones), there arose in the 1940s and 1950s most of the main colony-wide movements for national liberation which took the battle to Britain in the 1950s and 1960s, and most of their leaders. The situation was ripe for them in many ways. They had friends: powerful friends among the Great Powers, especially Russia (who was supposed to be against empires) and the United States (who, in a way, after the emancipation of the Philippines and before Vietnam was between empires); friends also among their African neighbours, especially in the French colonies which were sprouting nationalist movements of their own; and friends even in Britain, among the left, which prominent African nationalists like Kwame Nkrumah and Hastings Banda had spent most of the war and some time afterwards cultivating. They took encouragement from India, and from the general tide of world opinion at the time which seemed to be swimming with them. Very early after the war they showed their teeth. There was a six-week general strike in Nigeria in 1945, another one in the Sudan in 1947, and serious riots in Accra in the Gold Coast in 1948: not nationalist uprisings in origin, but used and exploited by nationalists after they had begun. By 1950, African nationalism was already a power on the west coast, and pushing through in East Africa too.[53]

None of this could the British ignore, though they widely disapproved of it. They disapproved of it mainly (they said) because the new nationalists were trying to push things too fast, to achieve in one jump what the government claimed to be preparing them for in easy stages, and far in advance of the opinion of the bulk of the people they professed to represent. An issue on which the two sides frequently collided head-on was the position of the traditional chiefs in Africa, whom nationalists regarded as little better than British puppets, about as representative of modern democratic African opinion as dukes and earls were of the English, but who continued to play a large role in British plans for Africa's future well on into the 1950s, because (said the Labour government about the Gold Coast in 1948) 'a large part of the country' still regarded them as 'essential to an ordered society', and considered the nationalists as parvenus.[54] Some in Britain resisted the nationalists because they resisted the whole idea of colonial independence. But for many of those who did not, who had reconciled themselves to losing Africa, it was still to be some years before they would accept the 'extreme' nationalists, the 'power-seekers',[55] as their proper successors. In some colonies they were very slowly forced to. The first democratic elections held in Ghana and Nigeria in 1951–52 seemed fully to vindicate all the nationalists' claims to represent the people. The British government took the lesson to heart, and acted on it: releasing from gaol the Gold Coast's leading 'extremist', Kwame Nkrumah, to make him 'prime minister' for the interim period before independence; and in both countries negotiating thereafter with the nationalists, and letting the chiefs alone. Elsewhere the argument that nationalists were unrepresentative agitators and that the people's true friends were their feudal lords, which went back at least as far as nineteenth-century India, was slow to die. It was still vigorous in Rhodesia in the 1970s. But as time went on and the nationalist virus spread, it became less and less convincing, and more and more impractical to act on.

The Conservatives' empire, 1951–59

By October 1951, when Labour left office, nationalist demands were already beginning to run on far ahead of Britain's willingness to concede them, and colonial policy was taking on the appearance of a power struggle between government and nationalists, which, for a very short period in the later 1940s, it had not had. The next eight or nine years were the most difficult of all for the post-war empire, as nationalist demands became bolder and their methods more drastic, and as the new Conservative government, a father brought in to hang his own child, came to terms only very slowly and painfully with the full reality of the situation and all its implications. Conflict sometimes erupted violently. To the colonial wars which were characteristic of the decade, Britain contributed her own: in Malaya (1948–58), Kenya (1952–56) and Cyprus (1954–59), and lesser skirmishes elsewhere. In 1956, in a late flourish of imperial self-assertion, she sent troops to the Suez Canal to safeguard her interests there in the old proprietary kind of way: with humiliating results. All this was in a desperate scramble to find some sort of handhold, a defensible position, to halt the fall from imperial eminence which had started in 1947. The attempt failed. Yet it may still have been necessary for the Conservatives' peace of mind to make it.

It was not a blind, intransigent resistance which they offered to the nationalist onslaught. They were not a reactionary government, though they had some reactionary supporters. They did not mean to reverse the trend, or even to halt it entirely. They professed, at the beginning of their term, an intention to continue the process towards 'self-government within the Commonwealth',[56] and they put no great obstacles in the way of this process in those colonies – like the West African colonies, the Sudan and the West Indies – where it was already too far advanced. For other colonies, they planned the same kind of progress, but in a slow and 'orderly' manner. Where their residual imperialism showed through, the evidence that their change of heart was less than complete, was in their continued belief that Britain still had a world role to maintain, and the right to keep hold of certain foreign territories in order to maintain it; and in their conception of self-government, which frequently fell short of the nationalists' – in East and Central Africa, for example, where it stopped far short of majority rule while there were still settlers there, and elsewhere where it stopped short of economic self-government while there were British firms and shares to defend. From the wreck of the old empire they tried to salvage what was essential: a role in the world, their new white dominion in Central Africa, and the means still to exploit countries they no longer ruled. Their inability to take in the full extent of their loss was reflected too in the conception they had of the new multi-racial Commonwealth just beginning to form from the pieces of the old empire, which some Conservatives still saw, in much the same way as Leopold Amery had, as a way of preserving Britain's interests in her colonies, and her status in the new Cold War world. In a way what they hankered for was a return to a still older imperialism, the 'informal' imperialism of the mid-nineteenth century, with all the rights and none of the responsibilities of empire, which was hopeless, because that kind of imperialism required an even stronger base of power in the world than 'formal' empire had required, and that kind of power now belonged only to the USA.[57]

But the attempt was made. In the 1950s, on the fronts it had decided to fight on, the new government fought hard. In some colonies it fought to keep them, in others to be able to give them to the right people. In the latter category it had two notable successes. In Malaya, a costly and sometimes dirty jungle war against communist guerrillas, which had begun in 1948, was effectively won by 1955, and power handed over two years later to a native government whose point of view on all essential matters, such as Britain's rubber interests there, was entirely satisfactory.[58] In British Guiana, in 1954, when the local inhabitants used the freedom of choice Britain had just bestowed on them to choose what looked to her like a communist administration, the government thought better of it and suspended the constitution until the colony's radical ardour had cooled. In both these cases, there was considerable doubt as to how much support among the people the communists really had, and radical cleavages which Britain could exploit, so that she was not entirely friendless, and not arrayed against a whole people. Elsewhere she failed because she falsely assumed that the same situation pertained, that the 'extremists' were a minority whom the 'people' would help them to pick off: which was a common Conservative mistake.

The success in Malaya gave the government heart in Cyprus, which was the scene of Britain's next colonial war, and her most dispiriting one. Cyprus exported almost nothing to Britain, and imported little from her, yet had become by the 1950s one of the most vital of Britain's possessions, essential if any remnant at all was going to be retained of her old imperial role, because of what recently had been happening around it. By the 1950s, Britain's interest in the oil of the Middle East, which was by far her largest and, for what it did for her industry, her most valuable import, was at least as vital as her interest in the sea-lanes to India had been in the 1880s, and as vulnerable to political instability, for which the Middle East was notorious. Since 1947 and (for Britain) the disastrous conclusion to the Palestine problem, everything had conspired to undermine the influence Britain felt was essential for her to safeguard her interests there, culminating in increasingly violent demonstrations and riots in Egypt against the British garrisons, which forced them to withdraw in 1954. With Palestine and Egypt gone, Cyprus became almost the last bastion of British influence in the east Mediterranean, the focus for all her Middle Eastern strategy and intelligence capability: the point therefore where the slide had to be halted. In July 1954, a junior minister at the Colonial Office announced that this was where their stand was going to be made: 'Nothing less than continued sovereignty over this island can enable Britain to carry out her strategic obligations to Europe, the Mediterranean and the Middle East.'[59] The garrisons were moved in: only to find themselves taken up, not with defending British interests in the seas and air around them, but with holding Cyprus itself, which proved as hot a seat as Egypt had been. For some time past there had been a movement (Eoka) among the majority population of the country to unite it to Greece; with these new discouraging developments Eoka took stronger hold. Very soon the island was in the throes of a full-scale guerrilla war.

Cyprus was a more difficult guerrilla war for the British than Malaya, because they had a smaller local minority (Turkish) to ally with, and the opposition of most world opinion. It was made more difficult by the continuing toppling of other old imperial pillars around them: in friendly Jordan where the King dismissed his army's British commander, John Glubb, in March 1956, and in Egypt where President Nasser nationalised the Suez Canal in July. The latter provoked a petulant and enraged reaction by the British government, who, in secret collusion with France and Israel, invaded Egypt in November, only to be pulled up very unceremoniously by political realities. Suez should have been the moment of truth for British imperialists and for many of them it was. It provoked as no other of their recent escapades had done an agonised and bitter conflict of opinion in Britain, the disapproval of nearly every other nation in the world, including much of the Commonwealth, and the active opposition of the United States. With this latter, especially, British imperialism could not live. The crunch appears to have come when America refused help for the critically ailing pound unless a truce were signed. For whatever reason, the cabinet did sign. It was a vivid lesson for every Briton, both in the general relationship between power and freedom of international action, and in the realities of world power then.[60]

Cyprus fell very soon afterwards. It had been intended as a base from which to guard the Suez Canal. During the Suez War it had proved less than useful as a base, because it had no deep-water harbour; and after Suez there was little left in that part of the world for it to guard anyway. Even with a massive army of 30,000 ranged against it, Eoka remained intransigent, and grimly effective. In 1957, the British government started negotiating, and looking around for new homes for its strategic forces. Britain's hand had slipped again, the slide continued: and the search recommenced for handholds further down.[61]

The Mediterranean and the Middle East were, and always had been, an area of worldwide concern. Every great power as well as Britain had vital interests there: consequently, everything that happened there was likely to happen in the full glare of international attention, and any noise would awaken and irritate the giants. This was why Cyprus was so stormy, and the Suez adventure just not on. By contrast, East–Central Africa, which was the imperialists' other main fighting front, was more of an international backwater, less sensitive, more hidden. It was a country behind the giants' backs where, it was to be hoped, Britain might still be able to play uninterrupted, if not unseen; which for a while she did.

Imperialist ambitions for East–Central Africa remained lively right through the 1950s, and long after Suez had undermined them elsewhere: indeed, when Cyprus began to crumble, the first place the British government thought of to replace it as their main military base for the Middle East was Kenya. In East–Central Africa, their allies, the nucleus around which they intended to consolidate their hold, and to maintain a British presence in the continent, were the settlers: a small minority everywhere, but one which in many of the colonies already had taken on many of the functions and responsibilities of government. The main problems were that: (1) in none of the colonies except Southern Rhodesia were there enough of them really to make a Southern Rhodesian-type transference of power to them viable; and (2) liberal opinion in Britain and African opinion there made this solution impolitic anyway. On the other hand, there was fairly widespread concern in Britain, which the government shared and could work on, that established settler interests should not be entirely abandoned to unpractised African politicians without safeguards. The government's answer to the problem centred around two approaches. The first was to try to federate the six East–Central African colonies into two groups, each of which would contain one strong element – a colony where the settler interest was substantial – which would dominate, and two weak, black ones. For the three northern colonies – Kenya, Tanganyika, Uganda – this idea never left the ground; for the other group – the Rhodesias and Nyasaland – it did fly but soon crashed. The other, concurrent, approach was the devising of some kind of formula whereby power in the colonies appeared to be shared between Europeans and Africans, while the Europeans in fact, for a generation at least, remained dominant. This came to be called variously 'partnership' or 'multi-racialism'.

The British government's support of the settler cause in Kenya had to contend with what turned out to be the most ferocious of all the nationalist movements which confronted her in Africa, mainly among dispossessed and desperate Kikuyu, whose violent methods and association with pagan rituals brought out the worst in what was probably the most backward, bigoted and also vulnerable of all the privileged settler minorities in British Africa, supported atrociously by the contemporary colonial authorities. The precise number of Africans who died as a result of what was euphemistically called the Mau Mau 'Emergency' of the 1950s is not known; estimates range from 20,000 to over 100,000 (some of them killed by other Africans), as against 32 white settlers killed by Mau Mau. More than 1,000 of those were judicially murdered: that is, hanged after peremptory trials, often by judges brought out from Britain and effectively bribed to convict. In addition, tens of thousands were kept in appalling conditions in detention camps, many of them subjected to tortures so savage and obscene that accounts of them make difficult reading today. At the time this was kept quiet in Britain, or overshadowed by press concentration on the more comprehensible evils of Mau Mau. ('Savagery' was expected from Africans.) When one particular atrocity came to the surface in 1959 – the Hola Camp incident, in which 11 Mau Mau detainees were beaten to death by guards – it provoked even Enoch Powell to protest. Imperialist he may have been; but his more naïve, idealistic kind of imperialism (as of so many others) had no place for this. After Kenyan independence (1963) (Figure 10.2), both sides conspired to brush the full story of this baleful episode under the carpet, helping to perpetuate the myth that somehow British decolonisation was smoother, wiser and gentler than – for example – France's. In fact, Kenya was Britain's Algeria, with this single difference: that its settlers had far less impact on domestic politics. What would have been the situation if Kenya (or Rhodesia) had been just over the water from Britain, as North Africa was from France, is anyone's guess.[62]

Figure 10.2 Decolonisation. Independence Day in Kenya, 12 December 1963. Jorno Kenyatta,
        recently imprisoned by the British for 'terrorism', takes over his country from the
        Duke of Edinburgh, representing the Queen.
Source: © Keystone Press/Alamy Stock Photo.

In the meantime, Britain struggled on with her new approach, designed to combine
slow and safe political reform with the maintenance of essential control. In troubled
Kenya, this involved communal elections against a background of very restricted African political activity; and a constitution carefully devised to ensure 'parity', by allowing
its 50,000 Europeans the same number of elected representatives to the colony's legislature as 5 million Africans, and greatly to outnumber them in the inner council of
ministers.[63] In the Rhodesias and Nyasaland, the ramshackle Federation set up in
August 1953, in which the administration of Northern Rhodesia (with its booming
copper belt) and Nyasaland was shared by colonial officials and white Southern Rhodesians, staggered on until the end of the decade despite the fact that almost every
African who was asked for his opinion opposed it: 'It is good for you,' the Colonial
Secretary told them in 1957, 'and you must accept it.'[64] If there had been any genuine
resolve by its architects to achieve a genuine 'partnership' between whites and blacks, it
was not borne out in practice, certainly not in social practice, by a white population
which had little intention of narrowing any of the gaps between themselves and people
they considered and treated as inferior. The endemic racial arrogance of the Europeans
in the Federation, and the Africans' resentment of Britain's 'betrayal' of them, sparked
off a fiery nationalist reaction in Nyasaland and Northern Rhodesia, which a hurricane
of mass arrests and deportations and bannings and baton charges and worse failed to
douse. Yet still the British government persisted in backing Federation: to save the
copper belt from the nationalisers, or the Europeans from the Africans, or the Africans
from their own ineptitude, or the continent from 'communism'; or just themselves from
the humiliation of retreat.[65]

The wind of change, 1960–70

It was a brave rearguard action, and in the short run, it was not unsuccessful. In the late 1950s, despite all the reverses, there was a sizeable empire left for Britain to save, if she still wanted to. As well as this great slice of Africa, there were a score of smaller colonies all over the world which it was thought could never be viable on their own, and therefore would always be content to let Britain keep them, rather than have Russia or China grab them (which in the current view of the international political game, it was assumed happened to all small states on their own). There were the larger colonies, especially in West Africa, Malaya and the West Indies, whose progress towards independence could not be prevented now, but which might still be 'guided' towards a form of independence which suited Britain. There was the Commonwealth, and the strength which might still be drawn from it with imperial preferences and defence co-operation and the like. And, finally, there was Britain's remaining network of *strategic* bases in the world: Malta, Aden, Singapore, and so on. That made her a world power still, even without the more substantial colonies in between. As well as this, she had the nuclear bomb, which was supposed to confirm that status; and – surprisingly and even a little confusingly, after all that had been said before – the active support of the Americans for her continuing 'east of Suez' role. Indeed, in the 1960s, the United States became quite insistent over this. Could not Britain have stuck there, with a scaled-down empire, but a position of worldwide influence still?[66]

On the other side of this equation, however, there were clear disadvantages. One was financial. Britain's was not a strong economy in the 1960s. The period was bedevilled with balance of payments issues, runs on the pound, and the more fundamental problems underlying these. There were other insistent calls on the public purse. Governments, especially latterly, felt strapped for cash. It was this that persuaded them eventually to cut their losses overseas; reluctantly, even in the case of Labour ministers, who were generally no less wedded to Britain's great power status than the Conservatives were, but who when they 'examined the figures', as James Callaghan put it, decided that they had no real choice other than to submit to 'the costly realities'.[67] The Tories grumbled at the time, but then quietly accepted the situation too when they came to power. This was undoubtedly the major single motive for Britain's final stepping down from her former world role.

There were also, however, others. Some of them can be classed as 'moral'. The current did seem to be running against Britain. Trying to dam it in this way built up pressures which she had not been used to in more flexible times, and might not now be able to contain long. In East–Central Africa the effort to hang on had recently resulted in a series of overtly oppressive measures, and several atrocities, which were widely felt to have been uncharacteristic and shaming: not just the Hola camp incident in Kenya, but also a 'state of emergency' throughout the Central African Federation which a government Commission, no less, likened to a 'police state'; 50 African rioters shot in Nyasaland; and other clear symptoms of stress. Here and elsewhere the authorities increasingly found themselves resorting to methods which would have been considered unacceptable in earlier times: sophisticated and intrinsically amoral techniques of what was now called 'counter-insurgency', for example, which were developed and perfected in places like Kenya and Malaya, and later (though this is another story) shipped back to the British Isles.[68] This undermined the old basis – or pretence of a basis – of British colonial rule. Of the native 'collaboration' that had bolstered that rule in the past, there was very little now remaining (although to the end the white settlers in Africa continued to persuade themselves that there was, but that it was too frightened to speak). Britain was having to impose her will by an open display of force, which by this time she was not able to do comfortably.

Realists as well as moralists were turning away from empire. The men of industry and finance, who, by necessity, were the hardest realists of all, had for some little time been aware of the trend, and begun to make their own arrangements with the trend-setters, the empire's successor states, to protect and further their interests in the best ways they could. They might have regretted the loss of their imperial padding but they came to terms with it. They dealt with whoever was in command: in South Africa while they still looked to have firm control, it was the white supremacists, but in tropical Africa, it was the new black nationalists. Where there were still capitalists who considered continued colonial control to be vital to their interests, like the British South Africa Company in Northern Rhodesia, they were becoming too few to comprise a convincing lobby. Britain's trading position as a whole was altering, edging back away from the empire and ex-empire, and towards Europe again.[69] For more and more people in Britain, their real economic destiny now appeared to lie in a closer association with the European continent, which was already in the process of organising itself into a great 'Common Market', and which could make its own terms with the politically independent 'Third World' outside. The empire, by which was meant the old type of colonial control over satellite economies, was no longer necessary, or worth fighting for.

What was left when the 'interests' began leaving the sinking ship was a residue of mainly emotional commitments to the glory of empire, which were just not strong enough to persuade a realistic government, which is what Harold Macmillan's was, to resist all the material pressures pushing the other way. Iain Macleod, who became Colonial Secretary in October 1959, always excused his surrender to colonial nationalism by pleading necessity, though he probably had a genuine liberal commitment to independence too.

> We could not possibly have held by force to our territories in Africa. We could not, with an enormous force engaged, even continue to hold the small island of Cyprus. General de Gaulle could not contain Algeria. The march of men towards their freedom can be guided, but not halted. Of course there were risks in moving quickly. But the risks of moving slowly were far greater.[70]

Macmillan was of the same mind. In a famous speech in Cape Town in February 1960, he told of the 'striking impression' a tour of tropical Africa had given him of 'the strength of this African national consciousness'. The man who, three years earlier, had been chosen to succeed Sir Anthony Eden as Prime Minister because he was thought to be firmer on the Suez issue than his main rival, seemed himself to have changed bearings. A little later he was making for Europe. His party turned with him, though not without protests. Slowly and painfully it acquired new habits. To Macleod was entrusted the task of breaking the old habits, the imperial habits of a lifetime.

It was more than a matter of merely persuading people that they could no longer hold on to their empire, though there were still some who needed to be persuaded of that. It required a change of heart on the part of more liberal men too, the adherents of the old 'trusteeship' principle. It had been the declared aim of trusteeship to *prepare* colonies for self-government, on the assumption that if they started to govern themselves before they had been fully prepared for it, they would govern themselves badly. Those who thought this way had to be converted too, to the nationalists' demands for self-government *now*, sooner than the liberals thought was good for them. This was perhaps the hardest pill of all to swallow: to accept that their efforts were not appreciated and not wanted, that their better judgement should be ignored, that the empire was to be ungratefully snatched from them right at the moment when they were preparing and wrapping it to give graciously. To some paternalistic liberals it seemed a dereliction of duty, just as to some imperialists it appeared to be a surrender of right. Yet, because expediency demanded it, the conversion was made: of enough of both kinds of men to get decolonisation through.

Of course, the conversion was never a complete one. Realism might have reconciled most Conservatives to decolonisation, but it did not reconcile all of them, and those it did reconcile to it did not warm to the prospect. Occasionally their non-enthusiasm for the task strewed rocks in a path which could have been made smoother, and generated ill-will without any tangible return. In East Africa, where the change of heart went most against the grain, the work of disentangling the imperial factor was done more messily than anywhere, and left more bad feeling. The bad feeling was perhaps inevitable: for years past Britain had backed the white settlers, given them guarantees which they had felt honourable people *must* stick by; now she reneged. The mess was caused by Britain's reluctance for some time to admit to the settlers, and perhaps to herself, that she *was* reneging, which gave birth to a confusing assortment of 'multi-racial' devices and constitutions designed to delay the full impact of black majority rule, before at last she bowed to the principle of the latter in Kenya and Nyasaland in 1961 and in Northern Rhodesia a little later. Africans were alienated by the delays; Europeans could not but feel betrayed by the eventual outcome. In Southern Rhodesia, which was all that was left of the white-dominated Federation after Nyasaland and Northern Rhodesia had left it in 1963, the European population in November 1965 raised the flag of rebellion rather than submit to the fate of their northern neighbours. The British (Labour) government did not stop them: either because it lacked the will, or because it thought it lacked the power, as it always had against kith and kin in southern Africa. For some years Rhodesia survived a very ineffectually imposed trade boycott, an African guerrilla campaign, the tottering of one friend and ally to the east of her, and pressure from another in the south, to provide a last rallying point for some of Britain's old imperialists, a sole surviving altar at which those of the old religion whose faith was most resilient could worship still.[71]

Elsewhere the task was assumed with a better grace, and performed almost without people in Britain noticing. It was not always done well. In some colonies it was almost impossible to do well: colonies like those of East–Central Africa, for example, which it had always been tacitly assumed would be given to white settlers to govern if they were given to anyone at all, and in which as a consequence scarcely any preparation had been made until now for self-government by the Africans. When the change in intention came, it was sometimes almost too late. Crash-courses in public administration furnished a scanty framework of very green civil servants, who had to rely for some years afterwards on British colonial administrators staying behind to help them. Then there were sometimes political difficulties, obstacles arising, for example, out of the British government's reluctance to treat with one or other particular group of nationalists, even when they (the government) were firmly committed to emancipation, because they disapproved of them. Colonial nationalism still seemed to puzzle many British statesmen, and its excesses to shock them easily. Sometimes they fell back on the old dogmas: attributing movements of protest to devils of their own imagining – usually a 'communist conspiracy'; and persuading themselves that Kenyatta and Kaunda and the like were unrepresentative 'agitators'. A pattern seemed to be created, whereby any national leader had to be officially vilified and then imprisoned before he was negotiated with and given in to. It became a standing joke that an essential qualification for any prime minister of an emerging nation was a spell in a British prison. These barren detours from the straight path were wasteful and costly, though they may at the time have seemed worthwhile. When Britain came finally to negotiate, more shades of the past rose up to make the bargaining harder for her. Still she clung to hopes of salvaging something from the wreckage, some vestige of colonial control: economic control in the form of oil installations in Aden or copper royalties in Zambia; or political control by backing 'moderate' parties against extremists: parties which could too easily be branded as British 'stooges' and could not hope to retain power when their patrons had gone. Sometimes this backing may have gone to the lengths of rigging pre-independence elections.[72] There was some hard bargaining: but usually Britain lost because (as with India in 1947), she had nothing really substantial to bargain with, except the financial aid which she granted fairly liberally (but more grudgingly later). She could not threaten to withhold independence. In most cases (again as in India), independence raced forward inexorably: a date set, then brought closer, then independence granted sooner still. It was not the most dignified way to go.

Yet it was done. Britain in the 1960s was hustled and harried out of most of her old colonies, including many of the tiny ones like Gambia which very recently had been considered unfit for independence ever; and without too much bloodshed. The roll-call was an impressive one. In the 1950s, the Sudan, the Gold Coast (Ghana) and Malaya had been the only colonies to escape. In the 1960s, it quite suddenly became a stampede (Table 10.2).

And so it went on into the 1970s, with Fiji becoming independent in October 1970, the Bahamas in July 1973, Grenada in February 1974 – until almost everyone was out. Soon after the governors and district commissioners came home, the soldiers and sailors followed them, booted out usually by newly assertive national governments who put their pride – or tribute from elsewhere – before the money the bases brought them. In 1969, Libya demanded that the 1,700 British troops stationed there go, and they went. On 12 January 1968, the Labour cabinet decided to pull the considerable British contingents out of the Persian Gulf and Singapore, which was done by 1971, to the great annoyance of the Americans: and that was an end to Britain's role 'east of Suez'. (For anyone looking for a firm date to mark the end of the British empire, 12 January 1968 fits the bill better than most.) The fabric of the old empire had gone; now the frame which had taken its weight had gone too. There was nothing left but a few bricks, and some shadows.[73]

The response

None of the shadows was substantial enough to make up fully for what had been lost. At first, it was thought that the Commonwealth might. In the 1950s, the fact that so many ex-colonies had elected to stay within the Commonwealth led some imperialists to assume a substantive continuity between it and the old empire: with the black and brown nations joining Australia and Canada in an extended family cemented by common bonds of tradition, friendship and mutual interest, and the whole structure a force to be reckoned with in the world still. Leopold Amery, in 1953, speculated that 'other nations now outside it may well decide to join it in course of time ... Who knows but what it may yet become the nucleus round which a future world order will crystallise?'[74] This vision compensated a little for the loss of empire, provided a kind of empire-substitute. And

Table 10.2 Colonial independence

Year	Month	Location	
1960	June	British Somaliland (joined Somalia)	
	August	Cyprus	
	October	Nigeria	
1961	April	Sierra Leone	
	June and October	Cameroons (joined Nigeria and Cameroun)	
	December	Tanganyika (with Zanzibar became Tanzania in December 1963)	
1962	August	Jamaica	
	October	Trinidad and Tobago	
		Uganda	
1963	September	Singapore	(joined Malaya to
		North Borneo	become Malaysia;
		Sarawak	Singapore broke away 1965)
	December	Kenya	
		Zanzibar (joined Tanganyika to become Tanzania)	
1964	July	Nyasaland (Malawi)	
	September	Malta	
	October	Northern Rhodesia (Zambia)	
1965	February	Gambia	
1966	May	British Guiana (Guyana)	
	September	Bechuanaland (Botswana)	
	October	Basutoland (Lesotho)	
	November	Barbados	
1967	February	Leeward Islands	
	March and June	Windward Islands	
	November	Aden (People's Republic of South Yemen)	
1968	March	Mauritius	
	September	Swaziland	

while it seemed to do this, old imperialists retained their affection for it, and sought (as in the past) to cement its parts more tightly together, for example, by trade preferences for Commonwealth countries, and by preserving a definition of 'British nationality' (laid down in 1948) which allowed all Commonwealth citizens the right to enter Britain freely, without restriction.

'Common citizenship' was meant to symbolise the continuing unity, and hence the strength, of the 'Empire-Commonwealth'. But by the 1960s, it was abundantly clear that the Commonwealth was turning out to be something less (or more) than had been hoped. Its members did not have common interests, not even the 'white' Dominions, which were too far apart to do so. For the black and brown nations, their membership was not an expression of filial gratitude and loyalty. Rather it provided merely a convenient platform on the world stage, from which they could air their grievances, especially their grievances against Britain; and an entitlement to a share of what British aid there was going. The Commonwealth was never united at all. Its new members fought each other, broke off diplomatic relations with each other and with the 'mother country'; *abused* the mother in a most unfilial way. In 1961, they forced out of the family one of its oldest members, South Africa, because of apartheid, much to the indignation of her white sisters. In 1971, at a Commonwealth conference in Singapore, they put the British Prime Minister in a huff by trying to teach him his business over the issue of supplying arms to South Africa. Clearly this new organisation was of little use as a means of exerting British power and influence in the world. As a substitute for empire, it was a disappointing failure: the emperor's new clothes a sham. It was not long before the old imperialists had given it up as a dead loss.

There were some in public life who continued to value the new Commonwealth, but as something rather different from the old empire: as an informal debating club for widely divergent cultures, a possible means of scaling the barriers of racism and chauvinism going up all over the world, an example to the world of how different countries and continents could get along together even if they could not agree together, a corrective to the contemporary consolidation of the world into continental blocs – perhaps a kind of moral pressure-group in world affairs, if it were used aright. These men included some idealistic old imperialists, and one or two anti-imperialists of the old Fabian Colonial Bureau type, who were genuinely interested in questions of international co-operation and foreign aid. They came *not* to include the majority of either of the main political parties, who in the past had been imperialists or connived in imperialism mainly for what it did for Britain, and who abandoned the empire's successor when it ceased to be valuable to Britain. Parliament very soon lost interest in empire free trade, which was always a euphemism for imperial protectionism, and turned instead (in 1962, when the first serious overtures to the European Economic Community were made) to European free trade, which was similarly a euphemism for European protectionism. That was the first snub to the Commonwealth. Then (in 1962 again), it abandoned its noble conception of 'common citizenship' by restricting coloured immigration from the Commonwealth: which was the second snub. First, John Bull had started flirting with a new mistress; then he refused to let his old bride into his bed. Both actions might possibly have been justified in Britain's national interest. But what they seemed to betray, coming at this time, was a sudden loss of interest in the Commonwealth the moment it ceased to be materially useful to Britain. For imperial idealists, it was a sad end.[75]

For those same idealists, however, there might have been some comfort in the thought that decolonisation had gone through at all, and as relatively smoothly as it had. In the minds of some people, for years past, the prospect of decolonisation had provided – somewhat paradoxically – the *raison d'être* of the empire. Like Marx's proletarian state, or a plaster cast around a broken leg, the empire's whole function had been to make itself dispensable. Britain ruled other people because they could not rule themselves; her justification for ruling them had been that she was teaching them to rule themselves. She would have fulfilled her task, therefore, when they could rule themselves and began to. The death of empire would be its culmination, its glorious climax. Historically, this was a lot of nonsense. Just as 'trusteeship' had never really been the motive for Britain's imperial expansion in the past – and few people seriously tried to maintain that it was – so it was not the reason for contraction now. In cold reality, decolonisation was a defeat, not a victory. But it softened the blow a little for some imperialists to believe the contrary; and there was just enough substance in the 'trusteeship' idea to make it a sturdy enough bandwagon to carry all those imperialists who now wanted to jump on to it. By doing so, they could justify both the empire and its demise in retrospect, and save face. The empire had *not* been a failure, but a great success: decolonisation proved it. They had recourse again, for the last time, to their favourite 'father and child' analogy. Before, it had justified their arbitrary rule. Now it explained its relaxation. Britain's adopted children had come of age. Her duties as parents had been completed, she had prepared them for the future, they could now stand on their own feet, so she let them go. Of course, there were regrets: no parent ever relinquishes power over his or her children without them. But the object of parenthood was just this, to fit your children for an independent existence. This Britain had done, and she should not be dismayed at their majority, but proud of it, and of the imperialism which had made it possible.

This was how some people made decolonisation easier for themselves to bear. Most people, however, did not think very much about it at all, at any rate, after the first shock. There was not much thought either given to what had gone, the old empire: very little public nostalgia, for a few years at least, though there may have been a great deal of nostalgia among ex-Indian Army officers and district commissioners in private. No party or political group ever thought even half-seriously of restoring the empire, except for very fringe right-wing organisations like the League of Empire Loyalists and the National Front. No-one seemed even to want to remember it. Public memorials were rare: one to the Indian Army was unveiled in Camberley in 1971, and a museum of the Indian raj was opened in the same year – not in London or Edinburgh or even Cheltenham, where the officers of the raj were popularly supposed to retire, but in Colne in Lancashire. It was not until 2002 that the British Empire and Commonwealth got a museum of its own, on the edge of Bristol (Temple Meads station); this closed in 2008 and originally planned to move to London, although this has yet to materialise. (Little Belgium got *its* Empire museum in 1910.[76]) Until then, the Empire appeared almost invisible. One prominent ex-imperialist even went to the lengths of trying ingeniously to show that it had in a way never existed at all, that it had all been a 'myth', because the thought of having lost it upset him so much.[77] Yet there were some who were faithful still. When sometimes Britain's past colonial record was attacked in some detail or other, there was nearly always found an old imperialist somewhere who was moved to set the record straight, in Parliament or the correspondence columns of *The Times*. That there were strong feelings being bottled up became clear when a fairly mild and not very profound television documentary series about the British empire in 1972 provoked a flood of letters to the newspapers and a lengthy debate in the Lords, most of the letters and many of the speeches betraying an almost personal sense of injury, that 'the noblest Empire the world had ever seen' should have been so 'denigrated' and 'smeared'.[78] But apart from such occasions, when they felt publicly affronted, such men nursed their grievances privately; and the mass of people, as they had all along, cared very little.

Notes

1 N. Mansergh, *The Commonwealth Experience* (Weidenfeld & Nicolson, 1969), p. 186; and see F. W. Perry, *The Commonwealth Armies: Manpower and Organization in Two World Wars* (Manchester UP, 1988).

2 Lord Elton, *Imperial Commonwealth* (Collins, 1945), p. 521.

3 *Parliamentary Debates*, 5th series, 361 (1940), c. 42.

4 R. Hinden, *Empire and After* (Essential Books, 1949), pp. 143–4.

5 See E. Monroe, *Britain's Moment in the Middle East* (Chatto, 1963), pp. 89–94; J. Marlowe, *The Seat of Pilate* (Barrie & Jenkins, 1959), Chapter 11.

6 V. P. Menon, *The Transfer of Power in India* (Longman, 1957), p. 60.

7 I include myself in this. I was unaware of the Bengal Famine until I came to the fourth edition of this book.

8 C. H. Philips (ed.), *The Evolution of India and Pakistan, 1858–1947: Select Documents* (Oxford UP, 1962), p. 339.

9 See H. V. Hodson, *The Great Divide* (Hutchinson, 1969), Chapters 8–10; Menon, *op. cit.*, Chapters 1–8; S. C. Bose, *The Indian Struggle, 1920–1942* (Asia Publishing House, 1964), Chapters 22, 29–38.

10 D. Day, *The Great Betrayal: Britain, Australia and the Onset of the Pacific War, 1939–42* (Angus & Robertson, 1988); and D. Day, *Menzies and Churchill at War* (Angus & Robertson, 1987).

11 *Parliamentary Debates*, 5th series, 407 (1945), cc. 2168–9.

12 The Watson Commission (1948), in G. E. Metcalfe (ed.), *Great Britain and Ghana: Documents of Ghana History, 1807–1957* (Nelson, 1965), p. 682.

13 R. D. Furse, *Aucuparius: Recollections of a Recruiting Officer* (Oxford UP, 1962), p. 294.

14 See M. Crowder, *West Africa under Colonial Rule* (Hutchinson, 1968), pp. 490–2; J. Hatch, *A History of Post-War Africa* (Deutsch, 1965), Chapter 2; R. I. Rotberg, *The Rise of Nationalism in Central Africa: The Making of Malawi and Zambia, 1873–1964* (Harvard UP, 1966), pp. 168–98.

15 Hinden, *op. cit.*, p. 146.

16 W. K. Hancock, *Argument of Empire* (Penguin, 1943), p. 7.

17 L. Barnes, *Soviet Light on the Colonies* (Penguin, 1944), p. 9.

18 See *ibid., passim*; Hancock, *op. cit., passim*; A. Campbell, *It's Your Empire* (Gollancz, 1945) *passim*; Lord Hailey, *The Future of Colonial Peoples* (Princeton UP, 1943), *passim*; M. Perham, *Colonial Sequence, 1930 to 1949* (Methuen, 1967), pp. 189–275 *et passim*.

19 *Parliamentary Debates*, 5th series, 361 (1940), c. 42.

20 *Ibid.*, 361, cc. 79–80, 1210.

21 See R. A. Callahan, *Churchill: Retreat from Empire* (Scholarly Resources Inc., 1984), *passim*.

22 On the Empire in the Second World War, see Perry, *op. cit.*; Wm R. Louis, *Imperialism at Bay: The USA and the Decolonisation of the British Empire, 1941–45* (Clarendon Press, 1977); Christopher Thorne, *The Issue of War* (Hamilton, 1985).

23 D. Goldsworthy, *Colonial Issues in British Politics, 1945–1961* (Oxford UP, 1971), section 20.

24 M. Barratt Brown, *After Imperialism* (Heinemann, 1963), p. 294.

25 G. B. Shaw, *Fabianism and the Empire* (1900).

26 See F. Lees, *Fabianism and Colonialism: The Life and Political Thought of Lord Sydney Olivier* (Defiant Books, 1988).

27 *Parliamentary Debates*, 5th series, 361 (1940), c. 55.

28 R. Hinden (ed.), *Fabian Colonial Essays* (Allen & Unwin, 1945), p. 13.

29 R. Hyam (ed.) *British Documents on the End of Empire*, Series A, *The Labour Government and the End of Empire, 1945–1951*, Volume 2, Part II, p. 467.

30 Hinden, *Empire and After*, p. 164.

31 See Hinden, *Empire and After*, and R. Hinden (ed.), *New Fabian Colonial Essays* (Allen & Unwin, 1959); P. S. Gupta, *Imperialism and the British Labour Movement, 1914–1964* (Macmillan, 1975); Goldsworthy, *op. cit.*; Barnes, *op. cit.*; Ronald Hyam, 'Africa and the Labour government, 1945–51', *Journal of Imperial and Commonwealth History*, 16 (1988), 148–72, and his Introduction to R. Hyam, *The Labour Government and the End of Empire* (University of London Institute of Commonwealth Studies, 1992), p. 467.

32 *Parliamentary Debates*, 5th series, 156 (1922), c. 221.

33 On 'colonial development', see S. Constantine, *The Making of British Colonial Development Policy, 1914–40* (Cass, 1984); J. M. Lee and M. Petter, *The Colonial Office, War and Development Policy, 1939–45* (Temple Smith, 1982); J. M. Lee, *Colonial Development and Good Government* (Clarendon Press, 1967), and J. M. Lee, 'Forward thinking and the war: the Colonial Office during the 1940s', *Journal of Imperial and Commonwealth History*, 6 (1977), 64–79; D. J. Morgan (ed.), *The Official History of Colonial Development*, 5 vols (Macmillan, 1980); Michael Havinden and David Meredith, *Colonialism and Development: Britain and its Tropical Colonies, 1850–1960* (Routledge, 1993).

34 Hyam, *The Labour Government and the End of Empire*, p. 59.

35 *Ibid.*, pp. 273–82; and see D. Silverfarb, *The Twilight of British Ascendancy in the Middle East: A Case Study of Iraq, 1945–1950* (Macmillan, 1994).

36 See W. Roger Louis and R. E. Robinson, 'The imperialism of decolonization', *Journal of Imperial and Commonwealth History*, 22 (1994), 462–511.

37 P. Foot, *The Rise of Enoch Powell* (Cornmarket, 1969), p. 19; A. Roth, *Enoch Powell* (Macdonald, 1970), p. 51.

38 M. D. Wainwright, 'Keeping the peace in India, 1946–7', in C. H. Philips and M. D. Wainwright (eds), *The Partition of India: Policies and Perspectives* (Allen & Unwin, 1970), p. 130.

39 C. R. Attlee, *As it Happened* (Heinemann, 1954), p. 214.

40 Hodson, *op. cit.*, p. 200.

41 A. Campbell-Johnson, *Mission with Mountbatten* (Hale, 1951), p. 221.

42 *Ibid.*, p. 29.

43 Mansergh, *op. cit.*, Chapter 12; R. J. Moore, *Making the New Commonwealth* (Clarendon Press, 1987).

44 On the 'transfer of power' in India, see B. N. Pandey, *The Break-Up of British India* (Macmillan, 1969), Chapters 5–8; Hodson, *op. cit.*; E. Penderel Moon, *Divide and Quit* (Chatto & Windus, 1961); Menon, *op. cit.*; E. W. R. Lumby, *The Transfer of Power in India* (Allen & Unwin, 1954); C. H. Philips and M. D. Wainwright, *The Partition of India: Policies & Perspectives* (Allen & Unwin, 1970); Philip Ziegler, *Mountbatten* (Collins, 1985); R. J. Moore, *Escape from Empire: The Attlee Government and the Indian Problem* (Clarendon Press, 1983); Anita Inder Singh, *The Origins of the Partition of India, 1936–47* (Oxford UP, 1987); Chaudhri Muhammed Ali, *The Emergence of Pakistan* (Columbia UP, 1967); K. K. Aziz, *The Making of Pakistan* (Chatto & Windus, 1967).

45 W. R. Louis; *The British Empire in the Middle East, 1945–51* (Clarendon Press, 1984), M. Jones, *Failure in Palestine: British and United States Policy after the Second World War* (Mansell, 1986); R. Ovendale, *Britain, the United States and the End of the Palestine Mandate, 1942–48* (Boydell, 1989).

46 W. Woodruff, *The Impact of Western Man* (Macmillan, 1966), pp. 158, 289, 317.

47 Barratt Brown, *op. cit.*, p. 111.

48 Woodruff, *op. cit.*, facing p. 302.

49 *Ibid.*, p. 317.

50 Rotberg, *op. cit.*, p. 158.

51 F. J. Pedler, *West Africa* (Methuen, 1951), p. 87.

52 T. Hodgkin, *Nationalism in Colonial Africa* (Muller, 1956), p. 67.

53 On African nationalism, see Hodgkin, *op. cit.*; Rotberg, *op. cit.*; R. I. Rotberg and A. A. Mazrui (eds), *Protest and Power in Black Africa* (Oxford UP, 1970); D. J. Barnett and K. Njama, *Mau Mau from Within* (MacGibbon & Kee, 1966); C. G. Rosberg and J. Nottingham, *The Myth of Mau Mau* (Praeger, 1966); Tabitha Kanogo, *Squatters and the Roots of Mau Mau* (James Currey, 1987); David Throup, *Economic and Social Origins of Mau Mau, 1945–53* (James Currey, 1987); F. Furedi, *The Mau Mau War in Perspective* (James Currey, 1989); Karen Fields, *Revival and Rebellion in Colonial Central Africa* (Princeton UP, 1985); Frederick Cooper, *On the African Waterfront: Urban Disorder and the Transformation of Work in Colonial Mombasa* (Yale UP, 1987).

54 Metcalfe, *op. cit.*, p. 686.

55 Goldsworthy, *op. cit.*, pp. 17, 21; Hinden, *Empire and After*, Chapter 13.

56 Goldsworthy, *op. cit.*, p. 24.

57 See *ibid.*, Chapters 5, 8; and David Goldsworthy, 'Keeping change within bounds: aspects of colonial policy during the Churchill and Eden governments, 1951–57', *Journal of Imperial and Commonwealth History*, 18 (1989), 81–108; L. D. Epstein, *British Politics in the Suez Crisis* (Pall Mall Press, 1964), Chapters 2 and 4, *passim*.

58 R. Stubbs, *Hearts and Minds in Guerrilla Warfare: The Malayan Emergency, 1948–60* (Singapore: Oxford UP, 1989).

59 C. Cross, *The Fall of the British Empire* (Hodder & Stoughton, 1968), p. 310.

60 On the Suez affair, see Hugh Thomas, *The Suez Affair* (Weidenfeld & Nicolson, 1967); Epstein, *op. cit.*; H. Macmillan, *Riding the Storm* (Macmillan, 1971), Chapter 4; Sir Anthony Eden, *Memoirs*, Part 2: *Full Circle* (Cassell, 1960); A. Nutting, *No End of a Lesson* (Constable, 1967).

61 See H. D. Purcell, *Cyprus* (Benn, 1969), Chapter 6; R. Stephens, *Cyprus: A Place of Arms* (Pall Mall Press, 1966), Chapters 8–12.

62 On all this, see David Anderson, *Histories of the Hanged* (Weidenfeld & Nicolson, 2005); and Caroline Elkins, *Britain's Gulag* (Jonathan Cape, 2005).

63 See Rosberg and Nottingham, *op. cit.*; Barnett and Njama, *op. cit.*; Throup, *op. cit.*

64 Rotberg, *op. cit.*, p. 282.

65 See T. M. Franck, *Race and Nationalism* (Allen & Unwin, 1960); W. M. Macmillan, *The Road to Self-Rule* (Faber, 1959), Chapter 11; Rotberg, *op. cit.*, Chapters 9–11; E. Clegg, *Race and Politics* (Oxford UP, 1960).

66 See D. Reynolds, *Britannia Overruled* (Longman, 1991), p. 231. On Anglo-American relations generally, see R. Ovendale, *The English-Speaking Alliance: Britain, the United States, the Dominions and the Cold War, 1954–61* (Allen & Unwin, 1985); W. R. Louis and H. Bull (eds), *The 'Special Relationship': Anglo-American Relations Since 1945* (Clarendon Press, 1986); and D. Reynolds, 'A "Special Relationship"? America, Britain and the international order since 1945', *International Affairs*, 62 (1985), 1–20.

67 J. Callaghan, *Time and Chance* (Collins, 1987), p. 169.

68 T. R. Mockaitis, *British Counter-Insurgency, 1919–60* (Macmillan, 1990).

69 Barratt Brown, *op. cit.*, p. 225; M. Beloff, *The Future of British Foreign Policy* (Secker & Warburg, 1969), Chapter 3.

70 Goldsworthy, *Colonial Issues in British Politics*, p. 363.

71 On UDI Rhodesia, see E. Windrich, *Britain and the Politics of Rhodesian Independence* (Croom Helm, 1978); D. Martin and P. Johnson, *The Struggle for Zimbabwe* (Faber & Faber, 1981); P. Godwin and I. Hancock, *'Rhodesians Never Die': The Impact of War and Political Change on White Rhodesia, c.1970–1980* (Oxford UP, 1993).

72 Harold Smith, 'Appointment in Lagos', unpublished ms, Chapter 14.

73 On decolonisation, see W. P. Kirkman, *Unscrambling an Empire* (Chatto & Windus, 1966); Richard Symonds, *The British and Their Successors* (Faber & Faber, 1966); R. F. Holland, *European Decolonisation 1918–1981: An Introductory Survey* (Macmillan, 1985); John Darwin, *Britain and Decolonisation* (Macmillan, 1988), and John Darwin, *The End of the British Empire: The Historical Debate* (Basil Blackwell, 1991); A. N. Porter and A. J. Stockwell, *British Imperial Policy and Decolonisation, 1938–64*, 2 vols (Macmillan, 1987, 1989); Prosser Gifford and William Roger Louis (eds), *The Transfer of Power in Africa: Decolonization, 1940–1960* (Yale UP, 1982), Chapter 6; J. Hargreaves, *Decolonisation in Africa* (Longman, 1988); Nicholas Tarling, *The Fall of Imperial Britain in South-East Asia* (Oxford UP, 1993); and later works listed in Further reading.

74 L. S. Amery, *My Political Life* (Hutchinson, 1953), i, 16.

75 On the modern Commonwealth, see P. N. S. Mansergh, *The Commonwealth Experience* (Weidenfeld & Nicolson, 1969), Chapters 12, 13; M. S. Rajan, *The Post War [sic] Transformation of the Commonwealth* (Asia Publishing House, 1963); D. Judd and P. Slinn, *The Evolution of the Modern Commonwealth, 1902–80* (Macmillan, 1982); W. David McIntyre, *The Significance of the Commonwealth, 1965–90* (Macmillan, 1991).

76 Strictly, the Congo Museum, at Tervuren. Matthew Stannard, 'Learning to love Leopold', in John MacKenzie (ed.), *European Empires and the People* (Manchester UP, 2011), p. 132.

77 E. Powell, *A Nation Not Afraid: The Thinking of Enoch Powell*, ed. J. Wood (Batsford, 1965), Chapter 13.

78 House of Lords debate, 6 July 1972, reported in *The Times*, 7 July 1972, p. 8; see also the correspondence columns of *The Times* and the *Daily Telegraph* from January to April 1972.

11 A sudden shift: 1970–95

The remains

That the empire was almost forgotten in Britain did not mean that it had left no marks at all, or even that it was quite gone. In a strictly legalistic sense, Britain still had overseas colonies in the mid-1970s. She had Rhodesia, though for years she had been powerless to do anything there; she had Hong Kong, with four million inhabitants, partly on lease from China until 1997; she had Gibraltar at the southern tip of the Iberian peninsula; she had a little piece of central America, British Honduras, until it became the independent state of Belize in 1981; she had the snows and penguins – and the potentially fabulous mineral resources, if they could be ripped out of it – of British Antarctica; and she had a scattering of tiny islands all over the world.[1] The total population of all her overseas colonies apart from Rhodesia and Hong Kong was well under a million. Most of them she did not rule directly, but only protected or subsidised. Yet still they could give her problems, which were in a way all the more onerous now that she seemed to be getting nothing back from the empire in exchange.

Rhodesia was the biggest problem throughout the 1970s – at home, where it continued to arouse enormous controversy especially among Conservatives; in the Third World, where its non-resolution provoked great bad feeling; and of course in Rhodesia itself. It was eventually settled in April 1980, when the colony achieved proper legal independence as Zimbabwe. Robert Mugabe, who was the man to whom Britain handed over power, was a Marxist, which would have horrified most British Conservatives just a few years or even months before, and indicates both Britain's impotence and her pragmatism in the face of it. (It was almost the last pragmatic thing that particular government did.) Rhodesia was Britain's last really big colonial burden, apart from 'Fortress Falklands', which was partly self-imposed; and so to most people it was a relief when it was shed. Her other main colony, Hong Kong, imposed problems of a different kind: internal problems of government, and diplomatic problems with the Chinese arising out of their imminent resumption of the lease. Gibraltar and the Falkland Islands caused problems because they were claimed by other governments (Spain and Argentina), and so poisoned Britain's relations with those states. The poison turned into war in April 1982 between Britain and Argentina over the Falklands, in which 2,000 men (on both sides) died. That was an awful price to pay for almost the least significant of all Britain's imperial remnants: or would have been, if so many people at home had not seemed to enjoy it so much. No other post-colonial crisis was anything like so dramatic. The island of Anguilla in the Caribbean, which was not a real colony but part of a British 'Associated State' with St Kitts and Nevis, caused a flurry in March 1969 when it wanted to break away from

St Kitts, and at its own request was invaded by a force of London police to protect it. There were residual problems too over pensions for retired colonial civil servants, which for years Britain tried to saddle the ex-colonies with; and over East African Asians who, under an earlier dispensation, had been allowed to retain British passports after their countries of domicile had become independent, but who when they were thrown out of Uganda in 1972 were let only reluctantly into a Britain which in the meantime (perhaps out of chagrin at the way some of her other ex-subjects now treated her) had become more narrow-minded and less generous. These traces of empire could be irritating, but they were little more. They were not the significant remains of the empire (Map 12).

The empire left behind it more than a few stragglers. For both Britain and the ex-colonies the whole imperial experience, from its beginning to its end, had been arguably one of the most important things that had happened to them over the last 100 years. For the ex-colonies, things might have been very different had it not been for the experience of conquest and domination and national liberation they had just gone through. For Britain, though now people tried to dismiss it, her empire had once been thought to be the thing which marked her off from ordinary nations, the proof and the source of her power and prosperity, the reason why she was of so much more account than her mere 50 millions. If none of these things was quite true, nevertheless the imperial interests and habits of a lifetime could not have been shrugged off as if they were mere toys that could be taken up for distraction and just as easily put down again. For all parties concerned, the British empire left a legacy which was substantial, and in all probability lasting: though it was not a legacy which was altogether predictable, or intended.

The results

Both Britain and her ex-colonies came out of all this very much altered, but not necessarily because of what the empire had done to them. For the ex-colonies their conquest and rule by Britain were significant, but it was only one aspect of a wider phenomenon which was of more moment. What had happened to them over the past 100 years was this: that they, the 'under-developed world', had been brought into the ambit of Europe's world market, and concurrently into the stream of a wide range of European ideas and values. In this process it had nearly always been Europe which had taken the initiative: that is, Europe, and especially European capitalism, which had been expanding outwards to take in the under-developed world, and not the under-developed world which had been out foraging in search of Europe. This was certain; as were some of its effects.

A general effect was the wide and rapid diffusion of European people, money, technology, religion, weapons and many other things throughout the world. A more particular but widespread effect, which was much criticised later, was that under-developed countries, whose economies previously had been relatively poor (in the sense that they created very little surplus to provide for anything beyond mere subsistence) but also fairly balanced (meaning that they could at least provide for themselves most of the things they subsisted on) now became usually – but not always – richer, but also more dependent for their prosperity on single products, almost always primary products, which they exported. The advantage of this for under-developed countries was that it promoted economic growth. The disadvantages were that it tended to put their fates in the hands of the European buyers of their staples, which, if the price of those staples slumped (or was deliberately kept low by the buyers), could be disastrous; and that it discouraged manufacturing industry and so kept growth sluggish. It happened for two reasons. First, the

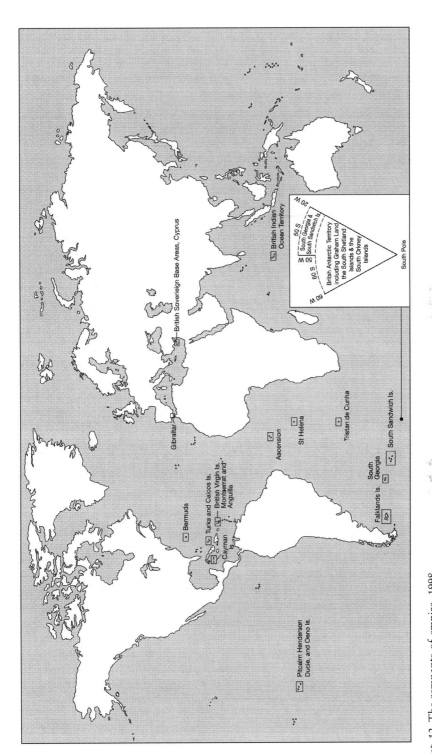

Map 12 The remnants of empire, 1998

Source: After Brown, J. and Louis, W. R. (eds), *The Oxford History of the British Empire*, vol. IV (Oxford University Press, 1999, p. 695), reprinted with permission of Oxford University Press via PLS Clear.

European market was only interested in what the under-developed countries produced best and cheapest, which climate and other factors usually determined was just one or two crops or minerals. Second, local producers, whether native or immigrant, were only interested in producing what they could sell most profitably. The size of the market had created a division of labour between different areas on a worldwide scale. It happened naturally and almost inevitably, to nearly every country in the world which had something to sell that Europe wanted.[2]

The British empire was all part of this. In origin, though indirectly, it was a consequence of the broader expansion of Europe, most of its extensions of authority being designed to safeguard and consolidate some of the material advantages Britain got from this expansion. By creating favourable conditions for capitalists, and also for the purveyors of European culture (which the British called 'civilisation'), it was a factor in the diffusion of both. It did this far more often than it *obstructed* the spread of capitalism and 'civilisation', though it did that occasionally. But it was not the only or necessary diffuser of capitalism and 'civilisation': clearly not in countries which did not become colonies, nor even in those which did. There were countries which adapted quite comfortably to the expansion of Europe and to Europe's demands on them without having to become European colonies. Indeed, it required a positive effort – such as, for example, China and Korea and Tibet made – to resist the contagion. Some of the countries which did become European colonies might have been able to adapt without, and in some cases *were* adapting before they were taken over. They did not require necessarily to be colonised before they were 'civilised', and sometimes the fact that they were colonised was quite incidental to their 'civilisation'. The British empire's contribution, therefore, to the 'development' or 'exploitation' or 'civilisation' of the world was not a straightforward one. All these things came about through contact between continents. One kind of contact was colonial contact. Whether it was the colonial aspect of the contact which was the vital factor in diffusing anything anywhere could be debated, but not presumed.

What the empire did do quite clearly, and what other and more ubiquitous kinds of contact and diffusion did *not* do to the same degree, was to take out of its colonies' hands the control of their own responses to the demands made on them by the expansion of Europe. This was the automatic effect of overtly replacing indigenous governments by an alien one imposed from outside, and ultimately responsible to an external power, which was the distinguishing mark of an empire, even of one like the British which probably relied less on external direction and more on internal collaboration than any other empire of its time. The result of this was to create at once an artificial, contrived situation, in which whatever happened was no longer determined by local realities, by the strengths and weaknesses of forces and interests on the spot, but by a reality, a strength and an interest external to it. Immediately, the natural development of a society, the way it would have gone if it had had to respond on its own, was suspended. Whatever happened afterwards, whether or not it was what the government in authority wanted to happen, was likely to be distorted by the very presence of that authority. There was no way of getting away from this, except by the removal of that authority.

For a time, this was not supposed to matter. It was not supposed to matter because it was vaguely but widely assumed that, whatever the 'natural' way of development for a society was likely to be, there was a *best* way of development and Britain knew what that best way was. She knew it from her own national experience, which if not typical was supposed to be a model, and consequently of universal application. From the most proselytising days of the East India Company before the Mutiny, to the years of 'development and welfare' after the Second World War, there was always at least a trace of this assumption in Britain's colonial policy: that she knew what was best for her colonies. She had the plans, the designs, the working drawings of the Great Architect in the sky.

It was this assumption which it was most difficult to shift throughout the history of the empire, though it was questioned at various stages all along. It was questioned by some colonial nationalists. It was also questioned by some colonial administrators, who from their experience of the colonies they worked in, and not their experience of home, deduced that British society might have some peculiarities of its own, for example, its homogeneity, which made it unsuitable as a model for societies everywhere. The problem then was that if you no longer had a plan, it was difficult to know how to proceed. The critics suggested by returning colonial societies to their natural paths of development. But this was a tall order. In the first place, much of the old fabric, which might possibly have given clues as to the direction of that development, had been trampled down by the men with their architects' drawings. In the second place, colonial societies could not evolve 'naturally' while they had this great artificial scaffolding supporting and shielding and distorting them still. It was like trying to teach a lion in a zoo to live naturally.

Probably there were some things which could be taught to a colonial people, which were good for them and would help them to live in the wild, yet which could as well be taught in a colonial context as in any other. What became fairly clear towards the end, however, was that certain things, and perhaps the most important things, were better taught by experience than by instruction, for two reasons. First, self-government was the kind of skill which needed practice to inculcate it. A British liberal early in the twentieth century likened it to swimming: 'If a child could not be taught to swim on the land, let it, with proper precautions, get into the water.'[3] Edwin Montagu believed that representative government required not only representative institutions to thrive, but also 'conventions and customs and habits' which no Act of Parliament could teach or impose, and which nations best learned on their own: consequently, the Indians, he felt, should be given 'a chance at once to work out their own destiny. Chaos, revolution and bloodshed will occur, but the result years afterwards might be a more vigorous, more healthy, more self-created [plant] than the plant we have in view.'[4] The point was also that, while the artificiality of colonial rule still remained, the teachers were in no position to know exactly what needed to be taught. They were guessing: guessing at what would be needed by their pupils for survival in the outside world, and guessing at what would be acceptable to them in those very different conditions. Left on their own, just because they were on their own, their pupils were much more likely to find out: though the lesson for them might be a painful one.

The results, when the colonial peoples were allowed to find out for themselves, were new polities and customs which in every case owed much to their colonial masters, but not always in a direct, straightforward kind of way. Some of the things which had been offered to them they assimilated whole, like styles of dress, and some of the forms of parliamentary government, and cricket (Figure 11.1) (which, curiously, went with formal empire as football did not: perhaps because it was an acquired taste and required a few centuries of settled domination to take hold; or because colonial rulers, who were gentlemen and therefore usually batsmen, needed to teach natives to bowl to them). Direct transmission of cultural traits like these was common, but it was not the only way in which the colonial relationship could make its mark. More often it was not the example or the teaching of the colonial power which moulded an institution, but the situation

Figure 11.1 Cricket. An early 'Grand Intercolonial Cricket Match' between Victoria and New South Wales, played in Melbourne, 1858.
Source: Henry H. Glover. Courtesy of the National Library of Australia, available at: https://nla.gov.au/nla.obj-136081365.

itself. Colonial nationalism, for instance, was partly copied from European precept or example, and partly remembered from the pre-colonial past; and it frequently made appeals to both. Yet it, and especially the style of nationalist leadership, owed far more to the particular (and contrived) colonial situation in which it arose and to which it was a response, than it did to either of these; and so consequently did the forms of politics and leadership which pertained after independence, which in most cases were retained almost intact from the 'freedom fighting' days.[5] The empire might have helped to mould individual colonial attitudes too, not by precept but by provocation.[6] In ways like this, British imperialism fundamentally affected the development of the countries it conquered, but not as it intended. The dams it built diverted history, but not always into the channels it had dug for it.

From colonial rule to self-rule the transition was consequently sometimes a bumpy one. Where it was bumpiest was where, in the artificial conditions created by colonial rule, plants had taken root which resisted adaptation: like minority communities whose establishment had been permitted, but whose natural assimilation to their hosts had been discouraged, by the fact of there being an external authority to shelter them. With someone there protecting them – not necessarily partially, and perhaps reasonably – minorities were freed from the necessity of bringing their attitudes and ambitions into line with their own real numerical strength; freed, that is, from the need to accommodate, adjust and compromise. 'They will be arrogant and quarrellous,' wrote an observer in 1870, 'believing that whatever they do they will be pulled through.'[7] Consequently, situations were fostered which were compatible only with the presence of the imperial authority, and could not have lived, initially at any rate, without it. What happened in these cases when the dam was taken away could be nasty. If while it had been there, the minority had not managed to accrue to itself enough power of its own to defend its position without it, it would have to try to swim with the rushing waters, or else drown. This is what happened in 1947 in India, and also to the white settlers in Kenya and the Asians of Uganda. Where the minority had managed to build itself up, or perhaps to find help from another source, then it might survive, but at a price. In Ireland, in Palestine and in Rhodesia there were settler communities (Protestant, Jewish, European) which only existed as dominant races because of Britain's artificial suspension of the natural course of events sometime in the past. Because they had managed in these artificial conditions to take strong root, they still held out when conditions returned to 'normal'. But it was always against the embittered and determined opposition of the indigenous crop, of those who had been there before and who, if it had been left to them, would have had things different. In this way, at least three of the world's main trouble spots in the last quarter of the twentieth century could be directly debited to the account of the British empire: to its inevitable interference with the natural evolution of smaller, weaker communities.[8]

On the colonies, therefore, the empire was likely to have made a considerable impact, but in a very hit and miss kind of way, like a blind man with a box of paints. Much of what was attributed to the empire, by critics and apologists alike, was not the empire's doing at all, but the effect of a broader movement of culture contact, which the empire may have helped along, or not. Where it did help it along, it was just one way among others of doing it, and not necessarily the best way. What particularly distinguished it from others was that it was an 'artificial' way, which may not always have been a bad thing, but did have certain results which were peculiar to it. Those results were not often the results which Britain had intended for her colonies, because her control over their destinies was always imperfect. This was, first, because of her defective understanding of the materials she had in her hands; and, second, because the British empire itself was as much affected by realities and forces outside its control as it affected them. Which was why, in the beginning, the empire had been acquired; and why in the end it failed to do for Britain what she wanted it to do.

The residue[9]

On Britain herself her imperial experience appeared to have left less of a mark than it had on her ex-colonies. On the cultural surface this was certainly so. Englishmen did not walk the streets of London in turbans or even pith helmets in the way that Africans were supposed to sport top hats in Accra. In the creative arts there were a few odd instances of composers toying with Indian harmonies and novelists writing against South Sea backgrounds, but they were not many, and not evidence of any very profound acculturation. The cultures and civilisations which the empire brought Britain into such intimate contact with were recorded and studied seriously and with affection, but always as things apart from British life, academically. The relics which did find their ways to Britain were displayed as curios, or kept firmly away from life in museums. There were exceptions, but the exceptions were usually regarded as aberrant and regrettable. On the whole, there was no more cultural traffic from east to west than would have been expected in a country which just traded with the east occasionally: much less than the familiarity of the imperial connection seemed to make likely. Which was unusual, for it was a common characteristic of other colonising peoples in the world's history that they were changed as much by the people they colonised as they changed them:

> Conquering Mongols are partly civilized by conquered Chinese and Persians; a like good fate befell the Arab hosts in Persia, India, and Egypt; the earliest Median invaders were civilized in Mesopotamia; and throughout the first century we can watch the struggle at Rome between *simplicitas romana* and the refinements of the conquered East.[10]

British civilisation was very much more resilient and sure of itself than these; and, besides, the British exerted themselves to make sure they were *not* contaminated by other cultures, which was what all the nonsense about dressing for dinner in the African bush was about. It was part of the style of British imperialism that it kept its distance from its subjects, and very much disapproved, for example, of the laxer Portuguese, who did not. Acculturation in this direction was called 'going native'.

Nevertheless, there were ways in which the empire had changed Britain, and which were to affect her adjustment to the post-imperial age too. After all, the empire, while it had been there, had taken up a good deal of the time of a large number of Britons, and provided also a kind of spiritual comfort for them and for many others: which, though it was difficult to measure, was of some account, and must have had repercussions when the empire was taken away. An institution which had gone on so long, and entangled itself so deeply into the fabric of British upper- and middle-class society, and whose loss had been preceded by so little warning, was bound to leave sores, if nothing else, when the ties were broken. For those who had run the empire, and were good for little else, there were the problems of adapting to very different, and perhaps uncongenial, lives and life-styles. For those for whom the empire had been an integral part of their world always, decolonisation must have left frustrations which substitutes could not satisfy, emotional urges which could not be channelled elsewhere, loves unrequited; a whole range of attitudes and aptitudes evolved over the years in the service of the empire, and now left without an object. Some of these people managed to adjust. Some did not, but were content to take their old worlds with them into private retirement. Some may have brought them with them into other streams of British public life, like politics or industrial management, so that these things became infused with attitudes left over from the empire. Others managed to find new berths which still suited them without having to change much, sometimes abroad in the service of their old subjects if they were agreeable (as many were); or if that was too hard a pill to swallow, in southern Africa, where the old world still lasted remarkably long. Some of the old idealism which had previously found its outlet in the empire was now diverted to other forms of overseas service, like Voluntary Service Overseas (VSO), which sent young adventurous altruists abroad to help the less fortunate to help themselves. In these ways the old paths merged into new ones, and the traces of empire were lost.

If the upper echelons of British society were able to shrug off their imperial losses so easily and conveniently, others were not. One of the more apparent aftereffects of the empire was the immigration into Britain of so many of its ex-subjects during and after decolonisation: a few white settlers fleeing from what they saw as a horrendous future, and many thousands (132,000 between 1955 and 1957) of non-whites, mainly West Indians and Pakistanis, escaping from a stifling present. By 2001, the number of Asian-origin Britons had risen to 2.3 million. This was almost unprecedented.[11] For most of the empire's long life, at least after the eighteenth century, people from the colonies had only rarely been seen in Britain; unless they were 'white' (European-origin), in which cases, of course, they tended to melt into their surroundings. It was only when the empire entered its final stages that significant numbers of its old subjects started appearing, physically, in the metropole. Their cultural impact was enormous. One obvious (if perhaps trivial) example was the proliferation of 'Indian' (usually, in fact, Bangladeshi) and Chinese restaurants in British cities, where they had scarcely ever featured – certainly for the native clientele – while the raj was still on the go. (By 2001, according to Foreign Secretary Robin Cook, chicken tikka had come to qualify as a 'British national dish', no less – once masala sauce had been added to it 'to satisfy the desire of British people to have their meat served in gravy'.[12]) Immigrants also contributed disproportionately to British sporting life. But they were perceived to bring cultural dissonances and social problems too, in the working-class communities they settled among: men and women who had had very little direct contact with the empire while it had been alive, but now (as they thought) bore the full brunt of its dying legacy. A multi-racial Britain was one of the main results of empire, but one for which the empire, despite all its high multi-racial pretensions, had very poorly prepared her people.

The loss of empire had an effect on Britain's national morale too, though this was as intangible as the others. Dean Acheson, a former US Secretary of State, described her predicament in 1962 as having 'lost an empire and not yet found a role'. At the time that was rather resented, but with hindsight it can be seen to have been profoundly true. The problem was that the empire had defined Britain's role for so long now that it was difficult to conceive of alternatives: so she was left floundering. It was not only her part in world affairs that this affected, but also her view of herself. Without the empire, Britain as a whole, and England within it, had no clear sense of national identity. That had been hijacked by the imperialists long before, with their 'imperial race' braggadocio, their appropriation of the Union flag to their creed, and all the propagandist paraphernalia of empire they had been trying to foist on their social inferiors for decades. Not all of the last, as we have seen, stuck, but they did enough to confuse the picture. What, apart from the empire, made Britain distinctively British? For some, it was simply her history, up to and including, but not going beyond, her 'finest hour'. That was all right up to a point – every national identity needs a history to sustain it – and a useful revenue-spinner, through museums, historical theme parks, 'heritage trails' and the rest to entice visitors to view Britain's history, or a version of it; but in itself it gave few clues as to what distinguished Britons *today*. There were some attempts to re-create a more positive non-imperial national identity, based on Britain's fabled 'tolerance', for example, or 'moderation', or 'sense of fair play', which might possibly have sufficed were it not for the fact that none of these qualities seemed specially applicable to Britain in these latter years. In 1992, Margaret Thatcher staked a claim for 'enterprise' and 'anti-socialism' as the defining British characteristics,[13] but that was a partisan view, at best. There was no agreement over this. Everyone had a different idea of Britishness. That was a source of weakness, certainly, when it came to Britain's new place in world affairs.

At worst, it could make the country parochial and bitter. Professor Max Beloff, a distinguished imperial historian, warned of this in 1969. 'We now face,' he wrote, 'the danger of a sudden and total revulsion against anything that reminds us of past advantages and past glories, a sudden shift into an isolationist little-Englandism with unhealthy overtones of xenophobia and even racialism accompanying it.'[14] There were plenty of signs of that in the following years. Immigrants and Europe got the main brunt of it. Racism directed at coloured immigrants or their descendants was a constant problem in Britain from the 1950s onwards, provoking two kinds of legislative response – immigration controls, and anti-discrimination laws – which may have forestalled what Enoch Powell once notoriously prophesied would be a racial blood bath, but never succeeded completely in cutting the cancer out.[15] Anti-European xenophobia was seen on two main levels: among young thugs and neo-fascists on the streets and (typically) the terraces of continental football stadia, and on the Conservative anti-European Community Right. This was one way of re-defining Britishness in the post-imperial era. Whether it had anything to do with the loss of empire more directly is problematic. Social and cultural factors mainly accounted for the thuggery. Large-scale black immigration was new; if it had happened in imperial days, maybe Britons would have behaved similarly. And they had always looked down their noses at Europeans.[16] That was nothing new.

It may be, in fact, that 'imperialism' was too easy a scapegoat for many of the ills that afflicted Britain in the 1960s and 1970s. People seized on it unfairly. It became the accepted view, that clinging nostalgically on to outworn imperial glories had held Britain back ever since the Second World War. It was supposed to have had two major adverse effects. The first concerned Europe. Britain's destiny lay in union with Europe, it was said; had lain there ever since 1945, for those with eyes to see. What prevented more eyes from seeing was their fixation on the patterns of the past. Hence Britain missed the boat when it first raised steam, in the 1940s: 'we had every western European government eating out of our hand in the immediate aftermath of war. For several years our prestige and influence were paramount and we could have stamped Europe as we wished' (that was Sir Nicholas Henderson, a retiring ambassador);[17] and failed to catch up with it until it was well out to sea. When she did board it eventually, in January 1973, it was singularly unenthusiastically so far as most Britons were concerned, and on terms set – inevitably – by those who were already on deck. There were a number of reasons for the blunder, but the chief ones – it was said – were Britain's loyalty to her Commonwealth, and the illusion that she had a world role still. The damage did not stop in 1973, but continued thereafter, explaining Britain's always uncomfortable and frequently fractious position within what later became the European Union (EU).

Obviously, there was a great deal of truth in this. Those who argued this way knew what they were talking about: in many cases they were speaking for their former selves. Britain was full of overblown Great Power illusions in the 1950s and 1960s, especially; not only in the corridors of power but outside them too. Whether those illusions were essentially responsible for her failure to join Europe earlier, however, is another matter. Some of the fault for that lies outside Britain entirely: with the French government of Charles de Gaulle, for example, who frustrated both Macmillan's and Wilson's genuine efforts to climb on board, chiefly because of their American – not imperial – paraphernalia. So far as Britain was reluctant, it was for understandable reasons, even possibly good ones, which had little to do with the empire *per se*. One was the pattern of her trade, which was entirely different from her later European partners' – far more extra-European, for example – and consequently bound to make the adjustment more painful for her than it was for them.[18] It was real material and political *interests* which made Britain wary of the European connection, not simply a foolish atavistic dream. That being said, however, the dream was an element in it. Pro-Europeans seized on it.

It helped them to make the cause of Europeanism seem so much more progressive: the modern, liberal and internationalist antithesis to imperialism. That was another – very different – way in which the shade of the old empire continued to be a factor in British politics, long after imperialism proper came to an end.

It was also widely blamed for Britain's economic decline. That decline, as we have seen, was no new thing. Britain had been falling behind other industrial powers for very many years before 1970. After 1970, however, the situation got worse. In the first place, after 30 years of full employment, minimal inflation and rising standards of living, which buffered the social impact of Britain's relative decline, it became associated with massive unemployment, high inflation, and lower living standards overall. As well as this, it became absolute. In the 1980s, graphs of production did not merely level off: they started to dip. In 1983, a symbolic turning-point was reached when, for the first time in centuries, Britain began importing more manufactured goods than she exported. Except for those who refused to measure 'progress' in material terms, the facts of her decline were stark. A sizeable literature grew up to try to account and prescribe for it: a kind of new science of 'declinology'.[19] (In a small way, the first edition of this book in 1975 was a part of it.) Diagnoses varied widely, from capitalism's inner contradictions to the abuse of trade-union power. But the empire played a prominent role in some of them. Its main offence was supposed to be that it had artificially protected Britain from the salutary wages of her economic sins. Like a sticking plaster over a cut, after a while it had prevented the air from reaching and healing her wounds.

It had happened this way. Britain (as we have seen) had been declining industrially for years. But it did not seem to matter, or to be very widely noticed, while she had her wider-world markets and fields for investment to compensate. When her industry got into difficulties, which it did fairly frequently after 1870 because it never was as efficient as some others, it used the under-developed world as an easy way out. Instead of competing in Europe and America, it went for softer markets outside. This way, it maintained a reasonable growth rate, without having to modernise. As well as this, Britain's massive foreign investments overseas produced an additional income which made up the deficit that remained on her visible trade. This was how her economy was padded, until about 1945. After then, however, the padding started falling away. It was not just a question of *imperial* decline: if it had been, it would not have been as serious as it was. But the loss of the empire was merely a symptom. Underneath Britain had lost far more, most of it not to her ex-colonies but to the United States. Chiefly she had lost her premier trading and financial position in the world, with which had gone – and it had been the wars that had done most to take them from her – many of her markets, and a great deal of the capital she had used to invest abroad. That loss itself was serious; more disturbing, however, was what it had left behind. For the main trouble was that Britain had done much more than trade and invest in the under-developed world: she had traded and invested there as an alternative to making her own industry more efficient and competitive in tighter markets; and she had allowed her trade and investment there to obscure that inefficiency and uncompetitiveness at home. When her overseas clothes started being shed, what was left was not only a naked body but also a chronically sick one: industrial and commercial deficiencies which had been there for decades, even when the 'workshop of the world' had appeared to be doing best, but which Britain had been able to get away with until now. If the empire had any real lasting effect on Britain, therefore, it may have been this: to make it more difficult for her to do without.

Britain's wider-world preoccupations were also blamed for diverting investment capital away from her own industry, which could have done with it; though an alternative way of looking at this was to regard it as British industry's own fault, for not being efficiently managed enough to *attract* capital.[20] Even this explanation, however, did not exonerate the empire entirely. For another common ploy in the 1970s was to put the blame on the empire – among other factors – for Britain's *managerial* shortcomings too. The argument was that the service of the empire had somehow displaced the running of manufacturing industry as an object of ambition for the British middle-class young. This was encouraged by the public schools, which the bourgeois took over from the aristocracy in the later nineteenth century but then proceeded to de-bourgeoisify. Second-generation capitalists had their capitalist values brainwashed out of them and replaced by patrician values of an older vintage. Industry, consequently, was starved of able captains, who all went off overseas to become platonic guardians instead. Eventually the guardianships dried up, but their values were perpetuated in the schools, the older universities, the civil service, and the low status accorded to industry and to capitalist acquisitiveness generally in Britain, by contrast with those in America, Germany and Japan. That was the thesis. It was a beguiling one. The Left took it up initially, mainly because they rejected empire first: Tony Benn, for example, blamed Britain's economic decline on the fact that in the later nineteenth century she had 'opted to become an imperial country instead of continuing as an industrial one', as early as 1966.[21] Then, in the 1980s, the 'New' post-imperial Right cottoned on to it, as a convenient explanation for Britain's relative industrial decline before socialism was sufficiently strong to take the blame,[22] The empire – the theory went – drained industry of talent, and was still doing this, even after it had gone.

The argument can be taken further. The empire not only enervated Britain's industry; it also stultified, or diverted, her whole national development as a capitalist state. Late nineteenth-century imperialism may have been capitalist in origin, at least in part, but it also had the effect of perpetuating certain pre-capitalist trends in British society. This is because it could not be *governed* by capitalists, who are classically uninterested in government and even antipathetic towards it. Their preferred form of empire, of course, was what today is called the 'informal' sort, which obviated the need for government almost entirely, but we have seen that towards the end of the nineteenth century this became less and less viable, because of rivalries and pressures outside. The result was the progressive formalisation of Britain's empire, and a consequent demand for new bureaucracies and bureaucrats. There were other contemporary factors encouraging bureaucracy in Britain too, like social reform (or 'social*ism*', as it was sometimes called), but the expanding formal empire was a major one. To an orthodox 'political economist', or free market capitalist, this was a thoroughly retrograde step. Bureaucracies were an incubus on enterprise, and consequently on progress, which is why so much Liberal and also Conservative effort in mid-Victorian times had been devoted to trying to whittle them down. More pernicious still may have been the effect of all this on *values*. Practical imperialists – as we have seen – had mental attitudes different from those of capitalists. They tended to be paternalist, and aware of social duties, rather than individualistic and motivated by material gain. This brought them close to certain kinds of socialist, with whom they formed an important bond in the 1940s, contributing to the colonial 'development and welfare' legislation of that time.[23] That bond spilled over into domestic policy. One reason for the Conservative Party's broad acceptance of Labour's *domestic* welfare measures after 1951 was its domination by old-fashioned paternalist Tories, rather than by the free marketist sort. That compounded the damage. This may well have been the most important domestic effect of the empire on Britain while it lasted: to hold up the march of the pure capitalist ethos, and hence allow all kinds of plants to flourish – welfareism, consensus, the spirit of public service – which without it would almost certainly have withered by then.

At the time, this significance was not clear. Later it became more so, when the empire went, leaving the paternalists without their chief source of sustenance, and consequently diminishing their influence within the Conservative Party. This, at any rate, is one way of explaining what happened not only to Britain's external role, but also to her domestic situation, from the 1970s on. That must be counted a revolution. As with all revolutions, there were individuals on hand to claim credit for it; especially Margaret Thatcher, who came on to the scene shortly after it had started, and whose later recollections made it appear that she was solely responsible for it: that she had somehow single-handedly seized history by the scruff and turned it round. That was an exaggeration. History was turning in any case, helped by the removal of this imperial obstruction to what now appeared to be the natural development of capitalism, which was thus enabled to resume its previous course.

With Thatcher herself, scarcely any trace of the old imperial spirit remained: far less than in the case of most of her Conservative predecessors, with the possible exceptions of Edward Heath and Stanley Baldwin; and less even than with Harold Wilson, who had always, for example, had a soft spot for the Commonwealth. Thatcher regarded the latter with a mixture of puzzlement and contempt, mainly because of its ethos, which must have seemed dangerously *social* to her (the word 'common' in the title will have jarred somewhat), and because she could not see any utilitarian point to it.[24] Her obligatory attendances at Commonwealth Prime Ministers' Conferences always seemed to spark rows. She did, it is true, once go to war over a remnant of empire, but that was an accident. There was no imperial *rationale* to it. Britain did not fight the Argentines over the Falkland Islands for profit, or for the security of her sea-lanes, or for the material or spiritual good of anyone. She fought them for a principle (to resist aggression), to restore her government's injured *amour propre*, and possibly for electoral profit – though that was a less certain advantage at the time than it afterwards turned out to be. The 'jingoism' released by the affair was, equally, not at all an imperial one, one, that is, that revealed a particular imperial as against a merely national pride: any more than popular jingoism had been in the 1870s, when the word had been coined. This whole adventure, in other words, was a typically Disraelian ploy, shot through with Disraelian motives, touching Disraelian chords, and mainly, like most of Disraeli's actions, for show. It did not indicate in the least that 'imperialism' proper was about to be resurrected, even if that had been practicable; or that anyone intended it should be.

On the narrowly domestic front, too, the repercussions of empire faded fast. The values it had bolstered gradually disappeared. Those who dared espouse them in Margaret Thatcher's early cabinets were disparagingly referred to by her as 'wets', and one by one removed. Thatcher's own litany of prime public virtues – for which she adopted the collective name 'Victorian values' in January 1983 – strikingly omitted those that had been associated with the best aspects of the empire in Victorian times. Hard work, thrift, self-reliance, personal responsibility and patriotism were found places, for example, but not service, loyalty and fair play.[25] This reflected the new contemporary spirit, which was, be it noted, not just a British one, but spreading rapidly worldwide. It almost certainly reflected something greater than Thatcher's personal influence: the triumph, perhaps, for the time being at any rate, of international capitalism, through its own inherent dynamic, and against *most* of the barriers erected against it hitherto. The Soviet Union, which was even more protective of its people against this kind of thing than the British empire had been, followed the latter into oblivion in 1991. Society generally was disintegrating: internationally into nation states bound together only by alliances; domestically into individuals relating to each other only through cash. Is it fanciful, or necessarily reductionist, to see all those phenomena as parts of a single great historical trend? The fall of empires and the decline of the more social human values were related; almost certainly in Britain, and possibly elsewhere too.

So far as the empire itself was concerned – our main focus here – few Britons cared at all for what remained. They were, most of them, proud to have defended the Falklands; but none was particularly proud of *having* them to defend. Most of Britain's other colonial responsibilities were regarded now as burdens she would much rather be without, and would have been, if she could have got away with scuttling them without loss of honour or face. In her new straitened circumstances they stretched her defence resources grievously, and to the detriment of what in most people's eyes was her main defence commitment, to the NATO alliance. They also no longer reflected her real position in the world. When Hong Kong and the Falklands and all the rest had originally been acquired, it had been as part of a larger pattern of commercial penetration and naval ascendancy. They had been pieces in a jigsaw, and made sense in relation to the pieces around them. Now the pieces around them had gone, most of the surviving ones either made very little sense, or else made a different kind of sense from before. Hong Kong is an example of the latter, acting as it did now as a kind of cat-flap into communist China until its reversion in 1997; the Falklands is probably the best example of an overseas commitment which, partly because it never had had very much value to Britain, now had none at all. Even if oil had been found off its shores, or South Georgia could have been used as a base from which to exploit Antarctica, Britain was no longer the sort of power which could afford to sustain these kinds of operations so very far from home. The almost ludicrous measures that had to be resorted to in order to supply the Falklands after May 1982 illustrate this: with Ascension Island being called into service as a mid-way base, and Hercules transport aircraft having to be refuelled twice in the air between there and Port Stanley, at a dive because the Hercules' maximum speed was slower than the Victor tankers' stalling speed, and with the Victor tankers themselves having to be refuelled in the air by *more* Victor tankers in order to be able to get back: all at a cost of millions, and because Britain could not depend on the South American mainland for more convenient facilities.

But it was not only a question of power. Britain's material interests had contracted too: especially her commercial ones. For decades, as we have seen, Britain's external trade had once had a number of distinctive features, two of which were that it far exceeded any other country's foreign trade, and that most of it was carried on outside Europe. This was the rational justification (in among the irrational ones) for Britain's initial reluctance to join the EEC: the difficulty was, as a leading 'anti-Marketeer' wrote in 1973,

> that for 400 years our interests in commerce, the flow of our money, our trade and our people have been oceanic not continental; Europe, for us, has only been one of five continents with which we are linked as closely as we are to Europe itself.[26]

Which was true of the previous 400 years, but was rapidly becoming much less so. Between 1960 and 1980, Britain's pattern of trade shifted enormously, towards Europe and away from the 'wider world'. In 1960, only 31.7 per cent of her exports went to western (non-communist) Europe, and 30.7 per cent of her imports came from there; by 1980, these figures had rocketed to 56.9 per cent and 55.7 per cent respectively.[27] Of course, this may not have been a 'natural' shift – one that would have taken place, that is, if Britain had not been forced into a more Eurocentric commercial pattern by the EEC. Nevertheless it had happened. So had the much more gradual relative decline of her foreign trade generally, by comparison with that of America, Japan, Germany and even France. In 1980, Britain was no longer a worldwide trading nation to anything like the extent she had been before. It followed that it was inappropriate for her still to have substantial political responsibilities outside her own particular corner of the globe.

Of course, there remained her *financial* interests overseas, which had not contracted – so far as it was possible to tell – to the same degree. Britons still invested hugely outside Europe; and British companies like Unilever and Dunlop and Imperial Tobacco, which under imperialism had grown to the positions they had of dominance over certain colonial (or semi-colonial) economies, managed in many cases to continue dominating, though by agreement now, and on less one-sided terms. This was sometimes called 'neo-colonialism'. But it was not the same. For one thing, there were some very big exceptions to the neo-colonial rule. The biggest was oil, where the West's domination of the market did not survive decolonisation, and the oil-producing countries banded together to raise prices to the very great detriment of those economies – which meant most industrial economies, including Britain's – which had grown dependent on cheap imported petroleum to a vulnerable degree. This was one area in which Britain's economic decline could be traced directly to the loss of her empire, for the oil crisis of 1973–74, which partly triggered that decline, could not have happened, obviously, if Britain had still been able to dictate policy in the Persian Gulf. This kind of table-turning was unusual, but not unique, in a world that had grown rather harder than it had used to be to manipulate in the interests of the West.[28] This was one limitation to Britain's neo-colonial capacities. Another was that she was no longer at the butt end of every neo-colonial gun. In a way – with her own dependence now on foreign capital and loans, and so much of her industry owned from abroad – she was almost a 'neo-colony' herself. She was a beneficiary as well, but a very minor one now by the side of the United States, for example, whose own financial domination of Britain might well, if it could have been measured, have outweighed Britain's financial domination of anywhere else. Again, the material facts of Britain's situation did not justify a world power role. It was not just that she was too weak; a world role was functionally wrong for her now.

British imperialism, therefore, was totally and irrevocably finished, except as a myth, or a metaphor for other kinds of alleged domination (like that of England over Scotland or Englishmen over women), or a bequeather of unwanted legacies to its heirs. Its infrastructure had crumbled away almost to nothing – the reef which in Chapter 1 was described as connecting Britain's old colonial outcrops under the surface of things. Scattered around above the surface there remained one or two little boulders, 'survivals' (as the anthropologists would call them) from the past, but survivals that were no longer valuable to Britain or valued by her. The imperial spirit had gone too, despite some misleading signs to the contrary (like Falklands jingoism), and whatever might be said by supercilious foreigners who could not credit Britain with having put her imperial past behind her so soon. In fact, she had, to a remarkable degree. Asked by some Gallup pollsters whether they thought it was important for Britain to retain her status as a major power, only 30 per cent of a sample of Britons replied 'yes' in 1975, as against 55 per cent ten years before,[29] which indicates that people were very quickly becoming acclimatised to their new national role. The pain which the death of empire had left in the breasts of some of its devotees in the 1950s and 1960s faded mercifully away, to be replaced by the sort of warm but distant and consequently unregretful nostalgia which pervades the books about the empire by Jan Morris, its most lyrical modern chronicler,[30] and certain rose-coloured feature films. The effects of this change were reflected too in British public life, as the old imperial patrician element in the Conservative Party, for example, began to be frozen out by the newly dominant caste of estate agents and tax lawyers and marketing executives; and in other areas, like cricket, which, in the 1970s and 1980s, became commercialised and vulgarised in the wake of the decline of the old imperialist fuddy-duddies in the MCC. Every year the ruins of the imperial edifice were obliterated further, as the undergrowth crept up and covered them stone by stone. People ceased to relate to the empire, and then to remember it: in schools and universities, for example, where it was squeezed out of most history curricula.[31] It was done, past, finished; a chapter of Britain's history that had now – surely – definitely come to an end.

Retrospect

It was not a very long chapter, as these things go, but it is difficult to see how it could have been. The magnificent show that the British empire made at its apogee should not blind us to its considerable weaknesses all through. Those who believe that qualities like 'will' and 'leadership' can mould events might not accept this, of course, but there was nothing that anyone in Britain could have done in the twentieth century to stave off the empire's decline. It was just too riddled with contradictions. The one that gave rise to most uneasiness at the time was between *imperium* and *libertas*: just how could Britons square their domestic libertarianism with the frankly authoritarian nature of some of the regimes they were imposing abroad? Ways were found around this, chiefly the 'trusteeship' idea, by which Britain was supposed to be using her authority to nurture future colonial liberties, but the dichotomy remained, and at the crunch, when it seemed to be a matter of choice between them, it was a source of weakness to her. Another contradiction was military, and is very simply put: Britain expanded territorially in order to defend vulnerable interests and frontiers, but every inch of expansion extended her frontiers, and so multiplied her vulnerable points. This put an increasing burden on her military forces, and consequently on her budget: which highlighted a third, and probably the most serious, contradiction implicit in her imperial situation. For another reason for Britain's expansion in the nineteenth century had been the protection of her commercial and financial interests in the world, which the paraphernalia of empire in other ways was inimical to. The cost of empire, both financial and, as we have seen, through its effects on the societal values of the day, undermined the health of the economic system it was also seeking to defend. In this sense it can be said that late nineteenth-century British imperialism was both capitalist and anti-capitalist, at one and the same time.[32]

These contradictions made nemesis inevitable at some period; and the only reason why it did not come sooner was that circumstances were kinder to Britain before 1945. Before 1880, she was operating in a kind of power vacuum outside Europe, with none of her major rivals greatly interested in competing with her there. After 1880, they did begin competing, which caused problems, but not half the problems that would have arisen had they *combined*. Until the early 1920s, the rebellions that periodically broke out against British colonial rule also generally came singly, and unaided by powerful outsiders, which made them manageable, if sometimes only just. Lord knows what might have happened if the Boers and the Indians had mutinied at the same time, with the Germans and the Russians coming – as they sometimes threatened to do – to their aid. That this sort of conjunction never took place was due partly to some clever diplomacy on Britain's part, partly to some skilful governing, and partly to sheer luck. The British empire's achievement in keeping the world at bay during the nineteenth and much of the twentieth centuries was a reflection, therefore, not so much of its relative power at that time, as of the indulgence, for various reasons, of other states.

This may seem to belittle it, but really it is only belittling some of the pretensions that used to surround it. Even stripped of those pretensions, it was a remarkable phenomenon: the most extensive formal empire ever known to man, with constructive achievements to its credit which only the much less scrupulous Romans probably ever exceeded. The men who were the agents of its acquisition and then its administration were a mixed bunch of villains, adventurers and idealists, with motives ranging from Christian philanthropy to pure greed, and more than a touch of madness, perhaps, about some of them, but all of them were privileged, and most of them aware of it, to be involved in something considered out of the ordinary, even 'great'. The *principle* may have been wrong: the subjugation by the natives of one state of the natives of others without consent but, in a way, that was inevitable with the world as it was, and if it was taken advantage of to Britain's benefit, it was not taken advantage of as much as it might have been. If the dependent empire was a standing temptation to some Britons to exploit it mercilessly, it also furnished an inspiration to others to acts of heroism and lives of self-sacrifice which subsequent generations must both admire, and envy their perpetrators the opportunities for. It was men like this who saved the empire from being *merely* a milch-cow for voracious capitalists, or a vast open-air seraglio of sexual opportunity, or an adventure playground for retarded public schoolboys to test their macho mettle in. It was always something more than that.

Is it not also arguable – today, in the early twenty-first century, more than it was, perhaps, almost 40 years ago, when the first edition of this book appeared – that empires may not necessarily be the worst things to befall their subjects, if they protect them from the kinds of forces that fill the vacuums that are left when they disband? Governments are not always the most powerful or cruel of masters. They can protect people from other cruelties: their own among themselves, for example; foreign aggressors; or natural afflictions, like an unreliable climate, or wild beasts; or a free-roaming capitalism, red in tooth and claw. When Britain departed from her colonies, their people were not left simply to themselves, but more vulnerable than they had been to exploitation by others: home-grown tyrants, local mafias, multinational corporations, the hand of God revealed through drought and famine, and the basic instincts of xenophobia and war. These can be resisted, but are not always resisted successfully. Since the British empire fell, the collapse of other empires has reiterated those dangers; in particular, of course, the Soviet Union (or Russian empire) and the Yugoslav confederation (or Serb empire), neither of whose peoples was left demonstrably better off under 'freedom' than they had been when they were in chains. It may be that this was, or will turn out to be, a price worth paying for national independence. The point is, however, that there *is* a price – in instability, exploitation, violence and death – to be paid.

This is probably the sunniest slant one can put on the legacy of the British empire, in so far as it affected its subjects; the best case that can be made out for it. It is an idealised way of looking at it, of course; but that is because so many of the empire's agents were idealists. That should not be forgotten, in the general rush to condemn imperialism since the fall of the European empires – and in the light of its resuscitation by the United States (of which more in Chapter 12). Many of the people who ran the British empire – it is impossible to say how many, but it may have been most of them – were honourable men (usually men), who were not out for their own profit or gratification, but wished to benefit humanity, as the Good Book had told them to, and believed that selflessly serving 'their natives' was a way to do this. Many of them were not even racist. The fact that things often turned out badly should not necessarily be ascribed to their motives, as is often done: perhaps because people need to think that bad things must be done for bad reasons. (So, for example, if you opposed the invasion of Iraq, you had to believe it was done to grab Iraq's oil.) The converse of this, of course, is to think that if you do something for a pure motive, it must be right. Tony Blair ('God will be my judge') was like that. In fact, bad results very often follow from the best of motives: because of the law of unintended consequences; because, in this case, alien societies are complex and sensitive things to start interfering with – those are the two main reasons for most of the messes created by British imperialism; and because the practice and experience of imperialism can be corrupting. Henry Morton Stanley offered the last as his best excuse for the appalling atrocities committed by two upper-class members of one of his expeditions in Uganda in 1888. One of them, James Sligo Jameson, of the Irish whiskey family, had, as Tim Jeal describes it, 'purchased an eleven-year-old girl and given her to cannibals so that he could watch her being stabbed to death, cut up, cooked in a pot and eaten, while he made sketches'. These men were 'not originally wicked', claimed Stanley. But

> circumstances had changed them ... They were suddenly transplanted to Africa and its miseries. They were deprived of butcher's meat & bread & wine, books, newspapers, the society & influence of their friends ... until they became but shadows, morally & physically, of what they had been in English society.[33]

Whether or not this is adequate as an excuse, there is some truth in it as an explanation of why white men could 'go bad', as E. M. Forster put it in *A Passage to India*, 'in the tropics'. Maybe it helps explain many of the other most atrocious acts of the British in Kenya, say, or India; or of the American military in Iraq. Together with all those other reasons for not relying too much on 'motives' to guide your actions – generally judgement is a better guide than morality – it must constitute a powerful argument against imperialism, however well-intentioned; possibly *the* most powerful one.

Another was its impact on Britain; most of whose own people had also been subjects of her empire in a sense, and, as we have argued above, been victimised by it to a great extent. It had also – as in the Soviet and Yugoslav cases – protected them from something: capitalism, or the full rigours of the market, or the consequences of their own industrial inefficiency, or whatever (it comes to the same thing really), which consequently then hit Britain forcibly – whether for good or ill is a contentious issue – when that protection was withdrawn. This was probably the empire's greatest significance, so far as Britain was concerned. It cushioned her from the implications of her decline in the world, both diplomatic and industrial, which began around 1870 and continued steadily from then on. In a way, it was a symptom of that decline, acquired (much of it) to stave it off; it also aggravated the decline ultimately, by enabling Britain to postpone the economic measures that seemed to be necessary to arrest it. By so doing, however, it also saved her, albeit temporarily, from some of the more unpleasant and even possibly destructive consequences of those measures (for who can tell how successful red-in-tooth-and-claw capitalism will be in the long term?); and gave an added lease of life to a certain set of social values which seemed admirable at the time, and for which some people afterwards still felt a sneaking regard, although it stood little chance, in this new age, of surviving the teeth and the claws.

Without this protection, Britain inevitably declined. This had been foreseen decades back, especially by the imperialists of the empire's great heroic age, who – however wrong they may have been in other ways – were nearly always the most *prescient* men and women of their time. One of their prophesies is worth quoting at length, because of its accuracy, which is almost uncanny. It comes from an article Lord Curzon published in January 1908, in which he painted this picture of a Britain (or England) of the future, bereft of her empire, and so left to fend against the teeth and claws for herself.

> England, from having been the arbiter, would sink at the best into the inglorious playground, of the world. Our antiquities, our natural beauties, our relics of a once mighty sovereignty, our castles and cathedrals, our mansion houses and parks, would attract a crowd of wandering pilgrims. People would come to see us just as they climb the Acropolis at Athens or ascend the waters of the Nile. A congested population, ministering to our reduced wants, and unsustained by the enormous demand from India and the Colonies, would lead a sordid existence, with no natural outlet for its overflow, with no markets for its manufactures beyond such as were wholly or partially barred to it by hostile tariffs, with no aspiration but a narrow and selfish materialism, and, above all, with no training for its manhood. Our emigrants, instead of proceeding to lands where they could still remain British citizens and live and work under the British flag, would be swallowed up in the whirlpool of American cosmopolitanism, or would be converted into foreigners and aliens. England would become a sort of glorified Belgium. As for the priceless asset of the national character, without a world to conquer or a duty to perform, it would rot of atrophy and inanition. To use Wordsworth's splendid simile – 'the flood of British freedom would perish in bogs and sands, and to evil and to good be lost for ever'.[34]

There we have it almost all: the economic decline, the narrowing of horizons, the loss of national identity, the tourists, consumerism, Americanisation, Australian republicanism. It must have appeared a bleak prospect in 1908. But one can get used to such things.

So, the British empire both stemmed from Britain's history, and diverted it, but not for long. It also diverted other countries' histories, to different degrees and for varying lengths of time. What its contribution overall was to human progress, or regression, or whatever is difficult to say. In its final days, some extreme views of this were expressed. A few were surprisingly self-denigrating. In 1965, one Colonial Governor, no less (Sir Richard Turnbull of Aden), told Denis Healey, the visiting Defence Secretary, that when the empire did finally sink 'beneath the waves of history', it would leave just 'two monuments' behind it: 'the game of Association Football, and the expression "Fuck Off"'.[35] That was a dispiriting assessment. It was also a faulty one. Association Football has no place among the legacies of the empire. Cricket was the imperial game (and arguably the greatest of all Britain's gifts to the civilisation of the world). Football spread in the wake of Britain's *informal* influence. It represents the elemental forces that gave rise to the empire originally, and which still survive. *They* did not 'fuck off', even though they were often told to. In this sense, whatever happened to the substance and the trappings of the British empire, imperial*ism* – the underlying motto of this book, though we have concentrated on its more formal manifestations – never did truly sink beneath history's waves.

Notes

1 In the Caribbean: Bermuda, St Vincent (independent 1979), Dominica (independent 1978), Montserrat, the Virgin Islands, the Cayman, Turk and Caicos Islands, Antigua (independent 1981), St Lucia (independent 1979), St Kitts and Nevis (independent 1983), Anguilla; in the South Atlantic Ascension Island, St Helena, Tristan da Cunha and the Falkland Islands; in the Indian Ocean: the Seychelles (independent 1976) and the (uninhabited) British Indian Ocean Territory; in the Pacific: the Solomon Islands (independent 1978), Pitcairn, the New Hebrides (independent as Vanuatu, 1980), and the Gilbert and Ellice Islands (independent as Tuvalu and Kiribati, 1979). In 1955, Britain annexed her last colony: the island of Rockall in the north Atlantic.

2 On the economic effects of imperialism on the ex-colonies, see D. R. Headrick, *The Tentacles of Progress: Technology Transfer in the Age of Imperialism, 1850–1940* (Oxford UP, 1988); D. K. Fieldhouse, *Black Africa 1845–1980: Economic Decolonisation and Arrested Development* (Allen & Unwin, 1986).

3 *Parliamentary Debates*, 4th series, 179 (1908), c. 419.

4 E. S. Montagu, *An Indian Diary* (Heinemann, 1930), p. 136.

5 Fatma Mansur, *Process of Independence* (Routledge, 1962), *passim*.

6 F. Fanon, *The Wretched of the Earth* (Allen & Unwin, 1965), *passim*.

7 Sir Frederic Rogers, quoted in W. D. McIntyre, *The Imperial Frontier in the Tropics, 1865–75* (Macmillan, 1967), p. 230.

8 See L. H. Gann and P. Duignan, *Burden of Empire* (Pall Mall Press, 1968), Chapter 22; M. Perham, *The Colonial Reckoning* (Collins, 1963), *passim*; D. A. Low, *Lion Rampant* (Cass, 1973), Chapter 6.

9 On all this, see Bernard Porter, *The Absent-Minded Imperialists* (Oxford UP, 2004), especially Chapter 12.

10 Clive Bell, *Civilisation* (Chatto, [1928], 1938 edn), p. 209.

11 Taken from en.wikipedia.org/wiki/British_Asian

12 Speech reported in the *Guardian*, 19 April 2001.

13 M. Thatcher, 'Don't undo what I have done', *Newsweek*, April 1992; reprinted in the *Guardian*, 22 April 1992.

14 M. Beloff, *The Future of British Foreign Policy* (Secker & Warburg, 1969), pp. 3–4.

15 C. Holmes, *John Bull's Island: Immigration and British Society, 1871–1971* (Macmillan, 1988); Panikos Panayi, *Immigration, Ethnicity and Racism in Britain, 1815–1934* (Manchester UP, 1994). Powell's speech, prophesying 'rivers of blood', was delivered at Birmingham in April 1968.

16 B. J. Porter, '"Bureau and barrack": early Victorian attitudes towards the continent', *Victorian Studies*, xxvii (1984), 407–33.

17 *The Economist*, 2 June 1979, p. 34.

18 See B. J. Porter, *Britain, Europe and the World 1850–1982: Delusions of Grandeur* (Allen & Unwin, 1983), pp. 127–31.

19 See, for example, W. B. Gwyn and R. Rose (eds), *Britain: Progress and Decline* (Macmillan, 1980), especially the first chapter, by Gwyn; I. Kramnick (ed.), *Is Britain Dying? Perspectives on the Current Crisis* (Cornell UP, 1979); A. Gamble, *Britain in Decline* (Macmillan, 1981); and T. Nairn, *The Break-Up of Britain* (NLB, 1977).

20 G. C. Allen, *The British Disease* (Institute of Economic Affairs, 1976), p. 33.

21 T. Benn, *Out of the Wilderness: Diaries 1963–67* (Arrow, 1988), p. 461.

22 For example, Lord Young of Graffham, *Enterprise Regained* (Conservative Political Centre, 1985), pp. 5–6.

23 See above, pp. 247f.

24 Margaret Thatcher's lack of empathy with her fellow Commonwealth prime ministers is illustrated in her memoirs: *The Downing Street Years* (HarperCollins, 1993), pp. 167, 517–24.

See also B. J. Porter, 'Wealth or Commonwealth? The history of a paradox', in R. Maltby and P. Quartermaine (eds), *A Common Culture?* (University of Exeter Press, 1989).

25 *Weekend World* (LWT), 16 January 1983, reported in *The Times*, 20 January 1983.

26 P. Shore, *Europe: The Way Back*, Fabian Tract 425 (1973), p. 11.

27 Calculated from tables in *Annual Abstract of Statistics 1969* (HMSO, 1970), pp. 239–40; and *Annual Abstract of Statistics 1983* (HMSO, 1984) pp. 253, 255.

28 See T. Smith, *The Pattern of Imperialism: The United States, Great Britain, and the Late-industrializing World Since 1815* (Cambridge UP, 1981); B. R. Tomlinson, 'The contraction of England: national decline and the loss of empire', *Journal of Imperial and Commonwealth History*, xi (1) (1982), 58–72; and L. Freedman, 'Whose crisis? Britain as an international problem', in Kramnick, *op. cit.*, p. 206.

29 Quoted in Gwyn and Rose, *op. cit.*, p. 20, n. 10.

30 J. Morris, *Heaven's Command* (Faber & Faber, 1973); J. Morris, *Pax Britannica* (Faber & Faber, 1968); and J. Morris, *Farewell the Trumpets* (Faber & Faber, 1978).

31 Although the new National Curriculum in History published in 1990 did find a minor place for it, as an optional study unit at 'Key Stage 3'.

32 This theme is elaborated in Porter, *Britain, Europe and the World*, Chapter 12.

33 Tim Jeal, *Explorers of the Nile* (Faber & Faber, 2011), pp. 372–3.

34 Lord Curzon, 'The true imperialism', *Nineteenth Century*, lxiii (1908), 157–8.

35 D. Healey, *Time of My Life* (Penguin, 1990), p. 283.

12 Coming out of the closet: *circa* 2000

Beginning this new chapter nearly ten years after writing the last sentence of Chapter 11, I was glad I made that proviso about imperialism's never really going away. It meant that I did not leave readers totally unprepared for the extraordinary events of the start of the twenty-first century, in Kosovo, Sierra Leone, Afghanistan and Iraq in particular, which were widely interpreted at the time as a continuation or revival of precisely the phenomenon that had been the subject of this book. 'It was an old colonial war,' wrote the novelist John le Carré of the 2003 'Coalition' invasion of Iraq, 'dressed up as a crusade for Western life and liberty.'[1] Certainly, there were many similarities. Because Britain was intimately involved in these events, there is a case for saying that they should be included here, as part of our main narrative. Opinions can differ over whether they really do qualify as 'imperialism', rightly understood. In some ways, it is still too early to say. It certainly depends on what becomes of those countries in the future as to *how* 'imperialistic' these adventures can be considered. (The longer the occupying forces remain, the more obviously colonial the situation will be.) But the question is at any rate worth considering, against the perspective provided by Britain's earlier imperialism, as described in the previous chapters: whether we then decide to regard these recent events as an integral part of the British imperial story, or as just an odd little epilogue. That will be up to readers to judge.

An American empire?

The leading actor in these events, of course, was the United States of America; whose own 'imperialist' credentials, therefore, need to be considered first.[2] Of course, it was not new for her to be seen in this way. Leftists had been characterising America's expanding capitalism as 'imperialistic' for decades: in the sense, that is, that early and middle nineteenth-century British 'informal' imperialism had been. There was also fairly widespread agreement, at any rate outside America, that most of her military, political and secret intelligence interventions in the world ostensibly against communism – Vietnam, for example, and Chile – were essentially 'imperialistic' too. This was common currency. The difference now was that it was coming to be acknowledged by the political Right. People began actually defending American imperialism – even flaunting it. This *was* new.

It started after the USA's invasions of Afghanistan in 2001 and Iraq in 2003. The rationale for both those adventures – plausible in the former case – was that she was defending herself against a repetition of the Al-Qaeda terrorism of '9/11', the murderous attacks of September 2001 on the New York Twin Towers and the Pentagon. But most observers accepted that an invasion of Iraq had been on the books of the

'Neo-Conservatives', the people who rose to power with President George W. Bush, long before then. It was part of a broader agenda, of American global domination in the future; its source is usually traced to a think-tank called the 'Project for the American Century', which was supposed to be influential in high quarters then.[3] There was always going to be a response to 9/11, of course; but this group's rise to power (it was said) determined that it would be responded to in this 'imperialist' way. It was not called that at first. There was some pussyfooting. The columnist Mark Steyn suggested that the squeamish could 'give it some wussified Clinto-Blairite name like "global community outreach"', if they preferred. But it was still imperialism, he insisted; and all the better for it.[4] Others were less diffident. 'People are now coming out of the closet on the word "empire"', wrote the right-wing commentator Charles Krauthammer early in 2002.[5] Sure enough: 'I prefer the more forthright if also more controversial term American Empire,' said former Bush speechwriter David Frum a little later, '– sort of like the way some gays embrace the "queer" label.'[6] People even started making favourable historical comparisons with the old British empire. 'Afghanistan and other troubled lands today cry out for the sort of enlightened foreign administration once provided by self-confident Englishmen in jodhpurs and pith helmets,' exclaimed a particular admirer.[7] The Roman empire also came back into favour. (Ancient historians suddenly found themselves 'relevant'.[8]) That was a striking change, for a people that had always prided itself on its unique purity in this regard, as a nation – as one commentator put it in 2000 – 'with imperial capabilities but without an imperial mind'.[9]

But was this really imperialism? Most other Americans still seemed reluctant to admit it. Their public leaders certainly were. 'We don't do empire,' asserted Defense Secretary Donald Rumsfeld, quite simply.[10] 'If we were a true empire,' agreed Vice-President Dick Cheney in January 2004, 'we would currently preside over a much greater piece of the earth's surface than we do. That's not the way we operate.'[11] And from the very top: 'we have no desire to dominate, no ambitions of empire': that was President Bush in his 2004 State of the Union Address.[12] The nearest anyone in the contemporary US administration came to accepting the word was the fine distinction that National Security Adviser Condoleezza Rice drew on one occasion between 'imperial', which the US was perforce, and 'imperial*ist*', which implied, she thought, something entirely different.[13] No-one in authority would admit to *that*. It would have been difficult for them to. One of the things that obviously stood in its way was the Americans' great founding myth, that their nation had actually been forged on the anvil of a struggle *against* an empire. As well as this, 'imperialism' had accrued a sackful of new negative connotations to itself over the past half-century, in relation to both the old European empires (including Britain's) and what President Reagan had called the 'evil' Soviet one. It was a slur to be avoided if possible.

Historians, however, should not be discouraged by slurs. If the cap fits, they should insist that it be worn, whatever disreputable wearers it may have had previously. A case can certainly be made out for regarding America as a genuine successor of those earlier empires. As early as the late eighteenth century, she had been widely tipped to replace Britain eventually as the world's great global imperial power.[14] Between then and the twenty-first century, she showed her imperial slip quite frequently: westward expansion, the 1812 war (for Canada), the Mexican war, Cuba and the Philippines, and so on. That was at least as powerful a national tendency as the more bruited 'republican' one. So its re-emergence in the early twenty-first century should not have come as a complete surprise. After the collapse of the Soviet Union, the USA dominated the world economically and militarily, probably to a greater extent than any single nation had ever dominated it before. One count of American military and naval bases in the world in 2002 found them in 40 different countries.[15] 'A political unit that has overwhelming superiority and uses that power to influence the internal behavior of other states, is called an empire,' wrote American national security expert Stephen Peter Rosen in June 2002. 'Because the United States does not seek to control territory or govern the overseas citizens of the empire, we are an indirect empire, to be sure, but an empire nonetheless.'[16] That was probably the kindest construction to put on all this. It fits Condoleezza Rice's formulation quite neatly. There was widespread agreement among impartial commentators that America had indeed become an 'empire'. (An exception was Martin Woollacott of the *Guardian*, who urged his readers not to 'call this empire, lest it become one', but that seems somewhat delphic.[17]) The question remained, however: was she also imperial*ist*? The two do not have to go together, though they usually do.

That depends on two things. The first is America's intentions. Did she *wish* to rule or dominate, and for what reasons? The second is semantics. Can these intentions be *defined* as 'imperialist'? On the first point, American leaders made a great deal of their reluctance to rule other peoples directly, but we have shown in this book, that this does not necessarily preclude imperial motives, by other ways of looking at them. Hence 'informal imperialism'. That could have taken two forms in America's case. One was a desire to dominate other countries economically. One way of doing that, it is sometimes said, is through 'globalisation', which is supposed to be fair and a means of prosperity for all participating countries, but in fact advantages (say the critics) the strong.[18] This is no place to go into that debate, important though it is; suffice it to say that very similar arguments could – and were – put on both sides of the question of 'free trade', which underlay what is now generally taken to be Britain's 'informal' empire in the early and mid-nineteenth century. Much more specifically, some critics accused America of having gone to war with Iraq in 1993 and 2003 in order to acquire or at least secure its oil fields; a suspicion that was supposed to be borne out by the very close ties the Bush administrations (I and II) had with the American oil industry. If that were true, it must obviously count as 'capitalist imperialism', in a much more direct way.

Even if not, however, the USA is not necessarily off the hook. The reasons her leaders gave for invading Iraq in the second (2003) case were, first, self-defence, against the threat of Iraq's supposed 'weapons of mass destruction' (or 'WMDs'); and, second, 'regime change': the toppling of a brutal dictator, and the spreading of democracy in the Middle East. Self-defence should clearly *not* count as 'imperialism', although Bush II's extension of the notion to allow it to be 'pre-emptive' muddied the waters here rather; especially when after the second Iraq War there turned out to be probably no threat – no WMDs – that required to be pre-empted at all. Stopping genocide, as in Kosovo, is also not in itself imperialistic. The problem comes when that slides into what was called 'regime change'. The question here, of course, is not whether or not this was 'right', but whether or not it can be regarded as 'imperialistic'. The first is a matter of judgement, which has no place here; the second, a question of definition.

Bush, in his 2004 State of the Union message, admitted that America had what he called a 'mission', to spread 'democratic peace' in the world. This meant imposing her values. That might be regarded as a form of 'cultural' imperialism in itself. The only way of possibly avoiding this implication is if the values that are being imposed can also be presented as 'universal' ones. Then it would be a question of 'enlightenment', or 'liberation', rather than a genuine imposition. This was a widespread American view. It was bolstered by the belief of some Americans that their own polity and society marked the peak of human development, the 'End of History', no less,[19] to which the rest of mankind (and womankind) was progressing in any case. So they knew the way. That qualified them to lead others along it. This of course is what many other empires in history have also maintained, and probably genuinely believed, including certainly the British,[20] which means that the mere *claim* to be 'enlightening' or 'liberating' people does not acquit a nation of 'imperialism' in itself. Americans sometimes spoke as though it did. Unlike real imperialists, their motives were pure. All America's foreign interventions had 'a high moral purpose';[21] her power was only used 'for the benefit of mankind';[22] 'America is the most *magnanimous* of all imperial powers that have ever existed';[23] ... and so on. But that is another common imperial delusion. (Britain also thought that hers was kinder than other empires.) Whether America really was different in this regard – less 'imperial' – depends not on this particular self-perception, but on whether *we* believe the values she was spreading, unlike the Romans', for example, or Spain's, or Napoleon's, or the British, or the Soviets', really were as 'universal' as she claimed they were. If they were, it either detracts from America's 'imperialism', or, by another way of looking at it, may justify it. But there are two further possibilities. The first is that what she believed to be universal values were in fact culture-specific constructs. The second is that universal values underlay her motives, but encrusted and distorted by cultural prejudices. The latter seems at least possible. Otherwise what was *capitalism*, for example, doing among the 'basic freedoms' she claimed to be spreading? 'Evangelical enthusiasm for open economies, western democratic norms and globalisation is not shared by all', pointed out the *Guardian* newspaper in January 2002.[24] Objectively, these would seem to be less a matter of fundamental principle than of permissible choice. Early imperial Britain, of course, had made exactly the same mistake – if mistake it was – of confusing this particular ideology with a universal truth. This is one of the closest parallels between the two imperialisms.

Obviously, this is a semantic question too. The problem with the word 'imperialism', and the reason why some do not like to apply it directly to the modern Americans, is that 'it carries so much baggage with it'.[25] Underneath the baggage, however, it is – we must constantly remind ourselves – *only* a word. People can define it as they like. It is perfectly permissible to use it in a way that excludes modern America's foreign policy adventures entirely, on the grounds, for example, that America did *not* seek territory. If so, then much of early- and mid-nineteenth-century British 'informal imperialism' would need to be exempted also; but that need not be problematic. By any broader sort of definition than this, however, American foreign policy in the early twenty-first century probably *should* be described as 'imperialistic', but not *as* imperialistic, perhaps, as it is possible to be. Questions *of degree* come in here. A long-term *de facto* occupation of Iraq and Afghanistan would be regarded as more – or at least more overtly – imperialist than a brief one. That is what had happened to Gladstone in Egypt. He wanted to withdraw, but found he could not. If he had been able to, his original invasion of Egypt would not today be seen as such a key imperialist act. (The two events are often compared.) America might well prove luckier than 1880s Britain in this regard. In that case, she could indeed claim to be different from earlier imperial powers. She would have managed to stick, broadly, at the 'informal' stage of imperialism, without moving on – as Britain did – to the more territorial kind. An imperial power, however, and probably an imperial*ist* one, she would remain. 'Domination', in various forms, has been taken as the essential defining quality of an 'empire' in this book. Only if she relinquished that – which came to look a possibility after the financial crashes of 2007–08 – would her underlying informal 'imperial' role go.

Comparisons have been made in this chapter between America's modern 'empire' (if that is what it was) and Britain's during much of the nineteenth century. Many of the similarities are striking, including, of course, this very debate about whether or not they should be *called* 'imperialist'. We shall return to this later, but before then we should consider one intriguing possibility that it opens up. Could there have been a direct connection between them, something linking the two 'empires'; a racial element, perhaps, each of them representing a separate stage of a single 'Anglo-Saxon–Celtic' imperialism, with America taking over the reins of world domination *from* Britain when the latter's grip slackened in the second half of the twentieth century? By this hypothesis, British imperialism did not die when it was thought to have done, but simply lived on, in Uncle Sam's clothes. Some earlier British imperialists would have welcomed this, incidentally; those who had always retained their affection for their American 'daughter', for example, and thought it the most natural thing in the world that she should carry the 'Anglo-Saxon' flame on when mother became too weak to do so. Kipling himself had urged the then President of the United States to 'Take up the white man's burden' (in partnership with Britain) in 1899.[26] Some twenty-first-century opponents of American imperialism also saw things in this light. One pointed out how many of the propagandists for it were not American-born, but came originally from Britain or ex-British colonies, obviously intent on foisting their bad old-world ways on the great Republic.[27] (Interestingly, a similar point could be made of a number of the leading imperial propagandists in Edwardian Britain. Foreigners often take to empires more than natives.[28]) What others took to be a 'new' American imperialism, therefore, was in fact a foreign incubus; nothing less than the old British empire, transplanted across the sea. If this is so, then it clearly merits a significant place on its own account in this book.

The reason it will not get this attention is that, underneath the rhetoric, American imperialism clearly had its own material and cultural roots, which differentiated it widely from the British. For a start, there is no real comparison to be made between nineteenth-century Britain and twenty-first-century America in terms of strength, with the US enormously more powerful than Britain ever was, particularly in military terms, even allowing for 'power inflation'. (Britain was never a *lone* superpower.) She was also far more milita*ristic*. There were other significant differences. America had no genuinely imperialist – 'jodhpur and pith helmet' – class. That could have been a disadvantage when it came to ruling the 'colonies' she conquered – or maybe not. The religious ('crusading') element may have been stronger than in Britain's case. 'Democracy' made a difference. So did 9/11. And so on.[29] Quite apart from all this, as a general rule, empires are not inherited or passed on from one power to another in this way. They arise out of circumstances, both domestic and international, peculiar to each in its time. It is easy to see the circumstances that gave rise to the modern American empire, without needing to resort to this idea of a 'continuation' from the British. So this is not why this short discussion of the former has been included here.

A new British imperialism?

The main reason is Britain's close *attachment* to it, during the premiership of Tony Blair (1997–2007). The chief manifestation of this was her strong support for America's war in Iraq, almost alone among the middling-sized powers of the world. That was bound to tar her with the new American imperialism to some extent. But questions about her own motivations remain. Was she imperialist in this sense – by association – for genuinely imperial reasons? And if she was, were these the *same* imperial reasons as America's? Is this really proof of the survival or resurrection of the old imperialism in Britain, therefore, quite apart from in America? For that does not automatically follow. The fact that Britain became hitched to an imperial power in the early 2000s did not necessarily make her one too.

Certainly, the material conditions for an imperial policy, which we have argued were usually crucial, seemed no longer to apply in her case. Britain's original imperialism had been the product of a brief moment in history when she had been economically preeminent, which could not be expected to last. Long before the end of the twentieth century she had clearly become a second-rank economy, and consequently only a middle-ranking 'power'. Her trading patterns had altered drastically from the time when the wider world had been more important to her than her European neighbours, which had been one of the reasons for her nineteenth-century political expansion overseas. Her late twentieth-century relationship with those neighbours, now her equals, was less happy than it might have been: a situation which, as we have seen, was sometimes blamed on imperial nostalgia. But no-one believed that a viable alternative now to her membership of the European Union was to go after another empire, to replace the one she had recently lost. She simply did not have the capacity, or, it seemed, the will. Though her army was larger than her neighbours', and with recent overseas experience (the Falklands, the first Gulf War), which may have indicated a post-imperial desire to punch above her weight, she certainly could not have invaded Afghanistan or Iraq successfully on her own. (Sierra Leone she could manage.) It could only be done 'piggy-back', as one contemporary commentator put it,[30] that is, on the shoulders of the nation that *did* have the material infrastructure to support a proper imperial role. Otherwise Britain should have grown out of – or been too small for – this kind of thing. Which is what makes it more surprising for her than for America that she went along with it. To some people, it appeared so incongruous as to be 'crazy'.[31]

Non-imperial motives for this course of action are not difficult to find. Blair obviously valued the American alliance *per se*. This – the 'special relationship' – was a policy with a long (if interrupted) pedigree in modern British history. Some of it was 'family' (America seen as Britain's 'daughter'); some derived from a shared anti-Europeanism; some of it had to do with common economic values, especially from Thatcher onwards: Britain being at least *more* free-marketist than continental European countries; and some was probably simply a matter of wanting to keep on the right side of the biggest beast in the jungle. This confuses the picture. It is conceivable that Blair could have supported American imperialism for non-imperial reasons. Not all commentators thought so, however. Some saw the corpse of the old British imperialism, long thought to be dead, breaking through the earth here.

Martin Jacques, former editor *of Marxism Today*, took this line early on. They had used to believe, he wrote, that they had 'laid the colonial ghost to rest', but they had turned out to be wrong:

> Once an imperial nation, always an imperial nation, even when the substance of power has long since disappeared. It is a mentality, a way of being and thinking. As a nation we still have a desperate need to believe that we still matter … Buried deep in the national psyche, in a way that affects each and every one of us, is a desperate desire to believe that we are the best: it is a part of our imperial genetic make-up, shared only by other imperial nations like the US and France.[32]

This went far to explain the imperial behaviour of nearly all Britain's prime ministers, 'especially those who dream of a place in history', long after the formal empire had dissolved. Blair was merely the most recent and blatant example (Figure 12.1). It was part of Britain's 'imperial hangover', shared by the whole people, as well as him.[33]

In Blair's case, the argument for this rests not only on his actions, but also on three important speeches he gave in the middle of his premiership: in Chicago in April 1999, in Brighton in October 2001 (the Labour Party Conference), and in Bangalore in January 2002. In the first – during the Kosovo campaign, and long before 9/11, incidentally – he urged the USA, at that time still under Clinton, to use its military power in harness with Britain to 'defend' and 'spread' throughout the world the 'values' they both cherished. His main concern there was to wean Americans away from 'isolationism' by persuading them that the dissemination of their values would also make them 'safer'. Another was to question the traditional United Nations principle (almost a sacred cow) of 'non-intervention', which had always, of course, been the latter's main bulwark against imperialism before. His excuse for this was that 'globalisation' had rendered it obsolete.[34] The Labour Party Conference speech advocated intervention in Africa specifically, in order to prevent genocide (like the recent episode in Rwanda) and other evils there. It also gave a promise not to 'walk away' from Afghanistan after the evil there had been dealt with, which implied, of course, a term of foreign occupation.[35] In Bangalore, Blair went further with this, claiming that they now knew how to put 'failed' states like Afghanistan together again, which answered those critics who argued that foreign occupations usually made things worse. (Free markets were the main solution.) As well as this, the Bangalore speech mused about the place of this new policy in the history of

Figure 12.1 Post-imperial imperialism. Steve Bell's take on the 'new' British imperialism of the early twenty-first century, specifically, in this instance, the invasion of Afghanistan.
Source: Guardian, 19 March 2002. © Steve Bell/All Rights Reserved.

British foreign relations generally, especially its continuity from imperial times, which may be thought to back up the 'old imperialism still alive' (or revived) scenario:

> For Britain, there is both challenge and opportunity. The days of Empire are long gone ... Britain has the fourth largest economy in the world but our land mass and population inevitably constrain us. We are not a superpower today, but we can act as a pivotal partner, acting with others to make sense of this increasingly global interdependence and make it a force for good, both in the interest of Britain and the wider world. In doing so, in being that partner with others, in this world coming increasingly closer together, I believe we have found a modern foreign policy role for Britain.
>
> In part, this is by virtue of our history. Our past gives us huge, perhaps unparalleled connections with many different regions of the world ...[36]

The disavowal of imperialism – 'the days of Empire are long gone' – was obligatory, of course. (We have seen how Bush did it too.) The word was still too provocative. Nonetheless, there are obvious *ingredients* of the kind of British imperialism that have been the subject of this book so far to be found in these remarkable statements. It is no wonder that these were widely picked up in Britain and elsewhere at the time.

It was ex-colonial subjects and leftists who first spotted the imperial signs, and predictably used them to lambast Blair. 'In essence,' wrote a Sri Lankan commentator just a week after the Chicago statement, '... he wants to go back to the era of the British empire on which the sun did not set'. He also objected to Blair's 'imperialist' assumption that western 'values' were good for everyone. 'Like everything else, human rights ... are not absolute and are relative. They are relative to culture. The present day human rights are relative to the west.' He saw Blair's project as less of an 'internationalist' one than a ganging up of 'the West' against the others, as part of the 'clash of civilisations' (between the West and Islam) that was going on at that time.[37] The *New Statesman* also thought that the speech, taken in conjunction with the intervention in Kosovo, meant 'in effect the revival of imperialism, with the liberal humanitarian's burden replacing the white man's burden'. (That Kipling phrase came up repeatedly in the months that followed.) But, reminded the *New Statesman*, 'imperialism is not usually a pretty thing'.[38] The strident anti-imperialist Richard Gott anticipated Martin Jacques in seeing this as part of a 'powerful imperial drive' that 'still survives in the British cultural make-up'; though he also remarked on how little this seemed to reflect the *popular* mood at this time.[39] Soon more specific and sophisticated comparisons were being made with nineteenth-century British imperialism. Gladstone in Egypt was a common one. The latter's well-known moralism also seemed to find an echo in the piously Christian Blair. Richard Shannon, a distinguished biographer of Gladstone, used this to try to warn Blair against following Gladstone too closely, in the light of the cropper the latter had come in Egypt.[40] The other popular comparison was with turn-of-the-century 'liberal imperialism'.[41] 'Liberals,' as another historian pointed out, truly, 'are often the best imperialists of all.'[42] What was common to all these analyses was a recognition of the 'sincerity' of Blair's motives (unlike Bush's, perhaps), but also of their naïvety.[43] 'At heart, he is one of those thoroughly decent, clean-limbed, former prefects who once found themselves manning the outposts of empire,' wrote another imperial historian, Lawrence James, just before the Iraq invasion. There was the line of descent. But history should have taught Blair that things were not as simple as that.[44]

At the same time as this, however, some others were coming to believe that maybe they *were*. A school of assertive pro-imperialists emerged, as in America, but perhaps more predictably than there, in view of Britain's more openly imperial history and the strain of nostalgia that still existed for it on the political Right. Defenders of the old empire had been poking their heads over the battlements intermittently for a few years now, usually only to be met by a fusillade of fire by the massed anti-imperialist guns ranged against them, but surviving these onslaughts bravely.[45] This may have helped fuel the new movement. (Not all 'new imperialists' were Rightists, however. A number of commentators noted how many of them had originally come from the Left.[46] Peter Hitchens even cited the 'fact' that its 'hottest-eyed supporters on both sides of the Atlantic' were 'ex-Marxists' as a reason why true Conservatives should not support the Iraq War.[47]) This happened in Britain at about the same time as in America. An article by the Economics Editor of the *Financial Times* in October 2001 is fairly typical; entitled 'The need for a new imperialism', its main argument was that there was no other way to solve the 'problem' of what he also called 'failed states'.[48] That last expression appears to have emanated from a British Foreign Office official called Robert Cooper, who in March 2002 published an influential essay that actually used the 'i'-word in this context: '[w]hat is needed ... is a new kind of imperialism, one acceptable to a world of human rights and cosmopolitan values'. The significance of this is supposed to have been enhanced by Cooper's former position, apparently, as a close policy adviser to Tony Blair.[49] Others joined in, including some more historians (Niall Ferguson: 'Welcome the new imperialism'),[50] and even a novelist (Philip Hensher: 'Let's be honest: we need to impose our imperial rule on Afghanistan').[51] The 'new imperialism' was becoming respectable in Britain too, albeit not in every quarter. (The fusiliers were still heavily armed and trigger-happy. Most of these pro-imperial declarations provoked lively responses, reminding people of the bloody record of Britain's original empire, which made her – as one anti-imperialist put it – 'the last country on the planet' fit to intervene in other nations' problems now.[52]) The obvious inference to draw from this was that old British imperialism had never really died. It was merely lying doggo, until this time.

There was clearly something in this. Of course, imperialism as an ideology never completely disappeared in Britain after decolonisation, any more than Naziism did in Germany since denazification, for example, or communism in Russia after the fall of the Berlin Wall. (These are not intended as analogies in any other ways. British imperialism should certainly not be equated with Naziism.) You can never get rid of every trace of history, even where the conditions have entirely changed. Britain even has its druids still. In Blair's personal case, the argument – that he represented a kind of extension of the older imperialism – is compelling: partly because of the striking similarities between his views of the place of morality in international affairs and Gladstone's; and partly because of that assertion of his in Bangalore that he had found a new 'role' for Britain (as 'pivotal partner') to replace or succeed her imperial one, at last. That must have been a reference to the notorious Dean Acheson gibe of 1962, which had riled her statesmen for decades, that she had 'lost an empire and not yet found a role';[53] its special attraction in this context was that it showed that Britain had *not* 'lost' her empire entirely, but was still making use of what was left of it: her long 'shared history' (!) with India, for example, and those other 'huge, perhaps unparalleled connections with many different regions' that could be made so useful now.[54] So it had not all been wasted. It is difficult not to detect here, as well as the 'sincerity', a certain post-imperial delusion of national grandeur. Blair could be regarded as a very late-born child of the empire in that sense.

This was one of the factors that encouraged him to string along with Bush. After 9/11, America abandoned her non-interventionism, just as Blair in Chicago had asked her to. British and American 'imperialisms' coalesced. They were not identical, however. It was sometimes hard to tell them apart, simply because the British sort was so swept along by the American, but there were important differences. There is much less suspicion in the British government's case, for example, of an 'oil' motive. There appears to have been genuine friction between Bush and Blair over a number of issues: the Israel/Palestine conflict; Guantanamo Bay (in Cuba, where the US was detaining hundreds of suspected 'Al-Qaeda' operatives, including some British, illegally, according to most international lawyers); and the much broader question of 'internationalism', and particularly the place of the United Nations, despised by the American administration but which Blair seems to have rated more. One of Blair's defences of the 'special relationship' was that it gave Britain the chance to put her *distinctive* input into American policy. His own best-known effort in this direction was his persuading of Bush in March 2003 to seek a specific UN mandate for his planned invasion of Iraq. That failed: the UN declined to sanction it, but Bush went ahead regardless, with Britain accepting the situation and following, but the episode may exemplify a real contradiction between the 'imperialisms' of the two of them. In the end, it signified very little, because American imperialism easily trumped the British sort when it came to the final deal. But it was there.

It consisted in this. America's imperialism was, broadly speaking, unilateralist: a matter of the USA alone – or at least in the lead – imposing her will on the world. That 'will' did not need to be intentionally oppressive, as we have seen. (This does not mean that it might not have been oppressive in effect.) America sought only, she said, to rescue peoples from tyranny, spread the blessings of freedom, and at the same time ensure the whole world's – including her own – 'security'. All this, especially the spread of 'free' values and security, was inter-connected. This was also Blair's message in Chicago, as we have seen; which then, two and a half years later, seemed to be dramatically confirmed by 9/11. (If 'they' had shared our values, they would not have attacked.) It was because he believed that America had taken on this message, presumably, that he so lavished his support on her thereafter. But America's view of it may not have been quite the same as his. First of all, it appeared – certainly in most official expressions of it in the post-9/11 months – to be a great deal cruder than Blair may have intended; metamorphosed into the doctrine that only American *forms* of freedom, security and the like were worthy of being imposed. This gave rise to a second difference. Because America was the only model of freedom and the rest, she was entitled to determine the whole process of global intervention, or imperialism, on her own: what should be the targets for it (Bush's 'Axis of Evil'); the means of intervention; and the 'nation-building' that followed from that. She welcomed co-operation, required it, in fact, both to give her actions moral legitimacy in the eyes of those who could not take that for granted, and to share the burdens with her, but only on her terms. Hence her contempt for United Nations' attempts – which turned out to have been much more successful than she had credited – to contain Saddam Hussein in Iraq. This was to be an American empire, in *this* sense: of the whole world moulded to the (free) American ideal. That was because America was not merely a nation, but much more. She was the 'shining city on the hill', the model for everyone. That was why she did not need to take account of others' views. We have seen that this, once again, is a common imperial myth.

It will have been harder for modern Britons to fall for it, except the most extreme philo-Americans among them. Britain *was* clearly 'merely' a nation now. No sane person thought *she* could be a model for the world. (It would have been difficult to, with the state of her railways.) She did not have America's self-confidence. In part, of course, this was a result of her long-term post-imperial decline, but it may also have reflected her people's greater knowledge and therefore appreciation of other countries compared with of most Americans.[55] This is one of the factors that are supposed to have made her administration of the part of Iraq she was given to look after at the end of the war (around Basra) more sensitive than the Americans' in Baghdad. Her former colonial experience and present Commonwealth ties could also have helped here. There is nothing like *ruling* a people to teach you to understand them, runs the argument; no amount of 'informal' imperialism can give you this. (On the other hand, the Basra–Baghdad contrast was exaggerated.)

Another result was to make British governments more genuinely internationalist than – at any rate – Bush's in America; more anxious, that is, to co-operate genuinely with other countries, respecting their different outlooks, rather than either insisting they follow you, or refusing (as the USA did over Kyoto) to play. The Blair 'doctrine' of foreign relations certainly talked the language of internationalism: '[b]y necessity we have to co-operate with each other across nations … We are all internationalists now … We are witnessing the beginnings of a new doctrine of international community …' and so on.[56] The role he saw for Britain in this was not as leader, or (early on) a whipper-in for America, but as – as we have seen – 'a pivotal partner, acting with others' for the mutual benefit of all. 'I stress the role is as *partner*.'[57] That rhetoric, at any rate, is very different from Bush II's. It is another thing putting Blair much closer to Gladstone: *vide* the latter's 'Concert' idea.[58] As with Gladstone, it may make Blair no less 'imperialistic'. But it was a different sort of imperialism. Its base was spread wider: with several nations sharing in it, rather than just one. (Some commentators suggested a revival of the old League of Nations mandates system to take care of it.[59]) That is why Blair used his more 'wussified' words for it. This gave it a different feel from Bush's *Pax Americana*, even if its impact might have been the same. We shall never know that for sure, because it was never allowed its head.

Nor can we be sure that the British people more generally went along with even this more liberal form of imperialism, as Martin Jacques thought they did. Even Blair's own party and government seem not to have shared it, at least with his (Blair's) degree of enthusiasm. This was *so personal* a policy to him that it is difficult to imagine any alternative Labour prime minister espousing it. No other leading politicians made speeches of the Chicago or Brighton or Bangalore kind. Jack Straw, Blair's second Foreign Secretary, was far plainer and more practical. (Robin Cook, his predecessor, had also talked of a 'moral' foreign policy; but in his case it seemed to refer chiefly to where Britain sold arms. He later resigned from the government over Iraq.) Straw's main contribution to the broader debate over imperialism was an interview in the *New Statesman* in which he attributed many of the world's present ills to British colonial intervention in the past, which was greatly resented by the old imperialists, of course ('the Foreign Secretary traduces the British empire: surely this must be the last Straw', chaffed one old soldier[60]); and it does seem difficult to square, without a great deal of special pleading, with the sort of interventionism with which he was loyally supporting his leader over in Afghanistan and Iraq. Perhaps it was a ploy to confuse the government's enemies, by distancing the government from the kind of imperialism they were explicitly accusing it of. That may have been necessary. The Iraq intervention was certainly not widely popular, apart from a few weeks at the peak of the fighting. (People tend to rally round when their 'boys' are under fire.) It actually attracted the largest anti-government demonstrations ever seen in British history, in London and elsewhere, on 22 March 2003. That the British people were unreliable on the quasi-imperial aspects of the policy ('regime change') was tacitly acknowledged by the government when it put 'weapons of mass destruction', threatening Britain (and within '45 minutes', it was implied), at the forefront of its public case for going to war. We have suggested already that WMDs could have made it a defensive (and so, by definition, not an imperialist) affair. It is worth noting that across in America George W. Bush did not need to emphasise this *casus* so much; with the result that his administration was less embarrassed than the British government was when, after the war, the WMDs were not found. That may be a measure of the relative degrees of true 'imperial' feeling generally in each country. The fact that Blair survived both this and the demonstrations was more an indication of his personal power in the country, and the weakness, perhaps, of the latter's democracy, than it was a reflection of any residual imperial feeling in Britain on a large scale. But then, had it not always been thus?

History and empire

The Iraq War seemed to show that imperialism was alive and well still in the twenty-first century, in ways that its nineteenth-century practitioners would certainly have recognised. The similarities between the two imperialisms are striking; not least, as we have remarked already, the debates that went on in both periods over whether 'imperialism' really was the right word for them. Attentive readers of the first four chapters of this book in particular may well feel that they have passed this way before. The later or 'new' imperialists were also very aware of these precedents. 'History' in fact became a key element in the contemporary debate over the phenomenon. It helped define it, for example, American foreign policy was 'imperialistic' because it resembled earlier imperialisms, or – alternatively – should be considered free of the stigma because it did not. Practical lessons were drawn from it: examples to emulate – all those jodhpur-clad young Englishmen – or, more often, warnings of what could follow from even the most tentatively imperial interventions, ranging from an Egyptian-type imbroglio (in Iraq), to ultimate 'decline and fall'. Even if one believed one's own empire could avoid these pitfalls – and every empire in history has contained optimists who foolishly took this view – one still needed to be aware of them. In this way, British imperial history suddenly came to be considered 'relevant' to the early twenty-first century; much as ancient Roman imperial history had been considered by the old British empire builders.

Academic historians are generally wary of attempts like this to 'learn' from their subject, probably because they are more aware than amateurs of its complexities.[61] Usually when people make direct comparisons between present and past events, it is with ulterior political motives, and crassly: think of all the ways the example of 'appeasement' has been misappropriated, for instance, in the years after 1938. (It cropped up in connection with Iraq, too.) Most historical parallels are more misleading than otherwise. Take, for instance, that favourite one between Iraq in 2003 and Egypt 121 years earlier: a seductive one, chiefly because of Bush's insistence, like Gladstone's, that he only intended to restore self-government, then withdraw; which was then stymied in the latter case, as it *may* be in the former's, by nationalist resistance, Muslim fundamentalism, and – possibly – a more acquisitive agenda underneath. These resemblances are striking. But they *are* only superficial. The differences between the two situations are arguably far greater. Ismael

Pasha, whom Lord Cromer considered 'a thief and a murderer',[62] was no Saddam Hussein; Egypt possessed no equivalent of 'WMDs' (even imaginary ones); the 'Mahdi' was not the same kind of threat as Osama bin Laden; and neither Blair nor Bush (emphatically) is a Gladstone. America's and Britain's domestic circumstances today, and the general situation of the world, are also hugely different. So it would be wrong to hazard any guesses at all about the future of Iraq from the Egyptian case. Because Gladstone got bogged down in Egypt, it did not at all mean that Bush and Blair *must* suffer the same misfortune in Iraq. America might even have found a way to buck the general 'decline and fall of empires' law. History does not teach us anything certain about that. Every historical situation is (mainly) unique.

If there are practical present-day lessons to be learned from these earlier manifestations of imperialism, then they will not be predictive ones. If history has any 'uses' in this context, they will be of other kinds. One thing it can do is drive out *bad* history: assumptions based on false readings of the past, such as littered the thoughts in the early twenty-first century of some American imperialists. We have met these already: the ideas that the only sort of empire is territorial, which is based on a historical misunderstanding; that you could not be an empire if you did not want to be: ditto; that America was the only great power in history with 'a high moral purpose': obvious historical nonsense; and that armies that invaded countries for honourable and benevolent reasons were invariably greeted by grateful populations throwing flowers. That last expectation, in particular, common before the Iraq invasion but sorely disappointed afterwards, showed a sorry state of historical ignorance. For that to have happened in Iraq (or Afghanistan) in the early 2000s would have been, as Anatol Lieven put it, 'contrary to historical precedent'.[63] That does not mean it is impossible: things do happen contrary to historical precedent; only that a study of history would have shown that it could by no means be relied upon.

The reasons for this are fairly straightforward, and may point out a more general lesson to be learned from past imperialisms – one we have alluded to more than once: that they may not *work*, even if their motives are of the best. Of course, motives are suspect in most cases – modern America is no exception here – but even the most genuinely benevolent ones may not have *beneficent* effects. We have seen this countless times in the history of the British empire: Christian proselytism in pre-Mutiny India, for example; 'indirect rule' in Africa;[64] and the forcing of free trade on many countries – all of them policies that were genuinely believed to bring huge blessings to the people they were directed at – having mixed results, at best. The road to post-colonial chaos is as paved with good imperial intentions as with bad. There are three common explanations for this. The first is that the 'benevolence' may in fact be a sham, or outweighed by more dubious and damaging motives. Second, it can be genuine, but misdirected: based on a faulty or biased view of what is 'good' for other people. (We have touched on this, too.) Third, even if it is neither of these things, imperialism may not be the best way to deliver it. People do not like even 'universal values' being forced on them by outsiders, especially at gun (or missile) point. There is, truth to tell, something of a contradiction at the heart of this. 'How could you simultaneously claim to be the enlightened banner bearer of civilisation and employ ferocious methods of coercion?', asks the historian Lawrence James, rhetorically, referring in particular to aerial bombing by the British in their mandated territories in the 1920s and by the British and Americans in modern Afghanistan. 'The old dilemma of imperialism remains unresolved.'[65] 'I know of no instance in history,' wrote the traveller and writer Alfred Lyall way back in 1882, 'of a nation being educated by another nation into self-government and independence; every nation has fought its way up the world as the English have done.'[66] Now, this may not be a general rule. It could even be claimed that certain events since Lyall's time have confounded it. The Americans in Iraq may manage to do the same. But these historical precedents at least illustrate the difficulties of 'nation building', at all times; and the cultural *sensitivity* required, at the very least, to carry it out. They may be a good additional reason – there are many others – for being wary of imperialism, even as an instrument of 'good'.

The great problem, however, is that it is difficult to avoid. Its recent reappearance corroborates this; a lesson that historians can learn from the present, perhaps, to set against all those other vice versa ones (learning from the past). In an imperfect world – it is a cliché, but obviously a true one – there are going to be inequalities of power and wealth, differences of ideology, national ambitions, historic grievances, insecurities, greeds and needs – the old Adam, perhaps – which will incite or encourage powerful nations to try to dominate others, and, in Lord Salisbury's 'age of the merest *Faustrecht*',[67] sometimes to succeed. For those who worry about such things, and over the obvious potential evils of imperialism, there are really only two possible grounds for optimism. The first would be some kind of international agreement or system of regulation that would act to prevent or at the very least police the current forms of imperialism. It would also need, of course, to address the problems that sometimes make imperialism necessary. That was one of the main objects of both the League of Nations and the UN when they were founded. Before then, in Britain's time, it was not yet an option. In the early twenty-first century, it was perceived – particularly by the Americans – as an inadequate one. The second best hope is that the dominant imperialism of the day – whatever its provenance – is at least relatively mild and benevolent. Then it might even be preferable to some of the alternatives, as we have suggested before, for example, in defending minorities. In Britain's case, the jury is divided over this (and the present book will offer no verdict). In America's, of course, we have not heard all the evidence yet.

'Benevolence' is a matter of opinion and judgement. 'Progress' may not be. Another 'historical' way of looking at present-day imperialism is as a vehicle for progress in the world: the means by which the inexorable development of humanity is carried along, whether we believe the direction in which it is being taken is a desirable one or not. That does not necessarily follow. (Only the Victorians believed 'progress' had to be 'good'.) There could be broad trends in history that are inevitable, yet may also be regrettable, and could even lead to our destruction. One likely-looking one these days, of course, is global capitalism, whose 'progress' appears unstoppable just now; and – just possibly – self-destructive. American imperialism is in the forefront of this trend – possibly pushed along *by* it. Back in the nineteenth century, British imperialism had very much the same kind of role. The main difference there was that Britain also had an unprogressive class on hand – the jodhpurred one – to soften the impact of the trend. The present-day USA, a purer capitalist society, lacks this. Consequently, one assumes, the 'progress' now will be all the faster. Nonetheless, this *is* something that links the two imperialisms historically. The continuity does not lie in the imperialisms *per se* – America simply inheriting Britain's imperialism from her, as we posited earlier – but in the underlying process that carried both of them. That was the 'progress' of the world towards globalisation, free markets, consumerism, liberalism and all the rest: the '*end* of history', *perhaps*. This is the fundamental historical trend. Modern imperialisms are just corks, bobbing along on the surface. This may be how to understand them best.

Notes

1 John le Carré, *Absolute Friends* (Hodder & Stoughton, 2003), taken from Robert McCrum's review of it in the *Observer*, 7 December 2003.
2 On this topic, see Bernard Porter, *Empire and Superempire: Britain, America and the World* (Yale UP, 2006).
3 Easily accessible through the Internet.
4 Mark Steyn, 'Imperialism is the answer', *Chicago Sun-Times*, 14 October 2001.
5 Quoted by Emily Eakin in '"It takes an empire," say several US thinkers', *New York Times*, 2 April 2002.
6 Quoted in Jeet Heer, 'US takes on burden of empire', *National Post* (Canada), 29 March 2003.
7 Max Boot, 'The case for American empire', *Weekly Standard*, 15 October 2001.
8 For the Roman comparison, see Robert Kaplan, *Warrior Politics* (Random House, 2001); and (in Britain) Jonathan Freedland, 'Hail, Bush. Is America the new Rome?', *Guardian*, 18 September 2002. Paul Kennedy made an unusual comparison with the Spanish empire, in 'Enemies on all fronts', *Guardian*, 16 January 2003. Very few commentators took Eastern empires as their comparators.
9 Charles Maynes, quoted in Philip S. Golub, 'Westward the course of empire', *Le Monde diplomatique* (English version), September 2002.
10 Reported in *Guardian*, 2 March 2003.
11 In answer to a question after his speech to the World Economic Forum, Davros, 24 January 2004; reported in *New York Times*, 25 January.
12 As reported in *The Washington Post*, reprinted in *Guardian Weekly*, 29 January–4 February 2004.
13 Quoted in Peter Beaumont, 'Now for the Bush Doctrine', *Observer*, 22 September 2003.
14 See Linda Colley, 'What Britain taught Bush', *Guardian*, 20 September 2002.
15 Jonathan Freedland, 'Rome, AD … Rome, DC?', *Guardian*, 18 September 2002.
16 Stephen Peter Rosen, 'The future of war', *Harvard Magazine*, May–June 2002.
17 Martin Woollacott, 'Something is being born, but let's not call it empire', *Guardian*, 20 June 2003.
18 Michael Hardt and Antonio Negri, *Empire* (Harvard UP, 2000), is one of many books equating globalisation with imperialism.
19 A reference to Francis Fukuyama's best-selling *The End of History and the Last Man* (Hamish Hamilton, 1992), which argued that modern American free market liberalism represented the culmination of the historical process.
20 See above, p. 274.
21 Paul Krugman, 'White man's burden', *New York Times*, 24 September 2002.
22 Heer, *op. cit.*
23 Dinesh D'Souza, 'In praise of American empire', *Christian Science Monitor*, 26 April 2002 (italics added).
24 *Guardian*, 7 January 2002, commenting on Tony Blair's Bangalore speech of 5 January.
25 Timothy Garton Ash, interview in *Frontline* (India), 28 May 2003.
26 See above, p. 46.
27 Heer, *op. cit.* These included, according to Heer, Dinesh D'Souza (India), Paul Johnson (UK), Mark Steyn, Charles Krauthammer and Michael Ignatieff (all Canada); plus Max Boot (born in Russia).
28 See Bernard Porter, *The Absent-Minded Imperialists* (Oxford UP, 2004), Chapter 10.
29 For a good overview of the similarities and differences, see Linda Colley, 'What Britain taught Bush', *Guardian*, 20 September 2002.
30 Kirsty Milne, 'Blair's like-it-or-lump-it message for the sceptics', *Scotsman*, 2 October 2002.
31 For example, Eric Margolis, 'Is Tony Blair crazy, or just plain stupid?', *Toronto Sun*, 16 March 2003.
32 On this last point, one wonders whether Jacques had ever visited Sweden.
33 Martin Jacques, 'The age of selfishness', *Guardian*, 5 October 2002.
34 Tony Blair, 'Doctrine of the International Community'; address delivered to the Chicago Economic Club, 22 April 1999.

35 Blair's speech to the Labour Party Conference, 2 October 2001.

36 Blair's speech to the Partnership Summit, Bangalore, 5 January 2002.

37 'The bare doctrine of Blair the bear', *Kalaya* (Sri Lanka), 28 April 1999. 'The clash of civilisations' refers to Samuel Huntington's celebrated book of that name (Simon & Schuster, 1996).

38 Leading article, 'Blair revives imperialism', *New Statesman*, 10 May 1999.

39 Richard Gott, 'The drive to intervene', *Guardian*, 20 May 1999.

40 Richard Shannon, 'History lessons', *Guardian*, 4 October 2001.

41 The first reference I have found is Seumas Milne, 'Throwing our weight about', *Guardian*, 11 September 2000. Thereafter the 'liberal imperialist' label becomes ubiquitous. An article in *Frontline* (India), 28 May 2003, asked three leading authorities – Timothy Garton Ash, Paul Berman and David Rieff – to comment on the term specifically.

42 Hywel Williams, 'The danger of liberal imperialism', *Guardian*, 4 October 2001.

43 For example, *Guardian* leader, 'Doomed to irrelevancy', 7 January 2002: 'his idealism and sincerity are persuasive, but …'; and Hugo Young, 'Blair has one final chance to break free of his tainted fealty', *Guardian*, 1 April 2003.

44 Lawrence James, 'The revival of benevolent imperialism', *Independent*, 20 March 2003.

45 Examples are Robert Rhodes James, 'Now that the sun has gone down', *The Times*, 3 November 1995; Trevor Lloyd's defensive *Empire: The History of the British Empire* (Hambledon, 2001); and Niall Ferguson's 'Empire' series on Channel 4 TV, 2003.

46 For example, Henry Porter, 'Radical mistakes', *Guardian*, 9 June 1999, and Tariq Ali, 'The new empire loyalists', *Guardian*, 16 March 2002.

47 Peter Hitchens, 'Not in our name', *Spectator*, 29 March 2003.

48 Martin Wolf, 'The need for a new imperialism', *Financial Times*, 10 October 2001.

49 This originally appeared as 'The post-modern state' in a collection of essays published by the Foreign Office, *Re-ordering the World: The Long-term Implications of September 11*. It was summarised in the *Observer*, 7 April 2002 (which describes Cooper as 'Tony Blair's foreign policy guru'), and is printed in full on that paper's website.

50 Niall Ferguson, 'Welcome the new imperialism', *Guardian*, 20 October 2001.

51 Philip Hensher, 'Let's be honest: we need to impose our imperial rule on Afghanistan', *Independent*, 17 October 2001. Hensher had recently published a novel, *The Mulberry Empire*, featuring the Anglo-Afghan wars of 1838–42, which he himself described as 'A slightly unusual thing these days – a 600-page epic in praise of imperialism and the British Empire in particular': University of Cambridge Press Release, 8 May 2001.

52 Milne, 'Throwing our weight about', *op. cit.* Other examples are: Seumas Milne, 'An imperial nightmare', *Guardian*, 8 November 2001; Maria Misra, 'The Empire strikes back', *New Statesman*, 12 November 2001 (this is the best argued of these); Mahmood Mandani, 'Misrule Britannia', *Guardian*, 8 February 2002; Randeep Ramesh, 'Amnesia with intent', *Guardian*, 18 November 2002, and Randeep Ramesh, 'Imperial history repeats itself', *Guardian*, 3 July 2003.

53 See above, p. 271.

54 See above, p. 298.

55 This is a familiar observation among Europeans who visit America: that their news media, for example, ignore the rest of the world (unless Americans are fighting there). It ties in with my own impressions from living and working (fondly) in America. I should like to get an exact figure for the number of adult Americans who carry passports; I have been told it is only 5–10 per cent.

56 Speech in Chicago, 22 April 1999 (see above, note 34).

57 Speech in Bangalore, 5 January 2002 (see above, note 36). Italics added.

58 See above, p. 83.

59 For example, Max Boot, 'The case for American empire', *Weekly Standard*, 15 October 2001; Ferguson, 'Welcome the new imperialism', *op. cit.*; David Rieff interviewed in *Frontline* (India), 28 May 2003.

60 See the *Sunday Telegraph*, 15 November 2002; and Sir Robin Ross's letter, from the Army and Navy Club, printed in the *Daily Telegraph*, 16 November.

61 See, for example, *Guardian*, 19 February 2003, in which several leading historians were asked which was the closest parallel with the contemporary Iraq situation, 'Munich' or 'Suez'. Most of them haughtily dismissed both.

62 Roger Owen, *Lord Cromer* (Oxford UP, 2004), p. 326.

63 Anatol Lieven, 'A trap of their own making', *London Review of Books*, 8 May 2003.
64 See Mandani, 'Misrule Britannia', *op. cit.*, showing how harmful the legacy of 'indirect rule' in particular was for Africa.
65 Lawrence James, 'The revival of benevolent imperialism', *Independent*, 20 March 2003.
66 Quoted in Owen, *op. cit.*, p. 169.
67 See above, p. 110.

13 After-image

Old empires do not die, nor even fade away – for a while, at least. Chapters 11 and 12 of this book have made this clear in the case of the British empire. Signs of the lasting impact of nineteenth- and early twentieth-century imperialism are all around us, in a thousand guises. Recognisably imperial attitudes still survive in certain circles, especially governing ones. Many of Britain's external policies in the first decade of the twenty-first century can be seen as mere extensions of the imperialism – military, economic or humanitarian – of her earlier years. American 'imperialism', in places like Afghanistan and Iraq, looks uncannily like an extension of that. A direct and unbroken line can also be drawn between what is often called Britain's 'informal' or 'free trade' empire in the nineteenth century, and 'globalisation' today. The creature is not dead yet.

It is also still with us in another way. When any great historical event or movement comes to an end, it leaves behind it certain myths. Sometimes those myths can be as powerful as the ideas that informed the event in the first place; bearing in mind that – certainly in this case – 'ideas' were arguably less important in determining the nature of the phenomenon (imperialism) than the material circumstances that lay beneath it. Freed from the trappings of the genuine article, and increasingly distant from memories of it, several ideas about British imperialism have taken on lives of their own in modern times. Many of these bear little relation to the reality of the old empire. Almost none takes any account of its complexity, which it has been one of the objects of this book to emphasise. This may be why they are often so potent. Grand and simplistic versions of events carry a peculiar attraction, with which more nuanced histories cannot hope to compete. This, then, is the newest manifestation of British imperialism in the modern world; as a ghost of past events, obscurely seen, but effective nonetheless.

Forgotten

One reason why these myths were able to take such hold is that they appeared in a virtual vacuum. During the 1960s and 1970s, Britons were largely ignorant about their empire. Its history was hardly taught at all in their schools; had not been, in fact, for most of the past century. (Hence Sir John Seeley's complaint in 1883, that from its invisibility in the school syllabuses of his day one would have thought that the empire had been acquired 'in a fit of absence of mind'.[1] Seeley is often misread here. *He* didn't think it had been acquired absent-mindedly.) The neglect of the subject in universities and colleges has been noted here already.[2] The general public seemed to take little intelligent interest in their empire, apart from the crises and scandals it threw up, plus cricket, and as an alternative to the 'Western' scenario for adventure films; and none at all in its history. For any who might wish to find out more, there were few reasonably objective books around for them to consult; most that existed were either polemical, for the politically committed, or anodyne, usually by ex-colonial hands. When a few more reliable general histories of British imperialism did start appearing in the 1970s, they were rarely directed to a lay readership: by their authors in some cases, and their publishers in others. (I initially conceived this book for the general reader. It came to be marketed, however, as a niche textbook.) For the mythmakers, who appeared on the scene in the later years of the twentieth century, therefore, there was no solid ground of popular knowledge to build on, or to inform their own ideas. (Most of them were approaching the topic from outside.) This made it easy – indeed, almost inevitable – for misunderstandings and over-generalisations to catch on.

Abroad, there were other reasons for this general ignorance, and more excuses. Being the subject of an empire, or its jealous rival, is bound to skew your understanding of it – as well, it has to be said, as enhancing your knowledge and empathy of how it works at its sharp end. You are unlikely to gain an overall view of an empire whose agents are, at that moment, taunting you with racist insults in one corner of it. (That was Edward Said's formative experience in Egypt.[3]) Your treatment is a crucial part of the picture, and often a criminally neglected one, in top-down histories of British imperialism, for example – and also of other empires: what a boon it would have been if a Said had been around to describe the atrocities of England's own Roman and Norman conquests, which both tended to get off rather lightly in the versions of them taught in English schools! – but it is probably not representative, and obviously not complete. On the other hand, what more can imperialists expect? This kind of reaction is a normal, even natural, concomitant of colonial conquest, and one reason – among others – for thinking twice before embarking on it.

It was no more reasonable to expect balance and sophistication from (non-colonial) foreigners. Foreigners see us as we present to them. (The same is true, of course, the other way around.) In the nineteenth and for most of the twentieth centuries, Britain's dominant image abroad was of a globe-straddling behemoth (those *circa*-1900 red-besplattered world maps had much to do with this), seeking to impose its will everywhere, and frequently coming into conflict with them – the other nations of the world, some of them with imperial ambitions of their own – along the way. In other words, it was *as* an empire that Britain appeared to everyone else; and as an *ex*-empire that she mainly presents today. Looking out from France, say, or Sweden, or Japan, quite apart from Australia or India or West Africa, it was (and is) difficult to view her in any other way. Of course, like her colonial subjects' or victims' perceptions of Britain, this approach contained a great deal of truth, often not seen or else pushed aside by stay-at-home Britons themselves. It is part of the picture. But it is still only a partial part.

Recalled

To this likely recipe for misunderstanding, or imperfect understanding, was added one further important ingredient in the 1960s and 1970s. Radicals discovered 'imperialism'. Some of them had known about it for years before, of course: indeed, my own first book dealt with the emergence of certain 'anti-imperial' ideologies as early as the 1890s,[4] and the story could be traced much further back.[5] Now, however, there were two differences. The first was that hostility to imperialism became almost universal, usually predicated on an analysis of it as a malevolent development of capitalism – this was the 1890s critics' particular contribution to the debate over empire – with pro-imperialists so far margin-alised as to become laughing stocks (quite literally; 'Major Bloodnok' in the 1950s BBC Radio comedy *The Goon Show* is an example). Not only was pro-imperialism rejected. Any nuanced view of the phenomenon was, too.

The second new development was that 'imperialism' came to the front of the stage as the fashionable explanation for almost every kind of – again malevolent – political, eco-nomic and social development in the world at that time. In order to perform this role, the word had to undergo something of a broadening in semantic terms, to cover kinds of domination beyond the merely 'formal' one. This built on work that had been done in the 1950s by imperial historians who had already pushed the definition of 'empire' out some way, by coining such terms as 'free trade' and 'cultural' imperialism, if only to enable them to understand better the dynamics of the 'formal' sort. That was entirely justifiable. (It has been the approach of this book.) But it also opened up a barrel-load of worms. 'Imperialisms' began to be spotted everywhere. A Google search today, for example, throws up – all these intended as serious uses of the word – internal imperial-ism (one part of a nation lording it over another); religious imperialism; linguistic imperialism; gender imperialism; adult imperialism (or 'adultism'); species imperialism (our poor subjected pets); educational and academic imperialisms; football imperialism; *reverse* cricket imperialism (Australia and the Indian subcontinent beating England); Starbucks imperialism (of course); and probably many more. There is even an anti-imperial imperialism, usually referring to the US takeover of the Philippines (from the Spaniards) around 1900. Some of these are perfectly valid extensions of the word – the last especially, as it happens. The point is, however, that diluting the term to cover almost any kind of 'domination' limited its usefulness as an analytical tool, as has been noted before; and encouraged the notion that 'imperialism' was ubiquitous. Combined with the almost universal opprobrium that by now was attached to the original phe-nomenon, this proved a seductive, but also obfuscating, mix.

You would expect this sort of thing abroad. What may be more surprising, however, was the way it caught on in Britain. The 'vacuum' was partly responsible for this. With imperial historians thin on the ground, and often suspected of imperial*ism* for simply taking an interest in the subject (I was, when I began teaching it at university in 1968), others stepped in. They came from all over. Some were from the political Left, their anti-imperialism re-energised in most cases by what they saw (rightly) as modern American 'imperialism', who were the ones who first came to regard both that and the old British variety as the source of most of the contemporary world's ills, and also of Britain's domestic reactionism. (Two good examples are John Newsinger's evocatively titled *The Blood Never Dried* (2000); and Richard Gott's more exhaustive *Britain's Empire: Resis-tance, Repression and Revolt* (2011), which stops, however, just after the Indian Mutiny.[6]) Others were 'straight' academic historians of Britain who were puzzled by the neglect of the imperial dimension to their subject as it had been taught to them at school and college, and suspected – rightly – that there must be more there than met the eye. So they set about uncovering it; often by looking in places that previous historians had been unaware of, or simply not thought worth bothering with. 'Propaganda' was one such area, pioneered by John MacKenzie in his path-breaking *Propaganda and Empire* of 1984, which revealed some of the traces left by the empire on popular culture in Britain after 1880; and was then followed up by a whole series of works teasing out others.[7] The sheer quantitative impact of this – quite apart from the quality of much of it – seemed over-whelming. The effect was to push imperialism from the dim background to the vivid foreground of the British historical picture for a while, obscuring the topics and themes that had traditionally taken the historians' eye, or else colouring them with its own patina.

To this was added the contribution of certain literary and cultural scholars who began doing the same thing as MacKenzie, but with 'high' culture: that is, exposing the previously neglected imperial or colonial dimensions to it.[8] This culminated with Edward Said's *Culture and Imperialism* (1993), following on his critique of western literary *Orientalism* (1978), and these two books laid the grounds of an immensely influential school of thought, interpreting almost every aspect of British nineteenth- and twentieth-century culture in imperialist terms. The idea here – a 'theoretical' one (that is, it had no empirical foundation) – was that the imperial 'discourse' of that time must have been impossible to escape. (Famously, even Jane Austen could not struggle free.[9]) So, not only was there more domestic 'imperialism' about than earlier historians had credited – this was the valuable contribution of MacKenzie and his school, but it also dominated, and so explained in retrospect, everything else.

Most of this new attention paid to British imperialism was critical of it, implicitly at least. But not all. While the Leftists, the MacKenzie-ites and the Saidists (MacKenzie's word) were busy building up the imperial edifice from one side, another team was approaching from around the back. These were the pro-imperialists: marginalised, as we saw, in the 1950s and 1960s, when imperialism had been damagingly associated with 'capitalist exploitation', but now riding the reaction in *favour* of capitalism that had begun (so far as Britain was concerned) in the 1970s, and came to fruition under Margaret Thatcher in the following decade. With capitalism rehabilitated, in some circles at any rate, historians like Niall Ferguson (whose original expertise was in the history of banking) began celebrating British imperialism (albeit with qualifications) for the very qualities and effects it had been denigrated for previously; seemingly unaware, incidentally, that these were emphatically *not* the qualities that had fired the last cohort of empire defenders, the 'Major Bloodnoks': old colonial paternalists who believed that what they had been doing was protecting their subjects *against* what was now being called 'modernisation'. Ferguson's book *Empire* was subtitled 'How Britain Made the Modern World'. It seemed to represent the opposite viewpoint to that of the 'post-colonialist theorists' (as the Saidists were more properly called); and did in fact do so in one very obvious way: in its more positive take on the legacy of imperialism. This was the aspect of it that was generally taken up in reviews, and most vigorously contested. Had the British empire been a force for good, or a force for evil? Behind this apparently stark dichotomy, however, there lay a common assumption. Both the antis and the pros agreed that the empire was a 'force'. It was this that confirmed the impression that was gaining ground, that imperialism had used to be a dominant aspect of Britain's national identity, and a means by which she had used to dominate the world. The 'after-image' of empire had grown to full size.

One other reason might be adduced to account for it. In one way at least, the empire actually became far more visible in Britain *as* a ghost, than it had been when it was 'alive'. This was largely the effect of the relatively mass migration of people from the ex-colonies into Britain that took place from the 1950s on, mentioned before in this book,[10] and of the cultural exoticisms the new settlers brought with them, especially their cuisines. Add to this the films, books and television documentaries featuring aspects of British imperialism that poured out in the last quarter of the twentieth century, and the stream of high-profile reminders by its former subjects of the harm it had done to them, usually accompanied by demands for retrospective apologies or material compensation; and it may not seem so very surprising that the British empire came to impinge more consciously as a cadaver, or ghost, than it almost ever had as a living and breathing creature.

Misunderstood

Although all this served to bring the British empire back into the limelight, which was much needed, little of it was necessarily conducive to any very subtle analysis. Subtle analyses of imperial history *were* going on at this time, in university History departments in Britain and the United States, in the hands of scholars who had worked at the various coal-faces of the relationship between Britain and her colonies, and who were aware also of the broader contexts of the imperial events and beliefs they described. Much of their work is to be found in the five volumes (and several 'Supplements') of the *Oxford History of the British Empire*, edited by Wm Roger Louis and published (the main volumes) in 1998–99; one of whose clear lessons was that nothing was as simple as the anti-imperialists, the pro-imperialists or the post-colonial theorists tended to assume, and especially with regard to Britain's supposed *power* to impose her will on her colonies. Imperial historians had always been aware of this. It is what the coal-face had taught them – and what the present book has tried to convey. The trouble was that these more nuanced approaches suited neither party in the major contemporary debate over British imperialism. Imperialists thought they denigrated or diminished their empire; anti-imperialists that they were providing excuses for it: giving 'comfort' to British reactionaries and even 'balm' to present-day American imperialists, for example, according to two critics of my own gentle attempt to 'revise' the fashionable view of a ubiquitous British popular imperialism in 2004.[11] Another problem could simply be (as suggested already) that versions of history with big 'themes' are easier to swallow and therefore to sell than sophisticated ones. Or, lastly, it may simply be, of course, that the imperial historians had got it wrong – were too narrowly empirical, perhaps, so that they couldn't see the wood for the coal.

For whatever reason or combination of reasons, this became the dominant 'after-image' of the British empire once it had come to an end (formally); the next and latest of its successive materialisations over the centuries. It had been a huge thing – supposedly. Estimates varied from a fifth of the world's land surface or population to the *Observer*'s ridiculous 'nearly half the planet' in 2011.[12] But in any case, it was the biggest empire in history (though this is debatable: it depends how you measure them); dominant; changing the world irreversibly; and profoundly altering Britain's own 'national character', of course. This myth (bearing in mind that 'myths' can be partially true) continued to have repercussions for years. Some were intangible, but still might have been important. One was a sense of regret, even grief, among certain classes in Britain for what they thought they had lost, which there were a number of alternative ways of expressing or exorcising: Enoch Powell, for example, did it by switching to a narrow 'English' nationalism combined (bizarrely) with free marketism.[13] For others, the knowledge of the scale of their nation's guilt provoked shame; a tendency to forgive the empire's successor-states for their worst failings or crimes ('who can blame them, after what we did to them?'); and constant efforts to make amends: through 'good works' in Third World countries, for example, sometimes in neo-colonial guises. Abroad, the collapse of her once-great empire aroused a definite sense of *Schadenfreude*, often directed at post-colonial Britons travelling or living there. This probably matters little on a personal level (most of us expatriates manage to cope with it), and can anyway hardly be compared with the racial abuse that many of Britain's imperial forebears used to heap on their colonial subjects, for which this could be regarded as a poetic payback. But who is to say what effect it still might have on higher, diplomatic relations between Britain and other countries? There were concerns that it might adversely affect US President Barack Obama's attitude to Britain, in view of his own Kenyan grandfather's experience at the sharp end of some of the declining British empire's worst atrocities.[14] Fortunately most of the signs – during a friendly and flattering US state visit to Britain in 2011,[15] for example – suggested that Obama was too big a man to let that influence him. But this might not be true of his successor, or of every other foreign leader.

Blaming Britain, still, was one thing. Some ex-colonial politicians, however, went further than that. Building on this idea of British imperialism as a 'huge' thing in the past, they came to see it, or at least present it, first, as an ever-present danger; and, second, as a convenient brush with which to tar any *value* that they saw as 'western', and so imperially imposed. The most flagrant example of the former was Robert Mugabe's repeated claims, either because he believed them or in order to curry votes, that Britain's criticisms of his regime hid an ambition to take back Zimbabwe as a colony.[16] That of course was unlikely, and based on a misunderstanding of Britain's relationship with 'Rhodesia', as it was called then, in colonial times. As we have seen, she had never run it as a proper colony, but had left that to the white prospectors and settlers.[17] That dereliction of duty was highly culpable, and might be thought to make Britain the last country in the world with the moral right to criticise Mugabe's regime, but it gave no ground for believing that she had any new 'imperial' designs – in the conventional sense – on Zimbabwe. And Mugabe wasn't the only African leader to exploit the 'imperial' bogey in this way. Omar Al-Bashir, President of Sudan, raised the same cry against critics of his allegedly genocidal suppression of Darfur in the mid-2000s.[18] When Colonel Muammar Gaddafi sought to stiffen his people's resolve against UN-backed intervention in the Libyan revolt of March 2011, he did it by traducing it as 'crusader colonialism'.[19] (That 'crusader' slant, in a Muslim country, gave it an even more potent spin.) Of course, these charges were bound to resonate among people with fairly recent experience of formal European imperialism, and reasonable suspicions of the more modern, American 'informal' sort. But they also testified to the exaggerated importance that may have been attached to imperial power at this time, with all Third World struggles being regarded, still, in terms of that, *versus* 'nationalism'.

It was when this anti-imperialism impinged on ideas and values, however, that it became most problematical. This stemmed in part from the old imperialists' belief, or pretence, that they were bringing western 'civilisation' – the only sort of civilisation, natch – to the '*un*civilised'. (Niall Ferguson's book *Civilization: The West and the Rest*, 2011, perpetuates the same idea today.) The questions this raises are legion. First, many imperialists did not *want* to spread western 'civilisation', because they were simply out for what they could get (or worse); because they feared it might unsettle the 'natives' and so pose problems of order; because they thought the natives were incapable of being civilised; or, in a few cases, because they came to prefer non-western civilisations when they grew familiar with them. Second, even when they might have liked to spread 'civilisation', they very often couldn't, because they didn't have the human resources to do so. (The British colonies in particular were run on a shoe-string.) Third, some of the features of westernisation they *did* spread were difficult to regard as 'civilised' by most meanings of that word: capitalist exploitation, European diseases, guns and alcohol, to mention just a few. Fourth, many of the others were at least arguably culturally spe-cific – the products of particular European societies – and hence not 'universal' enough to merit forcing on other societies. Free market capitalism may have been an example. Lastly, many of what *could* be regarded as 'universal' marks of civilisation or 'progress' were not 'western' alone, but were found in other cultures too, side-by-side with some admirable values that the West rather lacked. 'Enlightened' thinking never was a monopoly of the West, as the anthropologist Jack Goody has demonstrated in a number of books about India and China, the title of one of which – *The Theft of History* (2007) – makes plain what he thinks of the West's attempts to appropriate it. In other words, the idea that the 'West' was bringing 'civilisation' to the rest of the world was debatable, at best.

But it was *not* widely debated – and this had one unfortunate effect. Third World anti-colonialists, taking the imperialists at their word, came to see all 'western values' as simply that, and a tool of imperialism to boot, and to reject them outright for these reasons. That is easy to understand. No-one with any self-respect likes to have even virtue forced on him or her. So, for example, militant Islamists turned against anything *they* associated with the 'Great Satan'; 'human rights' appeared to one Sri Lankan com-mentator in 1999 (in response to Tony Blair's efforts to spread them) as 'not absolute', but 'relative to the present West, which has been successful in establishing their hege-mony over the entire world',[20] and so eminently resistible; and African Anglican bishops came to see their mother church's generally more tolerant line on homosexuality as an attempt to impose Canterbury's liberalism on them imperially.[21] In Uganda, it was widely believed that homosexuality itself had been brought there by the colonisers. Before the British came, they were all 'straight'.[22] (This could be confusing, with Europeans blaming the empire for the opposite. In 2011, for example, a *Guardian* columnist claimed it was Britain that had *outlawed* homosexuality in the colonies, on the misunderstanding that English laws automatically covered them too.[23] So Britain was responsible for colo-nial homosexuality *and* homophobia.) In these instances at least, the 'civilising mission' appears to have been counter-productive. Of course, we cannot know this, but the pos-sibility is that the more genuinely 'universal' of the values that the West regarded as 'civilised' might have taken hold more quickly and easily – grafted on to indigenous roots – if they hadn't been championed by the imperialists.

Why this was so mistaken has been made clear, I hope, in this book. The main error was to see imperialism as overwhelming: the factor in recent British and world history that trumped all others, and left its mark on most of them. That may have had something to do with the sonority of the word itself – especially if you knew your Latin.[24] It also suggested that 'imperialism' was a single and active 'thing', objectified it, in other words. The word is certainly problematical, used as it generally has been as an umbrella term for what was – even before its meaning was extended to cover trade, culture, Starbucks and the like – a confusing variety of relationships between Britain and her colonial periphery. Many of those relationships were consensual and essentially equal, hardly involving 'power' at all, except as providing protection for colonial settlers; this was broadly the nature of the connections between Britain and Australia, for example, once the latter had served its original purpose as a penal colony; and between Britain and the thirteen American colonies long before. (For modern 'white' Australians to claim historical soli-darity with Britain's other subjected peoples, now it has become a badge of honour, is perverse. The same could be said of the Scots.) Even in more 'directly' ruled colonies, like the Indian empire and in Africa, Britain depended hugely on collaboration with native elites, or on native societies more broadly. And how many millions of colonial subjects could hardly have been aware that they were part of the British empire, at all?

Appraised

All this was a reflection of the empire's essential vulnerability throughout its existence, which was also the main obstacle standing in the way of Britain's professed 'civilising mission' in the world, whether that be seen as a boon or a curse. That civilising mission itself varied greatly from colony to colony: generally involving Christianity, but not always, and sometimes in the face of dogged obstruction from colonial governments; often favouring capitalism, but usually only in those colonies where the colonial government's writ – as opposed to the white settlers', or over-mighty planters' – did not really run (elsewhere governors sought to protect 'their' natives *from* capitalist exploitation); and with cricket and football generally in there somewhere – but with most of its victims seemingly turning a blind eye to *their* imperial provenance. (Even Afghanistan has an international cricket XI.) Cricket, in fact, serves to corroborate an important point about what is called 'cultural imperialism' in the nineteenth and twentieth centuries, which was alluded to at the start of this book: that it was most effective when it clearly resonated with the culture it was being spread among; was a matter of '*in*culturation', that is, at least in part.[25] In the case of football, this is more obvious, because – more closely associated as it was with 'informal' empire – there was rarely any question of its having been 'imposed'. (The same applies to the imperial spread of all those Indian 'takeaways' in Britain.)

If the colonies were not all colonised to the same degree, neither was Britain – the metropole – evenly imperialised. Although nearly all Britons were implicated in the empire to some extent, if only through consuming its products (and it was perfectly possible to escape that), and significant numbers were engaged in it more actively, as soldiers, missionaries, explorers, prospectors, administrators and the like, still these latter only comprised a minority; and the evidence that the broader majority of the English population, at any rate, was even aware of its empire before (say) the 1880s, or much interested in it thereafter, or coloured by it in any way (for example, racism), is questionable.[26] Even those who *were* aware, were not necessarily supportive of it; and those who did support the empire – through 'Mafficking', for instance[27] – may have been fooling themselves. They were certainly not part of the imperial ruling set. In most ways they had less in common with it, than with their colonial subjects. (Many were aware of this, which was why so many socialists latterly came to support colonial liberation movements; the nationalists' cause was theirs.) This was certainly how the ruling classes regarded the situation. It is well known that they were trained for ruling their colonial subjects at their 'public' schools, but not any differently from the ways they were taught to rule their own working classes, which was what more of them went on to do. Take into account the complicated situation on the ground in the empire, with most Australians freer than their compatriots in Britain, and all those 'collaborators' helping out in the more directly governed colonies, and the familiar empire–colony dichotomy begins to break down. There were rulers and subjects on both sides of the equation. My working-class grandfather was as much a colonial subject, essentially, as Barack Obama's. It is only the resonance of the word 'imperialism' that obscures this.

The trouble with that kind of argument, at a time when British imperialism is still a live political issue (the Italians don't have this problem with the Roman empire), is that it might give the impression of trying to avoid responsibility – on my part, that is, as an Englishman – for Britain's past colonial crimes. If they were uneven, they weren't so bad; if my forebears can in this Jesuitical kind of way be painted as colonial victims, then I sneak safely on to their side; if they can be seen as collaborating in their own oppression and exploitation, then their descendants must share at least some of the guilt with 'us' (or rather, with my granddad's oppressors' descendants). You occasionally see this suspicion voiced explicitly; for example, by the sociologist Paul Gilroy in an attack in 2004 on the historian Linda Colley, who had dared to argue that the impact of British imperialism in the eighteenth century was 'uneven … shallow and … slow' – exactly the point that has been made in this book for the nineteenth century, and which is incontrovertible, surely, for the eighteenth – which Gilroy resented on the grounds that it sought to 'usurp' colonial victims' 'honoured place of suffering'. (He also inferred from it that Colley was trying to place the blame for imperialism on its victims, and that she wanted the British empire back again.[28]) That was obviously unfair – even, arguably, to the colonial subjects whose 'honoured place of suffering' he was protecting. (Some of us might think that painting them as weak, helpless victims, rather than as active agents, did them scant justice.) It certainly flew in the face of the evidence; which should be the historian's only concern, irrespective of any judgements that might be adduced from that.

On the other hand the evidence of the damage done by British imperialism, where it did have the power to inflict it, is clear: far clearer indeed than the evidence for 'good', not necessarily because there *was* no good, but because the latter by the nature of things is bound to be more controversial. With one or two exceptions – the spread of cricket is one – it is invariably difficult to assess the British empire's positive achievements: to disentangle them from its many failures, for example, and from unintended consequences of even the best-laid plans (like the reaction against 'western values'); to agree on what constitutes a 'success' ('modernity'?); and to be certain that any 'successes' one might want to attribute to imperialism might not have happened anyway, as the results of quite independent historical forces, which the British empire was merely riding, like the 'corks' mentioned at the close of Chapter 12.

By contrast, the reverse side of the coin is usually more straightforward. 'Atrocities', for example, (those inverted commas, incidentally, are not intended to suggest that there can be any doubt about their atrociousness) are easier to identify and quantify (in dead bodies); and also to lay directly at the door of British imperialism. It was, after all, the colonial authorities that generally perpetrated them, or at least permitted them on their watch. (On the other hand, many of them may not have been *essentially* imperialist; Britain could be atrocious in other circumstances too.) Shooting from guns, the massacre at Omdurman, Denshawi, Amritsar, aerial bombing in Iraq, the Bengal famine, the Kenya death camps, lots of stuff in Ireland …: of course, stringing them all together like this gives a misleading impression of the totality of the British imperial experience, but they need to be acknowledged, if only to show where empire is likely to lead. (America has discovered this, too.) Whether they need to be apologised and compensated for is another question, raising certain philosophical issues: like whether it is rational to apologise for what your generation hasn't actually done (I'm still waiting for Denmark – or is it Norway? – to say sorry for all that rapine and pillage inflicted on my part of England in Viking times), but it obviously can't do harm. As well as easing the pain for Britain's most recent victims (in Kenya, for example), it is good for Britons to be reminded that, in certain circumstances, they can be as horrid as foreigners. (Horridness is a human, not a national, tendency after all.) Taught in schools, this might not do much for children's patriotism, which many politicians seem to regard as the main function of history teaching; but history should aim higher than that.

A final reason for acknowledging the downside of British imperialism is that so many of its contemporaries did. This is an aspect that hardly ever appears in any of the empire's more popular 'after-images': the extent and passion of the debate that invariably surrounded both the empire and the broader question of 'imperialism' in Britain, from the American War of Independence – which many British supported – to our own time. Empire was never uncontroversial. Throughout the nineteenth and twentieth centuries, it always had opponents, and critics; those who wanted to see Britain withdrawing from her colonies entirely and immediately, and those who wished to see them better run. In general, the latter were the more intelligent, because they knew that Britain's withdrawal would not lead to their colonies' independence, in any meaningful sense, but merely to their thralldom to other *kinds* of imperialism: rival imperial powers', or local 'big men's', or else exploitation by unfettered global capitalism; which could be worse. The alternative to imperialism was not non-imperialism – and never would be – thought the greatest imperial critic of them all, J. A. Hobson, until an international body could be created to police a genuinely non-imperial world.[29] The critics were also the more effective of the two traditions (the out-and-out antis merely washed their hands of the whole thing); modifying the impact of colonialism in a hundred ways, and eventually helping to subvert it from within. Their impact on the British empire may not have been as powerful as that of external events and great historical trends, like the development of capitalism – the waves on which the empire bobbed; or as internal events, like resistance, in the colonies; or as the effect of its own inherent and chronic weaknesses. But it was at least as important as the influence of the committed 'imperialists' in Britain; illustrating once again the bewildering complexity of the 'imperial' situation in Britain, as well as in her colonies. It is for this reason that simplistic analyses and judgements of the British empire, or of British imperialism, just won't do; and why the debate over their 'legacy' will probably go on and on.

Notes

1 J. R. Seeley, *The Expansion of England* (Macmillan, [1883]; 2nd edn 1895), p. 10.
2 See above, Preface to the fifth edition.
3 Edward Said, *Out of Place: A Memoir* (Granta, 1999), p. 4.
4 B. J. Porter, *Critics of Empire* (Macmillan, 1968).
5 See Gregory Claeys, *Imperial Sceptics* (Oxford UP, 2011).
6 John Newsinger, *The Blood Never Dried: A People's History of the British Empire* (Bookmarks, 2000); Richard Gott, *Britain's Empire: Resistance, Repression and Revolt* (Verso, 2011).
7 Manchester University Press's 'Studies in Imperialism' series, edited by John MacKenzie.
8 See Martin Green, *Dreams of Adventure, Deeds of Empire* (Routledge, 1979).
9 Jane Austen, *Mansfield Park* (1814); interpreted by E. W. Said in *Culture and Imperialism* (1994 Vintage edn), pp. 100–16.
10 See above, p. 165.
11 See B. J. Porter, 'Further thoughts on imperial absent-mindedness', *Journal of Imperial and Commonwealth History*, 36 (1) (2008), p. 104. 'Gentle' is tongue-in-cheek.
12 David Croft, *Observer*, 2 October 2011.
13 See above, pp. 250, 279.
14 See *The Times*, 3 October 2008.
15 24 May 2011.
16 One out of many references is 'Internet a tool of British imperialism', says Mugabe, in *Daily Telegraph*, 11 December 2003.

17 See above, p. 217.
18 See, for example, 'The hunt for Al-Bashir', in the *Yale Globalist*, quoted in *The Perspectivist* (www.perspectivist.com), 30 January 2011.
19 *Guardian*, 21 March 2011.
20 From an article, 'The bare doctrine of Blair the bear', in *Kalaya* (Sri Lanka), 28 April 1999.
21 See, for example, the statement by the Most Revd Peter Akinola reported in *Episcopal News Service* (www.episcopalchurch.org), 19 October 2004.
22 See Elizabeth Day, 'Why was I born gay in Africa?', *Observer*, 27 March 2011.
23 Zoe Williams, 'Rights and wrongs', *Guardian*, 14 September 2011.
24 'Imperium': power, dominion.
25 See above, p. 4.
26 See B. J. Porter, *The Absent-Minded Imperialists* (Oxford UP, 2004).
27 See above, p. 115.
28 Paul Gilroy, *After Empire: Melancholia or Convivial Culture* (Routledge, 2004), p. 13. The book by Colley referred to here is *Captives* (Cape, 2002).
29 J. A. Hobson, *Imperialism, a Study* (Allen & Unwin, 1902), pp. 362–3; and J. A. Hobson, *Towards International Government* (Allen & Unwin, 1915), *passim*.

14 Epilogue

Brexit and the empire

Since the fifth edition of this book was published, Britain has passed through one of her major national crises: one that will determine her very identity for decades to come. Many regard it as the most existential decision she has made since her entry into the Second World War in 1939. On 23 June 2016, her people voted in a referendum to leave the European Union they had joined 46 years before, by the narrow margin of 51.9 to 48.1 percentage points on a vote of 71.8 per cent of the total electorate (which was a good turnout for Britain), and so set about the process of organising the practical details of the divorce. This turned out to be far more painful than those who had campaigned for 'Brexit' (as it was called: the word was coined in 2012) had warned anyone, maybe because they really thought it would be, in the words of one pro-Brexit minister, 'the easiest negotiation in history'.[1] In fact, as a more experienced politician commented three years later, after three or four 'deals' with the remaining EU had foundered in the British Parliament: 'the trouble with Brexit is that at a certain level it *is* rocket science'.[2] Even after the decision to leave the EU had been rubber-stamped in a General Election in December 2019, there remained plenty to do, especially in terms of new commercial treaties, before anyone could know for sure how the country would look afterwards. Along the way to this, Brexit gave rise to perhaps the most divisive period in British and Anglo-European politics since the English Civil War, such that some predicted it might well lead to the break-up of Britain, and possibly even of Europe, and to a Civil War Mk II, no less. Because it came so relatively soon after the demise of the British empire, it may be worthwhile investigating the possible relationship between the two.

Much of what follows will be speculative. Obviously too little time has passed to reach any definitive judgements, or to moderate my own prejudices, which will surely appear in what I write below.[3] And then, of course, one always has to allow for the unexpected to happen in history – 'events, dear boy, events', as Harold Macmillan once pithily put it – one of which in particular, the great corona virus pandemic, raging at the very moment this sixth edition is being prepared for press, could throw all our calculations out.

***

Strictly speaking, and at first glance, Brexit had little to do with the empire (Figure 14.1). After all, it all happened 40 or 50 years after British imperialism as it is usually understood had come to an end. It directly involved Europe alone, not the colonies or ex-colonies. That is, with three important exceptions: parts of Britain that were both British and European. The first was the 'colony' of Gibraltar on the southern tip of Spain, whose status was quite clearly endangered by the new dispensation. But Gibraltar scarcely featured in the public

Figure 14.1 Brexit nationalist isolationism. Overt references to the British empire during the Brexit campaign are exceedingly rare. Here is one: satirical.
Source: Monte Wolverton, Cagle Cartoons.

discussions over Brexit. (Obviously at the Foreign and Commonwealth Office, it will have featured more.[4])

Ireland, however, was another matter. The problem here arose out of *Northern* Ireland's Union with Great Britain, which was believed to be existentially imperilled by the vote. That was partly because, in the referendum of 2016, Northern Ireland and Scotland (as well as Gibraltar) had voted predominantly to 'remain' in the EU, which put them at odds with the rest of the UK. Northern Ireland, of course, was originally a product of English settler colonialism. In 2019, it suddenly emerged as a controversial issue in the negotiations with the remaining EU over a divorce settlement (or 'deal') between them, because of the undesirability of a border between it and the Republic of Ireland – still an EU member – whose removal had been generally credited with the success of the 'Good Friday' agreement of 1998 which had brought an end to the bloody 'Troubles' of the previous 20 years. One eventual result of this, though it seemed unlikely at the time, might be a reunion of the two parts of Ireland, to the UK's – and the Ulster Unionists' – loss.[5]

Scotland's situation vis-à-vis the empire was different. She had always been an indigenous rather than a settler nation. Her imperial credentials rested mainly on the prominent part her people had played in the *overseas* British empire, to share in the profits of which is supposed to have been one of the motives behind her formal adhesion to the kingdom of Britain in 1707. When Scotland had decided in her own 'independence' referendum in 2014 to stay within the UK (the margin of difference there was about 10 per cent), it was at a time when Britain was still in the EU, which many thought had been a factor behind her vote. Now the UK's situation looked likely to change, into an entity the Scots had *not* opted to be part of, which Scottish nationalists used as an argument in support of a further (Scottish) referendum, which in these new circumstances they might well win. (Her loss of the imperial pickings that had attracted her to unite with her southern neighbour in the first place was not widely offered as another reason. The Scots didn't like to regard themselves as implicated in, rather than a victim of, imperialism.[6])

If in one or other of these ways an unsought effect were to smash up what Theresa May called (tearfully) her 'precious Union',[7] the very 'heart' of the old Empire would have been broken. 'England' alone, with what many argued was a weaker explicit sense of national identity than 'imperial Britain' had had, and far weaker than those of any of her three erstwhile partners, would struggle to survive. (Already there were movements afoot for her northern counties, feeling little affinity with the 'Home Counties' they felt dominated and exploited by, to be allowed to hive off and join Scotland.) If any of this were to happen, then it could be said to be the most serious 'imperial' repercussion of the whole affair. But we are still waiting on that. Ireland, Scotland and 'Gib' were the three places in which Brexit and Britain's imperial inheritance directly clashed. Otherwise the empire was merely a part of 'history' by this time.

Self-evidently, Brexit mainly involved Britain's relations with Europe. Yet even in this respect, it could be said that it wasn't really *about* Europe, in so far as the causes and motivations behind it were concerned. There are good reasons for thinking – backed up by public opinion polls[8] – that very few Britons were significantly concerned about their connections with Europe, before the question was put before them in the summer of 2016. They had long appeared pretty relaxed about a relationship and a status which had been theirs now for more than 40 years. Several commentators, including the present author,[9] preferred to attribute the surprising and even shocking result of the June Referendum to purely domestic issues: the current Conservative-Liberal policy of 'austerity'; the decline of public services, especially the National Health Service (NHS); perceived neglect of the North of England and the 'marginal' nationalities of Britain; an electoral system that didn't reliably represent electors' views; domination of public life by various – often hidden – 'elites', including of course all those posh ex-public schoolboys in the government, but not confined to them (sometimes nearly anyone with education was included); foreign immigration (most of it not from Europe, but never mind); the tyranny of 'political correctness'; a Labour opposition that wasn't really helping, either because it was now too 'Tory-lite', in the guise of 'New Labour', or alternatively – and contradictorily – too 'extreme'; politicians continually denigrated by the popular press as self-serving and corrupt, which not all of them were, but which fed the anti-'Establishment' prejudice; and a general fed-upness with life generally. Given almost their first opportunity to cast votes which might actually *impact* on something, because the referendum was on a single issue, supposedly, and votes would be counted proportionately, English voters used it to poke a collective finger in the Establishment's eye. When dedicated anti-Europeans came along and told them that the European Union was at the root of all their complaints, they went for it, whether they really believed it or not. Europe was, in other words, a convenient scapegoat, exploited by those who wished to lead them into Brexit, for their own very different reasons. In considering the broad motivations for Brexit, these two groups of people, the leaders and the led, need to be kept well apart.

***

It is among the former that it may be worth examining whether residual post-imperial feelings had any influence on their views. That was a common construction put on the whole Brexit phenomenon at the time, especially by foreigners who may have been misled about the extent to which the empire had impinged on British national identity and culture when it was at its height. The general idea appears to have been that much of the backing for Brexit in the referendum came from people who had not yet reconciled themselves to the loss of their empire, or shed the disdain for 'Johnny Foreigner' that the empire was supposed to have encouraged. Continental Europeans, especially, favoured this explanation, which offered a convenient if well-worn stick with which to beat the Brits. If there was anything in it, then it would make the legacy of the empire an important factor behind this 'historic' decision.

One of the arguments of this book has been that popular enthusiasm for the empire even when it was a going concern has been exaggerated. Nonetheless, it was a natural mistake for foreigners to make, in view of the public face that Britain had long presented to them. And, indeed, there was some evidence to support it, among those classes and generations of society which had always thrilled to the sounds of the imperial trumpets, had perhaps even pursued careers in the colonies many years before; who resented (with some justice) the almost universal obloquy that was poured on their motives and achievements post-imperially; and who felt genuinely and even painfully nostalgic for the world they believed they had lost. The elderly, who of course remembered the empire best, voted more heavily for Brexit in the 2016 referendum than the young.[10] Indeed, this was presented by 'Remainers' as one of their best arguments for a second referendum on the issue in 2019, by which time the most elderly cohort in the 2016 plebiscite would, they thought, have had died out, and been replaced by a new generation of sprightly young Europhiles. After all, it was the youngsters who would have to live longest with the result.

Among the leaders of the Brexit charge in the 2010s, Boris Johnson and Jacob Rees-Mogg could be said to fit this template most comfortably: well-off, upper-middle-class Old Etonians both, who weren't quite old enough to have experienced the empire directly, but whose respect for it may well have been nurtured at their school. (On the other hand, Eton's preference for Classical over 'modern' history might indicate that it was not.[11]) In both these cases their imperialism was rarely explicitly stated, due probably to the bad odour into which the word and the realities behind it had almost universally fallen over the past 50 years. 'Defending' empire by then had become almost as disreputable as denying the Holocaust. Nonetheless, it takes very little in the way of 'deconstruction' to espy hidden 'imperialist' tropes behind the thinking of these two men, and of other upper-middle-class Brexit spokespeople.

The clearest hint of this is the appeal that all of them made to extending Britain's commercial ties with the world, beyond the limits that it was felt the EU was imposing on them. The term for this – the ultimate ambition of the Brexiteers – was a 'Global Britain', defined thus by Boris Johnson in July 2018:

> By Global Britain I meant a country that was more open, more outward-looking, more engaged with the world than ever before. It meant taking the referendum and using it as an opportunity to rediscover some of the dynamism of those bearded Victorians; not to build a new empire, heaven forfend.[12]

'Heaven forfend', indeed; but the 'informal imperial' resonances of 'Global Britain' will be obvious to anyone familiar with almost any recent reading of the British empire's history. Historians have long abandoned the idea that 'formal' control alone defines 'empire', as have most of those who use the 'e' and 'i' words more loosely and metaphorically. Other substitutions for the word 'empire', felt to be more sensitive to post-imperial feelings, were some older ones, revived, like 'Greater Britain' and the 'Commonwealth', favoured because they did not seem to imply British 'control'; and a brand-new term, the 'Anglosphere', which was felt to be more acceptable on this same ground, but could also be regarded as 'racist', or what has been called 'culturist' in this book.[13] It also, conveniently in the light of Britain's much-bruited post-war 'Special Relationship', embraced the USA. Then, regardless of Johnson's and Rees-Mogg's disavowals, civil servants began using another expression for it: 'Empire 2.0',[14] which might be thought to have rather given the game away. Indeed, there can surely be little doubting the surviving 'imperialist' resonances in much of the leading Brexiteers' rhetoric, whether or not these justified the critics' suspicion that the whole thing was essentially powered by imperial nostalgia.

To the extent that it was, however, it needs to be pointed out that it was a particular form and era of old British imperialism that the Brexiteers felt nostalgic towards: the kind that is described and explained in Chapter 2 of this book, called by historians the 'imperialism of free trade'. And that may only have attracted them because of what were thought to be its other advantages, especially in relation to their material interests; in other words, nothing essentially to do with the 'glory' side of Empire, but more venal. One of the underlying arguments of this book, and indeed of most imperial histories since the appearance of Robinson's and Gallagher's seminal work on the phenomenon in the 1950s,[15] has been that Britain's early nineteenth-century economic expansion overseas was defended ethically on the grounds that it was *not* 'imperialistic' by the normal contemporary definition of that word, which implied force, conquest, protectionism and control, but was indeed 'free' on all sides, in fact, the very opposite of 'empire' in its literal sense. It was only later, when 'free trade' proved difficult to sustain without elements of pressure or compulsion, that it was supposed to have morphed into 'empire' as the word was – and still is – generally understood. Brexiteers like Johnson and Rees-Mogg appear to have disavowed empire – 'heaven forfend' – only in this later, formal sense. Which is why when they ever used the 'e'-word in its derogatory sense, it was to sully the European Union they wished to escape from, which was at least a formal, legal entity, although its 'imperialness' in other respects must be open to doubt.

The earlier 'free trade' ideal also fitted in with the leading Brexiteers' other basic political and economic principles, which were what by now had come to be bundled together as 'neoliberalism': an idea that by now was coming to dominate economic debate, and Conservative, or 'Liberal', politics, all over the Western world. It was their neoliberalism – the idea that economic activities, or the workings of supply and demand, should not be 'artificially' restricted – that seems to have lain behind the leading Brexiteers' turn to this kind of 'imperialism' in the early 2000s. One of the models they most admired was Singapore, where market freedoms – at the same time as strong social and political discipline – had created the kind of booming economy they wished to see in 'Global Britain'. As an ex-colony, Singapore was of course another link with the historical empire. For those of a conspiratorial turn of mind, the imminence of a new EU law to regulate or even outlaw the extra-European 'tax havens' into which the rich were reputed to be squirreling their wealth, away from the regulators, to come into force in January 2020, which was why Brexit had to be done before then, may have been the final straw. Many of these tax havens, too, were in 'British overseas territories' like the Cayman Islands; which formed another connection with Britain's imperial past.[16] This could have been the 'venal' motive underlying their 'imperialism'. Another of these links may be the fact that many of the proprietors of Britain's right-wing press, crude propaganda sheets for Brexit, in the main, heavily availed themselves of these ex-colonial tax-dodging facilities; and in many cases were from the wider 'Anglosphere' themselves.[17]

And that is without taking account of the massive financial investments that Britain still possessed in her former colonies, gathered together and serviced expertly in the City of London's new, gleaming modern and post-modern palaces. The empire had gone; but its paw-prints remained all over the place.

When glorifying these nineteenth-century overseas achievements Johnson and Rees-Mogg generally attributed them to heroic individuals; which was how they had been presented at the height of the empire too. In 2014, Johnson published a biography of Winston Churchill which was subtitled *How One Man Made History* (2014), which was followed in 2019 by Rees-Mogg's *The Victorians: Twelve Titans Who Forged Britain*; both subtitles clearly indicating their approach. The 'great man' theory of history had rather fallen out of favour among academic historians by the 2000s, but here it was again, dusted off for patriots in these new 'Global British' times, and perhaps an inspiration for Johnson in particular. (A number of reviewers read his biography of Churchill as being basically about himself.[18]) It fitted in well with another feature that was even more central to Brexit: its *insular* view of Britain, proudly seeing off the Spanish Armada, Napoleon's armies and the German Luftwaffe *on her own*, with no assistance from any allies, and consequently no need for European help as she set off on her great global adventure to repeat the glories of her past. A favourite – but historically misleading – term for it was 'splendid isolation'. Insularity was connected too with ideas of British 'exceptionalism'; *her* exceptional feature, of course, being her peculiar and superior 'liberties', later bequeathed as her lasting gift to the Anglosphere. The flaws in both these approaches have been pointed out again and again in books that the Brexiteers won't have read, but which are out there, and so do not need to be retailed here.[19] The interesting question for our purposes is whether both may have been inherited from an earlier era of *imperial* story-telling, the heroic 'empire-builders' approach (*vide* Kipling and C. R. Leslie, *A History of England*, 1911); or from a more modern account written in a similar, or complementary, vein: Niall Fergusson's celebratory *Empire: How Britain Made the Modern World*. (Most on the Right had read this. The subtitle, of course, pandered to their patriotism.) If this was so, then it might furnish yet another link between Brexit and Britain's imperial past.

There is one more possible connection. Britain's famous Public schools – her own 'peculiar institution' – had relied significantly from the mid-nineteenth century onwards on servicing the empire, by furnishing it with 'proconsuls' and a particular ethos to guide them. It was this that, in part, gave them their rationale and their popularity among the patrician classes; and hence their domination of British 'high' society and politics, at home as well as in the colonies. After the empire fell, it looked for a while as though they would lose this advantage, with proconsular jobs drying up, and a succession of British prime ministers being recruited from more 'ordinary' schools, until the Public schools quite suddenly in the 2000s made a comeback, with the Old Etonians David Cameron and Boris Johnson becoming prime ministers, and the British cabinet and Conservative Party again filling up with 'Old Boys'. Many of these were involved in the financial or 'capitalist imperialism' that had both preceded and succeeded the classical, 'formal', sort. We have seen that one other pro-Brexit cabinet minister, Jacob Rees-Mogg, was also an old Etonian, with most of the rest coming from other elite schools; and being financiers to boot. (They included the Brexiteers' influential wild card, Nigel Farage; never an MP but leader over the referendum period of the United Kingdom Independence Party, or UKIP.) This might be thought to make nonsense of many Brexiteers' common refrain, that they represented the 'people' *against* the elite, but of course elites can change their spots: as can any of us, otherwise all our lives would be determined by our social class. (Clement Attlee was a Public schoolboy. And George Orwell went to Eton.) The question remains, however, how much of the imperial element of the old Public school ethos remained to influence these men in the post-imperial period. (We have seen that Attlee was certainly influenced by the sense of patrician duty that Haileybury – originally founded specifically to train up the rulers of India – instilled.) Of course, it is impossible to tell, except by having sat in their classes with them. But it's another possible link between the empire and Brexit.

If nostalgia for the British empire *was* a factor behind Brexit, therefore, it probably only affected the elite of the movement, was generally imagined falsely,[20] and even in these cases may have been merely a cover or excuse for other deeper motives, rather than a fundamental one in itself. Among these men's (they were mostly men) more plebeian followers, one could hear the very occasional patriotic reference to the empire – boasts like 'we used to rule half the world' (*we? half?*) – but mostly as ill-considered slogans, and not as indicative of the proletariat's true feelings and motives for supporting Brexit as were the grievances outlined near the beginning of this chapter. But then, imperialism had rarely cut much ice with the plebs.

***

Imperialism hadn't; but 'independence' had. Britons' feelings for independence – or 'freedom', or 'sovereignty', which goes a long way back: 'Britons never never never shall be slaves' – may well have been forged and tempered, in part, by their long history of (supposed) imperial dominance, which nurtured the belief in them that they had everything (again, supposedly) under their own national control. One of the most powerful slogans in the referendum campaign, in fact, was 'Let's Take Back Control'. That carried resonances of a very different – indeed contradictory – aspect of the imperial period, which was the British *anti*-imperialism it had provoked. The Brexiteers were mostly *nationalists*, which is what the empire's enemies, too, had called themselves. There are of course nationalists and nationalists – Garibaldi and Hitler – but few people believed that Brexiteers were likely to morph into the latter sort. Now, some of them claimed, the colonial shoe was on the other foot, with Britain being *subjected* to this new empire, run from Brussels. Sir Bill Cash, a prominent anti-European for decades, believed it was an essentially 'German' empire, which indicates another trope filtering into these older xenophobes' attitudes. (Cash was 79 in 2019.[21]) This was powerful in other ways: the idea, that is, that Britain's essential history was a succession of battles against *other* empires – Roman, Danish, Spanish, French, Nazi German – from which she had always emerged victorious and unscathed. These – rather than her own imperial exploits – set the scenes for most of the war books, films and TV series that the British (especially British men) were so fond of; with even the more imperial ones, *Zulu*, say, or *North-West Frontier*, highlighting plucky Britons defending themselves against native 'hordes'. Of course, you don't need to have had an imperial history to value your national independence. But the loss of control over others might, in this case, have heightened that feeling. Who can tell?

Another effect of having ruled, or at least administered, an empire for so long may have been to take away from (some) Britons, the habit of *compromise*, which is always necessary in order to build effective alliances. Mind you, if they had – again – read any reliable imperial histories, they would have been aware of how important compromise, or 'appeasement', had always used to be in sustaining an empire whose administrators were so dangerously outnumbered. (Hence 'indirect rule'.) When the empire started showing signs of fatal weakness early in the last century, some enlightened imperialists had thought to prolong its life by turning it into such a collaborative enterprise, which was how the Commonwealth had come about: an essentially egalitarian and multi-racial idea – 'common/wealth' – with its other, ex-colonial, members regarded as truly equal to their Mother. Even then, however, there could only be one Mother. This at any rate was the ideal, and why the (socialist) Fabian Society was so keen on it. Until 'Europe' came along (that is, the EU and its predecessors), Britain had rarely been in the situation she found herself in now, as a mere ally with others. Even the Second World War was presented to her people, misleadingly, as a British-*led* victory. This was especially true on the political Right, whence Brexit recruited most of its officer class; and in the government which first tried to negotiate Britain's exit, whose prime minister, Theresa May, scarcely knew the meaning of the word 'compromise'. (Hence her repeated but singularly unhelpful slogan, 'Brexit means Brexit'.) Again, 'we used to rule half the world'. Which is what made pooling their sovereignty with some of that world, or becoming a 'colony' of Brussels (or Germany) especially galling.

A colony of Brussels? Well, in a way she was; but of Brussels as the centre of a *co-operative* empire, or more strictly 'commonwealth', in which Britain had equal say with all its other 'colonies', and several valuable bespoke opt-outs from its rules. If the EU was an 'empire' (and it did occasionally display some of the characteristics of more conventional, expansionist empires, for example its interference in the ex-Soviet east), it was only one of many such in the world, most of them 'informal', between which Britain was bound to have to choose. Readers of this book will be familiar by now with this notion of 'informal empire' – later it came to be called 'soft empire'; the problem was, however, that few people in the early 2000s apart from imperial historians and political scientists were. The majority still imagined the old British empire with clear boundaries, and coloured in red; which we now know was not really the sum of it, and doesn't define 'imperialism'. Nearly every colonial relationship, as we have seen, was *negotiated*, as were many quasi-colonial relationships outside. A 'Brexit' Britain could probably avoid being taken in by a more 'formal' kind of empire, but that would not leave it truly 'sovereign'. In fact, absolute national independence in most circumstances, certainly in a global world, is virtually impossible. 'No man is an island, entire unto himself', as John Donne poetically put it; to which we might add that no island, or group of islands, is an island either, in Donne's sense.

If Britain had cut herself off entirely from the European Union, which the extreme Brexiteers hankered for (it was called a 'hard Brexit'), she still would not have been 'free'. Commercial arrangements have to be negotiated, and negotiations create their own bonds. Those who thought that the 'Anglosphere' could 'freely' compensate for the European markets Britain might lose after Brexit were swiftly disabused.[22] The best hope seemed to be the USA, with its President keen to see the EU split apart, so that he could pick up some of the pieces: Britain's national health system for the profit of American pharmaceutical firms, for example, or a market for US farmers' by now notorious 'chlorinated chicken'. But this would have tied Britain into a new 'informal empire' in effect. Up until then, the EU had given Britain the possibility of resisting this, co-operatively, with the combined strength provided by its size and numbers. Left to herself, and desperately needing these new commercial deals, Britain would be as dependent – as *un*-sovereign, therefore, in a practical sense – as any colony. Some of the early liberal and socialist critics of old-fashioned imperialism, incidentally, had already woken up to this, and had given it as a reason for protecting newly independent colonies from their own weakness in the face of the potentially oppressive world market that 'colonial emancipation' would cast them into: international protection if possible (a League of Nations), but if not, then by means of a more gentle form of 'empire'. Another of those vultures circling the EU, equally eager for its dismemberment, and probably plotting for it, was Vladimir Putin, who was just then in the process of rebuilding the rival empire that *Russia* had recently lost. It seems that there will always be empires, of one kind or another. The trick, for a medium-sized country, is to seek the shelter of the empire that suits it best. Some Brexiteers – the 'free marketists' on the Right of the Conservative Party – thought that was America: Boris Johnson seems to have been one of them (it so happened that he had been born there),[23] but they couldn't say it too loudly, for fear of alarming those who didn't like the sound (just the sound, maybe) of 'chlorinated chicken', or the prospect of their beloved NHS being stolen from them by the Americans.

***

In fact, very few of those who voted for Brexit in June 2016, as distinct from their spokespeople, really cared about the EU, any more than their forebears had cared about the empire; or were even conscious of it, beyond the tales that their millionaire-owned popular newspapers spun about it. (It was Boris Johnson, again, as the *Daily Telegraph*'s correspondent in Brussels for a while, who originated the myth that the EU was going to ban 'bendy bananas'.) The press, in fact, may have been crucial here, originating as it had in its present 'yellow' and 'jingoistic' form at the hottest period of assertive British imperialism (the *Daily Mail* was started in 1900), in order to plug the empire, and later to push its proprietors' views on 'Europe'.[24] So this could be said to provide another albeit indirect link between the empire and Brexit. Without these propagandist newspapers, it must be doubtful whether the majority of people – the voters, that is, not their leaders – would have cared one way or another about the European Union. Questioned in the streets, it was exceedingly rare for any of them to be able to name a single material way in which 'Europe' had disadvantaged them; Brexit-voters' answers generally either fell back on vague abstractions like 'sovereignty' and 'Brussels bureaucracy', or missed the target altogether. (Many believed that 'Europe' was the cause of all those 'darkies' coming in.) In other words – and this is yet another way in which it could be said that Brexit and the empire were linked – most Britons were simply not generally interested in any sort of 'foreign' affairs.

What they *were* interested in, in the years leading up to 2016, was their material situation in the new post-George Osborne era of crippling 'austerity' brought about by a banking collapse in 2008, although the Conservatives blamed it on over-spending under the previous Labour government. This created that large pool of discontent in parts of Britain, whose specific grievances were listed at the start of this chapter, together with people's feeling of electoral helplessness. This may be why they reacted as they did when they were offered a *referendum*, on a single issue, in which every vote would 'count'. The referendum could have been on almost any issue, and the result would probably have gone against what the electorate surmised the government of the day wanted, simply as a protest. This social discontent was then exploited, as we have seen, by the ideological Europhobes to realise their decades-old ambition to gain their independence from the 'Brussels empire'. As we are looking for 'imperial' links here, a historical comparison could be drawn with the 'tariff reformers' of the turn of the twentieth century, who similarly used the issue of 'empire' to address the social problems of that time. (In 2016, it was the National Health Service that was allegedly going to gain £350 million a week if the Brexiteers won – that was an example of clear dishonesty; in 1906, it was State pensions, which the Conservatives maintained could be funded by tariffs on imported goods. That didn't work. The Liberals won.) In both cases, a 'foreign' issue was linked with a more pressing domestic one.

It could be argued that the old empire had contributed to this economic and social misery in a number of, albeit indirect, ways. One was by cushioning Britain's economy against extra-imperial competition while it was still a going concern, making manufacturers complacent, and so (together with the trade unions, claimed the manufacturers themselves) contributing to the decline in British industry that was widely observed from the post-imperial 1960s onwards; and then ultimately to the revolution in business practices that was associated with Margaret Thatcher in the 1980s. On the other hand, the Thatcher reforms could have themselves contributed to Britain's decline subsequently; together with the inevitable global trend of late-stage capitalism that she so successfully rode. (Leftists had long predicted that capitalism was bound to become redder in tooth and claw, through its own internal contradictions, until – as Karl Marx had fondly wished – it imploded. Thatcher could be said to have helped that on.) Another legacy of the empire was the transformation, long before Thatcher, of Britain's economy from a mainly industrial into a financial one, dependent on banking, investment and other 'invisibles', much of it in the colonies (there's the link again), which marked the latest stage of British capitalism; and could be seen as a version of 'imperialism' in itself. If it had not been for this reliance on finance, for example, Britain would not have been hit quite so hard as she was by the banking crisis of 2008.

Last of all, Brexit could be seen as the event that marked the true end of Britain's long imperial journey symbolically, rather than literally. As the formal empire was in the process of declining and falling, from 1947 on, if not earlier, many people had marvelled at the smoothness of the whole process, when contrasted with other empires in history. London was never sacked like Rome had been. The Visigoths stayed away – unless you counted immigrants. There were no riots in British streets over Rhodesia, as there were currently in France over Algeria. The idea was put out that in Britain's case decolonisation had been a voluntary and consensual process, a peaceful *transference* of power, agreed on by all sides in order to create as little chaos as possible, and little ill-will after the deed had been done. The empire's evolution into the Commonwealth was part of this, and was sometimes presented as a deliberate culmination of the imperial process all along. (So it hadn't declined and fallen at all.) That was largely a nonsense, as we have seen; but it was supposed to make people feel better about it all.

Another sign of the wisdom and maturity of Britain's way of extricating herself from her empire was reckoned to be her willingness, in 1973, to exchange her ruling and dominating position in the world for the co-operative one that joining the EEC represented. It was not always frictionless: there was controversy over Britain's entry at the time, though nothing like that provoked by Brexit; and Britain was always seen as a somewhat awkward (or 'semi-detached') member of the Community. But the move was regarded as having given her a 'role', at last, to replace the one that in 1962 Dean Acheson famously felt she had 'lost' when her colonies fell away.[25] By this way of looking at it, entry into Europe marked a surprisingly gentle 'end of empire', and with as convincing a historical pedigree as her 'imperial' one; a soft landing, and the prelude to another way of international living. Few Britons below a certain class appeared to regret it, or to hanker after past glories. For those brought up on earlier editions of this book, that is where the story ends.

***

Until, that is, 2016, and the Brexit campaign; which came out of an almost clear blue sky to bring to the surface some post-imperial regrets that had clearly been well hidden before, as well as some imperial-era prejudices among the political elite, and what might be regarded as imperial-style – that is, authoritarian – behaviour from some of them. One clear example was the British Home Office, under the vicar's daughter Theresa May before her short-lived premiership, which quite suddenly became far less 'Homely' than its title implied, more like one of those 'Ministries of the Interior' that were so reviled in Eastern European countries, especially in its treatment of Commonwealth immigrants, who were an obsession of May's. The '*Windrush* scandal' over the Home Office department's sudden expulsion of ex-colonial workers and others originally recruited in order to provide much-needed labour, and having lived legally in Britain for several decades, was the most notorious. There were many others: long-settled families separated, scholars kicked out, foreign partners of Britons threatened with exclusion,[26] and almost certainly hundreds more who didn't have the advantages that academics have in pleading their cases. One way of getting around this was to seek British citizenship; but that process was so gruelling, expensive and unfriendly as to put many off.[27] All this was the product of the new migration policy which May announced at the start of her draconian term at the Home Office, to turn Britain into a 'hostile environment' (her words) for unwanted incomers. That was *very* un-Commonwealth. But it was in line with other shifts in the ethos of Britain that followed the fall of the empire. Or maybe they were survivals *from* that imperial age, kept under wraps then so far as the domestic scene was concerned, only to break out at home when they could less easily be diverted abroad. Bearing in mind the long divergence in imperial times between Britain's liberal conduct at home and her more authoritarian policies in her colonies, and especially with regard to Ireland, that seems possible. But it would be difficult to prove. Many other things had happened in between that could explain the new 'toxicity' of her public life.

There were, for example, ominous threats against prominent 'Remainers', necessitating special police protection for most of their MPs; the shocking murder of one of them, Jo Cox, by an 'English nationalist' just a few days before the referendum; an upsurge of racism and other far-Right or even quasi-Fascist ideologies; rioting in the streets; explosive devices with pro-Brexit messages laid on underground railway lines; and threats of bloody insurrection on the Brexit side (including by one of its most prominent leaders: Nigel Farage talked of picking up a rifle if Brexit was 'betrayed');[28] a poisonous national discourse generally, mainly in the media but also in Parliament, where a new prime minister openly and unconstitutionally took the 'populist' side against his own 'Establishment', and even proposed limiting the influence of Parliament in favour of the Executive, i.e., *him*; all of it fed and fanned by a reactionary popular press (inherited, as we have just seen, from the empire), a new out-of-control 'social media', and some clever propagandists ('Cambridge Analytica'); all intent on forcing on the nation a 'hard' – or hardish – Brexit,[29] which most 'experts' (though Brexiteers didn't set much store by 'experts'[30]) believed would harm the country domestically, and had already all but destroyed its dignity and reputation among foreigners.[31] By this time several commentators were talking seriously of the possibility of 'Fascism' in Britain. They included even a former US Presidential candidate.[32] Why, after all, had Britain largely escaped conventional Fascism before? Perhaps it was *because* of her empire. Fascism generally appeals to nations – or national leaders – who feel their countries are hard done by. That could be said to be the situation of Britain now. Fascism, or neo- or quasi- or proto-fascism, might be said to have filled the political hole left on the Right of British politics by the fall of the empire. All of which led some to wonder whether the post-imperial settlement really had been as successful and civilised as it had once seemed. The final sack of Rome had only been delayed.

Of course, not all the shenanigans over Brexit can be attributed to the empire, even indirectly. We need to be aware of the foreign context of all this discontent and protest before we attribute too much to it. 'Populism', as it was called, was not confined to post-imperial Britain but was springing up all over Europe and the Americas, and maybe on other continents too; each of its manifestations bearing striking resemblances to all the others, if you allowed for national variants, of which, for Britain, the post-imperial factor was one. It was aided by an international network of Far Right thinkers, often working subversively and with new Internet-based tools, which helps explain their common features. Their first great success, and an early sign of the weakness of existing political institutions in the face of this threat, was the election of the nativist Donald Trump to the US Presidency, in the same year as the British Brexit referendum; which took the established political classes by complete surprise, feeding as it did on perceptions of 'decline' and anti-elite prejudice, and yet headed by as elite a person (in American capitalist terms) as you could hope to meet. 'Make America Great Again' was his more boastful version of Brexit's 'Take Back Control'. Again, as in the case of Brexit, anti-intellectualism was taken to the point of rejecting all authority and many established 'truths'. (The famously untruthful Boris Johnson was a fan of Trump's.) All the other Right-wing popular movements that sprang up – the *Front Nationale* in France, *Alternativ für Deutschland* in Germany, *Sverigedemokraterna* in Sweden, *Fidesz* in Hungary, *Vox* in Spain, *Law and Justice* in Poland – targeted immigrants as the main visible manifestation of the dangers they felt were threatening their nations (or 'Christian civilisation' in the case of Hungary), and advocated excluding them, in Trump's case, notoriously, with a 1,954-mile-long wall to keep the Mexicans out of his southern States. Even the state of Israel started exhibiting increasingly racist and authoritarian tendencies, despite its peoples having been the victims of such tendencies, magnified to the most grotesque degree, in the recent past; and to the despair of many of its own people and of genuine philo-semites all over the world. It may be that some of these movements, the French one, in particular, were also tinged, like UKIP, with post-imperial regrets.[33] But clearly there were other large common factors lying behind this almost universal phenomenon, besides which Britain's imperial legacy, such as it was, appears to have been a fairly minor local one. The empire's apparent importance in modern British history, as signified by those old red-besplattered world maps, for example, which we have seen were misleading even at the height of the empire, should not distract us from the other – possibly deeper – causes of Britain's post-imperial traumas.

The deepest of them all *may* have been the 'crisis of capitalism', one of many, of course, over the past two hundred years, which hit Britain and much of the rest of Europe and the world in the 2000s. We have seen in this book how the British empire was never self-generating, 'imperialism' never a fundamental motive power or agency on its own, but always rode on the back of Britain's economic development, which for the whole imperial period was underpinned by the evolution of her capitalism, quite independently, however much it may have been modified by other factors, like the public school ethos, religion, and the best and worst of purely human traits. When from the later nineteenth century onwards, Britain's capitalist prosperity began its long relative decline, the task of sustaining the empire became more and more difficult; with the only surprise being that Britain managed to sustain it at all, and with it the illusion, largely, of her still being a 'world power'. That was down to some clever diplomatic tricks, including various measures of 'appeasement' to colonial nationalists which in themselves reflected her true weakness, and sheer luck, like powerful rivals fighting with one another, or else, like the USA after the First World War, dropping out of the competition temporarily. After 1945, and her last great struggle for national survival (so far), her economic weakness by comparison with a now more interventionist America and the USSR meant that she could no longer bear the weight of an empire which was in any case rejecting her. So she scurried off to Europe. Which seemed to work until tensions within the global capitalist system, possibly Marx's predicted *final* crisis of capitalism, gave rise to economic, social and political problems at home, which helped revive Britons' illusions about their imperial or at least 'independent' past, and set them scampering back to those.[34]

***

Which, finally, leaves the Commonwealth, which is still a (fairly) going concern. In this connection, it is worthwhile pointing out that there are good liberal and internationalist arguments, *in principle*, for wider and free-er relationships between countries than a regional, racially fairly homogeneous and essentially protectionist grouping such as the European Union represents. In Britain's case, this idea also had clear imperial roots. It was how some of our more idealistic late nineteenth- and early twentieth-century imperialists had hoped their empire would ultimately evolve, into a kind of United Nations in embryo. Some of these imperialists were active in the foundation of the League of Nations, which is why it is grossly unfair to tar all of them retrospectively with the blackest of imperial brushes, and to regard Britain's colonial legacy as *only* malevolent. (Its bequest to its colonial subjects is similarly mixed, but is not the subject of this book.) I believe, though I cannot remember for sure, that I personally may have voted against British membership of the 'Common Market' in the 1975 referendum on those grounds; preferring to join on equal terms with the many Asian and African friends I had lived and worked among at university, in preference to what I do remember characterising then as a 'White Man's Club'. The EU is usually lauded for its 'internationalist' qualities, but it is not as internationalist as it might be, or as the worldwide free multiracial Commonwealth of nations of the old imperialists' dreams. If that had been the direction British imperialism had taken after, say, 1945, then this book would have ended very differently.

But times change, and naïve illusions can be pricked. That wonderful 'Commonwealth' ideal was obviously largely a last-ditch response to the inevitable decline of the other sort of British empire, the more strictly 'imperial' one (*imperium*); whose fierce underlying *nationalism* was the aspect of it that was carried through into the Brexit movement, making the latter a creature of the political Right rather than of the liberal (as distinct from 'neoliberal') and internationalist Left. Even when the former – men like Boris Johnson – referenced the old Commonwealth, it was nearly always the 'white' bits they meant by it, once called 'kith and kin', and not the 'black, brown and yellow' parts that had been embraced by the original ideal. As a result, during the Brexit debates of the 2010s, it was people of a far Right disposition who led the charge, with their following consisting mainly, but certainly not exclusively, of popular nationalists, 'Britain First' mobs, and old-fashioned racists. If some of the roots of these people's attitudes could be traced back to the old British empire, it was to a very different side – the xenophobic rather than the internationalist one – of what had always been, as this book has hopefully exemplified, a confusingly multifarious and multi-layered phenomenon. That's why there are no broad, simple 'theories of imperialism' offered here; and why that should be the ultimate 'lesson' to be drawn from Britain's relatively brief imperial moment.

Perhaps the last word on all this should be left to one of Britain's partners in the EU, Donald Tusk, a Pole by nationality and President of the European Council from 2014 to 2019, who, shortly before his retirement, remarked that 'one of my English friends is probably right when he says with melancholy that *Brexit is the real end of the British Empire.*'[35] Some Brexiteers, of course, would disagree. On the contrary, they would say, the 'real end' had come with Britain's *entry* into the EEC. Brexit was thus a means of *renewing* Britain's imperial greatness, in one form or another. Maybe the 'global Britons' will succeed in this, and the doubters – or 'Remoaners' – will be proved wrong. In that case, you never know, *The Lion's Share* might even go into a seventh edition.[36] But it doesn't look like it presently. Signing off on this sixth edition in the middle of 2020, the judgement of Tusk's English friend appears to be more on the ball, and consonant with the broad argument of the earlier editions of this book. That makes it a fitting quotation with which to conclude this sixth edition.

Notes

1 Liam Fox, quoted in www.mirror.co.uk/news/politics/tory-liam-fox-doesnt-regret-11387919.
2 This was Tony Blair: www.thenational.scot/news/uk-news/17985738.tony-blair-brexit-rocket-science-even-experts-struggle-follow/.
3 I should here declare my own leaning, which is towards what is called the 'Remain' side of the debate; feeling strongly enough about the loss of my European citizenship under Brexit, in fact, to have recently taken on another European (dual) nationality in order to reclaim it. Obviously, I like to think that my current political view has been informed by my study of history, rather than the other way around.
4 On Gibraltar, see Jennifer Ballantine Perera's chapter in Stuart Ward and Astrid Rasch (eds), *Embers of Empire in Brexit Britain* (Bloomsbury Academic, 2019).
5 Discussed in Fintan O'Toole's chapter, 'England and the Irish question', in Stuart Ward and Astrid Rasch (eds), *Embers of Empire in Brexit Britain* (Bloomsbury Academic, 2019).
6 See Neal Ascherson's chapter, 'Scotland, Brexit and the persistence of empire', in Stuart Ward and Astrid Rasch (eds), *Embers of Empire in Brexit Britain* (Bloomsbury Academic, 2019).
7 See www.bbc.co.uk/news/uk-scotland-scotland-politics-39151250. The tears welled up as she repeated the phrase during her announcement of her resignation in front of 10 Downing Street on 24 May 2019.
8 See www.theguardian.com/politics/2016/mar/20/britons-on-europe-survey-results-opinium-poll-referendum.
9 See, for example, https://bernardjporter.com/2016/06/16/is-it-really-about-the-eu/.
10 See www.ipsos.com/ipsos-mori/en-uk/how-britain-voted-2016-eu-referendum.
11 In the course of writing this chapter, I emailed the Head of History at Eton asking for a view of the school's History syllabus and reading lists at that time, and got no reply. But in any event it is possible that, as Classical scholars, Johnson and Co. studied virtually no British history at all. And the present Headmaster of Eton, in a recent interview, pointed out, somewhat defensively, how much Eton has changed – for the better, he implied – since the era of Johnson and Rees-Mogg. See www.theguardian.com/education/2019/sep/23/head-of-eton-hits-back-at-labour-plans-to-abolish-private-schools.

12 Quoted in Ward and Rasch, *op. cit.*, p. 3.

13 See James Belich, *Replenishing the Earth: The Settler Revolution and the Rise of the Anglo-World, 1783–1939* (Oxford UP, 2009); and Michael Kenny and Nick Pearce, 'Brexit and the Anglosphere', Chapter 3 in Stuart Ward and Astrid Rasch (eds.), *Embers of Empire in Brexit Britain* (Bloomsbury Academic, 2019).

14 See www.thetimes.co.uk/article/ministers-aim-to-build-empire-2-0-with-african-commonwealth-after-brexit-v9bs6f6z9.

15 J. A. Gallagher and R. E. Robinson, 'The imperialism of free trade', *Economic History Review*, 6 (1953), 1–15.

16 On Britain's 'Dependent Territories' generally, see Robert Aldrich and John Connell, *The Last Colonies* (Cambridge UP, 1998).

17 The best-known examples are Rupert Murdoch, born in Australia, but now an American citizen (*The Times* and *Sun*); and, some years ago, William Maxwell Aitken, 1st Baron Beaverbrook, born in Canada (*Daily Express*). To whom might be added the Barclay Brothers, resident (for tax purposes) in the Channel Islands (*Daily Telegraph*).

18 See, for example, www.spectator.co.uk/2014/10/the-churchill-factor-by-boris-johnson-review/.

19 See David Reynolds, *Island Stories: Britain and its History in the Age of Brexit* (HarperCollins, 2019).

20 See the chapter by Bill Schwarz, 'Forgetfulness', in Stuart Ward and Astrid Rasch (eds), *Embers of Empire in Brexit Britain* (Bloomsbury Academic, 2019).

21 Speech in the House of Commons, 3 April 2019.

22 See Philip Murphy, *The Empire's New Clothes: The Myth of the Commonwealth* (Hurst and Co., 2018), available at: www.newstatesman.com/politics/uk/2018/04/commonwealth-delusion-why-empire-20-no-substitute-eu; and www.theguardian.com/commentisfree/2018/jul/10/past-boris-johnson-colonial-brexit-colony.

23 In New York.

24 I'm grateful to John Field for this suggestion. See his *Towards a Programme of Imperial Life: The British Empire at the Turn of the Century* (Greenwood, 1982).

25 Quoted above, p. 300.

26 My own Australian daughter-in-law, married with a new baby, was one.

27 By contrast, Swedish *Migrationsverket* charged me almost nothing for my dual citizenship with them.

28 See www.independent.co.uk/news/uk/politics/nigel-farage-brexit-rifle-pick-up-uk-eu-withdrawal-ukip-leader-liberal-democrat-a7741331.html.

29 Depending on what happens …

30 See www.ft.com/content/3be49734-29cb-11e6-83e4-abc22d5d108c.

31 This is hearsay (from my Continental European friends); but very widely expressed.

32 See www.thetimes.co.uk/article/hillary-clinton-britain-is-on-the-path-to-fascism-cffskmk90?fbclid=IwAR0A6vHc00N6OivBd-LcZXrEgJs_3H-CiMdBIQeAAJTTf8ftZwCu5NyLayY.

33 Elizabeth Buettner's chapter in Stuart Ward and Astrid Rasch (eds), *Embers of Empire in Brexit Britain* (Bloomsbury Academic, 2019) discusses the colonial components of other ex-imperial European countries' relationships with the EU.

34 Evidence of this appears in a survey undertaken by YouGov in June 2019, in which 32 per cent indicated that they believed the empire was 'more something to be proud of' than otherwise; and only 19 per cent that it was 'more to be ashamed of'; but 49 per cent that it was 'neither one thing nor the other', or else that they 'didn't know', which seem to me to be the most reasonable boxes to tick. YouGov's sample, however, was only of 1,684 adults.

35 Quoted in the *Independent* Newsletter (online), 14 November 2019.

36 Someone else will have to do it. I'll be dead by then.

Further reading

The endnotes (*supra*) contain references to the sources used in writing this book. Some of these are quite old, which does not mean of course that they are no longer of any use. This is a bibliography mainly of works that have appeared since the first edition. Some of them relate to areas of imperial history that are covered only marginally in the book, or even not at all.

General surveys

The new *Oxford History of the British Empire* (general editor Wm Roger Louis, 5 vols, Oxford University Press, 1998–99) is a valuable compendium of information and approaches to British imperial history. Vol. iii (ed. Andrew Porter) covers the nineteenth century; vol. iv (ed. Judith M. Brown and Wm Roger Louis) the twentieth. There are chapters here bearing on most of the particular topics listed below. Equally useful are volume v, *Historiography* (ed. Robin W. Winks); and the massive *Bibliography of Imperial, Colonial and Commonwealth History since 1600* (ed. Andrew Porter, Oxford University Press, 2002), which was published to accompany the *Oxford History*. Together these should make up for the deficiencies in this Further reading section.

The best recent general histories of British imperialism are probably John Darwin, *The Empire Project: The Rise and Fall of the British World-System* (Cambridge University Press, 2009), complementing his even more ambitious *After Tamerlane: The Global History of Empire since 1405* (Bloomsbury, 2008); and – albeit approaching the subject from an entirely different direction – James Belich, *Replenishing the Earth: The Settler Revolution and the Rise of the Anglo-World* (Oxford University Press, 2009).

Good shorter accounts of long periods of British imperial history are Bill Nasson, *Britannia's Empire* (History Press, 2006); Lawrence James, *The Rise and Fall of the British Empire* (Little, Brown, 1994); Peter Marshall (ed.), *Cambridge Illustrated History of the British Empire* (Cambridge University Press, 1996); Denis Judd, *Empire: The British Imperial Experience from 1765 to the Present* (HarperCollins, 1996); Simon C. Smith, *British Imperialism, 1750–1970* (Cambridge University Press, 1998); Trevor Lloyd, *Empire: The History of the British Empire* (Hambledon, 2001); Niall Ferguson's popular *Empire: How Britain Made the Modern World* (Allen Lane, 2003), written to accompany a controversial (because supposedly imperialist) TV documentary series; and, on a broader front, Andrew Porter, *European Imperialism, 1860–1914* (Macmillan, 1994). Among older texts that have worn well are Ronald Hyam, *Britain's Imperial Century* (2nd edn, Macmillan, 1993); and James (Jan) Morris's evocative trilogy, *Heaven's Command, Pax Britannica*, and *Farewell the Trumpets* (Faber & Faber, 1973, 1968, 1978).

These can be supplemented by Andrew Porter (ed.), *Atlas of British Overseas Expansion* (Routledge, 1991), which is much more than a mere atlas.

The best way of keeping up with the latest scholarship in this field is through the *Journal of Imperial and Commonwealth History* (Frank Cass, 1972–present).

Trade, investment and empire

The main works on this are Lance E. Davis and Robert A. Huttenback, *Mammon and the Pursuit of Empire: The Political Economy of British Imperialism, 1860–1912* (Cambridge University Press, 1986); and P. J. Cain and A. G. Hopkins, *British Imperialism*, originally published in two volumes: *Innovation and Expansion, 1688– 1914*, and *Crisis and Deconstruction, 1914–1990* (Longman, 1993). The classic early text is J. A. Hobson, *Imperialism: A Study* (1902; 3rd edn, 1938; re-issued with an Introduction by J. Townshend, Unwin Hyman, 1988). Peter Cain, *Hobson and Imperialism: Radicalism, New Liberalism, and Finance, 1887–1938* (Oxford University Press, 2002) deals both with Hobson and with the wider issues raised by his famous book. For statistics, see B. R. Mitchell, *British Historical Statistics* (2nd edn, Cambridge University Press, 1988).

The classic text on 'free trade imperialism' is J. A. Gallagher and R. E. Robinson, 'The imperialism of free trade', *Economic History Review*, vi (1953), 1–15, and anthologised since elsewhere.

Emigration and 'diaspora'

A good starting point is Carl Bridge and Kent Fedorowich (eds), 'The British world: diaspora, culture and identity', a special issue of the *Journal of Imperial and Commonwealth History*, 31 (2) (2003). The following are two good works on British emigration in the nineteenth century: David Fitzpatrick, *Oceans of Consolation: Personal Accounts of Irish Emigration to Australia* (Melbourne University Press, 1995); Robert F. Haines, *Emigration and the Labouring Poor: Australian Recruitment in Britain and Ireland, 1831–60* (Macmillan, 1997).

Travel, exploration, missions and empire

See Tim Jeal, *Explorers of the Nile* (Faber & Faber, 2011); Steve Clark (ed.), *Travel Writings and Empire: Postcolonial Theory in Transit* (Zed Books, 1999); Felix Driver, *Geography Militant: Cultures of Exploration and Empire* (Blackwell, 2000); and, on missionaries, Andrew Porter, *Religion versus Empire? British Protestant Missionaries and Overseas Expansion, 1700–1914* (Manchester University Press, 2004).

Imperial ideology

There is an extensive older literature examining nineteenth- and early twentieth-century ideas (and ideals) about empire, going back to A. P. Thornton, *The Imperial Idea and its Enemies* (Macmillan, 1959). Two recent books are Duncan Bell, *The Idea of Greater Britain* (Princeton University Press, 2007); and Theodore Koditscheck, *Liberalism, Imperialism, and the Historical Imagination* (Cambridge University Press, 2011).

The self-governing dominions

Canada, Australia, New Zealand and South Africa all have their own national histories. Brief, convenient and sound ones include Stuart Macintyre, *A Concise History of Australia* (Cambridge University Press, 2000); John L. Finlay and Douglas Sprague, *The Structure of Canadian History* (3rd edn, Prentice-Hall Canada, 1989); Keith Sinclair, *A History of New Zealand* (new edn, Penguin NZ, 1991); and T. R. H. Davenport, *A Short History of South Africa* (5th edn, Macmillan, 2000).

India

General accounts of the raj include Stanley Wolpert, *A New History of India* (Oxford University Press, 1977, and later editions); Judith Brown, *Modern India* (Oxford University Press, 1985); Lawrence James, *Raj: The Making and Unmaking of British India* (Little, Brown, 1997); and the much shorter Denis Judd, *The Lion and the Tiger: The Rise and Fall of the British Raj* (Oxford University Press, 2004). The excellent *New Cambridge History of India*, ed. Gordon Johnson (Cambridge University Press, 1987–), organised by topics, is still ongoing. Also recommended are David Omissi, *The Sepoy and the Raj: The Indian Army, 1860–1940* (Macmillan, 1994); C. Dewey, *Anglo-Indian Attitudes: The Mind of the Indian Civil Service* (Hambledon, 1993); E. Stokes, *The Peasant Armed: The Indian Rebellion of 1857* (Clarendon Press, 1986); and (perhaps eccentrically) Henry Yule and A. C. Burnell, *Hobson-Jobson: The Anglo-Indian Dictionary* (1886; reissued by Wordsworth Reference, 1996): a treasure-house of Anglo-Indian culture.

Mid-Victorian colonialism and its crises (excluding India)

James Belich, *The New Zealand Wars and the Victorian Interpretation of Racial Conflict* (Auckland University Press, 1986); B. Semmel, *The Governor Eyre Controversy* (McGibbon & Kee, 1962); G. Heuman, *Between Black and White: Race, Politics and the Free Coloureds in Jamaica, 1792–1865* (Clio, 1981); Thomas C. Holt, *The Problem of Freedom: Race, Labor and Politics in Jamaica and Britain, 1832–1938* (Johns Hopkins University Press, 1992); Philip Curtin, *Death by Migration: Europe's Encounter with the Tropical World in the 19th Century* (Cambridge University Press, 1989).

Africa: later nineteenth century

The starting point for any consideration of the 'scramble' for Africa is still Ronald Robinson and John Gallagher, *Africa and the Victorians: The Official Mind of Imperialism* (1963; 2nd edn, Macmillan, 1981); the latest general Europe-wide account is H. L. Wesseling, trans. Arnold J. Pomerans, *Divide and Rule: The Partition of Africa, 1880–1914* (Praeger, 1996).

On Egypt and the Sudan, two important works are Edward M. Spiers, *Sudan: The Reconquest Reappraised* (Frank Cass, 1998); and Roger Owen, *Lord Cromer: Victorian Imperialist, Edwardian Proconsul* (Oxford University Press, 2004).

The South African War

A flood of books and collections on the Anglo-Boer war of 1899–1902 appeared to mark its various anniversaries. They included W. R. Nasson, *The South African War,*

1899–1902 (Edward Arnold, 1999); Martin Marix Evans, *Encyclopaedia of the Boer War* (ABC-CLIO, 2000); Donal Lowry (ed.), *The South African War Reappraised* (Manchester University Press, 2000); John Gooch (ed.), *The Boer War: Direction, Experience and Image* (Frank Cass, 2001); Denis Judd and Keith Surridge, *The Boer War* (John Murray, 2002); David Omissi and A. S. Thompson (eds), *The Impact of the South African War* (Palgrave, 2002); and Greg Cuthbertson, Albert Grundlingh and Mary-Lynn Suttie, *Writing a Wider War: Rethinking Gender, Race and Identity in the South African War, 1899–1902* (Ohio University Press, 2002).

Among earlier works, the following are particularly valuable: Andrew Porter, *The Origins of the South African War: Joseph Chamberlain and the Diplomacy of Imperialism, 1895–99* (Manchester University Press, 1980); Iain R. Smith, *The Origins of the South African War, 1899–1902* (Longman, 1995); Peter Warwick, *Black People and the South African War 1899–1902* (Cambridge University Press, 1983), and (ed.), *The South African War: The Anglo-Boer War, 1899–1902* (Longman, 1980); W. R. Nasson, *Abraham Esau's War: A Black South African War in the Cape 1899–1902* (Cambridge University Press, 1991); and Stephen Koss (ed.), *The Pro-Boers: The Anatomy of an Anti-War Movement* (University of Chicago Press, 1973).

For Britain's relations with South Africa apart from the Boer War, see Timothy J. Keegan, *Colonial South Africa and the Origins of the Racial Order* (Leicester University Press, 1996); and Ronald Hyam and Peter Henshaw, *The Lion and the Springbok: Britain and Africa since the Boer War* (Cambridge University Press, 2003).

The empire and the Great War

Earlier books on this are listed in a note at the appropriate place. The best modern survey is Robert Holland's chapter, 'The British Empire and the Great War, 1914–1918', in *The Oxford History of the British Empire*, vol. iv, *The Twentieth Century* (ed. Judith Brown and Wm Roger Louis, 1999). David Omissi (ed.), *Indian Voices of the Great War: Soldiers' Letters, 1914–18* (Palgrave, 1999) provides a fascinating insight into a neglected contribution.

Colonial government

Anthony Kirk-Greene, *On Crown Service: A History of HM Colonial and Overseas Civil Services, 1837–1997* (IB Taurus, 1999), and *Britain's Imperial Administrators, 1858–1966* (Macmillan, 2000) are the latest on this. Of older books, Robert Heussler, *Yesterday's Rulers: The Making of the British Colonial Service* (Oxford University Press, 1963), and 'Philip Woodruff', *The Men who Ruled India: The Guardians* (Jonathan Cape, 1954), are still revealing. For a direct insight into the mind of some of the British rulers of Africa, see Anthony Kirk-Greene, *Gold Coast Diaries: Chronicles of Political Officers in West Africa, 1900–1919* (Radcliffe Press, 2000): one of a number of diaries and memoirs that have been published. A different angle is provided by Barbara Bush, *Imperialism, Race and Resistance: Africa and Britain, 1919–1945* (Routledge, 1999).

The ethos of the British empire's rulers is well described in David Cannadine, *Ornamentalism: How the British Saw their Empire* (Allen Lane, 2001); Kwasi Kwarteng's highly original *Ghosts of Empire: Britain's Legacies in the Modern World* (Bloomsbury, 2011); J. A. Mangan, *The Games Ethic and Imperialism: Aspects of the Diffusion of an Ideal* (2nd edn, Frank Cass, 1998); and many of the memoirs referred to above.

Culture and empire

This is an area not much covered in the present work, but important nonetheless. The two key texts are John MacKenzie, *Propaganda and Empire: The Manipulation of British Public Opinion, 1880–1960* (Manchester University Press, 1984); and Edward Said, *Culture and Imperialism* (Chatto & Windus, 1993), though they deal with different 'levels' of culture. Each has given rise to something of a 'school', with scores of follow-up studies. In MacKenzie's case, many of these are published in his own Manchester University Press 'Studies in Imperialism' series. A major recent contribution to this genre is Catherine Hall, *Civilizing Subjects: Metropole and Colony in the English Imagination, 1830–1867* (Polity Press, 2002). Some of this 'cultural' research claims to link the empire intimately with literature, art, music, theatre, museums, exhibitions and zoos. Worth citing in this connection are Martin Green's pre-Said *Dreams of Adventure, Deeds of Empire* (Routledge, 1979); Jeffrey Richards, *Imperialism and Music: Britain 1876–1953* (Manchester University Press, 2001) and (ed.), *Imperialism and Juvenile Literature* (Manchester University Press, 1989); Annie E. Coombes, *Reinventing Africa: Museums, Material Culture, and Popular Imagination in Late Victorian and Edwardian England* (Yale University Press, 1994); Marty Gould, *Nineteenth-Century Theatre and the Imperial Encounter* (Routledge, 2011); John MacKenzie, *Orientalism: History, Theory and the Arts* (Manchester University Press, 1995), which marks out the difference between him and the 'Saidists' (MacKenzie's neologism); and his (ed.), *Imperialism and Popular Culture* (Manchester University Press, 1986). A critical overview of this whole field is provided by my own *The Absent-Minded Imperialists: The Empire in British Society and Culture* (Oxford University Press, 2004).

The empire, politics and the 'people'

The main empirical study of Boer War jingoism appeared some years ago: Richard Price, *An Imperial War and the British Working Class* (Routledge, 1972). Since then, the following have appeared: R. H. MacDonald, *The Language of Empire: Myths and Metaphors of Popular Imperialism, 1880–1918* (Manchester University Press, 1994); and Andrew Thompson, *Imperial Britain: The Empire in British Politics, c. 1880–1932* (Longman, 2000) and *The Empire Strikes Back?* (Longman, 2005). Many of the works cited in the previous ('Culture and empire') section, especially John MacKenzie's and my own, also bear on this.

Science and technology

The classic works are both by Daniel R. Headrick: *The Tools of Empire: Technology and European Imperialism in the Nineteenth Century* (Oxford University Press, 1981, 1991); and *The Tentacles of Progress: Technology Transfer in the Age of Imperialism, 1850–1940* (Oxford University Press, 1988). Since then, Helen Tilley, *Africa as a Living Laboratory* (Chicago University Press, 2011), has put a revisionary slant on their work.

Women, gender and empire

Neglected as participants in the empire until recently (and in this book), the distinctive place of women is now receiving the attention it deserves. Ronald Hyam's *Empire and Sexuality: The British Experience* (Manchester University Press, 1990), explores one aspect, albeit controversially. (Most feminists do not like it.) Upper-class metropolitan women's imperialism around the turn of the century is covered in Julia Bush, *Edwardian Ladies and Imperial Power* (Leicester University Press, 2000), and in a number of articles by Eliza Riedi: for example, 'Options for an imperialist woman: the case of Violet Markham, 1899–1914', *Albion*, 32 (2000), 59–84; and 'Women, gender and the promotion of empire: the Victoria League, 1901–1914', *Historical Journal*, 45 (2002), 569–99. The part women played in the colonies is the subject of Antoinette Burton, *Burdens of History: British Feminists, Indian Women, and Imperial Culture, 1865–1915* (University of North Carolina Press, 1994); Helen Callaway, *Gender, Culture and Empire: European Women in Colonial Nigeria* (Macmillan, 1987); Margaret Strobel, *European Women and the Second British Empire* (Indiana University Press, 1991); Nupur Chaudhuri and Margaret Strobel (eds), *Western Women and Imperialism: Complicity and Resistance* (Indiana University Press, 1992); Clare Midgley (ed.), *Gender and Imperialism* (Manchester University Press, 1998); Mary Ann Lind, *The Compassionate Memsahibs: Welfare Activities of British Women in India, 1900–1947* (Greenwood Press, 1988); and Mary A. Procida, *Married to the Empire: Gender, Politics and Imperialism in India, 1883–1947* (Manchester University Press, 2002). A pioneering work on one aspect of imperial 'masculinity' is Mrinalini Sinha, *Colonial Masculinity: The 'Manly Englishman' and the 'Effeminate Bengali' in the Late Nineteenth Century* (Manchester University Press, 1995).

Anti-imperialism

For years, virtually the only work on this was Bernard Porter, *Critics of Empire* (Macmillan, 1968; republished by IB Tauris, 2008). Recently, however, that has been supplemented, if not quite supplanted, by Gregory Claeys, *Imperial Sceptics* (Cambridge University Press, 2011); and Mira Matikkala, *Empire and Imperial Ambition* (IB Tauris, 2011).

Colonial liberation movements and decolonisation

The best general surveys are John Darwin, *Britain and Decolonisation* (Macmillan, 1988), and *The End of the British Empire: The Historical Debate* (Blackwell, 1991); W. D. McIntyre, *British Decolonisation, 1946–1997* (Macmillan, 1998); A. N. Porter and A. J. Stockwell, *British Imperial Policy and Decolonisation, 1938–64*, 2 vols (Macmillan, 1987, 1989); and Ronald Hyam, *Britain's Declining Empire* (Cambridge University Press, 2006). Other key works are W. R. Louis, *Imperialism at Bay: The USA and the Decolonisation of the British Empire, 1941–45* (Clarendon Press, 1977); W. R. Louis and R. E. Robinson, 'The imperialism of decolonisation', *Journal of Imperial and Commonwealth History*, xxii (1994), 462–511; Frank Heinlein, *British Government Policy and Decolonisation, 1945–1963: Scrutinising the Official Mind* (Frank Cass, 2002); A. N. Porter and A. J. Stockwell (eds), *British Imperial Policy and Decolonisation, 1938–64*, 2 vols (Macmillan, 1987, 1989); and the series *British Documents on the End of Empire*, published by HMSO, especially the editors' Introductions to Series A, vols 2 and 4 (1992, 2000), by Ronald Hyam and Wm Roger Louis. In addition, three 'special issues' of the *Journal of Imperial and Commonwealth History* have been devoted to the topic: R. F. Holland and G. Rizvi (eds), 'Imperialism and decolonization', xii (2) (January 1984); Robert Holland (ed.), 'Emergencies and disorder in the European empires after 1945', xxi (3) (September 1993); and Kent Fedorowich and Martin Thomas (eds), 'International diplomacy and colonial retreat', xxviii (3) (September 2000).

Regional studies include Prosser Gifford and William Roger Louis (eds), *The Transfer of Power in Africa: Decolonisation, 1940–1960* (Yale University Press, 1982); J. Hargreaves, *Decolonisation in Africa* (Longman, 1988); Caroline Elkins, *Britain's Gulag* (Jonathan Cape, 2005); David Anderson, *Histories of the Hanged* (Weidenfeld & Nicolson, 2005) (the last two both on the Kenya 'Emergency'); Nicholas Tarling, *The Fall of Imperial Britain in South-East Asia* (Oxford University Press, 1993); T. N. Harper, *The End of Empire and the Making of Malaya* (Cambridge University Press, 1999); Christopher Bayly and Tim Harper, *Forgotten Wars: The End of Britain's Asian Empire* (Allen Lane, 2007); Greet Kershaw, *Mau Mau from Below* (James Currey, 1997); Robert Holland, *Britain and the Revolt in Cyprus, 1954–1959* (Clarendon Press, 1998); Yiannis D. Stefanidis, *Isle of Discord: Nationalism, Imperialism and the Making of the Cyprus Problem* (Hurst, 1999); Sucheta Mahajan, *Independence and Partition: The Erosion of Colonial Power in India* (Sage, 2000); and Michael Cohen and Martin Kolinsky (eds), *The Demise of the British Empire in the Middle East: Britain's Responses to Nationalist Movements, 1943–1955* (Frank Cass, 1998).

On the 'residue' – the colonies left over after the main decolonisation process – there is Robert Aldrich and John Connell, *The Last Colonies* (Cambridge University Press, 1998). Stuart Ward (ed.), *British Culture and the End of Empire* (Manchester University Press, 2001), discusses the impact of decolonisation on Britain.

The modern Commonwealth

The key general works are Denis Judd and Peter Slinn, *The Evolution of the Modern Commonwealth 1902–80* (Macmillan, 1982); Margaret Doxey, *The Commonwealth Secretariat and the Contemporary Commonwealth* (Macmillan, 1989); and W. David McIntyre, *A Guide to the Contemporary Commonwealth* (Palgrave, 2001).

The 'imperial aspects of Brexit'

Books that bear specifically on the 'imperial' aspects of Brexit include: Stuart Ward and Astrid Rasch (eds), *Embers of Empire in Brexit Britain* (Bloomsbury Academic, 2019); David Reynolds, *Island Stories: Britain and its History in the Age of Brexit* (HarperCollins, 2019); and Philip Murphy, *The Empire's New Clothes: The Myth of the Commonwealth* (Hurst and Co., 2018).

Index

Page numbers in italics refer to figures or maps. Page numbers in bold refer to tables. Page numbers followed by 'n' refer to notes.